■ THE RESOURCE FOR THE INDEPENDENT TRAVELER

"The guides are aimed not only at young budget travelers but at the indepedent traveler; a sort of streetwise cookbook for traveling alone."

—*The New York Times*

"Unbeatable; good sight-seeing advice; up-to-date info on restaurants, hotels, and inns; a commitment to money-saving travel; and a wry style that brightens nearly every page."

—*The Washington Post*

"Lighthearted and sophisticated, informative and fun to read. [Let's Go] helps the novice traveler navigate like a knowledgeable old hand."

—*Atlanta Journal-Constitution*

"A world-wise traveling companion—always ready with friendly advice and helpful hints, all sprinkled with a bit of wit."

—*The Philadelphia Inquirer*

■ THE BEST TRAVEL BARGAINS IN YOUR PRICE RANGE

"All the dirt, dirt cheap."

—*People*

"Anything you need to know about budget traveling is detailed in this book."

—*The Chicago Sun-Times*

"Let's Go follows the creed that you don't have to toss your life's savings to the wind to travel—unless you want to."

—*The Salt Lake Tribune*

■ REAL ADVICE FOR REAL EXPERIENCES

"The writers seem to have experienced every rooster-packed bus and lunar-surfaced mattress about which they write."

—*The New York Times*

"A guide should tell you what to expect from a destination. Here Let's Go shines."

—*The Chicago Tribune*

"[Let's Go's] devoted updaters really walk the walk (and thumb the ride, and trek the trail). Learn how to fish, haggle, find work—anywhere."

—*Food & Wine*

LET'S GO PUBLICATIONS

TRAVEL GUIDES

Alaska 1st edition **NEW TITLE**
Australia 2004
Austria & Switzerland 2004
Brazil 1st edition **NEW TITLE**
Britain & Ireland 2004
California 2004
Central America 8th edition
Chile 1st edition
China 4th edition
Costa Rica 1st edition
Eastern Europe 2004
Egypt 2nd edition
Europe 2004
France 2004
Germany 2004
Greece 2004
Hawaii 2004
India & Nepal 8th edition
Ireland 2004
Israel 4th edition
Italy 2004
Japan 1st edition **NEW TITLE**
Mexico 20th edition
Middle East 4th edition
New Zealand 6th edition
Pacific Northwest 1st edition **NEW TITLE**
Peru, Ecuador & Bolivia 3rd edition
Puerto Rico 1st edition **NEW TITLE**
South Africa 5th edition
Southeast Asia 8th edition
Southwest USA 3rd edition
Spain & Portugal 2004
Thailand 1st edition
Turkey 5th edition
USA 2004
Western Europe 2004

CITY GUIDES

Amsterdam 3rd edition
Barcelona 3rd edition
Boston 4th edition
London 2004
New York City 2004
Paris 2004
Rome 12th edition
San Francisco 4th edition
Washington, D.C. 13th edition

MAP GUIDES

Amsterdam
Berlin
Boston
Chicago
Dublin
Florence
Hong Kong
London
Los Angeles
Madrid
New Orleans
New York City
Paris
Prague
Rome
San Francisco
Seattle
Sydney
Venice
Washington, D.C.

COMING SOON:
Road Trip USA

LET'S GO

HAWAII
2004

HADLEY ABERNATHY EDITOR
ELLA M. STEIM ASSOCIATE EDITOR

RESEARCHER-WRITERS
ANNA BYRNE
LUCY EBERSOLD
SARAH JESSOP
KENNY SHIRLEY

CHRISTINE YOKOYAMA MAP EDITOR
ARIEL FOX MANAGING EDITOR

MACMILLAN

HELPING LET'S GO

If you want to share your discoveries, suggestions, or corrections, please drop us a line. We read every piece of correspondence, whether a postcard, a 10-page email, or a coconut. **Address mail to:**

Let's Go: Hawaii
67 Mount Auburn Street
Cambridge, MA 02138
USA

Visit Let's Go at **http://www.letsgo.com,** or send email to:

feedback@letsgo.com
Subject: "Let's Go: Hawaii"

In addition to the invaluable travel advice our readers share with us, many are kind enough to offer their services as researchers or editors. Unfortunately, our charter enables us to employ only currently enrolled Harvard students.

Published in Great Britain 2004 by Macmillan, an imprint of Pan Macmillan Ltd.
20 New Wharf Road, London N1 9RR
Basingstoke and Oxford
Associated companies throughout the world
www.panmacmillan.com

Maps by David Lindroth copyright © 2004 by St. Martin's Press.

Published in the United States of America by St. Martin's Press.

ISBN: 1 4050 3307 X
First edition
10 9 8 7 6 5 4 3 2 1

Let's Go: Hawaii is written by Let's Go Publications, 67 Mount Auburn Street, Cambridge, MA 02138, USA.

CONTENTS

LIST OF MAPS

HOW TO USE THIS BOOK

INTRODUCTORY MATERIAL. The first chapter, **Discover Hawaii,** will introduce you to the Hawaiian islands and get you primed for an unforgettable adventure. If you grow so anxious to get going that you can barely think straight, fear not! Our **Suggested Itineraries** have a little something for everyone, and make planning the perfect trip a no-brainer.

ESSENTIALS. All the practical information involved in traveling can get downright pesky. Flip to this section to get the quick and easy guide to Hawaii, including getting there, getting around, finding a place to stay, and staying safe.

LIFE AND TIMES. This chapter holds the answers to all your burning questions about Hawaii. Why do so many Hawaiian words sound the same? Who was Kamehameha the Great? What's the deal with Spam? History, culture, music—you name it. It's all here.

COVERAGE. There is a chapter dedicated to each one of the major Hawaiian islands—Oahu, Maui, Molokai, Lanai, Big Island, and Kauai. The Northwestern Hawaiian Islands, Kahoʻolawe, and Niʻihau also have their own, shorter chapters. The **black tabs** in the margins will help you navigate the book quickly and easily.

SOLO TRAVELERS. All of our accommodations and transportation information is geared toward the options for the solo traveler; we do, of course, also report on accommodations for travelers in larger groups, but the default is one person. Also, transportation prices are one-way unless otherwise noted.

GLOSSARY. Once in Hawaii, you'll find that although the islands are technically a part of the US, they have a language all their own. In our Hawaiian and pidgin glossaries, we've included many commonly used words and phrases to help you avoid looking (and sounding) like a tourist.

PRICE RANGES AND RANKINGS. Our researchers list establishments in order of value from best to worst. Our absolute favorites are denoted by the Let's Go thumbs-up (🖼). Since the best value does not always mean the cheapest price, we have incorporated a system of price ranges for food and accommodations into the guide on p. IX and inside the back cover. These are indicated by ❶❷❸❹❺ symbols in the text.

GRAYBOXES AND ICONBOXES. **Grayboxes** provide facts about historical events and information on Hawaiian culture. **Whiteboxes,** contain important practical information, such as warnings, helpful hints, and further resources.

PHONE CODES AND TELEPHONE NUMBERS. The area code for phone numbers is 808, unless noted otherwise. Phone numbers are preceded by the ☎ icon.

FEATURES. Find recent news items, hidden deals, big splurges, interviews with locals, major celebrations, regional cuisine, local lore, and (our favorite) researchers' tales from the road, in our black-sidebar features throughout the book.

SCHOLARLY ARTICLES. We hired the experts to share information on hula dance, Hawaii's beaches, and the sport of surfing. See p. 34, 289, 447, and 448.

A NOTE TO OUR READERS The information for this book was gathered by *Let's Go* researchers from January through August of 2003. Each listing is based on one researcher's opinion, formed during his or her visit at a particular time. Those traveling at other times may have different experiences since prices, dates, hours, and conditions are always subject to change. You are urged to check the facts presented in this book beforehand to avoid inconvenience and surprises.

ABOUT LET'S GO

GUIDES FOR THE INDEPENDENT TRAVELER

Budget travel is more than a vacation. At *Let's Go*, we see every trip as the chance of a lifetime. If your dream is to grab a knapsack and a machete and forge through the jungles of Brazil, we can take you there. Or, if you'd rather enjoy the Riviera sun at a beachside cafe, we'll set you a table. If you know what you're doing, you can have any experience you want—whether it's camping among lions or sampling Tuscan desserts—without maxing out your credit card. We'll show you just how far your coins can go, and prove that the greatest limitation on your adventure is not your wallet, but your imagination. That said, we understand that you may want the occasional indulgence after a week of hostels and kebab stands, so we've added "Big Splurges" to let you know which establishments are worth those extra euros, as well as price ranges to help you quickly determine whether an accommodation or restaurant will break the bank. While we may have diversified, our emphasis will always be on finding the best values for your budget, giving you all the info you need to spend six days in London or six months in Tasmania.

BEYOND THE TOURIST EXPERIENCE

We write for travelers who know there's more to a vacation than riding double-deckers with tourists. Our researchers give you the heads-up on both world-renowned and lesser-known attractions, on the best local eats and the hottest nightclub beats. In our travels, we talk to everybody; we provide a snapshot of real life in the places you visit with our sidebars on topics like regional cuisine, local festivals, and hot political issues. We've opened our pages to respected writers and scholars to show you their take on a given destination, and turned to lifelong residents to learn the little things that make their city worth calling home. And we've even given you Alternatives to Tourism—ideas for how to give back to local communities through responsible travel and volunteering.

OVER FORTY YEARS OF WISDOM

When we started, way back in 1960, Let's Go consisted of a small group of well-traveled friends who compiled their budget travel tips into a 20-page packet for students on charter flights to Europe. Since then, we've expanded to suit all kinds of travelers, now publishing guides to six continents, including our newest guides: *Let's Go: Japan* and *Let's Go: Brazil*. Our guides are still annually researched and written entirely by students on shoe-string budgets, adventurous travelers who know that train strikes, stolen luggage, food poisoning, and marriage proposals are all part of a day's work. Even as you read this, work on next year's editions is well underway. Whether you're reading one of our new titles, like *Let's Go: Puerto Rico* or *Let's Go Adventure Guide: Alaska*, or our original best-seller, *Let's Go: Europe*, you'll find the same spirit of adventure that has made *Let's Go* the guide of choice for travelers the world over since 1960.

GETTING IN TOUCH

The best discoveries are often those you make yourself; on the road, when you find something worth sharing, please drop us a line. We're Let's Go Publications, 67 Mt. Auburn St., Cambridge, MA 02138, USA (feedback@letsgo.com).

For more info, visit our website: www.letsgo.com.

PRICE RANGES >> HAWAII

Our researchers list establishments in order of value from best to worst; our favorites are denoted by the Let's Go thumbs-up (🖐). Since the best value is not always the cheapest price, we have incorporated a system of price ranges for quick reference. Our price ranges are based on a rough expectation of what you will spend. For **accommodations,** we base our price ranges off the cheapest price for which a single traveler can stay for one night. For **restaurants** and other dining establishments, we estimate the average amount that you will spend in that restaurant. The table below tells you what you will *typically* find in Hawaii at the corresponding price range; keep in mind that a particularly expensive ice cream stand may still only be marked a ❷, depending on what you will spend.

ACCOMMODATIONS	RANGE	WHAT YOU'RE *LIKELY* TO FIND
❶	under $25	Camping; most dorm rooms, such as HI or other hostels or university dorm rooms. Expect bunk beds and a communal bath; you may have to provide or rent towels and sheets.
❷	$25-65	Upper-end hostels or small hotels. You may have a private bathroom or a sink in your room.
❸	$65-110	A small room with a private bath. Should have decent amenities, such as phone and TV. Breakfast may be included in the price of the room.
❹	$110-150	Similar to 3, but may have more amenities, be in a more touristed area, or near the beach.
❺	above $150	Large hotels or upscale chains, almost always near the beach.

FOOD	RANGE	WHAT YOU'RE *LIKELY* TO FIND
❶	under $7	Mostly street-corner stands, pizza places, or fast-food joints. Rarely ever a sit-down meal.
❷	$7-10	Sandwiches, appetizers at a bar, or low-priced entrees (like a good local plate lunch). You may have the option of sitting down or getting take-out.
❸	$10-15	Mid-priced entrees, possibly coming with a soup or salad. Tip'll bump you up a couple dollars, since you'll probably have a waiter or waitress.
❹	$15-20	A somewhat fancy restaurant or a steakhouse. Either way, you'll have a special knife.
❺	above $20	Food with foreign names and a decent wine list. Wear your best *aloha* shirt and don't order PB&J.

RESEARCHER-WRITERS

Anna Byrne   *Honolulu, Waikiki, Windward/Leeward Oahu*

Anna landed in Hawaii via Europe, where she was traveling after studying in London. Anna is a self-described surfing neophyte who loves Mai Tais, but we also know her to be a fantastic researcher and great with deadlines. An associate editor for both *Let's Go: Europe 2002* and *Let's Go: Western Europe 2002*, and editor of *Let's Go: Barcelona 2003*, this was Anna's first researching gig, and she was, in short, the bomb.

Lucy Ebersold   *Maui, Lanai, North Shore Oahu*

Lucy was our offseason researcher, and our shopping, art, and drink menu sleuth. Having been an associate editor for *Let's Go: Spain, Portugal, and Morocco 2003*, she is now an assistant editor for two technical business-to-business publications. Future Let's Go researchers will love to hate her flawless map edits in their training manuals—she set the standard for the series. If only they had access to her marginalia about cute boys...

Sarah Jessop   *The Big Island*

Having researched for *Let's Go: Italy 2001*, and *Let's Go: Ireland 2003*, and associate edited for *Let's Go: Spain 2002* and *Let's Go: South Africa 2002*, Sarah knew the gig. She shared her love of Hawaiian sun, *lilikoi* (passionfruit) smoothies, and Hawaii Volcanoes National Park with fellow History of Science concentrator Deema Baha Arafah *(Let's Go: Middle East 2002)*. Sarah was tirelessly upbeat, despite those pesky "deadlines."

Kenny Shirley   *Kauai/Molokai*

Otherwise known as Kenny "Baaah, I'm a mountain goat" Shirley, we couldn't help but forgive him for his late copy when he sent us a coconut. Kenny wrote our favorite features: **As Sure Footed as a What, Golf on a Shoestring**, and one on the Milwaukee Bucks (which didn't quite fit). His undergraduate degree in math didn't help him with his computer problems (there's a reason the "reset" button is hard to push), but maybe his PhD in statistics will.

CONTRIBUTING WRITERS

Maren Lau researched for *Let's Go: California and Hawaii 1997*.
Stephen "Dr. Beach" Leatherman is a professor and Director of the Laboratory for Coastal Research at Florida International University in Miami.
Christine Yokoyama is the map editor for *Let's Go: Hawaii 2004, Let's Go: Australia 2004, Let's Go: Boston 2004*, and *Let's Go Road Trip USA: 2005*.
Sarah Rotman edited *Let's Go: Boston 2001*, served as Publishing Director for the *Let's Go* 2002 series, and researched for *Let's Go: Hawaii 2003*.
Bryden Sweeney-Taylor researched for *Let's Go: Southwest USA 2002, Let's Go: South Africa: 2003, Let's Go Hawaii: 2003*, and *Let's Go: Southwest 2004*.

ACKNOWLEDGMENTS

LET'S GO

TEAM ALOHA SAYS: Ariel, we really do aspire to be you. Thanks for your skills, speed, and care. Christine, good luck with the route next summer. Dusty, we don't know how you're so patient, but thanks for *every bit* of your help. Mapland, here's to windows with natural light and Matchbox 20. Again. Jesse, we're still on for kickball, right? Jeff and Julie, thanks for helping us find a last-minute researcher.

HADLEY SAYS: *Mahalo nui loa* to Ella for being my partner in processed-sugar crime, and for being the organized one with the flawless handwriting. Thanks also to: the rockin'est lot of RWs; to Ariel, for being the best ME ever; to Christine, for being a mapper *and* a scholar; to my Hawaiian *ohana* who put the islands in my heart: Rianne and family, Pohai, Cathy, Kumu, Uncle Joe, and Liz; to Mom, Charley and Meghan for long phone calls; and to Matt, for flower, bagel, and Red Sox hat deliveries, and for encouragement, with both the book and my wiffle ball swing.

ELLA SAYS: *Mahalo* to Hadley for putting up with my fits of organization, for Bend it Like Beckham (yeah, Sporty Spice), and for frequent Finagling. Thanks to: Ariel, our fearless leader; who now knows how to pronounce Kauai; to all our RWs; to Mapland, our surrogate home; to Megan, for putting it all in perspective; to Zahra, for the real low-down; to Liz, Alex, Will, and Em, for inspirational emails; and to my family, for letting me go (but still come home on weekends), and for taking me to Hawaii in the first place.

CHRISTINE SAYS: *Mahalo* to Hadley and Ella for being helpful and cheerful and for writing in glittery pen. Also many thanks to Kate, Jess and Kath for putting up with me; to Brian "Miss Independent" for the map proof; to Matt for reminding me to eat lunch; to my family for always being supportive and for taking me to Hawaii and to my extended family in Hawaii for letting us visit often.

Editor
Hadley Abernathy
Associate Editor
Ella M. Steim
Managing Editor
Ariel Fox
Map Editor
Christine Yokoyama
Typesetter
Jeffrey Hoffman Yip

Publishing Director
Julie A. Stephens
Editor-in-Chief
Jeffrey Dubner
Production Manager
Dusty Lewis
Cartography Manager
Nathaniel Brooks
Design Manager
Caleb Beyers
Editorial Managers
Lauren Bonner, Ariel Fox,
Matthew K. Hudson, Emma Nothmann,
Joanna Shawn Brigid O'Leary,
Sarah Robinson
Financial Manager
Suzanne Siu
Marketing & Publicity Managers
Megan Brumagim, Nitin Shah
Personnel Manager
Jesse Reid Andrews
Researcher Manager
Jennifer O'Brien
Web Manager
Jesse Tov
Web Content Director
Abigail Burger
Production Associates
Thomas Bechtold, Jeffrey Hoffman Yip
IT Directors
Travis Good, E. Peyton Sherwood
Financial Assistant
R. Kirkie Maswoswe
Associate Web Manager
Robert Dubbin
Office Coordinators
Abigail Burger, Angelina L. Fryer,
Liz Glynn

Director of Advertising Sales
Daniel Ramsey
Senior Advertising Associates
Sara Barnett, Daniella Boston
Advertising Artwork Editor
Julia Davidson

President
Abhishek Gupta
General Manager
Robert B. Rombauer
Assistant General Manager
Anne E. Chisholm

Hawaii

0   20 miles

0   20 kilometers

PACIFIC OCEAN

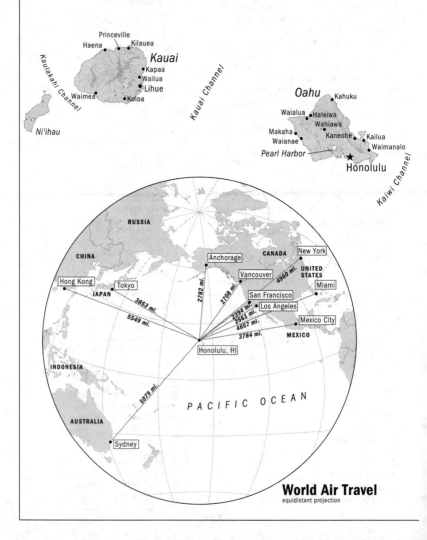

Kaulakahi Channel

Princeville
Kilauea
Haena

Kauai

Kapaa
Wailua
Lihue
Waimea
Koloa

Kauai Channel

Ni'ihau

Oahu

Kahuku

Waialua   Haleiwa
Wahiawa
Makaha   Kaneohe   Kailua
Waianae   Waimanalo
Pearl Harbor

Honolulu

Kaiwi Channel

RUSSIA

CHINA

Hong Kong
Tokyo
JAPAN

Anchorage

CANADA

New York

Vancouver

UNITED
STATES

Miami

San Francisco
Los Angeles

Mexico City

MEXICO

3853 ml.
5549 ml.
2782 ml.
2708 ml.
2394 ml.
2561 ml.
4857 ml.
3784 ml.
4960 ml.

Honolulu, HI

INDONESIA

5079 ml.

PACIFIC OCEAN

AUSTRALIA

Sydney

World Air Travel
equidistant projection

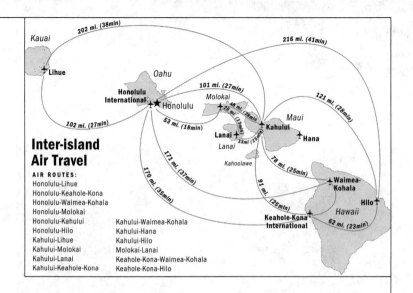

Inter-island Air Travel

AIR ROUTES:
Honolulu-Lihue
Honolulu-Keahole-Kona
Honolulu-Waimea-Kohala
Honolulu-Molokai
Honolulu-Kahului
Honolulu-Hilo
Kahului-Lihue
Kahului-Molokai
Kahului-Lanai
Kahului-Keahole-Kona

Kahului-Waimea-Kohala
Kahului-Hana
Kahului-Hilo
Molokai-Lanai
Keahole-Kona-Waimea-Kohala
Keahole-Kona-Hilo

DISCOVER
HAWAII

The most remote island group in the world, the Hawaiian islands are separated from the mainland US by over 2000 miles. Hawaii is composed of eight major islands— "The Big Island" (distinguishing the largest island actually named Hawaii), Maui, Molokai, Lanai, Oahu, Kauai, and Ni'ihau—and over 120 other small islands and atolls. Due to the islands' location, the so-called "crossroads of the Pacific" has developed into a unique environment of tropical enticements and a melting pot of cultures. Hawaii is a geological wonder, encompassing within its shores a wide variety of climates and ecosystems. The awe-inspiring landscape— including rainforests with tropical fruit and desolate remnants of lava flows, all backed by the thundering Pacific—is alive, in every sense of the word, with the forces of creation. The heartbeat of the Earth is so strong here that it is almost palpable, a sense that perhaps explains the strong ties that Hawaiians feel to their land. The allure of the land has enticed voyagers from Polynesia, Europe, Asia, and beyond; today Hawaii is the most ethnically diverse state in the US. Residents of radically different backgrounds are united under the affectionate term *kama'aina* (local), adding to the mosaic of the islands. The culture is an amalgamation of Hawaiian tradition, laid-back surfer lifestyle, the influence of an on-going military presence, waves of international tourists, and more, all united by the *aloha* spirit. Generalizations are few and far between in this dynamic, colorful state, however. Along every beach there is another more secluded stretch of sand, and beyond every stunning vista there is an even more breathtaking sight. The diversity of land, people, and cultures ensures that, in Hawaii, the journey never ends.

FACTS AND FIGURES

CAPITAL: Honolulu.

STATE POPULATION: 1,211,537.

STATE MOTTO: *Ua mau ke ea o ka 'aina i ka pono* (The life of the land is perpetuated in righteousness).

STATE SPAM CONSUMPTION RATE: 1100 cans per day.

NUMBER OF LETTERS IN THE HAWAIIAN ALPHABET: 12.

PERCENTAGE OF THE WORLD'S REEFS IN HAWAIIAN WATERS: 70%.

WHEN TO GO

How soon can you leave? With year-round temperatures rarely straying far from 80°F, Hawaii's climate is always welcoming. Even the hotter summer months are kept in check by cooling trade winds, and the ocean averages a pleasant 75°F. Though wind and rainstorms are more common in the winter, they usually pass through the islands quickly and without incident. Hawaii's mountainous regions and valleys are often rainy and damp. Weather is often localized, however, and beach-goers are almost always able to find sunny patches on the drier, leeward sides of the islands.

Depending on the focus of your vacation, there may be specific times when you should travel. Winter is surf season, when hard-core boardriders and their groupies pilgrimage to Oahu's North Shore for the biggest waves of the year. Families with young children should consider a summer vacation, when swimming conditions are generally safer than at other times of year, and there are guaranteed to be plenty of other tykes cavorting in the waves. December through April is considered high season in Hawaii; accommodation prices generally drop a bit at other times of year, but flights are consistently expensive.

THINGS TO DO

Hawaii is a veritable smorgasbord of activities, sights, and experiences. Outdoorsy types will be pleasantly overwhelmed by the sheer number of hikes to tackle and mountains to tame. Hedonists will find more than enough sand and surf to occupy the days, and ample frozen concoctions to fill the nights. If one too many Mai Tais isn't slowing you down, Hawaii's cultural and historical sights provide a contrast to the seemingly endless parade of white-, black-, and red-sand beaches. Throughout this adventure, Hawaii's local culture provides a vivid backdrop, wooing travelers with colorful tales of Old Hawaii, tasty island treats, and a genuinely welcoming attitude.

ADVENTURE SPORTS. Hawaii takes sports to a new level. Across the islands, there are athletes and travelers toeing the edge, pushing the limits, and expanding the scope of what is possible. At the same time, adventure sports aren't necessarily just for the most gung-ho of them all—for every grueling hike, there's an equally pleasant one and for every big surf beach, there's a handful of innocuous "learning" beaches. Whatever your level of expertise, Hawaii has you covered.

On **Oahu,** surfing reigns supreme. Every year, countless people catch their first waves at **Baby Queen's** (p. 130) in Waikiki, and many others perfect their technique on Oahu's innumerable beaches. The winter months bring mammoth waves to the **North Shore** (p. 158) and the Leeward Coast's **Makaha Beach** (p. 177), as well as the surf junkies who roam the globe in search of the perfect wave. The rest of the island is also not without appeal. **Kailua Beach** (p. 153), with its seemingly constant breeze, is a windsurfer's paradise and on the eastern coast, **Sandy Beach** (p. 141) and **Makapu'u** (p. 142) are to body boarding what the North Shore is to surfing.

The Big Island offers opportunities for on-land adventures, with mountain bike and ski tours on **Mauna Kea** (p. 320) as well as biking, horseback riding, and ATV-ing in **Waipi'o Valley** (p. 352). Snorkelers will delight in the underwater treats of **Kealakekua Bay** (p. 341) and **Lapakahi State Historical Park** (p. 362). Big Island is also the site of the most extreme event of them all—the **Ironman Triathlon** (p. 29) held annually in October.

Maui beckons adventurers. Helicopter tours run out of **Kahului** (p. 182), dolphin- and whale-watching cruises leave from **Ma'alaea** (p. 190) and snorkel trips to **Molokini** are popular in **Kihei** (p. 191). **Pa'ia** beaches (p. 220) are prime surfing and wind-surfing spots and within **Haleakala National Park** (p. 239), several companies offer bike tours. The surf spot **Jaws** is known for its immense waves that are too big to paddle over—extreme surfers have jet-skis tow them in.

On **Kauai**, beginners can get an easy introduction to the art of surfing on **Hanalei's** (p. 400) gentle waves. Advanced kayakers navigate the **Na Pali Coast** (p. 406) and snorkelers drift happily among the native fish at **Tunnels Beach** (p. 402).

ROPE 'EM AND RIDE 'EM. While Stetsons and spurs may not figure into your vision of a typical Hawaiian holiday, *paniolo* **(cowboy)** culture is alive and well in America's westernmost state. Since John Palmer Parker established the Parker Ranch on the Big Island in the early 19th century and hired Mexican *paniolos* to help him run it, a number of other ranches have sprung up on the islands, creating an interesting part of Hawaiian life. If you're looking to break from the monotony of sun, sand, and surf, visit one of Hawaii's **working cattle ranches.** At **Molokai Ranch** (p. 274) you can play cowboy and still enjoy all the amenities of a luxury resort. The **Kualoa Ranch** (p. 156) on Oahu allows visitors to explore its grounds on **horseback** (or, for equi-phobes, on ATV). Here, you can tour the stunning **Waipi'o Valley** (p. 353) on **horseback** or in a **mule-drawn covered wagon.** The historic **Parker Ranch** (p. 358) merits a visit by any wannabe cowpoke. Check out the **Parker Ranch Museum** and tour the property in a **covered wagon.** If you'd rather just watch, swing by the annual **July 4th Horse Races and Rodeo** for a taste of a real Hawaiian showdown. The **Makawao Rodeo** (p. 244) on Maui takes place the 1st weekend in July and features **steer roping, barrel racing,** and **bareback riding,** all done with classic *paniolo* flair.

■ LET'S GO PICKS

BEST PLACE TO HANG TEN: Take a lesson at **Waikiki Beach,** where the gentle rollers make every wave a party wave (p. 135).

BEST PLACE TO LOOK BEYOND THE BEACHES: The impressive **Bishop Museum** in Honolulu (p. 109) holds an extensive collection of Hawaiian art and artifacts.

BEST PLACE TO FEEL ATHLETICALLY INFERIOR: The **Ironman Triathlon,** a three-part test of true grit, held annually in Kailua-Kona on the Big Island (p. 29).

BEST PLACE FOR A CAFFEINE BUZZ: Get your fix at **Kauai Coffee,** a working coffee farm and museum on Kauai (p. 420), with a conveniently well-stocked gift shop of coffee-related products.

BEST PLACE TO WITNESS THE FURY OF PELE: The lava flows of **Kilauea,** the Big Island's active volcano, in Hawaii Volcanoes National Park (p. 307).

SWEETEST TESTAMENT TO A FRUIT: **Guava Kai,** a plantation and agronomic engineering center for the guava fruit, on Kauai (p. 395). The **Dole Plantation Gardens**, on Oahu (p. 138), pays homage to that famed island fruit, the pineapple.

BEST SUNSET: Polihale State Park (p. 431) on Kauai, or any expanse of open sky on the islands.

BEST WHALE WATCHING: With a certified naturalist on a **Pacific Whale Foundation**—a non-profit dedicated to marine research and conservation—tour on Maui (p. 179).

SUGGESTED ITINERARIES

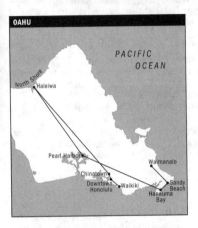

158). Soak up sun at Sunset Beach, Pipeline, or Waimea Bay (jump off the cliff!). Keep an eye out if you're there in the winter (Dec.-Apr.)—you may spy professional wave riders. Stay overnight in bohemian **Haleiwa** (p. 162), and use the next morning to poke around its various shops and galleries. Head toward **Pearl Harbor** (p. 136), stopping at a fruit stand along the way. Even if you're not a history buff, an afternoon visit to the memorial and museum is certainly worthwhile. For the next day or two, pack a beach bag and drive along the eastern coast. Snorkel with the fish at **Hanauma Bay** (p. 139), catch a few waves at **Sandy Beach** (p. 141), and enjoy the spectacular drive. End up in **Waimanalo** (p. 142), picking up an authentic plate lunch and shave ice before returning to Honolulu for your flight home.

OAHU (1 WEEK). From the Honolulu International Airport, get your bearings by driving around the perimeter of the island—with the windows wide open. Spend a day or two indulging in the whirlwind of **Waikiki** (p. 116). Sip a frosty drink (or 3), buy a $4 t-shirt, catch a free concert, and enjoy tourism at its best. Next, take a day to explore the historical sights in **Downtown Honolulu** (p. 104), popping into **Chinatown** (p. 101) for a quick bite and a stroll through the markets. Throw on your best surf bum outfit and road trip up the **North Shore** (p.

WHIRLWIND TOUR (2 WEEKS ON OAHU, THE BIG ISLAND, MAUI, AND KAUAI). Start your trip with a condensed version of our **Oahu** itinerary (see above). Spend one day driving around the island and hit the beaches on the **North Shore** (p. 158). After a night of the club scene in **Waikiki** (p. 123), take it down a notch and wander the historical and cultural sights of **Downtown Honolulu** (p. 104) and **Pearl**

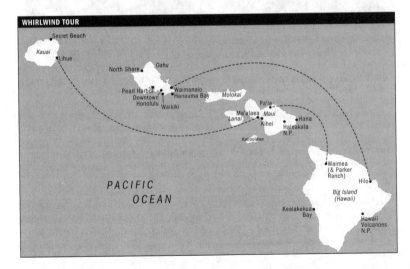

Harbor (p. 136). On day 3, steer east to **Hanauma Bay** (p. 139), **Sandy Beach** (p. 141) and **Waimanalo** (p. 142). Camp under the stars, grab a plate lunch or shave ice, and return to Honolulu for your flight to **Big Island.** Drop your bags in **Hilo** (p. 299) and meander through the town's colorful streets, taking in a museum or two and refueling at the **Hilo Farmers' Market** (p. 303). The next day, set out for **Hawaii Volcanoes National Park** (p. 307). Tour the natural wonders of the park along **Crater Rim Drive** and **Chain of Craters Road** (p. 311). The next day, put your snorkel to good use at **Kealakekua Bay** (p. 341). Take a boat cruise or explore the protected reef on your own. On your final day, pretend you're a *paniolo* (cowboy) in **Waimea** (p. 354) and **Parker Ranch** (p. 354), then brush the dust off and hop on the next plane to **Maui.** Centrally-located **Pa'ia** (p. 220), with its budget-friendly prices and laid-back attitude, is a perfect home base. Use the afternoon to scout out the town and hit one of the beaches. View the varied sights of **Haleakala National Park** (p. 239) in a day by driving up the switchback road to the summit, then take the next couple of days to explore—marvel at the sights on the **Road to Hana** (p. 233), soak up the sun at the pristine beaches near **Kihei** (p. 191), and catch a dolphin or whale-watching tour out of **Ma'alaea** (p. 190). Next, head to **Kauai.** After a brief stop in **Lihue** (p. 372) to find a hotel, follow the sounds of Hawaiian music to **Smith's Tropical Paradise** (p. 385). Enjoy the boat tour to **Fern Grotto** (p. 385), then return to Smith's to gorge yourself at their *luau.* The next day, find your way to **Secret Beach** (p. 393) for sunbathing and swimming. Return to Lihue and pack your bags—it's time to go home.

OFF THE BEATEN PATH (2 WEEKS ON MOLOKAI, MAUI, LANAI, AND THE BIG ISLAND). Shake off all the tourist trappings as you head for a 5-day stay on **Molokai.** You can hang your hat in **Kaunakakai** (p. 253), the island's major town, before hiking down to the **Kalaupapa Peninsula** (p. 259), a former leper colony and one of the most awe-inspiring spots on the island. Rub elbows with locals at a Little League game back in Kaunakakai, and get the inside scoop on **Wailau Valley** (p. 273), a rugged locale where Molokians go for *their* vacations. If your vacation-within-a-

vacation has you looking for some excitement, spend a night in **One Ali'i Beach Park** (p. 256), and party local-style. The next day, get closer to Native Hawaiian history and culture at the **'Ili'ili'opae Heiau** (p. 269), the second-largest Hawaiian temple in the islands. Three days in the islands and not yet a day dedicated to sun and sand? Pack your bathing suit and hiking boots, and set off for **Mo'omomi Preserve** (p. 266). A hike through the preserve encounters a number of rare and endangered plant species, before unfolding into a series of white sand beaches. Last but not least, spend a day at **Halawa Valley** and **Moa'ula Falls** (p. 272). Next, fly out for a 3-day stay on **Maui.** You can head to **Haiku** (p. 247), a lush and sleepy town near the North Shore and on the Road to Hana. Stay in a local B&B for real Hawaiian hospitality. Four miles north of Hana, **Waianapanapa State Park** (p. 231) merits a day's excursion, with a number of unique sights including a heiau, lava tube caves, lava arches, and a small black-sand beach. Overlook the tourist glut of **Lahaina,** and instead take one of the **Maui Nei** organization's historical-cultural tours (p. 213) of the city. Equipped with your newfound knowledge, hop a ferry from Lahaina to **Lanai.** Go for an off-road adventure along the **Munro Trail** (p. 283), then park yourself at a local campground to spend a night under the stars. Step into the otherworldly **Garden of the Gods** (p. 284), an area of red earth and rock formations, before sailing back to Maui, then a 4-day stint on the **Big Island.** Touch down in **Hilo** (p. 299), the island's low-key metropolis. From there, drive north through the unspoiled **Hamakua Coast** (p. 349) to North Kohala. Explore the abandoned ancient village at **Lapakahi State Historical Park** (p. 362), and snorkel from its coral beach. Next you can make a pilgrimage to **Mo'okini Heiau** (p. 363), the birthplace of Kamehameha I. Continue east along the coast to South Kona. Seek the spirit of the ancients at the extensive **Pu'uhonua o Honaunau National Historical Park** (p. 343). Round out your tour with a jaunt through the diverse **Ka'u** district on your way back to the airport in Hilo.

DISCOVER

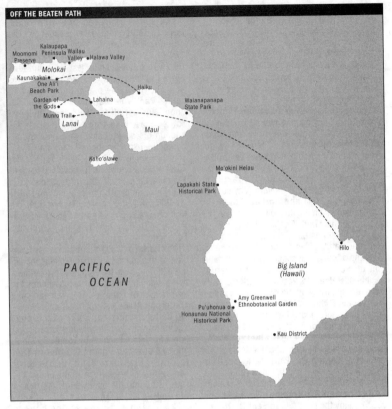

OFF THE BEATEN PATH

Kalaupapa Wailau
Moomomi Peninsula Valley Halawa Valley
Preserve
Molokai
Kaunakakai
One Ali'i
Beach Park Haiku
Garden of Lahaina
the Gods Waianapanapa
Munro Trail State Park
Lanai
Maui

Kaho'olawe

Mo'okini Heiau

Lapakahi State
Historical Park

Hilo

PACIFIC Big Island
OCEAN (Hawaii)

Amy Greenwell
Ethnobotanical Garden
Pu'uhonua o
Honaunau National
Historical Park

Kau District

BACK TO NATURE (12 DAYS ON THE BIG ISLAND, MAUI, AND KAUAI).

Ready to cast off the 9-to-5 drudgery and commune with Mother Nature? From Honolulu, head to the **Big Island** for 5 days, stopping first in **Hawaii Volcanoes National Park** (p. 307). During your 3-day stay in the park, spend at least one night backcountry camping on **Mauna Loa.** (Get a free **permit** at the park **Visitor Center.**) See how the Hawaiian Islands were formed at **Kilauea,** the world's most active volcano, which has been spewing molten lava continuously for the past 20 yr. Stargaze from the slopes of **Mauna Kea** (p. 320), where amateur and professional astronomers alike enjoy some of the best viewing conditions on the planet. In **Akaka Falls State Park** (p. 307), about 4 mi. up Mauna Kea, trek though lush rainforest and check out the park's two spectacular waterfalls. Next,

leave the park and head to the northern tip of the island, where you can hike the verdant **Waipi'o Valley** (p. 352) or satisfy your inner equestrian by exploring the valley on horseback. Drive south along the **Hamakua Coast** toward Hilo, being sure to stop at the **Hawaii Tropical Botanical Garden** (p. 307), home to over 2000 different plant species, along the way. Further south in Puna, the otherworldly forms at **Lava Tree State Park** (p. 325) are a testament to nature's powers of creativity. Head back to **Hilo** (p. 299), then to **Maui** for 3 days. Stop first at **Kipahulu Valley** and **Ohe'o Gulch** (p. 233), both of which are within the confines of **Haleakala National Park.** Take a hike to the dazzling **Makahiku** and **Waimoku waterfalls** (p. 233), and pass the splendid **Pools of Ohe'o** (p. 233) along the way. Next, travel to **Kihei** (p. 191) and take a snorkeling trip to **Molokini**, where

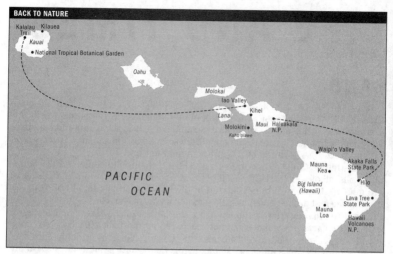

many of the species you will encounter exist nowhere else in the world. From there, head north to the sacred **Iao Valley** (p. 189), the site of countless ancient battles, and the final resting place of *ali'i* (royalty). The last leg of your journey takes you to **Kauai,** and some of Hawaii's most untamed wilderness. Don't miss the world-famous **Kalalau Trail** (p. 406), which runs 11 mi. along Kauai's **Na Pali Coast** (p. 405). This strenuous 3-day **hike** or **kayak** has incredible **views** and **beaches.** Apply for a **camping permit** in advance (p. 370). During the final day of your journey, visit the historic **Kilauea lighthouse** at the **Kilauea Point National Wildlife Reserve** (p. 394) in Kilauea. Glimpse of some of the many endangered species that call the reserve home, including **humpback whales, nene geese, monk seals,** and **sea turtles.** Finally, the fragrant blossoms at the **National Tropical Botanical Garden** (p. 414) in Lawa'i will provide you with a last breath of island air before you have to leave for Honolulu and then head for home.

LIFE AND TIMES

LAND

Hawaii is located in the Pacific Ocean, 2400 mi. (3860km) off the coast of the continental US; it is the most isolated populated landmass in the entire world. At approximately the same latitude as central Mexico, it is the southernmost state and the 4th smallest in area, spanning 6,450 sq. mi. (16,706 sq. km). The average temperature on Hawaii is 85°F (29°C) in summer and 78°F (26°C) in winter. Hawaii stretches 1523 mi. (world's longest island chain) and contains 132 islands and atolls, all of which are the result of volcanic activity. Only seven of the islands are inhabited, and with the exception of the large but uninhabited Kaho'olawe, most of the rest are too small to make human occupancy viable.

Hawaii (or **The Big Island**), the youngest and largest of the Hawaiian islands, is home to two active volcanoes, Mauna Loa and Kilauea. Kilauea has been erupting continuously since 1983, and visitors to the Hawaii Volcanoes National Park can observe her lava flows up close. Mauna Kea is the highest point in the state at an altitude of 13,796 ft. (4208m) above sea level. The high cliffs along the northern and southeastern coasts of Big Island make its many waterfalls spectacular. In addition to its natural wonders, The Big Island is known for being the world's leading producer of macadamia nuts and orchids.

Of the two volcanoes on **Maui,** only one, Haleakala, is still considered active, though it hasn't erupted for some time. The remains of the second volcano are known as Halemahina, or the West Maui Mountains. A great deal of sugar cane is cultivated in the fertile valley between Haleakala and Halemahina, while much of eastern Maui is covered by tropical rainforest.

Molokai has three distinct geographical regions: the mountainous east, the arid west, and the verdant central plain. The island also boasts some of the world's tallest sea cliffs, which soar up to 3000 ft. above the ocean.

Castle & Cooke Co., the maker of Dole pineapple products, owns 98% of the island of **Lanai.** Historically a center for commercial pineapple production, Lanai is aptly nicknamed "the Pineapple Island." Lanai is the only Hawaiian island from which five of the other main islands are visible.

Considerable pineapple and sugar production also takes place on **Oahu,** in the central valley between the eastern Koolau Mountain Range and the Waianae Range in the west. One of the most famous sights on the island is Diamond Head, an extinct volcanic crater on the southeastern coast. At 760 ft. in height and 3520 ft. in diameter, it's impressive but all bark and no bite—it hasn't erupted in 150,000 years. Oahu is also the home of Honolulu, the state capital, and Waikiki, an extremely popular tourist destination.

Kauai is home to the rainiest spot on earth, Mount Wai'ale'ale, which averages 460 in. (1143cm) of rain per year. Thanks to this heavy rainfall, a number of spectacular canyons have been eroded into the mountains of Kauai. The northernmost and geologically oldest of the Hawaiian islands, Kauai is also the most verdant, earning it the nickname "The Garden Island."

Ni'ihau, "The Forbidden Island," has been privately owned by Kauai's Robinson family since 1864. The semi-arid island functions mainly as a cattle ranch, but is better known for its isolation from the outside world. To prevent the modernization of the island, visitors are not allowed on the island except with express permission from the Robinson family or a resident. The least racially diverse island with the fewest non-Hawaiians, Ni'ihau is also the only place where Hawaiian is the primary language.

LAVA ME TENDER When Dr. Evil plotted to cover the Earth with "liquid hot magma" in 1999's smash *Austin Powers: The Spy Who Shagged Me*, the would-be world dictator erred in his geological calculations. While the volcanic substance made of liquid and solid rock remains below ground, it is known as **magma**. Once magma is exposed to the air, either through a volcanic eruption or a fissure in the earth, it becomes **lava**. How lava behaves once it breaks the surface depends on its chemical composition. **Low silica lava**, which is common in Hawaii, flows and can travel for great distances. **High silica lava** (also called pyroclastics) explodes in ash or cinders when it leaves the volcano. The most famous example of this type of lava was the 1980 eruption of Mount Saint Helens in Washington, where the force of the magma being released caused the volcano to self-destruct. In addition to having varying silica levels, lava also comes in three different forms:

Pahoehoe: This type of lava can be found at almost all volcanoes. Fast-flowing, it hardens into a smooth, ropy solid. The outside of lava channels can solidify before the interior lava, forming lava tubes; lava can flow within these tubes for long distances.

Pillow: A type of *pahoehoe* lava, pillow lava is found under water or ice. This form of lava is named for the distinctive way it occurs: newly erupted lava is immediately surrounded by a temporary crust before the next wave of lava breaks through (like toothpaste!), forming another "pillow."

A'a: Some attribute the name of this form of lava to an old tale of how Captain Cook walked barefoot across the lava, screaming, "Ah! Ah!" Slow-moving, *a'a* lava is characterized by its rough and jagged appearance. Its flows are much thicker and have been known to pile up (sometimes to heights over 100 ft.). *A'a* lava is formed from Pahoehoe lava that is traveling fast and losing gas at the same time.

FLORA AND FAUNA

None of the plants and animals that exist in Hawaii today originated there, because Hawaii was never part of a larger landmass. Rather, they are the product of migration and transformation. Since the islands of Hawaii were formed from volcanoes on the Pacific floor, it was not until after the lava cooled that tides, winds, and birds carried seeds to the islands. Later, when **Polynesian settlers** arrived in canoes, bringing plant and animal species from their native lands, much of the flora and fauna on Hawaii developed special adaptations to their new home and evolved into brand new species. Today about 90% of the plants and animals on Hawaii are endemic, meaning that they exist nowhere else in the world.

Since Hawaii's native plants and animals evolved in the absence of predators or competitors, they did not develop natural defenses like thorns or camouflage. As a result, many native species have been pushed to the brink of extinction by alien plants and animals that have been introduced to the islands in the past few hundred years. Considered the endangered species capital of the US, Hawaii is home to more endangered species per square mile than any other place on the planet. In spite of all this, however, Hawaii still boasts an astounding degree of biodiversity.

PLANTS

There are more than 2500 species of native plants in Hawaii, as well as a consider-able number of non-native species. There are 139 different types of **ferns** in Hawaii. These lush, green plants were some of the first to arrive on the islands, sprouting up on the cooled lava flows; they form much of the ground cover in Hawaii's for-ests. Hawaii's most abundant native tree, the **'o'hia lehua,** is also among the first to spring up on fresh lava flows. Highly distinctive, the *'o'hia lehua* can identified by its crooked branches and bright red, pompom-like flowers. It is also highly adapt-able, and can survive in a multitude of environments, including elevations between 1000 and 9000 ft. above sea level.

Hawaii's second most prominent native tree is the **koa,** which, like the *'o'hia lehua,* is indigenous to the islands. Capable of growing up to 100 ft. tall, the *koa* has sickle-shaped leaves and yellow flowers clustered into puffballs. Ancient Hawaiians used the reddish wood of the *koa* tree to fashion canoes, surfboards, weapons, and other items. The hard wood is highly sought-after today as a mate-rial for making household furniture. Cattle and other feral animals have destroyed thousands of acres of Hawaiian *koa,* but fortunately the tree is highly resilient, and has thrived under recent reforestation programs.

The **Haleakala silversword,** a spherical flowering plant that grows close to the ground, nearly became extinct in the 1920s due to grazing by goats and cattle. The silversword is still very rare due to its limited range; the only place in the world it can be found is on the Haleakala volcano on Maui. However, protection programs within the Haleakala National Park have saved the species from extinction. Its thin, spiny leaves are covered with tiny silver hairs, and at the end of its 15- to 50-year life span it produces a tall stalk covered with maroon blossoms.

Ki, the **ti** plant, was a symbol of power in ancient Hawaii and was also used as a good luck charm. Sacred to the fertility god Lono and the goddess of the hula, Laka, *ki* was introduced to Hawaii by Polynesian settlers. A member of the lily family, the *ti* plant has shiny green leaves, which were used as roof thatching, food wrappers, and decoration. The leaves are still used in religious ceremonies and in floral arrangements. *Ki* grows abundantly throughout Hawaii, thriving in areas of low elevation where moisture is plentiful.

Hawaii's state flower is the **yellow hibiscus** (*pua aloalo* or *ma'o hau hele*). Ubiq-uitous throughout the islands, there are five endemic species of hibiscus in Hawaii. These brightly-colored tropical blossoms can measure up to a foot in diameter and have become a popular symbol of the state. **Orchids, plumeria, bouga-invillea,** and **birds of paradise** are also commonly found in Hawaii.

Sugarcane, pineapples, guavas, mangoes, papayas, coconuts, avocados, bananas, limes, passion fruit, macadamia nuts, *taro* (*poi*), breadfruit (*'ulu*), and ginger (*'awapuhi*) are all cultivated on Hawaii. The endangered **sandalwood** tree (*'iliahi*), famous for its aromatic oil, also grows on the islands.

ANIMALS

There are no snakes, crocodiles, or large cats on Hawaii. In fact, Hawaii boasts only two native mammals: the **Hawaiian monk seal** and the **hoary bat.** The hoary bat is Hawaii's only native land mammal. Found on the Big Island and in Koke'e State Park on Kauai, hoary bats feed on insects and, like all bats, they are nocturnal.

Unlike most seals, Hawaiian monk seals are solitary animals. They are a very old species; scientists believe that they have not evolved in 15 million years. They are primarily found in the remote regions of the Northwestern Hawaiian islands. Like many species native to Hawaii, they evolved in the absence of predators and are naturally tame. This spelled disaster for the monk seal during the 19th century, as they were killed in large numbers for their oil and pelts. Today they are considered the most endangered marine mammal in the US, with a population of around 1300-1400. Because the survival of these gentle creatures remains precarious, it is important that visitors not disturb them—please stay a safe distance away.

Humpback whales were among the first species to discover the joy of wintering in Hawaii. Each autumn they travel 3000 mi. from their arctic feeding grounds to the tropical waters of Hawaii to mate and give birth. These baleen whales grow to over 50 ft. in length and weigh 30-50 tons. They are known for their spectacular acrobatics, as well as their complex underwater mating songs. They are now an endangered species, with between 15,000 and 20,000 humpbacks worldwide, only 15-20% of the original population. Maui is the best island from which to see humpback whales, particularly in the winter, from November to February.

Hawaii's state bird, the highly endangered **nene,** or Hawaiian goose, is the rarest goose in the world—fewer than 900 exist in the wild. As they tend to nest low to the ground, their low numbers are in part attributed to predation by mongooses, as well as destruction of nests by pigs and other feral animals. Capable of living up to 4000 ft. above sea level, most *nene* live on the slopes of volcanoes on the Big Island, though they can also be found on Maui and Kauai. Thought to be closely related to the Canadian goose, the *nene* developed long toes and reduced webbing on their feet for climbing on lava flows.

Kauai has the most varied bird population of any of the Hawaiian islands. The **honeycreeper, puaiohi** (thrush), and **'o'u** (a kind of honeycreeper) are some of the more magnificent. The Big Island is also home to a number of rare birds, including several varieties of honeycreeper and the endangered **'io** (Hawaiian hawk).

There are an estimated 700 different species of fish in Hawaiian waters, many of which exist nowhere else in the world. Impress your friends by telling them about Hawaii's state fish, the **humuhumunukunukuapua'a** (pronounced HOO-moo-HOO-moo-NEW-coo-NEW-coo-AH-poo-AH-ah), or the **reef triggerfish.** This tiny tropical fish is 8-9 in. long and has a trigger-shaped, blue-and-yellow dorsal fin. There are also about 40 different species of **shark** inhabiting Hawaiian waters. The most commonly seen are **tiger sharks, reef sharks,** and **hammerheads.** Of these, the tiger shark is considered the most dangerous to humans (see **Wilderness Safety,** p. 59).

The **mongoose** was introduced to Hawaii in the late 19th century in an attempt to exterminate the rats that were overrunning sugar plantations. Unfortunately, this solution was highly ineffective, as rats are nocturnal, while mongooses are diurnal. Today mongooses abound on all of the islands except for Kauai, and they are considered pests because they prey on the eggs of ground-nesting birds, many of which are very rare. For more information on the land, plants, and animals of Hawaii, please see **Additional Resources,** p. 32.

HISTORY

EARLY HISTORY (AD 500-1778)

The original inhabitants of the Hawaiian islands are believed to have been descendents of Asiatic peoples who migrated over land and water routes, eventually landing in the Central Pacific. **Polynesian voyagers** were probably the first to discover the islands, landing near Ka Lae on the Big Island around AD 500-750. Archaeological and cultural evidence indicates that these voyagers originated from the Marquesas, an island group north of Tahiti. They navigated the South Pacific seas in double-hulled canoes, using the stars and ocean currents as guides.

500-750 AD
Polynesians arrive
from the Marque-
sas Islands

Bands of warlike **Tahitians** were the next groups of people to reach Hawaii. Hawaiian culture reflects this early Tahitian influence. Around 1175 a Tahitian *kahuna* (priest), known as Pa'ao in ancient oral histories, arrived in Hawaii. He brought with him **Pili**, the first in the royal line which led to Kamehameha. Pa'ao is thought to have founded the *kahuna nui* (high priest) line, initiating a new system of rule which lasted for the next several hundred years. One *ali'i nui*, the most powerful *ali'i* (royal) of the region, headed each island and distributed land to the chiefs below him (who then allowed the commoners to work on, but not purchase, that land) in a feudal-style system. The *ali'i* were believed to have been chosen by the gods, and served as a link between the people and the deities they worshipped. Below the *ali'i* and the priest class were the *maka'ainana* (commoners), and a third class of citizens known as *kaua*. The *kaua* were most often those who had broken *kapu* (taboo) and had neither rights nor property. The Hawaiians used little writing, and preserved most of their history in chants, known as *mele*, and legends. Much of Hawaiian history was lost with the deaths of *kahunas* and others whose duty it was to pass on the knowledge of the ancients.

1000 AD
Tahitian settlers
arrive

REDISCOVERY AND WESTERN TRADE (1778-1872)

THE BRITISH ARE COMING. The first known European to arrive in the Hawaiian islands was **Captain James Cook,** who happened upon the islands in 1778 during his third and final quest for the Northwest passage. His first glimpse of Hawaii was the island of Oahu, but it was at Kauai that he went ashore for the first time. Here he provisioned his ships by trading metal objects for food, water, and other necessities. After only a brief stop in Hawaii, Cook sailed north. He dubbed his new find the Sandwich Isles in honor of the English Earl of Sandwich.

1778
Captain Cook "dis-
covers" Hawaii and
names it the Sand-
wich Islands

About a year later, on his way back from Alaska, Cook once again spotted the Hawaiian islands, this time landing on The Big Island. Here Cook's arrival coincided with the Hawaiians' *makahiki* festival, an annual celebration of the fertility god Lono. It is possible that the islanders mistook the white sails of Cooks' ships for Lono's white *kapa* flags, and interpreted his arrival at Kealakekua Bay on The Big Island as the earthly descent of the their god. Whether or not the Hawaiians thought Cook to be an incarnation of the god Lono, Cook and his men were welcomed to the islands and allowed to trade with the islanders.

The Captain and his crews departed after two weeks of festivities, only to meet fierce storms which resulted in damage to their vessels. When they returned to Kealakekua Bay a week after having left, they found the festivities ended and the area deserted. Upon Cook's return, the Hawaiians began to lose faith in a god who could sustain such sizeable damage in his own domain. With their respect for Cook diminished, the natives helped themselves to items from Cook's ships in exchange for the supplies and gifts which they had given the British sailors upon their arrival. Cook and a small party of his men went ashore to take the island chief hostage and demand the return of their goods. The plan went awry, however, and Cook and several of his men were killed in a skirmish with the Hawaiians on Valentine's Day, 1779. Some debate has arisen among historians regarding the true manner of Cook's reception; see **Additional Resources** (p. 32) for further readings.

KAMEHAMEHA THE GREAT. At the time of Cook's discovery, the islands were under the rule of a number of warring kings. Kahekili ruled Maui, Kaho'olawe, Lanai, and later Oahu; Kahekili's brother, Kaeo, ruled Kauai; and Kalaniopuu ruled The Big Island and the Hana district of Maui. When Kalaniopuu died in 1782, he left his kingdom to his son, Kiwalo, but he left possession of the family war god, Kuka'ilimoku, to his nephew, **Kamehameha** (1758-1819), thus dividing the chiefs of the island into two factions. Although Kamehameha and his forces were ultimately victorious in a nine-year conflict with his cousin over the Big Island, it began what would become a decade of civil war throughout the Hawaiian islands. The end of the struggle came with Kamehameha's **unification** of the islands under his sole rule in 1810. His 9 yr. rule as king of all Hawaii was marked by a simple peace.

During Kamehameha's reign, the export of highly-prized **sandalwood** to China increased, facilitating trade with other nations, most notably the US and Britain. In 1819 the first whaling ships arrived in Kealakekua Bay. The **whaling industry** became profitable for the Hawaiian economy as Hawaii became a stop on New England-based whaling routes through the Pacific. The Westerners brought more with them than tools, provisions, and luxury items, however. The introduction of infectious diseases, and the spread of Western ways had a profound impact on the health and habits of the natives. Even as Kamehameha was creating peace and a strong culture for Hawaii, *haoles* (foreigners) were quietly eating up his progress.

THE KAMEHAMEHA DYNASTY. With the death of Kamehameha in 1819, power passed to his son, **Kamehameha II, Liholiho** (1796-1824). To some extent, power was really passed to Kamehameha's favorite wife, **Ka'ahumanu,** the queen regent. Under Liholiho, many changes occurred in the established religion of the islands. At Ka'ahumanu's urging, Liholiho overthrew the ancient *kapu* system by allowing men and women to eat at the same table, and announcing the destruction of *heiaus* (temples) along with the old idols. 1820 saw the arrival of the first Christian missionaries to the islands from the United States. The missionaries took advantage of the changes that had been occurring in the Hawaiian lifestyle over the previous decades to spread their Christian teachings. The missionaries established schools, developed the Hawaiian alphabet into the 12-letter form known today, and used this alphabet to translate the Bible into Hawaiian. Moving with the changes coming to his country, Liholiho

1810
Kamehameha the Great unites the islands into one kingdom

1813
Spanish explorers introduce the pineapple to Hawaii

1819
Kamehameha dies; Prince Liholiho ascends the throne, does away with the *kapu* system

1820
Missionaries arrive from Boston

became the first Hawaiian king to venture out of the islands. In 1823, he and his wife made their first and only official state visit to England, where they both contracted measles and died not long after.

On the occasion of Liholiho's death in 1824, Kamehameha's second son, **Kauikeaouli, Kamehameha III** (1813-1854), became king. Only nine when he received the crown, Kamehameha III was raised amidst the changing Hawaiian culture. His actions during his lifetime represent this cultural confusion. In 1839, Kamehameha III introduced Hawaii's first constitution, the Declaration of Rights, which is regarded as the Hawaiian Magna Carta. With this declaration, Hawaii ceased to be an absolute monarchy. Eight years later, Kamehameha III enacted The Great *Mahele* (division), effectively ending the traditional feudal style of land ownership. True to its name, the edict divided land between the *ali'i* and the *maka'aina* (commoners), and provided the first legal basis for private land ownership. The division opened the door for the purchase of land not only by previously disenfranchised Native Hawaiians, but also by *haoles* and commercial investors.

Kamehameha IV (1834-1863) ruled from 1855-1863. His was a short reign, marked by a further deterioration of traditional Hawaiian culture in favor of the Christian model. **Kamehameha V** (1830-1872), who reigned from 1863-1872, established a controversial constitution in 1864 that gave more power to the king, taking away power from elected officials at the same time. Both Kamehameha IV and Kamehameha V were heirless, and when Kamehameha V died in 1872, his genetic line died with him. All Hawaiian kings were thereafter elected.

SUGAR AND PINEAPPLES (1840-1940)

The freeing up of land in Hawaii in 1848 coincided with the beginning of the decline of the whaling industry and a subsequent movement toward the development of agriculture. By the end of the 19th century, sugar and pineapple plantations run by American businessmen had overtaken much of Hawaii's land and the crops were the two most important sources of revenue for the Hawaiian economy. The first sugar plantation in Hawaii, the **Koloa Plantation** on Kauai, was founded in 1835, initiating an explosion in the sugar industry as mills began to appear all over the islands. In 1850, the Hawaiian legislature approved the hiring of immigrant laborers from Japan, China, the Phillipines and Portugal to work in the booming **sugar industry.** The inhabitants of today's Hawaii reflect the diversity of these immigrant laborers. Ultimately, the importation of workers and the changes in land ownership laws took land away from natives, land used instead for sugar mills.

The massive Hawaiian **pineapple** industry began as a one-man operation but today Hawaii produces one-third of the world's commercial supply of pineapples. James D. Dole planted his first pineapple trees near Wahiawa on Oahu in 1901, and founded the **Hawaiian Pineapple Company.** In 1922, Dole purchased the island of Lanai for the purpose of large-scale pro-

1825
Kamehameha III comes to power

1835
First sugar plantation started at Koloa on Kauai

1839
Declaration of Rights and Edict of Toleration

1840
First constitution of Hawaii established

1848
The Great Mahele

duction; by 1950 his was the largest pineapple company in the world. Dole was eventually bought out by the **Castle & Cooke** company, which still owns much of Lanai. Pineapples were the state's second-biggest industry until the mid-1940s.

ANNEXATION AND AMERICAN INFLUENCE (1875-1900)

THE END OF THE MONARCHY. David Kalakaua (1836-1891) was elected king in 1874. The "Merrie Monarch" began his reign with a world tour to meet other heads of state, including an 1881 visit to the United States which marked the first time a Hawaiian king had visited the mainland. Kalakaua was proud of Hawaiian culture, and promoted traditional Hawaiian customs and heritage at home and abroad. He reintroduced the hula and wrote the lyrics for the Hawaiian national anthem, *Hawaii Ponoi*, which is now the state song. The end of his reign was not so joyous; rather, it was marred by corruption and contention.

Among the controversial acts enacted under Kalakaua's reign was the **Reciprocity Treaty of 1875.** Under the treaty, Hawaiian sugar was admitted tax-free into the US, and in return a number of American products could enter Hawaii duty-free. The treaty appeared to give Hawaiian sugar a favorable position in US markets, but it also consolidated American economic supremacy in Hawaiian trade. This influenced the course of events in changes in the power of Hawaiian monarchy by strengthening the influence of American sugar interests in the kingdom.

In 1887, Kalakaua signed the **Bayonet Constitution,** which revised Kamehameha V's Constitution of 1864. The act, so named because it was signed under threat of armed disturbance, undermined the king's authority, transferring much of his power to the cabinet. Stipulations of the Constitution included the election of the nobility rather than their appointment by the king, and a provision allowing foreigners with at least one year of residency in Hawaii the right to vote, if they paid taxes and pledged to honor the constitution. The act enfranchised foreign businessmen, increasing their control over politics in the islands.

Controversy over the constitution and struggles for political power under Kalakaua carried over into the reign of his sister, **Queen Liliuokalani.** Hawaii's last monarch and only reigning queen ascended to the throne in 1891 following the death of her brother. The 1892 session of the legislature was made up of three political parties: the National Reform Party which supported the Queen; the Reform Party which opposed strengthening the crown and therefore opposed Liliuokalani; and the Liberal Party. The major concerns of the 1892 session of the Hawaiian legislature were the themes of the Bayonet Constitution—control of the cabinet and changes in the constitution.

Upon gaining power, Liliuokalani appointed members of the National Reform Party to the cabinet; they were promptly voted out of office. Undaunted, Liliuokalani appointed

1864
David Kalakaua becomes king

1875
Hawaii and US enter into the Reciprocity Treaty

1881
Macadamia nuts first introduced to Hawaii

1885
First large group of Japanese immigrant workers arrive to work in sugar plantations

1887
Bayonet Constitution

1889
Father Damien dies on the Kalaupapa leper colony on Molokai (see p. 259)

HAWAII

another set of National Reform Party members who met the same unfortunate fate as their predecessors. Working under the third-time's-the-charm hypothesis the Queen then appointed a cabinet of Reform Party members, in order to get the state moving. This plan backfired, however, as frustrated Liberal Party members joined the National Reform Party in a move to overthrow the Reform Party instead. The Queen again appointed members of the National Reform Party to the cabinet right before the legislature adjourned.

Bills to amend the constitution and expand suffrage to the common people were rejected for the second time when the legislature reconvened in 1892. This denial of voting rights elicited widespread protest. Queen Liliuokalani, slowed by ministers who feared a backlash from the white business community, failed to move quickly enough to ratify the proposals. In the meantime, the **Annexationist Club,** a group of white plantation owners who had banded together earlier that year, held a secret meeting to discuss the proceedings in government. The group formed a Committee of Public Safety, and decided on a plan to get rid of the monarchy, set up a provisional government, and put forth a bid for US annexation of the islands.

AMERICAN RULE BEGINS. Queen Liliuokalani abdicated and the provisional government gained power in 1893, thanks to the force and manipulations of the Annexationist Club. The Queen stepped down under protest with the belief that the United States would not enforce the annexation. Representatives from the provisional government and Queen Liliuokalani went to Washington to plead their respective cases. Queen Lili-uokalani's representatives were delayed, however, as they were denied passage on a plantation-owned ship while the representatives from the annexationists proceeded to Washington, an incident which reflects the relative political power and influence of white planters in Hawaii at the time.

US President Grover Cleveland did not immediately ratify the annexation since it appeared that most Hawaiians were opposed to the revolution. President Cleveland sent **James Blount,** a former chairman of the House Foreign Affairs Committee, to investigate the conditions of the overthrow of the monarchy. Blount's report indicated that the majority of Hawaiians had not favored the move, and that American plantation owners had incited the revolt in order to further their own business interests. Blount charged that the uprising had been the result of pressure from revolutionary leaders and United States Minister John L. Stevens.

The annexationists succeeded in establishing a provisional government headed by Sanford B. Dole in 1894, despite the US government's subsequent attempts to restore Queen Lili-uokalani. In 1898, under President Cleveland's successor William McKinley, a joint resolution of the US Congress approved **official annexation** of Hawaii. Native Hawaiians made a silent protest to the action by boycotting the ceremonies. The islands were made a US **territory** in 1900, with Dole as governor.

1893
Queen Liliuokalani overthrown; provisional government established, led by Sanford B. Dole

1900
Hawaii made a US territory

1912
Duke Kahan-amoku participates in the Olympics in Stockholm

1921
Hawaiian Homes Commission Act passed

1927
First non-stop flight to Hawaii from the US mainland

1941
Japanese forces attack US military base at Pearl Harbor

WORLD WAR II (1941-1945)

A DAY THAT WILL LIVE IN INFAMY. In 1941, on the other side of the world European nations were caught in the horror of **WWII.** The US had yet to be drawn into the war, although their eventual participation seemed inevitable. For the Japanese, the war provided an opportunity to capitalize on European preoccupation with war to make a bid for supremacy in Southeast Asia through the capture of former European colonial holdings. One of the few obstacles left in their way was the sizeable American fleet that lay within striking distance of the South Pacific—the fleet based at **Pearl Harbor,** Hawaii (see p. 136).

At 7:55am on the morning of December 7, 1941, Japanese fighter jets swooped through the still air of the military base at Pearl Harbor, initiating a surprise strike that would prove to be one of the single most destructive attacks in naval history. The Japanese objective was the obliteration of the fighting capacity of the seven US battleships moored there, and the American military strength in the Pacific as a whole. As air strikes rained on the battleships, Japanese fighter pilots also targeted the American bombers at nearby airfields.

Many on board the ships and on the shore thought the attack was nothing more than another military drill until they saw the marks of the "rising sun" on the sides of the Japanese planes and witnessed the destruction. Of the seven battleships, the **USS Arizona** suffered the most severe damage, taking seven bombs and hits from an aerial torpedo. One of the bombs fell through the steel decks, detonating stored ammunition; the twisted hull of the ship lies as a poignant monument to the 1102 men still entombed within. The attack seriously weakened American air strength in the Pacific and took the lives of over 2400 American military personnel and civilians. Despite the destruction, the attack on Pearl Harbor ultimately propelled the United States into the conflict, in both the Pacific and European theaters.

HAWAII'S ROLE IN THE PACIFIC THEATER. As the United States reeled from the attack and began to prepare itself for war, Hawaii, a territory annexed by the US, was ruled by **martial law.** Martial law was declared directly following the attack on Pearl Harbor, and was not lifted until October of 1944. During this time the writ of *habeas corpus* was suspended, and all those considered suspicious were rounded up and placed in custody at immigration stations.

Hawaii continued to serve as a base for military operations in the Pacific following the attack at Pearl Harbor. The next notable clash in the Pacific islands was the **Battle of Midway** in June of 1942. The battle—a victory for the US—was a turning point for the American forces in the Pacific and marked Hawaii's movement from a combat zone to a training facility and military base. Today Hawaii hosts the largest combined American military presence in the world.

Hawaiian citizens stepped up to take part in the war effort. Some civilians participated in domestic defense and administration; island-born Japanese served as language interpreters

1941
US enters WWII

1941
Martial law declared in Hawaii; Japanese citizens are held suspect

1942
Battle of Midway

1944
Martial law lifted in Hawaii

HAWAII

for the military. Many others took up arms. Among these were a contingent of Americans of Japanese descent (AJAs) who were discharged from the Hawaii Territorial Guard, most likely as a result of paranoia regarding those of Japanese descent. About 1400 of these Hawaiian men banded together to form the **100th battalion,** which fought valiantly in the European theater, earning itself the nickname the "Purple Heart Regiment."

War continued to rage in the Pacific for several months after the European theater ended on **V-E Day** (Victory in Europe), May 8, 1945. The Pacific theater closed with the Japanese surrender on September 1, 1945 **(V-J Day)** following the dropping of two atomic bombs on Japan.

CONSUMER CULTURE TO TOURIST CULTURE (1945-1970)

LABOR UNIONS. World War II brought changes to the Hawaiian lifestyle, including military restrictions and shortages, as well as an influx of *haoles* from the mainland. Following the war, whites employed by the military vacated the islands and locals returned, but development continued. Immigration restrictions, high wages, and the end of the war reduced the labor force and resulted in an increased reliance on mechanization in the sugar and pineapple industries. A labor freeze in 1944 and discontent among workers led the way to a mass unionization in Hawaii's major industries, headed by the International Warehousemen's and Longshoremen's Union **(IWLU)**. The momentum of the labor movement pushed the National Labor Relations Board to pass the Hawaii Employment Relations Act in 1945, which granted the same rights to agricultural workers as those granted to industrial workers. IWLU's regional director, **Jack Hall,** was a prominent figure in Hawaii's labor movement during the post-war years.

Union supporters joined with AJAs and Democrats to shift the political dominance in Hawaii from the Republican party, electing a number of Democrats to political office and expanding the ethnic diversity of the party ticket. In 1956, **Jack Burns,** a force in Hawaiian politics during the last half of the 20th century, became Hawaii's first Democratic Congressman since the 1930s.

THE QUESTION OF STATEHOOD. In 1937 the first bill promoting Hawaii's conversion to statehood was put forth in the US Congress. It and bills like it were defeated for a number of reasons including the problem of distance, concerns with destruction of traditional Hawaiian ways of life, and the interest of the population in becoming part of the United States. In the islands, the sugar industry and other businesses were concerned with the move to statehood and doubts about the balance in representation between the islands' ethnic groups existed as well.

A proposal for Hawaiian statehood was originally presented as part of a combined bill for both Hawaiian and Alaskan statehood. The combination complicated the congressional political processes during the debate of the plan, and progress stalled.

1945
V-E Day
V-J Day

1946
Devastating tsunami hits Hilo on the Big Island; "Great Sugar Strike" organized by the ILWG

1953
First bikinis seen on Waikiki beach

1959
Hawaii becomes 50th US state

Hawaiians favored the move to statehood, and in 1954 over 110,000 islanders signed a **petition** urging Congress to act. Hawaii and Alaska were eventually put on separate bills, and in 1959 Hawaii became the **50th US state.**

THE GROWTH OF TOURISM. Advances in air travel and increased investment in the islands during World War II helped to expand the tourism industry in the islands. Once Hawaii became a state, it was marketed on the mainland as the **"American Paradise,"** and tourists flocked to experience it. By the 1970s, tourism had a firm position as the state's **top industry,** surpassing the military.

THE HAWAIIAN RENAISSANCE

HAWAIIAN HOME LANDS. In the early 1920s, **Prince Kuhio,** a member of the nobility and a Republican delegate to Congress, spearheaded the passage of the **Hawaiian Homes Commission Act.** The Act, which became law in 1921, was meant to protect Native Hawaiians by releasing public lands for the purposes of agricultural development and homesteading, much of it on the island of Molokai. The Act also set up a Commission to administer the program. The success of the program itself was questionable, since much of the land was leased to corporations. It was, however, a part of the movement that gained particular significance in the wake of the tourism boom during the post-war years.

1969
Hawaii Five-O debuts on TV

Hawaiian activism in the 1970s focused on *aloha'aina,* or love for the land. One of the first markers of the movement was a confrontation over land use in Kalama Valley in 1970. A group of 5000 Hawaiians near Waimanalo formed **The Hawaiians,** and lobbied in protest of the **Department of Hawaiian Home Lands** administration of the Home Lands Act. Up to that time, the Department had appropriated only 20% of its 200,000+ acres to Native Hawaiians. The group was successful in its bid to obtain more lots for natives. Continuing in the tradition of the Hawaiian Homes Commission Act, the **Office of Hawaiian Affairs (OHA)** was founded in 1978 for the protection of the interests of Native Hawaiians, using revenue from public lands.

1976
Voyage of the outrigger canoe *Hokule'a*

KAHO'OLAWE. The tiny island of Kaho'olawe has been another focal point of the *aloha'aina* movement. During the 19th century, goats and sheep roamed the island, devastating plant life and causing massive erosion. The US Navy seized the island at the start of World War II to use it as a target and training area for bombing practice. The Navy failed to return the island at the end of the war, and in 1953 an Executive Order placed the island under the control of the Secretary of the Navy on the condition that it would be returned in a "habitable condition" once the Navy no longer needed it. The island lay littered with military wreckage for another 20 years until the formation of **Project Kaho'olawe 'Ohana** in 1976. Kaho'olawe 'Ohana challenged the Navy and the government by carrying out a series of occupations which brought national attention to the move-

1978
Office of Hawaiian Affairs established

1980
Magnum P.I. debuts on TV

HAWAII

1983
Kilauea volcano begins erupting on the Big Island. It's still going.
Hurricane Iniki hits Kauai

1993
US Congress passes the Apology Resolution

ment. Kahoʻolawe ʻOhana settled a federal suit against the Navy in 1980 with a Consent Decree that allowed access to the island for educational, scientific, and cultural purposes.

In 1993, the Hawaii State Legislature established the **Kahoʻolawe Island Reserve,** consisting of the island proper and all the waters around it in a 2 mi. radius. The area was preserved solely for Native Hawaiian cultural, spiritual, environmental, educational, and historical purposes; commercial usage is strictly prohibited. Congress also passed a law requiring the Navy both to return the island to the state and to conduct a cleanup and environmental restoration of the area. Under the bill, federal funding is allocated to the project through November 2003. Rounding out the list of major legislative events in 1993 was the **"Apology Resolution"** passed in the US Congress, which apologized to Native Hawaiians for the overthrow of the monarchy in 1893, and for the deprivation of rights to self-determination.

HOKULEʻA. On May 2, 1976 a double-hulled canoe, a replica of the kind that brought the first Polynesians to Hawaii, departed from the islands to begin an overseas voyage recreating the route of those ancient mariners. The vessel, the *Hokuleʻa* ("star of gladness") was named in honor of Hawaii's **zenith star,** also known as **Arcturus.** The 17-man crew traversed the seas using ancient navigational methods, relying only upon the stars and ocean currents as guides. When they arrived in Tahiti, there were more than 25,000 spectators waiting to greet them.

The voyage was not only a physical triumph, but a cultural one as well, creating a focal point for Hawaiian pride. After its successful journey, the vessel was taken to schools throughout Hawaii and used as an educational tool to promote knowledge of Hawaiian heritage. The boat ultimately capsized in a storm off the coast of Molokai in 1978, but not before making a lasting impact on the Hawaiian renaissance movement.

HAWAII TODAY

THE END OF THE TWENTIETH CENTURY. Within the last decade, there have been moves to rectify the injustices of Hawaii's past. Both Dole's Iwilei pineapple cannery and the last sugar plantation on the Big Island closed in 1992 and 1995, respectively. The US government also recognized their own role in the disenfranchisement of Native Hawaiian peoples, and in the destruction of Hawaiian land during the 19th century. **Tourism** remained the primary industry of the state, despite a slump in economic and population growth. In 1992, **Hurricane Iniki** hit the island of Kauai and the western shores of Oahu. The storm was the strongest hurricane to hit the islands in a century and caused mass destruction.

1995
The last sugar plantation in Hawaii closes

2000
US Supreme Court decides *Rice v. Cayetano*

THE NEW MILLENNIUM. The US Supreme Court case of **Rice v. Cayetano** (2000) was another seminal event in the series of legislative moves regarding the rights of Native Hawaiians. The ruling declared that the restriction of voting in the Office of Hawaiian Affairs to Native Hawaiians violates the 15th Amendment. The issue of ethnicity regulations gained another dimension in 2002, when **Kamehameha Schools**

admitted a non-Hawaiian student to their Maui campus. Heated debate erupted over the schools' admissions policies, which have traditionally limited the acceptance pool to students of Hawaiian blood. Many critics of the school's actions claim that they are an attempt to protect the school from claims of discrimination and, in turn, safeguard its tax-free status. (See **The Kamehameha One**, p. 214.)

Air travel suffered following the tragedy on **September 11, 2001,** when hijacked planes crashed into the World Trade Center in New York City, the Pentagon in Washington, D.C., and in Pennsylvania, claiming thousands of lives. Hawaii saw a significant decline in tourism, as it is primarily accessible by plane. However, tourism in Hawaii has been returning to normal levels throughout 2003.

PEOPLE

DEMOGRAPHICS

The people of Hawaii are world-famous for their spirit of *aloha*. This attitude of friendly acceptance is characterized by a sense of warmth, kindness, generosity, humility, and patience.

The secret to Hawaiian harmony may lie in the fact that Hawaii is one of the few places in the US, and perhaps the world, where there is no racial or ethnic majority. The state population of 1.2 million (2000) is 24% white (*haole*), 19% Hawaiian, 17% Japanese, 14% Filipino, 5% Chinese, 2% Korean, 2% black, and 20% mixed. Less than 1% of those who identify themselves as Hawaiian are pure Hawaiians, and the high incidence of intermarriage among people of different races and ethnicities makes the population even more diverse.

Among the Hawaiians who have made a name for themselves on the mainland are entertainer **Don Ho;** politician **Hiram L. Fong,** the first Chinese-American senator, elected in 1959; astronaut **Ellison Onizuka**, a member of the ill-fated 1986 Challenger crew; legendary **Duke Kahanamoku,** Olympic swimmer and gold medalist who introduced surfing to the non-Hawaiian world; 6'9", 510 lb. **Akebono** (Chad Rowan), the first foreign grand champion in sumo wrestling's 2000-year history; and actress **Tia Carrere,** of *Wayne's World* and *Lilo and Stitch*.

LANGUAGE

ʻŌleo Hawaiʻi, the Hawaiian language, belongs to a family of Polynesian languages which also includes Tahitian, Maori, Tumotuan, and Rarotongan. Hawaiian's reduplication, apparent in words like *wikiwiki* (fast), its application of glottal stops (symbolized by the *ʻokina* (ʻ) and similar to what comes between the "uh" and the "oh" in "uh-oh"), and the prolific use of vowels make it particularly distinctive. The key to speaking Hawaiian is to pronounce every vowel: the Likelike Hwy. is pronounced "lee-kay-lee-kay."

ʻŌleo Hawaiʻi was a strictly oral language until the arrival of Captain James Cook in 1778 and the Protestant missionaries who flocked to the island thereafter. The missionaries' primary

HAWAII

2001
Terrorist attacks on the mainland claim the lives of thousands, sending shockwaves through the nation

2002
Hawaii passes a bill to become the first state to put a cap on gasoline prices. First edition of *Let's Go Hawaii* begins production

goal was to teach the islanders to read the Bible, so they set about giving the Hawaiian language a written form. What emerged was a 12-letter alphabet that became the official **writing system** of the Hawaiian government.

When Hawaii was annexed by the US in 1898, ʻŌleo Hawaiʻi was banned from schools and government and English became the state's official language. ʻŌleo Hawaiʻi dwindled to near-extinction until the 1970s, when a Hawaiian cultural renaissance (see **History,** p. 19) rekindled interest in the language. In 1978, ʻŌleo Hawaiʻi again became an official language of the State of Hawaii (along with English), and it remains the only Native American language that is officially used by a state government. By 1987, public schools were teaching the language, and the number of speakers continues to grow today.

Hawaii's *unofficial* language is **Hawaiian Creole** or **Pidgin.** A by-product of Hawaii's tremendous diversity, Pidgin developed as a means of communication between people who spoke different languages for use in business transactions. It integrates elements from Hawaiian, English, Chinese, and Japanese, among others. Nearly all Hawaiians incorporate some Pidgin into their daily conversation, though it is primarily used by teenagers. While Native Hawaiians often appreciate attempts by visitors to speak ʻŌleo Hawaiʻi, it is inadvisable for visitors to try to speak Pidgin, as it is usually considered condescending.

HOOKED ON EH*BRAHN*ICS Few foreigners can pull off speaking Pidgin, but here are some fun translations so you can understand local-speak, at least. Find more translations and jokes submitted by local Hawaiians, at www.e-hawaii.com/fun/jokes/.

English: Hello. How are you?
Pidgin: Howzit?
English: Excuse me. You seem to be blocking my path of travel. Would you mind stepping to the side, please?
Pidgin: Try move.
English: Please, officer, I give you my word that I will no longer travel in excess of the speed limit. I beg you not to write that ticket.
Pidgin: Eh, you know my uncle?
English: That is an excellent idea. I am in full concurrence with your plan. Let us do the deal.
Pidgin: Shoots!

RELIGION

Prior to contact with the West, life in Hawaii was governed by the system of **kapu,** or taboo, meaning literally "obey or die." Every aspect of the early Hawaiians' daily life was regulated by this strict set of rules and customs. The *kapu*, while often restrictive and unfair, was largely responsible for the high degree of order in early Hawaiian society. **Kahunas** (priests) wielded considerable power in early Hawaii and were responsible for enforcing the *kapu*. Among their other responsibilities were healing, canoe-building, and leading the islands' chiefs in elaborate religious ceremonies carried out in meticulous detail, as the slightest deviation from *aha* (perfection) would incur the wrath of the gods.

Hawaiians believed that all natural phenomena were controlled by the gods, whose aid and protection they sought through offerings and worship. Particularly in times of trouble, sacrifices—sometimes even human sacrifices—would be made in order to appease the gods and encourage them to look upon the people with favor. Idols were a key element of early Hawaiian religion, as it was believed that they represented a link between mankind and the gods. Every home had a *kuaʻaha* (altar) where families worshipped their *aumaka* (guardian deities). *Akua* (greater gods) were worshipped in more complex ceremonies in *heiaus* (open-air temples), which were presided over by *kahunas*. Among the *akua* are: **Kane,** god of creation; **Ku,** god of war; **Lono,** god of peace, prosperity, wind, rain, and fertility; **Kanaloa,** god of the ocean; and **Pele,** goddess of the volcano.

The **Kumulipo,** an ancient Hawaiian *mele oli* (chant), tells the Hawaiian version of the story of creation. Handed down from generation to generation in the oral tradition, the *kahunas* would memorize the poem, which consists of over 2000 lines, and recite it on special occasions, such as the birth of a first-born child or at festivals honoring the gods. The early Hawaiians believed that the night gave birth to *kumulipo*, the source of all life. Interestingly, it appears that they also believed in some degree of evolution, as the *Kumulipo* describes how organisms were created, starting with the simplest and gradually progressing to the complex.

After the death of Kamehameha around 1820, just before the arrival of missionaries from the West, the cult of the ancient Hawaiians dissolved. *Heiaus* and idols were destroyed, and the *kapu* was abolished, making way for the new religion—Christianity—that was soon to arrive. Elements of this earlier belief system persist in Hawaii today, however, as evidenced by the proliferation of miniature idols. Many people—locals and tourists alike—still make offerings to Pele and other deities in attempts to win their favor.

As one would expect, religion in Hawaii today is as varied as its colorful and diverse population. Protestants, Catholics, Jews, Buddhists, Hindus, and a melange of others exist peacefully alongside one another. Travelers will have no difficulty finding services to meet their spiritual needs, regardless of their faith. For more reading on the people of Hawaii, please see **Additional Resources,** p. 32

CULTURE

VERTICALLY CHALLENGED The *menehune* legends are a colorful part of Hawaii's culture. Stories about these fabled "little people" abound. The *menehune* are credited with being superior builders who could construct impressive structures overnight; **Kauai's Alekoko Fishpond** and **Menehune Ditch** are said to be examples of their handywork.

According to scholars, the *menehune* lore has historical roots. Though the theories vary slightly, most agree that the name "menehune" comes from the Tahitian word for slaves or people of small status, *manahune*. Polynesians from the Marquesas Islands settled Hawaii sometime around the 6th century. Roughly 600 years later, conquerors from the Tahitian Islands arrived in Hawaii. Before long, they succeeded in subjugating the Marquesans and forcing them north, to Kauai. The Tahitians looked down upon the original settlers, contemptuously calling them *manahune*. Some historians speculate that the *menehune* legends were born when Western writers heard of the *manahune* and misconstrued the term to mean people of small size. With their active imaginations and a little help from amused Hawaiian contacts (who obligingly revised and expanded their knowledge of the "little people"), the *menehune* tradition was born.

FOOD

Hawaiian culture is intricately tied to food. In many ways, the confluence of backgrounds and ethnicities that makes up Hawaii's unique population is most evident in local culinary favorites. Most popular dishes combine elements of several cultures and incorporate unique island ingredients. Much like Hawaii residents, island fare is unpretentious and low-key; anything that isn't beach-friendly is immediately suspect.

The epitome of local cuisine is the **plate lunch**. It's practically sacrilegious to leave the islands without trying this meal. Plate lunches are available almost everywhere, from roadside stands to fast-food chains. The meal is a descendant of the Japanese plantation worker's **bento**, a bucket lunch consisting of rice, meat, and pickled vegetables. A typical plate lunch is a combination of two scoops of white rice, one scoop of macaroni salad, and an entree. For the entree, most places offer an overwhelming array of choices. At the very least, most menus list Japanese teriyaki or *katsu*, Korean short ribs, Filipino *adobo*, Chinese soy-sauce chicken, hamburgers, and chili. Quantity often trumps quality in this island version of comfort food. Most plate lunches (inexpensive at $6-8) can usually feed two people.

Many other local favorites have been taken from outside cultures and adapted over the years. **Saimin,** Japanese noodle soup known as Ramen on the mainland, is so common that even McDonalds offers a fast-food version. Locals turn the packaged noodles into more of a stew, adding vegetables, tofu, leftover meat, or dumplings—whatever is handy. **Crack seed,** residents' preferred snack, is a generic term that refers to a type of preserved fruit that was brought to Hawaii by Chinese plantation workers. Many generations of kids and teenagers have flocked to neighborhood crack seed shops for afterschool snacks. The little stores are packed with island delicacies—Japanese rice crackers (*arare*), peanuts, coconut candy, dried squid—in addition to the huge glass jars filled with varieties of crack seed. The most popular versions of the treat are **li hing** (a distinct sweet-sour seasoning), plum and mango.

Some other local treats are Hawaiian to the core. **Shave ice** comes from the old days, when islanders would shave blocks of ice into a fine powder and top it with fruit juice. Since then, electricity has taken the grunt work out of the process, but the idea remains the same. Toppings include the basic flavored syrups as well as fancier options such as ice cream, condensed milk, shaved *li hing mui*, and *azuki* beans. **Spam,** the lovable spiced ham in a can, rounds out any true Hawaiian's diet. After being introduced to Spam by the military during World War II, islanders quickly incorporated the food into their cooking. Despite mainland conceptions of Spam as pedestrian and unappealing, islanders are addicted. Hawaii now boasts the highest Spam consumption in the world (1100 cans daily). **Spam musubi,** sticky rice topped by Spam and wrapped in dried seaweed, is one of the most popular forms of the food's preparation. **Poi** is another unique island dish. Made out of pounded *taro* root, *poi* is a thick, purplish-grey paste. Though it has no strong flavor, *poi's* unfamiliar consistency and appearance make it an acquired taste. However, locals swear by it, their children grow up on it, and some even rave about its semi-magical healing powers.

In recent years, Hawaii-based chefs have developed a style of cooking they call **Hawaii Regional Cuisine.** Led by **Sam Choy, Alan Wong,** and **Roy Yamaguchi,** the chefs have taken advantage of Hawaii's unique ingredients to create a type of cuisine that honors Hawaii's diverse culture while meeting the highest culinary standards.

LUAUS

Under *kanawai*, the ancient Hawaiian system of laws, certain things were *kapu*, or forbidden. *Kapu* dictated that women eat separately from the men; in addition, women were prohibited from eating many island delicacies. However, in 1819, King Kamehameha II held a huge feast, during which he ate with women. With the event, the ancient religious traditions died and the **luau** was born.

The *luau* takes its name from the young *taro* (see *poi*, above) leaves that are used in the preparation of many *luau* dishes. Originally a celebration giving thanks to the gods, the *luau* has become one of the most well-known aspects of

Hawaiian culture. Birthdays, anniversaries, and any other significant events are marked with these feasts. The tourist industry has capitalized on the marketability of the *luau;* almost every major hotel and restaurant offers some version.

Historically, *luau* guests sat on woven mats laid on the floor and used their fingers to devour the feast. Many modern-day *luaus* are still held on the grass, though bigger celebrations might have tents and picnic tables. There is almost always some form of musical entertainment, whether it is a cousin strumming a guitar or an entire group complete with ukulele, steel guitar, and bass. The main focus of any *luau* is the traditionally-prepared **kalua pig.** The meat is covered in *ti* or banana leaves and roasted in an **imu** (underground oven). The meat is supplemented by other island dishes, such as **poi, poke** (raw, seasoned sashimi), **lau lau** (meat wrapped in *taro* leaves and coconut milk, then steamed), and **lomi salmon** (salted salmon with tomatoes and Maui onions). The meal is finished with a dessert of **haupia** (coconut pudding), **pineapple,** and **coconut cake.**

HAWAIIAN DRESS

On any given day, locals look beach-ready. The preferred style of dress often incorporates one or more of the following: **slippers** (plastic flip-flops), **board shorts,** other **surf-inspired clothing,** and anything **aloha print.** One of the most popular elements of Hawaiian dress, the **aloha shirt,** actually owes its inspiration to both Western and Asian cultures. Supposedly a descendant of the thick "thousand-mile" shirt worn by pioneers and missionaries, the *aloha* shirt came into its familiar form in the late 1920s at the hands of Waikiki tailor **Ellery J. Chun.** The style only became common, however, after **Herbert Briner** began mass-manufacturing the shirts in the late 1930s. During the 1950s, the *aloha* shirt craze spread to the mainland when audiences saw icons like Elvis Presley, John Wayne, and Frank Sinatra wearing them in feature films. In response to the widespread mimicking of the *aloha* shirt, the Hawaii Chamber of Commerce ruled in the 1960s that a true *aloha* shirt must be made in Hawaii. Currently, the only company to design and produce shirts entirely in Hawaii is **Reyn Spooner.**

CUSTOMS & ETIQUETTE

Hawaii residents place so much stock in the **aloha spirit** that there is an actual law in the Hawaii Revised Statutes (section 5-7.5) that requires residents to abide by the spirit of ancient Hawaiians. And, for the most part, locals do. Smiles abound and islanders are quick to wave hello, usually in the form of **shaka,** a greeting made by extending the pinkie and thumb and curling up the middle three fingers of the right hand. It is especially popular with young people in Hawaii; the gesture is a way of saying, "hang loose" or "relax." The word **aloha** is also used extensively throughout the islands. Don't be afraid to use it to say hello; it's not regarded as corny. The **lei,** a garland of flowers, shells, leaves, or even candy, is a traditional Hawaiian symbol of love or friendship. Visitors entering and leaving Hawaii are often gifted with the fragrant necklaces. *Leis* are also given to mark special occasions like anniversaries, birthdays, and graduations.

While Hawaii is extremely laid-back, there are a few things that travelers should keep in mind. Hawaii is inhabited by an exceptionally diverse group of people, but the only people who are referred to as **Hawaiian** are those of Hawaiian blood. Anyone born in the islands, except Caucasians, is a **local.** The term **haole** for Caucations is not necessarily offensive. Residents who were born outside of Hawaii but have lived in the state for a considerable amount of time are known as **kama'aina.**

Respect is a key word in Hawaiian culture. It is especially important to treat sacred sites, such as *heiaus*, with appropriate consideration. When entering a person's home, it is polite to remove your shoes. Lay off the horn when driving and follow the speed limit. Don't litter.

YOU KNOW YOU'RE LOCAL IF...

You give directions using *mauka* and *makai*.

Your only suit is a bathing suit.

You let other cars ahead of you on the freeway and give *shaka* to others letting you in.

You call everyone older than you "Auntie" or "Uncle."

You drive barefoot.

You can correctly pronounce Kalanianaole, Kalakaua, and Aiea.

You raise your chin in greeting, instead of nodding (like one *haole*).

It's 70° and you're freezing.

You say "shave ice," not "snow cone" or "shaved ice."

The only time you honk your horn is once a year during the safety check.

Find more jokes and local Hawaiian lore at the web site whose goal is to reflect Hawaii and the aloha spirit: www.e-hawaii.com/fun/jokes/.

THE ARTS

ARCHITECTURE. Hawaii's architecture reflects its varied past. **Heiaus** are a remnant of ancient Hawaiian religion. These simple structures were built as temples to the gods and typically consist of altars and taboo houses enclosed by lava or limestone walls. Many, albeit in varying stages of disrepair, still stand today and there have been initiatives to restore them to their original state.

Plantation-style houses are another throwback to Hawaii's past. Built to house immigrant workers from China, Japan, and the Phillipines, the houses were grouped in villages. They stood on lava rock foundations and featured single-wall construction and cedar shingle roofs. The **plantation-style commercial structures** of this era were much more elaborate, often consisting of multiple buildings grouped around a courtyard. The main building would sometimes be modeled in mainland-style, with wide canopies extending over the sidewalk. The **Honolulu Hale** and the **Hawaii State Public Library** are examples of this design.

Along with Christianity, missionaries also brought a more ostentatious style of architecture. Neo-classical edifices like the **Iolani Palace** and gothic structures like the **Cathedral of Saint Andrew's** were built in the late 19th century and strongly reflect Western influences. Most residential houses in Hawaii have been built with regard to the islands' tropical climate. They are typically low, airy structures that make full use of tradewinds.

ARTS. Though it may never rival New York City or Paris, Hawaii has a healthy art community. Along with numerous private galleries, Oahu has two notable art museums. The **Honolulu Academy of the Arts** recently celebrated its 75th birthday. The museum has a permanent stock of over 35,000 pieces, including a celebrated collection of Asian art. The less conventional **Contemporary Museum** has two locations on Oahu. Part of the organization's mission dictates that a significant portion of its exhibitions must focus on art created in Hawaii. Maui too has a strong coalition of artists and art lovers. Each year, the island hosts **Art Maui**, a prestigious exhibition of about 100 new works by Maui County artists.

Hawaii has inspired a number of extraordinary artists. Though prominent oil painter **John Young** died in 1999, he is remembered by a museum within the University of Hawaii. The **John Young Museum of Art** was Young's pet project, fostered out of his belief that all college students should have access to a campus museum. Prior to settling down in Honolulu, Paris-born **Jean Charlot** (1898-1979) worked as Diego Rivera's assistant in Mexico. During his time in Hawaii, Charlot applied the techniques he learned with Rivera to a number of fresco murals that residents can enjoy in various Oahu locations, including the University of Hawaii at Manoa. **Madge Tennent** (1889-1972) concentrated on capturing the beauty she saw in the Hawaiian people. She is best known for her oil paintings of Hawaiian women, many of which hang prominently in buildings around Honolulu. Other notable Hawaiian artists include: watercolor artist **Hon-Chew Hee;** painter and print-maker **Yvonne Cheng;** and potter and watercolor artist **Charles Higa.**

Art takes on a practical form in the distinctive **Hawaiian quilts.** After learning quilting techniques from New England missionaries, Hawaiian women translated the images from their daily lives onto fabric. The quilts, with their flower, leaf, and vine designs, are still popular today. A full-size quilt can take up to a year to finish.

LITERATURE. Until recently, Hawaiian literature has consisted of tales written by curious outsiders looking in. Early in his career, **Mark Twain** journeyed from San Francisco to Hawaii for a month-long sojourn that became four months. It was Hawaii that helped Twain achieve his mammoth literary stature. Chronicles of his trip were published in the *Sacramento Union* and scholars hold that it was in Hawaii that Twain first began to develop his singular descriptive and interpretive style. Twain later compiled his personal and professional writings from this period into *Roughing It.* Intrigued by the islands and people of the Pacific, **Robert Louis Stevenson** explored the area extensively and lived the last years of his life in Samoa. Much of his writing from that period is compiled in *Travels in Hawaii.* One of the most well-known novels about Hawaii is James Michener's 1,036-page epic titled, simply, *Hawaii.* A combination of fact and fiction, the book begins with the creation of the islands and follows their growth until the year 1955.

Hawaiian authors have begun to assert themselves on the literary scene. Nurtured by local organizations, such as *Bamboo Ridge,* the journal of Hawaiian literature and arts, local writers are gaining exposure and (some) critical acclaim. The leader of this generation of authors is Hawaiian-born novelist **Lois-Ann Yamanaka,** who tackles the themes of Asian-American families and local culture in Hawaii. Yamanaka's work addresses the reality of living in paradise; she eschews flowery word painting for authentic pidgin dialogue between her (often dysfunctional) characters. Other authors who are a part of this reinvention of Hawaiian literature include: **Milton Murayama, Darrell Lum, Sylvia Watanabe,** and **Nora Okja Keller.**

MUSIC. Hawaiian music instantly conjures up images of swaying palm trees and crashing waves. Traditional musicians record songs almost entirely in Hawaiian and use the **ukulele, steel guitar** and **slack key guitar** extensively. Legends hold that the ukulele was introduced to Hawaii in 1879 by a Portuguese immigrant named **Joao Fernandes.** The islanders dubbed Fernandes's *braguinha* (a type of guitar) a ukulele (literally, "jumping flea") because of the way the musician's fingers jumped across the strings of the instrument. The ukulele quickly gained popularity; even Hawaiian royalty became proficient. The ukulele became a symbol of Hawaiian beach culture during the 1920s and 30s thanks to a group of men who lived and worked on Waikiki. The **Waikiki Beachboys,** as they were called, serenaded locals and tourists with their ukuleles. The Beachboys included such renowned Hawaiian musicians as **Squeeze Kamana** and **Chick Daniels.**

The steel guitar was developed on Oahu by local **Joseph Kekuku** in the late 19th century. Kekuku's instrument was able to achieve a previously-unthinkable range of sound, and to this day remains a centerpiece of Hawaiian music. Hawaiian musicians round out the distinctive island sound using a guitar technique called slack key, or **ki ho'ai.** Literally, "loosen the key," this method of playing consists of relaxing the strings of an acoustic guitar and picking them with the fingers. The guitar is reputed to have come to the islands via early 19th-century cowboys. However, Hawaiians developed the unique slack-key sound themselves.

With the Hawaiian renaissance of the 1970s, traditional artists, such as **Israel "IZ" Kamakawiwo'ole** (recently known on the mainland for his "Somewhere Over the Rainbow/What a Wonderful World" remake), the **Sons of Hawaii,** and **Keali'i**

Reichel, all experienced a boost in their popularity. There remains a large demand for "Island Contemporary" recordings, music that is billed as an "updated Hawaiian sound." Notable artists include: **Teresa Bright, Keola and Kapono Beamer,** and the **Makaha Sons of Ni'ihau** (the original group of "Cousin Iz").

DANCE. The **hula** has long been a symbol of Hawaiian culture. Though the precise origins of hula are unknown, the most commonly cited legend holds that the dance began when Pele, the Hawaiian goddess of fire, commanded her younger sister, Laka, to dance. The dances and chants of ancient hula were an integral part of the Hawaiians' oral tradition; through them, elders ensured that their traditions, customs, and history would live on in a younger generation. For a short period in the early 19th century, Christian missionaries convinced the reigning monarchs to outlaw the dance. However, in 1874, **King David Kalakaua** ascended to the throne. The new king, nicknamed the **"Merrie Monarch,"** became hula's greatest patron and during his rule, the dance flourished. The ukulele and the steel guitar were used to accompany dancers, who began wearing ti leaf skirts for the first time. Kalakaua is remembered each year in the **Merrie Monarch Festival,** which showcases both ancient hula and the more modern versions that have developed.

FILM. Despite the difficulty of transporting film-making equipment, movie producers have never been able to resist Hawaii's allure. The islands are reputed to have made their onscreen debut as early as 1898, when a film crew stranded by a layover shot footage of the tropical paradise. In the early 1900s, Hawaii was used in numerous silent films, including *Hawaiian Love* (1913) and *The Shark God* (1913).The advent of "talkies" added a new dimension to Hawaiian-set films. In 1937, Bing Crosby starred in *Waikiki Wedding,* playing a crooning press agent for a pineapple cannery. The film's hit song, "Sweet Leilani" garnered an Oscar and earned Crosby his first gold record.

Though WWII put filmmaking in Hawaii on hold for a few years, it also provided the industry with its most enduring subject: war. *From Here to Eternity* (1953) chronicled the days leading up the Pearl Harbor attack but is probably best remembered for Burt Lancaster and Deborah Kerr's passionate embrace on the sand (and in the water) of Halona Cove. Kauai was used to film the musical *South Pacific* (1958), in which Mitzi Gaynor plays a lovestruck Army nurse who tries, unsuccessfully, to wash a captivating man out of her hair. Elvis Presley fastened the gaze of his adoring fans on Hawaii when he starred in 1961's *Blue Hawaii.* As an island boy back from the war, Presley spends much of the movie strumming the ukulele and wooing beach bunnies with his signature dance moves. The film yielded several musical hits, including "Blue Hawaii" and "Can't Help Falling In Love."

Filmmakers switched gears in 1976, when Hawaii was featured in the blockbuster *King Kong.* Following the movie's release, Hawaii increasingly became the filming site of action-packed crowd-pleasers. In 1980, George Lucas and Steven Spielberg joined forces to produce the first of the Indiana Jones series, *Raiders of the Lost Ark,* filmed partly in Kauai. Spielberg continued his blockbuster trend with *Jurassic Park* (1992), also filmed in Hawaii. The 1997 dino-sequel, *The Lost World,* faltered in the wake of its predecessor's success, though it still featured gorgeous shots of Kauai's lush scenery. Other crowd-pleasers filmed in Hawaii include *George of the Jungle* (1997), *Mighty Joe Young* (1998), and *6 Days, 7 Nights* (1998).

Hawaii continues to be a popular site for movie-making. In 2001, producer Jerry Bruckheimer let loose his biggest (and longest) film yet, the epic *Pearl Harbor.* Director Tim Burton also used Hawaii for part of his remake of *Planet of the Apes* (2001). Director John Woo, originally of Hong Kong, returned to the World War II theme in *Windtalkers* (2002). In addition to sweeping shots of the Hawaiian islands, the film features Nicholas Cage as US Marine Sergeant who must protect a Navajo codetalker. The Hawaii Visitor's and Convention Bureau joined forces with Disney to market *Lilo & Stitch* (2002), which is set in the islands, and the recent *Blue Crush* (2002) celebrates the subculture of female Hawaiian surfers.

Hawaii hosts a few **film festivals** each year. The **Hawaii International Film Festival** began at the University of Hawaii (Manoa) in 1981 as a means of cultural exchange between North America, Asia, and the Pacific. It is now a state-wide event, with screenings on the six major Hawaiian islands. The **Maui Film Festival** is still in its infancy—it began in 2000—but seems like the event is around to stay.

ON LOCATION IN THE ISLANDS Hawaii has had its share of television excitement. From 1968 to 1980, **Hawaii 5-0,** one of the longest-running series on television, was filmed almost exclusively in Hawaii. During the 80s, Tom Selleck charmed viewers across the nation as a dashing Hawaii-based private investigator in **Magnum, P.I.** The **Baywatch** cast packed up its itty-bitty wardrobe and suntan oil in 1999 to relocate from California to Hawaii. The new series, **Baywatch Hawaii,** lasted only two seasons.

RECENT DEVELOPMENTS. In 2000, the Hawaii Television and Development Board was created to facilitate film and TV production in the islands. In a move to encourage the use of Hawaii in film and television, the Hawaii Film Office is working to secure the necessary funds to revamp the Hawaii Film Studio at Diamond Head. The studio was built in 1976 for **Hawaii 5-0** and has since been the site for number of projects, including *Final Fantasy* and *The Matrix Reloaded.*

SPORTS & RECREATION

With myriad outdoor activities available, Hawaii vacations are more about hopping from activity to activity than they are about passively soaking up sun. Water sports reign here—some of the world's best surfing and windsurfing spots are in Hawaii. Golf is the chosen sport of many tourists, and manicured greens are spread across the islands. Sports in Hawaii run the gamut from the extreme to the tame; other popular activities include paddling, kayaking, snorkeling, surfing, scuba diving, swimming, hiking and biking.

COLLEGE SPORTS AND FOOTBALL. Water polo, volleyball, and sailing are among the most popular high school and college competitive sports in Hawaii. The **University of Hawaii at Manoa** Rainbow Warriors boast a nationally-ranked sailing program, and the 2002 Men's Volleyball team were National Champions. Since 1997, the **Hula Bowl All-Star Football Classic** has been held each year on Maui. Recent negotiations between bowl officials and the **NFL** have resulted in a decision to link the Hula Bowl and the **Pro-Bowl.** The Hula Bowl will move from January to the first weekend in February, the date of the Pro-Bowl. In addition, the newly-created NCAA **Hawaii Bowl** will be played in the Aloha Stadium on Christmas Day.

GOING THE DISTANCE. Laid-back lifestyle aside, Hawaii is home to hundreds of running events and triathlons, from 1 mi. fun-runs to a 100 mi. ultramarathon on the Big Island. Among these is one of the world's most badass multi-sport events—the **Ironman Triathlon.** Held every fall in Kailua-Kona on the Big Island, the event draws 1500 qualifiers from all 50 US states and over 50 countries to compete in the grueling race. Competitors start with a 2.4 mi. ocean swim, followed by a 112 mi. bike race, and cap the whole thing off with a full 26.2 mi. marathon. The course is open for 17 hours; the current record time is 8:04:08 set by Luc Van Lierde in 1996. Over 50 million viewers world-wide tune in to witness the event each year.

Hawaii also has five official **marathons.** The Honolulu Marathon, held each December, is the 6th-largest marathon in the world. The Maui Marathon, held in March, was the first of the pack as the oldest continuously-held running event in Hawaii. The other official marathons are the Kilauea Volcano Marathon in July, the Kona Marathon in August, and the Big Island International Marathon in October.

PADDLING. Outrigger canoe paddling is widespread throughout the Hawaii. By all accounts, the phenomenally popular sport originated in the islands. The **outrigger canoe** differs from a regular canoe in that it has a rig, known as an **outrigger**, extending from one or both sides of the vessel. The outrigger acts to balance the hull of the boat. Early Hawaiians used the outrigger canoes extensively in their daily lives, and paddling eventually became a means of recreation.

Encouraged by King Kalakaua, paddling enthusiasts formed the first official outrigger club in 1908. **The Outrigger Canoe Club of Hawaii** was followed shortly after by **Hui Nalu** and, in 1910, canoe racing began. Formal regattas began in the 1940s and there are now over 60 outrigger clubs throughout the islands. Paddlers are typically grouped into divisions by age. There is a separate junior season (Jan.-March) to ensure that younger athletes get as much attention as possible. Though paddling had previously been dominated by males, the number of women competing in the sport has increased steadily since the 1980s.

Participants race in six-person canoes in both sprint and distance events. Sprints are held in sheltered water, usually rivers, lakes, or bays, and can range from 250m to 3000m in length (though 250m to 500m is most common). Distance races differ from between age groups. In open divisions, courses can be anywhere from 8km to 60km (the famed Molokai to Oahu race). In extremely long races, regattas actually allow fresh rowers to switch into the boat.

The **International Polynesian Canoe Federation** promotes the sport within the Pacific region, though there is no set of official rules. Each state or country develops its own body of regulations. In the Hawaiian islands, the **Hawaii Canoe Racing Association (HCRA)** is organized by geography into smaller regulatory bodies. At the end of each season, regional events qualify paddlers to the state championships, which rotate between the islands.

Sailing canoes are a variation on the outrigger canoes. Though not nearly as common as paddling, sailing canoe races have been gaining popularity. Each May, participants race the 75 mi. between Maui and Oahu in canoe sailing's most well-known competition, the **Steinlager Ho'omana'o Sailing Canoe Race.**

SURFING. Surfing was born in Hawaii, and the sport stays true to its homeland. There is no impeding continental shelf surrounding the islands to slow incoming waves, so they arrive huge and powerful on Hawaiian shores in the form of magnificent, world-renowned surf. The two surf seasons constitute the entire year and are differentiated by wind and storm patterns. Storms in the South Pacific generate Hawaii surf in the summer (May-Aug.). Summer surf is dominated by northeast trade winds and occurs on the southern shores of the islands. In the winter (Sept.-Apr.), storms in the northern Pacific create surf on the northern shores of the islands. The seasons' overlap allows for nearly year-round surfing.

The so-called "sport of kings" began as the ancient sport of *he'e nalu* (wave-sliding) and later perfected by the kings of Hawaii. The revival of interest in surfing in the early 20th century is attributed to Hawaii's **Duke Kahanamoku.** His Highness was a talented swimmer, representing the United States at four Olympic Games between 1912 and 1924, winning three gold medals and two silvers to become Hawaii's first Olympic medalist. His first love was surfing, however, and he organized one of the first amateur surfing clubs in 1908. He also invented **windsurfing**—which has become one of Hawaii's most popular sports—and **wakesurfing** (surfing in the wake of a motorboat).

Since then, the evolution of **board design** and material has made major changes to surfing, both as an activity and as a culture. The first boards were made of wood; their weight and lack of maneuverability was part of what limited the sport to men. The first big breakthrough in board design came in 1958 when construction changed to lightweight foam and fiberglass, making surfing accessible to everyone. Surfing gained popularity in California during the surfing craze of the

1950s and 60s, which included surfing fashion, music, and movies. The lighter boards made surfing more accessible to women in particular. Surfing is now the second-fastest growing sport among women.

Today, surfers use one of two types of boards: **long boards** (traditional style of board that can range as long as 10-12 ft.) and **short boards.** Short boards are less than 9 ft. in length, are faster, and have better maneuverability. Although beginning surfers generally start off on long boards, most surfers use short boards as well, as they are better for riding larger waves. Surfboards have two to three fins, called **thrusters,** which provide greater maneuverability. The addition of a **leash** improved both the safety of surfing and its style. Before leashes were added, surfers spent a lot of time swimming out to retrieve lost boards after getting knocked off by waves. Lost boards would collide with reefs and rocks as well, resulting in significant damage. With leashes, surfers can ride waves near rocks and reefs and try radical tricks with greater security.

A SURFING STATE OF MIND For many locals, surfing is not just an activity, but a way of life. Surfers range from the hard-core pro surfers, to local *bruddahs,* to 9-5ers who keep a board in their trunks to catch a post-work wave. While tourists are welcome to pick up a board and try their hand on a curl, don't expect to be inducted into surfer culture fresh off your first wave. Surfers are secretive about the best spots, have their own slang, and abide by their own code. A few tips on **surfer etiquette** for novice wave-riders: never "drop-in" on a wave. The surfer closest to the curl (the breaking part of the wave) has the right of way on that wave, and all other surfers should back up out of it (failure to do so is dropping in). Be careful of body boarders and other surfers—collisions can cause serious injuries.

HOLIDAYS & FESTIVALS

Late January: Chinese New Year: This celebration is best seen on Oahu, in Chinatown. Highlights include a lion dance, fireworks, and all the Chinese food you can handle.

Late January: Pacific Islands Arts Festival: In Waikiki. Highlights include local culinary favorites, "make n' takes" for kids, and demonstrations by local artists.

Mid-February: Polynesian Festival: In Waikiki. Highlights include *poi*-pounding, coconut-husking, fire-making, and more! Food, entertainment, and crafts from various Polynesian islands.

March 26: Prince Kuhio Day: In celebration of the birthday of Prince Jonah Kuhio Kalanianaole, Hawaii's 2nd delegate to Congress.

Early April: Merrie Monarch Festival: In Hilo. A week of cultural events culminating in Hawaii's most prestigious hula competition.

April 15: Father Damien DeVeuster Day: In celebration of Father Damien DeVeusteur, highly-regarded Christian missionary to the Kalaupapa Peninsula leper colony.

May 1: Lei Day

June 11: King Kamehameha Day: In celebration of Kamehameha the Great

Mid-June: Maui Film Festival: In Wailea. Film premieres under the stars, as well as food and wine events.

Late June: Taste of Honolulu: In Honolulu. An outdoor wine, food, and entertainment festival benefiting Easter Seals Hawaii.

Third Friday in August: Statehood Day

September 2: Queen Liliuokalani Day: In celebration of Hawaii's last monarch and only ruling queen, Liliuokalani

September-October: Aloha Festival: State-wide. Hawaii's largest cultural festival, spanning two months and featuring events on all the major islands.

Early October: Ironman Triathlon World Championships: In Kailua-Kona. Hardcore athletes from around the world flock to The Big Island for this ultimate test of endurance.

Late October: Macadamia Nut Festival: In Hilo. Yummy macadamia nut concoctions, plus local music and entertainment.

November: Hawaiian International Film Festival: State-wide. Screenings of (mostly) Pacific Rim films in various locations across the state.

ADDITIONAL RESOURCES

HISTORY

A Concise History of the Hawaiian Islands. Phil Barnes (Petroglyph Press Ltd., 1999).

Ancient Hawaii. Herb Kawainui Kane (Kawainui Press, 1998).

The Apotheosis of Captain Cook. Gananath Obeyesekere (Princeton University Press, 1992).

Day of Infamy: The Classic Account of the Bombing of Pearl Harbor. Walter Lord (Henry Holt & Co., 2001).

In the Shadow of the Pali: A Story of the Hawaiian Leper Colony. Lisa Cindrich (Penguin, 2002).

Niihau: The Last Hawaiian Island. Ruth M. Tabrah (Booklines Hawaii Ltd., 1987).

Paradise Remade: The Politics of Culture and History in Hawaii. Elizabeth Buck (Temple University Press, 1994).

THE GREAT OUTDOORS

A Field Guide to the Birds of Hawaii and the Tropical Pacific. Douglas Pratt (Princeton University Press, 1987).

Hawaii Best Beaches. John R.K. Clark (University of Hawaii Press, 1999).

Hawaii's Best Hiking Trails. Robert Smith and Kevin Chard (Hawaiian Outdoor Adventure, 1999).

Hiking Maui: The Valley Isle. Robert Smith (Hawaiian Outdoor Adventure, 1999).

Kauai Trails: Walks, Strolls and Treks on the Garden Island. Kathy Morey (Wilderness Press, 2002).

Plants and Flowers of Hawaii. Seymour H. Sohmer (University of Hawaii Press, 1994).

Remains of a Rainbow: Rare Plants and Animals of Hawaii. David Littschwager, et. al. (National Geographic Society, 2001).

SPORTS

The Big Drop: Classic Big Wave Surfing Stories. John Long, ed. and Hai Van K. Sponholz, ed. (Falcon Publishing, 1999).

Girl in the Curl: A Century of Women's Surfing. Andrea Gabbard (Seal Press, 2000).

The Hawaiian Canoe. Tommy Holmes (Editions Limited, 1993).

Sleeping in the Shorebreak and Other Hairy Surfing Stories. Don Wolf (Waverider Publications, 1999).

The Ultimate Guide to Marathons. Dennis Craythorn and Rich Hanna (Marathon Publishing, 1997).

CULTURE

The Aloha Shirt: Spirit of the Island. Dale Hope and Gregory Tozian (Beyond Words Publishing, 2000).

The Food of Paradise: Exploring Hawaii's Culinary Heritage. Rachel Laudan (University of Hawaii Press, 1996).

The Hawaiian Lei: A Tradition of Aloha. Ronn Ronck (Mutual Publishing Company, 1999).

Hawaiian Dictionary. Mary Kawena Pukui and Samuel H. Elbert (University of Hawaii Press, 1986).

The Kahuna. Likeke R. McBride (Petroglyph Press, 2000).

FICTION AND TRAVEL NARRATIVES

A Hawaii Anthology. Joseph Stanton, ed. (University of Hawaii Press, 1997).

Blu's Hanging. Lois-Ann Yamanaka (Avon Books, 1998).

da word. Lee Tonouchi (Bamboo Ridge Press, 2001).

Growing Up Local: An Anthology of Poetry and Prose from Hawaii. Eric Chock, ed., et al. (Bamboo Ridge Press, 2000).

Hawaii. James A. Michener (Random House, 1973).

Hawaii One Summer. Maxine Hong Kingston (University of Hawaii Press, 1998).

Hawaii Reflections: Writings of Mark Twain, Jack London, Robert Louis Stevenson, and Charles W. Stoddard. (Mauna Loa Publishing, 1995).

Roughing It. Mark Twain (N A L, 1976).

Travels in Hawaii. Robert Louis Stevenson (University of Hawaii Press, 1991).

FILM

Blue Hawaii. (Dir. Norman Tauroq. 20th Century Fox, 1961).

From Here to Eternity. (Dir. Fred Zinneman. Columbia TriStar, 1953).

Gidget Goes Hawaiian. (Dir. Paul Wendkos. Columbia TriStar, 1961).

Hawaii (Dir. George Roy Hill. MGM, 1966).

Molokai: The Story of Father Damien. (Dir. Paul Cox. Unapix, 1999).

Ride the Wild Surf. (Dir. Don Taylor. Columbia TriStar, 1964).

Tora! Tora! Tora! (Dir. Richard Fleischer. 20th Century Fox, 1970).

Pearl Harbor. (Dir. Michael Bay. Buena Vista, 2001).

Lilo and Stitch. (Dir. Chris Sanders and David DeBlois. Disney, 2001).

Blue Crush. (Dir. John Stockwell. Universal Studios, 2002).

HAWAIIAN MYTHS AND LEGENDS

Hawaii Magic and Spirituality. Scott Cunningham (Llewellyn Publications, 2000).

Hawaiian Mythology. Martha Warren Beckwith (University of Hawaii Press, 1977).

The Legends and Myths of Hawaii: The Fables and Folklore of a Strange People. David Kalakaua, R.M. Dagget, ed. (Charles E. Tuttle Co., 1972).

une in, turn on, mellow out. Local radio isn't just about surf conditions anymore—it's a way to get inside info on community happenings—from island politics to farmers' markets to drum circles. Keep an ear open for Jawaiian jams, reggae with a Hawaiian twist as smooth and sweet as a Mai Tai at sunset. So skip the CDs in the rental car and crank the radio dial to the *real* Hawaii. All frequencies are FM unless otherwise noted.

OAHU

89.3 KIPO Hawaii Public Radio—Need your National Public Radio or BBC fix? Here it is—international news and erudite pondering at its best (www.hawaiipublicradio.org).

90.3 KTUH University of Hawaii Radio—Java jive jazz, far-out funk, and freaky free-form. Tune in to "Monday Night Live" for live performances by up and coming local acts, M 9pm-midnight. Also at **91.3** on the North Shore, and **89.7** in Hawaii Kai (www.ktuh.org).

100.3 KCCN "FM 100"—Extraordinarily popular island music station that plays *da kine* tracks, *bruddah!* The #1 station in Honolulu, owing in no small part to the morning drive-time stylings of Billy V and PP, M-F 5-10am (http://kccnfm100.com).

102.7 KDDB "Da Bomb"—Hip-hop, rap and urban jams (www.dabombhawaii.com).

105.1 KINE Tune in for the Aloha Morning Show 5-10am, or Bruddah Wade 3-7pm. Also check their web site for upcoming entertainment events (http://hawaiian105.com).

MAUI

91.5 KEAO Mana'O Radio. An eclectic, irreverent station established by deadheads and karate black belts. On-air daily 6am-midnight. (http://www.manaoradio.com)

93.5 KPOA Island Music. Think Neil Diamond meets Don Ho. The "music you listen to when you clean da house!" Surf reports M-F 7, 9am and 3pm (www.kpoa.com).

94.3 KDLX Maui's Country—Hey *paniolo*, KDLX ropes in the big ones all the way from Nashville. Grab your cowboy hat and get ready to ride.

95.1 KAOI—Jazz, adult contemporary, and Hawaiian. May the jet-lagged rejoice: jazz great Ramsey Lewis has his own show at the ungodly hours of 6-8am on Su.

101.1 KLHI The Point—A fraternity of mainland transplants bring you alternative rock. Sponsors bikini contests and "the island's wildest parties" (www.thepointfm101.com).

103.7 KNUQ "The Rhythm of the Islands"— Smooth Jawaiian jams (www.q103maui.com).

BIG ISLAND

94.7 KWXX—Jawaiian and island music, as well as a shot in the arm of mainland pop. Stays true to its roots with *"Alana i Kai Hikina,"* an all-Hawaiian language primetime show purported to be the first of its kind, Su 6-8pm (http://www.kwxx.com).

99.1 Kona / 100.3 Hilo KAPA—"All Hawaiian, all the time." Many a local declares this their fave rave. (www.kapafm.com)

105.1 KINE—Traditional island music. For 20+ years, Harry B. Soria, Jr. has hosted the "Territorial Airwaves" show, featuring vintage Hawaiian vinyl, Su 5-6pm. (http://hawaiian105.com)

AM 530—Volcanoes National Park pre-recorded Park and eruption information. Warning: static-laden transmissions are eerie when you're driving through cooled lava flows.

KAUAI

90.9 KKCR Kauai Community Radio—The last bastion of free speech in the Hawaiian islands, at least they'll make you think so. Don't miss Manulele's community calendar, M-F 7:30am; or Western Front with Jones, F 8-10pm (www.kkcr.org).

93.5 KQNG Kong Radio—Top 40 fix for those homesick for the mainland. (www.kongradio.com)

98.9 KITH "Travelhost Radio"—A siren's song of classic Hawaiian tunes laced with real estate commercials designed to lure unsuspecting mainlanders into staying.

99.9 KTOH "Oldies Radio, Hits 99.9FM"—Plays a "continuous history of rock 'n' roll."

ESSENTIALS

FACTS FOR THE TRAVELER

ENTRANCE REQUIREMENTS

Passport (p. 36). Required for citizens of all foreign countries except Canada.
Visa (p. 37). A visa is usually required to visit the US, but can be waived.
Work Permit (p. 37). Required for all foreigners planning to work in the US.
Driving Permit (p. 53). Required for all those planning to drive.

EMBASSIES AND CONSULATES

Contact your nearest embassy or consulate for information regarding visas and passports to the United States. The **US State Department** provides contact info for US embassies and consulates abroad at http://usembassy.state.gov. For more detailed info on embassies, consult www.embassyworld.com.

AMERICAN CONSULAR SERVICES ABROAD

US EMBASSIES

Australia: Moonah Pl., Yarralumla **Canberra** ACT 2600 (☎02 6214 5600; fax 6214 5970; http://usembassy-australia.state.gov/embassy/index.html).

Canada: 490 Sussex Dr., **Ottawa,** ON K1N 1G8 (☎613-238-5335; fax 688-3091; www.usembassycanada.gov).

Ireland: 42 Elgin Rd., **Dublin** 4 (☎1 668 8777 or 668 7122; fax 668 9946; www.usembassy.ie).

New Zealand: 29 Fitzherbert Terr., Thorndon, **Wellington,** Mailing Address: P.O. Box 1190, Wellington (☎4 462 6000; fax 499 0490; http://usembassy.org.nz).

South Africa: 877 Pretorius St., **Pretoria,** Mailing Address: P.O. Box 9536, Pretoria 0001 (☎342 1048; fax 342 2244; http://usembassy.state.gov/pretoria).

UK: 24 Grosvenor Sq., **London** W1A 1AE (☎020 7499 9000; fax 491 2485; www.usembassy.org.uk).

US CONSULATES ABROAD

Australia: 553 St. Kilda Rd., **Melbourne** VIC 3004 (☎03 9526 5900; fax 9525 0769); 16 St. George's Terr., 13th fl., **Perth** WA 6000 (☎08 9202 1224; fax 9231 9444); MLC Centre, 19-29 Martin Pl., 59th fl., **Sydney** NSW 2000 (☎02 9373 9200; fax 9373 9184).

Canada: 615 Macleod Trail SE, **Calgary,** AB T2G 4T8 (☎403-266-8962; fax 264-6630); Suite 904, Purdy's Wharf Tower II, 1969 Upper Water St., **Halifax,** NS B3J 3R7 (☎902-429-2480; fax 423-6861); 1155 St. Alexandre St., **Montréal** QC H3B 3Z1, Mailing Address: P.O. Box 65, Station Desjardins, Montréal, QC H5B 1G1 (☎514-398-9695; fax 398-9748); 2 Place Terrasse Dufferin, **Québec City,** QC G1R 4T9 (☎418-692-2095; fax 692-4640); 360 University Ave., **Toronto,** ON M5G 1S4 (☎416-595-1700; fax 595-0051); 1095 W. Pender St., **Vancouver,** BC V6E 2M6 (☎604-685-4311; fax 685-5285); 860-201 Portage Ave., **Winnipeg,** MB R3B 3K6 (204-940-1800).

New Zealand: Citibank Building, 3rd fl., 23 Customs St., **Auckland,** Mailing Address: Private Bag 92022, Auckland, (☎9 303 2724; fax 366 0870).

South Africa: Broadway Industries Center, Heerengracht, Foreshore, **Cape Town,** Mailing Address: P.O. Box 6773, Roggebaai 8012 (☎021 421 4280; fax 425 3014); Old Mutual Building, 31st fl., 303 West St., **Durban** 4000 (☎031 305 7600; fax 305 7691); 1 River St., Killarney, **Johannesburg,** Mailing Address: P.O. Box 1762, Houghton 2041 (☎011 644 8000; fax 646 6916).

UK: Queen's House, 14 Queen St., **Belfast,** N. Ireland BT1 6EQ (☎028 9032 8239; fax 9024 8482); 3 Regent Terr., **Edinburgh,** Scotland EH7 5BW (☎0131 556 8315; fax 557 6023).

CONSULAR SERVICES IN THE US

IN WASHINGTON, D.C.

Australia, 1601 Massachusetts Ave., 20036 (☎202-797-3000; fax 797-3168; www.austemb.org). **Canada,** 501 Pennsylvania Ave. NW, 20001 (☎202-682-1740; fax 202-682-7701; www.canadianembassy.org). **Ireland,** 2234 Massachusetts Ave. NW, 20008 (☎202-462-3939; fax 232-5993; www.irelandemb.org). **New Zealand,** 37 Observatory Circle NW, 20008 (☎202-328-4800; fax 667-5227; www.nzemb.org). **South Africa,** 3051 Massachusetts Ave. NW, 20008 (☎202-232-4400; fax 265-1607); www.saembassy.org). **UK,** 3100 Massachusetts Ave., 20008 (☎202-588-6500; fax 588-7870; www.britainusa.com/consular/embassy).

DOCUMENTS AND FORMALITIES

REQUIREMENTS. All foreign visitors except Canadians need valid **passports** to enter the US and to re-enter their own country. Canadians must demonstrate proof of Canadian citizenship, such as a citizenship card with photo ID. Returning home with an expired passport is illegal and may result in a fine. The US does not allow entrance if the holder's passport expires in under six months.

PHOTOCOPIES. Be sure to photocopy the page of your passport with your photo, passport number, and other identifying info, as well as any visas, travel insurance policies, plane tickets, or traveler's check serial numbers. Carry one set of copies in a safe place, apart from the originals, and leave another set at home. Consulates also recommend that you carry an expired passport or an official copy of your birth certificate in a part of your baggage separate from other documents.

LOST PASSPORTS. If you lose your passport, immediately notify the local police and the nearest embassy or consulate of your home government. To expedite the replacement process, you will need to know all info from the previous passport; you must also show ID and proof of citizenship. In some cases, a replacement may take weeks to process, and it may be valid only for a limited time. Any visas stamped in your old passport will be irretrievably lost. In an emergency, ask for immediate temporary traveling papers that will permit you to re-enter your home country. Your passport is a public document belonging to your nation's government. You may have to surrender it to a US government official, but if you don't get it back in a reasonable amount of time, inform your country's nearest mission.

NEW PASSPORTS. File any new passport or renewal applications well in advance of your departure date. Most passport offices offer rush services for a steep fee. Citizens living abroad who need a passport or renewal should contact the nearest consular service of their home country.

Australia: Citizens must apply for a passport in person at a post office or an Australian diplomatic mission overseas. New adult passports cost AUS$144 (for a 32-page passport) or AUS$216 (64-page), and a child's or senior's is AUS$72/AUS$108. Adult passports are valid for 10 years and child passports for 5 years. Adults can request passport renewal forms by phone or online. For more info, call toll-free (in Australia) ☎ 13 12 32, or visit www.passports.gov.au.

Canada: Citizens may enter Hawaii with any proof of citizenship.

Ireland: Citizens can apply for a passport by mail to the Department of Foreign Affairs, Passport Office, Setanta Centre, Molesworth St., Dublin 2 (☎ 01 671 1633; fax 671 1092; www.irlgov.ie/iveagh). Residents of the Munster counties of Clare, Cork, Kerry, Limerick, Tipperary, and Waterford can apply to 1a South Mall, Cork (☎ 021 494 4700). Obtain an application at a local *Garda* station or post office, or request one from a passport office. 32-page passports cost €57 and are valid for 10 years. 48-page passports cost €69. Citizens under 16 or over 65 can request a 3-year passport (€12).

New Zealand: Application forms for passports are available online or from any travel agency or Link Centre. Applications should be sent to the Passport Office, P.O. Box 10-526, Wellington, New Zealand (☎ 0800 225 050 or 04 474 8100; fax 474 8010; www.passports.govt.nz). Adult passports (NZ$80) are valid 10 years; passports for children under 16 (NZ$40) are valid 5 years. Recent proposals would reduce the adult fee to NZ$71 and the children fee to NZ$36.

South Africa: Citizens must bring a completed application and accompanying information to a domestic Home Affairs office or a consulate abroad. Processing takes at least 6 weeks. Adult passports (ZAR120) are valid for 10 years. Passports for children under 16 (ZAR90) are valid for 5 years. Information and application documents are available at www.home-affairs.pwv.gov.za.

United Kingdom: Application forms are available at passport offices, main post offices, travel agencies, and online (www.ukpa.gov.uk). Apply by mail, in person at a passport offices, or at one of the High Street Partners. Adult passports (UK£33) are valid for 10 years; under 16 (UK£19) are valid for 5. The process takes about 2 weeks. The UK Passport Agency advice line is at ☎ 0870 521 0410.

VISAS

Citizens of most European countries, Australia, and New Zealand can waive US visas through the **Visa Waiver Pilot Program.** Visitors qualify if they are traveling only for business or pleasure (*not* work or study) and are staying for fewer than 90 days. In addition, travelers must provide proof of intent to leave (such as a return plane ticket) and an I-94 form. Citizens of South Africa and some other countries need a visa in addition to a valid passport for entrance to the US. To obtain a visa, contact a US embassy or consulate (see p. 35). The US charges $100 to apply for a visa.

All travelers planning a stay of more than 90 days (180 days for Canadians) need to obtain a visa; contact the closest US embassy or consulate. US citizens can take advantage of the **Center for International Business and Travel (CIBT),** 23201 New Mexico Ave. NW, #210, Washington, D.C. 20016 (☎ 202-244-9500 or 800-929-2428), which secures **B-2** (pleasure travel) visas to and from all possible countries for a variable service charge (six month visa around $45). If you lose your I-94 form, you can replace it at the nearest **Bureau of Citizenship and Immigration Services (BCIS)** office (☎ 800-375-5283; www.bcis.gov). **Visa extensions** are sometimes attainable with a completed I-539 form; call the forms request line at ☎ 800-870-3676. Be sure to double-check on entrance requirements at the nearest US embassy or consulate, or consult the Bureau of Consular Affairs' web site (www.travel.state.gov).

Entering Hawaii to **work** or **study** requires a special visa. For more information, see **Alternatives to Tourism** (p. 75).

IDENTIFICATION

When you travel, always carry two or more forms of identification on your person, including at least one photo ID; a passport combined with a driver's license or birth certificate is usually adequate. Many establishments, especially banks, may require several IDs in order to cash traveler's checks. Never carry all your forms of ID together; keep them in separate places in case of theft or loss.

TEACHER, STUDENT & YOUTH IDENTIFICATION. The **International Student Identity Card (ISIC)** is the most widely accepted form of student ID, provides discounts on sights, accommodations, food, and transportation. The ISIC is preferable to an institution-specific card (such as a university ID) because it is more likely to be recognized (and honored) abroad. The card also offers access to a 24hr. emergency helpline (☎44 20 8762 8110); and insurance benefits for US cardholders (see **Insurance,** p. 8). Applicants must be degree-seeking students of a secondary or post-secondary school and must be of at least 12 years of age. Because of the proliferation of fake ISICs, some services (particularly airlines) require additional proof of student identity.

The **International Teacher Identity Card (ITIC)** offers teachers the same insurance coverage as well as similar but limited discounts. For travelers who are 25 years old or under but are not students, the **International Youth Travel Card** (**IYTC**), also called the **GO25 card,** offers many of the same benefits as the ISIC.

Each of these identity cards costs US$22 or equivalent. ISIC and ITIC cards are valid for roughly one and a half academic years; IYTC cards are valid for one year from the date of issue. Many student travel agencies (see p. 50) issue the cards; for a list of issuing agencies, or for more information, contact the **International Student Travel Confederation (ISTC),** Herengracht 479, 1017 BS Amsterdam, The Netherlands (☎31 20 421 28 00; fax 421 28 10; www.istc.org).

CUSTOMS

Upon entering Hawaii, you must declare certain items from abroad and pay a **duty** on the value of those articles that exceed the allowance established by the US Customs Service. Upon returning home, you must likewise declare all articles acquired abroad and pay a **duty** on the value of articles that exceed the allowance established by your country's customs service. Keeping receipts for larger purchases made abroad will help establish values when you return. Note that goods and gifts purchased at **duty-free** shops abroad are not exempt from duty or sales tax at your point of return; you must declare these items as well. "Duty-free" merely means that you need not pay a tax in the country of purchase. For more specific information on customs requirements, contact the following info centers.

AMERICAN CUSTOMS DECLARATIONS Entering the **US** as a *resident,* you may claim $800 worth of goods and merchandise. If 21, you may bring in 1L of wine, beer, or liquor. 200 cigarettes, 50 cigars (steer clear of Cubans), or 2kg of smoking tobacco are also permitted. As a *non-resident,* you may claim up to $100 worth of goods and merchandise only if you remain in the US for at least 72hr. and the goods accompany you.

Australia: Australian Customs Information Centre (in Australia ☎1 300 363 263, from elsewhere ☎61 2 6275 6666; www.customs.gov.au).

Canada: Canadian Customs (in Canada ☎800-461-9999, from elsewhere ☎1 204-983-3500; www.revcan.ca).

Ireland: Customs Information Office (☎01 877 6200; www.revenue.ie).

New Zealand: New Zealand Customs Service (☎0800 428 786; www.customs.govt.nz).

South Africa: South African Revenue Service, Pretoria Customs and Excise, (☎012 334 6400; www.sars.gov.za).

UK: Her Majesty's Customs and Excise, National Advice Service (☎0845 010 9000; www.hmce.gov.uk).

US: US Customs and Border Protection Service (☎ 202-354-1000; www.customs.gov).

MONEY

No matter how small your budget, if you plan to travel for more than a couple of days, you will need to keep handy a larger amount of cash than usual. Carrying it around with you, even in a money belt, is risky, and personal checks from another country, or even another state, will probably not be accepted no matter how many forms of identification you have (some banks don't even accept checks).

CURRENCY AND EXCHANGE

The main unit of currency in the US is the **dollar ($)**, which is divided into 100 **cents (¢)**. Paper money is green in the US; bills come in denominations of $1, $5, $10, $20, $50, and $100. Coins are 1¢ (penny), 5¢ (nickel), 10¢ (dime), 25¢ (quarter), and $1. The chart below is based on rates published in August 2003. Check the currency converter on web sites such as www.americanexpress.com and www.xe.com, or a large newspaper for the latest exchange rates.

DOLLAR ($)		
CDN$1 = US$0.72		US$1 = CDN$1.40
UK£1 = US$1.61		US$1 = UK£0.62
AUS$1= US$0.65		US$1 = AUS$1.53
NZ$1 = US$0.58		US$1 = NZ$1.72
ZAR1 = US$0.14		US$1 = ZAR7.25
EUR€1 = US$1.13		US$1 = EUR€0.88

Banks generally have the best rates. Elsewhere, you can expect steep commission rates. A good rule of thumb is to use banks or money-exchanging centers that have at most a 5% margin between buy and sell prices. Convert in large sums to avoid numerous penalties, but don't exchange more than you'll need. ATM and credit cards (see p. 40) often get very good rates.

If using traveler's checks or bills, carry some in small denominations ($50 or less), especially for times when you are forced to exchange at poor rates. Also carry a range of denominations since charges may be levied per check cashed. Ideally, at any given time you will be carrying some cash, some traveler's checks, and an ATM and/or credit card.

TRAVELER'S CHECKS

Traveler's checks (**American Express** and **Visa** are the most widely recognized) are one of the safest and least troublesome means of carrying funds. Several agencies and banks sell them for a small commission. Each agency provides refunds if your checks are lost or stolen, and many provide additional services, such as toll-free refund hotlines, emergency message services, and stolen credit card assistance.

ESSENTIALS

While traveling, keep check receipts and a record of which checks you've cashed separate from the checks themselves. It also helps to leave a list of check numbers with someone at home. Never countersign checks until you're ready to cash them, and always bring your passport with you to cash them. For lost or stolen checks, immediately contact a refund center of the company that issued your checks to be reimbursed; they may require a police report verifying the loss or theft. Ask about toll-free refund hotlines and the location of refund centers when purchasing checks, and always carry emergency cash.

American Express: Checks are available with commission at select banks, at AmEx offices, and online (www.americanexpress.com; US residents only). American Express cardholders can also purchase checks by phone (☎888-269-6669). AAA (see p. 53) offers commission-free checks to its members. *Cheques for Two* can be signed by either of 2 people traveling together. For purchase locations or more information contact AmEx's service centers: In the US, Canada, and Puerto Rico ☎800-221-7282; in the UK ☎0800 587 6023; in Australia ☎800 68 80 22; in New Zealand ☎0508 555 358; elsewhere call US collect.

Travelex/Thomas Cook: In the US and Canada call ☎800-287-7362; in the UK call ☎0800 62 21 01; elsewhere call UK collect ☎44 1733 31 89 50.

Visa: Checks available (generally with commission) at banks worldwide. For the location of the nearest office, call Visa's service centers: From the US and Puerto Rico ☎800-227-6811; from the UK ☎0800 51 58 84; elsewhere UK collect ☎44 020 7937 8091.

CREDIT CARDS

Credit cards are generally accepted in most of Hawaii. However, establishments in more rural areas are sometimes not equipped for credit card transactions. Major credit cards—**MasterCard** (along with its European counterparts **Euro Card** and **Access**) and **Visa** (with its European counterparts **Carte Bleue** or **Barclaycard**) are the most widely accepted—and can be used to extract cash advances in dollars from associated banks and teller machines. Some places do not accept **American Express,** so make sure to have an alternate method of payment. Credit card companies get the wholesale exchange rate, which is generally 5% better than the retail rate used by banks and other currency exchange establishments. American Express cards also work in some ATMs, as well as at AmEx offices and major airports. All such machines require a **Personal Identification Number (PIN).** You must ask your credit card company for a PIN before you leave; without it, you will be unable to withdraw cash with your credit card outside your home country. If you already have a PIN, check with the company to make sure it will work in Hawaii.

CREDIT CARD COMPANIES. Visa (☎800-336-8472) and **MasterCard** (☎800-307-7309) are issued in cooperation with banks and other organizations. **American Express** (☎800-843-2273) has an annual fee of up to $55. AmEx cardholders may cash personal checks at AmEx offices abroad, access a 24hr. emergency medical and legal assistance hotline (in North America call ☎800-554-2639, elsewhere call US collect ☎715-343-7977), and enjoy American Express Travel Service benefits (including plane, hotel, and car rental reservation changes; baggage loss and flight insurance; mailgram and international cable services; and held mail). The **Discover Card** (in US ☎800-347-2683, elsewhere call US ☎801-902-3100) offers cash back bonuses on most purchases.

CASH CARDS (ATM CARDS)

Cash cards—popularly called **ATM** (Automated Teller Machine) cards—are widely used on most islands. Islands with less of a tourism industry, however, such as Molokai and Lanai, have ATMs in only a few locations. Depending on the system that your home bank uses, you can most likely access your personal bank account from abroad. ATMs get the same wholesale exchange rate as credit cards, but there is often a limit on the amount of money you can withdraw per day (around $300). There is typically also a surcharge of $1-2 per withdrawal. Also, if your PIN is longer than four digits, ask your bank whether you need a new number.

The two major international money networks are **Cirrus** (☎800-424-7787) and **VISA/PLUS** (☎800-843-7587). To locate ATMs around the world, call the above numbers, or consult www.visa.com or www.mastercard.com. Most ATMs charge a transaction fee that is paid to the bank that owns the ATM.

DEBIT CARDS

Debit cards are a hybrid between credit and cash cards. They bear the logo of a major credit card, but purchases and withdrawals made with them are paid directly out of your bank account. Using a debit card like a credit card often incurs no fee (contact the issuing bank for details), gives you a favorable exchange rate, and frees you from having to carry large sums of money. Be careful, though: debit cards lack the theft protection that credit cards usually have.

GETTING MONEY FROM HOME

If you run out of money while traveling, the easiest and cheapest solution is to have someone back home make a deposit to your credit card or cash (ATM) card. Failing that, consider one of the following options.

WIRING MONEY. It is possible to arrange a **bank money transfer,** which means asking a bank back home to wire money to a bank in Hawaii. This is the cheapest way to transfer cash, but it's also the slowest, usually taking several days or more. Note that some banks may only release your funds in local currency, potentially sticking you with a poor exchange rate; inquire about this in advance. Money transfer services like **Western Union** are faster and more convenient than bank transfers, but also much pricier. Western Union has many locations worldwide. To find one, visit www.westernunion.com, or call in the US ☎800-325-6000, in Canada ☎800-235-0000, in the UK ☎0800 83 38 33, in Australia ☎800 501 500, in New Zealand ☎800 27 0000, or in South Africa ☎0860 100031. To wire money within the US using a credit card (Visa, MasterCard, Discover), call ☎800-225-5227. Money transfer services are also available at American Express offices.

COSTS

The cost of your trip will vary considerably, depending on where you go, how you travel, and where you stay. For foreign travelers, the single biggest cost of the trip will probably be the round-trip **airfare** to Hawaii (see **Getting There**, p. 49). A car is necessary for traveling in many parts of Hawaii, and travelers who plan on renting must also figure this expense into account (for information on car rental, see p. 22). It is a good idea to plan a daily **budget** for your trip before leaving.

STAYING ON A BUDGET. In Hawaii, **accommodations** start at about $17 per night in a hostel bed, while a basic sit-down meal costs about $8-12 depending on the region. A slightly more comfortable day (sleeping in hostels/guest houses and the occasional budget hotel, eating one meal a day at a restaurant, going out at night) would run $50-65; for a luxurious day, the sky's the limit. Transportation costs will increase these figures. **Gas** prices have risen significantly in the US over the past year. In Hawaii a gallon of gas now costs about $2.00 per gallon, but prices vary widely according to state gasoline taxes. Finally, don't forget to factor in emergency reserve funds (at least $200) when planning how much money you'll need.

TIPS FOR SAVING MONEY. Considering that saving just a few dollars a day over the course of your trip might pay for days or weeks of additional travel, the art of penny-pinching is well worth learning. Learn to take advantage of freebies: for example, museums will typically be free once a week or once a month, and cities often host free open-air concerts and/or cultural events (especially in the summer). Bring a sleep sack to save on sheet charges in hostels, and do your **laundry** in the sink (unless you're explicitly prohibited from doing so). You can split **accommodation** costs (in hotels and some hostels) with trustworthy fellow travelers; multi-bed rooms almost always work out cheaper per person than singles. The same principle will also work for cutting down on the cost of **restaurant** meals. You can also buy food in supermarkets instead of eating out. These simple tactics make the occasional splurge feel all the more rewarding.

TIPPING AND BARGAINING

In the US, it is customary to tip waitstaff and cab drivers 15-20% (at your discretion). Tips are usually not included in restaurant bills, unless you are in a party of 6 or more. At the airport and in hotels, porters expect at least a $2 per bag tip to carry your bags. Except at flea markets or other informal settings, bargaining is generally frowned upon and fruitless in Hawaii.

TAXES

In Hawaii, the state sales tax is 4%. There are often reduced rates for some types of items. Usually these taxes are not included in the prices of items. There is a transient accommodations tax of 11.42%.

INSURANCE

Travel insurance generally covers four basic areas: medical/health problems, property loss, trip cancellation/interruption, and emergency evacuation. Although your regular insurance policies may well extend to travel-related accidents, you may consider purchasing travel insurance if the cost of potential trip cancellation/interruption or emergency medical evacuation is greater than you can absorb. Prices for travel insurance purchased separately generally run about $50 per week for full coverage, while trip cancellation/interruption may be purchased separately at a rate of about $5.50 per $100 of coverage.

Medical insurance (especially university policies) often covers costs incurred abroad; check with your provider. **Canadians** are protected by their home province's health insurance plan for up to 90 days after leaving the country; check with the provincial Ministry of Health or Health Plan Headquarters for details. **Homeowners' insurance** (or your family's coverage) often covers theft during travel and loss of travel documents (passport, plane ticket, rail pass, etc.) up to $500.

ISIC and **ITIC** (see p. 38) provide basic insurance benefits, including US$100 per day of in-hospital sickness for up to 60 days, $3000 of accident-related medical reimbursement, and $25,000 for emergency medical transport. Cardholders have access to a toll-free 24hr. helpline (run by the insurance provider **TravelGuard**) for medical, legal, and financial emergencies overseas (US and Canada ☎ 877-370-4742, elsewhere call US collect ☎ 715-345-0505). **American Express** (US ☎ 800-528-4800) grants most cardholders automatic car rental insurance (collision and theft, but not liability) and ground travel accident coverage of $100,000 on flight purchases made with the card.

INSURANCE PROVIDERS. STA (see p. 50) offers a range of plans that can supplement your basic coverage. Other private insurance providers in the US and Canada include: **Access America** (☎ 800-284-8300); **Berkeley Group/Carefree Travel Insurance**

(☎800-323-3149; www.berkely.com); **Globalcare Travel Insurance** (☎800-821-2488; www.globalcare-cocco.com); **Travel Assistance International** (☎800-821-2828; www.europ-assistance.com). Providers in the **UK** include **Columbus Direct** (☎020 7375 0011). In **Australia,** try **AFTA** (☎02 9264 3299).

SAFETY AND SECURITY

Hawaii is generally considered a safe place; however, travelers should be sure to exercise the basic precautions described below. For more specific tips and information, see **Specific Concerns** (p. 67) or **Wilderness Safety** (p. 59).

PERSONAL SAFETY

EXPLORING. To avoid unwanted attention, try to blend in as much as possible and familiarize yourself with the area before you set out. The gawking camera-toter is a more obvious target for thieves and con artists than the low-profile traveler. Carry yourself with confidence; if you must check a map on the street, duck into a shop. If you are traveling alone, be sure someone at home knows your itinerary, and *never admit that you're traveling alone.*

Whenever possible, *Let's Go* warns of unsafe neighborhoods and areas, but there are some good general tips to follow. When walking at night, stick to busy, well-lit streets and avoid dark alleyways. Do not attempt to cross through parks, parking lots, or other large, deserted areas. Buildings in disrepair, vacant lots, and unpopulated areas are all bad signs. Keep in mind that a district can change character drastically between blocks and from day to night. Look for children playing, women walking in the open, and other signs of an active community. If you feel uncomfortable, leave as quickly and directly as you can, but don't allow fear of the unknown to turn you into a hermit. Careful, persistent exploration will build confidence and make your stay even more rewarding.

SELF DEFENSE. There is no sure-fire way to avoid all the threatening situations you might encounter when you travel, but a good self-defense course will give you concrete ways to react to different types of aggression. **Impact, Prepare,** and **Model Mugging** can refer you to local self-defense courses in the US (☎800-345-5425). Visit the web site at www.impactsafety.org for a list of nearby chapters. Two- to three-hour workshops start at $50; full courses (20hr.) run $350-500. Both men and women are welcome.

GETTING AROUND. If you are using a **car,** learn local driving signals and wear a seat belt. Children under 40 lbs. should ride only in a specially-designed carseat, available for a small fee from most car rental agencies. Study route maps before you hit the road. If your car breaks down, wait for the police to assist you. For long drives in desolate areas, invest in a cellular phone and a roadside assistance program (see p. 53). Be sure to park your vehicle in a garage or well-traveled area, and use a steering wheel locking device in larger cities. **Sleeping in your car** is one of the most dangerous (and often illegal) ways to get your rest. When at the beach, never leave valuables in your car, as thieves often target crowded beach parking lots.

Public transportation is generally safe. Occasionally, bus stations can be unsafe; *Let's Go* warns of these stations where applicable. Within major US cities, the quality and safety of public transportation vary considerably. It is usually a good idea to avoid buses late at night; if you must use these forms of transportation, try to travel in a large group. **Taxis** are usually safe. *Let's Go* does not recommend **hitchhiking** under any circumstances, particularly for women—see **Getting Around,** p. 52 for more info.

TERRORISM. In light of the September 11, 2001 terrorist attacks in the eastern US, the US government frequently puts the nation, and its territories, on an elevated terrorism alert. Hawaii has not had any attacks, or threats of attacks, but like the rest of the US the islands have taken necessary precautions. Allow extra time for airport security and do not pack sharp objects in your carry-on luggage, as they will be confiscated. Monitor developments in the news and stay on top of any local, state, or federal terrorist warnings, but do not let fear of terrorism prevent you from enjoying your vacation.

TRAVEL ADVISORIES. The following government offices provide travel information and advisories by telephone, by fax, or via the web:

Australian Department of Foreign Affairs and Trade: ☎13 00 555 135; fax back service 02 6261 1299; www.dfat.gov.au.

Canadian Department of Foreign Affairs and International Trade (DFAIT): In Canada and the US call ☎800-267-8376, elsewhere call ☎613-944-4000; www.dfait-maeci.gi.ca. Call for their free booklet, *Bon Voyage... But.*

New Zealand Ministry of Foreign Affairs: ☎04 439 8000; fax 494 8506; www.mft.govt.nz/travel/index.html.

United Kingdom Foreign and Commonwealth Office: ☎020 7008 0232; fax 7008 0155; www.fco.gov.uk.

US Department of State: ☎202-647-5225; fax back service 202-647-3000; http://travel.state.gov. For *A Safe Trip Abroad*, call 202-512-1800.

FINANCIAL SECURITY

PROTECTING YOUR VALUABLES. There are a few steps you can take to minimize the financial risk associated with traveling. First, **bring as little with you as possible.** Second, buy a few combination **padlocks** to secure your belongings either in your pack or in a hostel. Third, **carry as little cash as possible.** Keep your traveler's checks and ATM/credit cards in a **money belt**—not a "fanny pack"—along with your passport and ID cards. Fourth, **keep a small cash reserve separate from your primary stash.** This should be about US$50 sewn into or stored in the depths of your pack, along with your traveler's check numbers and important photocopies.

CON ARTISTS AND PICKPOCKETS. In large cities **con artists** often work in groups, and children are among the most effective. Beware of certain classics: sob stories that require money, rolls of bills "found" on the street, mustard spilled (or saliva spit) onto your shoulder to distract you while they snatch your bag. **Don't ever let your passport and your bags out of your sight.** Beware of **pickpockets** in city crowds, especially on public transportation. Also, be alert in public telephone booths: If you must say your calling card number, do so very quietly; if you punch it in, make sure no one can look over your shoulder.

ACCOMMODATIONS AND TRANSPORTATION. Never leave your belongings unattended; crime occurs in even the most demure-looking hostel or hotel. Be particularly careful on **buses;** horror stories abound about determined thieves who wait for travelers to fall asleep. Carry your backpack in front of you where you can see it. When traveling with others, sleep in alternate shifts. Do not leave valuables in your car. If you must, however, place them in an area where they are not easily visible.

DRUGS AND ALCOHOL

As in the continental US, the drinking age in Hawaii is a strictly-enforced 21. The youthful should expect to be asked to show government-issued identification when purchasing any alcoholic beverage. Most localities restrict where and when alcohol can be sold. Drinking and driving is prohibited everywhere, and it is illegal to have an open container of alcohol inside a car, even if you are not the driver and even if you are not drinking it. Those caught drinking and driving face fines, a suspended license, imprisonment, or all three.

Narcotics such as marijuana, heroin, and cocaine are highly illegal in the US. If you carry prescription drugs while you travel, it is important that you keep a copy of the prescription with you.

HEALTH

Common sense is the simplest prescription for good health. Travelers complain most often about their feet and their gut, so take precautionary measures: drink lots of fluids to prevent dehydration and constipation, wear sturdy, broken-in shoes and clean socks, and use talcum powder to keep your feet dry. To minimize the effects of jet lag, "reset" your body's clock by adopting the time of your destination as soon as you board the plane. It also helps to avoid caffeine and alcohol on the flight; stick to water instead.

BEFORE YOU GO

Preparation can help minimize the likelihood of contracting a disease and maximize the chances of receiving effective health care in the event of an emergency. For minor health problems, bring a compact **first-aid kit** (see p. 49). In your **passport**, write the names of any people you wish to be contacted in case of a medical emergency and list any **allergies** or medical conditions of which you would want doctors to be aware. Allergy sufferers might want to obtain a full supply of any necessary medication before the trip. Matching a prescription to a foreign equivalent is not always easy, safe, or possible. Carry up-to-date, legible prescriptions or a statement from your doctor stating the medication's trade name, manufacturer, chemical name, and dosage. While traveling, be sure to keep all medication with you in your carry-on luggage.

IMMUNIZATIONS AND PRECAUTIONS

Travelers over two years old should make sure that the following vaccines are up to date: MMR (for measles, mumps, and rubella); DTaP or Td (for diptheria, tetanus, and pertussis); OPV (for polio); HbCV (for haemophilus influenza B); and HBV (for hepatitis B). For recommendations on immunizations and prophylaxis, consult the CDC (see below) in the US or the equivalent in your home country, and check with a doctor for guidance.

USEFUL ORGANIZATIONS AND PUBLICATIONS

The US **Centers for Disease Control and Prevention (CDC;** ☎877-FYI-TRIP or 394-8747; toll-free fax 888-232-3299; www.cdc.gov/travel) maintains an international travelers' hotline and an informative web site. The CDC's comprehensive booklet *Health Information for International Travel*, an annual rundown of disease, immunization, and general health advice, is free online or available for $30 via the Public Health Foundation (☎877-252-1200). Consult the appropriate government agency of your home country for consular information sheets on health, entry requirements, and other issues for various countries. For quick information on health and other travel warnings, call the **Overseas Citizens Services** (8:15am-5pm EST ☎202-647-5225; after-hours ☎202-647-4000), or contact a passport agency, embassy, or consulate abroad. US citizens can send a self-addressed, stamped envelope to the Overseas Citizens Services, Bureau of Consular Affairs, #4811, US Department of State, Washington, DC 20520. For information on medical evacuation services and travel insurance firms, see the US government's web site at http://travel.state.gov/medical.html or the **British Foreign and Commonwealth Office** (www.fco.gov.uk).

For detailed information on travel health, including a country-by-country overview of diseases and a list of travel clinics in the US, try the **International Travel Health Guide,** by Stuart Rose, MD ($25; www.travmed.com). For general health info, contact the **American Red Cross** (☎800-564-1234; www.redcross.org).

MEDICAL ASSISTANCE ON THE ROAD

Medical services in Hawaii are available 24hr. at hospitals throughout the islands. Some more rural towns may be driving distance away from the nearest hospital but, for the most part, medical care is readily available. In an emergency, dial ☎**911** from any phone and an operator will send out paramedics, a fire brigade, or the police as needed. Alternatively, if there is an emergency room near by, go directly there for immediate service. Almost all cities and towns have standard pharmacies.

If you are concerned about obtaining medical assistance while traveling, you may wish to employ special support services. The *MedPass* from **GlobalCare, Inc.,** 6875 Shiloh Rd. East, Alpharetta, GA 30005 (☎800-860-1111; fax 678-341-1800; www.globalems.com), provides 24hr. international medical assistance, support, and medical evacuation resources. The **International Association for Medical Assistance to Travelers (IAMAT;** US ☎716-754-4883, Canada ☎519-836-0102; www.cybermall.co.nz/NZ/IAMAT) has free membership, lists English-speaking doctors worldwide, and offers detailed info on immunization requirements and sanitation. If your regular **insurance** policy does not cover travel abroad, you may wish to purchase additional coverage (see p. 8).

Those with medical conditions (such as diabetes, allergies to antibiotics, epilepsy, heart conditions) may want to obtain a **Medic Alert** membership (first year $35, annually $20 thereafter), which includes a stainless steel ID tag and other benefits, including a 24hr. collect-call number. Contact the Medic Alert Foundation, 2323 Colorado Ave, Turlock, CA 95382 (☎888-633-4298; outside US ☎209-668-3333; www.medicalert.org).

ONCE IN HAWAII

ENVIRONMENTAL HAZARDS

SURFING AND SWIMMING PRECAUTIONS Hawaiian waves make for some of the world's best surf, but they can also be deadly. High surf can bring strong currents and rip tides, and each year lives are lost and endangered when surfers and swimmers fail to heed precautions. In Hawaii waters, know your limits and use extra caution whenever you swim or surf. The following are a few simple precautions:

Never swim alone.

Swim and surf only in **lifeguarded** areas.

Do not struggle against a **current** or **riptide;** swim diagonally across it.

Signal for help if you are unable to swim out of a strong current.

Use a **leash** for surf and boogie boards.

Keep your distance from other surfers and swimmers—a loose board can deliver a lethal blow.

Familiarize yourself with **beach and surf conditions,** as well as beach safety signs and symbols before you head out.

If you see **sharks,** get out of the water.

Heat exhaustion can lead to fatigue, headaches, and wooziness. Avoid it and **dehydration** by drinking plenty of fluids, eating salty foods (e.g. crackers), and avoiding dehydrating beverages (e.g. alcohol and caffeinated beverages). Continuous heat stress can eventually lead to heatstroke, characterized by a rising temperature, severe headache, and cessation of sweating. Victims should be cooled off with wet towels and taken to a doctor.

The sunshine of paradise comes at a price if you're not careful. Remember that you can get **sunburned** even on a cloudy day. Be sure to apply sunscreen of SPF 15 or higher before you go out for the day and after swimming. If you do get sunburned, drink more fluids than usual and apply an aloe-based lotion. Severe sunburns can lead to sun poisoning, a condition that affects the entire body, causing fever, chills, nausea, and vomiting. Sun poisoning should always be treated by a doctor.

In **high altitudes,** allow your body a couple days to adjust to less oxygen before exerting yourself. Note that alcohol is more potent and UV rays are stronger at high elevations.

INSECT-BORNE DISEASES

Many diseases are transmitted by insects—mainly mosquitoes, fleas, ticks, and lice. Be aware of insects in wet or forested areas, especially while hiking and camping; wear long pants and long sleeves, tuck your pants into your socks, and buy a mosquito net. Use insect repellents such as DEET and soak or spray your gear with permethrin (licensed in the US for use on clothing).

FOOD- AND WATER-BORNE DISEASES

Travelers in Hawaii experience food and water-related illness much less often than in most parts of the world, thanks to good water-treatment facilities and fairly well-maintained restaurant standards. The tap water in Hawaii is treated to be safe for drinking. There are, however, a few campsites that require the water be treated before drinking. Purify water by bringing it to a rolling boil or treating it with iodine tablets; boiling, however, is more reliable.

Leptospirosis is a bacterial disease that is caused by exposure to fresh water contaminated by the urine of infected animals. Most common in tropical climates, it has been known to be present in Hawaii's fresh water. Symptoms include a high fever, severe headaches, chills, nausea, and vomiting. If not treated it can lead to liver failure and meningitis. Protective clothing and footwear should be worn by all those who might be exposed. Consult a doctor for treatment.

OTHER INFECTIOUS DISEASES

Hepatitis B is a viral infection of the liver transmitted via bodily fluids or needle-sharing. Symptoms may not surface until years after infection. Vaccinations are recommended for health-care workers, sexually active travelers, and anyone planning to seek medical treatment abroad. The three-shot vaccination series must begin 6 months before traveling.

Hepatitis C is similar to Hep B, but the mode of transmission differs. IV drug users, those with occupational exposure to blood, hemodialysis patients, and recipients of blood transfusions are at the highest risk, but the disease can also be spread through sexual contact or sharing items like razors and toothbrushes that may have traces of blood on them.

AIDS, HIV, & STDS

For detailed information on **Acquired Immune Deficiency Syndrome (AIDS)** in Hawaii, call the **US Centers for Disease Control's** 24hr. hotline at ☎ 800-342-2437, or contact the **Joint United Nations Programme on HIV/AIDS (UNAIDS),** 20, avenue Appia, CH-1211 Geneva 27, Switzerland (☎ 41 22 791 3666; fax 22 791 4187). According to US law, HIV positive persons are not permitted to enter the US. However, HIV testing is conducted only for those who are planning to immigrate permanently. Contact the US consulate for information (see p. 35).

ESSENTIALS

Sexually transmitted diseases (STDs) such as gonorrhea, chlamydia, genital warts, syphilis, and herpes are easier to catch than HIV and can be just as deadly. **Hepatitis B** and **C** can also be transmitted sexually (see above). Though condoms may protect you from some STDs, oral or even tactile contact can lead to transmission. If you think you may have contracted an STD, see a doctor immediately.

WOMEN'S HEALTH

Women traveling in unsanitary conditions are vulnerable to **urinary tract** and **bladder infections,** common and very uncomfortable bacterial conditions that cause a burning sensation and painful (sometimes frequent) urination. Over-the-counter medicines can sometimes alleviate symptoms; if they persist, see a doctor.

Vaginal yeast infections may flare up in hot and humid climates. Wearing loosely fitting trousers or a skirt and cotton underwear will help, as will over-the-counter remedies like Monistat or Gynelotrimin. You may want to bring supplies from home if you are prone to infection.

PACKING

Pack lightly: lay out only what you absolutely need, then take half the clothes and twice the money. If you plan to do a lot of hiking, also see the section on **Camping & the Outdoors** (p. 59).

LUGGAGE. If you plan to cover most of your itinerary on foot, a sturdy **frame backpack** is unbeatable. (For the basics on buying a pack, see p. 60.) Toting a **suitcase** or **trunk** is fine if you plan to live in one or two cities and explore from there or plan to rent a car, but is a very bad idea if you're moving around a lot. In addition to your main piece of luggage, a **daypack** (a small backpack or courier bag) is a must.

CLOTHING. Dress in Hawaii is like the Hawaiian lifestyle—casual and laid-back. Almost everyone, from grandparents to preschoolers, swears by plastic **flip-flops** ("slippers" or "slippahs" in local speak). If you want to blend in, pick up a pair at any drugstore or supermarket. Otherwise, shorts and light t-shirts or tank tops can suffice for almost any occasion. A light sweater or jacket can come in handy for cooler nights, though during the summer they're almost never needed. No matter when you're traveling, it's always a good idea to bring a **rain jacket** (Gore-Tex® is both waterproof and breathable) and if you're planning on hiking, sturdy shoes or **hiking boots** are a must. Long pants may also come in handy. You may want to add one nicer outfit beyond the jeans and t-shirt uniform. Luckily, women can almost always get away with wearing sundresses and sandals and all men typically need is a pair of khakis and an aloha shirt. If you are planning on splurging on a chi-chi dinner at an expensive restaurant, you may need to upgrade your wardrobe a smidgen; a nicer sundress for a woman and a jacket for a man.

CONVERTERS, ADAPTERS, AND TRANSFORMERS. In Hawaii, as in the rest of the US, electrical appliances are designed for 120V current. Canadians, who use 120V at home, will be able to use electrical appliances in the U.S. with no problem. Visitors from the U.K., Ireland, Australia, New Zealand (who use 230V), as well as South Africa (who use 220-250V), won't need a converter, but will need an adapter to use anything electrical. In addition, they will need to purchase a transformer to convert the lower American voltage to the higher voltage required for most appliances; however, certain electrical devices may accept both 230V and 120V. For further details, check out http://kropla.com/electric.htm.

TOILETRIES. Toothbrushes, towels, soap, talcum powder (to keep feet dry), deodorant, razors, tampons, and condoms are readily available, but it's a good idea to bring extras along. The same goes for contact lenses. Bring your glasses and a copy of your prescription in case you need emergency replacements. If you use heat-disinfection, either switch temporarily to a chemical disinfection system (check first to make sure it's safe with your brand of lenses), or buy an adaptor and a transformer to 120V.

FIRST-AID KIT. For a basic first-aid kit, pack: bandages, pain reliever, antibiotic cream, a thermometer, a Swiss Army knife, tweezers, moleskin, decongestant, motion-sickness remedy, diarrhea or upset-stomach medication (Pepto Bismol or Imodium), an antihistamine, sunscreen, insect repellent, burn ointment, and a syringe for emergencies (get an explanatory letter from your doctor).

CELLULAR PHONES. Cellular coverage in Hawaii varies from island to island. Oahu, the Big Island, Maui, and Kauai all have some coverage, but as large parts of these islands are National Parks and other uninhabited areas, there is no coverage on any entire island. If you are a domestic traveler, check with your service provider before you leave to see if your phone will work. If you are coming from abroad, your phone will most likely not work. Companies like **Cellular Abroad** (www.cellularabroad.com) rent cell phones for a variety of destinations around the world.

FILM. Less serious photographers may want to bring a **disposable camera** or two rather than an expensive permanent one. Despite disclaimers, airport security X-rays *can* fog film, so buy a lead-lined pouch at a camera store or ask security to hand-inspect it. Always pack film in your carry-on luggage, since higher-intensity X-rays are used on checked luggage.

OTHER USEFUL ITEMS. For safety purposes, you should bring a **money belt** and small **padlock**. Basic **outdoors equipment** (plastic water bottle, compass, waterproof matches, pocketknife, sunglasses, sunscreen, hat) may also prove useful. **Quick repairs** of torn garments can be done on the road with a needle and thread; also consider bringing electrical tape for patching tears. If you want to do laundry by hand, bring detergent, a small rubber ball to stop up the sink, and string for a makeshift clothes line. **Other things** you're liable to forget: an umbrella, sealable **plastic bags** (for damp clothes, soap, food, shampoo, and other spillables), an **alarm clock**, safety pins, rubber bands, a flashlight, earplugs, garbage bags, and a small **calculator**.

IMPORTANT DOCUMENTS. Don't forget your passport, traveler's checks, ATM and/or credit cards, and adequate ID (see p. 38). Also check that you have any of the following that might apply to you: a hosteling membership card (see p. 57); driver's license, and travel insurance forms.

GETTING TO HAWAII

Hawaii is primarily accessible by plane. Airfares can be quite expensive, so a little effort and research can save you a bundle. Tickets bought from consolidators and standby seating are good deals, but last-minute specials, airfare wars, and charter flights often beat these fares. The key is to hunt around, to be flexible, and to ask persistently about discounts. Students, seniors, and those under 26 should never pay full price for a ticket.

AIRFARES

Airfares to Hawaii are consistently high throughout the year. Holidays and the winter months are particularly expensive. It is slightly cheaper to travel in the fall and spring. Midweek (M-Th morning) round-trip flights run $40-50 cheaper than weekend flights, but they are generally more crowded and less likely to permit frequent-flier upgrades. Not fixing a return date ("open return") or arriving in and departing from different cities ("open-jaw") can be pricier than round-trip flights. Patching one-way flights together is the most expensive way to travel. Flights into Oahu are by far more common and, almost always, less expensive than flights into other islands.

If Hawaii is only one stop on a more extensive globe-hop, consider a round-the-world (RTW) ticket. Tickets usually include at least five stops and are valid for about a year; prices range $1200-5000. Try **Northwest Airlines/KLM** (☎800-447-4747; www.nwa.com) or **Star Alliance**, a consortium of 22 airlines including United Airlines (☎800-241-6522; www.star-alliance.com). **Circle Pacific** fares are another way to incorporate Hawaii into a larger itinerary. One fare allows you to visit various destinations around the Pacific Ocean. The web site www.justfares.com helps travelers create a custom itinerary with all their desired destinations and then spits out a quote for that trip. The **World Traveller's Club** (☎800-693-0411; www.around-the-world.com) also provides a similar service. Their web site lists the most popular Circle Pacific routes but also allows users to design their own trips. The tickets are valid for one year and travelers are (almost always) free to stay in each destination for as long as they desire.

Fares for roundtrip flights to Hawaii from the US or Canadian east coast range from $1000 to $2000, depending on how early you book your flight. From the US or Canadian west coast $500-700; from the UK £800-850; from Australia, AUS$3000-3500; from New Zealand NZ$3000-3500.

BUDGET AND STUDENT TRAVEL AGENCIES

While knowledgeable agents specializing in flights to Hawaii can make your life easy and help you save, they may not spend the time to find you the lowest possible fare—they get paid on commission. Travelers holding **ISIC and IYTC cards** (see p. 38) qualify for big discounts from student travel agencies. Most flights from budget agencies are on major airlines, but in peak season some may sell seats on less reliable chartered aircraft.

CTS Travel, 30 Rathbone Pl., **London** W1T 1GQ, UK(☎020 7290 0630; www.ctstravel.co.uk). A British student travel agent with offices in 39 countries including the US. Empire State Building, 350 Fifth Ave., Suite 7813, **New York,** NY 10118 (☎877-287-6665; www.ctstravelusa.com).

STA Travel, 7890 S. Hardy Dr., Ste. 110, Tempe AZ 85284, USA (☎800-781-4040; www.sta-travel.com). A student and youth travel organization with over 400 offices worldwide. Ticket booking, travel insurance, and more. US offices in Boston, Chicago, L.A., New York, San Francisco, Seattle, and Washington, D.C. In the UK, 33 Bedford St., Covent Garden, **London** WC2E 9ED (☎0870 1 600 599). In New Zealand, Shop 2B, 187 Queen St., **Auckland** (☎09 309 0458). In Australia, 260 Hoddle St., **Abbotsford** VIC 3067 (☎03 8417 6911). Check their web site for a complete list of offices. **Council Travel** is now a subsidiary of STA, but still has offices throughout the US.

Travel CUTS (Canadian Universities Travel Services Limited), 187 College St., **Toronto,** ON M5T 1P7 (☎416-979-2406 or 800-667-2887; www.travelcuts.com). Canada's main student travel agent has offices throughout Canada and a few in the US, including Boston, Seattle, New York, and San Francisco. Books budget plane tickets for students and non-students. Also in the UK, 295A Regent St., **London** W1B 2H9.

USIT, 19-21 Aston Quay, Dublin 2 (☎01 602 1600; www.usitworld.com). Ireland's leading student/budget travel agency has 22 offices throughout Northern Ireland and the Republic of Ireland. Offers programs to work in North America.

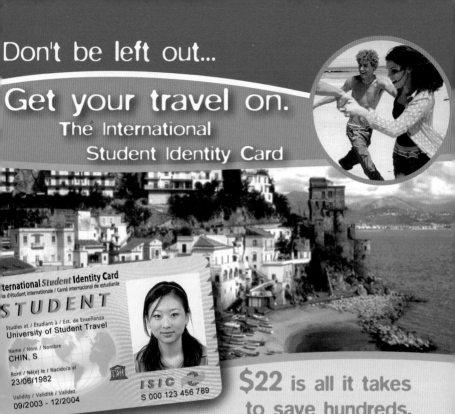

FLIGHT PLANNING ON THE INTERNET.
Many airline sites offer special last-minute deals on the Web. Aloha Airlines (www.alohaair.com) and Hawaiian Airlines (www.hawaiianair.com) often publicize low web fares on their sites. Other sites do the legwork and compile the deals for you—try www.bestfares.com, www.flights.com, www.onetravel.com, and www.travelzoo.com.

StudentUniverse (www.studentuniverse.com) and **STA** (www.sta-travel.com) provide quotes on student tickets, while **Expedia** (www.expedia.com), **Orbitz.com,** and **Travelocity** (www.travelocity.com) offer full travel services. **Priceline** (www.priceline.com) allows you to specify a price, and obligates you to buy any ticket that meets or beats it; be prepared for antisocial hours and odd routes. **Skyauction** (www.skyauction.com) allows you to bid on both last-minute and advance-purchase tickets.

An indispensable resource on the Internet is the *Air Traveler's Handbook* (www.cs.cmu.edu/afs/cs/user/mkant/Public/Travel/airfare.html), a comprehensive listing of links to everything you need to know before you board a plane.

COMMERCIAL AIRLINES

The commercial airlines' lowest regular offer is the **APEX (Advance Purchase Excursion)** fare, which provides confirmed reservations and allows "open-jaw" tickets. Generally, reservations must be made seven to 21 days ahead of departure, with seven- to 14-day minimum-stay and up to 90-day maximum-stay restrictions. These fares carry hefty cancellation and change penalties (fees rise in summer). Book peak-season APEX fares early; by May you will have a hard time getting your desired departure date. Use **Microsoft Expedia** (http://msn.expedia.com) or **Travelocity** (www.travelocity.com) to get an idea of the lowest published fares, then use the resources outlined here to try and beat those fares. For a complete list of airports and airlines that fly to the Hawaiian islands, go to http://www.state.hi.us/dot/airports.

STANDBY FLIGHTS

Traveling standby requires considerable flexibility in arrival and departure dates and cities. Companies dealing in standby flights sell vouchers rather than tickets, along with the promise to get to your destination (or near your destination) within a certain window of time (typically 1-5 days). You call in before your specific window of time to hear your flight options and to hear the probability that you will be able to board each flight. You can then decide which flights you want to try to make; show up at the appropriate airport at the appropriate time, present your voucher, and board if space is available. Vouchers can usually be bought for both one-way and round-trip travel. You may receive a monetary refund only if every available flight within your date range is full; if you opt not to take an available (but perhaps less convenient) flight, you can only get credit toward future travel. Carefully read agreements with any company offering standby flights as tricky fine print can leave you in a lurch. To check on a company's service record in the US, call the Better Business Bureau (☎ 212-533-6200). It is difficult to receive refunds, and clients' vouchers will not be honored when an airline fails to receive payment in time.

TICKET CONSOLIDATORS

Ticket consolidators, or **"bucket shops,"** buy unsold tickets in bulk from commercial airlines and sell them at discounted rates. The best place to look is in the Sunday travel section of any major newspaper (such as *The New York Times*), where many bucket shops place tiny ads. Call quickly, as availability is typically extremely limited. Not all bucket shops are reliable, so insist on a receipt that gives full details of restrictions, refunds, and tickets, and pay by credit card (in spite of the 2-5% fee) so you can stop payment if you never receive your tickets. For more info, see www.travel-library.com/air-travel/consolidators.html.

TRAVELING FROM THE US & CANADA

Travel Avenue (☎800-333-3335; www.travelavenue.com) finds the best available published fares and then uses several consolidators to attempt to beat that fare. Other consolidators worth trying are **Rebel** (☎800-227-3235; www.rebeltours.com) and **TravelHUB** (www.travelhub.com). Keep in mind that these are just suggestions to get you started in your research; *Let's Go* does not endorse any of these agencies. Be cautious, and research companies before you hand over your credit card number.

TRAVELING FROM THE UK, AUSTRALIA, & NEW ZEALAND

In London, the **Air Travel Advisory Bureau** (☎0207 306 3000; www.atab.co.uk) can provide names of reliable consolidators and discount flight specialists. From Australia and New Zealand, look for consolidator ads in the travel section of the *Sydney Morning Herald* and other papers.

CHARTER FLIGHTS

Charters are flights a tour operator contracts with an airline to fly extra loads of passengers during peak season. Charter flights fly less frequently than major airlines, make refunds particularly difficult, and are almost always fully booked. Schedules and itineraries may also change or be cancelled at the last moment (as late as 48hr. before the trip, and without a full refund), and check-in, boarding, and baggage claim are often much slower. However, they can also be cheaper.

   Discount clubs and **fare brokers** offer members savings on last-minute charter and tour deals. Study contracts closely; you don't want to end up with an unwanted overnight layover.

GETTING AROUND HAWAII

BY PLANE

There are three inter-island airlines: Hawaiian Airlines (☎800-367-5320), Aloha Airlines (☎800-367-5250) and Island Air (☎800-323-3345). All three offer competitive rates on inter-island flights. One-way flights from Honolulu to the outer islands start at $50. Aloha Airlines sells a pass for $336 that allows visitors unlimited inter-island air travel for seven days.

BY BUS

Public transportation on **Oahu** is generally safe, clean and relatively convenient. With 86 routes criss-crossing the island and over 4000 bus stops, it's safe to say that TheBus can get you where you're going. Adult one-way fare is $1.50, student one-way fare is $0.75. Monthly passes ($27 and $13.50, respectively) can be purchased at various supermarkets and drugstores. Contact **TheBus,** 811 Middle St., Honolulu 96819 (☎808-848-5555 or customer service 808-848-4500; www.thebus.org). The county of **Kauai** also maintains a decent bus system. Schedules and other information are available at the **County of Kauai Transportation office,** 3220 Ho'olako St., Lihue, Kauai 96766 (☎808-241-6410; fax 808-241-6417). The **Big Island** has limited bus service. Contact **County of Hawaii Mass Transit office,** 630 E. Lani-kaula St., Hilo 96720 (☎808-961-8744; fax 808-961-8745; http://www.hawaii-county.com/mass_transit/transit_main.htm). **Maui** offers only localized shuttle service through **Speedishuttle** (☎808-661-6667; www.speedishuttle.com). **Molokai** and **Lanai** have no form of public transportation.

BY CAR

Though car rental can be expensive, driving is the best and most efficient way to get around in Hawaii. "U.S." (as in "U.S. 1") refers to US highways, and "Rte." (as in "Rte. 7") to state and local highways.

INTERNATIONAL DRIVING PERMIT

If you do not have a license issued by a US state or Canadian province or territory, you might want an **International Driving Permit (IDP).** While the US allows you to drive with a foreign license for up to a year, it may help with police if your license is written in English. You must be 18 to obtain an IDP, it is valid for a year, and must be issued in the country in which your license originates. You must carry your home license with your IDP at all times. Contact these offices to apply:

Australia: Contact your local Royal Automobile Club (RAC) or the National Royal Motorist Association (NRMA) if in NSW or the ACT (☎08 9421 4400; www.rac.com.au/travel). Permits AUS$20.

Canada: Contact any Canadian Automobile Association (CAA) branch office or write to CAA, 1145 Hunt Club Rd., Ste. 200, Ottawa, ON K1V 0Y3 (☎613-247-0117; www.caa.ca). Permits CDN$13.

Ireland: Contact the nearest Automobile Association (AA) office or write to the UK address below. Permits €5.08. The Irish Automobile Association (☎353 01 617 9988), honors most foreign automobile memberships.

New Zealand: Contact your local Automobile Association (AA) or their main office at Auckland Central, 99 Albert St. Auckland City (☎9 377 4660; www.nzaa.co.nz). Permits NZ$12.

South Africa: Contact the Travel Services Department of the Automobile Association of South Africa at P.O. Box 596, Johannesburg 2000 (☎27 11 799 1000; fax 27 11 799 1010; http://aasa.co.za).

UK: To visit your local AA Shop, contact the **AA Headquarters** (☎0870 600 0371), or write to: The Automobile Association, International Motoring Documents, Fanum House, Basing View, Basingstoke Hampshire RG 21 4EA. For more info, see www.theaa.co.uk. Permits UK£4.

US: Visit any American Automobile Association (AAA) office or write to AAA Florida, Travel Related Services, 1000 AAA Dr., Heathrow, FL 32746, Attn: Mailstop #28 (☎407-444-7000; fax 444-7380). You don't have to be a member to buy an IDP/IADP. Permits $10. AAA Travel Related Services (☎800-222-4357) provides road maps, travel guides, emergency road services, travel services, and auto insurance.

AUTOMOBILE CLUBS

Most automobile clubs offer free towing, emergency roadside assistance, travel-related discounts, and random goodies in exchange for a modest membership fee. Travelers should strongly consider membership if planning an extended roadtrip.

▨ **American Automobile Association (AAA,** emergency road service ☎800-AAA-HELP/800-222-4357; www.aaa.com). Offers free trip-planning services, roadmaps and guide-books, 24hr. emergency road service anywhere in the US, free towing, and commission-free traveler's cheques from American Express with over 1000 offices scattered across the country. Discounts on Hertz car rental (5-20%) and various motel chains and theme parks. AAA has reciprocal agreements with auto associations in other countries which often provide full benefits while in the US. Membership costs vary depending on which branch you join, but hover between $50-60 for the first year; less for renewals and additional family members. Call ☎800-564-6222 to sign up.

ON THE ROAD

Tune up the car before you leave, make sure the tires are in good repair and have enough air, and get good maps. *Rand McNally's Road Atlas*, covering all of the US and Canada, is one of the best (available at bookstores and gas stations, $11).

While driving, be sure to buckle up—seat belts are **required by law** in Hawaii. The **speed limit** in Hawaii varies considerably from region to region. Most of the highways have a limit of 55 mph (89kph), while residential areas can post limits as low as 20 mph (32kph). Heed the limit; not only does it save gas, but most local police forces and state troopers make frequent use of radar to catch speed demons.

Hawaiian drivers are typically polite. Joggers, bikers, and pedestrians have the right-of-way and most drivers respect that rule. Mopeds, which travel at slower speeds than most cars, are common on most roads.

DRIVING PRECAUTIONS. Bring substantial amounts of water (a suggested 5L of **water** per person per day) for drinking and for the radiator. In extremely hot weather, use the air conditioner with restraint; if you see the car's temperature gauge climbing, turn it off. Turning the heater on full blast will help cool the engine. If radiator fluid is steaming, turn the car off for half an hour. *Never pour water over the engine to cool it.* Never lift a searing hot hood. For long drives to unpopulated areas, register with police before beginning the trek, and again upon arrival at the destination. Check with the local automobile club for details. When traveling for long distances, make sure tires are in good repair and have enough air, and get good maps. You might also want to consider renting a **car phone** or purchasing a **cell phone** in case of a breakdown. A **compass** and a **car manual** can also be very useful. You should always carry a **spare tire** and **jack, jumper cables, extra oil, flares,** and a **flashlight.** If you don't know how to **change a tire,** learn before heading out, especially if you are planning on traveling in deserted areas. Blowouts on dirt roads are exceedingly common. If you do have a breakdown, **stay with your car;** if you wander off, there's less likelihood trackers will find you. *Sleeping in a car or van parked in the city is extremely dangerous*—even the most dedicated budget traveler should not consider it.

CAR INSURANCE

Some credit cards cover standard insurance. If you rent, lease, or borrow a car, and you are not from the US or Canada, you will need a **green card,** or **International Insurance Certificate,** to certify that you have liability insurance and that it applies abroad. Green cards can be obtained at car rental agencies, car dealerships (for those leasing cars), some travel agents, and some border crossings.

RENTING A CAR

Car rental agencies fall into two categories: national companies with hundreds of branches, and local agencies that serve only one city or region. National chains usually allow you to pick up a car in one city and drop it off in another (for a hefty charge, sometimes in excess of $1000), and by calling their toll-free numbers, you can reserve a reliable car anywhere in the country. Generally, airport branches have more expensive rates. To rent a car from most establishments in Hawaii, you need to be at least 21 years old and have a major credit card. Some agencies require renters to be 25, and most charge those aged 21-24 an additional insurance fee (around $15-25 a day). Policies and prices vary from agency to agency. Small local operations occasionally rent to people under 21, but be sure to ask about the insurance coverage and deductible, and always check the fine print.

Depending on which island you plan to visit, the business of renting a car varies. **Molokai** and **Lanai** have only a few car rental agencies. In addition, some areas all but demand **4WD** (Lanai in particular). In general, cheaper cars tend to be less reliable and harder to handle on difficult terrain. Less expensive 4WD vehicles in particular tend to be more top heavy, and are more dangerous when navigating particularly bumpy roads. The following national agencies have locations in the Hawaiian islands.

Alamo (☎ 800-462-5266; www.alamo.com) rents to ages 21-24 with a major credit card for an additional $25 per day. With locations on Oahu, Maui, Kauai, and the Big Island.

Budget (☎ 800-527-0700; www.budget.com) rents to drivers under 25 with a surcharge that varies by location. With locations on Oahu, Maui, Kauai, the Big Island, and Molokai.

Dollar (☎ 800-800-4000; www.dollar.com) rents to customers ages 21-24 with a variable surcharge. With locations on Oahu, Maui, Kauai, the Big Island, Lanai, and Molokai.

Enterprise (☎ 800-736-8222; www.enterprise.com) rents to customers ages 21-24 with a variable surcharge. With locations on Oahu, Maui, and the Big Island.

Hertz (☎ 800-654-3131; www.hertz.com) policy varies by city. With locations on Oahu, Maui, Kauai, and the Big Island.

Rent-A-Wreck (☎ 808-632-0741; www.rent-a-wreck.com) specializes in supplying vehicles that are past their prime for lower-than-average prices; a bare-bones compact less than 8 years old rents for around $20-25; cars 3-5 years old average under $30. The only Rent-a-Wreck location in Hawaii is in Lihue, Kauai.

Thrifty (☎ 800-847-4389; www.thrifty.com) locations rent to customers age 21-24 for varying surcharges. With locations on Oahu, Maui, Kauai, and the Big Island.

You can generally make reservations before you leave by calling major international offices in your home country. However, occasionally the price and availability information they give doesn't jive with what the local offices in your country will tell you. Try checking with both numbers to make sure you get the best price and accurate information. Local desk numbers are included in town listings; for home-country numbers, call your toll-free directory.

LOCAL AGENCIES
Hawaii also has a number of locally-owned rental services. Be aware that their selection of vehicles may be more limited than that of national chains. Local car rental agencies are listed in the **Transportation** section of towns and cities.

AA Aloha Cars-R-Us (☎ 800-655-7989; www.hawaiicarrental.com). Researches the lowest rates for cars from major rental agencies. Also offers special Hawaii promotions.

Aloha Rent a Car (☎ 877-452-5642; www.aloharentacar.com). Maui-based, airport pickup.

Car Rentals in Hawaii (☎ 888-292-3307; www.carrentalsinhawaii.com). Travelers can search available rentals online.

Harper Car and Truck Rental (☎ 800-852-9993; www.harpershawaii.com). Kauai and Hawaii locations; rents motorhomes as well.

Kihei Rent a Car (☎ 800-251-5288; www.kiheirentacar.com). Family-owned business located in Kihei, Maui. Also a certified travel agency.

ESSENTIALS

COSTS & INSURANCE

Rental car prices start at around $25-30 a day from national companies, $20-25 from local agencies. Expect to pay more for larger cars and for 4WD. Cars with **automatic transmission** are common.

Most rental packages offer **unlimited mileage,** although some allow you a certain number of miles free before the charge of $0.25-0.40 per mile takes effect. Quoted rates do not include gas or tax, so ask for the total cost before handing over the credit card; many large firms have added airport surcharges not covered by the designated fare. Return the car with a full tank unless you sign up for a fuel option plan that stipulates otherwise. And when dealing with any car rental company, be sure to ask whether the price includes **insurance** against theft and collision. There may be an additional charge for a collision and damage waiver (CDW), which usually comes to about $12-15 per day. Remember that if you are driving a conventional vehicle on an **unpaved road** in a rental car, you are almost never covered by insurance; ask about this before leaving the rental agency. Major credit cards (including MasterCard and American Express) will sometimes cover the CDW if you use their card to rent a car; call your credit card company for specifics. Insurance plans almost always come with a **deductible** of around $500 for conventional vehicles. This means you pay for all damages up to that sum, unless they are the fault of another vehicle. The deductible you will be quoted applies to collisions with other vehicles; collisions with non-vehicles ("single-vehicle collisions"), such as trees, will cost you even more. Generally, there is a sliding scale with regard to deductible—the more you pay, the more you're covered. Hawaii is a no-fault state which means that if you don't have collision damage insurance, you have to pay for all the damages before you leave the state (regardless of whether or not you were at fault).

BY MOPED AND BICYCLE

Mopeds are a popular mode of transport in parts of Hawaii, especially Waikiki, although in areas with poor pavement quality or otherwise unsafe road conditions, mopeds are rarely used. A few major rental agencies are listed below.

A&B Moped Rental (☎808-669-0027), 3481 Lower Honoapiilani Hwy., Lahaina, Maui 96761.

Adventure Moped Rentals (☎808-941-2222), 1946 Ala Moana Blvd., Honolulu, Oahu 96815.

The Moped Zone (☎808-732-3366), 750-A Kapahulu Ave., Honolulu, Oahu 96815.

BY THUMB

Let's Go never recommends hitchhiking and strongly urges you to consider the significant risks before you choose to do so. On Kauai and the Big Island in particular, hitchhiking is fairly common among locals, but it can take a long time to get from place to place, and comes with the serious risks of riding with strangers.

ACCOMMODATIONS

HOSTELS

Hostels are generally laid out dorm-style, often with large single-sex rooms and bunk beds, although some offer private rooms for families and couples. They sometimes have kitchens and utensils for your use, bike or moped rentals, storage areas, and laundry facilities. There can be drawbacks: some hostels close during certain daytime "lockout" hours, have a curfew, don't accept reservations, impose a maximum stay, or, less frequently, require that you do chores. In Hawaii, a bed in a hostel will average around $15-20.

HOSTELLING INTERNATIONAL

Joining the youth hostel association in your own country (listed below) automatically grants you membership privileges in **Hostelling International (HI),** a federation of national hosteling associations. HI hostels are scattered throughout Hawaii, and are typically less expensive than private hostels. Most accept reservations via the **International Booking Network** (☎202-783-6161; www.hostelbooking.com), which takes worldwide reservations online and over the phone. HI's umbrella organization's web page (www.iyhf.org), which lists the web addresses and phone numbers of all national associations, can be a great place to begin researching hostelling in a specific region. Most student travel agencies (see p. 50) sell HI cards, as do all of the national hosteling organizations listed below. All prices listed below are valid for **one-year memberships** unless otherwise noted.

Australian Youth Hostels Association (AYHA), Level 3, 10 Mallett St., Camperdown NSW 2050 (☎02 9565 1699; fax 9565 1325; www.yha.org.au). AUS$52, under 18 AUS$16.

Hostelling International-Canada (HI-C), 205 Catherine St. #400, Ottawa, ON K2P 1C3 (☎613-237-7884; fax 237-7868; www.hostellingintl.ca). CDN$35, under 18 free.

Youth Hostels Association (England and Wales), Trevelyon House, Dimple Rd., Matlock, Derbyshire DE4 3YH (☎0870 870 8808; fax 01727 84 41 26; www.yha.org.uk). UK£13, under 18 UK£6.50.

An Óige (Irish Youth Hostel Association), 61 Mountjoy St., Dublin 7 (☎830 4555; fax 830 5808; www.irelandyha.org). €15, under 18 €7.50.

ESSENTIALS

Hostelling International Northern Ireland (HINI), 22 Donegall Rd., Belfast BT12 5JN (☎02890 31 54 35; fax 43 96 99; www.hini.org.uk). UK£10, under 18 UK£6.

Youth Hostels Association of New Zealand (YHANZ), P.O. Box 436, 193 Cashel St., 3rd Floor Union House, Christchurch (☎03 379 9970; fax 365 4476; www.stayyha.org). NZ$40, under 17 free.

Scottish Youth Hostels Association (SYHA), 7 Glebe Crescent, Stirling FK8 2JA (☎01786 89 14 00; fax 89 13 33; www.syha.org.uk). UK£6.

Hostels Association of South Africa, 3rd fl. 73 St. George's House, Cape Town 8001 (☎021 424 2511; fax 424 4119; www.hisa.org.za). ZAR70, under 18 ZAR40.

Hostelling International-American Youth Hostels (HI-AYH), 733 15th St. NW, #840, Washington, D.C. 20005 (☎202-783-6161; fax 783-6171; www.hiayh.org). $25, under 18 free.

BOOKING HOSTELS ONLINE One of the cheapest and easiest ways to ensure a bed for a night is by reserving online. Our web site features the **Hostelworld** booking engine; access it at **www.letsgo.com/resources/accommodations.** Hostelworld offers bargain accommodations everywhere from Argentina to Zimbabwe with no added commission.

OTHER TYPES OF ACCOMMODATIONS

YMCAS AND YWCAS

Young Men's Christian Association (YMCA) lodgings are usually cheaper than a hotel but more expensive than a hostel. YMCA rates may include TV, air conditioning, pools, gyms, access to public transportation, tourist info, safe deposit boxes, luggage storage, daily housekeeping, multilingual staff and 24hr. security. Many YMCAs accept women and families (group rates often available); some will not lodge those under 18 without parental permission. You can book online at Travel Y's International (www.travel-ys.com), for free.

YMCA of the USA, 101 N. Wacker Dr., Chicago, IL 60606 (☎888-333-9622 or 800-872-9622; www.ymca.net). Provides a listing of the nearly 1000 Ys across the US and Canada. Offers info on prices, available services, telephone numbers and addresses, but no reservation service.

YWCA of the USA, Empire State Building, #301, 350 Fifth Ave., New York, NY 10118 (☎212-273-7800; fax 213-273-7939; www.ywca.org). Publishes a directory ($8) on YWCAs across the US.

HOTELS AND GUESTHOUSES

Several major hotel chains have multiple locations within Hawaii. **Outrigger** (☎800-688-7444; www.outrigger.com) trumps the competition with its sheer number of offerings. Between its upscale resorts and the more moderately priced sister chain **Ohana Hotels** (☎800-464-6262; www.ohanahotels.com), there are over 30 Outrigger options. The chain offers myriad specials and packages, including discounts for seniors and military personnel. Call to inquire about promotions or see their web site. **Hilton** (☎800-774-1500; www.hilton.com) has a resort on Oahu and one on the Big Island. **Sheraton** (☎888-625-5144; www.sheraton.com), which includes the **Westin** and **W** hotel chains, has locations on each of Hawaii's islands. Sheraton rates range from high to higher, depending on the island and location. **Best Western** (☎800-780-7234; www.bestwestern.com) and **Marriott** (☎888-236-2427; www.marriott.com) also maintain a number of locations throughout Hawaii.

Hotel singles in Hawaii start around $65-90, depending on the island. Smaller **guesthouses** are often cheaper than hotels. If you decide to make **reservations** in writing, instead of by phone, indicate your night of arrival and how many nights you plan to stay. The hotel will send you a confirmation and may request payment for the first night. Not all hotels take reservations, and few take checks in foreign currency.

BED & BREAKFASTS (B&BS)

For a cozy alternative to impersonal hotel rooms, B&Bs (private homes with rooms available to travelers) range from the acceptable to the sublime. Rooms in B&Bs can cost anywhere from $50-150 in Hawaii. For more info on B&Bs, see **Bed & Breakfast Inns Online**, P.O. Box 829, Madison, TN 37116 (☎ 615-868-1946; www.bbonline.com), **InnFinder**, 6200 Gisholt Dr. Ste. 105, Madison, WI 53713 (☎ 608-285-6600; fax 285-6601; www.inncrawler.com), or **InnSite** (www.innsite.com). The **Hawaii Island Bed & Breakfast Association,** P.O. Box 1890, Honokaa 96727 (☎ 866-323-2248; www.stayhawaii.com) specializes in accommodations on the Big Island. You can also make reservations B&Bs throughout the state using **All Islands Bed & Breakfast** (☎ 800-542-0344 or 808-263-2342; fax 808-263-0308; http://home.hawaii.rr.com/allislands).

HOME EXCHANGES

Home exchange offers the traveler various types of homes (houses, apartments, condominiums, even villas), plus the opportunity to live like a native and to cut down on accommodation fees. For more information, contact **HomeExchange.Com** (☎ 800-877-8723; fax 310-798-3865; www.homeexchange.com), **Intervac International Home Exchange** (☎ 800-756-4663; www.intervac.com), or **The Invented City: International Home Exchange,** 41 Sutter St., San Francisco, CA 94404, USA (US collect ☎ 415-252-1141; www.invented-city.com).

CAMPING AND THE OUTDOORS

Camping in Hawaii can be a rewarding way to slash travel costs. Oceanfront campsites afford travelers the opportunity to enjoy a million-dollar view at a fraction of a hotel price. Hawaii's temperate climate only adds to the appeal of camping. Many beach parks have areas set aside for camping, though some are better equipped than others. The number of campsites varies; some parks offer as few as four spots while others can house up to 50. In addition, Hawaiian state parks are open year-round and issue permits for camping, lodging and group day-use for those who are at least 18 years of age. The fee for camping is generally $5 per campsite per night. Lodging in shelters and cabins is often available, for around $20-55 a night. Contact the **Department of Land and Natural Resources, Division of State Parks**, P.O. Box 621, Honolulu 96809 (☎ 808-587-0300; www.hawaii.gov/dlnr/dsp/index.html) for permit availability and further information. Guided ecotours are another way to explore Hawaii's natural beauty. Ask the local tourist bureau or look online at www.gohawaii.com. An excellent general resource for travelers planning on camping or spending time in the outdoors is the **Great Outdoor Recreation Pages** (www.gorp.com).

USEFUL PUBLICATIONS & RESOURCES

A variety of publishing companies offer hiking guidebooks to meet the educational needs of novice or expert. For information about camping, hiking, and biking, write or call the organizations listed below.

ESSENTIALS

Family Campers and RVers/National Campers and Hikers Association, Inc., 4804 Transit Rd., Bldg. #2, Depew, NY 14043 (☎/fax 716-668-6242; www.fcrv.org). Membership fee ($25) includes their publication *Camping Today*.

Hawaii Trail and Mountain Club, P.O. Box 2238, Honolulu 96804. Guests are welcome on their hikes (see quarterly schedule online at www.geocities.com/yosemite/trails/3660/skednewsl.html). Suggested $2 donation.

The Mountaineers Books, 1001 SW Klickitat Way #201, Seattle, WA 98134 (☎800-553-4453; fax 223-6306; www.mountaineersbooks.org). Over 600 titles on hiking, biking, mountaineering, natural history, and conservation.

The Nature Conservancy of Hawaii, 1116 Smith St., Honolulu 96817 (☎808-537-4508; fax 545-2019).

Wilderness Press, 1200 Fifth St., Berkeley, CA 94710 (☎800-443-7227 or 510-558-1666; www.wildernesspress.com). Over 100 hiking guides/maps.

Woodall Publications Corporation, 2575 Vista Del Mar Dr., Ventura, CA 93001 (☎877-680-6155; www.woodalls.com). Woodall publishes the annually updated *Woodall's Campground Directory* ($22).

WILDERNESS SAFETY

THE GREAT OUTDOORS. Stay warm, stay dry, and stay hydrated. The vast majority of life-threatening wilderness situations can be avoided by following this simple advice. Prepare yourself for an emergency, however, by always packing raingear, a first-aid kit, a reflector, a whistle, high energy food, and extra water for any hike. The sun can be brutal; be sure to take a hat, sunscreen, and sunglasses on any outdoor excursion.

Check **weather forecasts** and pay attention to the skies when hiking, since weather patterns can change suddenly. Whenever possible, let someone know when and where you are going hiking, either a friend, your hostel, a park ranger, or a local hiking organization. Do not attempt a hike beyond your ability—you may be endangering your life. See **Health,** p. 45, for information about outdoor ailments and basic medical concerns.

WILDLIFE. About 40 species of **sharks** inhabit Hawaiian waters, ranging in size from the 8 in. Pigmy Shark to the Whale Shark, which can measure over 50 ft. in length. There are eight species that are commonly sighted near shore, most of which pose little threat to humans. The Tiger Shark, recognizable by its blunt snout and the vertical stripes on its sides, is the most dangerous species of shark found in Hawaiian waters, and is known to attack humans. **Shark attacks** in Hawaii are actually quite rare—only two to three occur each year and few of these prove fatal. Surfers and spear fishers are at greatest risk of attack, and swimmers are advised to stay out of the water at dawn and dusk, when sharks move inshore to feed. Experts also advise against wearing high-contrast clothing or shiny jewelry and to avoid excessive splashing, all of which can attract sharks.

Transparent **Box Jellyfish** swarm to Hawaii's leeward shores 9-10 days after the full moon. The Box Jellyfish, which measures 1-3 in. with tentacles of up to 2 ft. long, administers a painful sting, which, in some cases, can cause anaphylactic shock. If you are stung by a box jellyfish, apply vinegar to the sting, pluck any tentacles out of the affected area using a towel or cloth (avoid using your hands), and apply a hot or cold pack. While not technically a jellyfish, the **Portuguese Man-of-War** is also endemic to Hawaiian waters. Purplish-blue in color with tentacles up to 30 ft. long, the Portuguese Man-of-War also has a painful and potentially dangerous sting, which has been known to cause anaphylactic shock, interference with heart and lung function, and even death. Unlike jellyfish stings, do not apply vinegar to a sting from a Portuguese Man-of-War. Instead, rinse the sting with salt or fresh water and apply a cold compress to the affected area. If pain persists or if breathing difficulty develops, consult a medical professional.

For more information on **Hawaiian wildlife,** consult *Pests of Paradise*, by Susan Scott and Craig Thomas, M.D. (University of Hawaii Press, $20). *How to Stay Alive in the Woods*, by Bradford Angier (Macmillan Press, $8) also provides valuable wilderness tips.

CAMPING AND HIKING EQUIPMENT

WHAT TO BUY...

Good camping equipment is both sturdy and light. Camping equipment is generally more expensive in Australia, New Zealand, and the UK than in North America.

Sleeping Bag: Most sleeping bags are rated by season ("summer" means 30-40°F at night; "four-season" or "winter" often means below 0°F). They are made either of **down** (warmer and lighter, but more expensive, and miserable when wet) or of **synthetic** material (heavier, more durable, and warmer when wet). Prices range $70-210 for a summer synthetic to $250-300 for a good down winter bag. **Sleeping bag pads** include foam pads ($10-30), air mattresses ($15-50), and Therm-A-Rest self-inflating pads ($45-120). Bring a **stuff sack** to store your bag and keep it dry.

Tent: The best tents are free-standing (with their own frames and suspension systems), set up quickly, and only require staking in high winds. Low-profile dome tents are the best all-around. Good 2-person tents start at $90, 4-person at $300. Seal the seams of your tent with waterproofer, and make sure it has a rain fly. Other tent accessories include a **battery-operated lantern,** a **plastic groundcloth,** and a **nylon tarp.**

Backpack: Internal-frame packs mold better to your back, keep a lower center of gravity, and flex adequately to allow you to hike difficult trails. **External-frame packs** are more comfortable for long hikes over even terrain, as they keep weight higher and distribute it more evenly. Make sure your pack has a strong, padded hip-belt to transfer weight to your legs. Any serious backpacking requires a pack of at least 4000 cubic inches (16,000cc), plus 500 cubic inches for sleeping bags in internal-frame packs. Sturdy backpacks cost anywhere from $125-420—this is one area in which it doesn't pay to economize. Fill up any pack with something heavy and walk around the store with it to get a sense of how it distributes weight before buying it. Either buy a **waterproof backpack cover,** or store all of your belongings in plastic bags inside your pack.

Boots: Be sure to wear hiking boots with good **ankle support.** They should fit snugly and comfortably over 1-2 pairs of wool socks and thin liner socks. Break in boots over several weeks first in order to spare yourself painful and debilitating blisters.

Other Necessities: Synthetic layers, like those made of polypropylene, and a **pile jacket** will keep you warm even when wet. A **"space blanket"** will help you to retain your body heat and doubles as a groundcloth ($5-15). Plastic **water bottles** are virtually shatter- and leak-proof. Bring **water-purification tablets** for when you can't boil water. Although most campgrounds provide campfire sites, you may want to bring a small **metal grate** or **grill** of your own. For those places that forbid fires or the gathering of firewood, you'll need a **camp stove** (the classic Coleman starts at $45) and a propane-filled **fuel bottle** to operate it. Also don't forget a **first-aid kit, pocketknife, insect repellent, calamine lotion, sunscreen,** and **waterproof matches** or a **lighter.**

...AND WHERE TO BUY IT

The mail-order/online companies listed below offer lower prices than many retail stores, but a visit to a local camping or outdoors store will give you a good sense of the look and weight of certain items.

Campmor, 28 Parkway, P.O. Box 700, Upper Saddle River, NJ 07458, USA. (US ☎888-226-7667; www.campmor.com.)

Discount Camping, 880 Main North Rd., Pooraka, South Australia 5095, Australia (☎08 8262 3399; fax 8260 6240; www.discountcamping.com.au).

Eastern Mountain Sports (EMS), 1 Vose Farm Rd., Peterborough, NH 03458, USA (☎888-463-6367; www.ems.com).

L.L. Bean, Freeport, ME 04033, USA (US and Canada ☎800-441-5713; UK ☎0800 891 297; www.llbean.com).

Mountain Designs, 51 Bishop St., Kelvin Grove, Queensland 4059, Australia (☎07 3856 2344; fax 3856 0366; www.mountaindesigns.com).

Recreational Equipment, Inc. (REI), Sumner, WA 98352, USA (☎800-426-4840 or 253-891-2500; www.rei.com).

YHA Adventure Shop, 19 High St., Staines, Middlesex, TW18 4QY, UK (☎1784 458 625; fax 1784 464 573; www.yhaadventure.com) The main branch of one of Britain's largest outdoor equipment suppliers.

CAMPERS AND RVS

Renting an RV will always be more expensive than tenting or hosteling, but it's cheaper than staying in hotels and renting a car (see **Renting a Car,** p. 54), and the convenience of bringing along your own bedroom, bathroom, and kitchen makes it an attractive option, especially for older travelers and families with children. Check out www.motorhomerentals.com, www.rvrentalnet.com, and www.rvamerica.com for more information on RVing in Hawaii.

ORGANIZED ADVENTURE TOURS

Organized adventure tours offer another way of exploring the wild. Activities include hiking, biking, kayaking, and sailing. Tourism bureaus can often suggest parks, trails, and outfitters; other good sources for info are stores and groups that specialize in camping and outdoor equipment like REI and EMS (see above).

Hawaii Activities, Aloha Tower 5th Floor, 1 Aloha Tower Drive, Honolulu, HI 96813, USA (☎877-877-1222 or 808-524-0008; www.hawaiiactivities). Service that books activities for tourists. Searchable web site with links to different tour companies offering every kind of adventure/excursion/activity under the sun.

The Real Hawaii (☎877-597-7325; www.therealhawaii.com). Eco-cultural excursions led by native Hawaiians.

Specialty Travel Index, 305 San Anselmo Ave., #313, San Anselmo, CA 94960, USA (☎800-442-4922 or 415-459-4900; fax 415-459-9474; www.specialtytravel.com). Tours worldwide.

Wild Side Eco-Adventures, 84-664 Upena St., Waianae, HI 96792, USA (☎808-306-7273; fax 696-0103; www.sailhawaii.com). Sailing and kayaking adventures on Oahu.

KEEPING IN TOUCH

BY MAIL

SENDING MAIL HOME FROM HAWAII

Airmail is the best way to send mail home from Hawaii. Aerogrammes, printed sheets that fold into envelopes and travel via airmail, are available at post offices. Write "air mail" or "par avion" on the front. Most post offices will

ENVIRONMENTALLY RESPONSIBLE TOURISM. The idea behind responsible tourism is to leave no trace of human presence behind. A camp-stove is the safer (and more efficient) way to cook than using vegetation, but if you must make a fire, keep it small and use dead branches or brush rather than cutting vegetation. Make sure your campsite is at least 150 ft. (50m) from water supplies or bodies of water. If there are no toilet facilities, bury human waste (but not paper) at least four inches (10cm) deep and above the high-water line, and 150 ft. or more from any water supplies and campsites. Always pack your trash in a plastic bag and carry it with you until you reach the next trash receptacle. For more information on these issues, contact one of the organizations listed below.

Earthwatch, 3 Clock Tower Place #100, Box 75, Maynard, MA 01754, USA (☎800-776-0188 or 978-461-0081; www.earthwatch.org).

International Ecotourism Society, 28 Pine St., Burlington, VT 05402, USA (☎802-651-9818; fax 802-651-9819; www.ecotourism.org).

National Audubon Society, Nature Odysseys, 700 Broadway, New York, NY 10003, USA (☎212-979-3000; fax 212-979-3188; www.audubon.org).

Tourism Concern, Stapleton House, 277-281 Holloway Rd., London N7 8HN, UK (☎020 7753 3330; fax 020 7753 3331; www.tourismconcern.org.uk).

ESSENTIALS

charge exorbitant fees or simply refuse to send aerogrammes with enclosures. Surface mail is by far the cheapest and slowest way to send mail. It takes one to three months to cross the Atlantic and two to four to cross the Pacific—good for items you won't need to see for a while, such as souvenirs or other articles you've acquired along the way that are weighing down your pack. Standard rates for mail from Hawaii (in US$) are:

Australia: Allow 4-7 days for regular airmail home. Postcards/aerogrammes cost $0.70. Letters up to 1 oz. cost $0.80; packages up to 0.5 lb. $7.10, up to 2 lb. $14.90.

Canada: Allow 4-7 days for regular airmail home. Postcards/aerogrammes cost $0.50. Letters up to 1 oz. cost $0.60; packages up to 0.5 lb. $2.35, up to 2 lb. $6.35.

Ireland: Allow 5-7 days for regular airmail home. Postcards/aerogrammes cost $0.70. Letters up to 1 oz. cost $0.80; packages up to 0.5 lb. $6.40, up to 2 lb. $13.30.

New Zealand: Allow 4-7 days for regular airmail home. Postcards/aerogrammes cost $0.70. Letters up to 1 oz. cost $0.80; packages up to 0.5 lb. $7.10, up to 2 lb. $14.90.

UK: Allow 5-7 days for regular airmail home. Postcards/aerogrammes cost $0.70. Letters up to 1 oz. cost $0.80; packages up to 0.5 lb. $6.40, up to 2 lb. $13.30.

US: Allow 3-7 days for regular airmail home. Postcards/aerogrammes cost $0.23. Letters up to 1 oz. cost $0.37; packages up to 0.5 lb. $3.50, up to 5 lb. $7.70.

SENDING MAIL TO HAWAII

Mark envelopes "air mail," or "par avion," or your letter or postcard will never arrive. In addition to the standard postage system whose rates are listed below, **Federal Express** (www.fedex.com; Australia ☎13 26 10; US and Canada ☎800-247-4747; New Zealand ☎0800 73 33 39; UK ☎0800 12 38 00) handles express mail services from most home countries to Hawaii; they can get a letter from New York to Hawaii in 2 days for US$16, and from London to Hawaii in 2 days for UK£26.

Australia: Allow 4-6 days for regular airmail to Hawaii. Postcards and letters up to 20g cost AUS$1; packages up to 0.5kg AUS$12, up to 2kg AUS$39. **EMS** can get a letter to Hawaii in 2-5 days for AUS$33. www.auspost.com.au/pac.

Canada: Allow 4-6 days for regular airmail to Hawaii. Postcards and letters up to 30g cost CDN$0.65; packages up to 0.5kg CDN$4.60, up to 2kg CDN$16. www.canadapost.ca

Ireland: Allow 4-6 days for regular airmail to Hawaii. Postcards and letters up to 25g cost €0.41. www.anpost.ie.

New Zealand: Allow 7 days for regular airmail to Hawaii. Postcards NZ$1.50. Letters up to 20g cost NZ$2-5; small parcels up to 0.5kg NZ$16, up to 2kg NZ$50. www.nzpost.co.nz/nzpost/inrates.

UK: Allow 4 days for airmail to Hawaii. Letters up to 60g cost UK£1.35; packages up to 0.5kg UK£4.55, up to 5kg UK£43. UK Swiftair delivers letters a day faster for UK£3.85 more. www.royalmail.com.

US: Allow 3-7 days for regular airmail to Hawaii. Postcards/aerogrammes cost $0.23; letters under 1 oz., $0.37. Packages under 1 lb. cost $3.50; larger packages cost a variable amount (around $10). **US Express Mail** can get it there overnight; 1 lb. parcel $17.85. http://ircalc.usps.gov.

RECEIVING MAIL IN HAWAII

There are several ways to arrange pick-up of letters sent to you by friends and relatives while you are abroad. Mail can be sent via **General Delivery** to almost any city or town in Hawaii with a post office. Address General Delivery letters like so:

Ella STEIM

General Delivery

City, HI Postal Code

USA

The mail will go to a special desk in the central post office, unless you specify a post office by street address or postal code. It's best to use the largest post office, since mail may be sent there regardless. It is usually safer and quicker, though more expensive, to send mail express or registered. Bring your passport (or other photo ID) for pick-up; there may be a small fee. If the clerks insist that there is nothing for you, have them check under your first name as well. *Let's Go* lists post offices in the **Practical Information** section for each city and most towns.

American Express's travel offices throughout the world offer a free **Client Letter Service** (mail held up to 30 days and forwarded upon request) for cardholders who contact them in advance. Address the letter in the same way shown above. Some offices will offer these services to non-cardholders (especially AmEx Travelers Cheque holders), but call ahead to make sure. *Let's Go* lists AmEx office locations for most large cities in **Practical Information** sections; for a complete, free list, call ☎ 800-528-4800.

BY TELEPHONE

 ☎ **AREA CODE** The area code throughout the Hawaiian islands is **808.**

CALLING HOME FROM HAWAII

A **calling card** is probably your cheapest bet. Calls are billed collect to your account. You can frequently call collect without even possessing a company's calling card just by calling their access number and following the instructions. **To obtain a calling card** from your national telecommunications service before leaving home, contact the appropriate company listed below (using the numbers in the first column). To **call home with a calling card,** contact the operator for your service provider in Hawaii by dialing the appropriate toll-free access number.

COMPANY	TO OBTAIN A CARD, DIAL:
AT&T (US)	800-288-4685
British Telecom Direct	800 34 51 44
Canada Direct	800-668-6878
Ireland Direct	800 40 00 00
MCI (US)	800-444-3333
New Zealand Direct	0800 00 00 00
Sprint (US)	800 877-4646
Telkom South Africa	10 219
Telstra Australia	13 22 00

You can also usually make **direct international calls** from pay phones, but if you aren't using a calling card, you may end up dropping your coins as quickly as your words. Where available, prepaid phone cards (see below) and occasionally major credit cards can be used for direct international calls, but they are still less cost-efficient. (See the box on **Placing International Calls** (p. 65) for directions on how to place a direct international call.)

Placing a **collect call** through an international operator is even more expensive, but may be necessary in case of emergency. You can place collect calls through the service providers listed above even if you don't have one of their phone cards.

 PLACING INTERNATIONAL CALLS. To call to and from Hawaii, dial:

1. The **international dialing prefix.** To dial out of **Australia,** dial 0011; **Canada** or the **US,** 011; the **Republic of Ireland, New Zealand,** or the **UK,** 00; **South Africa,** 09.
2. The **country code** of the country you want to call. To call **Australia,** dial 61; **Canada** or the **US,** 1; the **Republic of Ireland,** 353; **New Zealand,** 64; **South Africa,** 27; the **UK,** 44.
3. The **city/area code.** The city/area code for all of Hawaii is **808.** When calling internationally, if the first digit is a zero (e.g., 020 for London) omit the zero (e.g., dial 20 from Hawaii to reach London).
4. The **local number.**

CALLING WITHIN HAWAII

The simplest way to call within the country is to use a coin-operated phone. **Prepaid phone cards** available at newspaper kiosks and drugstores, which carry a certain amount of phone time depending on the card's denomination, and usually save time and money in the long run. The computerized phone will tell you how much time, in units, you have left on your card. Another kind of prepaid telephone card comes with a Personal Identification Number (PIN) and a toll-free access number. Instead of inserting the card into the phone, you call the access number and follow the directions on the card. These cards can be used to make international as well as domestic calls. Phone rates typically tend to be highest in the morning, lower in the evening, and lowest on Sunday and late at night.

TIME DIFFERENCES

Hawaii has its own time zone—**Hawaii Standard Time (HST).** HST is 10hr. behind **Greenwich Mean Time (GMT).** It is 6hr. behind New York and Boston (5hr. behind during daylight savings), 2hr. behind Vancouver and San Francisco, 12hr. behind Johannesburg, 3hr. ahead of Sydney, and 2hr. ahead of Auckland (NZ). Some countries (NOT the US) ignore **daylight savings time,** and fall and spring switchover times vary. The chart below gives the time in various cities around the world when it is midnight in Honolulu when daylight savings time is not in effect.

12AM	2AM	6AM	10AM	6PM	9PM
Honolulu	Vancouver Seattle San Francisco Los Angeles	Toronto Ottawa New York Boston	London (GMT)	China Hong Kong Manila Singapore	Sydney Canberra Melbourne

BY EMAIL AND INTERNET

Most medium to large cities in Hawaii have at least one Internet cafe. Otherwise, any one of the Hawaii State Public Libraries offers free Internet access with a library card (three-month passes are available for $10). In addition, copy stores such as Kinko's and Mail Boxes Etc. also have Internet access. Generally, the more rural a town, the less chance that email will be accessible.

Though in some places it's possible to forge a remote link with your home server, in most cases this is a much slower (and thus more expensive) option than taking advantage of free **web-based email accounts** (e.g., www.hotmail.com and www.yahoo.com). Travelers with laptops can call an Internet service provider via a **modem.** Long-distance phone cards specifically intended for such calls can defray normally high phone charges; check with your long-distance phone provider to see if it offers this option. **Internet cafes** and the occasional free Internet terminal at a public library or university are listed in the **Practical Information** sections of major cities. For lists of additional cybercafes in Hawaii, check out www.netcafeguide.com.

SPECIFIC CONCERNS

WOMEN TRAVELERS

In Hawaii, as everywhere in the US, a woman should expect to be treated just as a man would be; though sexism still exists, it is considered unacceptable behavior. If you are treated unfairly because you are a woman, this is grounds for complaint.

Women exploring on their own inevitably face some additional safety concerns, but it's easy to be adventurous without taking undue risks. Generally, it is safe for women to travel in the US, but common sense still applies; women are targeted for muggings and swindlings, as well as general harassment. Watch out for vendors who may try to take advantage of you. If you are camping in isolated areas or traveling in big cities with which you are unfamiliar, try to travel with partners. Wherever you go, walk purposefully and self-confidently; women who look like they know what they are doing and where they are going are less likely to be harassed.

When traveling, always carry extra money for a phone call, bus, or taxi. **Hitching** is never safe for lone women, or even for two women traveling together. Consider approaching older women or couples if you're lost or feel uncomfortable.

Your best answer to verbal harassment is no answer at all; feigning deafness, sitting motionless, and staring straight ahead at nothing in particular will do a world of good that reactions usually don't achieve. The extremely persistent can sometimes be dissuaded by a firm, loud, and very public "Go away!" Don't hesitate to seek out a police officer or a passerby if you are being harassed. *Let's Go: Hawaii* lists emergency numbers (including rape crisis lines) in the **Practical Information** listings of major cities, and you can always dial **911**. An **IMPACT Model Mugging** self-defense course will not only prepare you for a potential attack, but will also raise your level of awareness of your surroundings and your confidence (see **Self Defense**, p. 43).

For general information, contact the **National Organization for Women (NOW)**, 733 15th St. NW, Fl. 2, Washington, DC 20005 (☎202-628-8669; www.now.org), which has branches across the US that can refer women travelers to rape crisis centers and counseling services.

TRAVELING ALONE

There are many benefits to traveling alone, including independence and greater interaction with locals. On the other hand, any solo traveler is a more vulnerable target of harassment and street theft. As a lone traveler, try not to stand out as a tourist, look confident, and be especially careful in deserted or very crowded areas. If questioned, never admit that you are traveling alone. Maintain regular contact with someone at home who knows your itinerary. For more tips, pick up *Traveling Solo* by Eleanor Berman (Globe Pequot Press, $17) or subscribe to **Connecting: Solo Travel Network**, 689 Park Road, Unit 6, Gibsons, BC V0N 1V7, CAN (☎604-886-9099; www.cstn.org; membership $35). **Travel Companion Exchange**, P.O. Box 833, Amityville, NY 11701, USA (☎631-454-0880, or in the US ☎800-392-1256; www.whytravelalone.com; $48), will link solo travelers with companions with similar travel habits and interests. To link up with a tour group, try **Contiki Holidays** (888-CONTIKI; www.contiki.com), which offers a variety of packages designed for 18- to 35-year-olds. Tours include accommodations, transportation, guided sightseeing and some meals; most average about $75 per day.

OLDER TRAVELERS

Senior citizens are eligible for a wide range of discounts on transportation, museums, movies, theaters, concerts, restaurants, and accommodations. Almost all of Hawaii's major attractions offer some sort of discount for older tourists. If you don't see a senior citizen price listed, ask, and you may be delightfully surprised. The books *No Problem! Worldwise Tips for Mature Adventurers*, by Janice Kenyon (Orca Book Publishers, $16) and *Unbelievably Good Deals and Great Adventures That You Absolutely Can't Get Unless You're Over 50*, by Joan Rattner Heilman (NTC/Contemporary Publishing, $13) are both excellent resources. For more information, contact one of the following organizations:

Elderhostel, 11 Ave. de Lafayette, Boston, MA 02111, USA (☎877-426-8056; www.elderhostel.org). Organizes 1- to 4-week "educational adventures" in Hawaii on varied subjects for those 55+.

The Mature Traveler, P.O. Box 15791, Sacramento, CA 95852, USA (☎800-460-6676; www.thematuretraveler.com). Deals, discounts, and travel packages for the 50+ traveler. Subscription $30.

Walking the World, P.O. Box 1186, Fort Collins, CO 80522, USA (☎800-340-9255; www.walkingtheworld.com), organizes trips for 50+ travelers to Hawaii.

BISEXUAL, GAY, & LESBIAN TRAVELERS

Hawaii is one of the most progressive states when it comes to gay and lesbian travelers, though more so in cities than in rural areas. Listed below are contact organizations, mail-order bookstores, and publishers that offer materials addressing some specific concerns. **Out and About** (www.planetout.com) offers a bi-weekly newsletter addressing travel concerns and a comprehensive site addressing gay travel concerns.

ESSENTIALS

Gay's the Word, 66 Marchmont St., London WC1N 1AB, UK (☎44 20 7278 7654; www.gaystheword.co.uk). The largest gay and lesbian bookshop in the UK, with both fiction and non-fiction titles. Mail-order service available.

Giovanni's Room, 1145 Pine St., Philadelphia, PA 19107, USA (☎215-923-2960; www.queerbooks.com). An international lesbian/feminist and gay bookstore with mail-order service (carries many of the publications listed below).

International Lesbian and Gay Association (ILGA), 81 rue Marché-au-Charbon, B-1000 Brussels, Belgium (☎2 502 2471; www.ilga.org). Provides political information, such as homosexuality laws of individual countries.

▼ **FURTHER READING: BISEXUAL, GAY, & LESBIAN**

Spartacus International Gay Guide 2001-2002, Bruno Gmunder Verlag. ($33).

Damron Men's Guide, Damron Road Atlas, Damron's Accommodations, and *The Women's Traveller.* Damron Travel Guides ($14-19). For more info, call ☎800-462-6654 or visit www.damron.com.

Ferrari Guides' Gay Travel A to Z, Ferrari Guides' Men's Travel in Your Pocket, and *Ferrari Guides' Inn Places.* Ferrari Publications ($16-20). Purchase the guides online at www.ferrariguides.com.

The Gay Vacation Guide: The Best Trips and How to Plan Them, Mark Chesnut. Citadel Press ($15).

Gayellow Pages USA/Canada, Frances Green. Gayellow pages ($16). They also publish smaller regional editions. Visit Gayellow pages online at www.gayellowpages.com.

TRAVELERS WITH DISABILITIES

In large Hawaiian cities, most hotels and restaurants are wheelchair accessible, though this may not be the case in smaller towns or rural areas. Wheelchair-accessible vans are available to rent in most places, as are wheelchairs. Those with disabilities should inform airlines and hotels of their disabilities when making reservations; some time may be needed to prepare special accommodations. Call ahead to restaurants, museums, and other facilities to find out if they are handicapped-accessible. **Guide dog owners** should inquire as to the quarantine policies of each destination country.

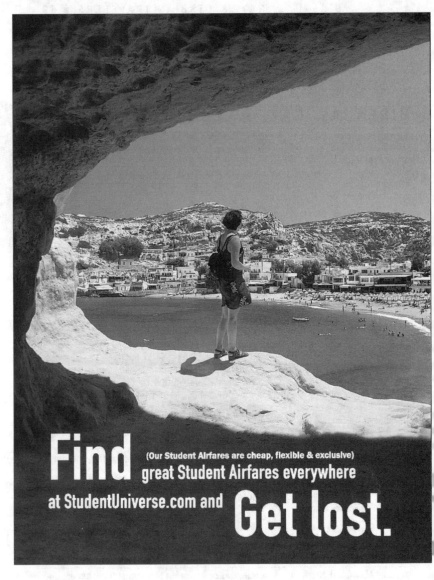

In the US, major airlines will accommodate disabled passengers if notified at least 72 hours in advance. For information on transportation availability in individual US cities, contact the local chapter of the Easter Seals Society.

If you are planning to visit a national park or attraction in the US run by the National Park Service, obtain a free **Golden Access Passport,** which is available at all park entrances and from federal offices whose functions relate to land, forests, or wildlife. The Passport entitles disabled travelers and their families to free park admission and provides a 50% discount on all campsite and parking fees.

USEFUL ORGANIZATIONS

Mobility International USA (MIUSA), P.O. Box 10767, Eugene, OR 97440, USA (voice and TDD ☎541-343-1284; www.miusa.org). Provides a variety of books and other publications containing information for travelers with disabilities.

Society for Accessible Travel and Hospitality (SATH), 347 Fifth Ave., #610, New York, NY 10016, USA (☎212-447-7284; www.sath.org). An advocacy group that publishes free online travel information and the magazine *OPEN WORLD* (US$18, free for members). Annual membership US$45, students and seniors US$30.

TOUR AGENCIES

Directions Unlimited, 123 Green Ln., Bedford Hills, NY 10507, USA (☎800-533-5343). Books individual and group vacations for the physically disabled; not an info service.

The Guided Tour Inc., 7900 Old York Rd., #114B, Elkins Park, PA 19027, USA (☎800-783-5841; www.guidedtour.com). Organizes travel programs for persons with developmental and physical challenges in the US, Canada, Ireland, Cancun, and Paris.

MINORITY TRAVELERS

Hawaii is such a mixed place that no ethnic group stands out as an obvious minority. Caucasians may be uncomfortable with being called a "haole," but in general, if you treat the island and its inhabitants with respect, the same respect will be afforded to you. While there are relatively few people of African descent on the islands, racial prejudice against blacks is extremely rare, especially in larger cities.

TRAVELERS WITH CHILDREN

Family vacations often require that you slow your pace, and always require that you plan ahead. If you rent a car, make sure the rental company provides a car seat for younger children. **Be sure that your child carries some sort of ID** in case of an emergency or in case he or she gets lost.

Museums, tourist attractions, accommodations, and restaurants often offer discounts for children. Children under two generally fly for 10% of the adult airfare on international flights (this does not necessarily include a seat). International fares are usually discounted 25% for children from ages 2 to 11. For more information, consult one of the following books:

Adventuring with Children: An Inspirational Guide to World Travel and the Outdoors, Nan Jeffrey. Avalon House Publishing ($15).

How to take Great Trips with Your Kids, Sanford and Jane Portnoy. Harvard Common Press ($10).

> *On the Go with Baby: A Stress Free Guide to Getting Across Town or Around the World,*
> Ericka Lutz. Sourcebooks Trade ($15).
>
> *The Penny Whistle Traveling-with-Kids Book,* Meredith Brokaw. Fireside ($14).
>
> *Trouble Free Travel with Children,* Vicki Lansky. Book Peddlers ($9).

DIETARY CONCERNS

With a little extra research, vegetarians should be able to find sufficient food options. Although local food tends to be centered around meat, many dining options are also Asian or Asian-inspired, using noodles, rice, and vegetables as ingredients. **The North American Vegetarian Society,** P.O. Box 72, Dolgeville, NY 13329 (☎518-568-7970; www.navs-online.org), publishes information about vegetarian travel. For more information, visit your local bookstore, health food store, or library, or consult *The Vegetarian Traveler: Where to Stay if You're Vegetarian,* by Jed and Susan Civic (Larson Publications, $16).

Travelers who keep kosher should contact synagogues in larger cities for information on kosher restaurants. Your synagogue or college Hillel should have access to lists of Jewish institutions in Hawaii. If you are strict in your observance, you may have to prepare your own food on the road. A good resource is the *Jewish Travel Guide,* by Michael Zaidner (Vallentine Mitchell, $17).

OTHER RESOURCES

Let's Go tries to cover all aspects of budget travel, but we can't put *everything* in our guides. Listed below are books and web sites that can serve as jumping off points for your own research.

USEFUL PUBLICATIONS

Aloha from Hawaii (www.aloha-hawaii.com/hawaii_magazine/magazine.shtml). Online magazine including features and a Hawaiian dictionary.

Hawaii Magazine (☎949-855-8822; www.hawaiimagazine.com). Monthly magazine with features on restaurants, events and community happenings.

Honolulu Magazine (☎808-537-9500; www.honolulumagazine.com). Articles on community figures and events.

Islander Magazine (www.islander-magazine.com). A web magazine specializing in the Hawaiian islands. Information on Hawaiian cuisine, books and history.

TRAVEL PUBLISHERS AND BOOKSTORES

Hawaii Book Publishers Association, P.O. Box 235736, Honolulu 96823 (☎808-734-7159; fax 808-732-3627; www.hawaiibooks.org). Publishes a free newsletter with information on literary events in Hawaii as well as other general information.

Hippocrene Books, Inc., 171 Madison Ave., New York, NY 10016, USA (☎718-454-2366; www.hippocrenebooks.com). Publishes foreign language dictionaries and language learning guides.

Hunter Publishing, 470 W. Broadway, Fl. 2, South Boston, MA 02127, USA (☎617-269-0700; www.hunterpublishing.com), has an extensive catalog of travel guides and diving and adventure travel books.

Rand McNally, P.O. Box 7600, Chicago, IL 60680, USA (☎847-329-8100; www.randmcnally.com), publishes road atlases.

Adventurous Traveler Bookstore, P.O. Box 2221, Williston, VT 05495, USA (☎800-282-3963; www.adventuroustraveler.com).

Travel Books & Language Center, Inc., 4437 Wisconsin Ave. NW, Washington, D.C. 20016, USA (☎800-220-2665; www.bookweb.org/bookstore/travelbks). Over 60,000 titles from around the world.

WORLD WIDE WEB

Almost every aspect of budget travel is accessible via the web. In 10 minutes at the keyboard, you can make a reservation at a hostel, get advice on travel hot spots from other travelers who have just returned from Hawaii, or find out exactly how much a surfboard rental in Kauai costs.

Listed here are some budget travel sites to start off your surfing; other relevant web sites are listed throughout the book. Because web site turnover is high, use search engines (such as www.google.com) to strike out on your own.

OUR PERSONAL FAVORITE...

Let's Go: www.letsgo.com. Our website, www.letsgo.com, now includes introductory chapters from all our guides and a wealth of information on a monthly featured destination. As always, our website also has info about our books, a travel forum buzzing with stories and tips, and additional links that will help you make the most of a trip to Hawaii.

THE ART OF BUDGET TRAVEL

How to See the World: www.artoftravel.com. A compendium of great travel tips, from cheap flights to self defense to interacting with local culture.

Rec. Travel Library: www.travel-library.com. A fantastic set of links for general information and personal travelogues.

Lycos: http://travel.lycos.com/destinations/. General introductions to cities and regions throughout Hawaii, accompanied by links to applicable histories, news, and local tourism sites.

INFORMATION ON HAWAII

Alternative-Hawaii: www.alternative-hawaii.com. "Your guide to the path less travelled." Self-described ecotourism site with links to accommodations and a section on Hawaii's special places.

Atevo Travel: www.atevo.com/guides/destinations. Detailed introductions, travel tips, and suggested itineraries.

Best Places Hawaii: www.bestplaceshawaii.com. An online travel planner with a virtual island tour and information on attractions.

DaKine: www.dakine.net. The local's guide to Hawaii. Reviews of Oahu plate lunch and shave ice establishments. Local humor!

Foreign Language for Travelers: www.travlang.com. Provides free online translating dictionaries and lists of phrases in Hawaiian.

Hawaii: www.hawaii.gov. Official web site of the state of Hawaii.

Hawaii Surf Report: www.surf-news.com. Up to the minute weather and surf information.

MyTravelGuide: www.mytravelguide.com. Country overviews, with everything from history to transportation to live web cam coverage.

PlanetRider: www.planetrider.com. A subjective list of links to the "best" web sites covering the culture and tourist attractions of Hawaii.

World Travel Guide: www.travel-guides.com. Helpful practical info.

TravelPage: www.travelpage.com. Links to official tourist office sites in Hawaii.

ESSENTIALS

ALTERNATIVES TO TOURISM

When Let's Go started in 1961, about 1.7 million people in the world were traveling internationally each year; in 2002, nearly 700 million trips were made, projected to be up to a billion by 2010. The dramatic rise in tourism has created an interdependence between the economy, environment, and culture of many destinations and the tourists they host.

Traveling from place to place around the world will be a memorable experience. But if you are looking for a more rewarding and complete way to see the world, you may want to consider alternatives to tourism. Working, volunteering, or studying for an extended period of time can be a better way to understand laid-back, *aloha*-style of life in Hawaii. From the sun-kissed sands of Waikiki to the awe-inspiring craters in Volcanoes National Park, Hawaii reveals many faces to its visitors. Its culture is a worldly blend, yet distinctly different from any other, and not without tension. Since tourism has long since surpassed the islands' agriculturally economic roots, it is important that travelers be aware and respectful of all that is unique to this small and remote island chain. This chapter outlines some of the different ways to get to know Hawaii and its varied landscapes and residents. In most cases, you'll feel that you partook in a more meaningful and educational experience—something that the average budget traveler often misses.

Two rising trends in **sustainable travel** are ecotourism and community-based tourism. **Ecotourism** focuses on the conservation of natural habitats and using them to build up the economy without exploitation or over development. **Community-based tourism** aims to channel tourist dollars into the local economy, by emphasizing tours and cultural programs that are run by members of the host community and that often benefit disadvantaged groups.

Those looking to **volunteer** in the efforts to resolve these issues have many options. You can participate in projects from helping preserve Hawaiian biodiversity through the Sierra Club, to researching geodesy in Volcanoes National Park, either on an infrequent basis or as the main component of your trip. Later in this section, we recommend organizations that can help you find the opportunities that best suit your interests, whether you're looking to pitch in for a day or a year.

There are many other ways that you can integrate yourself with the communities you visit. Studying at a college or language program is one option, and the University of Hawaii system has fantastic programs in tropical agriculture, tropical medicine, and oceanography, as well as in Hawaiian, Pacific Island, and Asian studies and languages, among others. Many travelers also structure their trips by the work that they can do along the way—either odd jobs as they go (helping clean a hostel in exchange for rent), or full-time stints in cities where they plan to stay for some time (working on an organic farm in exchange for room and board). For more on volunteering, studying, and working in Hawaii and beyond, consult Let's Go's alternatives to tourism website, **www.beyondtourism.com**.

FIND THE PATH. To read more on specific organizations that are working to better their communities, look for our **Giving Back** features throughout the book . (See p. 264, and 426.)

A NEW PHILOSOPHY OF TRAVEL

We at *Let's Go* have watched the growth of the 'ignorant tourist' stereotype with dismay, knowing that the majority of travelers care passionately about the state of the communities and environments they explore—but also knowing that even conscientious tourists can inadvertently damage natural wonders, rich cultures, and impoverished communities. We believe the philosophy of **sustainable travel** is among the most important travel tips we could impart to our readers, to help guide fellow backpackers and on-the-road philanthropists. By staying aware of the needs and troubles of local communities, today's travelers can be a powerful force in preserving and restoring this fragile world.

Working against the negative consequences of irresponsible tourism is much simpler than it might seem; it is often self-awareness, rather than self-sacrifice, that makes the biggest difference. Simply by trying to spend responsibly and conserve local resources, all travelers can positively impact the places they visit. Let's Go has partnered with **BEST (Business Enterprises for Sustainable Travel,** an affiliate of the Conference Board; see www.sustainabletravel.org), which recognizes businesses that operate based on the principles of sustainable travel. Below, they provide advice on how ordinary visitors can practice this philosophy in their daily travels, no matter where they are.

TIPS FOR CIVIC TRAVEL: HOW TO MAKE A DIFFERENCE

Travel by train when feasible. Rail travel requires only half the energy per passenger mile that planes do. On average, each of the 40,000 daily domestic air flights releases more than 1700 pounds of greenhouse gas emissions.

Use public mass transportation whenever possible; outside of cities, take advantage of group taxis or vans. Bicycles are an attractive way of seeing a community first-hand. And enjoy walking—purchase good maps of your destination and ask about on-foot touring opportunities.

When renting a car, ask whether fuel-efficient vehicles are available. Honda and Toyota produce cars that use hybrid engines powered by electricity and gasoline, thus reducing emissions of carbon dioxide. Ford Motor Company plans to introduce a hybrid fuel model by the end of 2004.

Reduce, reuse, recycle—use electronic tickets, recycle papers and bottles wherever possible, and avoid using containers made of styrofoam. Refillable water bottles and rechargable batteries both efficiently conserve expendable resources.

Be thoughtful in your purchases. Take care not to buy souvenir objects made from trees in old-growth or endangered forests, such as teak, or items made from endangered species, like ivory or tortoise jewelry. Ask whether products are made from renewable resources.

Buy from local enterprises, such as casual street vendors. In developing countries and low-income neighborhoods, many people depend on the "informal economy" to make a living.

Be on-the-road-philanthropists. If you are inspired by the natural environment of a destination or enriched by its culture, join in preserving their integrity by making a charitable contribution to a local organization.

Spread the word. Upon your return home, tell friends and colleagues about places to visit that will benefit greatly from their tourist dollars, and reward sustainable enterprises by recommending their services. Travelers can not only introduce friends to particular vendors but also to local causes and charities that they might choose to support when they travel.

VOLUNTEERING

VISA INFORMATION
Visa (p. 37). Visitors from most of Europe, Australia, and New Zealand can travel in the US for up to 90 days without a visa, although you may need to show a return plane ticket. Citizens of South Africa need a visa.
Work Permit (p. 37). Required for all foreigners planning to work in the US.

Though Hawaii is considered wealthy in worldwide terms, there is no shortage of aid organizations to benefit the very real issues the region does face, including endangered species, environmental destruction, and local poverty. Volunteering can be incredibly fulfilling, especially when combined with the thrill of travel.

Most people who volunteer in Hawaii do so on a short-term basis, at organizations that make use of drop-in or once-a-week volunteers. These are referenced both in this section and in our town and city write-ups themselves. The best way to find opportunities that match your interests and schedule may be to check with databases such as **Idealist** (www.idealist.org), **ServeNet** (www.servenet.org), or **VolunteerMatch** (www.volunteermatch.com). Short-term volunteer work is prevalent among the many environmental and wildlife conservation initiatives in Hawaii.

More intensive volunteer services may charge you a fee to participate. These costs can be surprisingly hefty (although they frequently cover airfare and most, if not all, living expenses). Most people choose to go through a parent organization that takes care of logistical details and frequently provides a group environment and support system. There are two main types of organizations—religious and non-sectarian—although there are rarely participation restrictions for either.

ENVIRONMENTAL CONSERVATION

Help preserve the view you came to see. Hawaii has over 2,500 native plant species, many of which are at risk of being overtaken by non-native species.

Department of Land and Natural Resources, Kalanimoku Bldg., 1151 Punchbowl St., Honolulu, HI 96813 (☎587-0400 (General), 587-0307 (State Parks), 587-0099 (Marine and Freshwater Wildlife), 587-0061 (Forestry and Wildlife), 587-0062 (Trails), 587-0063 (Natural Area Reserves); www.state.hi.us/dlnr/volunteer.html). Manages all of Hawaii's natural and cultural resources in the state's public lands and waters. Join a group of 10 or more for a weekend activity, or work individually with a staff member for an extended period of time in the state parks, harbors, trails, or historic buildings.

Earthwatch, 3 Clocktower Pl., Suite 100, Box 75, Maynard, MA 01754 (☎800-776-0188 or 978-461-0081; www.earthwatch.org). Arranges 1- to 3-week programs in Hawaii to promote conservation of natural resources. Fees vary based on program location and duration; costs average $1700 plus airfare.

Global Volunteers, 375 E. Little Canada Rd., St. Paul, MN 55117-1628 (☎800-487-1074; http://www.globalvolunteers.org/1main/hawaii/volunteer_hawaii.htm) runs "volunteer vacations," which are short-term service programs, to the Limahuli Gardens in the National Tropical Botanical Gardens and Koke'e State Park, both on the island of Kauai. Their aim is to help preserve the natural Hawaiian ecosystem. Programs run 1-2 weeks, almost continuously throughout the year. Prices range from $1400-1700, which includes meals, lodging, project expenses, and administrative costs, but not airfare.

Haleakala National Park, P.O. Box 369, Makawao, Maui, HI 96768 (volunteer information ☎572-4487; www.haleakala.national-park.com). Various volunteer positions available, including the **Student Conservation Association Conservation Crew,** which provides meals and lodging. Apply for SCA positions at least 1 year in advance.

Hawaii Volcanoes National Park, P.O. Box 52, Hawaii National Park, HI 96718-0052 (☎985-6000; www.nps.gov/havo). Various volunteer positions available, some of which provide meals and dorm-style housing.

Institute for Cultural Ecology, P.O. Box 991, Hilo, HI 96721 (☎866-230-8508; www.cultural-ecology.com) offers both experiential learning programs (a combination of internships and study that takes place in Hawaii, Fiji, and Australia) and a field studies program. Field studies run 6 weeks, 4 times per year, and provide exposure to Hawaiian culture, geology, ecology, and biodiversity. The program costs $2795 including housing, inter-island and ground transportation, and academic credit fees. Up to 15 academic credits are available through UC-Santa Barbara. Application fee $75.

Malama Hawaii, (www.malamahawaii.org; waiwaiohawaii@hotmail.com). Sponsors a number of programs to help the environment as well as a number of community-based initiatives. The web site lists both volunteer and work opportunities.

Sousson Foundation, 3600 Ridge Rd., Templeton CA 93465 (☎805-434-0299; www.sousson.org). Offers volunteer vacations to Volcanoes National Park. Aid in the conservation of rare and endangered species while learning about ecology and biodiversity. 8-day vacations run Apr.-Nov. Program fee $895 per person, $250 deposit.

USGS Hawaiian Volcano Observatory (HVO), US Dept. of the Interior, US Geological Survey, Menlo Park, CA (http://hvo.wr.usgs.gov/volunteer/), assigns each volunteer researcher a support group and HVO staff member. Opportunities include geochemistry, seismology, geodesy, electronics, carpentry, and web site or library support.

WILDLIFE CONSERVATION

Hawaii is known as "The Endangered Species Capital of the US," providing ample opportunities to make a difference in the preservation of global wildlife.

EarthTrust Windward Environmental Center, 1118 Maunawili Rd., Kailua, HI 96734 (☎261-5339; www.earthtrust.org), occasionally needs interns for its efforts to protect some of the world's threatened and endangered species.

Pacific Whale Foundation, 300 Maalaea Rd., Suite 211, Wailuku, HI 96793 (☎249-8811 or 879-8811; www.pacificwhale.org; internships@pacificwhale.org) is a nonprofit organization on Maui dedicated to marine conservation. Interns pay a fee for room and board, but get to assist marine biologists with research. 18+. Moderate to challenging physical demands. College credit available.

Sierra Club, Hawaii Chapter, P.O. Box 2577, Honolulu, HI 96803 (☎538-6616; www.hi.sierraclub.org), seeks to improve natural resource management, clean up pollution, and protect biodiversity in Hawaii.

COMMUNITY OUTREACH

Becoming involved with the cultural melting pot of these islands provides lasting and unique experiences and perspective.

Aloha United Way, 200 N. Vineyard Blvd., #700, Honolulu, HI 96817 (☎536-1951; www.auw.org/givinghelp/volunteerops.asp). Umbrella organization for a wide variety of community-oriented programs.

American Red Cross, 4155 Diamond Head Rd., Honolulu, HI 96816 (☎734-2101; www.hawaiiredcross.org/volunteer.htm). Volunteer opportunities in disaster relief, health and safety instruction, and first aid, among others.

Catholic Charities, 250 Vineyard St., Honolulu, HI 96813 (☎521-4357; www.catholic-charitieshawaii.org). Provides a range of social services.

Honolulu Habitat for Humanity, 2101 Nuuanu Ave., Honolulu HI 96817-1764 (☎245-1996; www.habitat.org), is a nondenominational, nonprofit group that builds affordable housing all over the US.

PBS Hawaii, 2350 Dole St., Honolulu, HI 96822 (☎973-1000 www.khet.org/support/volunteer_opportunities.htm), tries to find activities that match your interests and skills, with opportunities for all time commitments. Receptionist and clerical duties, data entry, and special events are a few options.

Volunteer Zone, (www.volunteerzone.org). A database of volunteer opportunities in Hawaii in a variety of fields, most of which are community-based.

World Horizons International LLC, P.O. Box 662, Bethelem, CT 06751 (☎203-266-5874 or 800-262-5874; www.world-horizons.com), designs volunteer vacation programs for high-school students interested in cross-cultural experience and community service. In Hawaii participants do a variety of service activities, as well as exploring Hawaii's history and biodiversity. One trip per year from late June to late July. Program fee, including airfare, approximately $5,000.

STUDYING IN HAWAII

VISA INFORMATION
Foreign students who wish to study in the US must apply for either an M-1 visa (vocational studies) or an F-1 visa (for full-time students enrolled in an academic or language program). If English is not your native language, you will probably be required to take the **Test of English as a Foreign Language (TOEFL),** administered in many countries. The international students office at the institution you will be attending has details. Contact **TOEFL/TSE Publications,** P.O. Box 6151, Princeton, NJ 08541 (☎609-771-7100; www.toefl.org).

Study abroad programs range from basic language and culture courses to college-level classes, often for credit. To choose a program, research all you can before making your decision—determine costs and duration, as well as what kind of students participate in the program and what sort of accommodations are provided.

In programs that have large groups of students who speak the same native language you do, there is a distinct trade-off. You may feel more comfortable in the community, but you will not have the same opportunity to practice a foreign language or to befriend other international students. For accommodations, dorm life provides a better opportunity to mingle with fellow students, but less chance to experience the local scene. If you live with a family, you can build lifelong friendships with locals and experience daily life, but conditions vary among families.

UNIVERSITIES

The **University of Hawaii (UH)** is composed of 10 independent university and community college campuses and five education centers throughout the islands. Students wishing to study in Hawaii may find it cheaper to enroll directly in one of the two major universities on Oahu (listed below), but check about obtaining college credit (www.hawaii.edu/welcome/campusmap.html). A good resource for finding programs that cater to your interests is www.studyabroad.com, which has links to semester abroad programs based on a variety of criteria, including desired location and focus of study. The following is a list of organizations that can help place students in university programs abroad or have their own branch in Hawaii.

Hawaii Pacific University, 1164 Bishop St., Suite 1100, Honolulu, HI 96813-9639 (☎543-8088; www.hpu.edu) offers masters programs in business administration, information systems management, hospitality management, and organizational change.

Pacific Whale Foundation, (☎249-8811 or 879-8811; www.pacificwhale.org), is a non-profit organization on Maui dedicated to marine conservation. Interns pay a fee for room and board, but get to assist marine biologists with research. 18+. Moderate to challenging physical demands. College credit available.

The University of Hawaii at Manoa, 2244 Dole St., Honolulu, HI 96822 (☎956-8111; www.uhm.hawaii.edu). A research institution with over 1700 people enrolled, has strengths in tropical agriculture; tropical medicine; oceanography; Hawaiian, Pacific Island, and Asian studies and languages, among others.

University of Hawaii at Hilo, 200 W. Kawili St., Hilo, HI 96720-4091 (☎800-897-4456; www.uhh.hawaii.edu), offers undergraduate liberal arts, professional programs and some graduate degrees.

Maui Community College, 310 Kaahumanu Ave., Kahului, HI (☎244-9181; www.hawaii.edu/about/mcc.html), is accredited by the Western Association of Schools and Colleges, with classes approved for veteran credit by the Veterans Administration.

LANGUAGE SCHOOLS

Unlike American universities, language schools are frequently independently run international or local organizations or divisions of foreign universities that rarely offer college credit. Language schools are a good alternative to university study if you desire a deeper focus on the language or a slightly less-rigorous courseload. These programs are also good for high-school students that might not feel comfortable with older students in a university program. Some good programs include:

Academia Language School, 1600 Kapiolani Blvd., Ste. 1215, Honolulu, HI 96814 (☎946-5599). Offers English and TOEFL prep classes starting every week.

EWA International Inc., 2555 Cartwright Rd., Honolulu, HI 96815 (☎922-1677). A 1-to-4-week homestay program. Costs include tuition and lodging.

Hawaii English Language Program (HELP), 1395 Lower Campus Rd. MC 13-1, Honolulu, HI (☎956-6636). Offers 10-week programs in English on the UH Manoa campus.

Institute of Intensive English, 2255 Kuhio Ave., Ste. 920, Honolulu, HI 96815 (☎924-2117). Offers both intensive and short-term English programs, and TOEFL prep courses.

WORKING

Some travelers want long-term jobs that allow them to get to know another part of the world as a member of the community, while other travelers seek out short-term jobs to finance the next leg of their travels. In the highly touristed areas of Hawaii, there are often jobs to be had on the staffs of hotels and resorts, or at local restaurants. Another possibility is to check with the national car rental agencies,

VISA INFORMATION

Work Permit (p. 37) Required for all foreigners planning to work in the US. Your employer must obtain this document, usually by demonstrating that you have skills that locals lack. It may be up to you, however, to apply for an **Employment Authorization Document** to prove that you may work in the US. Friends in the US can sometimes help expedite work permits or arrange work-for-stay exchanges. Obtaining a worker's visa may seem complex, but it's critical that you go through the proper channels. Visit the **Bureau of Citizenship and Immigration Services (BCIS)** web site (www.immigration.gov) for more information on the process for acquiring a work permit.

which may have jobs on their lots that need to be filled. Consult the help wanted sections of local newspapers for more listings—*Honolulu Star Bulletin* and *Hawaii Tribune Herald* on Oahu, *Kauai Garden News* on Kauai, *Maui Today* on Maui, and *West Hawaii Today* on the Big Island are good bets. For links to Hawaii **job banks,** check out **www.employmentspot.com/state/ha.htm,** as well as the classified sections of the aforementioned publications.

LONG-TERM WORK

If you're planning on spending more than about three months working in Hawaii, search for a job well in advance. International placement agencies are often the easiest way to find employment abroad. **Internships,** usually for college students, are a good way to segue into working abroad, although they are often unpaid or poorly paid (many say the experience, however, is well worth it). Be wary of advertisements or companies that claim the ability to get you a job abroad for a fee—often their listings are available online, in newspapers, or are even out of date. Some reputable organizations include:

AU PAIR WORK

Au pairs are typically women, aged 18-27, who work as live-in nannies, caring for children and doing light housework in foreign countries in exchange for room, board, and a small spending allowance or stipend. Most former au pairs speak favorably of their experience, and of how it allowed them to really get to know the country without the high expenses of traveling. Drawbacks, however, often include long hours of constantly being on duty and the somewhat mediocre pay (in Hawaii, this is usually between $120-200 per week, plus room and board). Much of the au pair experience depends on the family you're placed with. The agencies below are a good starting point for looking for au pair work.

Accord Cultural Exchange, 750 La Playa, San Francisco, CA 94121, USA (☎415-386-6203; www.cognitext.com/accord).

Au Pair in America, River Plaza, 9 West Broad St., Stamford, CT 06902 (☎800-928-7247; www.aupairinamerica.com; aupair.info@aifs.com).

Au Pair Homestay, World Learning, Inc., 1015 15th St. NW, Suite 750, Washington, DC 20005, USA (☎800-287-2477; fax 202-408-5397).

InterExchange, 161 Sixth Ave., New York, NY 10013, USA (☎212-924-0446; www.interexchange.org).

SHORT-TERM WORK

Traveling for long periods of time can get expensive; therefore, many travelers try odd jobs for a few weeks at a time to make enough extra cash for another month or two of touring around. Short-term work in exchange for room and board can be found at farms and hostels across Hawaii. Most often, these short-term jobs are found by word of mouth, or by talking to the owner of a hostel or restaurant. Many places, especially due to the high turnover in the tourism industry, are eager for help, even if only temporary. *Let's Go* tries to list temporary jobs like these whenever possible; look in the practical information sections of larger cities, or check out the list below for some of the available short-term jobs in popular destinations.

Evie's Natural Food, 79-7460 Mamalahoa Hwy. (☎322-0739), in Mango Court south of Kainaliu on the Big Island. A bulletin board lists current short-term work possibilities provided by the nearby Kona coffee industry. There are often farm jobs available that trade room and board for labor.

Kalani Oceanside Retreat, RR2 Box 4500, Pahoa-Beach Rd. (☎800-800-6886 or 965-7828; www.kalani.com), on the Big Island. Offers an interesting program where visitors can work as a part of the staff for 1 to 3 months. The volunteer staff handles a number of jobs from housekeeping to cooking, in exchange for room, board, and access to the center's activities. $900 for 1 to 3 months.

Margo's Corner, Wakea Ave. (☎929-9614), an organic farm in Ka'u on The Big Island, sometimes arranges work exchanges with travelers. In such an arrangement, visitors spend a few hours each day working in the garden or on other projects, in return for room, board, and an insiders look at Ka'u. Be sure to contact Margo's well in advance if you are interested in this option.

Willing Workers On Organic Farms (WWOOF), (www.wwoofusa.com/hawaii) matches visitors with host farms. Program applicants are required to fill out a short form and pay a small fee ($15). They then receive a booklet of all the available hosts in their desired destination; travelers are expected to contact farms and arrange a situation with the host. Most volunteers stay at the farms for 1-3 weeks. There are WWOOF farms on 5 of Hawaii's islands: Big Island, Kauai, Maui, Molokai, and Oahu.

HOSTELS

The following hostels offer the possibility of trading room and board for part-time work around the establishment, in maintenance and housekeeping.

Arnott's Lodge, 98 Apapane Rd., Hilo (☎969-7097; www.arnottslodge.com), acts as a clearinghouse for travelers looking for temporary jobs around the Big Island, particularly in the Hilo area. Work is generally on organic farms, in exchange for room and board.

Backpackers, 59-788 Kamehameha Hwy., Waimea (☎638-7838; www.backpackershawaii.com), in Waimea on Oahu's North Shore, exchanges short-term work for room and board.

Banana Bungalow, 310 N. Market St., Maui (☎800-846-7835 or 244-3678; www.mauihostel.com), a few blocks from Central Wailuku in Maui. Short-term work is available; email for more information.

Hostelling International Honolulu, 2323A Seaview Ave., Honolulu (☎946-0591; www.hiayh.org). Turn onto Seaview Ave. from University Ave. opposite the University of Hawaii campus just 4 blocks north of H-1. The hostel is on the left down a short driveway. Contact Mrs. Aiku.

Patey's Place, 75-195 Ala Ona Ona St., Kailua-Kona (☎326-7018; www.hawaiian-hostels.com) in Kailua-Kona on the Big Island. Sometimes needs people to help run the hostel.

Pineapple Park B&B, 81-6363 Mamalahoa Hwy., (☎877-865-2266 or 323-2224; www.pineapple-park.com), north of downtown Captain Cook on the Big Island. Trades a bed in the hostel for a few hours of housekeeping a week, and may be able to work out some other flexible work exchange arrangements.

Pineapple Park Hostel, 11-3489 Pikake St., Mountain View (☎877-865-2266 or 968-8170) in Mountain View near Hawaii Volcanoes National Park on the Big Island. Often offers a dorm bunk in exchange for a few hours of housekeeping a week. If you're volunteering at the park and need a place to stay, look no further.

Waikiki Beachside Hostel, 2556 Lemon Rd., Honolulu (☎923-9566; www.hokondo.com) offers short-term work in exchange for accommodations. Follow Kalakaua Ave. east toward Diamond Head.

YMCA Camp Erdman, 69-385 Farrington Hwy. (☎637-4615; www.camperdman.net), in Waialua on Oahu. Short-term work can be arranged for room and board. For more information, contact Bridget (ext. 30).

Waikiki Beachside Hostel, 2556 Lemon Rd., Honolulu (☎923-9566; www.hokondo.com), offers short-term work in exchange for accommodations. Follow Kalakaua Ave. east toward Diamond Head.

FOR FURTHER READING ON ALTERNATIVES TO TOURISM

Alternatives to the Peace Corps: A directory of third world and U.S. Volunteer Opportunities, by Joan Powell. Food First Books, 2000 ($10).

How to Get a Job in Europe, by Sanborn and Matherly. Surrey Books, 1999 ($22).

How to Live Your Dream of Volunteering Oversees, by Collins, DeZerega, and Heckscher. Penguin Books, 2002 ($17).

International Directory of Voluntary Work, by Whetter and Pybus. Peterson's Guides and Vacation Work, 2000 ($16).

International Jobs, by Kocher and Segal. Perseus Books, 1999 ($18).

Overseas Summer Jobs 2002, by Collier and Woodworth. Peterson's Guides and Vacation Work, 2002 ($18).

Work Abroad: The Complete Guide to Finding a Job Overseas, by Hubbs, Griffith, and Nolting. Transitions Abroad Publishing, 2000 ($16).

Work Your Way Around the World, by Susan Griffith. Worldview Publishing Services, 2001 ($18).

Invest Yourself: The Catalogue of Volunteer Opportunities, published by the Commission on Voluntary Service and Action, 2001 ($8).

OAHU

As the gateway to the islands, Oahu is where most visitors catch their first captivating glimpse of Hawaii. It's known as "the gathering place" for good reason—Oahu is the seat of the state government, as well as Hawaii's financial and business center. Though it is only the third largest of the inhabited Hawaiian islands, nearly three-quarters of the state's total population make their home here. Over half of these residents are concentrated in Honolulu, Hawaii's state capital and premier city. This bustling metropolis is the nexus of Oahu, with all the glitz and glamour of a big-time urban center. Waikiki, the southeastern quarter of the city, is one of the most famous tourist destinations in the world, a magical mile of beachfront hotels, shops, restaurants and endless entertainment.

Oahu's urban nature makes it a less scenic island than the others, but the commercialism and mass tourism industry do have their benefits. Visitors need look no further than Waikiki to get their fill of tropical *kitsch* and frenzied nightlife, and Downtown Honolulu offers myriad opportunities to explore Hawaii's historical and cultural past. However, Oahu isn't all souvenir shops and guided tours. With minimal effort, visitors can uncover the island's less obvious treasures. On the Windward side, a pleasant drive passes by rickety fruit stands and acres of pineapple fields on the way to the fabled North Shore, one of the world's best surf spots. Drive ten or so miles up the Leeward Coast and both the scenery and the mood change dramatically; you're in rural Hawaii, where inhabitants embrace a slower, more traditional way of life. The luxuriant Manoa Valley overflows with fragrant blossoms and tropical fruit, and hikers have their pick of countless intertwined trails that lead to pockets of unspoiled Hawaiian rainforest.

On Oahu, visitors can discover the multifaceted appeal of Hawaii. There is a trace of Big Island's hippie culture on the sands of the North Shore, some of Maui's beauty and opulence in the Windward Coast's resorts, a dash of Kauai's natural splendor in the lush interior valleys, and a little bit of rustic Molokai in the streets of Waimanalo. Oahu contains distilled versions of the best her sister islands have to offer. Consider this your crash course in Hawaiian appreciation.

HIGHLIGHTS OF OAHU

PAY YOUR RESPECTS at the Pearl Harbor memorials (p. 136).

RECREATE THE CARNAGE at the Nu'uanu Pali Lookout, the site of Kamehameha's 1795 victory and turning point in his campaign to unite all the islands (p. 155).

SNORKEL ALONGSIDE TROPICAL FISH of all colors at Hanauma Bay (p. 139).

HULA at the Polynesian Cultural Center, representing seven different cultures (p. 155).

RELIVE THE GLORY DAYS of the Hawaiian monarchy at Iolani Palace (p. 106).

CATCH A WAVE at Waikiki Beach, the perfect spot to learn to surf (p. 129).

LOUNGE at Kailua Bay while extreme windsurfers perform acrobatics (p. 153).

CLIFF JUMP into the crystalline waters of North Shore's Waimea Bay (p. 160).

Oahu

OAHU

Labels on map

Kaiwi Channel

Kauai Channel

PACIFIC OCEAN

Makapu'u Lighthouse

Koko Head / Hanauma Bay

Waimanalo Bay State Recreation Area

Waimanalo

Kalanianaole Hwy. 72

Diamond Head 760 (232m)

WAIKIKI

HONOLULU RANGE

Kailua

Maunawili

Mokapu Peninsula

Kaneohe Bay

Kaneohe

Nuuanu Pali State Park

Manoa Falls

Honolulu

Malaekahana State Recreation Area

WINDWARD COAST

Kualoa Regional Park

KOOLAUPOKO

Pali Hwy. 61

Likelike Hwy. 63

78

Honolulu International Airport

Mamala Bay

Kahana Valley State Park

Kahekili Hwy.

KOOLAU RANGE

Keaiwa Heiau State Park

Pearl City

Pearl Harbor

Laie

Polynesian Cultural Center

Hau'ula

Sacred Falls State Park

Punalu'u

Kamehameha Hwy.

Kahuku

KOOLAULOA

Waimea

Waimea Falls

Dole Plantation

WAHIAWA

Wahiawa

WAIALUA

Waipahu

EWA

Barber's Point

Kauai Channel

Haleiwa

Waialua

Mokuleia Natural Area Reserve

Mt. Kaala Natural Reserve

Makakilo

NORTH SHORE

WAIANAE RANGE

Waianae

Makaha

Maili

Nanakuli

LEEWARD COAST

Farrington Hwy.

Barber's Point Harbor

Karena Point State Park

Highway markers: 83, 830, 99, 801, 80, 803, 930, 93, 76, 750, H1, H2, H3, 92, 72

5 miles

5 kilometers

■ **INTERISLAND TRANSPORTATION**

Oahu is the major hub for transportation to the Hawaiian islands, as international flights, flights between Hawaii and the mainland, and interisland flights depart from **Honolulu International Airport** in Honolulu (see p. 86). See each city's **Transportation** sections for local transportation.

▚ **CAMPING**

In order to camp at any park on Oahu, you need a **permit.** Where you get the permit depends on whether you wish to camp at a City and County Park or a State Park. Camping permits for City and County Parks are obtainable from the Department of Parks and Recreation, on the ground floor of the **Honolulu Municipal Building,** 650 S. King St., Honolulu, 96813-3078; open M-F 7:45am-4pm, or at any **Satellite City Hall** in the county. A conveniently located Satellite City Hall is at the Ala Moana Shopping Center (p. 111). Camping at City and County Parks is allowed from 8am Friday to 8am Wednesday, though certain campsites are only open on weekends. City and County permits must be obtained in person. Reservations must be made at least one week in advance, but no more than two Fridays prior to camping date. Campsites fill quickly in summer, so have an alternate plan for accommodation in case campsites are full. For more information on camping, call ☎ 523-4525.

Camping at a State Park requires a permit from the State Parks office. Permits can be requested by mail, but must be picked up in person. *(1151 Punchbowl St. ☎ 587-0300; fax 587-0311. Open M-F 8am-3:30pm. $5 per campsite per night.)*

The state of Hawaii's **Division of Forestry and Wildlife** provides all manner of information concerning Oahu trails, including trail maps and descriptions. They also provide camping permits for areas within forest reserves. *(1151 Punchbowl St., Rm. 325. ☎ 587-0166; www.hawaiitrails.org. Open M-F 7:45am-4:30pm.)*

HONOLULU

As Hawaii's commanding capital and largest city, Honolulu is the point of entry for most visits to the islands. Although the tourist throngs often pass over Honolulu proper en route to the resorts of its Waikiki district, Waikiki's status as holiday playground par excellence is the result of only the most recent wave of newcomers that have changed the face of Hawaii's biggest city. The historical sights in the Downtown area and Civic Center illustrate the complex history of Hawaii's religious and economic modernization due to Western influence. Today's Hawaiians inherit a cosmopolitan city of almost 400,000 as their capital—Downtown bustles with *aloha* shirt-clad businesspeople every weekday, and Chinatown is crammed to the gills with daytime shoppers in search of its markets, giftshops, and authentic Asian restaurants. The mellow residential areas of Kaimuki and the University of Hawaii at Manoa contrast the hectic urban lifestyle. Locals in these areas avoid the fast pace of Honolulu by slipping away to Manoa's tropical mountains, Waikiki's beaches, or barbecuing *ohana*-style at Ala Moana Beach Park. Honolulu alternates as a beach resort, urban center, commercial hub, international port, and living landmark of Hawaiian history. To the adventure-seeking tourist, it is all of these at once, a capital city paradoxically unlike anywhere else in the state.

■ **INTERCITY TRANSPORTATION**

Honolulu International Airport (☎ 836-6413; www.honoluluairport.com) is off the Airport Exit from H-1, 9 mi. west of Waikiki. The airport is also accessible via **Ala Moana Boulevard.** Take Ala Moana west until it becomes **Nimitz Highway** and continue west. Turn left into the airport just west of the **Roger's Boulevard** intersection

Honolulu and Vicinity

THE LOCAL STORY

BEYOND WAIKIKI

Nani Loui, 19, was born and raised on Oahu. In 2002 she had a brief stint as a hostess at popular Waikiki restaurant Cheeseburger in Paradise.

LG: Waikiki: Tourist trap or Hawaiian haven?
A: Waikiki has a lot to offer. It's well-kept, fun, and has interesting people, but don't spend your whole vacation here.
LG: What does the rest of the island have to offer?
A: Everything in Waikiki tends to be more commercialized and stereotyped than anywhere else. It isn't a good representation of Hawaii. Tourists will come in and ask if there are any good restaurants in the area, and I'll just tell them to get out of the area. Little holes-in-the-wall are a better representation of our culture and the importance of food in Hawaii. Rather than sitting on Waikiki Beach, drive 20min. away and you'll find a private beach.
LG: What advice do you have for someone vacationing on Oahu?
A: Hawaii is an active place. Don't waste time in your hotel room! Take surfing lessons. Eat plate lunch or Spam musubi. Drive to the North Shore and stop at all the corn shacks and fruit stands. Real Hawaii is white sand beaches, mountains, rainforest hikes, laidback towns, and plate lunch stands. Do things you can't do anywhere else. Get in your rental car and just GO.

underneath H-1 and follow signs to Arrivals, Departures, or the many opportunistically-placed *lei* stands outside the airport.

Inside the airport, **ATMs** are available in the Interisland Terminal, the central lobby of the main terminal, and near gates 12-13. **Currency exchange** services are available in the central lobby of the main terminal, near gates 12-13 and 24-25. **Lost and found** (☎836-6547) is on the ground level in the parking structure, opposite the Main Terminal. Visitors can make photocopies, buy flight insurance, use postage and mail services, fax, and rent workstations at the **Airport Business Center.** (☎831-3600. Open daily 8am-5pm.) **Airport parking** (☎861-1260) costs $1 for the first 30min., $1 each additional hr., $10 per 24hr., and $100 per month, non-prorated. If you leave your car longer than 30 days, it can be towed unless you notify the parking company. Cars may be security-screened. **Reliable Shuttle** (☎924-9292) runs between the airport and hotels in Waikiki and Honolulu (approx. $6), as well as the *USS Arizona* Memorial. Make reservations by phone at least one day in advance. Shuttles run daily 6am-10pm. See **Interisland Transportation** at the start of each chapter for information on flights between the islands.

FLIGHTS

Honolulu International Airport operates most incoming flights to Hawaii, both international and domestic, as well as connecting flights to the other islands. See **Essentials** (p. 52) for more information. The following are a few major US carriers.

Aloha Airlines (☎800-367-5250 or 484-1111; www.alohaair.com) has ticket offices across Oahu. Service from Burbank, Oakland, Orange County, CA, and Vancouver, Canada. Also operates interisland flights from Honolulu to: Hilo and Kona on the Big Island; Lihue, Kauai; Lanai City, Lanai; Kapalua and Kahului on Maui; and Hoolehua, Molokai.

American Airlines (☎800-433-7300; www.aa.com) has flights from the continental US via Dallas-Ft. Worth, Los Angeles, San Francisco, San Jose, St. Louis, and Chicago.

American Trans Air (☎800-435-9282; www.ata.com) provides service from Los Angeles, Phoenix, and San Francisco.

Continental Airlines, Ala Moana Center Ste. 2230 (☎800-214-1469 or 946-9786; www.continental.com), offers service from Houston, Los Angeles, and Newark, and on partner airlines from Minneapolis/St. Paul, Seattle/Tacoma, and San Francisco. Ticket office open M-F 9am-6pm, Sa 9am-5pm.

Delta Airlines (☎800-221-1212; www.delta.com) provides service from Los Angeles and San Francisco.

OAHU

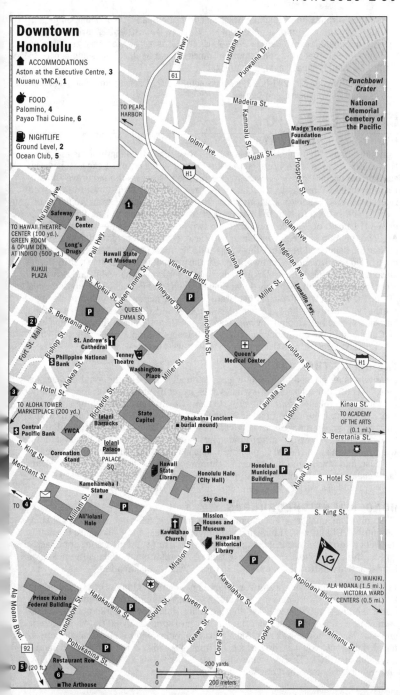

Downtown Honolulu

ACCOMMODATIONS
Aston at the Executive Centre, **3**
Nuuanu YMCA, **1**

FOOD
Palomino, **4**
Payao Thai Cuisine, **6**

NIGHTLIFE
Ground Level, **2**
Ocean Club, **5**

Pali Hwy.
61
TO PEARL HARBOR
Lusitana St.
Puowaina Dr.
Madeira St.
Kammalu St.
Iolani Ave.
Huali St.
Madge Tennent Foundation Gallery
Prospect St.
Punchbowl Crater
National Memorial Cemetery of the Pacific
H1
Iolani Ave.
Magellan Ave.
Lunalilo Fwy.
Nuuanu Ave.
Safeway
Pali Center
TO HAWAII THEATRE CENTER (100 yd.), GREEN ROOM & OPIUM DEN AT INDIGO (500 yd.)
Long's Drugs
Hawaii State Art Museum
KUKUI PLAZA
Vineyard Blvd.
Vineyard St.
Lusitana St.
Miller St.
S. Kukui St.
Queen Emma St.
QUEEN EMMA SQ.
Punchbowl St.
Lusitana St.
H1
S. Beretania St.
Fort St. Mall
St. Andrew's Cathedral
Bishop St.
Philippine National Bank
Alakea St.
Tenney Theatre
Washington Place
Miller St.
Queen's Medical Center
Lauhala St.
Lisbon St.
S. Hotel St.
TO ALOHA TOWER MARKETPLACE (200 yd.)
Central Pacific Bank
YWCA
Richards St.
Iolani Barracks
State Capitol
Pohukaina (ancient burial mound)
Kinau St.
TO ACADEMY OF THE ARTS (0.1 mi.)
S. Beretania St.
S. King St.
Merchant St.
Coronation Stand
Iolani Palace
PALACE SQ.
Hawaii State Library
Honolulu Hale (City Hall)
Honolulu Municipal Building
Alapai St.
S. Hotel St.
TO 4
Kamehameha I Statue
Milliani St.
Ali'iolani Hale
Sky Gate
S. King St.
Mission Houses and Museum
Kawaiahao Church
Hawaiian Historical Library
Mission Ln.
South St.
Queen St.
Kawaiahao St.
Kapiolani Blvd.
TO WAIKIKI, ALA MOANA (1.5 mi.), VICTORIA WARD CENTERS (0.5 mi.)
Ala Moana Blvd.
Prince Kuhio Federal Building
Punchbowl St.
Halakauwila St.
Keawe St.
Coral St.
Cooke St.
Waimanu St.
92
Pohukaina St.
Restaurant Row
TO 5 (20 ft.)
6 The Arthouse

0 200 yards
0 200 meters

Hawaiian Airlines has additional ticket offices inside Sears at Ala Moana and Pearl-ridge Shopping Centers and Windward Mall. (☎800-367-5320 or 838-1555; www.hawaiianair.com.) Service from: Anchorage, Las Vegas, Los Angeles, Phoenix, Portland, San Diego, Sacramento, San Francisco, and Seattle. Interisland service to The Big Island, Kauai, Lanai, and Molokai.

United Airlines (☎800-241-6522; www.ual.com) provides service from San Francisco, Los Angeles, Vancouver, and Denver.

✚ ORIENTATION

HIGHWAYS AND BYWAYS

Honolulu's main highway, **H-1**, runs east and west along the length of the city from Hawaii Kai, past the airport, and on to Pearl Ridge. Getting onto H-1 can be an ordeal, as some streets only provide access to one direction, either eastbound or westbound. Drivers can avoid the hassle, as well as downtown rush hour traffic, by using alternate roads. Access is available via: **Ala Moana Boulevard,** which stretches from Waikiki to the airport, and turns into Nimitz Hwy. west of Nu'uanu River; and **King Street,** which leaves H-1 north of Waikiki and splits into two one-way streets between University Ave. and the Aala Park edge of Chinatown. The one-way streets formed from the split of King St., **Beretania Street** (heading west) and **King Street** (heading east), are the back-bone of Downtown and Chinatown, and bear the brunt of intra-Honolulu traffic. Beretania and King St. also front a large portion of greater Honolulu's sights and activities. Most **TheBus routes** ply their way down King St., then head east and back up Beretania St. for the return trip. **Kapiolani Boulevard** is another major thoroughfare, slicing a northeast-southwest passage from Wailae Ave. and H-1, intersecting Waikiki's **Kalakaua Avenue** before plunging westward to the Civic Center at King St. Kapahulu, McCully, and Piikoi northbound one-way, Pensacola southbound one-way, and Ward Ave. are the biggest streets that intersect the east-west usual suspects.

THE LEI OF THE LAND

Honolulu is an abused place-name geographically, and like the local phrase "da kine," it is often used to refer to whatever is presently under discussion. To many, Honolulu means the urban and suburban sprawl that stretches along the south shore of Oahu, from Koko Head at the extreme eastern end of the island to Kalihi and the airport on the western end. Others consider Honolulu to be the compara-tively small Downtown area surrounded by the diverse districts of **Chinatown** to the west, **Ala Moana** and **Waikiki** to the south, **Kaimuki** and the revitalized **Wailae** area to the east, and **Manoa** and the valley neighborhoods to the north. The **Koolau Moun-tain Range** creates the city's backdrop, and fixed in the east is **Diamond Head Crater,** which provides a perfect vantage point for some of the best views on Oahu.

HONOLULU NEIGHBORHOODS

Honolulu is an amalgamation of a number of small neighborhoods, but Ala Moana, Downtown, Chinatown, Manoa and the University Area, and Waikiki are the major districts referred to in this guide, although some listings fall near, but not exactly within, the established boundaries of their given districts. **Waikiki** is the nexus of tourist activity in Honolulu. (See p. 116 for all Waikiki information.)

ALA MOANA. Occupying waterfront Honolulu along Ala Moana Blvd. from Down-town to Waikiki, Ala Moana is a shopper's paradise. A number of malls and complexes throw their hats into the capitalist ring, including Aloha Tower Marketplace and Res-taurant Row in neighboring Kaka'ako, Ala Moana's sprawling Victoria Ward Centers, and Ala Moana Shopping Center. Ala Moana Shopping Center is also a major bus ter-minal; if the route you need doesn't stop in front of the mall at Kona Street or behind it on Ala Moana Blvd. (TheBus routes #6, 8, 11, 12, 19, 20, 40, 42, 43, 52-58, 62, 65, 86A, and 88A do), it's just a short connection away.

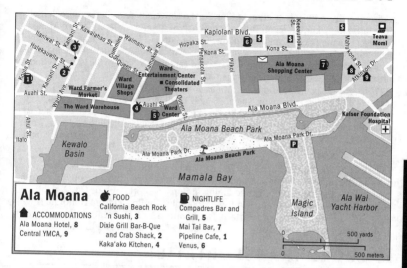

Ala Moana

🏠 ACCOMMODATIONS
Ala Moana Hotel, **8**
Central YMCA, **9**

🍴 FOOD
California Beach Rock
'n Sushi, **3**
Dixie Grill Bar-B-Que
and Crab Shack, **2**
Kaka'ako Kitchen, **4**

🍸 NIGHTLIFE
Compadres Bar and
Grill, **5**
Mai Tai Bar, **7**
Pipeline Cafe, **1**
Venus, **6**

DOWNTOWN. Downtown Honolulu is Hawaii's financial center, and at its center, Bishop Square houses Oahu's captains of industry. Weekday work hours find the area teeming with businessfolk, although at any other time of the week it feels more like a ghost town. Downtown draws only a small crowd with the historical sights of the Civic Center; few tourists venture into the financial district, which is host to some of the city's best restaurants, public art, and fountains. The Downtown area is located between Ala Moana and Chinatown, and is bordered by the Fort St. Mall, South St., and Kaka'ako. It has some of the most expensive parking in the country; avoid the headache of parking and one-way streets by taking TheBus #2, 13, or B CityExpress to Hotel St. and exploring on foot.

CHINATOWN. Chinatown assaults all the senses with its pungent fish markets, incense-surrounded shrines, vocal Chinese-speaking bargain hunters, and sizzling, claustrophobic food markets. Originally the red light district for sailors, Chinatown is now home to a diverse Asian population, as well as a destination for tourists in search of a cultural experience complete with shopping bargains and inexpensive food. All are readily available in Chinatown, but bargain hunters should come early to beat the crowds. Chinatown itself is a small grid a few blocks square, bordered by Downtown to the east and Aala Triangle Park to the west. Chinatown's shop-lined streets are River St., Maunakea St., Smith St., Nu'uanu Ave., and Bethel St. before Fort St. Mall. Kukui St. is the northern border of the area, which continues to Nimitz Hwy. on the harbor to the south. Begin pedestrian exploration at the intersection of Hotel and River St.; take TheBus #2, 13, or B CityExpress. Visitors should not travel to Chinatown alone after dark, when most businesses are closed and it may be unsafe.

MANOA AND THE UNIVERSITY AREA. The University of Hawaii hangs its scholarly hat in the pleasant Manoa Valley district, north of central Honolulu. Manoa itself is a peaceful valley overflowing with greenery, lava rock walls, and fruit trees. The higher up one travels in the valley, away from the city center and toward the Honolulu Watershed Forest Reserve, the more cheerful and tranquil the streets become. Two of Honolulu's main arteries, University Ave. and Punahou St., become Oahu Ave. and Manoa Rd. respectively once they hit Manoa. Manoa Rd. splits just north of Punahou School into Manoa Rd. and E. Manoa Road. E. Manoa Road veers to the Manoa Marketplace; Manoa Road continues on to Lyon Arboretum and Manoa Falls. A series of strip malls radiates out from the intersection of King St. and University Ave., in the more densely populated area known as Moiliili, at the base of Manoa Valley. West of Manoa, between Punahou School and Punchbowl Crater north of H-1, is the highrise-clogged neighborhood of Makiki. Excellent hiking and scenic drives are found at the extreme ends of Makiki Heights Dr., Round Top Dr., and Tantalus Dr., where the latter two loop into the Forest Reserve and the area near Mt. Tantalus, to the west.

TheBus #4 picks up westbound on Kuhio Ave. in Waikiki and continues up University Ave. and on to Downtown. The #5, 6, and 18 all pick up at Ala Moana Shopping Center and head to Manoa. The #80A is an express from Hawaii Kai from 6-7:30am to lower Manoa and Downtown weekdays during school, going as far into Manoa as Dole St. and UH. In the afternoon, the #80A runs from Punahou School at Punahou St. and Wilder Ave. back to Hawaii Kai.

KAPAHULU/WAIALAE. Kapahulu/Waialae and the blocks adjacent to these avenues in the amiable **Kaimuki** area are the cradle of a revitalized neighborhood known for its multitude of diverse dining options, a short walk or Our Neighborhood Trolley ride away from Downtown Honolulu. TheBus #9 from Honolulu travels from S. King St. up Kapiolani Blvd. and on to Waialae and 4th Ave. Alternatively, the #1 goes from west Honolulu to Kahala Mall and Hawaii Kai.

☰ LOCAL TRANSPORTATION

BY BUS. Oahu's public transit system, **TheBus** (☎848-4500; www.thebus.org), was voted "America's Best Transit System," in 2000. It offers safe and reliable service across the island. If you are not sure you are getting on the correct bus or off at the correct stop, the bus drivers are eager to help you find your way. Buses have the same number going in both directions, but the title of the bus changes depending on direction. Throw the driver a friendly signal if you wish to board an approaching bus, and push the yellow tape or pull the cord to signal your stop when riding.

Routes and Fares: One-way fare $1.75; senior citizens, the disabled, and students 18 and under $0.75; children under 6 free. Free transfers are good for 2hr., available by request from bus driver. **The Oahu Discovery Passport,** available at ABC Stores, is good for 4 consecutive days of unlimited travel ($20). Monthly passes are available at 7-Eleven stores and select ABC stores for $30, youth $13.50. **Route A,** the CityExpress, goes from Kalihi and Waipahu in the west, down King/Beretania to University Ave. and Manoa. **Route B,** the other CityExpress, stops short of University Ave. in Waikiki. **Route C,** the CountryExpress, makes it all the way out from Makaha to Ala Moana Shopping Center. These are just a few of TheBus's many routes; see the web site or information lines for details. *Let's Go* lists nearby TheBus stops for sights and towns, where applicable. See **Waikiki Transportation** (p. 116) for Waikiki-based routes.

Information Lines: Call **TheBus Information Service** (☎848-5555) with your location, a time of departure, and destination points, and they will find the best route to get you there. The 24hr. **Recorded Information from Waikiki** (☎296-1818) hotline offers an automated directory of bus routes to sites across the island, on buses that pick up from Kuhio Ave. TheBus also publishes the helpful **Map and Guidebook** ($5 English, $7.50 Japanese), available in convenience stores in the Honolulu area.

BY CAR. Driving is the easiest way to get around Oahu, despite traffic congestion and limited parking. The major **national car rental** chains have branches by the airport (listed below). From within the airport, follow the signs to car rentals. To return the vehicle from Honolulu, take H-1 west to the Airport. Arrivals are on street level, to the extreme left—follow signs that say Car Rental/Car Returns. As the nexus of most tourist activity in Honolulu, Waikiki holds a number of excellent smaller car and moped rental companies (see **Waikiki Transportation,** p. 116). Car rental costs fluctuate by season and availability, even at national chains. Be sure to call well in advance to reserve a vehicle, and to check company web sites for online deals and promotions. See **Essentials** (p. 53) for more information on traveling by car in Hawaii. Call ☎529-3231 for **stolen vehicles.**

Alamo (☎800-462-5266 or 833-4585; Waikiki branch 947-6112; www.alamo.com), at the airport and at the Ilikai in Waikiki. Cars from $30 per day, $160 per week. CDW $19 per day. 21+. Under-25 surcharge $25 per day. Rentals must be returned to the airport location. Deposit can also be made with credit or debit card, with proof of departure. Open daily 5am-1am. AmEx/D/MC/V.

Avis (☎800-230-4898 or 834-5536; Waikiki branch 971-3700; www.avis.com), at the airport and at the Outrigger East Hotel in Waikiki. Cars from $38-56 per day, depending on season and availability. Monthly rates around $300 per week. Unlimited mileage. CDW $21 per day unlimited, liability $11 per day. Under-25 surcharge. Returns can be made at Waikiki branch. Open daily 5am-3am. AmEx/D/MC/V, no debit cards.

Budget (☎800-527-7000 or 836-1700; www.budget.com), at the airport and 7 other island locations. Cars from $30 per day, $195 per week. Unlimited mileage. 21+. Under-25 surcharge $20 per day. Rentals must be returned to the airport location. Open 24hr. AmEx/D/MC/V.

Dollar (☎800-800-4000 or 866-434-2226; www.dollar.com), at the airport. Branch at 2002 Kalakaua Ave., in Waikiki. Cars from $31 per day, $210 per week. Unlimited mileage. CDW $18 per day. Under-25 surcharge $20 per day. Open daily 4:30am-midnight.

Enterprise (☎800-736-8222 or 836-2277; Kalihi branch ☎836-7722; www.enterprise.com), at the airport and 16 other island locations. Cars from $30 per day, $150 per week, $650 per month. Unlimited mileage. CDW $15 per day. 21+. Returns can be made at Salt Lake Kalihi, Waikiki office, and other locations; all usually match airport rates. Open daily 7am-9pm.

Hertz (☎800-654-3011 or 831-3500; www.hertz.com), at the airport. Cars from $37 per day; no long-term deals. Unlimited mileage. CDW $20 per day. 25+. Rentals must be returned to the airport location. Pick up and return service. Open daily 4:30am-2am. AmEx/D/MC/V.

National Car Rental (☎800-227-7368 or 836-2213; www.nationalcar.com), at the airport and 2 other Honolulu locations. Cars from $33 per day, $170 per week. Unlimited mileage. CDW $19 per day. 21+. Under-25 surcharge $25 per day. Returns can be made at other Honolulu locations. Open 7am-9pm. AmEx/D/MC/V required.

Thrifty (☎877-283-0898; www.thrifty.com), at the airport. Branch at 325 Seaside Ave. in Waikiki. Compact 4-door $30 per day, $160 per week. Unlimited mileage. CDW $19 per day. 21+. Under-25 surcharge $15 per day. $30 Waikiki drop-off fee. Open daily 5:30am-midnight. AmEx/D/MC/V.

PRACTICAL INFORMATION

The central branches of many of Oahu's services are found in Honolulu. Many tourist services within the city are also based in Waikiki, the hub of the city's tourist activity. See also **Waikiki Practical Information** (p. 120).

TOURIST AND FINANCIAL SERVICES

Tourist Office: Hawaii Visitors & Convention Bureau Information Center, at Waikiki Shopping Plaza, 2250 Kalakaua Ave., Ste. 502 (☎924-0266; www.gohawaii.com). The office has statewide tourist information, as well as a number of local brochures and tourist magazines. Open M-F 8am-4:30pm, Sa-Su 8am-noon.

Pleasant Ticket Office, 1601 Kapiolani Blvd., Ste. 940 (☎800-654-4386 or 922-1515), the kiosk in front of 7-Eleven at the intersection of Kapiolani Blvd. and Kalakaua Ave. The tiny office specializes in air, room, and car packages to the outer islands, and cheaper mainland airfare. Open M-F 8am-6pm, Sa-Su 8:30am-5pm. AmEx/D/MC/V.

OAHU

Free Tours:

The Native Hawaiian Hospitality Association (☎737-6442) offers the Queen's walking tour of old Waikiki on the 2 mi. Waikiki Historic Trail. Meet the Trail Historian M-Sa at 9am at the Royal Hawaiian Shopping Center stage by the waterfall at Kalakaua and Seaside. M-Sa 9-11am.

The Clean Air Team (☎948-3299) volunteers lead a 2 mi., 3hr. pleasant stroll through Kapiolani Park and along the Diamond Head Coast, ending at the Diamond Head Lighthouse. Participants may wish to bring flashlights for caves near the coast. Leaves from the Gandhi statue near the Honolulu Zoo entrance, 151 Kapahulu Ave. Su 9am. Under 18 must be accompanied by an adult; groups of 5 or more must call ahead. Parking available at the Waikiki Shell. $5 per person.

The Diamond Head Story (☎948-3299), a field-trip-like walking tour about the history of Diamond Head that ends at the beginning of a 2 mi. hike to the top of the crater. Participants may try the hike, or return to the zoo on their own. Leaves from the Gandhi statue (see above). Sa 9am. Under 18 must be accompanied by an adult; groups of 5 or more must call ahead. Parking available at the Waikiki Shell. $5 per person.

The Program to Preserve Hawaiian Placenames, at the Liliha Public Library, 1515 Liliha St.; take H-1 west to School St. and take N. School St. west to Liliha St. Catch the free "Introduction to Hawaiian Words" lecture, the easiest and fastest (1½hr.) way to become acquainted with Hawaiian word structure. The lecture teaches how to pronounce Hawaiian placenames, step by step. 1st W of every month, 7pm. No late arrivals.

The Like Hike (☎455-8193; www.gayhawaii.com), a gay Honolulu hiking club, sponsors a monthly hike, usually on Su, to explore the wild outback of Oahu. Check web site or call for times.

Paid Tours:

Hawaii Tours and Travels, 339 Saratoga Rd. Ste. 21 (☎922-4884; www.hawaiitourandtravels.com). See the entire island via a 25-person bus with A/C and big windows on the 120 mi. Grand Island Circle Tour (2 per day, 8:20am-4:30pm or 9am-5:30pm, $16; $30 with a 1¼hr. excursion including entrance to Waimea Falls). 4hr. Jungle Rainforest Hiking trip (1:30-5pm, $19), Dr. Livingstone and machete not included. Inexpensive outer-island helicopter rides, swimming with dolphins, and more. Open daily 8am-6pm; orders by phone 7:30am-9pm. D/MC/V.

Affordable Tours, 334 Seaside Ave., Ste. 102 (☎921-2280), books tours at discounted prices. Circle Island Tour (8:45am-5pm; $16, with entrance to Waimea Falls $35). Exotic Beach Luau with all-you-can-eat dinner buffet and 3 drinks (5-10pm; $30, transportation $4). Open daily 8am-6pm, phone orders 7am-10pm. MC/V.

Equipment Rental: See **Waikiki Practical Information,** p. 120.

Embassies and Consulates: Australia, 1000 Bishop St., Ste. PHOUSE 96813 (☎524-5050). Handles Australian and some **British and Canadian** travel documents. Open M-F 8am-4pm. **New Zealand,** c/o Hawaiian Electric Industries, Inc. 900 Richards St. #414; P.O. Box 730 96808 (☎547-5117; fax 543-7523; plewis@hei.com). NZ consulate is a 1-person operation which mails visa and passport applications. No office hours. See **www.embassyworld.com** or Essentials, p. 35 for a complete listing of embassies and consulates throughout the US.

Banks and Currency Exchange: American Savings has offices at 180 S. King St. (☎523-6844; open M-Th 7:30am-3:30pm, F 7:30am-5pm) and at the Ala Moana Center, 1450 Ala Moana Blvd. (☎973-4864; open M-F 9am-6pm, Sa 9am-1pm). 3% currency exchange fee for non-account holders. **Bank of Hawaii,** 111 S. King St. (☎538-4171; open 7:30am-3pm) and in Ala Moana at 1441 Kapiolani Blvd. (☎942-6111; open M-F 8:30am-4pm, F 8:30am-6pm, Sa 9am-noon). $10 currency exchange fee for non-account holders, $2 by machine. **Central Pacific** provides 24hr. telephone banking (☎522-2222) and has its main office at 220 S. King St. (☎544-0500). Open M-Th 7:30am-3pm, F 7:30am-4:30pm. $5 currency exchange fee for non-account holders. **First Hawaiian Bank** has a 24hr. customer service line (☎844-4444) and offices at 999 Bishop St. (☎525-6340) and in Chinatown at 2 N. King St. (☎525-6888). Both are open M-Th 8:30am-4pm, F 8:30am-6pm and charge non-account holders a currency exchange fee of $3 for amounts under $300. **Hawaii National Bank,** 45 N. King St. (☎528-7711), is open M-Th 8am-4pm, F 8am-5pm. $5 currency exchange rate for non-account holders. **Philippine National Bank,** 1145 Bishop (☎521-1493). Open M-Th 8:15am-4pm. No currency exchange. With the exception of the Philippine National Bank, all banks have **ATMs** throughout Honolulu.

LOCAL SERVICES

Libraries: Hawaii State Library, 478 S. King St. (☎586-3500), just east of Iolani Palace, in the Civic Center—look for the huge white pillars. Added to the State and National Register of Historical Places in 1975, the Hawaii State Library anchors the only statewide library system in the United States, with over 500,000 catalogued books. Open Tu-W 9am-5pm, Th noon-8pm, F-Su 9am-5pm. The **McCully-Moiliili Public Library** is at 2211 S. King St. (☎973-1099). Open Tu-W and F-Sa 10am-5pm, Th noon-7pm. Temporary library passes are available at all library branches. 3 mo. pass $10, non-resident pass (good for 1 yr.) $25. **Manoa Public Library,** 2716 Woodlawn Dr. (☎988-0459). Open M, W, F-Sa 10am-5pm; Tu, Th 10am-8pm.

Laundromat: Manoa Laundry, 2855 E. Manoa Rd. (☎988-9015), next to the post office in Manoa. Self-service $1.50, drop-off service $0.90 per lb. Open daily 7am-8:30pm.

Department of Parks and Recreation, 1000 Uluohia St., Ste. 309 (☎692-5585), in Kapolei. Oahu **camping permits** available at the Main Permits Office, 650 S. King St. Both offices open daily 7:45am-4:30pm.

Hawaii Nature Center, 2131 Makiki Heights Dr. (☎955-0100; www.hawaiinaturecenter.org), in Makiki Valley. Hands-on programs, community events, and guided hikes. Schedule available online. Open daily 8am-4:30pm.

Hawaiian Trail and Mountain Club, 41-023 Pu'uone St. (☎674-1459; www.geocities.com/Yosemite/Trails/3660), in Waimanalo. Hikes a different trail every weekend; visitors are welcome. Quarterly hike schedules available online. All hikes meet at Iolani Palace at 8am. Under 18 must be accompanied by adult. Suggested donation $2.

Sierra Club, Beretania St. (☎538-6616), across from the police station. Hikes, outings, and service projects. Visitors and non-members welcome. Schedule available online. Unless otherwise noted, hikes leave at 8am from 2510 Bingham St. in Moiliili. Under 18 must be accompanied by adult. $3, Sierra club members and children under 14 $1.

Honolulu Gay and Lesbian Cultural Foundation: ☎941-0424.

Weather and Surf Conditions: See **Honolulu and Waikiki Information Lines** (p. 97).

LOCAL MEDIA

Television Stations: ABC (KITV, channels 4/12/13); **CBS** (KGMB, channel 9); **Fox** (KHON, channels 2/7/11); **NBC** (KHNL, channel 13); **PBS** (KHET, channel 11). **KIKU** (channel 20) has multicultural shows in up to 8 languages, with over 30 hrs. of Japanese language shows per wk. **KWHE** (channel 14) is family Christian programming, but shows Big 12 football and basketball and Pac 10 Conference collegiate sports.

National Public Radio: 88.1 FM plays classical music and NPR news; 89.3 FM has news, talk, world music, NPR, and the BBC.

Other Radio Stations: ■ **90.3 FM KTUH Honolulu** (91.3 FM Hawaii Kai, 89.7 FM North Shore), the University of Hawaii's excellent radio station, plays jazz to jungle, house to Hawaiian. **Urban/Rap/Hip-Hop,** "Da Bomb" KDDB 102.7 FM, KIKI 93.9 FM, KXME 104.3 FM. **Modern Rock,** 97.5 FM KPOI and 101.9 FM KUCD. **Hawaiian music,** KDNN 98.5, KHUI 99.5, KCCN 100.3 FM, KINE 105.1 FM. **Classic Rock,** KAHA 105.9 FM. **Oldies,** KGMZ 107.9 FM for 60s and 70s nostalgia or KQMQ 93.1 for old-school dance and rock hits from the 70s through the 90s. **Adult Contemporary,** KSSK 92.3 FM and KRTR 96.3 FM. **Christian,** K218CH 91.14 FM and KAIM 95.5 FM.

EMERGENCY AND COMMUNICATIONS

Emergency: ☎911.

Police: 801 S. Beretania St. (☎529-3111). Downtown/Chinatown substation (☎527-6990). Airport sheriff (☎836-6606).

Crisis Lines: Sex Abuse Treatment Center, ☎524-7273. **Crisis Response Team,** ☎832-3100. **Poison Center,** ☎941-4411. **Missing Child Center,** ☎753-9797. **Suicide and Crisis Hotline,** ☎800-784-2433.

Fire Department: ☎831-7771.

Red Cross: Hawaii Chapter ☎734-2101.

24hr. Pharmacies: Long's Drugs at 1330 Pali Hwy. (☎536-7302 or 536-5542), on the corner of Pali Hwy. and Vineyard Blvd. Another branch is located at 2220 S. King St. (☎949-4781 or 947-2651), across from Honolulu Stadium State Recreation Area.

Hospital: Queen's Medical Center, 1301 Punchbowl St. (☎538-9011). An **Emergency Services Department** (☎547-4311) provides pre-hospital emergency medical care and ambulance services. Their referral line (☎537-7117) can help visitors find a doctor.

Medical Assistance: Urgent Care Clinic of Hawaii, 2155 Kalakaua Ave., at Beachwalk (☎597-2860). **Straub Clinic and Hospital,** 888 S. King St. (☎522-4000). See **Waikiki Practical Information,** p. 120.

Planned Parenthood Clinic of Hawaii: ☎589-1149.

Internet Access:

etopia, 1363 S. Beretania St. (☎593-2050; www.theetopia.com), on the corner of Beretania St. and Keeaumoku St. Members get a better rate ($2.50 per hr.), and go to the front of the waiting lists that sometimes form for the fast machines. Monthly membership $10. Under 18 not allowed during school hours. Open 24hr. AmEx/MC/V.

Netstop, 2615 S. King St. (☎955-1020; www.netstopcafe.com), at the intersection of S. King St. and University Ave. in Manoa. Intel Pentium computers have fast connections and Japanese, French, German, Chinese, and Korean capabilities. Internet access $0.09 per min. for non-members. Color Inkjet printing $0.70 per page, B&W laser printing $0.20 per page. Large coffee $1.25. Open M-F 8:30am-midnight, Sa-Su 9:30am-midnight.

Teava Momi, 1726 Kapiolani #101B (☎946-8988), across Kapiolani from the Hawaii Convention Center. Cable access $1.50 per 15min. Open M and W-Su 11am-11:30pm.

Post Offices:

Airport branch, 3600 Aolele (☎423-6029). Offers the only general delivery *(poste restante)* services on the island. Open M-F 7:30am-8pm, Sa 8am-4pm. **Postal Code:** 96819.

Ala Moana branch, 1450 Ala Moana Blvd., Ste. 1006 (☎532-1987). Open M-F 8am-4:30pm, Sa 8am-noon for package pick-up. **Postal Code:** 96814.

Downtown Honolulu branch, 335 Merchant St. (☎532-1987), west of Ali'iolani Hale in the civic center. Open M-F 8am-4:30pm. **Postal Code:** 96813.

Kaimuki branch, 1130 Koko Head Ave. (☎737-8937). Open M-F 8am-4:30pm. **Postal Code:** 96816.

Makiki branch, 1111 Lunalilo St. (☎532-5689). Open M-F 8am-4:30pm. Package pick-up 6-8am and 2-5pm. **Postal Code:** 96822.

Manoa branch, 2754 Woodlawn Dr. in the mall behind Safeway. Open M-F 8:15am-3:30pm, Sa 8:30am-noon. **Postal Code:** 96839.

Moilili branch, 2700 S. King St., Ste. B (☎532-5689). Open M-F 8am-4:15pm. **Postal Code:** 96826

PUBLICATIONS

Honolulu Weekly (www.honoluluweekly.com) is a free community paper with incisive articles and reviews, as well as extensive events listings. Pick one up on street corners throughout Honolulu. **This Week Oahu** and **Oahu Gold** are weekly coupon and ad-laden brochure magazines omnipresent in Oahu. A good **map of Waikiki** is in the free tourist publications available on every street.

The weekly **Downtown Planet** (www.downtownplanet.com) lists downtown parking locations and their prices, as well as other local information and events. Hawaii Pacific University puts out a monthly award-winning student newspaper, **Kalamalama.** Pick up either paper anywhere in the Fort St. Mall.

The **Honolulu Advertiser** (www.honoluluadvertiser.com) is Honolulu's most esteemed daily paper, covering national and international news, business, technology, entertainment, sports, and island life, and classifieds. It is available in grocery and convenience stores and street vending boxes. (www.honoluluadvertiser.com.

HONOLULU AND WAIKIKI INFORMATION LINES.

National Weather Service Surf Report: (☎973-4381); Oahu beaches surf report (☎973-4383).

Surf News Network: ☎596-SURF/7873.

US Weather Service Recording (☎973-4380) might as well be a broken record saying, "It's 82-86°F and sunny."

Lifeguard Services: ☎922-3888. Call to find out about safety at a particular beach.

Elderly Information and Assistance Services: ☎523-4545. Open M-F 7:45am-4:30pm.

Pacific Gateway Center (Foreign Language Translation Service): ☎845-3918

HandiVan Reservations: Information ☎454-5050. Reservations ☎456-5955. ☎523-4083. TDD ☎456-5045.

Honolulu Gay and Lesbian Cultural Foundation: ☎941-0424.

Honolulu Job Information: ☎523-5301.

Mayor's Office of Culture and the Arts (MOCA): ☎523-4674.

Neal Blaisdell Center and Waikiki Shell Calendar of Events: ☎527-5400; Blaisdell Box Office ☎521-2211.

Parks and Recreation Department Information: ☎692-5561.

Camping Permits: ☎523-4527. **Fishing and hunting permits:** ☎587-0072.

M-Sa $0.50, Su $1.75.) The **Honolulu Star Bulletin** (www.starbulletin.com) is a competitive daily broadsheet with travel, sports, editorial, business, and features sections. (M-Sa $0.50, Su $0.75.) **TGIF,** in the Friday edition of the Honolulu Advertiser, is Hawaii's prime source for island entertainment listings and editorials. ($0.50.)

ACCOMMODATIONS

The majority of Honolulu's hotels are crammed together in the tourist jungle of **Waikiki** (p. 116), where you'll find the best deals. Accommodations in the city's other neighborhoods cater more toward business people and locals.

ALA MOANA

Ala Moana Hotel, 410 Atkinson Dr. (☎800-367-6025 or 955-4811; www.alamoanahotel.com), 2 blocks from Kapiolani Blvd. on Atkinson Dr. This hotel is in the perfect location, within walking distance of the Ala Moana Shopping Center, TheBus routes, Ala Moana Beach Park, and Waikiki, though at enough distance to duck the throngs. It also tops all but the best of Waikiki's hotels' services with a business center, fitness room, pool (including pool bar), and sundeck, as well as **Aaron's** fine continental dining and **Rumours** nightclub, all on the premises. Check-in 3pm. Check-out noon. Doubles $125-195, Torch Ginger floors 29-35 (which have slightly better views and tub jacuzzis) $215. Call for frequent specials. AmEx/D/MC/V. ❹

Central YMCA, 401 Atkinson Dr. (☎941-3344), across the street from the Ala Moana Hotel. Catering to budget tourists with a fantastic location just outside of Waikiki and 1 block from Ala Moana Beach Park. College dorm-style rooms with single bed, desk, chair, and storage closet. No A/C or fan. Pool and fitness room. $10 key deposit. Limited parking $5 per day. Check-out 10am. Internet access in lobby. Reservations must be made 2 wk. in advance. Must be 18+ and have a valid photo ID. Rooms with shared bath (male only) $30, $159 per week; singles (male or female) $38. AmEx/MC/V. ❷

OAHU

HONOLULU AND WAIKIKI ACCOMMODATIONS BY PRICE

UNDER $25 (❶)		$110-150 (❹)	
Hostelling International Honolulu (98)	M	Ala Moana Hotel (97)	AM
Waikiki Beachside Hostel (122)	W	Pagoda Hotel (99)	G
Polynesian Beach Club Hostel (122)	W	Pacific Marina Inn (99)	G
Seaside Hawaiian Hostel (122)	W	🏨 Aqua Bamboo (123)	W
		The Imperial of Waikiki Hotel (123)	W
$25-65 (❷)		Ilima Hotel (123)	W
Pat Winston's Waikiki Condos (123)	W	Holiday Inn Waikiki (124)	W
Central YMCA (97)	AM	Aqua Marina Hotel (124)	W
Nuuanu YMCA (98)	DC	Aston Aloha Surf Hotel (124)	W
$65-110 (❸)		**$150+ (❺)**	
🏨 Manoa Valley Inn (98)	M	Aston at the Executive Centre Hotel (98)	DC
🏨 Waikiki Grand Hotel (122)	W	Waikiki Beachcomber Hotel (123)	W
Waikiki Gateway HOtel (123)	W	Waikiki Terrace Hotel (124)	W
Waikiki Sand Villa (124)	W	Sheraton Waikiki Beach Resort (125)	W
Leisure Resorts at Honolulu (124)	W	Renaissance Ilikai Waikiki Hotel (125)	W
Aston Coconut Plaza Hotel (124)	W	Outrigger Waikiki Shore Resort (125)	W
Royal Grove Hotel (124)	W		

AM ala moana **DC** downtown/chinatown   **G** greater honolulu **M** manoa **W** waikiki

DOWNTOWN AND CHINATOWN

Aston at the Executive Centre Hotel, 1088 Bishop St. (☎800-949-3932 or 539-3000; www.astonexecutive.com). Convenient to Bishop Sq. banking center, on the corner of Bishop and Hotel streets. From H-1 east take Exit 21A and turn right onto Pali Hwy., which becomes Bishop St. Aston keeps this property gleaming. All rooms come with full amenities, including same-day laundry and dry cleaning for a fee, 24hr. business center, fitness center, sauna, outdoor whirlpool, and sundeck with a 20m lap pool, just to name a few. Breakfast included. Parking $10. Check-in 3pm. Check-out noon. Business suite $190, corporate rate $129. 1-bedroom executive suites with full kitchen $240-270, corporate rate $149-159. Ask about weekend discounts. ❺

Nuuanu YMCA, 1441 Pali Hwy. (☎536-3556; fax 521-1181), on the corner of Vineyard Blvd. and Pali Hwy. Sparse single rooms for men only, although female YMCA members come in to use the athletic facilities, including a lap pool and cardio room. Hall phones with free local calls. No A/C. **Tanaka's Tastebuds Cafe** in-house (*loco moco* $4, plate lunch $5-6). Key deposit $5. 24hr. reception. Check-in 3pm. Check-out noon. Reserve rooms at least 2 wk. ahead. Rooms $30 per night, $160 per week. AmEx/D/MC/V. ❷

MANOA AND THE UNIVERSITY AREA

🏨 **Manoa Valley Inn,** 2001 Vancouver Dr. (☎947-6019; manoavalleyinn@aloha.net). Take Kapiolani Blvd., S. King St., or H-1 to University Ave. *mauka* (toward the mountains) and turn left onto Vancouver Dr. 2 mi. from rainforest hiking and Waikiki, this cozy mansion-turned-inn is a perfectly situated hideaway from hectic Honolulu, boasting classic rooms decorated in authentic Victorian style and a sweeping view of the city and Diamond Head from its breezy veranda. Jacuzzi in the garden. Breakfast included. Check-in 3pm. Check-out 11am. Doubles with shared bath $99, private bath $140. ❸

Hostelling International Honolulu, 2323A Seaview Ave. (☎946-0591; www.hiayh.org). Turn onto Seaview Ave. from University Ave.; the hostel is opposite the University of Hawaii campus just 4 blocks north of H-1. The best-kept hostel in Honolulu is in a mellow residential neighborhood within walking distance of university nightlife and a short bus ride to Waikiki or Ala Moana. Free lockers. $2 linen deposit. Maid service daily. Communal bath, full kitchen, and TV lounge. Reception 8am-noon and 4pm-midnight. 7-day max. stay. Semester-long dorm-style housing for students available; costs vary depending on length of stay but semester lease is usually around $300. Single-sex 6-bed dorms $14 for members, non-members $17. AmEx/MC/V. ❶

GREATER HONOLULU

Pagoda Hotel, 1525 Rycroft St. (☎941-6611; www.pagodahotel.com). From Waikiki, take Kapiolani Blvd. west from McCully St. and turn right onto Kaheka St., the 2nd right after Kalakaua Ave. From Kaheka St. take the 3rd left or Kanunu St. to the 1st parking lot on the right. Pagoda has studios, 1- and 2-bedroom suites, and a pool in a lush garden setting. The Terrace rooms have kitchenettes, and all rooms have A/C, TV, and Internet access ($2 per 10min.). 24hr. reception. Check-in 3pm. Check-out noon. Doubles $110, top floors $120; suites $110-195. ❹

Pacific Marina Inn, 2628 Waiwai Loop (☎836-1131; fax 833-0851; pacific_marina_inn_2000@yahoo.com). Take the frontage road from Nimitz Hwy., outside of the airport, east to Lagoon Dr. Take the 2nd left off Lagoon onto Waiwai Loop, opposite Ualena St. Near the airport, this is the only place worth the price. Walking distance to Keehi Lagoon Beach Park, with a pool, cable TV, and an in-house restaurant. Free transportation to Hickam's MAC terminal and the Honolulu airport. 24hr. reception. Check-in 3pm. Check-out noon. Doubles $90, add an economy car rental for $25. $50 deposit required if paying in cash. Wheelchair-accessible. AmEx/D/MC/V. ❹

🍴 FOOD

ALA MOANA

California Beach Rock 'n Sushi, 404 Ward Ave. (☎597-8000). The place to get high-quality sushi without having to guess your way through a Japanese-only menu. The specialty rolls like Stuntman (spicy tuna and cucumber with seared *ahi* layered outside; $9.25) and Crunchy Roll (shrimp tempura, cucumber, yamagobo, kaiware, and spicy mayo coated with crunchy flakes and smelt roe; $8.95) are especially popular. Early Bird Special 5-6:30pm $11. Lunch specials $5.25-9. Open Su 5-10pm, M-Th 11am-2pm and 5-10pm, F 11am-2pm and 5-11pm, Sa 5-11pm. AmEx/V. ❷

Dixie Grill Bar-B-Que and Crab Shack, 404 Ward Ave. (☎596-8359). An open-air beach party shack on a busy street, Dixie's serves up real Southern BBQ that will dirty your hands, mouth, and chin, but leave you grinnin'. Bust Yo Belly 2 lb. cheeseburger is free if you eat it, plus all the other fixins, in 30min.; otherwise it's $20. Jumbo coconut shrimp appetizer $9. Trash Can buffet (ribs, BBQ chicken, snow crab, catfish, and sides) $39 for 2. Also a wide selection of meals $10 and under (baby back rib basket $10). Open Su-Th 11am-10pm, F-Sa 11am-11pm. AmEx/MC/V. ❸

Kaka'ako Kitchen, 1200 Ala Moana Blvd. (☎596-7488), at the Ward Center. Kaka'ako Kitchen tempts shoppers with a frequently changing, reasonably priced menu and shady outdoor seating. Plate lunches $6-7.25. Gourmet salads ($5.75-9.25) and sandwiches ($6.50-9.25). Open for breakfast M-F 7-10am, Sa-Su 7-11am; lunch and dinner M-Th 10:30am-9pm, F-Sa 10:30am-11pm, Su 11:30am-5pm. DC/MC/V. ❷

DOWNTOWN

The recently renovated **Restaurant Row,** 500 Ala Moana Blvd., between Punchbowl and South St., provides a number of dining venues. The varied casual and formal environments are competitive amid Honolulu's many other options at Aloha Tower Marketplace, Ala Moana Shopping Center, Victoria Ward Centers, and Waikiki. (☎432-4750. From Waikiki head west on Ala Moana Blvd., turn right onto South St., and park in the covered garage.)

OAHU

HONOLULU AND WAIKIKI FOOD BY TYPE

AMERICAN

Dixie Grill BBQ and Crab Shack (99)	AM❸
Kaka'ako Kitchen (99)	AM❷
Big Island Steak House (100)	D❺
Andy's Sandwiches and Smoothies (103)	M❶
Volcano Joe's Island Bistro (103)	M❶
Eddie's Burgers & Frozen Custard (103)	KW❶
Wisteria (104)	G❷
Rainbow Drive-In (126)	W❶
Shore Bird Beach Broiler (127)	W❸
Chuck's Cellar (127)	W❹
Top of Waikiki (127)	W❺
Teddy's Bigger Burgers (128)	W❶
Cheeseburger in Paradise (128)	W❶

ITALIAN

🏠 Palomino (100)	D❹
C & C Pasta Company (103)	KW❺
Verbano (103)	KW❹
🏠 Auntie Pasto's (104)	G❷
Arancino (126)	W❸
Ray's Famous Pizza (127)	W❷

OTHER

🏠 Cha Cha Cha (126)	W❷
🏠 Pyramids (126)	W❸
Marie's Health Foods (127)	W❶
Ruffage Natural Foods (128)	W❶

COFFEE AND/OR DESSERT

Bubbies (103)	M❶
Coffee Cove (103)	M❶
Eddie's Burgers & Frozen Custard (103)	KW❶
Cafe Laufer (103)	KW❷
The Patisserie (127)	W❶

ASIAN

California Beach Rock 'n Sushi (99)	AM❷
Indigo (100)	D❷
Payao Thai Cuisine (101)	D❷
🏠 Legends Seafood Restaurant (101)	C❷
To Chau Restaurant (101)	C❶
Mabuhay Cafe and Restaurant (102)	C❷
A Little Bit of Saigon (102)	C❷
Maharani Cafe (102)	M❸
Kit N' Kitchen (103)	M❸
O-Bok Korean Restaurant (103)	M❷
Ezogiku Noodle Cafe (103)	M❶
Hale Vietnam (104)	KW❷
Happy Day Restaurant (104)	KW❷
Pagoda Floating Restaurant (104)	G❺
Mekong Thai Restaurant (104)	G❷
Wisteria (104)	G❷
Yasoba (126)	W❸
Keo's (126)	W❸
Todai (128)	W❺

GROCERY STORES AND MARKETS

Safeway (102)	M
Down to Earth (102)	M
Kokua Market (102)	M
Star Market (102)	M
Food Pantry (125)	W
Daiei (125)	W
The People's Open Market Program (125)	W

AM ala moana, **D** downtown, **C** chinatown, **M** manoa, **KW** kapahulu/waialae, **G** greater honolulu

🏠 **Palomino,** 66 Queen St. (☎528-2400), on the 3rd fl. in Harbor Court. To park, drive west on Ala Moana Blvd. 1 block past Aloha Tower Marketplace. Turn right onto Bethel St.; parking is on the right. Palomino's beautiful facade is just a taste of the visual feast that lies within. The plush interior, with glass chandeliers and a bar that oozes class, are worth the trip. Affordable thin crust pizzas ($9-13.50), dreamy desserts ($6-7), and specials like lobster paella ($29). First seating (5-6pm) offers a 3-course dinner for under $20. Reservations recommended before 8:30pm. The bar (open M-Th 11:15am-11:30pm, F 11:15am-1am, Sa 5pm-1am, Su 5-11:30pm) serves the full menu during restaurant hours. Open for lunch M-F 11:15am-2:30pm; dinner daily 5-10pm. ❹

Indigo, 1121 Nu'uanu Ave. (☎521-2900), adjacent to the Hawaii Theater Center, amid the fountains and the trees. Starring Eurasian cuisine in a tastefully understated setting, Indigo is a show-stopper. Lunch $7-17. Grilled shrimp and Thai macadamia nut pesto $21. Its Green Room is also a hopping night spot Tu-Sa. Reservations recommended before 8:30pm. Open Tu-Th 6am-9:30pm, F-Sa 6-10pm. D/DC/MC/V. ❹

Big Island Steak House (☎537-4446), in the Aloha Tower Marketplace. Big Island brings a Hawaiian sensibility to the grill. $2 drafts and half-off *pupus* (Polynesian *Pupu* Platter $12) during Happy Hour from 4-7pm. Hearty sandwiches ($7-10.50) and grilled dishes ($9-20) for lunch (served daily until 4pm); Honolulu's best Hawaiian-style baby back ribs ($20) or the baked Mac Nut mahi mahi ($23) for dinner. Call ahead to reserve a table on the balcony and watch the ocean liners as you eat. Open Su-Th 10:30am-10pm, F-Sa 10:30am-1am. AmEx/D/DC/MC. ❺

Payao Thai Cuisine, (☎521-3511), in Restaurant Row, 500 Ala Moana Blvd. Known as the "home of sticky rice," Payao has affordable, varied vegetarian selections with appetizers $2-7.50 and entrees like Payao's Evil Tofu ($7.50). Open for lunch M-F 11am-2pm and for dinner daily 5-9:30pm. AmEx/D/MC/V. ❷

CHINATOWN

While this is *the* place to find the best Chinese restaurants, the true thrill of the Chinatown dining experience is in the markets and shops that sell ethnic specialties. This is not a mall, however. Many shops and markets do not accept credit cards, and be prepared to encounter jarringly fresh-cut meats hung about.

Legends Seafood Restaurant, 100 N. Beretania St. #108 (☎532-1868), in the Chinatown Cultural Plaza. Legends serves true dim sum, the traditional Chinese brunch where items are selected from a train of circling carts. The succulent dishes are meant to be shared family-style and come in small ($2.15), medium ($3), and large ($3.75). Open M-F 10:30am-2pm and 5:30-10pm, Sa-Su 8am-2pm. D/MC/V. ❷

To Chau Restaurant, 1007 River St. (☎533-4549). There's always a line of people out the door, waiting for the unbelievable *pho* noodle soup ($4-5). Open daily 8am-2:30pm. ❶

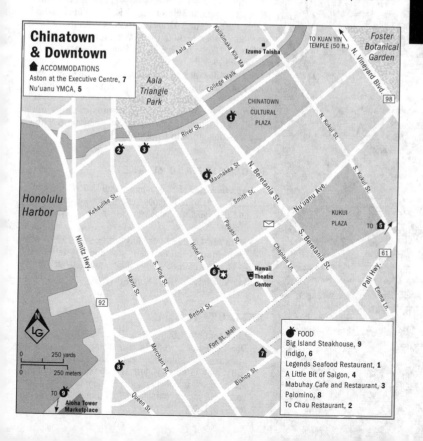

Chinatown & Downtown

ACCOMMODATIONS
Aston at the Executive Centre, **7**
Nu'uanu YMCA, **5**

FOOD
Big Island Steakhouse, **9**
Indigo, **6**
Legends Seafood Restaurant, **1**
A Little Bit of Saigon, **4**
Mabuhay Cafe and Restaurant, **3**
Palomino, **7**
To Chau Restaurant, **2**

OAHU

THE INSIDER'S CITY

CHINATOWN GALLERIES

There is an **official walk** (first Friday of the month 5-9pm), with receptions, refreshments, and entertainment, or you can go solo.

❶ **The ARTS at Mark's Garage,** 1159 Nu'uanu Ave. at Pahani St. (☎521-2903). Offers workshops to the local community as well as exhibitions in theatre, dance, sculpture, and painting. Open Tu-Sa 11am-6pm.

❷ **The Pegge Hopper Gallery,** 1164 Nu'uanu Ave. (☎524-1160). The largest collection of her renowned portraits of Polynesian women. Open Tu-F 11am-4pm, Sa 11am-3pm.

❸ **Ramsay Gallery,** 1128 Smith St. (☎537-2787). Quill and ink drawings and prints, so detailed you need a a magnifying glass. Open M-F 10am-5pm, Sa 10am-4pm.

❹ **The Contemporary Museum at First Hawaiian Center,** 999 Bishop St. (☎526-1322). Part of the Contemporary Museum in Makiki Heights, this museum has rotating exhibits of Hawaii-related art. Open M-Th 8:30am-4pm, F 8:30am-6pm.

Mabuhay Cafe and Restaurant, 1049 River St. (☎545-1956), next to Riverside Travel on the corner of N. Hotel and River St. Top-notch Filipino cuisine in a roomy eatery on the river. Fried pork $8. Shrimp *sari sari* $8. Open daily 10am-10pm. MC/V. ❷

A Little Bit of Saigon, 1160 Maunakea St. (☎528-3663), near the intersection of Maunakea and Puahi St. Serving Vietnamese entrees as *pupus*, with vegetables over *bun* (cold soft rice noodles), or as innovative roll-ups wrapped in rice paper and dipped in creative sauces. Try the *Ga Nuong* Chicken (*pupu* $5.50, roll-ups $8.50, *bun* or rice $6.50). BYOB. Open daily 10am-10pm. ❷

MANOA AND THE UNIVERSITY AREA

To get to **Manoa Marketplace,** take University Ave. north from H-1 past UH. Bear right to merge with Oahu Ave. and take a quick right turn onto E. Manoa Rd. The Manoa Marketplace parking lot is after Huapala St., the fourth street on the right. By bus, take Woodlawn Dr. #6 from Ala Moana Shopping Center. Nearby is a giant **Safeway,** 2855 E. Manoa Rd. (☎988-2058. Open 24hr.) Most establishments don't take credit cards, so head to the **ATM** in Safeway or at **Bank of Hawaii.** (Open M-Th 8:30am-4pm, F 8:30am-6pm, Sa 9am-1pm.)

Puck's Alley, at the intersection of University Ave. and King St., around the corner from the Moiliili post office, is a strip mall that perfects the collegiate triumvirate of cheap beer, cheap music, and cheap food, all with an appropriately ascetic hipness. The A Express bus stops in front of Puck's, or take TheBus #1, 4, 6, or 18.

GROCERIES AND MARKETS

Down to Earth, 2525 S. King St. (☎947-7678), is a full-service health food grocery store with wellness center and deli (vegan chocolate cream pie $3). Open daily 7:30am-10pm. AmEx/D/MC/V.

Kokua Market, 2643 S. King St. (☎941-1922), has natural foods and excellent bulk and vegetable sections. Open daily 8:30am-8:30pm. AmEx/D/MC/V.

Star Market, 2470 S. King St. (☎564-7666). Open daily 5am-2am. D/MC/V.

RESTAURANTS

Maharani Cafe, 2509 S. King St. (☎951-7447), next to Down to Earth grocery. Tasty, authentic Indian cuisine in a casual cafe atmosphere. The Shahi Chicken Korma ($8), marinated in yogurt and cooked in a creamy spice sauce, is delicious. Veg. options, including the vegetable *jalfrezi masala* ($8). Open daily 5-10pm. AmEx/D/MC/V. ❸

Andy's Sandwiches and Smoothies, 2904 E. Manoa Rd. (☎988-6161), across the street from Manoa Marketplace. This walk-up deli cooks healthy food, a rarity in Honolulu. Known for big sandwiches served on fresh homemade bread (fresh-roasted turkey sandwich $3.50) and plenty of vegetarian options (mushroom medley $3.75). Open M-Th 7am-6pm, F 7am-4pm, Su 7am-2:30pm. AmEx/MC/V. ❶

Volcano Joe's Island Bistro, 1810 University Ave. (☎941-8449), across the street from the UH campus. This new restaurant serves up an affordable, informal gourmet menu to the university crowd. Get your greens on with one of their salads ($5.25-7) or try their 9 in. pizza with 3 toppings of your choice included ($6). Many vegetarian options can be made vegan upon request. Coffee house and bakery next door. Open Su-Th 11am-9pm, F-Sa 11am-10pm. ❶

Kit N' Kitchen, 1010 University Ave. (☎942-7622), next to Varsity Theater. Brightly lit and clean, this modish East-meets-West fusion diner has a huge menu with diverse selections; try *sake*-drowned prawns ($9) or Crazy Red Seafood (spicy red sauce with shrimp, squid, scallops, and mussels served over pasta; $10). Open M-F 11am-2:30pm and 5-10pm, Sa-Su 11am-10pm. MC/V. ❸

O-Bok Korean Restaurant (☎988-7702), in the Manoa Marketplace. A tranquil, simple setting in which to enjoy O-Bok's Kalbi BBQ beef short ribs, champions of the Korean BBQ world, served in heaping portions with rice, *kimchi*, dried cuttlefish, and other Korean vegetable dishes ($8). Open Tu-Su 10am-8pm. MC/V. ❷

Ezogiku Noodle Cafe, 1010 University Ave. (☎942-3608), next to Varsity Theater. Ezogiku has been serving enormous portions of traditional Japanese ramen since 1968, prepared with a *miso* ($5.50), *shoyu* ($5.25), or *shio* ($5.50) base. ❶

Bubbies, 1010 University Ave. (☎949-8984), across from Varsity Theater. Heavenly homemade ice cream (1 scoop $2.50-3) and creative desserts. Try a nibble-sized Bite Me ($1 each or 12 for $9) or the Come Here Little Girl ice cream cake (thin mints and Bailey's Irish Cream ice cream with fudge and an oreo-raspberry crust; $4.25). Air conditioned and full of college students on weekends during the school year. Open M-Th noon-midnight, F-Sa noon-1am, Su noon-11:30pm. ❶

Coffee Cove, 2600 S. King St. #101 (☎955-2683), in Puck's Alley. A UH haven of wholesome food and Internet access. Huge made-to-order sandwiches ($4.25-6) and weekly plate lunch specials. Internet access $1 per 15min., printing $0.20 per page. Open M-Th 7:30am-11pm, F 7:30am-10pm, Sa 10am-11pm, Su 10am-11pm. ❶

KAPAHULU/WAIALAE

C & C Pasta Company, 3605 Waialae Ave. (☎732-5999). Filled with things that make you go mmmm, C & C Pasta Company serves rustic Italian fare. Warm up with the escargot appetizer ($8.50) or splurge on Chef's signature dish, tagliatelle with roasted duck ($19), and indulge in desserts like the tiramisu ($7.50). BYOB ($3.50 corkage fee). Open Tu-Th 11am-9pm, F-Sa 11am-10pm, Su 5-9pm. MC/V. ❺

Eddie's Burgers and Frozen Custard, 3607 Waialae Ave. (☎739-0033). This 50s-style burger joint makes its name with budget-friendly burgers ($4.25 and up). The velvety ice cream is technically called frozen custard because of its egg content, but you'll just call it heaven (small $3.25). Try the 🌊Tsunami Shake ($4.25), king of all disaster-dubbed ice cream treats. Open M-Th and Su 10:30am-9pm, F-Sa 10:30am-10pm. ❶

Verbano, 3571 Waialae Ave. (☎735-1777). One of a few reasonably priced Italian restaurants in Honolulu. Most entrees come in small or large sizes. The Ossobucco Cremolata has met acclaim ($17), and the seafood pasta dishes are budget-friendly ($11-16). Veggie pasta $8-13. Open M-F 11am-2:30pm and 5-10pm, Sa-Su 5-10pm. ❹

Cafe Laufer, 3565 Waialae Ave. (☎735-7717), is a fine pastry and coffee shop. The menu includes Brie cheese on a French baguette with fruit ($7.50). The chicken salad ($5.50-7.25) will win you over, but the pastries ($0.65-4) are what conquer. Cappucino $2.75. Open M, W-Th, Su 10am-10pm, F-Sa 10am-11pm. AmEx/D/MC/V. ❷

OAHU

Hale Vietnam, 1140 12th Ave. (☎735-7581), less than a block from Waialae Ave. Adding a delightful Vietnamese color to the Kaimuki culinary jigsaw, Hale Vietnam serves up the famous beef noodle soup, *pho* ($6-6.50), as well as entrees like tofu with eggplant ($9.50) and other vegetarian selections. Open daily 11am-10pm. D/MC/V. ❷

Happy Day Restaurant, 3553 Waialae Ave. (☎738-8666). This bright and spacious restaurant serves an incredible variety of Chinese dishes, from Chinese/American staples (lemon chicken $7) to the exotic (and expensive) delicacies (shark fin soup $33, bird nest soup $17). For big groups, Happy Day offers a dinner special for 10 for $179, including 3 lobsters. Seabass filet with snowpeas $8. Lunch special 11am-2pm $6. Open daily 8:30am-10:30pm. ❷

GREATER HONOLULU

🌊 **Auntie Pasto's,** 1099 S. Beretania St. (☎523-8855), on the corner of Beretania and Pensacola St. Auntie's has affordable pasta dishes ($7-9) big enough to fill a hungry *braddah* (brother) and authentic enough to satisfy any Italian. Reformed carnivores love the eggplant parmesan ($9). Its sister restaurant at 559 Kapahulu Ave. is equally good, and transforms nightly into one of Honolulu's hottest nightlife venues. Open M-Th 10:30am-10:30pm, F 10:30am-11pm, Sa 4-11pm, Su 4-10:30pm. MC/V. ❷

Pagoda Floating Restaurant, 1525 Rycroft St. (☎941-6611). On the grounds of the Pagoda Hotel, the restaurant's dining area is an archipelago of partially paned-in pagodas radiating out from a central island, all "floating" on a canal pond bridged by bamboo-railed walkways. Themed lunch buffets include Seafood M (11am-2pm; $13, children ages 5-10 $7), *Ohana* Sa (11am-2pm; $16, children $8), and the celebrated Su Brunch Buffet (10am-2pm; $18, children $9). Nightly dinner buffets 4:30-9:30pm ($21-23, children $10-11). Salad bar and dessert table included with all buffets. Reservations strongly recommended. Open daily 6:30am-2pm and 4:30-9:30pm. ❺

Mekong Thai Restaurant, 1295 S. Beretania St. (☎591-8841). Eastern-influenced menu includes many vegetarian specials ($5-8), noodles ($7.50-10), and soups ($7-11). Open M-F 11am-2pm and 5:30-9:30pm, Sa-Su 5:30-9:30pm. AmEx/D/MC/V. ❷

Wisteria, 1206 S. King St. (591-9276), at the corner of King and Piikoi St. This diner-style restaurant offers a Japanese and American menu in a no-frills, waitress named (insert-Hawaiian-equivalent-of-"Flo") setting. Sandwiches $3-8. Sushi $4-9. Open M-Th 6am-2pm and 4:30-10:30pm, F 6am-2pm and 4:30-11:15pm, Sa 6am-11:15pm, Su 6am-10:30pm. MC/V. ❷

🌊 BEACHES

The most popular sandy beaches in Honolulu are located near Waikiki (p. 128).

ALA MOANA BEACH PARK Ala Moana means "path to the sea," and the palm tree-dotted park does the name justice. The circuits, popular among joggers and roller bladers, connect to the calm bay which is perfect for an easy swim. Jutting out slightly into Mamala Bay, **Magic Island** is actually a peninsula, connected to Ala Moana Park Dr. by a large parking lot. Magic Island may be the best spot in the city to watch the sun dissolve into the sea and sky, throwing awe-inspiring color and beams of light visible through the hulking clouds that frequently roll over the Koolau Mountains. *(Park located in front of Ala Moana Shopping Center, on Ala Moana Park Dr. Access driveways are at the western end of the park just past Kamakee St., opposite Ward Entertainment Center. Alternately, take TheBus #8, 19, 20, 42, or 58 to the Ala Moana Center.)*

👁 SIGHTS

DOWNTOWN

🌊 **HONOLULU ACADEMY OF ARTS.** Comprised of over 30 galleries, this museum displays a wide variety of artwork, including works by international and local artists. The viewing experience is enhanced by the tranquil environment of the museum, which is dotted with outdoor courtyards, gardens, and fountains. The James A. Michener Collection of Japanese *Ukiyo-e* wood block prints features rotating exhibits, and the Kress Collection of Italian Renaissance paintings is equally impressive. Pieces by Picasso, Monet, Matisse, Van Gogh, Gaugin, and Cezanne are occasionally on display. The **modern theater** within the Academy's confines screens experimental, contemporary, and revival films. There's enough here to keep you all day; refuel at the **Pavilion Cafe ❷** (feta tapenade and *hau'ula* tomato sandwich $9) on the patio. *(900 S. Beretania St., in front of Thomas Sq. From Waikiki, take TheBus #2 toward town on Beretania. If driving or going to the theater, enter on Kinau St. ☎ 532-8700. www.honoluluacademy.org. Disabled visitors should call ahead to arrange access. Theater $5. Cafe open Tu-Sa 11:30am-2pm. Gallery open Tu-Sa 10am-4:30pm, Su 1-5pm. $7; seniors, students, and military $4; children under 12 and members free. AmEx/MC/V.)*

THE HAWAII MARITIME CENTER. Despite its small size, the Maritime Center has lots to offer, including one of only two humpback whale skeletons in the world. The 50min. audio tour of the museum chronicles Hawaii's maritime history, from the outrigger ships of ancient Polynesian explorers to the ocean sports of today. Admission includes passage aboard the *Falls of Clyde*, the last four-masted, fully-rigged ship in the world. *(On Pier 7 at Honolulu Harbor, across from Aloha Tower Marketplace, off Nimitz Hwy. ☎ 523-6151. Open daily 9am-5pm. $7.50, ages 6-17 $4.50, under 6 free.)*

CIVIC CENTER

The open, grassy areas surrounding the Civic Center's government buildings and historical sights are peaceful and sedate in comparison to Downtown's skyscraper-filled business district to the east. Parking can be tight, although there are metered spots in front of the Downtown post office at Richards and Merchant St., and also along King and other sidestreets. Avoid the hassle of parking and navigating street layout by taking TheBus #2, 13, or CityExpress B to S. Beretania and Punchbowl St., at the corner of the State Capitol's grounds.

⬛ SAINT ANDREW'S CATHEDRAL. This French Gothic cathedral is directly behind a 10 ft. bronze statue of St. Andrew. The rendering of the fisherman and missionary apostle stands in a fountain, surrounded by 10 bronze, water-spouting fish. The cathedral itself is awe-inspiring, with its bells rung the old-fashioned way, and the brilliant, stained glass Great West Window. The window is magnificent—it spans the entire western end of the church. Organ virtuoso Arlan Sunnarborg plays the enormous Aeolian-Skinner organ every Sunday after the 8 and 10am services, or you can come in early for the 7am Quick and Quiet Service. *(On the corner of Beretania and Alakea St., past the State Capitol in Queen Emma Sq. ☎ 524-2822. Mass M-F 7am, Su 7, 8, 10am. Historical tours are available after the Su 10am service. Call ahead to reserve. Open M-F 9am-5pm.)*

⬛ HAWAII STATE ART MUSEUM. In November 2002, the Hawaii State Art Museum opened its doors to great acclaim as the jewel of the Art in Public Places program, which began in 1967. The exhibit, Enriched by Diversity: The Art of Hawaii, houses 360 pieces by 284 Hawaiian artists, most of which date from the 1960s to the present, and has been hailed as one of the most sophisticated and powerful expressions of contemporary Hawaiian identity. Much of the work combines Western art forms with traditional Hawaiian and Pacific forms of expression. The unique focus of the museum and its beautiful setting in the old YMCA building make the museum a must-see for all those interested in Hawaiian culture, traditions, and art. *(No. 1 Capitol District Building, 250 South Hotel St., 2nd fl., west of the State Capitol building. Tours Tu-Sa 11am, 2pm. Open Tu-Sa 10am-4pm. Free.)*

HAWAII STATE CAPITOL. This unique building replaced Iolani Palace as Hawaii's capitol building in 1969, and is now the place of business for the state's governor, lieutenant governor, and legislators. The capitol's unusual architecture is meant to reflect Hawaiian geography—its conical legislative chambers mimic volcanoes, the surrounding concrete pillars are palms, and the pond encircling the structure symbolizes the ocean. Its open-air design is meant to encourage the winds that flow from mountain to sea, and the center lies open to sun, sky, and stars. *(On the corner of S. Beretania and Punchbowl St. ☎586-0178. www.hawaii.gov/sfca. 1½hr. tours M, W, F 1pm. Reserve ahead.)* Across Beretania St., stately **Washington Place** was the home of Hawaii's last reigning monarch, Queen Liliuokalani, and for many years after was the home of Hawaii's governors. Current governor Linda Lingle is the first governor not to live there, and officials are currently in the process of turning the home into a museum.

■ **IOLANI PALACE.** Hawaii's latter monarchs resided in the Florentine-style Iolani Palace, situated on lovely, coral-fenced grounds. Though you won't hear much about it on the tour, Iolani Palace is an important symbol for some Hawaiian sovereigntists who to this day decry the overthrow of Hawaii by Americans. The palace was originally built in 1883 as a show of the strength and independence of the Hawaiian Kingdom. It was the official residence of King Kalakaua and Queen Liliuokalani until American businessmen led a coup d'etat and abolished the monarchy in 1893. It was here that Liliuokalani was tried, convicted, and imprisoned for treason, after a failed loyalist retaliation in 1895 (see **History**, p. 11). After falling into disrepair while serving as the capitol of the subsequent Republic, Territorial, and State governments, the palace has been restored and maintained by the Friends of Iolani Palace and it gleams as it did in the monarchy's earlier days. The palace is of international interest too, with portraits of French, German, Russian, and British leaders, not to mention the Hawaiian monarchs. See one of Hawaii's first telephones, which ran a line to Honolulu Harbor, where King Kalakaua often held court on his party boat. Still on the grounds is the ancient burial site, Pohukaina, which holds the sacred remains of *ali'i* (royalty). The **Royal Hawaiian Band** plays a free concert in the Coronation Stand Fridays at noon.

The white-pillared building to the right of the palace is the **Hawaii State Library,** holding the private book collections of several of the latter monarchs. To the right of the library, further east down King St., is the old Spanish-style city hall, **Honolulu Hale.** *(364 King St. ☎538-1471; call ☎522-0832 for tour reservations. Purchase admission to the palace interior at the ticket office inside the Iolani Barracks, the white structure on the Richards St. side of the grounds. Open Tu-Sa 9am-2:15pm. 1hr. grand tour $20, military $15 (no children under 5). Self-guided gallery tour $10, children 5-17 $5, under 5 free. Gallery open 9am-4pm, last ticket sold at 3:30pm. No cell phones, photos, video cameras, or food. MC/V.)*

ALI'IOLANI HALE. Constructed in 1874, Ali'iolani Hale once housed both the legislature and the Supreme Court of the Hawaiian kingdom, and is the current seat of Hawaii's Supreme Court. Its name, Ali'iolani ("chief unto Heavens"), pays homage to King Kamehameha V, who initiated the planning and construction of this symbol of the stability and prosperity of an independent Hawaiian nation. **The Judiciary History Center** within chronicles 200 yr. of Hawaiian legal history, with a special focus on the *kapu* (forbidden) system and the evolution of the complex Hawaiian land laws. You can't miss the complex; it is fronted by one of Hawaii's most recognizable and beautiful landmarks, the golden-caped ■**King Kamehameha Statue.** Legend holds that Pai'ea Kamehameha (Kamehameha the Great; see **History,** p. 11) was born under Halley's Comet in 1758, a clear sign to the *kahunas* (priests) of his greatness. He went on to establish the Hawaiian kingdom from his home island of Hawaii, bringing Maui, Oahu, and Kauai under his sway by 1810. The original statue, cast in Paris at the commission of King Kalakaua, was lost in a shipwreck near the Falkland Islands on the way to Honolulu; a second one was cast, shipped, and installed at its present site in 1883. *(417 King St. ☎539-4994. Judiciary History Center open for self-guided tours M-F 9am-4pm. Guided tours available by reservation only. Free. Wheelchair access on the Punchbowl St. metered parking lot entrance.)*

KAWAIAHAO CHURCH. Possibly the most impressive feature of this, the first Christian church in Hawaii, is the effort undergone to construct it. Hawaiians dove 10-20 ft. to chisel out the 1000 lb. slabs of coral, 14,000 of which were hauled here and used as bricks for the foundation of the New England-style structure that was dedicated on July 21, 1842. The church gained its name from the legendary sacred spring called Kawaiahao ("the water of Ha'o"), where Chieftess Ha'o bathed. The church is also home to 21 portraits of various *ali'i* (royalty) and the tomb of King Lunalilo, the first democratically elected Hawaiian monarch. *(957 Punchbowl St. ☎ 522-1333. Open M-F 8am-4pm. Services Su 8, 10:30am, W 6pm; all welcome.)*

MISSION HOUSES AND MUSEUM. This collection of 19th-century buildings once formed the 1820-1863 headquarters of the Sandwich Island Mission. Recreated inside the climate-inappropriate Boston-style houses is the missionaries' printing press, birthplace of the written Hawaiian language. Admission may be purchased from the **Mission Houses Museum,** which leads tours of the mission as well as a Historic Downtown Walking Tour. *(553 S. King St., beyond the old stone church. ☎ 531-0481. 45min. tours of the mission Tu-Sa 10, 11:15am, 1, 2:45pm. Open Tu-Sa 9am-4pm. $10, seniors and military $8, students (all ages) $6, children under 5 free. Historic Downtown Walking Tour an additional $10; call for reservations. Free to all on selected Kama'aina Days. MC/V. Wheelchair-accessible ground floor only.)*

CHINATOWN

KUAN YIN TEMPLE. The beautiful, single-room temple is dedicated to Avalokitesvara, which is Sanskrit for Kuan Yin Boddhisattva. It is the personification of compassion, which is surrounded by a crowd of Buddhas. *(170 N. Vineyard Blvd., next to the Foster Botanical Gardens. Drive west on Vineyard from H-1 West to Exit 22 and turn right before Aala St. Free, donations recommended. Open 8:30am-2pm.)*

■ **FOSTER BOTANICAL GARDENS.** These amazing gardens are home to 26 of Oahu's "exceptional trees," so designated for their outstanding rarity, age, size, aesthetic quality, location, endemic status, or historical and cultural significance. Meeting nearly all of these criteria is the garden's great *Bo* tree, which Hindus consider sacred as the abode of Bhavani, and Buddhists honor as the tree under which Buddha attained enlightenment. This tree is an offshoot of the famous Sri Lanka *Bo*, planted there in 288 BC as an offshoot of Buddha's tree. Other worthwhile attractions include the beautiful bronze Dhaibatsu statue and the Mesozoic-era plants in the Prehistoric Glen. *(50 N. Vineyard Blvd. Take H-1 West or Ward Ave. north from Ala Moana Blvd. to Vineyard Blvd. Turn right into the parking lot after the Kuan Yin Temple, the last drive on the right before the river and Aala St. You can also take TheBus #4 from University to Nu'uanu Ave. and Vineyard Blvd. and walk up the block past Zippy's, towards the river. The entrance and visitor parking are on the right past the temple. ☎ 522-7066. Free guided tours M-F 1pm or by phone request. $5, ages 6-12 $1, under 5 free. Open daily 9am-4pm. MC/V.)*

IZUMO TAISHA. A distinctive peaked roof and pillared entrance mark Izumo Taisha, a Japanese Shinto Shrine. Erected in 1923 and held by the local government during WWII, the shrine is an important remnant of pre-WWII Japanese culture. Today it is the site of regular observances, usually on the 10th of the month at 7pm, for the members of the Izumo Taishakyo Mission next door. Monetary or other offerings are kindly accepted. Please respect the elaborate instructions for making a prayer and offering as posted at the shrine, and consult the minister or mission next door for instructions on proper shrine etiquette. In front of the shrine is **The Bell of Peace,** given to Honolulu by the city of Hiroshima in 1985 to celebrate 25 yr. of sister city affiliation. *(215 Kukui St. Mission ☎ 538-7778. Open daily 9am-4pm.)*

OAHU

MANOA AND THE UNIVERSITY AREA

THE CONTEMPORARY MUSEUM. Set at the base of Makiki Heights, the museum overlooks Honolulu, and terraced sculpture gardens cover much of its 3½ acres. Exhibitions address contemporary (1940-present) visual, performance, and media art, with a portion of the museum focusing on Hawaii. The Contemporary Cafe is a popular spot to grab a scenic lunch. *(2411 Makiki Heights Dr. Take Punahou St. past the YWCA at Vineyard toward Manoa Valley. Turn left on Nehoa St. and right on Mott Smith Dr. Drive until you see the signs for the museum's driveway. Or take TheBus #15 to Makiki Heights Dr. Cafe open Tu-Sa 11:30am-2:30pm, Su noon-2:30pm. Reservations recommended. Museum open Tu-Sa 10am-4pm, Su noon-4pm. $5, seniors and students $3, under 12 free. AmEx/D/MC/V.)*

UNIVERSITY OF HAWAII (UH) AT MANOA LIBRARIES. University of Hawaii at Manoa is a quiet, suburban campus attended by both locals and mainlanders. **Hamilton** and **Sinclair Libraries,** the main libraries for UH's flagship campus at Manoa and its 17,000 students, hold an impressive 3.1 million volumes in their collection. The libraries are open to anyone who wishes to use them, although certain resources are restricted to University students, faculty, and staff. Children under 13 must be accompanied by an adult. Visitors may use the Internet at the libraries for up to 1 hr. for free. *(2550 McCarthy Mall. Alternatively, take the #4 from Kuhio Ave. to UH Manoa. Hamilton ☎ 956-7205. Sinclair ☎ 956-8308. Both libraries open M-Th 8am-6pm, F 8am-5pm, Su noon-6pm; limited hours in summer. Children under 13 must be accompanied by an adult. Visitors may use the Internet at the libraries for up to 1 hr. for free. Parking entrance at the Dole St. and East-West Rd. entrance, accessible via University Ave.)*

LYON ARBORETUM. The University of Hawaii's impressive 194-acre refuge in the Koolau Mountains holds many tropical plant species, some of which are extinct in their native habitats. Formerly Manoa Arboretum, the botanical sanctuary begin in 1918 as a forest restoration project. Founder Harold L. Lyon rejuvenated the land—stripped bare by free-ranging cattle—with over 2000 tree species. The arboretum was renamed in 1957, when Lyon passed away. Today, in addition to being a beautiful spot to visit, the facility is highly regarded within the fields of horticulture, conservation biology, and ethnobotany. The park is open for visitors to explore on one of the featured self-guided tours or on one of the twice-weekly guided tours. *(3860 Manoa Rd. Leaving Waikiki on McCully St., take the 1st right after the Ala Wai Canal onto Kapiolani Blvd. From Kapiolani Blvd., turn right onto Kalakaua Ave., then right on King St. Take the 1st left onto Puou St. After Punahou St., Puou becomes Manoa Rd. Go left at the fork in the road, just after Kamehameha Ave. Or take TheBus #5 to the last stop, and walk the remaining ½ mi. up Manoa Rd. ☎ 988-0456. All visitors must sign in at the Visitor Center next to the parking lot. Open M-Sa 9am-3pm. Guided tours Tu 10am, Sa 1pm. Call a day ahead to reserve. Free. Suggested donation for all visitors to the park $5.)*

GREATER HONOLULU

PUNCHBOWL NATIONAL MEMORIAL CEMETERY. The cemetery lies within the Punchbowl crater north of town, which has one of the best views of Honolulu. From outside, the crater appears like a mountain in miniature; within, stairs pass through a grassy mall down to the monument where more than 5 million visitors pay their respects each year. The cemetery is the final resting place of over 33,000 veterans, from the Spanish-American War to the present. The memorial building has mosaics of WWII battle scenes. It is a 15min. stroll down to the cemetery and the memorial; the best view is from the path to the left of the memorial building. *(2177 Puowaina Dr. From Kuhio Ave., take the #2, 13, or B CityExpress away from Diamond Head to Beretania and Alapai streets, in front of the Honolulu Police Headquarters. Walk mauka (toward the mountain) 1 block to the bus stop on Alapai St. and transfer to the #15 Pacific Heights, which continues to the cemetery entrance. ☎ 532-3720. Open daily 8am-6:30pm. Free.)*

■ BISHOP MUSEUM. Designated the Hawaii State Museum on National and Cultural History in 1988, the Bishop Museum is the best place for tourists and scholars alike to learn about indigenous Hawaiian history and practices. The pricey admission is justified by the spectacular collection of nearly 25 million works of art and artifacts, including historical publications, photographs, films, audio recordings, manuscripts, and millions of species of plant and animal life, many of which are extinct. The Bishop Museum has the world's best collection of many ancient Hawaiian artifacts. Even more entertaining and just as educational is the program of guided tours, hula performances, planetarium shows, and garden tours every 30min. from 10am to 3:30pm. *(1525 Bernice St. From Kuhio Ave., heading away from Diamond Head, take the #2 School St./Middle St. bus to School St. and Kapalama Ave. Walk makai (toward the ocean) on Kapalama Ave. to Bernice St. ☎847-3511; fax 842-4703. $15, seniors and children ages 4-12 $12. Free with $30 membership.)*

HAWAII NATURE CENTER. The Hawaii Nature Center leads weekly programs for families and adults, and knowledgeable guides can answer your every question during the guided hikes. Visitors can also drop by and get advice and a free trail map or printed trail guide ($2) with flora information and location. The center is the trailhead of the popular Makiki Valley Loop trail. *(2131 Makiki Heights Dr. Drive away from Ala Moana Shopping Center on Keeaumoku St. at Kapiolani Blvd. Continue beyond H-1 until Nehoa St., then turn right. Take the 1st left onto Makiki St. and bear left at the fork in the road onto Makiki Heights Dr. At the 1st hairpin turn, where there is a row of 5 mailboxes, continue straight ahead onto the narrow 1-lane road. Park anywhere on the side of the paved street. Alternatively take TheBus #15 to Makiki Heights Dr. Continue along Makiki Heights Dr. Turn left up the 1-lane road at the 5 mailboxes and walk through a green gate, continuing approximately ¼ mi. The center is on the right. ☎955-0100. Open daily 8am-4:30pm. Free.)*

THE MADGE TENNENT FOUNDATION GALLERY. This charming gallery, one of Hawaii's registered historic sites, is dedicated to the artist Madge Tennent. Born in England and considered a child prodigy, Tennent moved to Hawaii in 1923, where she lived until her death in 1972. The large oils show the influence of Gauguin, and they glorify Hawaiian women as the embodiment of nature. Tennent is considered one of Hawaii's greatest artists, and some of her pieces are on permanent loan to the National Museum of Women in Washington, D.C. *(202 Prospect St. Take Ward Ave. away from Ala Moana Blvd. to the base of Punchbowl Crater and turn left onto Prospect St. Bear right at the intersection, hugging the crater on the left between Huali St. and Madeira St. ☎531-1987. Open Tu-Sa 10am-noon, Su 2-4pm, or by appointment. Donations accepted.)*

⬛ ARTS AND ENTERTAINMENT

THEATER, MUSIC AND DANCE

THE KENNEDY THEATRE. University of Hawaii at Manoa's theater opened in December 1963 and has the dual distinction of being beautifully designed by architectural phenom I.M. Pei (the man behind the John F. Kennedy Library in Massachusetts and the Meyerson Symphony Center in Dallas) and of being the first building named after the late president. The theater is acclaimed for its multicultural approach to the study of theater and dance. Here, Eastern and Western influences are synthesized in both venue and performance. The versatile facility hosts a number of productions each year, many of which are through UH's Department of Theatre and Dance. *(1770 East-West Rd. ☎956-7677; fax 956-4234. Take H-1 to University Ave. From University Ave. turn right onto Dole St. and follow it to the corner of East-West Rd. Or take the #6 Woodlawn Drive bus from Ala Moana shopping center. See www.hawaii.edu/theatre for calendar of events. Box office ☎956-7655; open M-F 10am-3pm, closed in summer. Visit www.ticketplushawaii.com for online ticket purchases.)*

HAWAII THEATRE CENTER. The Hawaii Theatre Center is in the homestretch of a fund-raising drive to give the dilapidated marquee a face-lift. It is the spearhead of the Honolulu Culture and Arts District, which sponsors a weekly gallery open house (Sa 11am-4pm). It also has an award-winning, volunteer-run gift shop selling theater merchandise. (1130 Bethel St. ☎ 528-0506. www.hawaiitheatre.com. 1hr. guided tours on the theater's history, art, and architecture Tu 11am, show schedule permitting. Tours $5, reservations recommended. $2 service charge on all tickets. Open Tu-Sa 9am-5pm and 2hr. prior to performances. AmEx/D/MC/V.)

HONOLULU SYMPHONY. Founded in 1900, the symphony is the oldest orchestra west of the Rocky Mountains. Performances are held at the Neil S. Blaisdell Hall. (777 Ward Ave., in Ala Moana. ☎ 792-2000; www.honolulusymphony.com. Box office open M-F 9am-5pm. Performances every other wk. Sept.-May $18-60. AmEx/MC/V.)

IONA PEAR DANCE THEATER. The toast of Honolulu's artistic community, Iona Pear Dance Theater presents captivating Japanese *Butoh* dance with dazzling costumes and inspiring performances. The company tours statewide twice annually; if you can make a performance, it's worth seeing. (P.O. Box 61633, Honolulu, 96839.)

FILM

MOVIE MUSEUM. The "museum" screens classic, modern, and foreign films as they should be seen—on the big screen, from the comfort of one of the intimate theater's 19 leather recliners. You can bring your own concessions; alcohol condoned but not encouraged. (3566 Harding Ave. In Kaimuki, 1 block from Waialae's restaurants on 12th Ave. Take the Our Neighborhood Trolley or TheBus #1 or 3. Showtimes vary depending on film length, but generally conform to M and Tu-Su 3, 5:30, 8pm. $5; members, seniors, and children under 13 $4. Reservations recommended. MC/V.)

VARSITY THEATER. The arthouse theater shows independent, foreign, and second run movies. (1106 University Ave., across from Puck's Alley in Manoa. ☎ 593-3000 or 973-5835. $8, seniors and children ages 2-12 $5.50. Matinee screenings before 4pm $6.)

THE ARTHOUSE AT RESTAURANT ROW. The theater shows Wallace Theaters' independent foreign and previously released films. (500 Ala Moana Blvd., in Restaurant Row downtown. ☎ 545-8635; www.hollywood.com. $7.75, matinee before 6pm $5.25, seniors and ages 3-11 $4.75.)

CONSOLIDATED THEATERS. Consolidated screens mainstream first-run movies in the highest-quality film venue in town, **Ward Stadium 16 Theaters,** in the Ward Entertainment Center (p. 111). All of the comforts you've come to expect from goliath multiplexes, including the hair-raising prices. Get discounts at many of the Victoria Ward Center establishments with a movie ticket stub. (1044 Auahi St. ☎ 593-300; www.victoriaward.com. F-Sa and holidays $9, Su-Th $8; military, seniors, and children $5.75. Before 4pm $6.50. MC/V.)

🔲 SHOPPING

PEOPLE'S OPEN MARKETS. The markets provide the chance to buy inexpensive produce from local farmers and fishermen, who offer local products not found in retail stores. The POM holds markets in Queen Kapiolani Park (in Waikiki, see p. 110, W 10-11am), Makiki District Park (1527 Keeaumoku Ave., next to the Makiki Public Library 1 block north of H-1, take TheBus #17, 18, or 83; M 8:30-9:30am), City Hall Parking Lot Deck at Alapai and Beretania St. (M 11:45am-12:30pm), Manoa Valley District Park (2721 Kaaipu Ave., 2blocks down Lowrey Ave. from the 5-way intersection of Manoa Rd. and Oahu Ave.; M 6:45-7:45am), and McCully District Park (831 Pumehana St., turn left on Citron, the 5th street after crossing the Ala Wai Canal on McCully St.; W 8:15-9:15am). The program is overseen by the City and County of Honolulu. (☎ 527-5167; www.co.honolulu.hi.us/parks/programs/pom/sked.htm.)

ALA MOANA SHOPPING CENTER. A 50-acre temple to commerce, Ala Moana is the US's largest open-air shopping center. Over 200 of the most famous purveyors on the globe intersect with over 56 million of the world's most sophisticated shoppers here each year. Many of the glitziest names in fashion make the roll call with their national or international flagship stores, including Banana Republic, Burberry, Diesel, Emporio Armani, Gianni Versace, Guess, Polo/Ralph Lauren, Ann Taylor, Chanel, Chistian Dior, Laura Ashley, and more.

Honolulu Satellite City Hall, on the first level, provides city job information, picnic and camping permits, TheBus pass sales, and more info. (Open M-F 9am-5pm, Sa 8am-4pm.) There's also a small post office inside the mall. (1450 Ala Moana Blvd., Suite 1006, 96814. Open M-F 8:30am-4:15pm, Sa 8am-4:15pm. Last collection M-F 5:30pm, Sa 5pm.) Makai Market, the mother of all mall food courts, is the largest international food court in Hawaii and among the largest in the US, with 20 international restaurants and seating for 1300. *(Between Ala Moana Blvd. and Kapiolani St. TheBus sends over 2100 buses to the center each day. From Waikiki, take the #8, 19, or 20. The shopping center's private shuttle service runs every 15min. M-Sa 9:30am-9:30pm and Su 10am-7:30pm through various stops, including many in Waikiki, $1.50. For shuttle wheelchair information, call ☎831-1555. The Customer Service Center (☎955-9517), near the main escalator on the ground floor, has maps and guides, rents free wheelchairs, and sells shuttle bus tickets and Ala Moana Gift Certificates. Open M-Sa 9:30am-9pm, Su 10am-7pm.)*

VICTORIA WARD CENTERS. This complex of shops, services, and markets aims to sell the true island experience to locals and visitors alike. On the corner of Ward Ave. and Auahi St., **Ward Warehouse** is a bi-level open-air mall peddling elegant Hawaiian souvenirs, clothes, and more. Inside the Ward Warehouse is an information kiosk where the staff can make you restaurant reservations, call a taxi, and answer all of your questions. **Ward Farmer's Market,** across Auahi St. from Ward Warehouse, is an indoor market where savvy (and strong-stomached) shoppers can buy fresh produce, seafood, and groceries from local vendors. (Markets generally open M-Sa 7am-5pm, Su 7am-1pm.) **Ward Entertainment Centers,** a block and a half from Ala Moana Park's western exit, holds both cinemas and upscale shops. (☎597-1243. Open W-Su noon-9pm.) **The Ward Village Shops,** on the corner of Kamakee St. and Auahi St., has recognizable shops like Pier One Imports. *(Between Queen St. and Ward Ave. From Auahi St. to Ala Moana Blvd., 1 block west of Ala Moana Shopping Center. Free parking in the lots and garages on Auahi and Kamakee St. and Ward Ave. TheBus #19, 20, or 42 from Kuhio Ave. in Waikiki, or the #6 from the University area. ☎593-2374; www.victoriaward.com. Shopping hours M-Sa 10am-9pm, Su 10am-5pm, with restaurants open later. Village Shops open M-Sa 10am-8pm, Su 10am-7pm. Information Center (☎593-2376) in Ward Warehouse has free brochures with maps.)*

🎵 NIGHTLIFE

Honolulu boasts a variety of nightlife archetypes including the laid-back budget dive, sports bars, ultra-swanky glamour courts, and live music venues whose schedules are packed with local reggae bands. Crowds of fickle Honolulu look-at-me social brahmins and the ever-changing tourist hordes ebb and flow from nightspots daily. Most bars close at 2am, although a few popular establishments stay open until 4am.

To keep up with the ever-evolving scene, visit **http://dj808.com** and **http://quadmag.com** for up-to-date event and venue listings, or pick up a copy of the monthly **Hype Hawaii**, filled with nightlife news, discounts, and events, free in stores throughout Honolulu. **DaKine magazine,** "the voice of Hawaii's Out Community," and **Odyssey** magazine frequently list gay-friendly events and nightlife. Both magazines are available in stores throughout Waikiki and Honolulu.

ALA MOANA

Compadres Bar and Grill, 1200 Ala Moana Blvd. (☎591-8307), on the 2nd floor of the Ward Center. Compadres is normally a calm cantina for enjoying a $2 draft beer, Mai Tai, or margarita, but *Dios mio!* it gets crowded for the $1 beef or chicken tacos Tu 4-7pm. *Aloha* F also draws a crowd with $2 margaritas and Mai Tais, $1 oysters, and live Hawaiian music. Open M-Th 11am-midnight, F-Sa 11am-midnight, Su 11am-10pm.

Pipeline Cafe, 805 Pohukaina (☎589-1999; call for detailed info on theme nights, dress code, and age requirements). Crowded with locals—especially on Tu (21+. Cover $6), when Pipeline breaks out $1 drinks, $1 Jell-O shots, and $2 *pupus*. Hit the dance floor until 4am. Ladies forego cover charge on Foreplay Fridaze (18+. Sex on the Beach $3). Happy Hour M-Sa 4-9pm $2 well, domestic drafts, house wine, and *pupus*). Pool tables, dart machines, foosball, and megatouch video in the sports bar. Strict dress code for men Tu, F, Sa nights. Cover Th-Sa $5. Open M-Sa 4pm-4am. AmEx/D/MC/V.

Venus, 1349 Kapiolani Blvd. (☎951-8671; www.venusnightclub.com), next to the Ala Moana Shopping Center. Venus indulges the sexy touch of *aloha* that scantily-clad Waikiki only hints at. Su's Playhouse event features Wild and Crazy Sex Games (with prizes) and a $2 price tag for a Sex on the Beach. Venus hosts various all-male review F-Sa nights; check the web site for special events. Sa and Th are predominantly gay nights, though it's always an open-minded crowd. No slippers, tank tops for men except on Sa. Cover: 18+ $10; 21+ $5-10. Open M-F and Su 10pm-4am, Sa 8pm-4am. MC/V.

Mai Tai Bar, 1450 Ala Moana Blvd. (☎947-2900), on the 3rd floor of the Ala Moana Shopping Center. Mai Tai brings herds of energetic young bargoers in with their late-night Happy Hour (M-Sa 8-11pm, Su 4-11pm; pitchers of Bud Light $5, well drinks $3, Icy Mai Tai $3), daily live music (4-7pm and 9:30pm-12:30am), and no cover. 21+. Open daily 11am-1am. AmEx/D/DC/MC/V.

DOWNTOWN

Kapono's, 1 Aloha Tower Dr. (☎536-2161), in the Aloha Tower Marketplace. Named after Hawaiian music legend Henry Kapono (who plays regularly W 5:30-8:30pm and F 6-9:30pm), Kapono's has excellent live Hawaiian contemporary music every night in its outdoor ampitheater. On *Pau Hana* F Kapono's rocks with pre-partyers in search of its multiple Happy Hours: from 11am on ($2 drafts), from 4-8pm (add 25% off wells and *pupus* $4-8, or *poke* for $10), and from 8pm-midnight. No cover. Open daily 11am-2am, kitchen open M-Sa 3pm-10pm, bands start around 5:30-7pm. AmEx/D/MC/V.

The Green Room and Opium Den & Champagne Bar at Indigo's, 1121 Nu'uanu Ave. (☎521-2900). Indigo suffers none of the malaise of the neighborhoods (Downtown and Chinatown) that host it. Busy Tu-Sa, especially during Martini Madness (M-F 4-7pm, free mini buffet of *pupus* 4-5pm and $2.75 Martinis). Food served 5pm-midnight. Live entertainment at least once a day. Open nightly 4pm-6am. D/DC/MC/V.

Ocean Club (☎526-9888), inside Restaurant Row at 500 Ala Moana Blvd. Bluntly reminding its guests "appropriate look overall necessary" and regulating with a 23+ entrance age most nights, Ocean Club attracts a throng hoping to see and be seen. Wildly popular Th 21+ night. Ultimate Cocktail Hour daily 4:30-8pm with $1.75 Ocean Ritas and Miller Lite drafts, and half-priced *pupus*. Fashionably casual attire (no shorts, torn or ripped jeans, or athletic attire for men; no beach wear, rubber slippers, or athletic attire for women). Cover $4-5 after 8pm. Open Tu-Sa 4:30pm-4am.

Ground Level, 1154 Fort St. Mall (☎546-9998). A good-times Hawaii Pacific University (HPU) crowd lends an international and communal atmosphere to this local-style college hang-out. Equipped with a Happy Hour (M-F 4-7pm; 48 oz. pitcher $5, wells $3) and all other necessary tools for constructing bar fun including billiards, darts, karaoke, satellite sporting events, and cheap *pupus* ($4-5). Open M-Sa 10am-2am. MC/V.

MANOA AND THE UNIVERSITY AREA

☒ **Anna Banana's,** 2440 S. Beretania St. (☎946-5190). A Manoa and UH institution, this dim, love-worn bar has been rocking live music for 33 yrs. Outstanding Happy Hour daily 3-6pm (beer $2). Live music upstairs 4 nights a week, with lots of reggae acts. Extremely busy Th-Sa after 10:30pm, especially during school year. 21+. Cover only for special events $5. Open daily 3pm-2am.

Magoo's, 1015 University Ave. (☎946-8830), plays Pied Piper to hard-working UH students with the sweet song of ☒ $7 pitchers of Newcastle Ale. Don't let the wall of patio plants out front deter you; the entrance is in the middle by the host's podium. Open-air Magoo's also bakes a mean pizza ($5.50-30) to justify another pitcher ($5 and up). 21+ after 9pm. Open daily 11am-1:30am. AmEx/MC/V.

Eastside Grill, 1035 University Ave. (☎952-6555), across the street from the Varsity Theater; get a discount at the grill with a ticket stub. A sports bar serving grill food with local flavors. Live music F-Sa, karaoke all other nights. Happy Hour daily 11am-6pm (beer $2-3). Try the extravagant crab dip ($9.25, $6 on Sa) or fish taco with fresh veggies and honey wasabi sauce ($6.25). Lunch specials from $5. Open daily 11am-1:30am. AmEx/D/MC/V.

Cheapo Music, 1009 University Ave. (☎943-0500), next door to Magoo's, sells no food but can fund it—pawn off those Backstreet Boys albums you bought "just to find out" and earn enough for another pitcher. Cheapo buys used CDs and DVDs (up to $5) for resale ($0.95 for singles to $11 for CDs). **Cheapo Books** around the corner on 200 S. King St. (☎943-0501) does the same, only with ☒ books. Check out the flyers near the door for nightlife information around Honolulu. Open daily 9am-midnight.

☒ HIKING

The connected rainforest trails that comprise the **Honolulu Mauka System** are a world away from the hustle and bustle of Honolulu. Because of the way the clouds cling to the mountains, trails can be home to diverse climates within a small area and numerous unique flora species. The most popular trails are the Manoa Falls Trail and the Makiki Valley Loop. At times, the bugs can be aggravating; pack **insect repellent** along with the standard **water** and **sunscreen.** Allow enough time to return with daylight to spare, never hike alone, and always **stay on the trail**— unmarked offshoots and access roads may be private and are not maintained as public recreation routes. Lastly, respect the land: remember to take out everything you took in. For more information, go to www.hawaiitrails.org.

MANOA FALLS TRAIL. (1 mi. one-way. Trailhead: Manoa Falls parking area. Elevation change: 800 ft. Level: easy.) This is one of Oahu's most popular trails, and for good reason. The well-marked path leads through eucalyptus groves, over bubbling streams, and by age-worn guava and mountain apple trees. Manoa Falls cascades down a stone face into a pool at the end of the trail. On any weekend, find groups of tourists posing for pictures, as well as a few brave souls testing the chilly waters. Small fissures in the rock wall contain stacks of rocks left by locals in respect for the *mana* (authority) of the area. Obey the posted landslide-warning signs at the falls viewing area. (*Leaving Waikiki on McCully St., take the 1st right after the Ala Wai Canal onto Kapiolani Blvd. From Kapiolani Blvd., turn right onto Kalakaua Ave., then right on King St. Take the 1st left onto Puou St. After Punahou St., Puou becomes Manoa Rd. Proceed straight ahead to the parking area and trailhead. Do not leave valuables in your car.*)

AIHUALAMA TRAIL. (1½ mi. one-way. Trailhead: From Manoa Falls trail. Elevation change: 1200 ft. Level: moderate.) This trail beckons more experienced hikers approximately 150 ft. before the end of the Manoa Falls Trail. Continuing up the western ridge of Manoa Valley, Aihualama features bamboo forests as well as spectacular vistas of Honolulu and the valley below. The trail also serves as a link between the Manoa Valley hikes and the Tantalus area hikes. To access these trails, keep going 1 mi. after the viewpoint to **Pauoa Flats** and the **Pu'u Ohia Trail.** Otherwise, turn back and return the way you came. *(Follow the directions through the Manoa Falls Trail to the marker for Aihualama, directly before a chain-link fence on the left.)*

MAKIKI VALLEY LOOP. (2½ mi. round-trip. Trailhead: Hawaii Nature Center. Level: moderate.) Combining three Tantalus area hikes—**Maunalaha, Kanealole,** and **Makiki Valley**—the trail offers a spectacular adventure. The trailhead for Maunalaha is clearly marked behind the **Hawaii Nature Center** (p. 109). Most people veer right and hike Maunalaha first, but to avoid the steep uphill climb on that side, head left and attack Kanealole first. This path heads uphill gradually for ¾ mi. The trail turns into Makiki Valley just before the **Kaneaole Stream.** Here the trail passes through a field of Job's Tears, a tall thick grass that can grow up to 5 ft. tall. The Makiki valley trail ends at a four-way intersection. To continue on the loop and onto Maunalaha trail, take the right fork. The middle *mauka* (mountain side) trail is the **Moleka Trail** (see below) and the right path is the **Ualakaa Trail,** an easy ½ mi. loop under canopied forest that ends at Round Top Dr. Maunalaha heads down the mountain through webs of tricky tree roots spreading out from immense Norfolk pines and eucalyptus trees. The steep ¾ mi. trail ends back at the trailhead above the Hawaii Nature Center. *(See directions to the Hawaii Nature Center, p. 109.)*

MOLEKA TRAIL. (¾ mi. one-way. Trailhead: Round Top Dr. or Makiki Valley Trail. Elevation change: 300 ft. Level: easy.) A short jaunt along the upper east edge of Makiki Valley, Moleka Trail ends at the Makiki Valley Trail. On the way, the path plunges through thick forest and passes by expansive vistas of Honolulu's skyscrapers and Tantalus. *(To reach the trailhead, take Keeaumoku St. past the Makiki Public Library. Turn right on Wilder Ave. and take the first left onto Makiki St., keeping right at the Makiki Heights Dr. Y-intersection. Continue left at the next split in the road, up Round Top Dr. There will be a trailhead sign and small parking lot on the left; actual trailhead is makai (toward the ocean). The trail can also be reached via the Makiki Valley Trail.)*

MANOA CLIFF TRAIL. (2½ mi. one-way. Trailhead: Tantalus Dr. Elevation change: 500 ft. Level: easy.) This trail is distinctive because of its native flora as well as its intersection with Tantalus area hikes. After gradually climbing through dense forest, the path emerges at amazing vistas of Manoa Valley. Approximately halfway through the hike, Manoa Cliff leads to the **Pu'u Ohia Trail.** The unchallenging hike, located off to the left, leads ¾ mi. to the highest point on Tantalus Crater and a **Nu'uanu Valley viewpoint.** Along the way, Pu'u Ohia features night-blooming jasmine, wild ginger, Christmas berry, and avocado trees as well as awe-inspiring views of Honolulu and Diamond Head. Continuing on Manoa Cliff past the Pu'u Ohia fork, there is another junction on the right to the **Pauoa Flats Trail.** Leading inland, the ¾ mi. Pauoa Flats Trail traverses through swamp mahogany, wild ginger, and eucalyptus trees before eventually connecting with **Nu'uanu Trail** (see below). If you stick to Manoa Cliff, you will find that the trail ends at a third junction, this time with **Kalawahine Trail.** This final trail delivers you to Tantalus Dr. via a 1 mi. trek through *koa* and banana trees, as well as other native and introduced vegetation. *(Follow directions to Moleka trailhead. The parking lot for Manoa Cliff is makai (on the ocean side), adjacent to the Moleka trailhead. The trail is across the street from the parking lot. To reach the Kalawahine trailhead, drive mauka (toward the mountains) on Tantalus Dr. There will be a sign for the trailhead on the left, adjacent to a private road that goes straight up the hill.)*

NU'UANU TRAIL. (1½ mi. one-way. Trailhead: via Kalawahine or Manoa Cliff trails. Elevation change: 600 ft. Level: moderate.) Climbing up the side of Pauoa Valley, Nu'uanu Trail features periodic vistas of Honolulu proper as well as Oahu's western region. After reaching its peak elevation atop the ridge, the trail drops down to the Nu'uanu Valley Floor. Before this, however, the path intersects with the **Pauoa Flats Trail** on the valley side and the **Judd Trail** on the cliff side. *(The trail can be accessed via the Kalawahine Trail or the Manoa Cliff Trail.)*

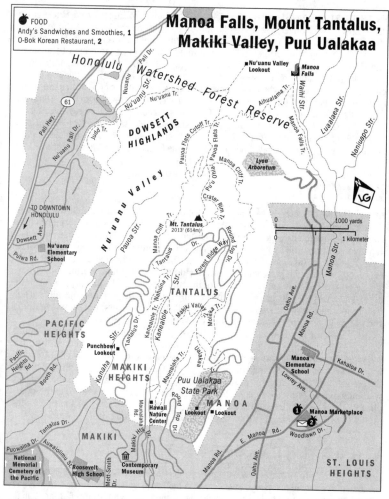

FOOD
Andy's Sandwiches and Smoothies, **1**
O-Bok Korean Restaurant, **2**

Manoa Falls, Mount Tantalus, Makiki Valley, Puu Ualakaa

JUDD TRAIL. (¾ mi. one-way. Trailhead: Nuʻuanu Trail. Elevation change: 200 ft. Level: easy.) After crossing a stream, Judd Trail becomes a loop that takes hikers through damp valley vegetation. The rocks can be slick, so mind your balance. About midway through the path, the trail connects with **Nuʻuanu Trail.** *(Take Pali Hwy. away from town and turn right on Nuʻuanu Pali Dr. Continue until you reach a concrete bridge. The trailhead is to the right, in the clearing. You can park here but be aware that it is a high theft area.)*

PUU PIA TRAIL. (1¼ mi. Trailhead: See below. Elevation change: 400 ft. Level: easy.) Featuring a gradual ascent through dense vegetation and beneath a nearly opaque tree canopy, Puu Pia is a painless hike suited for almost anyone. The climb begins at the heel of Manoa Valley and eventually features sweeping views of Honolulu and the surrounding area. *(Drive past Manoa Marketplace on E. Manoa Rd., heading mauka (toward the mountains). Turn left on Alani Dr. and continue ¾ mi. until the road takes a sharp right. From here, Alani Ln. continues straight. Park and walk down Alani Ln., past the houses and through a cable gate. A dirt road leads to the Forestry and Wildlife picnic shelter; the trailhead is to the left.)*

WAAHILA RIDGE TRAIL. (2½ mi. one-way. Trailhead: Waahila State Recreation Area. Elevation change: 500 ft. Level: moderate.) Skirting the Waahila Ridge above Manoa and Palolo Valleys, the trail offers amazing views at every turn. This hike is more demanding than others, as it sometimes tiptoes near the edge of the ridge and rises fairly quickly. However, adventurers will enjoy beautiful scenery along the way, including many native plants like *koa* and *'ohi'a lehua*. At the end of the path, there is a junction with the **Kolowalu Trail,** which is one of the area's most difficult hikes, rising 1100 ft. in a mere mile. *(Take Kapahulu Ave. away from Waikiki and turn right on Waialae. Take the first left, St. Louis Dr., following it up the St. Louis Heights residential area before turning right on Peter Pl. near the top. After the cul de sac, turn left on Ruth Pl. into Waahila Ridge State Recreation Area. The trailhead is at the rear of the park. The trailhead for Kolowalu is near the Puu Pia Trail, on the right side of the Forestry and Wildlife picnic shelter.)*

WAIKIKI

At any time of the day, there is something going on in Waikiki. People-watching is the best way to experience Hawaii's diversity amid the hectic, touristy commercialism of the area. European sunbathers flaunt their hard-earned bodies and tans, Japanese tourists mill around in huge groups spending their hard-earned yen, and local Hawaiians "talk story" and cruise on the beach, laughing at all the hard-earning going on. You can start your day as a wide-eyed and camera-toting tour group junkie on the Kalakaua Ave. strip, take up surf lessons and nihilism in search of the perfect wave on Kuhio Beach in the afternoon, and recreate yourself with a Mai Tai and a romantic encounter at nightfall. Idyllic sunsets, gorgeous weather, and plenty to do—this is paradise, and Waikiki is yours to perfect.

The center of tourism in Hawaii's biggest city, Waikiki is composed of equal parts genuine charm and manufactured gimmick. The tourist ephemerality that soaks modern Waikiki was assured in 1922 when the waters that flowed into what was a marsh at Waikiki were diverted into the then-new Ala Wai Canal. Waikiki beach was built by removing source waters and importing sand onto the Waikiki wetlands, which were formerly a Native Hawaiian gathering place. With the completion of the beach, tourism gained an early foothold here, and as a result, a significant portion of today's residents of Waikiki are only temporary visitors.

▐▀ LOCAL TRANSPORTATION

Bus: TheBus's (p. 92) 24hr. Waikiki information hotline (☎296-1818) offers an automated directory of bus routes to sites across the island on buses that leave from Kuhio Ave. For help on how to reach a specific destination, call ☎848-5555 5:30am-10pm. Listed below are a few convenient routes that leave from Waikiki. Consult a bus schedule or TheBus's web site (www.thebus.org) for more information.

#2 goes up Kuhio and Kalakaua Ave. through the heart of town and Chinatown and back through Waikiki to Kapiolani Park.

#4 goes by the University of Hawaii in Manoa west through Makiki and up Nu'uanu Ave. into Nu'uanu Valley via Downtown Honolulu.

#13 goes from the intersection at Kapahulu Ave. and Campbell Ave. up Kuhio and Kalakaua Ave., through Downtown, and up Liliha St.

#8 begins its island voyage at Kalakaua Ave. and Monsarrat Ave., and exits Waikiki at Kuhio Ave., finishing at the Ala Moana Shopping Center.

#19 leaves Monsarrat Ave. and Kalakaua Ave. for Kapahulu Ave., Waikiki and the Ala Moana Shopping Center, Downtown and finally the airport and Hickam AFB.

#20 follows the route of #19 to the airport, heading to Pearlridge Shopping Center, near the Pearl Harbor memorials and Aloha Stadium.

#22, known as the **Beachbus,** starts at the northwest end of Waikiki at Pau St. and Ala Wai Blvd., turns around at Niu St. onto Kalakaua Ave. and then Kuhio Ave. The Beachbus continues on to the intersection of Kapahulu and Paki Ave., up Diamond Head Rd. and by Kahala Mall. It then jumps on to the Kalanianaole Hwy. (designated H-1 West in the other direction) to Hanauma Bay, Sandy Beach, Makapu Beach, ending at Sea Life Park.

#42 leaves Waikiki via Ala Moana Blvd. and heads west through Downtown to Waipahu and Ewa.

#58 leaves Ala Moana and goes through Waikiki east to Hawaii Kai and Sea Life Park, around through Waimanalo and Kailua then back to Ala Moana.

Trolley: Our Neighborhood Trolley (☎ 792-4490), the system's newest line, is the one sensible exception to the over-priced $20-per day **Waikiki Trolleys.** It serves 25 stops in Waikiki, Kapahulu and Kaimuki, from the Waikiki Trade Center at Seaside and Kuhio to Liliuokalani Elementary up Waialae Ave., and is the cheapest ride to the dining and shopping options in Kapahulu ($2 for an all-day pass). There is a $1 one-way fare, but once you alight, you can't re-board unless you pay another $1. Runs every 30min. 10am-11pm.

Taxis: Waikiki is small—a ride across the district is around $6. Taxis to the airport are expensive ($25-30); arrange transportation through your hotel or hostel, or via the myriad airport shuttle services ($7). **Charley's Taxi and Tour** (☎ 955-2211) has 24hr. service to most of Oahu for $2.40 per mile, $2 per stop. **TheCab** (☎ 422-2222) offers 24hr. island-wide service, metered at $2.40 per mile, $2 per stop.

Car Rentals:

VIP Car Rental, 2463 Kuhio Ave. (☎ 924-6500). Other locations all over Waikiki, including 234 Beachwalk (☎ 922-4605) and 1944 Kalakaua Ave. (☎ 946-7733). VIP rents out older cars for the budget-minded, and exotic cars for the trendy. Mid-90s Nissan or Toyota coupe $13 first day, $24 per day after that, $89 per week and up. 3-day min. rental. Insurance not included. Ages 21-24 $10-15 surcharge, 18-20,$25 surcharge.

Ferrari Rentals, 2025 Kalakaua Ave. (☎ 942-8725). Rents expensive exotic cars, like the Ferrari F-355 Spyder ($650 per 24hr.), to customers over 21 years of age. Those 18+ can rent sporty Geo Trackers or Pontiac Sunfires for $55 per day. Discounts on longer rentals, free Waikiki pick-up. Open daily 8am-6pm.

Paradise Rent-a-Car, 1879 Kalakaua Ave. (☎ 946-7777), 355 Royal Hawaiian Ave. (☎ 924-7777). Paradise offers an unusually wide selection of cars, from compacts to Ferraris. Bicycle ($20) and moped ($32) rental as well. Compacts $30 per day, mid-size $35 per day, Jeeps $70 per day, Lamborghini Diablo VT Roadster $1500 per day. 3 day min. $20 surcharge for drivers under the age of 25. Open daily 8am-5pm.

Thrifty, 325 Seaside Ave. (☎ 808-971-2660). Compact from $22 per day. The under-25 surcharge at Thrifty is only $15 per day. Airport drop-off fee $30. Provides hotel pickups. Collision insurance $17. Open daily 7am-5pm.

Hertz, 1956 Ala Moana Blvd. (☎ 800-527-0700; www.hertz.com), with locations in the Hyatt Regency at 2424 Kalakaua Ave. and the Hilton Hawaiian Village at 2005 Kalia Rd. Economy cars from $36 a day. 25+. Credit card required.

Moped and Motorcycle Rentals:

Moped Direct, 750A Kapahulu Ave. (☎ 732-3366), just outside of Waikiki past the Ala Wai Golf Course on Kapahulu Ave. Generally has the lowest rates, and loans customers free helmets. Mopeds $1.50 per hr. Open M-F 9am-6pm, Sa-Su 9am-5pm.

Inter-Island Rentals, 234 Beachwalk (☎ 926-3356). Rents mopeds to customers 18+, and provides free maps, instruction, and helmet rental. $40-50 per day, $80 deposit required, includes insurance. Bike rental $20 per day. Open daily 8am-5pm.

OAHU

OAHU

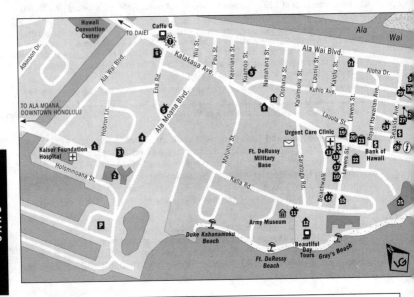

Waikiki

🏠 ACCOMMODATIONS
Aqua Bamboo, **46**
Aqua Marina, **1**
Aston Aloha Surf Hotel, **43**
Aston Coconut Plaza Hotel, **21**
Holiday Inn Waikiki, **4**
Ilima Hotel, **32**
The Imperial of Waikiki Hotel, **15**
Leisure Resorts at Honolulu, **33**
Outrigger Waikiki Shore Resort, **12**
Pat Winston's Waikiki Condos, **34**
Polynesian Beach Club Hostel, **51**
Renaissance Ilikai Waikiki Hotel, **2**
Royal Grove Hotel, **47**
Seaside Hawaiian Hostel, **31**
Sheraton Waikiki Beach Resort, **25**
Waikiki Beachcomber Hotel, **35**
Waikiki Beachside Hostel, **50**
Waikiki Gateway Hotel, **10**
Waikiki Grand Hotel, **52**
Waikiki Sand Villa, **44**
Waikiki Terrace Hotel, **9**

☀ ACTIVITIES
Aloha Beach Services, **38**
Hans Hedemann Surf School, **54**
Koa Board Sports, **45**
Outrigger Beach Services, **36**
Wave Riding Vehicles, **7**

🍽 FOOD
Arancino, **17**
Cha Cha Cha, **24**
Cheeseburger in Paradise, **49**
Chuck's Cellar, **42**
Keo's, **8**
Marie's Health Foods, **13**
Ono's Hawaiian Foods, **56**
The Patisserie, **14**
Pyramids, **55**
Rainbow Drive-In, **57**
Ray's Famous Pizza, **29**
Ruffage Natural Foods, **48**
Shore Bird Beach Broiler, **11**
Teddy's Bigger Burgers, **58**
Todai, **5**
Top of Waikiki, **26**
Yasoba, **18**

🍸 NIGHTLIFE
Diamond Head Grill, **59**
Duke's Canoe Club, **37**
Fusion Waikiki, **30**
Hula's, **53**
Kelly O'Neil's, **20**
The Maze, **28**
Moose McGillycuddy's Pub and
  Cafe, **19**
Nashville Waikiki, **41**
The Red Lion, **16**
Scruples, **40**
Snappers, **3**
Wave Waikiki, **6**
Zanzabar, **27**

🛍 SHOPPING
DFS Galleria, **23**
The International Market Place, **39**
Royal Hawaiian Shopping
  Center, **22**

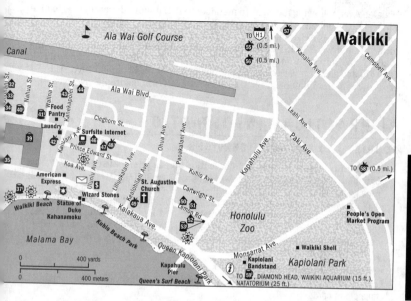

Hawaiian Peddler, 2139 Kuhio Ave. (☎926-5099 or 877-428-6386). Offers personal service and a wide selection of Jeeps ($59 per day, insurance not included). Their pride and joy is their collection of Harley Davidsons ($170 from 8am-4:30pm, $185 until 7pm; overnight not recommended), which make an odd contrast to their mopeds ($25 per day). Ask about bicycle and water activity equipment rentals. Open daily 8am-4:30pm.

Pineapple Cruzers, 305 Royal Hawaiian Ave. (☎924-0556) rents bicycles, mopeds, and motorcycles. Bicycle rental $15 for 8am-6pm. Open daily 8am-6pm. No deposit required. AmEx/D/MC/V.

✠ ORIENTATION

Waikiki is bordered on the north and west by the Ala Wai Canal, on the south by its famed beaches, and on the east by Diamond Head Crater. Three main thoroughfares run Waikiki's 2 mi. length from east to west: **Ala Wai Boulevard** parallels the canal with one-way traffic going west; **Kalakaua Avenue** fronts the ritziest hotels and beaches and carries one-way traffic east; **Kuhio Avenue** splits off from Kalakaua Ave. at the western end of Waikiki and bears the brunt of traffic all the way to **Kapahulu Avenue** on the east end of town. The three main east-west streets intersect numerous one-way sidestreets, necessitating many trips around the block for lost drivers.

The **Ala Wai Canal** is a scenic area, popular with joggers and walkers, although its distance from the action can make it the least safe part of Waikiki at night. Safety, mostly in the form of the hilarious, agile Kushman police buggy, increases closer to Kuhio Ave., which is noisy with unending bus traffic during the day, and the occasional pack of mopeds at night. Kalakaua Ave. is for show, with no bus traffic, lots of pedestrians, and all manner of street performers and vendors. Farther down Kalakaua, toward Diamond Head, the parks and beaches can become less safe after dark. Waikiki police response is impressively quick and thorough, however, and the area is considered fairly safe even at night.

Driving directions to H-1 West: From Kalakaua Ave. or Kuhio Ave., make a left onto Kapahulu Ave. Take Kapahulu past Kaimuki, under the H-1 overpass and left on

Waialae Ave., following the signs to merge onto H-1. A more direct route is to take Ala Wai Blvd. and turn right on McCully St. over the bridge. Stay on McCully (you'll drive over H-1), turn left on Dole St., and left on Alexander St. Yield and merge left onto the highway. **To H-1 East:** Take Ala Moana Blvd. over the canal, leaving Waikiki, and turn right on Atkinson Dr. Turn right on Kapiolani Blvd. toward H-1. Or take McCully St. over the canal and make a right on Kapiolani Blvd. The H-1 East on-ramp from Kapiolani Blvd. is a two-lane left turn before the overpass.

🛈 PRACTICAL INFORMATION

TOURIST AND FINANCIAL SERVICES

Tourist Office: Hawaii Visitors and Convention Bureau Information Office at Waikiki Shopping Plaza, 2250 Kalakaua Ave., Ste. 502 (☎800-GoHawaii or 924-0266; www.gohawaii.com). A friendly office that directs most visitors to 2 official tourist magazines—*Connections* and *Islands of Aloha Official Vacation Planner*. Open M-F 8am-4:30pm, Sa-Su 8am-noon. **Hale Aloha tourist information kiosks** in front of the Royal Hawaiian Shopping Center, on Kalakaua Ave.; in front of the Sheraton Princess Kaiulani Hotel, at 120 Kaiulani Ave.; and in front of the First Hawaiian Bank at Lewers St. and Kalakaua St.

Tours: See Honolulu Practical Information, p. 92.

Equipment Rental: Most rental agencies on the beach are fairly expensive, and don't take credit cards.

Koa Board Sports, 2420 Koa Ave. (☎923-0189). Surfboards $20 per day or $75 per week. Open 10:30am-4:30pm.

Wave Riding Vehicles, 1888 Kalakaua Ave. (☎979-4978). Sells surfboards and rents used boards for cheap, depending on availability. Long surfboards $35 per day, short $25 per day. Open M-Sa 10am-8pm, Su noon-5pm. MC/V.

Aloha Beach Services (call the Sheraton Moana Surfrider Hotel ☎922-3111, ext. 2341). Go straight onto the beach from Duke's Canoe Club, 2335 Kalakaua Ave., and turn left. For $30, you can get an instructor and a surfboard for an hr., as well as the guarantee that you'll be able to stand up. $10 for the first hr. for just the surfboard, $5 per additional hr. Body boards $7 per hr. Open daily from 8am, go early for lessons to avoid the crowds.

Outrigger Beach Services (☎926-9889), in front of Duke's under the blue umbrellas, rents surf boards at $10 for the first hr., $5 each additional hr. $30 per hr. for an instructor and board. Body boards $7 per hr. and $3 each additional hr. Open daily 7am-4pm; go before 11am to avoid a long wait for lessons.

Hans Hedemann Surf School, 2586 Kalakaua Ave. (☎924-7778), at the Park Shore Beach Hotel. Other locations at Sheraton Waikiki (booth on beach) or Outrigger Reef (sign says HH Surf School). The premier surf school in Waikiki, founded by famous surfer Hans Hedemann. Sign up here for a 2hr. group surfing lesson, $75 per person, including lesson and board. Surfboard rentals are $30 per 24hr., body boards $20 per day. Expect to pay more at their booths on the beach. They also rent bikes for $20 per day. Open daily 8am-5pm. AmEx/MC/V.

Banks and ATMS:

Currency exchange is available for 20 different currencies at the foreign exchange ATM on the first floor of Hibiscus Court in the Royal Hawaiian Shopping Center, on Royal Hawaiian Ave. Open daily 11am-10pm.

American Savings Bank, 321 Seaside Ave. (☎923-1102). Currency exchange fee $3 or 3% of transaction, whichever is greater. Open M-Th 9am-4:30pm, F 9am-5pm.

Bank of Hawaii, 2228 Kalakaua Ave. (☎800-643-3888). Currency exchange fee $2 by machine. Open M-Th 8:30am-4pm, F 8:30am-6pm.

First Hawaiian Bank, 2181 Kalakaua Ave. (☎931-3912). Currency exchange fee $3 for amounts under $300, $5 for amounts between $300 and $500. Open M-Th 8:30am-4pm, F 8:30am-6pm.

Central Pacific Bank, 105 Uluniu Ave. (☎971-3277). Currency exchange fee $5. Open M-Th 8:30am-4pm, F 8:30am-6pm.

American Express, 2424 Kalakaua Ave. (☎926-5443), in the Hyatt Regency, 2nd fl. Purchase or replace traveler's checks. Open daily 7am-7pm.

LOCAL SERVICES

Laundromats:

Waikiki Laundromats (☎923-2057) operates numerous self-serve, coin-operated laundromats in Waikiki which are on hotel premises, but open to the public.

Coin Laundry: in the basement of the Outrigger East at the corner of Kuhio and Kanikapolei. Wash $1. Dry $1 per 20 min. Open 6:30am-11pm.

Weather/Surf Conditions: See Honolulu and Waikiki Information Lines (p. 97).

EMERGENCY AND COMMUNICATIONS

Emergency: ☎911.

Police: Substation at **Duke Paoa Kahanamoku Building,** 2425 Kalakaua Ave. (☎529-3801), on Waikiki beach opposite the Hyatt Regency. Open 24hr.

Crisis Lines: Sex Abuse Treatment Center (☎524-7273). Crisis Response Team (☎832-3100).

Red Cross: American Red Cross, Hawaii Chapter (☎734-2101).

Medical Services: Urgent Care Clinic of Waikiki, 2155 Kalakaua Ave. (☎432-2700), at Beachwalk above the Planet Hollywood. Open daily 8am-8pm. Straub Doctors on Call Waikiki (☎971-6000). Planned Parenthood Clinic of Hawaii (☎589-1149).

Pharmacy: Good Neighbor Pharmacy, 2230 Kuhio Ave. (923-4466). Open daily 7am-10pm.

Internet Access:

Caffe G, 1888 Kalakaua Ave. C106 (☎979-2299; fax 979-7889). A comfortably hip Internet and sandwich joint. High Speed Internet at $1 per 10min., $1 minimum. B/W printing $0.25 per page; color $1 per page. Domestic fax $2 per page; international fax $3 per page. Fax hours M-F 8am-4pm. 12 oz. cup of joe $1.50. Open daily 8am-11pm.

Beautiful Day Tours, 2161 Kalia Rd., Ste. 110. (☎926-4700; fax 800-926-4701), behind the Outrigger Shore Resort on the 2nd floor landing facing the beach. High speed $3 per 20min., $1 each additional 10min. Copies and printing $0.24 per page, color print $0.96 per page. Local and domestic fax $0.96 per page, no international. Open M-Sa 9am-8pm, Su 10am-5pm.

Surfsite Internet, 159 Kaiulani Ave., #207. Walk down Kaiulani Ave. from Kuhio Ave. and take the first left to the mini mall on the right. In the savory company of a head shop, Smokey's, and Affordable Tattoos of Waikiki (#207-A, ☎923-7546), this haphazard Internet without cafe fits in well with its surroundings. $5 per hr., $5 minimum. Printing or copies $0.25 per page. Open daily 8am-10pm.

Post Office: Waikiki Station, 330 Saratoga Rd. (☎973-7515). Open M-F 8am-4:30pm, Sa 9am-1pm.

Postal Code: 96815.

▟ ACCOMMODATIONS

Hotels dominate the Waikiki skyline, choking up space along the beach and toward the Ala Wai Canal. Ironically, in most cases the impenetrable maze of edifices eliminates any real view, stealing the scene with industrial back-side views as often as with brightly-painted lanais. Wise travelers should ask to see the room before paying extra for any claims to a view, be it city, mountain or ocean. Most hotels offer rotating promotions and discounts that can add up to a significant savings. The prices listed below are standard (rack) rates, but be sure to ask about current deals at all establishments. In all cases, check internet prices before you book, as they are often substantially lower than the rack prices listed. Most hotels listed participate with internet wholesalers like priceline.com or expedia.com. Unless otherwise noted, all accommodations have A/C and 24hr. reception, 3pm check-in and check-out at noon.

ON THE MENU

GOT POI?

Though Hawaii is part of America, many mainlanders will have difficulty interpreting a traditional Hawaiian menu. Here is a short list of favorite Hawaiian dishes.

Plate lunch: the format of the traditional Hawaiian fast food. One entree (chicken teriyaki, deep-fried mahi mahi, beef stew, or *kalua* pig) with 2 scoops of rice and 1 scoop of macaroni salad.

Loco Moco breakfast: 2 eggs on 2 scoops of rice with 2 hamburger patties, all covered in gravy.

Shave Ice: not ice cream, and not a snow cone. Also not gritty or crunchy, shave ice has the taste of an icee minus the artificiality.

Kalbi Beef: short beef ribs, a staple of Korean barbecue.

Spam musubi: a fried slab of the favorite local spiced ham in a can, beached on a hunk of sushi rice and wrapped in *nori* (seaweed).

Kalua Pig: succulent pork roasted underground and shredded.

Lau Lau: pork wrapped in *taro (poi)* leaves and steamed. Eat the inner leaves, not the outer ones.

Malasada: a Portuguese donut.

Poi: a thick purplish paste made out of pounded *taro* root. Can be eaten alone, but more often is eaten with *kalua* pig or *lomi* salmon to cut the salty flavor.

Pipikaula: Hawaiian-style beef jerky.

Haupia: coconut-milk custard.

HOSTELS

Waikiki Beachside Hostel, 2556 Lemon Rd. (☎923-9566; www.hokondo.com). Follow Kalakaua Ave. east toward Diamond Head. Turn left on Kapahulu Ave., take your 1st left onto Lemon Rd. The young international travelers that populate the Waikiki Beachside are passionate about their destination. Guests share animated nighttime conversations on the patios, overlooking a parking lot-turned-courtyard (with big screen cable TV). All rooms have full kitchens. Breakfast included. Internet access $1 per 10min. A/C in some rooms. Cable TV in all rooms. Free Circle Island tour included with stay. 7th consecutive night free. 2 week advance reservations recommended in summer. 8-bed dorms $18 per person per night, $108 per week; 4-bed dorms $23 per person per night, $135 per week. Semi-private and private rooms also available. D/MC/V. ❶

Polynesian Beach Club Hostel, 2584 Lemon Rd. (☎877-504-2924 or 922-1340; fax 262-2817; reservation@hawaiihostels.com). See directions for Waikiki Beachside Hostel, above. The Polynesian Beach Club is probably the quietest hostel in Honolulu, as neighbors have mandated post-10pm quiet hours. Show them a neon flyer from the airport to get $3 off 1st night's stay and free pick-up with a 2-night stay. Continental breakfast included. Daily kayak tours $20. The guest services, including free use of boogie boards, snorkel gear, safety deposit boxes, and storage at the desk, may make up for the occasional lack of cleanliness. Check-out 10am. Dorms $17; semi-private double $39; private studio with kitchenette $55. 7th consecutive night's stay free. MC/V. ❶

Seaside Hawaiian Hostel, 419 Seaside Ave. (☎924-3303; www.seasidehawaiianhostel.com). Turn left onto Seaside Ave. from Kalakaua Ave. Take Seaside past Kuhio Ave. and turn right down the alley just before Manukai St. on the left. Turn left at the end of the alley; the Hawaiian Hostel is 50 ft. back. This hostel manages to survive among giants by offering cheap, basic accommodations to youth travelers. Communal kitchen, breakfast included. Snorkel and surf equipment rental $5-15 per day. Parking $5 per day. Visitors should be prepared to show both their passports and their tickets off the island. 6-bed dorms with full bath $17; double $20. MC/V. ❶

HOTELS

🏨 **Waikiki Grand Hotel,** 134 Kapahulu Ave. (☎923-1814 or 888-336-4368; www.queenssurf.com). Turn left on Kapahulu from Kalakaua Ave.; the Waikiki Grand is on the left before Lemon St. Queen's Surf Vacation Rentals lets out these privately-owned rooms, which offer more personality and thoughtful amenities than chain hotels. Some rooms have beautiful bamboo furniture and many have awesome views of Diamond Head and the ocean. Considering the quality of the rooms and the proximity of the beach, a room at the Waikiki Grand is a steal. Hosts Hula's gay bar on the 2nd fl. Doubles $85, with ocean view $105; studio with kitchenette $150. $20 discount Apr.-June and Sept.-Dec. 22 on the internet. Call to ask about last-minute discount rates. AmEx/D/MC/V. ❸

Aqua Bamboo, 2425 Kuhio Ave. (☎922-7777; www.aquabamboo.com). The trendy beige and black decor is dominated by a bamboo and Buddha motif. The small pool is surrounded by a beautiful garden area, spa and sauna. Guests receive discounts at fine dining restaurants across Waikiki. The management hosts a complimentary cocktail reception every Wednesday at 5pm. Doubles $145; studio with kitchenette $165. See web site for discounts and promotional rates. ❹

The Imperial of Waikiki Hotel, 205 Lewers St. (☎923-1827; www.imperialof-waikiki.com). Take Lewers St. toward the beach from Kalakaua Ave. The Imperial is part timeshare and part hotel, with a community feel and approachable management and staff. Rooftop sundeck with pool and jacuzzi, captivating ocean view above the 20th floor. Spacious and modern Ohia Suites (1-2 persons) have microwave, mini fridge, coffeemaker, and toaster with a (pull down) double bed and a queen-sized sofa bed, $140. Banyan suites (1-4 persons) add a bedroom with a queen-sized bed for $165. Seasonal $10 discount Apr.-June and Sept.-Dec. 19. AmEx/D/MC/V. ❹

Pat Winston's Waikiki Condos, 417 Nohonani St. (☎800-545-1948 or 922-3894; www.winstonwaikikicondos.com). Drive down Ala Wai Blvd., turn left on Nohonani. Whatever benefits are gained from being a condominium hotel rather than just a hotel, Pat Winston passes them on to his guests. These inexpensive accommodations are an even greater value during promotions. All rooms have a well-equipped kitchenette, full-sized refrigerator with freezer, a fold-out couch and a plush carpet. The astroturf pool deck and small pool are lorded over by an angry, 3 ft. tall Tiki statue. Deluxe rooms also available. Laundry facilities. 3 to 4 night min. stay. $25 one-time condominium cleaning fee. Budget room (fits 2-4) $79-109, each additional guest $10. AmEx/D/MC/V. 1 wheelchair-accessible room. ❷

Waikiki Gateway Hotel, 2070 Kalakaua Ave. (☎955-3741 or 800-247-1903; www.waikiki-hotel.com). On Kalakaua Ave. just after the Kuhio Ave. split, before Olohana St. Standard hotel rooms close to Ft. DeRussy Park at a lower price than you'll find elsewhere. Nick's Fish Market serves excellent seafood on-site, 5:30-10:30pm. Small pool with waterfall and pleasant view. Breakfast included. Doubles $99-129, but prices almost half online. All major credit cards. 1 wheelchair-accessible room. ❸

Ilima Hotel, 445 Nohonani St. (☎923-1877; www.ilima.com). The Ilima is centrally located but off Waikiki, 1 block from the Ala Wai down Nohonani Pl. Paintings by famous Hawaiian artist Ralph Kagehiro complement the well-kept pink hallways, doors, and mirrors. Good-sized private lanais and unobstructed Ala Wai views outside of some rooms, and nothing but cleanliness within. Free parking. Internet access available. Dec. 15-Mar. singles $129-165, doubles $139-175. Apr.-Dec. 14 save $10; ask about promotional rates. AmEx/D/MC/V. Wheelchair-accessible. ❹

Waikiki Beachcomber Hotel, 2300 Kalakaua Ave. (☎800-622-4646; www.waikiki-beachcomber.com). Sandwiched between the International Marketplace and Duke's Lane, the Waikiki Beachcomber Hotel is across the street from the Royal Hawaiian shopping center and Waikiki Beach. Location like this is pricey, but the Beachcomber rewards its guests with an attentive staff and an action-packed entertainment agenda. Hula, ukulele, or *lei*-making lesson $13. The Don Ho, Magic of Polynesia, and Blue

Hawaii shows are also held here. Singles and doubles $220. 3rd person or roll-away bed $25 per day. Check on the internet or call and ask for the value rate, which can go as low as $89, depending on occupancy. AmEx/DC/MC/V. ❺

Waikiki Sand Villa, 2375 Ala Wai Blvd. (☎922-4744; www.waikikisandvillahotel.com). Take Kalakaua Ave. to Kanekapolei St. and turn left. The Waikiki Sand Villa's clean, decent-sized rooms, wrap-around lanais, and 70 ft. pool are almost enough to make guests forget the distance to the ocean. Friendly staff, on-site bar, and rental shop. Free Internet access in lobby, data ports in rooms. Dec. 26-Mar. doubles $110, Apr.-Dec. 25 doubles $99; airport rate $54 (call from the airport; based on availability). AmEx/D/MC/V. 1 wheelchair-accessible room. ❸

Holiday Inn Waikiki, 1830 Ala Moana Blvd. (☎924-5454; www.holiday-inn.com). Turn right onto Ala Moana Blvd. from Kalakaua Ave. You may have seen the artwork in the rooms at 100 other Holiday Inns across America, but there's something comfortable about the standard, familiar rooms in the modern and impeccable chain hotel. Fitness center and pool. Doubles $140. ❹

Leisure Resorts at Honolulu, 431 Nohonani St. (☎923-7336; www.leisureindus-tries.com). Drive down Ala Wai Blvd., and take a left onto Nohonani Pl. These timeshare suites are frequently available to non-members for short stays, and are good options for small groups. Private lanai, full bath, and electric kitchenette with mini oven, stove, mini fridge, microwave, and coffee pot in every suite. Pool, jacuzzi and laundry facilities. 2-day minimum stay. Check-in 4pm. Check-out 11am. Suite (fits 4) $105, one-bedroom suite (fits 6) $125; during holiday season add $10 per room. ❸

Aqua Marina Hotel, 1700 Ala Moana Blvd. (☎942-7722; www.aquaresorts.com/marina). Take Kalakaua Ave. and turn right onto Ala Moana Blvd. A sleek high rise on the Ala Moana end of Waikiki, the Aqua Marina offers beautiful views of the marina through tinted windows on its upper floors. The condo format is convenient but probably won't make up for the distance from Waikiki Beach for the average tourist. Tennis court and swimming pool with sauna and whirlpool (9am-9pm daily). Front desk open Su-Th 7am-11pm and F-Sa 7am-midnight. Studio superior kitchenette $129, deluxe partial ocean $149. Discounts available based on occupancy and availability. AmEx/MC/V. ❹

Waikiki Terrace Hotel, 2045 Kalakaua Ave. (☎955-6000 or 800-367-5004; www.cas-tleresorts.com). On Kalakaua Ave. just after the Kuhio Ave. split. One of the few hotels that can live up to its claims of a view because of its relatively isolated position next to Ft. DeRussy Park. A sunny lobby greets the guests of this busy park-side hotel. Fitness room, pool with jacuzzi. All rooms have private lanais. Double occupancy $160. Kids 18 and under stay free. Significant discounts on the internet. Wheelchair-accessible. ❺

Aston Aloha Surf Hotel, 444 Kanekapolei St. (☎923-0222; www.alohasurfhotel.com). Turn left from Ala Wai Blvd. onto Kanekapolei St. The Aloha Surf is a healthy distance from Waikiki's noisier districts, as well as the beach. Thick carpets, gentle peach tones and a staff with *aloha* break the chain hotel mold. Parking $8 per 24hr. Wireless Internet access $11 per day, with own laptop. Doubles $135, $15 discount Apr.-June and Sept.-Dec. 22. Kids 17 and under stay free. Breakfast included. AmEx/D/MC/V. ❹

Aston Coconut Plaza Hotel, 450 Lewers St. (☎923-8828; http://astonhotels.com). Drive down the Ala Wai Blvd. and make an immediate left up the driveway after Lewers St. The clean Coconut Plaza is a corporate chain hotel on the Ala Wai Canal with afford-able rates, thanks to its distance from the bustle of central Waikiki. Standard rooms have a city view with private lanais, microwave, cable TV, and dataport. Tiny pool, valet parking ($9 per day). Breakfast included. Doubles $100, $10 discount Apr.-June and Sept.-Dec. 22. Studio (fits 3) $120, with mountain view $145; $10 and $15 discounts respectively during above dates. AmEx/D/MC/V. 1 wheelchair-accessible room. ❸

Royal Grove Hotel, 151 Uluniu Ave. (☎923-7691; www.royalgrovehotel.com). 2 blocks up Uluniu from glitzy Kalakaua, on the right before unglitzy Kuhio Ave. Like the vintage furniture and second-hand clothing that thrive within, the Royal Grove combines style and affordability in a great location for those who can resist pretensions. Small pool in courtyard. All rooms have kitchenettes, full bath, cable TV. Maid service twice weekly. Coin laundry. Parking $6. Check-in 2pm. Doubles $60 per night, $370 per week; 1-bedroom suites $75 per night, $450 per week. Weekly rates available Apr.-Nov.; monthly rates available Mar.-Dec. AmEx/D/DC/MC/V. ❸

RESORT HOTELS

Sheraton Waikiki Beach Resort, 2255 Kalakaua Ave. (☎922-4422; www.star-wood.com/hawaii). Turn right onto Royal Hawaiian Ave. from Kalakaua Ave., into the bowels of the avenue-spanning Royal Hawaiian Shopping Center. Make a right and an immediate left for parking, or continue on Royal Hawaiian Ave. to the hotel driveway. 80% of the rooms in the unique architectural layout have fabulous ocean views and 95% have private lanais. Every facility your heart could desire—and wallet can afford—all on the famed sands of Waikiki. 2 pools. 24hr. room service. Yoga, tai chi, aerobics and fitness center. Excellent children's program. 4 restaurants. City view $290, mountain view $360, partial ocean view $410, ocean front $495. ❺

Renaissance Ilikai Waikiki Hotel, 1777 Ala Moana Blvd. (☎949-3811; www.ilikaihotel.com). From the airport, take H-1 East to Nimitz Highway, which turns into Ala Moana Blvd. The Ilikai will be on the right past the Ala Moana Shopping Center. Due to its almost-but-not-quite Waikiki location, on the harbor and a stone's throw away from the tourist-clogged beaches, the recently renovated Ilikai offers competitive prices that make it the best value among upper echelon hotels. Torch-lighting ceremony daily at sunset. Kawika and Friends Hawaiian Hula Show Th-Sa 6-8pm; fireworks F 6-8pm, in the Chinn Ho Tree Courtyard. Canoes Restaurant on premises (open daily 6:30am-11pm; Bow Thai Pasta $20). Rack rates for standard rooms start at $300, but special 45-day advance specials on the internet go for $120. ❺

Outrigger Waikiki Shore Resort, 2161 Kalia Rd. (☎800-367-5004 or 952-4500; www.castleresorts.com). A resort condominium directly on the beach, all rooms have an amazing lanai sunset view of the Pacific and the Ala Wai Yacht Harbor's forest of masts. Unfortunately, there is no pool or recreation area. Full kitchens in all rooms. Studio deluxe ocean view $225. If you've got the money, honey, the 2-bedroom deluxe ocean view (1-6 persons) is one of the most beautiful hotel rooms in Waikiki for $425. ❺

◨ FOOD

Excellent dining options abound in Waikiki, as entrepreneurs rush to meet the demands of the area's many tourists. For those on a budget, stocking up at grocery stores and cooking in hotel kitchenettes provides a relatively inexpensive way to keep oneself fortified and beach-ready.

GROCERY STORES AND MARKETS

Food Pantry, 2370 Kuhio Ave., is relatively inexpensive and has a better selection compared to the ubiquitous ABC stores. Open daily 6am-1am.

Daiei, 801 Kaheka St. (☎973-4800), a cavernous Japanese grocery store stocking exotic Asian foods, is an even better deal for those looking to try out local cuisine. Cross the Ala Wai on Kalakaua Ave., take the 2nd left on Makaloa, and then the 2nd right onto Kaheka St. Open 24hr.

The People's Open Market Program (☎527-5167), in Kapiolani Park at Monsarrat and Paki St. Overseen by the City and County of Honolulu, the market sells fresh produce from local farmers and fishermen, and exotic ethnic ingredients not found commonly in retail stores. Open Wed. 10-11am.

THE FIRST TIME

Waiting for the van to the beach, others voiced our common ear: "I just know I'm going to be he only one who's not going to be able to stand up." The friendly beach boy instructors milled around, relaxed. "You'll do great! It's just for fun." I consoled myself by thinking that even if I was a horrible surfer, I would at least get some sun on my white legs.

When we arrived at the beach, we spent 15min. practicing on dry and how we would get up on our boards when we were actually out in the water. Everyone was so nervous that no one could do anything right. Calls for simple moves he instructors had shown us not 30 seconds before were met with blank stares. "Right turn?" Which foot goes back when I stand up?" "Where do I put my hands?" The instructors shook their heads. "It'll come to you in the water."

No one told me it was going to be so difficult just to get to the break. As the instructor pulled another girl and me out by pressing his toes on our boards, he encouraged us to "paddle! Paddle! Paddle!" The girl groaned "I don't think I'm going to have any energy left for the actual surfing."

When we got out to the break, he instructors lined us up facing he shore. I was chosen to be in he first group to catch a wave. As we waited for a set, my instructor old me helpful things to remember. I prayed that I wouldn't embarrass myself.

RESTAURANTS

■ **Cha Cha Cha,** 342 Seaside Ave. (☎923-7797). Turn left down Seaside Ave. from Kalakaua Ave. and look for the Tiki torches on the left. Culinary thrill seekers rejoice at the 2 Happy Hours (4-6pm and 9-11pm; lime margaritas $2.50) and the variety of hot sauces including the *Cholula, Jump up and Kiss Me,* and *Wrong Number Chipotle Habanero Sauce.* Ay yay yay. Authentic Caribbean-Mexican cuisine (grilled Jamaican jerk chicken $12, mahi mahi fish tacos $9.75). Show a copy of *Let's Go: Hawaii* for a free basket of chips and salsa. Open daily 11:30am-11pm. ❷

■ **Pyramids,** 758 Kapahulu Ave. (☎737-2900). Take Our Neighborhood Trolley from Waikiki to the Date St./Kapahulu Ave. stop and walk toward the mountains on Kapahulu. Authentic right down to its bazaar-inspired lanterns and dazzling live belly dancer, Pyramids offers high-quality Egyptian food in an exotic environment. Huge bowl of *hummus* $6. *Shwarma* with beef, lamb, chicken and rice $16. Belly dancer performs M-Sa 7:30 and 8:30pm, Su 7 and 8pm. Reservations recommended for dinner F-Su. Open M-Sa 11am-2pm and 5:30-10pm, Su 5-9pm. ❸

Arancino, 255 Beachwalk (☎923-5557), down Beachwalk from Kalakaua Ave., next to the ABC convenience store. Romantic (read: close) seating and traditional Italian music create an intimate atmosphere inside; the lines outside attest to the quality of the flavorful food. *Fettuccine alla Crema* with asparagus and ham $10. Pizzas $9-15. Reservations taken 5-6:30pm. Open daily 11:30am-2:30pm and 5-10pm. ❸

Rainbow Drive-In, 3308 Kanaina Ave. (☎737-0177). The Rainbow's walk-up window is the gateway to one of Hawaii's tastiest local dishes, plate lunch ($4-6). The meal is a favorite among locals who jam the parking lot, waiting patiently. (See **Got Poi,** p. 40) Try the Mix Plate ($6), with steak, mahi mahi, and chicken. Open daily 7:30am-9pm. ❶

Yasoba, 255 Beachwalk (☎926-5303), next to Arancino. Don't be alarmed when the entire staff turns and addresses you with *"irasshai"* (welcome), as you enter their authentic-as-*sake* ($6-10) Japanese restaurant. The *Tenmori Gozen* ($15) features both of the restaurant's specialties, assorted tempura and handmade soba noodles, as well as rice and dessert. Open daily 11:30am-2:30pm and 5:30-9:30pm. ❸

Keo's, 2028 Kuhio Ave. (☎951-9355). Go west on Kuhio Ave. and take a right before the Kalakaua Ave. junction on Kuamoo St. Amazing Thai and island cuisine served in an oasis of orchids. Panang Curry $12-15 with chicken, shrimp or seafood. Mango sorbet $6. Open daily 7am-2pm and 5-

10:30pm. Sister restaurant **Keoni's,** 2375 Kuhio Ave. (922-9888) serves American and Thai cuisine in a similarly tropical atmosphere. ❸

Shore Bird Beach Broiler, 2169 Kalia Rd. (☎922-2887), in the Outrigger Reef Hotel at the end of Beachwalk. Elevating beach BBQ to unprecedented heights, the Shore Bird sets up their huge grills and provides a 10 oz. *Kalua* Pork Chop ($15), Pulehu Pork Ribs with guava BBQ sauce ($16), or some other hunk of meat to cook yourself. Prices include an all-you-can-eat salad bar. The Shore Bird is all-inclusive, with an on-site beach bar, live Hawaiian entertainment 4pm-midnight, and stunning views of Diamond Head and the Waikiki sunset just over the top of your tropical drink umbrella. Lunch/lanai menu served 11am-1am, dinner served 4:30-10pm. Open M-F 7am-2am. ❸

Chuck's Cellar, 150 Kaiulani Ave. (☎923-4488), in the Ohana East hotel. Chuck's packs them in with live dinner music nightly from 7-10pm, an Early Bird special from 5:30-6:30pm ($10, includes all-you-can-eat soup and salad bar) and a prime rib and lobster dinner for $34. Mai Tai drink specials $4. Open nightly 5:30-10pm. ❹

Marie's Health Foods, 2155 Kalakaua Ave., (☎926-3900). Entrance on Beachwalk, behind the Planet Hollywood. The health-conscious patrons of Marie's can enjoy inexpensive, pesticide-free veggies under outdoor tables shaded by umbrellas and fragrant plumeria trees. Organic baby spinach salad $3-5, with chicken $7. Wraps $3. Smoothies $4. Marie's also sells vitamins, food supplements, and natural skin care products. Open M-Sa 11am-8pm. ❶

Ray's Famous Pizza, 2260 Kuhio Ave. (☎922-9221). Like the Tahitians, the Mormons, and the Japanese, Ray visited Oahu, fell in love with it, and decided to stay, bringing his successful New York-style pizza with him. All pizzas are made to order with fresh toppings. Lunch special $6. Thin crust pizzas $8-21. Sicilian-style pies $21-28. Su-Th 1 extra-large pizza and 25 wings $30. Free delivery and take-out. Open Su-Th 11am-11pm, F-Sa 11am-midnight. ❷

Top of Waikiki, 2250 Kalakaua Ave. (☎923-3877), on the 21st fl. of the Waikiki Business Plaza Building, in the flying-saucer-esque restaurant at the top. Boasting a 360° view of Waikiki, upscale food (Maine lobster $39; Hawaiian style mahi mahi $20), and a romantic atmosphere, the Top of Waikiki is a favorite among tourists. It's best to come during the Sunset Special (5-6pm, steak and lobster $20), when you can see the sun setting over the city. Reservations recommended on F-Su. Open daily 5-9:30pm. ❺

The Patisserie, 2168 Kalia Rd. (☎922-4974). Take Kalakaua Ave. to Beachwalk; the Patisserie is on the Ohana Edgewater Hotel premises. This unassuming lit-

As the wave came in, my instructor again yelled "Paddle! Paddle! Paddle!" I pulled with all my strength and as the wave reached me, my instructor gave me one big push and I felt the wave take over. Behind me I heard "Stand up! Stand up!" The wave felt powerful and solid underneath me, and I mindlessly pulled myself up. I was so surprised to be standing that I fell over almost immediately. "Good job! Next time stay lower!" I heard from behind me. I paddled back as fast as I could so that I could catch another wave, my fatigue forgotten.

As the lesson wore on, we progressed quickly. We all caught at least a couple waves and became reasonably comfortable in our stances. Toward the end my instructor even showed me how to turn left and right. I paddled in exhausted but happy. I'd done better than I could have possibly hoped and I felt initiated into the surf culture of Waikiki Beach. I began to understand the surfer's passion for the sport and the rush of riding the power of a wave. I felt like I'd accomplished something during that lesson that I could be able to remember for the rest of my life. And to top it off, I had gotten some sun on the backs of my legs. So much sun that I couldn't sit down for three days.

-Anna Bryne, 2003

tle shop has been serving fresh-baked breads, cakes and pastries for over 30 yr. Try a tasty sandwich ($2.50-7) or a smoothie ($3.50). Great for a Waikiki Beach birthday or other celebration, cakes ($10-14) must be ordered by 3pm the day before they are to be picked up. Open daily 6:30am-8:30pm. ❶

Ruffage Natural Foods, 2443 Kuhio Ave. (☎922-2042). This tiny hole-in-the-wall is half sandwich shop and half health-products store. Interesting clientele, from severely sun-burned tourists desperately looking for a cure for their folly to healthy-looking joggers dropping by for a protein shake after a run. The vegan burrito ($7) is a favorite. Try the (dolphin-friendly) tuna and avocado sandwich ($6). Open 9am-7pm. ❶

Teddy's Bigger Burgers, 3114 Monsarrat Ave. (☎735-9411), a ½ mi. stroll toward Diamond Head from Kapiolani Park on Monsarrat Ave. Take bus #13 or 22. The 100% chuck burgers ($4-6) are so juicy that Teddy's considerately provides moist towelettes with your meal. Cheese 40¢, pineapple or avocado 80¢ extra. Guests who tackle the Colossal Combo, with a Biggest burger, a heaping load of fries, and a large soda ($8), abandon all aspirations of surmounting Diamond Head afterward. The heart-stoppingly good peanut butter shakes ($3.75) are a favorite. Open daily 10:30am-9pm. ❶

Cheeseburger in Paradise, 2500 Kalakaua Ave. (☎923-3731), on the corner of Kalakaua Ave. and Kealohilani Ave. Loveable for its unabashed kitschy-ness, the restaurant is a tourist trap with worthwhile bait: a laid-back beach burger and view of the strip. Heaping basket of famous seasoned french fries $3.75. The namesake Cheeseburger in Paradise ($7.50) comes in beef or garden burger varieties. Live acoustic rock and Hawaiian music 4-11pm. Open daily 7am-11pm. ❶

Todai, 1910 Ala Moana Blvd. (☎947-1000). Turn onto Ala Moana Blvd. from Kalakaua Ave. Todai is at the end of the block on the right before Ena Rd., at Canterbury place. To park, turn right on Ena Rd; the garage is directly behind the building. Waikiki's installment of the all-you-can-eat Japanese seafood chain, shiny Todai offers 5 different buffet bars (sushi, seafood, hot food, salad and dessert) for the indecisive eater. Crab legs and over 40 different kinds of sushi available at lunch and dinner, lobster dinner only. M-F lunch $15, dinner $26; Sa-Su $16, $28. Under 11 ½ price. Open M-F 11:30am-2:30pm and 5:30-9:30pm, Sa-Su 10:30am-2:30pm and 5-10pm. ❺

🌊 BEACHES

Waikiki Beach is the general name that refers to any and all of the beaches on the south shore of Oahu. It begins on the Waikiki side of the Hilton Lagoon in the west, continues along the coastline of Waikiki's premier beach hotels, and stretches all the way to the fringes of Diamond Head Crater. Although the beach reaches moments of absolute saturation on busy weekends, the perpetual daytime crowds on Waikiki Beach can be enlivening—the throng of visitors excites a contagious stir and tangible buzz of enthusiasm. During the day, the Waikiki beaches are awash in aquatic activities as surfers paddle between catamarans, canoes paddle around snorkelers, and swimmers jostle into each other. Quieter, romantic moments occur on the bookends of the frenetic day, at dawn and sunset when the crowds have dispersed and calmed, and the plumeria breeze soothes burned skin.

DUKE KAHANAMOKU BEACH PARK. Duke Kahanamoku is the westernmost Waikiki beach, at the edge of the Hilton Lagoon. It houses several canoes that spend their days plying the waves, and experienced surfers can be seen in the distance, surfing the breaks out from the beach. On the fringes of the action, Duke Kahanamoku Beach is usually subdued and relatively quiet, making it a good place to escape the

BEACH SERVICES. Lifeguards are asked to watch over huge numbers of beachgoers; caution and common sense go a long way to ensure safety in the water. Never swim alone, always check with the lifeguard before entering unfamiliar water, and never dive into breaking surf. For those in need of wheelchairs, **Landeez All-Terrain Wheelchairs** (☎522-7034) can surmount the sturdiest of sand castles and are available free of charge from the Department of Parks and Recreation at Sans Souci Beach Park, 2863 Kalakaua Ave. (☎921-0110; open daily 9am-4pm) and Fort DeRussy Beach, off Kalia Rd. (☎949-8952).

multitudes farther down. *(There is limited free parking for the beach near the Hilton Lagoon; take Ala Moana Blvd. west to Hobron Lane and turn left after the Renaissance Ilikai Hotel. At the stop sign, turn left and follow the road past the yacht harbor to the lot on the left.)*

FORT DERUSSY BEACH PARK. Adjacent to Duke Kahanamoku Beach, in front of the Hale Koa military hotel and Fort DeRussy, is Fort DeRussy Beach Park. A wide stretch of sand littered with shells and coral near the shore, Fort DeRussy Beach is less than ideal for wading and swimming, but the neighboring park has shaded lawns for those fleeing the sun.

GRAY'S BEACH. East of the US Army Museum, stretching from the Outrigger Waikiki Shore to the jetty in front of the pink Sheraton Royal Hawaiian, is an area known as Gray's Beach, named after an inn that hosted some of Waikiki's earliest tourists. There's good surfing a long paddle out from the shore, and big daytime crowds begin there.

WAIKIKI BEACH. Tourists happily cram themselves together on the resort beachfront in between the two Sheraton Hotels, the Royal Hawaiian and the Moana Surfrider. This stretch of sand, at the Waikiki Beach Center, is often called **Royal Moana Beach,** or simply Waikiki Beach, and it sees almost as many tourists cavorting in its waters as lounging on its soft shores. Swimmers, surfers, catamarans, canoes, and all manner of pushed, pulled and wind-propelled potential water hazards dot the gently rolling Pacific all the way out to the surfers on the breakers.

Commemorative efforts in honor of Duke Kahanamoku continue at the section of beach between the Sheraton Moana and Kuhio Beach's two seawall-enclosed swimming pools on Kalakaua Ave. The towering **Duke Kahanamoku Statue** of the Hawaiian hero *cum* sheriff, Olympic champion, surfing popularizer, movie star and Ambassador of *Aloha* resides here, next door to the Honolulu Police's Waikiki Substation in the **Duke Paoa Kahanamoku Building.** The frequently *lei*-adorned, bronze Duke faces away from the Pacific, his board between him and the water as a tourist might pose for a picture on the beach. The position is considered improbable by many surfers and locals who adore his legacy.

Also nearby are the monuments to four ancient Tahitian soothsayers who visited Oahu and proved themselves to be healers and possessors of wisdom. The boulders—known as the **Wizard Stones**—were recently elevated to pop Hawaiian religious consciousness with their unearthing and by their current conspicuous replacement atop the sand. According to myth, the stones were to be a tangible reminder of the ministrations made and the suffering eased by the soothsayers. Kapaemahu, the leader, had his stone eponymously named, transferring his powers to it via incantations and the sacrifice of a lovely island chieftess. The beautifully landscaped strip between the beach and Kalakaua stretches from the Banyan tree by the police station east all the way to Kapahulu, and makes for a romantic sunset stroll when the Tiki torches are lit.

BABY QUEEN'S AND CANOES SURF BREAKS. A 50- to 100-yard paddle out from the next stretch of beach, between the Sheraton Moana and Kuhio Beach's two seawall-enclosed swimming pools, is a surf break favored by some locals as the safest spot to learn to surf. The area, known as Baby Queen's, is less dangerous and crowded than many of the sites favored by professional instructors. Just to the right of that area is another surf break called Canoes, which is often trafficked by outrigger canoes and novice surfers. Always consult the lifeguard.

KUHIO BEACH. Kuhio Beach extends beyond the recently-improved Kapahulu Pier (formerly known as Kapahulu Wall). Additions to the Kuhio Beach Park area in recent years have spruced up Waikiki. From the overlooking pier, beachgoers watch the surfers and body boarders tempt fate in waters that often conceal shallow coral. Swimming within the deep pools formed by the seawalls west of the pier is enjoyable, but inexperienced and unfamiliar boarders should not test the waves on the other side (to the right of the Kapahulu Pier), lest they be caught between the strong current and the slippery rock wall. **Queen's Surf Beach** is beyond the wall and across Kalakaua Ave. from Kapiolani Park. It is extremely popular with body boarders.

SANS SOUCI BEACH. Beyond the Waikiki Aquarium (p. 131), on the beach, is the **Natatorium,** a WWI monument and former Olympic training pool. The Natatorium perpetually awaits further renovation before reopening, despite a recent phase of refurbishment to improve its appearance. It does house the nicest public bathrooms on Waikiki's beaches. Next to the Natatorium is Sans Souci Beach, an adjacent grassy area toward the park. It's a favorite spot among local families for its proximity to beach and park recreation, and for its distance from the more urban part of Waikiki. Locals tell different stories about why Sans Souci beach is so named. Many link it to a no-longer extant hotel that occupied the site where the Kaimana Beach Hotel currently resides. Others say it is because of the high proportion of beauties and studs who flock to its sands to flaunt their looks. Regardless, Sans Souci affords a view of the Waikiki sunset at a distance from the cluster of hotels. Beyond Sans Souci is the **Outrigger Canoe Club Beach,** on the edge of Waikiki, which extends all the way to the beaches at Diamond Head's feet.

DIAMOND HEAD BEACH. Populated primarily by surfers and windsurfers, Diamond Head Beach is a narrow strip of sand below the highway. Most visitors come for the waves, not the sun, and few are beginners. This beach is better for experienced boarders and enthusiasts than for families, since the surf can be dangerous at times and there are better vistas at other beaches. (By car, take Kalakaua Ave. from Waikiki to Diamond Head Rd. Park just past the lighthouse and walk down to the beach on the trail beyond the lot. By bus, take the #14 from Waikiki, which stops near the lighthouse. Or, from the Diamond Head park entrance (see below), turn right as you exit and take Diamond Head Road all the way around the crater to the beach.)

◎ SIGHTS

▨ **DIAMOND HEAD.** The 350-acre Diamond Head crater was created about 300,000 years ago during a single, brief eruption that spewed ash and fine particles into the air. These particles eventually cemented together into a rock called **tuff;** geologists consider Diamond Head one of the world's best examples of a tuff cone.

Nicknamed *Le'ahi*, Diamond Head's 760 ft. summit resembles the *lae* (forehead) of the *'ahi* (tuna) when viewed from the west. The word can also be translated as "fire headland," referring to navigational fires built to guide canoes traveling along the shoreline. **Diamond Head Light** replaced the fires in 1917. The site finally earned the name "Diamond Head" when explorers from the West mistook calcite crystals in the rocks on the slope for diamonds in the late 1700s.

In 1904, Diamond Head was purchased by the federal government for defense purposes, due to the vast expanse of terrain visible from the top. The military built a fire control station at the summit in 1908, to aim mortar fire by triangulating from batteries at Fort DeRussy in Waikiki and Fort Ruger on the outer slopes of the crater. In 1915, long-range guns were installed, though they have never been fired.

At the park entrance, you'll find picnic tables, restrooms, a pay phone, and drinking water. The 30min. hike to the 560 ft. summit is relatively easy, but strenuous enough to give hikers of all ages a feeling of accomplishment once they've reached the top. Toward the end of the trail, after a set of 74 concrete steps, there is a dark, 225 ft. tunnel that is difficult to navigate without a **flashlight**, and may not be appealing for the claustrophobic. After the tunnel and another set of 99 steps, there is an equally poorly-lit spiral staircase, but the journey soon becomes worthwhile—the view at the top is simply spectacular. *(By bus, take the #22 or #58 from Waikiki (15min., every 30min.). It will let you off across from the entrance road, which leads through a tunnel to the park entrance. Be sure to walk against traffic in the tunnel— there is no sidewalk. By car from Waikiki, take Monsarrat Ave. to Diamond Head Rd. The park comes up quickly on the right and has an easy-to-spot sign. Open 6am-6pm. Last hike 4:30pm. Entrance fee single person $1, private vehicle $5.)*

WAIKIKI AQUARIUM. The aquarium specializes in coral reef exhibits and houses an impressive array of tropical fish, reef sharks and endangered Hawaiian monk seals. Though small, the aquarium does an extremely good job at showcasing over 2500 animals from Hawaii and the tropical Pacific. Hordes of schoolchildren mob the place on weekdays, contending with the aquatic wildlife for communication in high-pitched frequencies. *(2777 Kalakaua Ave. ☎923-9741. #2 bus stops directly out front every 10min. Limited free parking on the Aquarium side of Kalakaua Ave. Open daily 9am-5pm. $7; students, seniors and military $5; ages 13-17 $3.50; 12 and under free. Audio guide included with admission.)*

HONOLULU ZOO. Lions and tigers and bears: the Honolulu zoo has them all, as the focus of its exhibits is the African Savannah section. Chimps, giraffes, elephants, and cheetahs abound, but there is a surprising lack of focus on species indigenous to the Pacific islands. The zoo offers rotating daily talks by zookeepers about different animals. The Children's Zoo allows children to get up close and personal with the zoo's llamas, sheep, goats and cows. Family programs offer a more in-depth exploration of the zoo's exhibits, via Moonlight Tours and camping programs, among others. *($8-35 per person; visit the web site or call for info.)* One especially interesting program is Zoorotica, where adults can go at night and learn about the mating habits of different animals while munching on chocolate and sipping champagne. *(151 Kapahulu Ave., on the corner of Kapahulu and Kalakaua Ave. ☎971-7171; www.honzoosoc.org. Parking lot entrance on Kapahulu Ave., $0.25 per hr. Zoo open daily 9am-4:30pm except Christmas and New Year's Day. $6, ages 6-12 $1, under 5 free. Family Pass $25. Zoorotica $55 per couple.)*

ST. AUGUSTINE CHURCH. Staffed by the Congregation of the Sacred Hearts of Jesus and Mary, St. Augustine's beautiful interior is a Waikiki rarity worth seeing. The Father Damien Museum, behind St. Augustine Church, tells the story of a man who devoted the last 16 yr. of his life to the lepers on the island of Molokai. *(130 Ohua Ave., at Kalakaua and Ohua Ave. Church ☎923-7024. Museum ☎923-2690. Museum open M-F 9am-3pm.)*

🎵 ENTERTAINMENT

HULA SHOWS. In Waikiki, watching beautiful island girls shake their hips and surf-chiseled local men flex and posture is not only completely civilized, it's also free. The **Kuhio Beach Torch Lighting and Hula Show** has Hawaiian music and performance at the Kuhio Beach Hula Mound, near the Duke Kahanamoku statue at

Uluniu and Kalakaua Ave. (☎843-8002. *Hula show nightly 6:30-7:30pm. Waikiki style show with hula lesson M-Th. Hawaiian music and hula pageant by celebrated* halau *(hula troupes) F-Su. Free.*) Formerly the Kodak Hula Show, the **Pleasant Hawaiian Hula Show** has been continually enticing tourists with the sounds and sights of traditional Hawaiian music and dance performances since 1937. (*Blaisdell Center in Kapiolani Park. Tu-Th 10-11am. Free.*) Several **hotels** also offer free hula performances, many of which are open to guests and non-guests alike; earlier arrival ensures better viewing and more time to get another Mai Tai at the bar. The Hilton Hawaiian Village's popular hula show, near their **Tapa Bar,** occurs every Friday and is highlighted with a fireworks display visible from nearby beaches and roofs. (☎949-4321. *M-F 8-11pm.*) The Halekulani's **House Without a Key** restaurant has live Hawaiian music starting nightly at 5pm with a hula dancer. (☎923-2311. *Hula nightly 5:30-8pm*) The Renaissance Ilikai Waikiki's **Paddles Bar** is the place to go for a traditional sunset conch-blowing and torch-lighting ceremony. (☎949-3811. *Th-Sa 6-8pm.*) Farther from the beach the **Sheraton Princess Kaiulani Hotel** hosts pool-side entertainment nightly. (☎922-5811. *6:15-9:30pm.*) For the most up-to-date information on the free events held in Waikiki, check www.co.honolulu.hi.us/events.

FREE OUTDOOR FILMS. On weekends, The Kuhio Beach Torch Lighting and Hula Show (see **Hula Shows,** p. 131) is followed by **Sunset on the Beach.** The Honolulu Mayor's Office sets up a tall movie screen on the beach for a double feature of recent or classic family films. (☎523-2489. *Kuhio Beach Park. Sa-Su at sunset.*) Before the show, a wide variety of area restaurants set up portable booths just east of the Kapahulu Pier to sell mouth-watering (and not surprisingly, overpriced) concessions to the first-come, first-seated beach blanket crowd. (*Sa-Su 4-9pm.*)

BLAISDELL CENTER AND WAIKIKI SHELL. The Waikiki Shell in Kapiolani Park hosts concerts throughout the year. The **Kapiolani Bandstand,** next to the Waikiki Shell, hosts weekly concerts of mainly jazz and rock, alternated with Hawaiian music every week. (*F 5:30-6:30pm. Free.*) Full Moon Concerts are also held at the bandstand around 6pm on the evening of the full moon each month. (*Call* ☎523-CITY *for information. At sunset, around 6pm. Free.*) The Royal Hawaiian Band also performs at the Kapiolani Bandstand weekly. (*Su 2-3pm*) The Blaisdell Center hosts the Pleasant Hawaiian Hula Show (see **Hula Shows,** p. 131) as well as concerts and events. (*Blaisdell Center, 77 Ward Ave., between King St. and Kapiolani Blvd. King St. gate open M-Sa 5:30am-6pm, Su and holiday hours determined by events. Show information line and Box Office* ☎591-2211; *open M-Sa 9am-5pm. Waikiki Shell, 2805 Monsarrat Ave., at the Diamond Head end of Waikiki. Call Blaisdell Center or see visitor section of www.co.honolulu.hi.us for more information. Free.*)

▣ SHOPPING

Shopping in Waikiki has a dual nature, including in its scope 4-for-$1 Hawaiiana and knick-knacks in the International Market as well as chic, top-of-the-line designer items in the Royal Hawaiian Shopping Center or the proliferation of shops that populate the ground floors of Waikiki's myriad hotels.

THE INTERNATIONAL MARKET PLACE. The market is a maze of kiosk-like stands that hock the summer vacation trends you'll find in every kitschy tourist district around the world. It's also a prime place to get cheap *aloha* wear and Hawaiian souvenirs like carvings, macadamia nut *leis, puka* body ornaments, and jade Buddha statues and jewelry. There's even an Internet access booth. Prices are not set and bargaining is recommended. Remember to shop around—many booths sell the same things, so there is always the possibility of a better bargain elsewhere. (*At Kalakaua Ave. and Duke's Ln. Open daily.*)

THE MEANING OF ALOHA Tourism is the lifeblood of the Hawaiian economy, and the impact of this is varied and striking. Some friendly locals who would otherwise never miss the chance to offer *aloha* might raise an eyebrow and give the *stink eye* to the mere mention of Waikiki. However, anyone who gets beyond a service, transactional relationship with the many locals living, working, and playing in Waikiki can attest to the ready warmth and familiarity of local demeanor. Many locals earn their livelihoods in industries that contradict their Hawaiian cultural inheritance. If *aloha* is the "universal spirit of free hospitality and love," tourism is the practice of buying and selling hospitality. The commercialization of *aloha* brings with it a cultural ambiguity that robs it of its meaning. Many tourists in Waikiki understand *aloha* as little more than "a Hawaiian greeting," or worse, "good service."

When locals do extend *aloha*, the proper response is to do likewise, but that does not make *aloha* merely a social greeting. Waikiki brags about its world-class shopping, its world-famous beaches, its world-record tourist revenue, but what sets the tourist capital of Paradise apart from Cancun or Disneyland is that the *aloha* spirit dwells in commercial Waikiki as well. It is a central part of the attraction for millions of tourists, but real *aloha* cannot be bought or sold in Waikiki. It comes freely from locals genuinely happy to have you as a guest on their island. Waikiki has the most guests of the islands and, if you've noticed, the most accommodations, restaurants, bars, tours, buses, trolleys, ABC convenience stores, and shave ice stands. *Aloha* thrives not on the number of occasions for hospitality, but on the attitude of everyone—tourists and locals—involved. The spirit of *aloha* can transform the tenor of a local/tourist interaction. The *aloha* spirit makes Hawaii more than a tourist destination—it is a paradise.

ROYAL HAWAIIAN SHOPPING CENTER. The Royal Hawaiian presides over three buildings along Royal Hawaiian Ave., holding court with the nobility of the fashion world, including names like Armani, Cartier, and Chanel. Its East Asian-inspired interior is interesting if only for the impressive display of wealth it houses. *(On Royal Hawaiian Ave. Visitor Center on the first floor. Shopping Center open daily 11am-10pm.)*

KALAKAUA AVENUE. The avenue hosts many of the same glitzy, high-end offerings of the Royal Hawaiian shopping center, only with more crowds. At the crux of the avenue and the Royal Hawaiian is the **DFS Galleria,** a behemoth mall *cum* Duty Free Shop, which puts on free Hawaiian entertainment and features a 65,000 gallon walk-through aquarium. *(☎931-2655; www.dfsgalleria.com. On the corner of Kalakaua and Royal Hawaiian Avenues. Free hula show W, F 7pm. Open daily 11am-11pm.)* Twin towers scrape the sky over the little resort-spawned mall in the **Hyatt.** Check out the super-cool and popular Wyland Galleries, as well as the usual suspects, Gucci et al. *(Most Kalakaua Ave. stores open daily 10am-10pm.)*

■ NIGHTLIFE

CLUBS

The Maze, 2255 Kuhio Ave. (☎921-5800), on the second floor of the Waikiki Trade Center. Get lost in this cavernous dance club's 3 rooms: the audio-excellent Maze Arena, spinning house, hard house, and trance; bumping Red Room dropping hip-hop and crowd-pleasing Top 40; and Paradox Lounge with live instrumental, funk, disco, and house. Dress "absolutely fabulous," especially on bumping Friday nights. Cover M-Th $5, under 21 $10; F-Su $10, under 21 $15. 18+. On weekends, guys should wear pants and a nice shirt, no hats or slippers. Open nightly 10pm-4am. MC/V.

Diamond Head Grill, 2885 Kalakaua Ave. (☎922-3734), in the W Honolulu Hotel. The poshest place in town to see and be seen, the Diamond Head Grill offers 2 rooms—1 dance, 1 hip-hop—for the socially suave of Honolulu. Club open F and Sa nights only, though F is by far the most popular night to go. Domestic beer $4, mixed drinks $5.50. Dress to impress. No slippers, hats or tank tops (for men). Cover $10, $20 on special event nights. Open F-Sa 9pm-2am.

Zanzabar, 2255 Kuhio Ave. (☎924-3939), on the first floor of the Waikiki Trade Center. Rich and sultry Zanzabar hosts a hotter-than-thou local set *en masse* on F and Sa. Free salsa lessons Tu 8-9pm. Live DJs nightly. 18+ Su, Tu, Th; 21+ W, F-Sa $10 cover. No T-shirts, sandals or hats. Open Tu 8pm-4am, W-Su 9pm-4am. AmEx/D/MC/V.

Hula's, 134 Kapahulu Ave. (☎923-0669), on the 2nd fl. of the Waikiki Grand Hotel. The most legendary gay bar in Waikiki, the crowds start gathering to watch the sun set over the beach and stay for the fun, social atmosphere. Sophisticated dark interior with creative black lighting, pool table open-air views of the beach. F free pupus 3-9pm. F-Sa GoGo Boyz start performing at 10:30pm. Free Internet. $5 cover on promotional nights starting at 9pm. Open 10am-2am.

Wave Waikiki, 1877 Kalakaua Ave. (☎941-0424; http://wavewaikiki.com), on the right of Kalakaua Ave. from the Ala Wai Canal, before Ena Rd. Wave is Waikiki in microcosm—some consider it the most happening night spot around, others equate it with the worst of MTV's Spring Break. Tourist hordes and locals alike dance to hip-hop (Su-Th), or live DJs and bands (F-Sa). Happy Hour 9-10pm ($2.75 wells and domestics), but the action doesn't really get started until after midnight. Cover $5-7 after 10pm, $10-15 on promotional nights. Open nightly 9pm-4am.

Fusion Waikiki, 2260 Kuhio Ave. 2nd fl., across from the Waikiki Trade Plaza. Known best for its after-hours action, live DJs spinning house and hip-hop keep the dance floor of this gay bar throbbing, Su-Th starting at 9pm and F-Sa from midnight on. Female impersonator show (F at 11pm, cover $5). All-male strip show on Sa (11pm, cover $5; if you're feeling ballsy, contact Pat a night in advance for an audition). New pool table. Fusion opens up for the 18+ crowd on the 4th Su of the month for Hotsport, which includes a drag review. Beer $3.50. 21+. Open Su-Th 10pm-4am, F-Sa 8pm-4am.

Scruples, 2310 Kuhio Ave. A popular 18+ club in Honolulu, Scruples attracts all types of crowds. Plays hip-hop, oldies and top 40s. The scantily clad waitresses would probably do well in the Th night Bikini contest. Open daily 8pm-4am.

BARS

Duke's Canoe Club, 2355 Kalakaua Ave. (☎922-2268), inside the Outrigger Waikiki, on the beach. Parking at the hotel $2 per hr., or validate parking at the Ohana East Hotel on Kuhio Ave. A Waikiki institution, Duke's is a casual bar that mixes drinks with live contemporary Hawaiian music (F-Su 4-6pm nightly 10pm-midnight, on the lower lanai). Beachside seating is perfect for that sunset Mai Tai ($5). Duke's is also a thriving restaurant. Lunch buffet $10.50. Open daily 7am-midnight, bar open until 1am.

Moose McGillycuddy's Pub and Cafe, 310 Lewers St. (☎923-0751; www.moosewaikiki.com). Moose's serves 3 meals to slow the inebriation of the crowds that come for the ever-changing theme nights, listed on the web site. One staple is the bikini contest, webcast every Su. For those who want to start drinking early, Early Happy Hour stretches from 10am-4pm (Mai Tais $1.50). Restaurant downstairs, 21+ in the bar upstairs. No Cover. Open daily 7:30am-4am, food served until 10pm.

Kelley O'Neil's, 311 Lewers St. (☎926-1777), across from Moose's. A laid-back Irish bar where locals and tourists enjoy pints and live music in a comfortable atmosphere. Happy Hour 11am-8pm, domestic beer $3-4. Live music nightly 9pm-1am, Su Irish music 4-7:30pm, F-Sa additional live band 1:30-3:30am. Kitchen serves sandwiches ($4-7) and classics like corned beef and cabbage ($7.25). Open daily 11am-11pm.

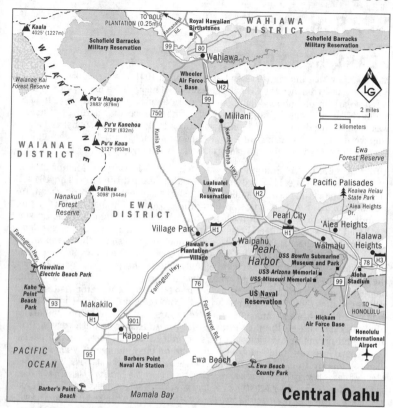

O A H U

Central Oahu

Nashville Waikiki, 2330 Kuhio Ave. (☎926-7911). Basement of the Waikiki West Hotel, on Kuhio Ave. between Walina and Nahua St. The Nashville Waikiki considers itself an authentic Texas-style bar—as authentic as one can get several thousand miles from the real deal. Line dancing and "real" cowboys complete the theme. Line dancing lessons M 7:30-10pm. Happy Hour daily 4-8pm. Open daily 4pm-4am. Wheelchair-accessible.

The Red Lion, 240 Lewers St. (☎922-1027), in the Ohana Waikiki Village basement. Mai Tais and well drinks ($1.50) during Happy Hour—and by "hour" they mean "day"— noon-9pm. Everyone, from angry sailors to Japanese tourists to broke college students, comes through the doors and ends up at the pool tables. Write your name on a Washington and they'll stick it to the ceiling forever and ever. Low ceilings and big crowds on promotional nights (M, W) lead to cramped, hot conditions, but you won't find a cheaper drink on the island. Cover $5 M, W, and F-Sa after 9pm. Open daily noon-4am.

Snappers, 1778 Ala Moana Blvd., Unit LL (☎947-3776). Snappers is a little bit of everything, with a pubby dark wood bar, lounge, pool room, and dance floor. 33 brews on tap, food served all day (fish and chips $7). Happy Hour 7am-7pm (domestic beer $2.50, margaritas $4). Live music F-Su 9pm-1am. 21+ after 9pm. Open daily 7am-2am, food served until 1:30am.

NEAR HONOLULU

PEARL HARBOR

At 7:55am on that infamous December morning in 1941, a wave of 350 Japanese fighter planes wrenched the US out of its steadfast neutrality and into the thick of WWII. Pearl Harbor, about 40min. outside of Honolulu, held the whole of the US Pacific Fleet, and was the target of Japan's swift surprise attack. The destruction was devastating; during the 2hr. onslaught, over 2400 military personnel and civilians were killed, 188 planes were demolished, and eight battleships were either damaged or destroyed. For more information, see **History,** p. 11.

ARIZONA MEMORIAL. Solemn and graceful, the *USS Arizona* Memorial is a fitting tribute to the 1177 crewmen who died aboard the ship. The 184 ft. memorial spans the partially sunken battleship's midsection, affording visitors a close, poignant view of the ship that still entombs 1100 men. Plans for the memorial began in 1943, but it wasn't until 1958 that President Eisenhower approved its creation. Alfred Preis designed the final structure, and it was dedicated in 1962. The structure features a unique concave shape that symbolizes America's great tragedy and the country's subsequent rise above it. There are three main sections: an entry room; a central area where visitors can observe the ship; and the shrine room, which has a marble wall engraved with the names of those who died on the *Arizona*. Sixty-four years later visitors can still see spots of oil that continue to leak from the ship. The on-shore **Visitor Center** has a historical museum and leads tours that include a documentary film and boat ride to the memorial itself. The tour is free, but every visitor must pick up his or her ticket in person on a first-come, first-served basis. Come early, as wait times can reach 2hr. and on busy summer days most tickets are gone by 1pm. (*From Honolulu, take H-1 West to the Arizona Memorial/Stadium Exit which will deposit you on Kamehameha Hwy. Follow the signs to the Battleship Missouri Memorial and USS Bowfin Park, turning left after ½ mi. TheBus #20, 42 or CityExpress A will also get you there; the bus stop is across the street from the Battleship Missouri trolley pick-up at Bowfin Park.* ☎ *422-0561. Open daily 7:30am-5pm. 1¼hr. tours every 15min., 7:45am-3pm. No bags, purses, backpacks or strollers with pockets and compartments. Baggage storage available in the parking lot, $2, cash only. Admission to Arizona memorial free.*)

BOWFIN PARK. One of 15 remaining WWII submarines, the *USS Bowfin* is the centerpiece of its own historical park. Called the "Pearl Harbor Avenger," the sub was set into action one year after the 1941 attack. In 1981, the *Bowfin* was pulled out of commission and given educational duty instead. In addition to the submarine, visitors can explore outdoor exhibits, like a waterfront memorial, as well as indoor exhibits of submarine-related paraphernalia, including paintings, photographs, battle flags, and models. (*The park is adjacent to the USS Arizona Visitor Center. See directions to USS Arizona above.* ☎ *423-1341. Open 8am-5pm, last tour of sub 4:30pm. Submarine and museum admission $8; military, senior citizens, Hawaii residents $6; ages 4-12 $3. Museum only $4, ages 4-12 $2. AmEx/D/MC/V.*)

BATTLESHIP MISSOURI MEMORIAL. After 5 decades of military service, the battleship *USS Missouri* was finally retired in 1999. The ship (nicknamed "Mighty Mo") was relaunched as a tourist attraction and has already attracted 1 million visitors in the past 2½ years. The 887 ft. *Missouri* is a veteran of World War II, the Korean War and, after an overhaul in the mid-1980s, the Persian Gulf War. Marvelously refurbished and preserved, the ship illustrates to visitors the claustrophobic monotony of the sailors' daily lives. There is a strong feeling of patriotism aboard the ship—among other historic spots, guests can visit the famed Signature Deck, where the Japanese signed and General Douglas MacArthur accepted the Instrument of Surrender on September 2, 1945, ending WWII. The entertaining **Chief's Guided Tour** *($22, children $14)*, takes visitors through the Combat Engagement Center for a real look at the room where all the drama occurred. The **Captain's Tour** *(1½hr.; $49, children $39)* gives visitors an inside look at the Captain's Cabin and combat centers of the ship as well as a detailed, formerly top-secret debriefing on the Desert Storm mission. Light refreshments are served on the commanding officer's authentic china. The newest attraction, the **Explorer's Tour** *(1½hr.; $49, children $39)*, outfits patrons with hard hats and flashlights so that they can delve into the previously closed and off-limits lower decks, viewing the circa-1943 mechanical analog super-computers. *(From Honolulu, take H-1 West to the Arizona Memorial/Stadium Exit which will deposit you on Kamehameha Hwy. Follow the signs to the Battleship Missouri Memorial and USS Bowfin Park, turning left after ½ mi. Or you can take TheBus #20, 42 or CityExpress A. From the USS Bowfin, take the free trolley. ☎ 973-2494; www.ussmissouri.com. Bags and backpacks are prohibited. Call for tour reservations within 24hr. of scheduled tour. Open daily 9am-5pm. Last ticket sold at the Bowfin 3:55pm. Admission, included with the tours, $14; ages 4-12 $7; under 4 free. AmEx/D/MC/V.)*

ALOHA STADIUM

When not hosting a major football event, Aloha Stadium is home to the largest flea market (or swap meet) on Oahu. Vendors sell everything from bathing suits to electronics to ukuleles. It's the place to go to get cheap jewelry or anything you could ever imagine in *aloha* print. Many vendors sell the same items so shop around; bargaining is recommended. *(One stop on the bus past Pearl Harbor. See directions above. Admission $0.50, 12 and under free. Open W and Sa-Su 6am-3pm.)*

WAIPAHU

HAWAII'S PLANTATION VILLAGE. Located in suburban Waipahu, Hawaii's Plantation Village documents the life of workers on sugar plantations throughout Hawaii in the early 1900s. The site is composed of several reconstructed residential buildings, each modeled after homes of mill workers from all the islands and representative of particular ethnic groups. Plantation owners recruited over 400,000 workers from nearly a dozen different nations between 1848 and 1946 after foreign diseases had ravaged the local workforce. The owners segregated the workers by race in order to prevent organized collective bargaining for wages. Much to the owners' chagrin, the different groups began sharing food, competing in athletic events, and intermarrying. From these initial exchanges arose the multiracial **International Longshore and Warehouse Union** (see p. 18), which successfully challenged the landowners and raised wages and quality of life for workers. Today, Waipahu's diverse ethnic makeup is a testament to the many Chinese, Portuguese, Japanese, Puerto Ricans, Okinawans, Koreans, Filipinos, Caucasians, and indigenous Hawaiians who came to the area to work in the mills.

Some sites of interest in the village include a 1930s-era barber shop, a public bathhouse, a 1940s-era RC Cola general store, and the last active shrine of the Inari, a minor sect of the Shinto religion often associated with the working classes. Admission to the village is allowed only with one of the guided tours which are scheduled every hour but visitors should call ahead to schedule a docent, as tours are often cancelled if there is not adequate demand. There's also a small **museum** that showcases artifacts from plantations and explains some of the historical information in greater detail. The Plantation Village is a good way to spend part of a non-beach afternoon, especially for travelers with children. *(94-695 Waipahu St. By car, take H-1 west to Exit 7. Turn left onto Paiwa St., then right on Waipahu St. The village is on the left about 1½ mi. from the highway; by car the center is ½hr. from Honolulu. By bus, take the #43 from the Ala Moana Shopping Center to the front gate (1hr., every 30min., 7am-5pm). ☎ 677-0110; fax 676-6727. Both the village and the museum are open M-F 9am-3pm, Sa 10am-3pm. Tours run every hr. on the hr. $7, seniors $4, college students $4, ages 5-18 $3, groups of 20 or more $4.)*

◪ DAYTRIPS FROM HONOLULU

KEAIWA HEIAU STATE PARK

By car, take Hwy. 78 west from Honolulu to the Stadium/Aiea Exit and continue onto Moanalua Rd. At the second light, make a right onto Aiea Heights Dr., which twists and turns its way to the park, about 3mi. up. By bus, take #11 from the Ala Moana Shopping Center hub (35min.; every hr. 6:48am-9:10pm, last return 8:03pm). Ask the driver to let you off at Kaamilo St. The park is a pleasant 25min. walk up 'Aiea Heights Dr. The Ala Moana Shopping Center is accessible via the #8 bus from Waikiki, or the #19 or #20 from elsewhere in Honolulu, all of which run frequently. ☎ 587-0300. The park is open Apr.-Sept. 7am-7:45pm; Oct.-Mar. 7am-6:45pm. Purchase camping permits ($5 per group) ahead of time at 1151 Punchbowl St.

Located above Aiea Heights, a quiet residential neighborhood north of Pearl Harbor, Keaiwa Heiau State Park is an excellent choice for those in search of a peaceful place to camp far from Waikiki's throngs, but close enough to the city for easy daytrips. Tall ironwood trees, pockets of eucalyptus, and its high elevation (880 ft.) give the place an impressive sense of scale. Great views of Honolulu and Pearl Harbor abound within the park's 350-odd acres of lush vegetation.

Although its natural beauty and tranquil atmosphere are the real attractions, the park's namesake gives it a degree of historical significance. In the late 15th century, *kahuna lapa'au*, herbal healers, practiced their craft in the *keaiwa heiau*, a squat stone structure, harnessing the natural energy of the site as well as the medicinal properties of nearby plants. Today, all that remains of the *heiau* are foot-high lines of rocks, placed where archaeologists believe walls once stood. The site is considered sacred by the Hawaiian people, and it is disrespectful (and illegal) to move stones or leave offerings of any kind.

The park has four good **campsites,** all of which can accommodate 10-20 people (though you'll rarely find more than five people at any given site). All campsites have restrooms and shower facilities. Those that have been recently renovated are spotless and modern; those that have not are a bit rusty.

All the campsites are accessible via a 1 mi. road that encircles the ridge near the entrance. The **Aiea Loop Trail,** an easy 4½ mi. hike through the forest, meanders between the restrooms at the park entrance and the second campsite, about ½ mi. down the road. In addition to striking views of the mountains and Pearl Harbor, the trail is home to hundreds of species of indigenous plants. Toward the end of the trail, the 1943 wreckage of a C-47 cargo plane is visible through the trees. The trail takes 2-3hr. to complete, and while shoes or lightweight hiking boots are suggested, sturdy sandals are adequate.

WAHIAWA

To reach Wahiawa by car from Honolulu, take H-1 west, then take H-2, which runs through the middle of town. Wahiawa is also on the #52 (2hr. every 30min.), and #62 (1¾hr., every 30min.) bus lines, just over 1hr. from the Ala Moana Shopping Center hub in Honolulu. Ala Moana is accessible via buses #19 and #20 from Honolulu, or #8 from Waikiki.

Wahiawa was once a strategically important town for Hawaiian royalty. The frequent thunder was thought to be divine voices welcoming the arrival of new Hawaiian royals. Today the thunder greets only the pawn shops, tattoo parlors, and bars that dominate the military town close to the Scholfield Barracks. Wahiawa is interesting mostly for its nearby sights; the town itself is best seen from the inside of an air-conditioned car.

About a mile from Wahiawa, the **Dole Plantation** offers more information about pineapples than the average person could hope to absorb. The brand new complex is becoming a major tourist attraction, with nearly one million visitors per year. The extensive gift shop serves fresh pineapples, dried pineapples, chocolate-covered pineapples, pineapple cake, and various pineapple-themed sorbets and beverages. (☎ 621-8408. Open daily 9am-5:30pm. Various pineapple foodstuffs $2-6.) The complex is also home to the world's largest maze, according to the *Guinness Book of World Records*. The maze is made out of local plants, and the goal is to reach each of six stations and exit in as short a time as possible; a list of best times is posted at the entrance. (Open daily 9am-5pm. Entrance $5, ages 4-12 $3.) Next door to the maze the brand new Dole Plantation Gardens offers a self-guided tour for visitors to learn about the various stages of pineapple growth, the history of pineapple plantations in Hawaii and the various indigenous and imported plants of the island. Also available are activities like *lei*-making and wood-carving. Entrance to the Gardens can be bought with a ticket for the Pineapple Express, a small train that ferries visitors around on a tour of a working pineapple plantation. The plantation is still developing, and while the 20min. ride is well-narrated, the actual views the train ride offers are often of red dirt and wild grasses rather than pineapples. (Open daily 9am-5pm. Train leaves every ½hr. beginning at 9am. Plantation Garden Tour $3.50, ages 4-12 $2.50. Train $7.50, $5.50. Combined train and garden ticket $9, $7.)

Fast-food establishments of all varieties abound in Wahiawa. To avoid them, head three blocks east from Kamehameha Hwy. on Kiliani Ave. to N. Cane St., where **Sunnyside ❶** serves super-cheap local eats. The cheeseburger ($1.40) is a good deal, and people come from all over central Oahu for the famous **cream and fruit pies** ($6.25), which tend to sell out by noon. (☎ 621-7188. Open M-F 6am-6pm, Sa 6am-4pm.)

SOUTHEAST OAHU

KOKO HEAD REGIONAL PARK AND ENVIRONS

The entire area west of Honolulu along **Highway 72 (Kalanianaole Highway)** from Koko Head to Sandy Beach is a county park that includes **Hanauma Bay**, the **Halona Blowhole and Cove,** and the **Koko Crater.** All these sites are easily accessible by car from the highway, and two major bus routes serve the area. **Bus #22,** affectionately referred to as the "Beach Bus," runs along the highway from Waikiki to **Sea Life Park,** and has stops at each of the destinations mentioned above, as well as Makapu'u point and beach. (Departs Waikiki 8:15, 9:15am, then every hr. at 5min. before the hr. Last return from Sea Life Park 5:40pm.) **Bus #58** serves a similar area, but it leaves the highway and runs through **Hawaii Kai,** a suburban residential community, serving all the same destinations with the exceptions of Hanauma Bay and Sandy Beach (every 30min., 8am-6:05pm, last return 7:06pm).

HANAUMA BAY MARINE LIFE CONSERVATION DISTRICT. Hanauma Bay is like Disneyland: a fun time, but the crowds are maddening. Nearly 10,000 people flock to this picturesque beach every day (over 1 million visitors annually), and while the snorkeling is among the best on the island, the legions of tourists and children can detract from the experience. Arrive as early as possible to avoid the crowds.

Hanauma means "Curved Bay." The wide, sandy beach is at the base of a ring of volcanic rock below **Koko Head,** and its waters are teeming with hundreds of species of brightly-colored fish. The concave bay is mirrored by an arc of rocky reef about 100 yards into the ocean; the space between the reef and the shore is shallow and encloses a beautiful latticework of coral.

Once a favorite local fishing spot, the bay has been a **conservation area** since 1967. In the past, overfishing has been a big problem. These days, however, the problem is overfeeding. The local fish population has become dependent on human handouts, and aggressive species foreign to the area, such as the Hawaiian Whitespotted Toby, have begun to move in and take over. Respect the bay (and the law) by not feeding the fish.

Be sure to read the **bulletin board** at the entrance to get the latest info on surf conditions, and to learn which parts of the bay are safe for swimming each day. Hanauma Bay has more serious injuries and deaths each year than any other beach on the island (admittedly, it also has the most visitors, which inflates the statistic somewhat). In 2002 12 people drowned. If you have health problems, are a weak swimmer, or a first-time snorkeler, take extra care. Everyone is encouraged to talk to the lifeguards about safety issues before they go into the water.

The largest of the open areas in the rock, **Keyhole,** is in the center of the bay. It is quite shallow and calm, which makes it a good spot for novice snorkelers. Snorkeling is better outside the reef, but the current is strong, and a surprise wave can throw even an experienced swimmer against the rocks. There is also a strong rip current called the **Molokai Express.** (Few make it to Molokai.) *Let's Go* does not recommend swimming beyond the reef.

The two most dangerous areas of the bay are **Toilet Bowl** and **Witches Brew,** both of which are closed to public access by chain-link fences and signs threatening fines and imprisonment for trespassing. Serious injury and death occur at both sites every year, so heed the warnings. Toilet Bowl is a natural pool about a 10min. walk along the left bank of the bay. It is connected to the sea by a submerged tunnel through the rock, and the water level rises with the surf and then drops 4-8 ft. almost instantly as the waves "flush" out. Witches Brew is a turbulent area on the right side of the bay near its mouth, with a notoriously strong rip current and powerful waves that have swept many unsuspecting beachgoers into the sea. Do not enter the water at either location.

The park has showers, restroom facilities, changing rooms, pontoon wheelchairs for the disabled, a picnic area, and various food cart vendors selling expensive eats. Snorkeling equipment is available for rent at the park but it is cheaper to rent in Waikiki. *(By car, take Kalanianaole Hwy. east from Honolulu. The entrance to the parking lot is on the right on top of the hill just past the Foodland shopping center. Parking costs $1, and the lot is usually full by midday. Bus #22 runs between Waikiki and Sea Life Park, and stops right in Hanauma Bay (30min.; every hr.; first departure 8:15am, last return 5:40pm). Most departures 5min. before the hour and returns 20min. before the hour; if you can't walk the steep slope to the beach, you can take a trolley down for $0.50 and up for $1; day pass $2. The park is open and lifeguards are on duty in summer M and W-Su 7am-7pm, in winter 7am-6pm. Parking $1. Admission $3, 12 and under free. Locker $5. Set of mask, fins, and snorkel $6 per day, plus car keys, credit card or a $30-50 per person deposit. Cash only, including deposit.)*

KOKO HEAD. Koko Head is the mountainous area to the southwest of Hanauma Bay, and should not be confused with Koko Crater (p. 141) several miles down the highway. The 642 ft. summit was accessible to hikers via a trail at the top of the entrance road for the Hanauma Bay parking lot until 1998, but the hike is now closed to the public. Determined hikers frequently disobey the signs in order to visit the two craters that make up Koko Head, and to catch a glimpse of the ocean view and radar facilities on the summit. *Let's Go* does not recommend this.

HALONA BLOWHOLE. About 2 mi. past Hanauma Bay is the Halona Blowhole, a lava tube submerged in the ocean. Passing waves push through the tube and create a geyser-like explosion of sea and sound. The quality of the spectacle depends on surf conditions; some days the water barely bubbles out of the blowhole, other days it shoots high into the sky. Do not climb over the fences to get a closer look, as people have been killed by falling.

To the right of the parking lot is the small, secluded **Halona Cove,** a quiet spot to sunbathe unmolested by the beach-going crowd. There is no easy path down, so be careful as you scramble through the rocks. Just before the blowhole is a stone wall and monument erected by the Honolulu Japanese Casting Club to please the Japanese god of protection, and to honor fishermen who have passed away at sea. *(Located along Kalanianaole Hwy. and the #22 bus route.)*

KOKO CRATER. Koko Crater contains a 60-acre **Botanical Garden** and a **stable** that offers morning horseback-riding lessons as well as pony rides. A two-mile **loop trail** leads visitors through collections of plants from various regions of the world, including the Americas, Hawaii, Madagascar, and Africa. The gardens are a worthwhile stop if you're in the area for the afternoon. *(408 Kealahou St. By car, take Kalanianaole Hwy. east from Honolulu until you reach a stoplight just past Sandy Beach at Kealahou St. Turn left, and then left again onto a dirt road after about a mile at the sign for the Koko Crater. The road leads directly to the stables and garden. The #58 bus runs along Kealahou St. and stops near the dirt road every half hr. Buses to Waikiki run to the left, away from the ocean; buses to Sea Life Park run to the right. ☎ 395-2628. Stables open Tu-Su 8am-6pm. 1hr. horseback tour through the crater $40, pony rides $25. Gardens open daily 9am-5pm. Free.)*

SANDY BEACH PARK. The best beach for **body boarding** on Oahu, Sandy Beach is a good spot to spend an afternoon whether you're an experienced boarder or just a fan of watching experienced boarders. The eastern part of the beach also has two breaks for experienced surfers, **Full Point** and **Half Point.** Surfers and body boarders should beware of a strong rip current when trade winds are strong. The beach itself is wide enough to accommodate the sunbathing crowd, and has a reputation for being a lively social center for the island's youth.

Despite the high quality body surfing, Sandy Beach is also among the most dangerous beaches on the island. Hanauma Bay may have more drownings, but Sandy has more broken necks and backs. Check with the lifeguards at either of the two stations for up-to-date surf information, and be sure to keep an eye out for red flags, which indicate dangerous water conditions.

The large grassy area to the left of the park entrance is a popular kite-flying destination, and is sometimes used as a landing strip for hangliders. There are usually a few food stands in the area, and the park has restrooms and showers. *(Sandy Beach is on the #22 bus route on Kalanianaole Hwy., just past the Halona Blowhole.)*

MAKAPU'U POINT. The lighthouse that sits atop the 647 ft. Makapu'u Point marks the easternmost point of Oahu and has been in operation for nearly 100 years. From the lighthouse, it is possible (but difficult) to scramble down to the beach below. Keep in mind the beach is there only at low tide.

A bit farther down the highway on the right is a lookout stop. Both the lookout and the lighthouse have fantastic views of **Manana** and **Kaohikaipu Islands.** Manana, the larger of the two, means "rabbit," and the island bears the name because it both resembles and is inhabited by rabbits. Kaohikaipu, the smaller island, was declared a bird sanctuary by the state in 1972. *(Entrance to the trail leading to the Makapu'u lighthouse is located on the right a quarter of the way up the hill just pass Sandy Beach. There is no parking lot, so cars must line up along the wide shoulder along the highway.)*

SEA LIFE PARK. A pretty standard aquatic-themed amusement park, Sea Life Park is expensive and full of children dragging their parents from tank to tank. It makes a good diversion if you're looking for something non-beach-oriented to do with the family—it has enough different parts to keep the kids amused for hours.

The park features a string of shows for families, including the Dolphin Cove Show and the Kolohe Kai Sea Lion Show. The park also has breeding programs for endangered animals like the Giant Sea Turtles and the Hawaiian Monk Seals, and capture and release programs for wounded animals and birds. The 300,000-gallon observation tank has thousands of species of fish, moray eels, stingrays, sharks and other indigenous reef life. A spiral walkway surrounds the tank, providing views of the mock-reef from different depths. There are also a slew of additional activities that aren't included with regular admission, including Sea Trek, an underwater photo safari in the big reef tank, and Dolphin Adventures, a pricey way to play with dolphins in person. *(41-202 Kalanianaole Hwy. By car, take Kalanianaole Hwy. east from Honolulu (approx. 35min.). The park is on the left just above Makapu'u Beach. Both the #22 and #58 buses run from Waikiki to Sea Life Park (just under an hour, every 30min.). The park also runs a shuttle service for those who advance purchase one of the extra adventures to major Waikiki hotels for $5. ☎ 259-7933; www.sealifeparkhawaii.com. Sea Trek $65; Dolphin Adventures $105. Park open daily 9:30am-5pm. $25, ages 4-12 $12.50.)*

MAKAPU'U BEACH PARK. Located below Sea Life Park, Makapu'u Beach Park is a favorite hangout of hangliders and surfers. The beach itself is surrounded by dark volcanic rock which contrasts pleasingly with the white sand. Makapu'u isn't all about vistas and pretty surroundings, however. Though the area is usually flat in the summer, in winter the waves range from 6 to 12 ft., attracting surfers and body boarders alike. Makapu'u is nearly as famous as Sandy Beach for neck and back injuries, so be on the lookout for **red flags** on signs, which detail dangerous surf conditions, strong tides or dangerous shore break.

WAIMANALO

Waimanalo is quintessentially Hawaiian. The residents of this small town are diverse, and they go about their daily lives in a slow-paced fashion. Some keep chickens, others quietly promote Hawaiian independence, and almost everyone is laid-back. The rougher neighborhoods add to the town's character, but valuables are best not left unattended here. Waimanalo's main attraction is its stunning ◼**beach,** the longest (and perhaps the best) on Oahu. Backed by the Koolau mountains, Waimanalo Beach stretches nearly 5 mi. in an arc of white sand against the green-azure waters of the Pacific.

■◼ ▣ **ORIENTATION AND PRACTICAL INFORMATION.** Waimanalo is located along **Highway 72 (Kalanianaole Highway),** about 50min. by car or 1hr. on the #57 bus (every 30min.-1hr.) from Honolulu. The town itself sits in the midst of the three beach parks listed below, and is spread thinly along the highway for about 2½ mi. There's a **Waimanalo Laundry** next door to KimoZ. (Wash $1.75, dry $0.25 per 5min., $0.70 per lb. drop-off service. Open M-Sa 6am-10pm, Su 6am-5pm.)

ACCOMMODATIONS. Kom A'ona Inn B&B ❹, 41-922 Laumilo St., is quite classy. The gated lawn and garden are lush and well-kept, and the place has a genuine Hawaiian feel. Most of the seven units are located in a clean, upscale house with a shared kitchen and pool table. All have handicapped bathroom access. (☎866-874-7244, or 225-3708; www.hawaii-beds-beaches.com. Reservations only. Rooms $105-200.)

FOOD. Locals and tourists alike flock to the window of ◪**Keneke's ❶**, 41-857 Kalanianaole Hwy., a drive-up plate lunch mecca, to sample the divine *kalua* pig and other authentic local eats. The mixed plate ($6.50) could satisfy even the biggest of appetites; the plate lunch ($5.75) and the mini plate ($3.75) are a bit more manageable. Sandwiches are a steal at $3 or less. (☎259-5266. Open daily 9:15am-5:15pm.) **KimoZ ❷**, 41-1537 Kalanianaole Hwy., is a bit pricier than Keneke's, but the dining experience is more relaxed. Try their specialty King Kal-Bi plate and sing karaoke. Enjoy the pool tables, dart boards and live entertainment Friday and Saturday nights. (☎259-8800. Open Su-Th 10am-11pm, F-Sa 10am-1:30am.)

Shima's Supermarket, 41-1606 Kalanianaole Hwy., is a one-stop market with a wide array of sundries. (☎259-9921; open M-Sa 8am-8pm, Su 9am-6pm.) **Bobby's,** 41-867 Kalanianaole Hwy., is a small grocery store with no sign and the coldest beer in Hawaii, located four doors down from Keneke's. (☎259-5044. Open M-Sa 7am-8:45pm, Su 7am-7:15pm.)

BEACHES AND CAMPING. Waimanalo Beach is one of the most beautiful beaches on the island with a very long shore and gentle surf ideal for less experienced ocean swimmers and beginning body boarders. Waimanalo Beach is divided into three areas, and some are better than others. The first beach on the right heading into town from Honolulu is **Waimanalo Beach County Park,** easily identifiable by the city of tents alongside the highway. Manana Island peeks around the southern portion of the beach, and the tall ironwood trees complement the beautiful mountains that stand tall on the inland side of the highway. **Camping ❶** here requires a state permit (see p. 86). The snorkeling is decent and the bathroom and shower facilities are adequate, though the area is not as beautiful as other parts of the beach. Lifeguards are on duty F-Su 9am-5:30pm.

Five minutes down the highway toward Waimanalo, the gorgeous ◪**Waimanalo Bay State Recreation Area** is less developed and more secluded than Waimanalo Beach County Park. The beach is wider and the view more striking than elsewhere along the bay. Helicopters from the nearby **Bellows Air Force Base** do maneuvers along the beach, sometimes to sunbathers' chagrin. The parking lot is nicknamed "Sherwoods" by the locals, and while there are fewer Robin Hoods frequenting the area today than there were in days past, you should still keep your valuables on your person rather than in your car. There are bathroom and shower facilities, and camping requires a state permit. The water is considered the bunny slope of body boarding in the summer, but the surf picks up significantly in winter, so be careful. The park is open daily 7:45am-6pm and lifeguards are on duty daily 9am-5:30pm.

Bellows Field Beach County Park ❶, a beach park within the Bellows Air Force Base, sits another 2min. along the highway toward Waimanalo. Enter at the first entrance to the base. The beach and campgrounds are open to the general public from noon on Friday until 8am on Monday morning only, and again, camping requires a state permit. Picnic, restroom, and shower facilities are spartan but neat. The water is relatively calm and safe for swimming all year, making it an ideal beach for young swimmers. The beach is open during daylight hours and lifeguards are on duty F-Sa 9:15am-5:15pm.

WINDWARD OAHU

As its name implies, the Windward coast of Oahu is rough, wind-swept country—the rural land along the highway is punctuated by towns and scattered with upturned barrels that house fighting roosters. Winding along Kamehameha Hwy. to the base of the Koolau Mountains, a trip through Windward Oahu provides a scenic cruise from Honolulu to the North Shore through towns like Lanikai and Laie, and by the well-known Polynesian Cultural Center. **Kailua,** the major tourist destination on the Windward coast, draws visitors with its famous turquoise bay and world-class windsurfing. Close enough to Honolulu to make it a convenient base for exploration, Kailua is an unspoiled community—paradise without having to prove it. **Kaneohe,** Honolulu's largest suburb on Kailua Bay, is the starting point for sightseeing tours of the Windward and North Shores from Honolulu. The smaller settlements along the Kamehameha Hwy. beckon with isolated charms, from sunny beach to rainy valley, barren oceanscape to rugged mountain vista.

✴ ORIENTATION

Driving directions along the Windward coast are confusing, to say the least. The first town is **Kailua,** north of Waimanalo. Kailua is just south of **Kaneohe** and the military's **Mokapu Peninsula,** and is bordered on the east by the windswept **Kailua Bay.** Three highways zip through here, over the Koolau Mountain Range, separating the Windward Coast from the south shore. These are **H-3, Highway 63 (Likelike Highway,** pronounced "lee-kay lee-kay"), and scenic **Highway 61 (Pali Highway).** Pali Hwy. is the most direct route from Waikiki, just 15 mi. away.

To reach Kailua from the Honolulu Airport, take H-1 West to Exit 1D, H-3 East/Kaneohe. Exit at Mokapu Blvd. and make the 3rd right onto Oneawa St., which becomes Kailua Rd. after the Kailua town center, eight blocks down Oneawa St.

From eastbound H-1, take Exit 21A, Pali Hwy., and turn left; from H-1 West take Exit 21B Pali Hwy. and bear right until you merge with the mountainbound Hwy. 61 (Pali Hwy.). After the mountains, Hwy. 61 intersects **Kamehameha Highway,** also known as **"Kam. Highway"** or **Highway 83,** which continues west to Kaneohe. Continuing beyond this intersection, Hwy. 61 is called the Kalanianaole Hwy. for 2 mi. until the right-hand junction with Hwy. 72, opposite the Castle Medical Center. **Highway 72,** which heads southeast to Waimanalo, is called the **Kalanianaole Highway** from here on.

Continue straight ahead on Hwy. 61, now called **Kailua Road.** Three miles farther is a complex intersection which marks the center of Kailua town. Left is **Oneawa Street,** and if you drive straight you will be on Kuulei Rd., which ends shortly at Kalaheo Ave. To stay on Kailua Rd., you must turn right at the Kailua town center intersection, and then left at the next intersection ½ mi. away. From the Wanaao Rd. intersection at the blinking yellow traffic light, Kailua Rd. heads straight for the western end of **Kailua Beach Park,** or over the canal on Kawailoa Rd. if you turn right at S. Kalaheo Ave.

Turning left at the end of Kailua Rd. onto **North Kalaheo Avenue** will take you past **Kalama Beach Park** to Kaneohe Marine Corps Base and **Kaneohe Bay Drive.** The right turn onto South Kalaheo Ave. will take you to the drainage canal bisecting Kailua Beach Park, with Kawailoa Rd. bridging it.

The **H-3** highway links Pearl Harbor to the **Kaneohe Marine Corps Base (KMCB),** which dominates the Mokapu Peninsula north of Kaneohe town. Highway 63 (Likelike Highway) travels from Honolulu over the Koolau mountains and through southern Kaneohe, becoming **Route 630 (Kaneohe Bay Drive).** Kaneohe Bay Dr. veers north to KMCB before changing names to **North Kalaheo**

Avenue and heading south into Kailua. Kaneohe's main artery, **Highway 83 (Kamehameha Highway),** runs north-south through the heart of Kaneohe to Castle Junction, where the Pali Hwy. becomes the Kalanianaole Hwy. The **Kaheliki Highway** parallels the Kamehameha Hwy. up the west side of Kaneohe, and is known as Hwy. 83 until its junction with Kamehameha Hwy. north of town. The Kamehameha Hwy. becomes Hwy. 830 through town, reverting to 83 when it absorbs the Kaheliki Hwy. near Kahaluu park. This unified Kamehameha Hwy. contours the scenic Windward coast.

⊑ TRANSPORTATION

Buses: From Ala Moana Shopping Center in Honolulu, #56 and 57 run to **Kailua.** The #55 Circle Island and #65 go to **Kaneohe.** The Circle Island route runs up the Windward Coast's Kamehameha Hwy. and returns to Ala Moana as the #52 via Wahiawa and central Oahu. $1.75; senior citizens, the disabled, and students $0.75.

Car Rental:

Enterprise Kailua, 345 Hahani St. (☎261-4282; fax 261-0037). From Hwy. 61 heading toward Kailua, turn right at the Kailua Center intersection, and turn right at Hahani St. The only car rental in town gives spring and fall weekend specials. CDW $15 per day. Compact $32 per day. 21+. Under-25 must have full insurance coverage and a major credit card. $30 fee to return car at the airport. Open M-F 8am-6pm, Sa 9am-noon. AmEx/MC/V.

Enterprise Kaneohe, 46-003 Alaloa St. (☎247-2909). Take the Kamehameha Hwy. northbound to Kahuhipa St., and turn right at the light, onto Alaloa St. CDW $15 per day, full coverage $26. Compact $30 per day. 21+. Must have a major credit card. Free pick-up and drop-off service within Kaneohe. Open M-F 8am-6pm, Sa 9am-noon. AmEx/D/MC/V.

◪ PRACTICAL INFORMATION

TOURIST AND FINANCIAL SERVICES

Kailua Information Center, 600 Kailua Rd. (☎261-2727 or 261-2676), in the Kailua Shopping Center. A friendly and helpful volunteer staff will answer questions. Bus schedules, maps of beach access, suggestions for activities in Kailua, phone numbers, and directions available. Open M-F 10am-4pm, Sa 10am-2pm.

City Halls: Kailua Satellite, 1090 Keolu Dr. (☎261-8575). **Kaneohe Satellite** (☎235-4571), in the Windward Mall, 2nd fl. next to Sears. Open M-F 9am-5pm, Sa 8am-4pm.

Banks: First Hawaiian Bank Kailua, 705 Kailua Rd. (☎261-3371). Open M-Th 8:30am-4pm, F 8:30am-6pm, Sa 9am-1pm. **Bank of Hawaii Kaneohe,** 45-1001 Kamehameha Hwy. (☎233-4670). Open M-Th 8:30am-4:30pm, F 8:30am-6pm.

LOCAL SERVICES

Libraries: Kailua Public Library, 239 Kuulei Rd. (☎266-9911), 2 blocks from Kailua town center, next to the police and fire stations. **Internet access** available with a visitor's card ($10). Open M, W, F 10am-5pm, Tu and Th 1-8pm. **Kaneohe Public Library,** 45-829 Kamehameha Hwy. (☎233-5676), in front of the police station, ½ mi. north of Likelike Hwy. Open M-Tu, Th, Su 10am-5pm, W noon-8pm.

Laundromats: U-Wash and Dry Center Kailua, on Hoolai St. off Kailua Rd. Clean and spacious. Wash $1.75, dry $0.25 per 6min. Open 24hr. **Kaneohe Washerette** (☎235-1238), next to the post office on Kamehameha Hwy., before the Windward Mall. Wash $1.75, dry $0.25 per 6min. Open 24hr.

Equipment Rental:

Kailua Sailboards and Kayaks Inc., 130 Kailua Rd. (☎262-2555). Rents kayaks (single $32, double $42 per day), surfboards ($25 per day), sailboards (starting at $39 per day), kiteboards ($25 per day), and bicycles ($25 per day). Guided kayak tour $79. Waikiki pickup and drop off available. Lessons also available: private windsurfing lessons $35 per hr. ($49 for 3hr. group lesson, including gear), kite surfing group introductory lesson $119. Weekly and ½ day rates available; $225 Funpak allows you to use any of Kailua Sailboards' water toys for a week. Open daily 9am-5pm. AmEx/D/MC/V.

Naish Hawaii, 155a Hamakua Dr. (☎262-6068), is the destination of choice for experienced windsurfers in Kailua. Though they operate as a B&B and vacation rental booking agency, their main business is renting equipment. Beginner boards from $20 for 2hr.; boards for beginner to advanced $30-45 per day. Windsurfing lessons for beginners and intermediates $55 for 1 person, $75 for 2 including 2hr. equipment rental. Kiteboard rental $25 per day, beginner lesson $100. Open 9am-5:30pm. AmEx/D/MC/V.

Aaron's Dive Shop, 307 Hahani St. (☎888-847-2822 or 262-2333). From Kailua Rd., turn right at the town center intersection and then take the 2nd right onto Hahani St. Aaron's will set you up with scuba gear for $30 per 24hr. plus $8 per tank, or bring you along on one of their daily dive trips ($125 for a 2-tank dive including equipment rental). Open M-F 7am-7pm, Sa 6:30am-6pm, Su 6:30am-5pm. AmEx/D/MC/V.

EMERGENCY AND COMMUNICATIONS

Emergency: ☎911.

Police: Kailua Substation, 219 Kuulei Rd. (☎262-6555). **Kaneohe Substation,** 45-270 Waikalua Rd. (☎247-2166). **Kahuku Substation,** 56-470 Kamehameha Hwy. (☎293-8565).

Medical Services: Braun Urgent Care Kailua, 130 Kailua Rd. Ste. 111 (☎261-4411), in the Kailua Beach shops. Walk-in patients welcome. Open daily 8am-8pm. **Castle Medical Center,** 640 Ulukahiki St. (☎263-5500; emergency services ☎263-5164), at the junction of Hwy. 61 and 72, 1½ mi. south of Kailua. **Straub Kaneohe Family Health Center,** 46-056 Kamehameha Hwy. (☎233-6200), inside the Windward Mall. Walk-in hours daily noon-7:30pm.

Fax Office: Island Printing Centers Kailua, 305 Hahani St. (☎261-8515). 1st page of fax to mainland $2, subsequent pages $1.25 plus $1 per min. of use. Black and white copies $0.08, color $0.95. Copy rates can vary. Mailboxes also available ($42 for 3 mo.). AmEx/D/MC/V.

Internet Access: Kailua Recreation Center, 21 S. Kainalu Dr. (☎266-7652) around the corner from the Kailua Public Library and the police station. Internet access free with registration. Available Th noon-2pm.

Post Offices: Kailua Main Office, 335 Hahani St. (☎266-3996). Last collection M-F 5pm, Sa 4pm. Open M-F 8am-4:30pm, Sa 8am-noon. **Postal Code:** 96734. **Kaneohe Main Office,** 46-036 Kamehameha Hwy. (☎235-1055). Last collection M-F 5:30pm, Sa 4:30pm. Open M-F 8am-4:30pm, Sa 8am-noon. **Postal Code:** 96744. **Kaawa Main Office,** 51-480 Kamehameha Hwy. (☎237-8372). Open M-F 8am-noon and 1-3:45pm, Sa 9:30-11:30am. **Postal Code:** 96730. **Laie Main Office,** 55-510 Kamehameha Hwy., Ste. 20 (☎293-0337). Open M-F 9am-3:30pm, Sa 9:30-11:30am. **Postal Code:** 96762.

⚑ ACCOMMODAT-IONS AND CAMPING

In general, the B&Bs in Kailua fill up weeks or months in advance, especially during the holiday season; it is essential to make reservations early.

BOOKING SERVICES

Many more B&Bs can be found in Kailua and Lanikai, as well as in Kaneohe and the rest of the Windward coast, through booking agencies.

All Islands Bed and Breakfast (☎800-542-0344 or 263-2342; www.all-islands.com), takes customized preferences for location, lodging types, and travel dates, and matches them with available B&B clients. Their list of clients numbers over 1000 from across the islands, including 95 establishments in Kailua. Reservations require a 20% deposit for the room. The balance must be paid to the B&B where you're staying. Reserve online or by phone. Open M-F 8am-5pm. AmEx/D/MC/V.

Hawaiian Islands Bed and Breakfast (☎800-258-7895 or 261-7895; www.lanikaibb.com) is run by the owners of the **Lanikai Bed and Breakfast.** They also reserve B&B and vacation rentals in Kailua and Lanikai. MC/V.

KAILUA

▨ **Hawaii's Hidden Hideaway,** 1369 Mokolea Dr. (☎877-443-2929 or 262-6560; www.ahawaiibnb.com). Take Kawailoa Rd. and make a left on Alala Rd. at the stop sign. Follow Alala as it changes its name to Aal-

Windward Oahu

TO TURTLE BAY (3 mi.)

Kahuku

Mormon Temple

Brigham Young University Hawaii Campus ■

Malaekahana State Recreation Area

0 — 4 miles
0 — 4 kilometers

Laie
Polynesian Cultural Center

83

Hauula

Kaipapau Forest Reserve

Hauula Forest Reserve

Hauula Beach Park

Sacred Falls State Park

Kahana Valley Beach Park

Swanzy Beach Park

Ahupua'a 'o Kahana

Kaaawa

Kaaawa Beach Park

KOOLAUPOKO DISTRICT

Kualoa Ranch

83

Kualoa Regional Park

Kualoa Point

PACIFIC OCEAN

Kahaluu

Ahuimanu

83

830

Valley of the Temples ■

Heeia State Park

Kahekili Hwy.

Kamehameha Hwy.

Heeia

H3

Kaneohe

Kaneohe Bay

Mokapu Peninsula

Hoomaluhia Botanical Garden

63

83

630

Kaneohe Bay Marine Corps Base

H3

630

Pali Hwy. ■ Nu'uanu Pali Lookout

Kailua Bay

61 Kailua

Kalama Beach Park

Kailua Beach Park

Ulupo Heiau

Lanikai Beach

Honolulu Watershed Forest Reserve

Kalanianaole Hwy.

Waimanalo

Bellows Field Beach Park

72

Waimanalo Bay Beach Park

OAHU

HE HIDDEN DEAL

PAMPERED IN PARADISE

As is fitting for a land renowned for its ability to relax the body and rejuvenate the soul, Hawaii is home to many of the most luxurious spas in America, but their services are prohibitively expensive for many travelers. For those looking for a pampering in paradise without the stress of spending last month's paycheck in a couple of hours, a trip to **Hawaii's Healing Arts College and Massage Professionals** in Kailua is in order. Students at the American Institute of Massage Therapy are going through their 11 mo. pre-certification at this richly appointed clinic. These future massage stars of Hawaii's 5-star resort hotel spas will rub all your cares away with a 1 hr. massage for only $25. The interns are trained in the basics of Swedish massage, and some have additional training in acupressure, trigger points, and the Hawaiian massage technique *lomi lomi*. The college will try to match up its clients with the best intern suited to their needs, but if you desire more flexibility and more experience, a massage with a professional at the center is still only $50 per hr., about half of what one might expect to pay at a hotel resort spa. *(In the Kailua Medical Arts Building, 407 Uluniu St., 2nd fl.* ☎ *266-2468; www.hhacdirect.com. Metered street parking. Open M-F 9am-9pm, Sa-Su 9am-5pm.)*

apapa Dr. After 1 mi. on Aalapapa Dr., turn right onto Mokolea Dr. A basket of fruit and a plate of cookies welcome guests to this hideaway; Japanese kimonos in the closets, carefully landscaped rock gardens, outdoor beach shower, and a plumeria tree complete the idyllic aesthetic. Private entrance, bath, lanai, cable TV, telephone, CD and DVD players, kitchenette, and a plethora of other touches in each unit—all just 1½ blocks from Lanikai Beach. Free laundry. 3-night min. stay. Check-in 3pm. Check-out 10am. Suites $95-175. ❹

🏖 **Akamai Bed and Breakfast,** 172 Kuumele Pl. (☎800-642-5366 or 261-2227; www.akamaibnb.com). Take Kuulei Rd. and turn right after the library onto Kainalu Dr. Make the 3rd left onto Kuukama St., and another left onto Kuumele Pl. and bear right. 2 spacious studios are decorated in a fun and tasteful Hawaiian theme. Each unit has a king-sized bed, private entrance, spotless bathroom, cable TV, radio, phone, full-sized fridge stocked with continental breakfast, and kitchenette with microwave. Take a dip in the large pool on the brick patio behind the units. 3-night min. stay. No children. Check-in 2pm. Check-out 10am. $95 per couple. ❸

Manu Mele Bed and Breakfast, 153 Kailuana Pl. (☎/fax 262-0016; www.pixi.com/~manumele). Units are immaculate and self-sufficient, with private entrances to the pool and patio, as well as a bath, mini fridge, microwave, coffee maker, cable TV, ceiling fans, and A/C. Assorted baked goods and fruit comprise the first morning's continental breakfast. This B&B is farther from the Kailua town center than the others, but beach access is a 3min. walk down a path that flanks the property. 5min. from Safeway and a few blocks from the #85, 86, and 70 bus stops. 2-night min. stay. No children. Fully refundable $100 deposit. Check-out 11am. Rooms $80-90. ❸

Papaya Paradise Bed and Breakfast, 395 Auwinala Rd. (☎/fax 261-0316; www.kailuaoahuhawaii.com). From Kailua Rd. continue straight onto Wanaao Rd. Turn right onto Awakea Rd. and make a quick left onto Auwinala Rd. Lovely units furnished in tropical rattan and wicker, each with a private entrance, private bath, A/C, cable TV, and telephone. Guests share a kitchenette with refrigerator and microwave, as well as a pool-side lanai with an amazing view of Olomana and the Koolau mountains. The knowledgeable hosts can tell you all there is to know about Kailua. Boogie boards, snorkels, masks, and beach gear available for loan to guests free of charge. 3-night min. stay. Check-in 3pm. Check-out 11am. Doubles $85-100, each additional person $15. ❸

Kay's Alii Vacation Rental, 232 and 237 Awakea Rd. (☎262-9545; www.kaysvacations.com). Heading toward town on Kailua Rd., continue onto Wanaao Rd., then turn left onto Awakea St. Kay's properties are across the street from each other, before Aumoe Rd. Rooming options include: a bedroom with shared bath and mini kitchenette; a studio with a king-sized bed and trundle, kitchenette, and private bath; a 1-bedroom cottage and 1-bedroom apartment that each sleep up to 4, each with full bath; the 8-person, 4BR house with 2 full baths (1 with jacuzzi), full kitchen, and dining and living rooms. All rooms have cable TV, as well as access to BBQ grill and coin-op washer and dryer. A/C in some rooms. 3-night min. stay. Check-in 4pm (call ahead). Check-out 11am. Bedroom $60; studio $75; cottage $85; house $235. Rates based on double occupancy; each additional adult $15, child $10. AmEx. ❸

Fairway View Bed and Breakfast, 515 Paumakua Pl. (☎263-6439; www.fairway-viewbnb.com). Take Kawailoa Rd. past Kailua Beach Park toward Lanikai and turn right onto Alala Rd. at the stop sign. From Alala Rd. turn left onto Paumakua Rd. True to its name, you can see the Mid-Pacific Country Club's 2nd fairway from the large windows in the living room of this well-kept B&B. 2 rooms, 1 with a queen-sized bed and small TV and the other with 2 double beds. Each has a mini fridge and shares a full bathroom. No A/C. 3-night min. stay. 2 guests max. per room. Check-in 2pm. Check-out 11am. High-season singles $60; doubles $65. Low-season singles $50; doubles $55. ❷

Sharon's Serenity Bed and Breakfast, 127 Kakahiaka St. (☎263-3634; www.sharons-serenity.com). Take Kailua Rd. to Wanaao Rd. and turn left at the blinking yellow light at the canal onto Kakahiaka St. Sharon's relaxed nature is evident in her home, where she keeps her poodles and cat, and prepares a delicious continental breakfast in her own kitchen. All 3 rooms have full private baths, ceiling fans, TV, and mini-fridge. No children under 8. 3-night min. stay. Check-in 1pm. Check-out 11am. Rooms $75-85. ❸

KANEOHE AND THE WINDWARD COAST

▨**Alii Bluffs Windward Bed and Breakfast,** 46-251 Ikiiki St. (☎800-235-1151 or 235-1124; fax 236-4877). Take Kamehameha Hwy. through Kaneohe, turn right onto Ipuka St. after King Intermediate School, then take an immediate left onto Ikiiki St. The influences of the house's owners (an artist and a real estate agent) are apparent in the artwork which graces the interior, as well as the home's choice bay view location. Standard double bed and private adjoined bath for Victorian-themed room. 2 single beds and private bath across the hall for the Circus-themed room. All are welcome at this gay-owned and gay-friendly establishment. Breakfast included. Laundry available. Seasonal prices. Victorian Room $70, Circus Room $60. MC/V. ❸

Camp Kokokahi YWCA, 45-035 Kaneohe Bay Dr. (☎247-2124; fax 247-2125). The simple single and multi-bunked cabins dating from the 1920s are available F-Su nights. Communal baths and showers inspire a summer camp feel. A common kitchen, heated lap pool, and full indoor gym with basketball court, ping-pong, foosball, and an outdoor volleyball net satisfy the whole troop. Hiking path and kayak rentals available ($10). Bedding $5. Office open M and Su 10am-3pm and Tu-Sa 8:30am-5pm. Check-in 4:30pm. Check-out 11am. Reservations recommended at least 1 wk. in advance. Private single cabin $25; private double $36. Open only F-Su nights. MC/V. ❶

CAMPING

Permits for camping at the beach and regional parks along Kamehameha Hwy. in Windward Oahu are available at the State Parks Office, 1151 Punchbowl St., Honolulu, or from any Satellite City Hall in the area for the County Parks. See **Camping,** p. 86 or **Windward Oahu Practical Information,** p. 145, for more permit information. The sites below are along Kamehameha Hwy.

Malaekahana State Recreation Area, 1 mi. north of the Mormon Temple on the coastal side of Kamehameha Hwy. This popular, isolated camping area features 3-bedroom, 2-bathroom beach houses, tent-cabins and campsites. Warm outdoor shower facilities,

24hr. security, and a swimming beach on Laie Bay make this a desirable spot to camp. Contact State Parks, 1151 Punchbowl St. (☎587-0300) for camping M-W and F-Su. and the Friends of Malaekahana (☎293-1736 M-F 10am-3pm) for camping W and Th and all beach house and tent-cabin reservations. Single camper $5 per night; beach house (up to 10 people) $60; tent-cabin (up to 6 people) $35. ●

Kualoa Regional Park, on Kaneohe Bay off Kamehameha Hwy. Extremely popular camp site. To reserve a space, 2 F before you intend to camp go to a Satellite City Hall that opens at 8am (like Kailua) to reserve a spot, as permits are usually gone by 9am. 30 sites. Camping M-W and F-Su. Free. ●

Swanzy Beach Park, north of Kualoa on Kamehameha Hwy., beyond Kaaawa Point and Beach Park. Swanzy Beach is not great for swimming, but it is popular among snorkelers. Basketball court on premises. Not gated. Conveniently located across the highway are the Kaaawa Main Post Office and a 7-Eleven. 9 designated sites. Make reservations 2 F in advance. Camping M and F-Su. Free. ●

Hauula Beach Park, north of Kaneohe, beyond Kahana Bay on Kamehameha Hwy. The park has restrooms, picnic facilities, and the occasional volleyball game, beach attendance permitting. Not gated. The park has a reputation among locals for attracting homeless. 15 undesignated campsites. Camping M and F-Su. Free. ●

◘ FOOD

Kailua and Kaneohe hold a wealth of dining options, and in comparison, the trip up the Windward coast to Turtle Bay is nearly devoid of good restaurants.

GROCERY STORES AND MARKETS

The Source, 32 Kainehe St. (☎262-5604), ½ block west of Kailua Rd. A small natural foods store in Kailua. Open M-F 9am-9pm, Sa 9am-6pm, Su 10am-5pm. D/MC/V.

Kalapawai Market, 306 S. Kalaheo Ave. (☎262-4359), at the intersection of Kalaheo Ave. and Kailua Rd., is a convenience store with the locals' favorite coffee ($1) and the closest **ATM** to Kailua Beach Park. Open daily 6am-9pm. MC/V.

Safeway, 200 Hamakua Dr. (☎266-5222). From Kailua at Castle Junction, turn right 1 block before the Kailua center intersection, onto Hamakua Dr. You can't miss the supermarket on the right, at the corner of Hahani St. Open 24hr. AmEx/MC/V. Another **Safeway** (☎254-2597) is located north of Kailua at 25 Kaneohe Bay Dr., 2 mi. up N. Kalaheo Ave. from the Kuulei St. intersection. As you cross the Kawainui Canal, where N. Kalaheo Ave. becomes Kaneohe Bay Dr., turn right on Mokapu Blvd. and make an immediate left into the Safeway Shopping Center parking lot. Open daily 5am-midnight. Yet another **Safeway** is at 46-065 Kamehameha Hwy. (☎235-5800) in Kaneohe. Large, bright and modern. Open 24hr.

Foodland, 108 Hekili St. (☎261-3211), in the Windward City Shopping Center in Kaneohe. Open 24hr.

Room Service in Paradise, 2639 S. King Suite 201 (☎941-3463; fax 942-5494). These saviors of Oahu's hungry, immobile masses charge $4-5 to deliver orders from participating area restaurants in Honolulu and Kailua town. If you're isolated on an idyllic beach far from civilization, fear not—they deliver island-wide for a $10 out-of-area fee and 15% gratuity (also mandatory on orders over $70). Delivery time varies, but is generally up to 1hr. Phone and fax orders daily 9am-10pm. Pick up a menu at restaurants around Honolulu and Kailua town. AmEx/D/MC/V.

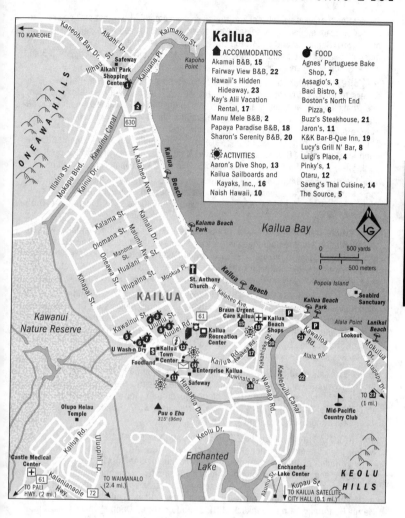

Kailua

ACCOMMODATIONS
Akamai B&B, **15**
Fairway View B&B, **22**
Hawaii's Hidden
  Hideaway, **23**
Kay's Alii Vacation
  Rental, **17**
Manu Mele B&B, **2**
Papaya Paradise B&B, **18**
Sharon's Serenity B&B, **20**

ACTIVITIES
Aaron's Dive Shop, **13**
Kailua Sailboards and
  Kayaks, Inc., **16**
Naish Hawaii, **10**

FOOD
Agnes' Portuguese Bake
  Shop, **7**
Assagio's, **3**
Baci Bistro, **9**
Boston's North End
  Pizza, **6**
Buzz's Steakhouse, **21**
Jaron's, **11**
K&K Bar-B-Que Inn, **19**
Lucy's Grill N' Bar, **8**
Luigi's Place, **4**
Pinky's, **1**
Otaru, **12**
Saeng's Thai Cuisine, **14**
The Source, **5**

OAHU

KAILUA

☒ **Luigi's Place,** 442 Uluniu St. (☎263-5678). Heading into Kailua on Kailua Rd., turn left onto Oneawa St. then right on Uluniu. Semi-hidden Luigi's is across from TCBY, set back from the street. This unassuming restaurant features 3 outdoor tables and a romantic interior in which to savor the masterful Italian-influenced cuisine. Vegetarian and seafood options only; tofu meatballs ($14.50) and lobster ravioli ($17) are both delicious and come with soup or salad. Appetizers $6.50-7.50. BYOB, $4 corkage fee. Open Tu-Sa 5:30-9:30pm. Reservations recommended F-Sa. MC/V. ❸

☒ **Buzz's Steakhouse,** 413 Kawailoa Rd. Take Kailua Rd. all the way to Kailua Beach Park and turn right onto S. Kalaheo; Buzz's parking lot is on the right after the bridge. People still buzz about the Clintons' unexpected drop-in visit in 1994; a plaque on the lanai commemorates the event. Locals flock to the all-you-can-eat salad bar that includes pickled onions, avocados, pineapple, spinach, bacon, tofu, pickled watermelon, and fresh-baked bread ($9). Salad bar and 10 oz. top sirloin $18. $9 min. order. Lunch serves a simpler menu of salads and burgers. Open daily for lunch 11am-3pm, drinks and *pupus* 3-5pm, dinner 5-10pm. Reservations recommended for lunch and dinner. ❸

Pinky's, 970 N. Kalaheo Ave. (☎254-6255). Head north of town on Kalaheo Ave. Access to Pinky's driveway is along the turnoff as you turn right onto Mokapu Blvd. Everything's bigger and better at this *pupu* bar and grill. The festive restaurant serves a huge menu of *pupus* (coconut crunchy calamari is the favorite, $7) and large entrees of mixed mainland/Hawaiian origin. Baby back ribs half rack $10, full rack $19. *Aloha* plate with grilled fresh fish, *kalua* pig, vegetable chow mein, and *lomi* salmon $13. The enormous, ice cold 18 oz. schooners of Bud Light, Sam Adams, or Newcastle set you back $3-4; 18 oz. Mai Tais or margaritas $6. Open M-Sa 4-10pm, Su 9am-10pm. ❸

Agnes' Portuguese Bake Shop, 46 Hoolai St. (☎262-5367), across the street from Boston's North End Pizza. Specialty baked goods and desserts served in an elegant cafe. Call 15min. ahead for fresh *malasadas*—divine, Portuguese-style doughnuts ($0.55 each, $5.40 per dozen). Open Tu-Sa 6am-6pm, Su 6am-2pm. ❶

Lucy's Grill N' Bar, 33 Aulike St. (☎230-8188). Aulike is the first left past the town center, approaching Kailua from the south. Lucy's serves gourmet *pupus* (oven roasted oysters $10), inexpensive pizzas ($9-12), and grill favorites with gumption (*kiawe* broiled baby back ribs with Mongolian BBQ sauce $16). All entrees come with a starch and vegetable. Open nightly 5-10pm. Reservations recommended 6-7:30pm. MC/V. ❸

Baci Bistro, 30 Aulike St. (☎262-7555), across the street from Lucy's. Emphasizing Old World know-how, Baci Bistro has earned its reputation as Kailua's best Italian restaurant. Gnocchi con Gorgonzola $14. *Saltimbocca di vitello,* layers of veal, mozzarella, and prosciutto sauteed in a wine and demi-glaze $20. For lunch, panini sandwiches start at $5.50. Wine by the glass $5.50-8.50. Open M-F 11:30am-2pm and daily 5:30-10pm. Reservations strongly recommended. AmEx/MC/V. ❸

Otaru, 600 Kailua Rd. (☎263-4482), in the Kailua Shopping Center. Otaru is known for its excellent Pacific Rim and Japanese-style cuisine. Sample the teriyaki and excellent shrimp tempura with *tsukemono, miso* soup, and salad ($16) or the live Maine lobster and *sashimi* ($32). A la carte sushi $5-7. Sake $4-13. Open M-F 11am-2pm and 5-9:30pm. AmEX/D/DC/MC/V. ❺

Jaron's, 201A Hamakua Dr. (☎261-4600). Hamakua Dr. is the last right from the Kailua town intersection, heading north on Kailua Rd. An excellent restaurant and popular Kailua nightlife spot known for showcasing local talent. Jaron's offers a well-rounded menu of steaks, seafoods, pasta, and salads. Tiger shrimp Lanikai linguine $16. Poached fresh salmon $15. Alternative rock jazzes up a local crowd Th 8:30pm-midnight, and everything from reggae to hip hop plays F and Sa 10pm-1:30am. Happy Hour daily 4-6pm (drinks $5.50). 21+ after 10pm. Open M-Th 11am-10pm, F-Sa 11am-1:30am, Su 9am-2pm and 4-10pm. D/MC/V. ❹

Saeng's Thai Cuisine, 315 Hahani St. (☎263-9727). Head toward the beach on Kailua Rd. from the Kailua town center intersection and turn right onto Hahani St. Fine Thai selections at budget prices. Spicy Evil Prince (beef, chicken or pork) $8. Seafood curry $10. Plenty of vegetarian options as well (Masman tofu, sauteed in Thai curry with peanuts, potatoes, onion, and coconut milk $7). Open M-F 11am-2pm and 5-9:30pm, Sa-Su 5-9:30pm. AmEx/MC/V. ❷

Boston's North End Pizza, 29 Hoolai St. (☎263-7757). Hoolai St. is the last left on Kailua-bound Kailua Rd. before Oneawa St. The 19 in. pizza pies weigh 3 lb., and that's just the plain variety ($13.25). Add a few toppings (including anchovy, green peppers, pepperoni, ham, and, of course, pineapple) and you have a fold-it-in-half-or-die slice of pizza paradise, which maximizes the value-volume curve at $3.25+ per huge slice. Open Su-Th 11am-8pm, F-Sa 11am-9pm. ❶

K & K Bar-B-Que Inn, 130 Kailua Rd. #102A (☎262-2272), in the Kailua Beach Shops. Fast local-style grinds, with breakfast 9-11am ($4-5), affordable sandwiches all day (BBQ cheeseburger $1.65), and the obligatory plate lunch in mini ($3.75-4.25) and regular ($5-6.15) sizes. Excellent Chinese specialties and spicy fried chicken wings (12 for $5.50). Open M-Sa 9am-9pm, Su 9am-4pm. ❶

Assaggio's, 354 Uluniu St. (☎261-2772). A premier establishment among Kailua's many Italian eateries, Assaggio's boasts an eager staff and a menu full of both typical and unexpected Italian dishes. The restaurant is well-known for its Caesar Salad, prepared table-side ($6), and huge martinis ($4.50). Specialties include the *Osso Buco Alla Romana* ($15-18) and the Chicken *Alla Saltimboca Romana* ($13-15). Hot homemade bread, free in a bottomless basket, is reason enough to head to Assaggio's. Wine $5 by the glass. Open for lunch M-F 11:30am-2:30pm; for dinner M-Th and Su 5-9:30pm, F-Sa 5-10pm. AmEx/D/DC/MC/V. ❸

KANEOHE AND THE WINDWARD COAST

🏖 **Zia's Caffe,** 45-620 Kamehameha Hwy. (☎235-9427). Zia's is a haven for the traveler weary of the wasteland of chop suey and fast food joints that cover Kaneohe. This breezy, casual restaurant serves fine Italian fare with friendly service. Seafood *arrabiatta* (shrimp, clams, and mussels sauteed in a spicy white wine garlic sauce, then tossed with pasta, bacon, fresh basil, and diced tomatoes; $15). Meat lasagna $10. Mandarin orange chicken salad $9. Open daily 11am-10pm. MC/V. ❸

🏖 **Pah Ke's,** 46-018 Kamehameha Hwy. (☎235-4505). Recently renovated, Pah Ke's sparkling interior is the perfect setting for their superb Chinese food. The extensive menu is cooked with an eye to the health-conscious, using canola oil, sea salt, and no MSG. Creative seasonal salads using fresh local ingredients $6-8. Entrees include black pepper steak sizzling platter ($9), braised black mushrooms with vegetables ($7), and Hong Kong-style fried chicken ($6). Open daily 10:30am-9pm. AmEx/MC/V. ❷

🏖 **Kaneohe Bakery,** 45-1026 Kamehameha Hwy (247-0474). Mmm . . . donuts ($0.65-2), cakes ($9-11.50), and custard and cream pies ($6-8.40) baked fresh daily and available around the clock. Open 24hr. M-Tu and Th-Su. MC/V. ❶

Masa and Joyce, 45-582 Kamehameha Hwy. (☎235-6129), in Kaneohe. Kaneohe locals crowd this haven of Hawaiian and Japanese favorites. Send your taste buds on an island marathon with the Squid *Luau* or Hawaiian Plate's *kalua* pork; both come with *poi* or rice, chicken or pork *lau lau*, chicken long rice, *lomi* salmon, and *shoyu poke* for only $7.50. Plate lunch $6 (locals favor the *kalua* pig and cabbage). Everything is made to order, so allow 15min. or call ahead. Open M and W-F 9am-6pm, Sa 9am-4pm, Su 9am-2pm. MC/V. ❶

Crouching Lion Inn, 51-666 Kamehameha Hwy. (☎237-8511). The classiest place to eat on the Windward side before Kaneohe, the Lion feeds famished road trippers with a gourmet bacon cheeseburger or mahi mahi melt (both $8.50) for lunch. Dinner brings out the superior house specialty: *kalua* pork with sweet steamed cabbage and *poi* bread pudding ($15). The house cocktail, Crouching on the Beach, is a rum, passion fruit, honeydew melon liqueur, and 7-Up concoction ($4.50). Craving mainland cuisine? You can't go wrong with the New York steak and lobster ($25). Open daily 11am-4pm and 5-9pm. AmEx/D/DC/MC/V. ❹

🏖 BEACHES

KAILUA BEACH. Though proclaiming a particular beach the nation's best is as subjective as naming its most beautiful woman, the delicately curving neck of white sand around Kailua Bay's splendid turquoise waters pleads a strong case. The winds in Kailua Bay harken from nearly all directions, making the bay the best **windsport** area on Oahu, especially during the winter. Spectators gather to gape at the expert **windsurfers** and **kiteboarders** who careen over the whipped-up waves. **Kayakers** also brave the surf, frequently crossing to the State Bird Sanctuary on **Mokulua Islands** offshore. The usually gentle surf makes the beach popular for **swimmers** and families. There are parking lots (which fill up early on weekends), bathrooms, showers, a small craft storage building, and, on the eastern end, a boat ramp in Kailua Beach Park. On the secluded northern half of Kailua Beach lies the grassy marsh of **Kalama Beach Park.** The virgin sand here has fewer visitors than the beach park, and the choppier waves are free of the watersport traffic farther south. Kalama is a good learning spot for novice **body boarders** and **body surfers.** Beach facilities include a restroom, showers, and picnic tables. *(Take the Lanikai-bound bus #70 from Kailua town center. By car, stay on Kailua Rd. through Kailua town to S. Kalaheo Ave., and turn right. S. Kalaheo will become Kawailoa Rd. to cross the drainage canal, and one of the parking lots is on the left just before the drainage canal. To reach Kalama Beach park, turn left on N. Kalaheo Ave. from Kuulei Rd.; the parking lot is on the right, before Kapaa St.)*

LANIKAI BEACH. Residential Lanikai is just around Alala Pt. from Kailua Beach Park, on the utterly romantic Lanikai Beach. You can live out your beachside cottage fantasies here in a warm, wealthy community comfortably crowded between the siren song of the beach and the Keolu Hills, which crown Lanikai's own little side of Oahu. Public beach access to these secluded sands is on Mokulua Dr. You may park streetside, but do not obstruct the bus stops (bus #70 makes a loop around Lanikai), driveways, or the bike path. *(See directions for Kailua Beach, above.)*

MALAEKAHANA STATE RECREATION AREA. This popular, isolated **camping** area (p. 149) features indoor and outdoor shower facilities, picnic areas, and a **beach** on Laie Bay that is safe for swimming. Studded with shady ironwood trees, the narrow beach is perfect for a leisurely stroll, and the mellow waves make good training grounds for novice body surfers. At low tide it is possible to wade through the coral to **Goat Island,** a state bird sanctuary just offshore beyond Kalanai Point. Kamehameha Hwy. leaves the coast north of Malaekahana, passing through the faded environs of Kahuku, with its dilapidated sugar mill, the last stop before Turtle Bay and the North Shore. *(Entrance to the park 1 mi. north of the Mormon Temple on the makai (ocean) side of Kamehameha Hwy.)*

◎ SIGHTS

HOOMALUHIA BOTANICAL GARDEN. This botanical garden encompasses 400 acres of plants, trees, and flowers, all organized by world geography—there are plants from the Philippines, Hawaii, Africa, Sri Lanka and India, Polynesia, Melanesia, Malaysia, and South America. Visitors to the gardens can join the guided walks Saturday at 10am, Sunday at 1pm, or hike on their own along the many trails. **Camping** is permitted in designated areas from noon Friday to 4pm Monday. Camping permits are available at the Visitor Center. Restrooms and showers are spread throughout the park, as are fire pits, picnic tables, and parking. Keep in mind that this is the Windward side, and campers should expect wet conditions in the rainforest-like setting. *(Driving northbound on Kamehameha Hwy., turn left onto Luluku Rd. at the Aloha Gas Station just before Kaneohe's Windward City Shopping Mall. Alternatively, take TheBus #55 or 56 to this junction. The garden is 2 mi. from Kamehameha Hwy. Gates open daily 9am-4pm, after which all cars staying in the park must be registered. The Visitor Center is 1 mi. beyond the entrance. ☎ 233-7323. Open daily 9am-4pm. Free.)*

VALLEY OF THE TEMPLES. A Christian chapel and a Buddhist temple on the grounds honor the followers of both religions who are buried in this unique, beautiful cemetery. Byodo-In, the Buddhist temple, is a perfect replica of the 900-year-old temple in Uji, Japan, which is built around an enormous statue of Buddha. The ring of the temple's three-ton brass bell echoes over the *koi*-filled pools and tranquil groves of the grounds, which are home to a number of swans and peacocks. *(North of Kaneohe on Kaheliki Hwy.; turn left on Valley of the Temples Dr. Open daily 8am-4:30pm. Entrance fee $2.)*

QUEEN EMMA SUMMER PALACE. This small palace, also known as **Hanaiaka-malama** (foster child of the moon), was once the retreat of Kamehameha IV's cosmopolitan Queen. It now houses furniture and memorabilia which once belonged to her, including Prince Albert Edward's elaborate cradle, and a bracelet with a lock of Queen Victoria's hair. *(2913 Pali Hwy., on the right going north from Honolulu, approximately 2 mi. north of H-1. ☎ 595-3167. Open daily 9am-4pm. $5, children free.)*

NU'UANU PALI LOOKOUT. As you creep up the Nu'uanu side of the Koolau Mt., imagine King Kamehameha's onslaught of Big Island warriors, aided by two Western cannons, savagely driving Oahu's warriors up the *palis* (cliffs), finally forcing them over the 980 ft. drop. The moment was a decisive victory in Kamehameha's campaign to unite the islands, completed 15 years later in 1810. This is the site of the Battle of the Nu'uanu Pali's dramatic finish, and where rural legend claims the wind is strong enough to knock a man from the cliffs and then blow him right back up. Apparently, the latter did not hold true for the unfortunate warriors from Oahu. The vista spans the Windward coast, beginning at the Koolau Mountain crater, the eroded remains of which now lie under Kailua, Kaneohe, and the Pacific.

Early improvements to the passage over the Nu'uanu Pali were made around 1825, so that wood for the Kawaiahao Church in distant Honolulu could be brought over from Kaneohe. During the 1830s and 40s, missionaries constructed steep stairs, and it is believed that the opening line to Liliuokalani's song *Aloha 'Oe* (*Ha'aheo ka ua i na pali*, or "proudly by the rain of the cliff") was composed as she descended the path on horseback. The first carriage road was built in 1898 after the overthrow of the monarchy. Jack London wrote of it in 1917: "we coasted the intricate curves of the road that is railed and reinforced with masonry, fairly hanging to a stark wall for the best part of two miles." The passage is easier now, thanks to the completion of tunnels bored through the mountain, the first of which was completed in 1957.

The tunnels exit immediately below the Pali Lookout, affording drivers the same sweeping bay view; if you're heading back to Honolulu from the Windward side, there is a roadside scenic overlook on the right as the highway begins to curve to the left to enter the tunnels. Coming from Honolulu to Kailua, there is a marked scenic overlook with excellent photographic opportunities, as well as parking for the **Maunawili Trail** (p. 158), just after the hairpin turn. The Pali Lookout has informative placards and plenty of parking. *(North of Honolulu on the Pali Hwy. Open daily 9am-4pm. Don't leave valuables in your car.)*

▧ THE POLYNESIAN CULTURAL CENTER. Equal parts cultural exhibit and amusement park, this mammoth tourist attraction employs an army of native and Polynesian performers, artisans, cooks, and other cultural conservators to display the rich traditions of Polynesian cultures. The islands of Tonga, Fiji, Tahiti, Samoa, Aotearoa (New Zealand), Marquesas, and Hawaii all have villages with surprisingly authentic and intriguing performances—see real Tahitian hula, or learn how Samoans start a fire with sticks, open coconuts with their bare hands, and climb palm trees of dizzying heights. The spectacular canoe pageant at 2:30pm gives a sampling of the music and dance from all of the islands. There's an IMAX screen, canoe rides, free tram tours of Laie town, a spectacular nighttime *luau* buffet and show (though because the park is owned by the Mormon church, there is no alcohol served), and much more, all accessible depending on the variety of high-priced

THE BIG SPLURGE

TURTLE BAY RESORT

A jewel of a resort on the northernmost shore of Oahu, **Turtle Bay** boasts 880 acres, over 5 mi. of legendary shoreline, and a garland of emerald golf courses. Thes resort commands a mesmerizing view of bayside sunsets, as it rests along the rural coastline between two tranquil white-sand beaches. All guestrooms enjoy views of the surrounding Pacific. Turtle Bay's first-class amenities include a recently renovated pool, horseback riding trails, a complete day spa, two golf courses (including the Arnold Palmer Course, home to an official PGA Tour event), and 10 plexi-pave tennis courts. Fine dining at 21° North restaurant completes the package; the helipad sends it to excess. Thourgh the resort is secluded in Kahuku on the North Shore of Oahu, Honolulu is only an hour's drive away. Even if you can't free up the budget to spend the night at Turtle Bay, you can still see how the other half lives by exploring the resort's grounds or by sipping a fancy cocktail. Specialty tropical drinks ($6) at the Hang Ten Bar well drinks $5.75, beer $4-5.50; open daily 11am-11pm) go down especially well with the sun. ❺

(*57-091 Kamehameha Hwy.* ☎ *800-203-3650 or 293-8811; www.turtlebay.com. Check-in 3pm. Check-out 11am. 24hr. reception. Standard rooms for 2-4 $295-400; suites $500+; cottages $550-700. AmEx/D/MC/V.*)

tickets purchased. Plan to spend all afternoon and evening at the park. (*55-370 Kamehameha Hwy. in Laie; you can't miss the 10ft. wooden Tiki statues that frown over the roadside just before the parking lot.* ☎ *877-722-1411; www.polynesia.com. Transportation can be arranged from around the island by calling* ☎ *800-367-7060. Open M-Sa 12:30-9pm; island villages open 1pm. $40-175, children ages 5-11 $24-115. AmEx/D/MC/V.*)

THE MORMON TEMPLE. Truly a sight to behold, this was the first Mormon temple built outside the continental US. The temple, built of crushed volcanic rock and coral, was dedicated on November 27, 1919 and sits on the 6000-acre plantation purchased in 1865 by The Church of Jesus Christ of Latter-Day Saints. Beyond the temple, the 11-acre site is comprised of well-manicured formal gardens and a Visitor Center with a 10 ft. marble replica of Thorvaldsen's *Christus.* The Center's guided tours explain the saints' beliefs with obvious but unobtrusive missionary overtones. (*55-645 Naniloa Loop. A tram line runs here from The Polynesian Cultural Center, through historic Laie (every 20min. 1-7pm, free). By car, turn left onto Hale La'a Blvd., the 2nd street after the Laie Shopping Center.* ☎ *293-9297. Open daily 9am-8pm. Free.*)

KUALOA RANCH AND REGIONAL PARK. The **Kualoa Ranch,** a privately owned 4000-acre working cattle ranch-turned-tourist attraction, stretches up Ka'awa Valley. The establishment gives visitors the chance to play cowboy with an hour of horseback riding ($45); those not so fond of animals can hop on an iron steed and cruise around Kualoa's many off-road trails in an ATV ($45). Package deals include transportation from Waikiki, lunch, and access to Kualoa's private Secret Island Beach (where you can kayak, canoe, or jet ski), as well as one adventure activity (e.g. horseback or ATV riding) for $57. Nearby **Kualoa Regional Park,** on the coastal side of the highway south of the ranch entrance, is a grassy flat leading to a narrow beach. This is the closest point to Chinaman's Hat, an offshore island and Windward landmark named for its tapering, peaked shape. **Kualoa Point,** at the extreme end of the park, marks the northern edge of Kaneohe Bay. (*49-560 Kamehameha Hwy.* ☎ *237-7321. The main entrance to the ranch is on the mauka (mountain) side of Kamehameha Hwy., north of Kualoa Regional Park. Open daily 9:45am-3:15pm. Sa-Su ATV and horseback riding only. For information on camping at Kualoa Regional Park, see Camping, p. 86. MC/V.*)

TROPICAL FARMS. Set in the midst of Kualoa Ranch, just before Kualoa Park, Tropical Farms is the only working macadamia nut farm on Oahu. The extensive gift shop offers ✷**free samples** of freshly harvested nuts, Kona-macadamia coffee, exotic locally grown fruits, and much more. The shop overlooks an 800-year-old fishpond and extensive variety gardens. *(49-227A Kamehameha Hwy. ☎877-505-6887.)*

ULUPO HEIAU. This sacred *heiau* (temple) is set on a peaceful plateau of lava rocks beside a shady grove with benches and a few placards. *Heiaus* were traditionally built at the orders of *kahunas* (priests) to ensure success in war and agricultural and aqua cultural fertility; from this *heiau* the *ali'i*, or chief, of the political and religious center in Kailua could survey his holdings at Kawainui. The holdings became a *taro (poi)* patch following the abolition of the native religion in 1819. Chinese buyers converted the same land into a rice paddy in the late 1800s, but it had been abandoned as marshland by 1920. Thick growth conceals the bottom of the morass, which is home to numerous endangered native waterfowl. *(Near Kailua. Turn right onto Uluoa St., from Kailua toward Pali Hwy., and take the 1st right onto Manu Aloha. Go to the end of the block. Park behind the Windward YMCA and walk around it to the heiau. Call the Oahu District division of the Department of Parks and Recreation for more info, ☎587-0300.)*

⬛ HIKING

HAUULA. The **Maakua Ridge Trail** and **Hauula Loop Trail** (2½ mi. Trailhead: Hauula Homestead Rd., across from **Hauula Beach Park** (see **Camping**, p. 149). Level: easy). The trail comes to a fork initially; take the right fork, climbing up the ridge to cross Waipilopilo Gulch. This path then turns back toward the ocean, overlooking Kipapau Valley, and loops to rejoin the beginning of the trail. The initial trail is easy, and well-suited for families. The Maakua Ridge Trail begins in a *hau* forest on the left side of the access road, beyond the Hauula Loop Trailhead. After a stream crossing, there is a switchback to a ridge-top shelter with benches overlooking seaside Hauula. The loop begins here, and you may proceed in either direction to rise 800 ft. in moderate to difficult terrain. Both trails are accessible for mountain bikers, so use caution when heading out on foot. This area is also a hunting ground and the water contains the bacteria leptospirosis; hike at your own risk. *(By car from Kamehameha Hwy. northbound, turn left on Hauula Homestead Rd. Where the road curves sharply to the left continue straight onto Maakua Rd. Park roadside before the cable gate. Hauula Loop Trail begins on the right, just beyond the hunter/hiker check-in station.)*

KAIWA RIDGE TRAIL. (2 mi. round-trip. Trailhead: Kaelepulu Dr. near Lanikai. Level: moderate.) Also known to locals as "Pillboxes," this moderately difficult hike climbs up the ridge behind Lanikai (see **Beaches**, p. 154) to WWII army bunkers overlooking the beach. From the top, 600 ft. up, you can see Molokai, Lanai, and, on a superbly clear day, Maui. Despite its popularity, the trail receives minimal maintenance, and hikers are advised to use caution and not to climb the bunkers. You may either return the way you came up, or continue along the trail to loop back around to Mokolea Dr. *(Take Aalapapa Dr. into Lanikai and then turn right on Kaelepulu Dr. At the Mid-Pacific Country Club, park in the turnout on the right side of the street. The dirt trailhead is across the street, to the left of the chainlink fence.)*

MAUNAWILI DITCH TRAIL. (2¾ mi. Trailhead: Waikaupanaha St. Level: easy.) This equestrian, bike, and hiking trail rises an easy 200 ft. and ends at the Waimanalo side of the **Maunawili Trail**. *(Driving north from Waimanalo on the Kalanianaole Hwy., turn left onto Kumuhau St. about ½ mi. north of the Waimanalo Shopping Center. Turn right on Waikaupanaha St. and park near the fence and gate on the right, after Mahiku Pl. at the bend in the road. Proceed through the fence, mauka (toward the mountains) along the dirt road.)*

MAUNAWILI TRAIL. (10 mi. round-trip. Trailhead: Pali Hwy. Elevation change: 500 ft. Level: moderate.) The terrain of the Maunawili ("twisted mountain") Trail varies from wet, overgrown gulches to open forest canopies as it traverses the Windward base of the Koolau Mountain Range. The voyage among *koa*, lobelia, *'o'hia*, and other vegetation ends with transcendent views of Olomana, the Koolaupoko watershed, and, at the south end, Waimanalo. *(Driving on Pali Hwy. to Kailua from Honolulu, as you come out of the tunnels, turn into the parking area marked "Scenic Overlook," just after the hairpin turn on the right. The trailhead is adjacent to this parking area.)*

MAUNAWILI FALLS TRAIL. (1¼ mi. Trailhead: Maunawili Rd. Level: moderate.) The wet and muddy Mauanawili Falls Trail crosses the Maunawili stream frequently and without the aid of bridges, which often necessitates some fancy footwork hopping across rocks. The trail passes through mountain apple and coffee trees and is popular with families with kids of elementary school age and older. There is a stair descent at the last stream crossing to reach the payoff: a cool, deep pool and a short cascading waterfall. Local teenagers who visit the spot sometimes jump off of the waterfall into the pool, but it is not recommended. Bring your own water—the falls water carries biological impurities. *(Driving toward Kailua on the Pali Hwy., continue through Castle Junction and past Kapa'a Quarry Rd. The next intersection on the right is Auloa Rd.; the road splits almost immediately, so be sure to take the left fork, Maunawili Rd. Follow this road until it ends in a residential neighborhood, and look for the trailhead signs. Make sure to park on the right. Do not leave valuables in your car.)*

NORTH SHORE

Oahu's North Shore has long been a relaxed destination for city dwellers to escape the bustle of urban life. With only 18,000 residents, the North Shore is relatively quiet, and remains rural and undeveloped in places, though the surf industry certainly attracts its share of visitors and traffic, especially in winter. The hotel and golf course at **Turtle Bay** is the area's sole resort, situated amid the corn fields and shrimp farms of **Kahuku,** the shore's northernmost village. Southwest of Turtle Bay, from **Sunset Beach** to **Waimea,** there is one spectacular beach after another; while some are quite popular for surfing and swimming, others are astonishingly empty. Past Waimea, **Haleiwa** (see p. 162) is the center of life on the North Shore, with its first-rate eateries, shops, and galleries, as well as plenty of places to stock up on surf gear. To the west of Haleiwa lie **Waialua** and **Mokule'ia,** two small towns known for their agriculture and their adventure sports.

To reach the North Shore by car, take H-1 from Honolulu to the end of H-2, then follow Rte. 803 or Hwy. 99. **Highway 83 (Kamehameha Highway)** is the main road that runs along the coast through each town from Haleiwa to Kahuku, and down the Windward Coast. The North Shore is also served by TheBus #52, which runs from Honolulu via Wahiawa to Haleiwa, and then up the coast on Kamehameha Hwy. to Turtle Bay. TheBus #76 runs between Haleiwa and Waialua along Farrington Hwy.

WAIMEA AND SUNSET BEACH

Along the coast northeast of Haleiwa, Kamehameha Hwy. meanders through the communities of Sunset Beach and Waimea. Though there are no real town centers, both have clusters of roadside food stands, surf shacks, and hostels, as well as miles of beaches. This is *the* place to stay if you're serious about winter surfing, but it's also worthwhile during the calmer summer months, when there is great snorkeling, swimming, and hiking up Pupukea (see p. 161).

Rollerbladers, bikers, joggers, and strollers alike enjoy the **bike path** that stretches for several miles between Sunset Beach and Waimea. Separated by thick

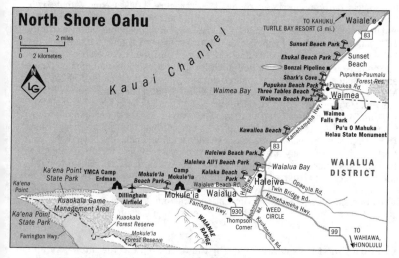

North Shore Oahu

trees and shrubbery from Kamehameha Hwy. and the houses that line it, the path provides a scenic yet secluded way to see the North Shore. For those who prefer public transportation, TheBus #52 shuttles back and forth from Turtle Bay Resort in Kahuku through Sunset Beach and Waimea to Haleiwa.

■ ● ORIENTATION AND PRACTICAL INFORMATION. Kamehameha Highway is the main road from Haleiwa through Waimea and Sunset Beach. There is an **ATM** and a Starbucks inside **Foodland,** at the intersection of Pupukea Rd. (Open daily 6am-11pm.) In the small plaza next to Sunset Pizza (see p. 160), you'll find Kammie's Market **convenience store** (open daily 9:30am-8:30pm) and **Sunset Beach Laundry.** (☎638-9138. Open daily 7am-9pm.) Since neither Waimea nor Sunset Beach are large enough to merit their own zip code, the nearest **post office** is in Haleiwa (see p. 163). Another option is the **Kahuku post office,** 56-565 Kamehameha Hwy., past Sunset Beach. (☎293-0485. Open M-F 8:30am-4:30pm, Sa 8:30am-11:30am.) **Postal Code:** 96731.

● ACCOMMODATIONS. There are numerous **vacation rentals** available along the beaches near Waimea; call the real estate agents listed in Haleiwa (see p. 162) for more information. Among them, the **Ke Iki Beach Bungalows ❸** have an unbeatable location directly on a long, sandy (and almost always empty) beach. The waves are only big during the winter but the view is spectacular year-round. The studio and one- and two-bedroom bungalows are newly renovated and landscaped, with patios and hammocks on the beach side. They are reasonably good values, but have high cleaning fees. (☎638-8829; www.keikibeach.com. Reservations strongly recommended. Cleaning $45-85. Streetside bungalows Apr. 23-June 15 and Sept. 4-Nov. 16 $65-140; otherwise $85-160. Beachside $130-199; $150-200. Discounts available if staying 1 week or more.)

Waimea also has a couple of budget accommodations. Both are right across from a beach and a #52 bus stop, and are within walking distance of Foodland. **■Shark's Cove Rentals ❷,** 59-672 Kamehameha Hwy., across from Sharks Cove snorkel and dive spot and Log Cabins surf spot. The owners live on the premises with their family and keep everything ship-shape, even providing homey touches like towels and shampoo in the rooms. There are three houses, each with its own living room (with cable TV), kitchen, and full bath. All rooms have bunk beds, and some also have a double-sized bottom bunk. BBQ, pay phone, soda machine, and coin-op laundry are located in the central courtyard. There is also free snorkel equipment for guests. (☎888-883-0001 or 638-7980; www.sharkscoverentals.com. An entire house can be rented for groups. 3-day minimum stay. Linen and key deposit $20. Apr.-Sept. shared doubles $25, private doubles $50-75. Oct.-Mar. shared doubles $30, private doubles $60-100.) **Backpackers ❶**, 59-788 Kamehameha Hwy., across from Three Tables beach, has 120 beds for relaxed surfers looking for the cheapest digs in town. There are a variety of accommodations, from 2- to 6-bed dorms to private beachfront cottages, but all are very basic. Dorms and some private rooms share kitchen and bath; cottages have their own. Perks include free daily airport shuttle (with reservations), nightly meals ($6), free snorkel equipment and boogie boards, discounts on activities (up to 50%), Internet access ($7 per hr.), and equipment storage. **Short term work** can be arranged in exchange for room and board. (☎888-628-8882 or 638-7838; www.backpackers-hawaii.com. Reception 8am-7pm. Check-in noon. Check-out 10am. Reserve dorms a day or so in advance in high season. Dorms $15-18; private doubles $45-60; cabins $80-200. MC/V.)

◘ **FOOD.** The **Foodland** in Waimea by the traffic light at the intersection of Kamehameha Hwy. and Pupukea Rd. has the largest selection of groceries on the North Shore, but the prices (1 lb. of tomatoes; $7) will shock you. (Open daily 6am-11pm.) Within Waimea and Sunset Beach, there are quite a few roadside food stands and take-out establishments that have earned solid reputations. **⧉Taste of Paradise ❷**, 59-25 Kamehameha Hwy., near Sunset Beach, packs a winning combination with flavorful food, cheery atmosphere, and service with a smile. They serve up Brazilian-style plates ($7-12) made with fresh, high-quality ingredients from a psychedelic food truck in the back of a giant rainbow tunnel. Eggplant, fish, shrimp, chicken, or beef come with brown or white rice, and are topped with grilled onions and pineapple, garlic toast, and organic greens. (☎638-0855. Open daily 11:30am-9:30pm. Live music on weekends.) **⧉Ted's Bakery ❶**, 59-024 Kamehameha Hwy., has been a North Shore favorite for 15 years. The pastry experts whip up donuts that make Krispy Kremes taste like hockey pucks, as well as tempting cakes and pies made with real butter, eggs, and cream. The home of the original chocolate-haupia cream pie opens at 7am, and the fresh, warm donuts are long-gone soon after. **Sunset Pizza ❶**, next to the laundromat and market, is known for its pizza but also makes a tasty mahi mahi burger. Mostly takeout with some outdoor seating. (☎638-7660. Slices $2.50-3. Open daily 10am-9pm.)

If you happen to be in Waimea on a Saturday morning, be sure to stop by the **North Shore County Market**, 59-530 Kamehameha Hwy., between Sharks Cove and Ehukai Beach Park. Local farmers gather at this community event to sell fresh organic produce including fruits, vegetables, flowers, and other plants. The market is a great opportunity for travelers to catch a glimpse of the local North Shore community. (☎638-7172. Open Sa 8am-2pm.)

◪ **BEACHES.** If the beach is your thing, you're in the right place—from Sunset Beach to Waimea, it's sand, sand, and more sand. Between **Sunset Beach Park**, 59-360 Kamehameha Hwy. (☎638-7051) and **Ekuhai Beach Park** there is one surf spot after another. While Ehukai breaks on a sandy bottom, Sunset Beach has a strong riptide, but that doesn't keep the crowds away from this world-famous spot. Both parks have parking, restrooms, and lifeguards. Between Ekuhai Beach Park and Kalalua Point, there is a long stretch of sandy beach that is practically always empty. The famous **Bonzai Pipeline** is a part of this beach, as is the **Log Cabins** surf spot, where the undertow can still be strong in summer. Shoreline access is marked along the walking path between Kamehameha Hwy. and the private beachfront homes; park wherever there is a pullout in the path and join the crowds scoping the surfers in peak season. On the other side of Kalalua Point and just before the Foodland in Waimea, **Pupukea Beach Park,** 59-727 Kamehameha Hwy. (☎338-7213) and **Shark's Cove** offer some of the best snorkeling on Oahu in the summer (masks can be rented at several kiosks and homes across the street). Between Foodland and Waimea, **Three Tables Beach** is named for the three plateaus of reef that emerge from the water at low tide. The reef makes for great snorkeling in summer and world-class surfing in winter. One of the most spectacular sites is **Waimea Beach Park,** a deep crescent of sand visible from the road above as it curves into the gulch toward Waimea Falls. Though Waimea Bay is impossibly flat during the summer, it morphs into an experts-only surf spot come winter. There's good snorkeling and cliff jumping off to the left when it's calm. The parking lot fills up quickly, and you may be ticketed if you park on the road above.

⚡🗺 HIKING AND SIGHTS The biggest tourist attraction in the area is **Waimea Falls Park,** 59-864 Kamehameha Hwy. (☎638-8511). Fairly pricey, but a better deal if you arrive after 4pm, when admission drops and the grounds are less crowded, though you'll miss the demonstrations. The park, across the highway from the Waimea Bay Beach Park, includes pleasant botanical gardens, a few Hawaiian cultural displays, and an anticlimactic waterfall that lies at the end of ¾ mi. of paved path. Cliff diving shows are performed five times daily, but you can't jump yourself. Horseback riding, mountain biking, and kayaking are also available within the park, but can be done more cheaply elsewhere. ($25, after 3pm $14, after 4pm $10. Open daily 10am-5:30pm.)

A more direct communion with nature can be reached hiking the trails of **Pupukea,** which begin at the end of Pupukea Rd. (next to Foodland). Follow the steep and winding Pupukea Rd. about 3 mi. up the hill until you see Camp Pupukea, the Aloha Council Boy Scout camp, on your left. Though you can't park in the camp, you'll have no problem leaving your vehicle roadside right before it. From the Boy Scout Camp, there are two excellent trails, the 6 mi. **Kaunala Loop** and the 9 mi. **Pupukea Summit Trail.** Conditions are frequently rainy and always muddy, so rain gear and sturdy hiking boots (and mosquito repellent!) are strongly recommended.

The Kaunala Loop trail winds through several gulches full of *ti* plants, sandalwood, and *koa* trees, as well as the occasional wild orchid. To reach the trailhead, follow the dirt road past the camp, around the locked gate, and sign in on the sheets inside the mailbox on the left. Take a peek at the trail map next to the mailbox to get an idea where you're going. Continue down the road, keeping to the left; there's a marked trailhead on the left side when you reach the first major fork. Follow the yellow hiker's arrows on the signs whenever there is an intersection or ambiguous fork. The trail connects with a dirt road; turn right onto it and follow the ridge along several ups and downs. On clear days, there are views of the shore along this leg. The road eventually loops back to the original dirt road you started on (turn right at the intersection and continue down the hill to return to the parking area). The Kaunala Loop is an intermediate level hike; the most strenuous part of it is maintaining your balance through mud puddles and over small streams. At a moderate pace, it should take you about 2hr. to complete. The Pupukea summit hike requires permission from the US Army, as they maintain the trail and train here. For information and permission, write to: Commander, U.S. Army Garrison, Schofield Barracks, HI 96857 (attn: APVG-GWY-O).

For a more spiritual connection with nature and history, stop by the **Pu'u O Mahuka Heiau State Monument,** off Pupukea Rd. About 1½ miles from Kamehameha Hwy. and Foodland, look for signs on your right. Follow the narrow speed-bump-covered road to the remains of an ancient Hawaiian *luakini heiau* (temple). Today only the rock walls and stone paved floor are left at the national historic landmark, but 250 years ago on the site stood a major temple that was dedicated as a sacrifice for success in war. High priest Ka'opulupulu presided over the temple in the 1770s, and Kamehameha I's *kahuna* (priest) Hewahawa oversaw it until 1819 when the ancient Hawaiian religion was abolished. Built on a bluff above Waimea Valley, the monument offers a commanding view of the shoreline and the channel between Oahu and Kauai. Signal fires built here used to provide visual communication between the islands. The site is considered very sacred to the Hawaiian people, and a visit here can be a spiritual retreat from the North Shore surfing frenzy.

HALEIWA

It's easy to see how folks can come to Haleiwa for a weekend and end up staying longer. Since its beginnings, Haleiwa has been a grand vacationland; Christian missionaries came to the North Shore in 1832 and established a small village that later became the seashore destination of choice for city dwellers who would ride the sugar train along Oahu's northern coast to Haleiwa. Renowned for its legendary beaches, Haleiwa is a favorite refuge for Oahu's residents and a must-see for visitors. For surfers and locals, the town is a place to refuel on tasty grinds and "talk story;" for vacationers, it's an opportunity to trade the chaos of the city for the leisurely tempo of the country. Many visitors make the trip up from Honolulu simply to peruse Haleiwa's distinctive galleries and shops, and to grab a rainbow-hued shave ice. Haleiwa is the undisputed center of life on the North Shore, and the double-arched Anahulu River bridge on the edge of town is the gateway to the world-famous beaches that are strung like pearls along the coast.

ORIENTATION

Haleiwa center is located along **Route 83 (Kamehameha Highway),** just north of the traffic circle where **Highway 99** meets Rte. 83. **Haleiwa Road** runs along the harbor toward Waialua, intersecting Kamehameha Hwy. by the **Anahulu Bridge.** Haleiwa is served by TheBus #52, which runs from Honolulu via Wahiawa up Kamehameha Hwy. to Turtle Bay, and #76, which shuttles between Haleiwa and Waialua.

PRACTICAL INFORMATION

Banks: American Savings Bank (open M-Th 9am-4:30pm, F 9am-6pm), **Bank of Hawaii** (open M-Th 8:30am-4pm, F 8:30am-6pm), and **First Hawaiian Bank** (www.fhb.com; open M-Th 8:30am-4pm, F 8:30am-6pm) are all located on Kamehameha Hwy. between Haleiwa Super Market and Aoki's Shave Ice. There are **ATMs** outside the 3 banks (open 24hr.), as well as in both supermarkets and the Coffee Gallery.

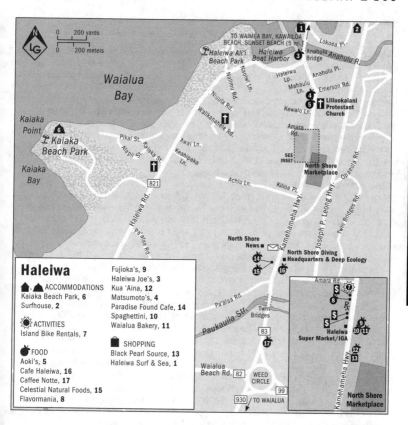

Haleiwa

▲, ▲ ACCOMMODATIONS
Kaiaka Beach Park, 6
Surfhouse, 2

☼ ACTIVITIES
Island Bike Rentals, 7

🍴 FOOD
Aoki's, 5
Cafe Haleiwa, 16
Coffee Notte, 17
Celestial Natural Foods, 15
Flavormania, 8

Fujioka's, 9
Haleiwa Joe's, 3
Kua 'Aina, 12
Matsumoto's, 4
Paradise Found Cafe, 14
Spaghettini, 10
Waialua Bakery, 11

■ SHOPPING
Black Pearl Source, 13
Haleiwa Surf & Sea, 1

Pharmacy: Haleiwa Pharmacy and PhotoLab/Valu-Rite, 66-145 Kamehameha Hwy. (☎637-2313), next to Flavormania Ice Cream. Fills prescriptions and has an extensive selection of first-aid supplies. Open M-Tu and Th 9am-6:30pm, W and F-Sa 9am-5:30pm. Closed daily for lunch 1-1:30pm.

Copy/fax services: At **North Shore News,** 66-437 Kamehameha Hwy. (☎637-3138, fax 637-8862), behind the post office on the 2nd fl. Copies $0.10. Open M-F 9am-5pm. AmEx/MC/V.

Internet Access: The **Coffee Gallery,** in the North Shore Marketplace, has 3 finicky terminals (☎637-5355. $1 per 10min. Open daily 7am-8pm.). **Surf Hawaii Surf School,** on the 2nd fl. of the peach and beige building in the back right corner of the North Shore Marketplace, has 2 relatively new computers. (☎637-2622. $1 for 15min., $5 for 55min.) Also in the Marketplace, **Kono's Big Wave Cafe** can likewise hook you up. (☎637-9211. $1 for 10min., $5 for 1hr. Open M-Sa 8am-6pm, Su 9am-6pm.)

Post office: 66-437 Kamehameha Hwy. (☎637-1711), in the buildings complex next to Celestial Foods on the southeastern edge of town. Open M-F 8am-4pm, Sa 9am-noon.

Postal Code: 96712.

ACCOMMODATIONS

There are numerous properties on the beaches near Haleiwa that are available as **vacation rentals.** Houses on the beach range from surfer shacks to luxurious homes. You can expect to pay $90-150 per bedroom per night for a moderate house, with a price break for weekly and monthly rentals. Rentals are a more economical option for those traveling in groups, as rates for multi-bedroom homes work out to be quite reasonable. **Sterman Real Estate** (☎877-637-6200; www.sterman.com) and **Team Real Estate** (☎800-982-8602, ext. 10; www.teamrealestate.com) are both based in Haleiwa with home offices in the North Shore Marketplace and handle vacation rentals all over Oahu's northern coast. Neither company charges a user's fee but they do require a deposit and one-time cleaning fee, in addition to the rent. For high season (Nov. 15-Feb. 15), reserve at least three to four months in advance.

The primary accommodation option in Haleiwa is the **Surfhouse ❶,** 62-203 Lokoea Pl., about a 5min. walk from the bus station at the Chevron, and a 10min. walk to the center of town. To reach the Surfhouse from Haleiwa center, take a right off of Kamehameha Hwy. immediately after the Anahulu Bridge onto Lokoea Pl. As the road turns from pavement to dirt and takes a sharp curve to the left, you'll see Surfhouse directly in front of you. The Surfhouse is a good choice if you want to pitch a **tent** in the midst of their citrus grove, or if you want to be within walking distance of town (other budget accommodations near Waimea are more comfortable and nearer to the big surf spots). Many of the guests are European backpackers, although several people stay semi-permanently while looking for employment and housing elsewhere. There is one private tin-roof cabin and a six-bunk dorm; neither have doors that lock but there is a safe in the office. All guests share an outdoor kitchen and one toilet, sink, and shower in a separate outbuilding. (☎637-7146; www.surfhouse.com. Dorms $15; tent site for 1 person $9, for 2 people $15; cabin for 1 person $40, for 2 people $45.)

The only other option for accommodations in Haleiwa is at **Kaiaka Beach Park,** about a mile west of town past the fire department on Haleiwa Rd., where free **camping ❶** with a permit is allowed from Friday to Tuesday nights. Kaiaka has seven sites, restrooms, showers, and picnic tables, and the scenery can't be beat as the park is directly on the beach. (See p. 64 in the **Essentials** section for information on obtaining camping permits. Gates lock daily 6:45pm-7am.)

FOOD

Haleiwa has plenty of burger grills and takeout joints, as well as a few excellent sit-down restaurants. Vegetarians will have no problem—surfer food tends toward the healthy and filling (and cheap), which means burritos, brown rice, and tofu galore. And, as Haleiwa is on the water, the fish is reliably good wherever you go.

There are also a number of markets in and around Haleiwa. **Fujioka's,** 66-190 Kamehameha Hwy., right in the center of town, sells liquor, basic staples, and produce. There's an ATM machine and a Western Union office inside. (Open M-Sa 8am-8pm, Su 8am-5pm. AmEx/D/MC/V.) Across the street, **Haleiwa Super Market/IGA,** 66-197 Kamehameha Hwy., has similar offerings, including an ATM machine. (Open M-Sa 8am-8pm, Su 8:30am-5:30pm. D/MC/V.) **Foodland,** in Waimea (p. 158), has a better selection but outrageous prices. You'd be better off buying fruit at the produce stands northwest of town. **Celestial Natural Foods,** 66-443 Kamehameha Hwy., next to the post office and across from Cafe Haleiwa, has a limited selection of organic produce, packaged foods, vitamins, and health care products. (☎637-4540. Open M-Sa 9am-6pm, Su 10am-6pm. MC/V.)

RESTAURANTS AND CAFES

■ **Haleiwa Joe's,** 66-011 Kamehameha Hwy. (☎637-8005). Formerly a Chart House restaurant, Haleiwa Joe's kept the Tiki torches but added its own local style. There may be a wait for sunset dining on weekends, but you can join the crowd at the bar for *pupus* (like *ahi* spring rolls and Thai fried calamari) and specialty drinks like the fruity Sandy Snorkel and provocative Naughty Angel ($6-7.50). Save room for the substantial entrees—the prime rib, garnished with an *aloha* flower, is about 2 in. thick and requires a team effort. The fresh fish is well-prepared—notable creations are the baked *ono* with coconut crust, mango chutney, and green curry ($19), and the guava-miso glazed salmon ($18). The wine selection is excellent and reasonably priced. Entrees $12-23. Aloha Hour M-F 4:30-6:30pm. Open daily 11:30am-2pm and 5:30-9:30pm. Bar stays open until 10:30pm on weekends, featuring live music on F night. AmEx/MC/V. ❸

■ **Caffee Notte,** 66-560 Kamehameha Hwy. (☎636-2285), at the southwesternmost edge of town near the 7-11. Opened by the owners of Cholo's (see below), this Italian restaurant has a comfortable and classy atmosphere. The pasta sauces are fresh and flavorful, with plenty of garlic and some real heat in the spicy marinara. The tomato and broccoli pasta goes well with a side of the Italian sausage, and the seafood specials are perfect with a glass of white wine. Entrees $10-17. Open daily 5-10pm. AmEx/MC/V. ❸

■ **Kua 'Aina,** 66-214 Kamehameha Hwy. (☎637-6067). Seats are hard to come by at this jam-packed sandwich and burger joint that has become so popular in its 28 years that there are now satellites in Honolulu and Tokyo. The acclaimed "world's best hamburgers" are quite possibly just that; try yours with avocado or pineapple. The mahi mahi sandwiches are legendary, and are perfectly accompanied by the crispy homemade fries ($1.65). Rumor has it that Kua 'Aina may be relocating within Haleiwa, so be sure to scope out its alleged new home. Burgers $5-6. Open daily 11am-8pm. ❶

■ **Coffee Gallery,** 66-250 Kamehameha Hwy. (☎637-5355), in the North Shore Marketplace. It seems as though everyone in Haleiwa comes here for their daily caffeine fix. Though the menu offers fresh mango smoothies ($3.75) and smoked *ahi* wraps ($5.50), the draw is more likely the winning combination of good conversation and top-quality beans roasted daily on the premises. See what all the buzz is about; small cups of the 5 varieties of 100% Hawaiian java will only set you back $1.30. **Internet access** ($1 per 10min.) and **ATM.** Open daily 7am-8pm. ❶

Cholo's Homestyle Mexican, 66-250 Kamehameha Hwy. (☎637-3059), in the North Shore Marketplace. Fun and festive Cholo's is always packed, and for good reason—the fish tacos are chock-full of grilled and spiced *ahi*, the tamales are moist and tender, and the chips and salsa are always fresh. Entrees run $6-10, though many dishes come a la carte for the meager of appetite or budget. Think of Cholo's fruit fajitas with cinnamon tortillas as an alternative breakfast option. Open daily 8am-9pm. AmEx/MC/V. ❷

Cafe Haleiwa, 66-460 Kamehameha Hwy. (☎637-5516). A Haleiwa institution for 2 decades, Cafe Haleiwa serves hearty breakfasts and lunches substantial enough to fuel a day of surf and sun. Contemplate the psychedelic surf paintings on the walls as you take on Breakfast in a Barrel (what less surf-minded folks might call a breakfast burrito) or plunge Off the Lip (an egg and veggie scramble). For your caffeine fix, enjoy some hot java from the Espresso Bar in back. Nothing is over $7. Open for breakfast M-Sa 7am-12:30pm and Su 7am-2pm, lunch (burgers and Mex plates) served M-Sa 11am-2pm. AmEx/MC/V. ❶

Paradise Found Cafe, 66-443 Kamehameha Hwy. (☎637-4540), in the back right corner of the Celestial Natural Foods Store. The wisdom of the hippie poetry on the walls is questionable, but there are no doubts as to the quality of the made-to-order vegetarian food. Salads are layered with creamy avocado, heirloom tomatoes and tangy feta, and the tofu curry scramble is big on flavor. If you'd rather not dine to the smell of incense and patchouli, you can take your meal to go. Everything is $5-6. Open M-Sa 9am-5pm, Su 10am-5pm. MC/V. ❶

Spaghettini, 66-200 Kamehameha Hwy. (☎637-0104). Don't be fooled by the modest facade—Spaghettini doesn't scrimp on quality ingredients in their homemade "New York style" pizzas and pasta sauces, and everything is cooked to order. The pizza crust is crisp, chewy and just thick enough. Plus, you can enjoy the sounds of classic American rock while you dine on the outdoor patio. Combo meals include pizza, salad, and soda for $5. Slices $2-3; large pizza $13, plus $1.50 for each topping. Pastas $6-9. Open daily 11am-8pm. ❶

Waialua Bakery, 66-200 Kamehameha Hwy. (☎637-9079), next to Fujioka's market. The fresh loaves of baked bread are soft and savory and make tasty sandwiches ($4-5). Look for special flavors like cheese and herb or sunflower wheat. Add a refreshing smoothie ($3.50) and you're good to go. Open M-Sa 8am-4pm. ❶

SHAVE ICE AND ICE CREAM

Shave ice is to Haleiwa what gelato is to Venice—you're doing yourself a disservice if you pass up these cheap, colorful, and tasty treats.

■ **Matsumoto's,** 66-087 Kamehameha Hwy. (☎637-4827), is by far the most famous (tour buses now stop directly outside), as evidenced by the huge lines. There is a strict protocol for ordering: state how many small or large cones you want, whether you want ice cream and/or sweet *azuki* beans (try them!), and only when they *ask* do you state your flavors. Plain with 3 flavors $1.20, with ice cream and beans $1.80. Shave ice can get pretty drippy, so consider shelling out an extra quarter for a reusable plastic shave ice catcher. Enjoy Matsumoto's unique and extensive selection of t-shirts; they make great gifts at $14 each. Open daily 9am-6pm. ❶

■ **Aoki's,** 66-117 Kamehameha Hwy. (☎637-7017), next door to Matsumoto's and just as good; owners Cathy and Michael also make their own syrups. The only difference is that Aoki's has fewer flavors (not by much!) and a much shorter line. The same ordering rules apply (see above). Plain with 3 flavors $1.20, with ice cream and beans $1.80. Open M-F "usually around" noon- "most of the time" 5:30pm, Sa-Su closes 6pm. ❶

Flavormania, 66-145 Kamehameha Hwy. (☎637-9362). If you're craving some creamy sweetness, Flavormania has over 30 varieties of ice cream that could take on both Ben *and* Jerry. All the flavors—from Kona Koffee to Bonzai Banana—are made on the premises. Single scoop $1.80. Open daily 11am-8pm. ❶

BEACHES

Although the most famous beaches and surf spots in the area are near **Waimea** and **Sunset Beach** (p. 158), there are a few decent spots right in Haleiwa, as well as northeast between Waimea and Haleiwa. The beaches east of Haleiwa off Waialua Beach Rd. are known spots for shark breeding, but there is excellent **kiteboarding** (see Kiteboarding to Extremes, p. 80) farther west in Mokule'ia.

HALEIWA ALI'I BEACH PARK. Haleiwa Ali'i Beach Park is placid during the summer, but the winter brings three good surf breaks offshore to the left. The one farthest left, if facing the water, is known as **Walls,** to the right of Walls is **Avalanche,** and **Haleiwa** is directly out from the beach park. The latter is a good place for beginners when the waves are small, but for experts only when they get big. The beach has restrooms, showers, and picnic tables. *(66-167 Haleiwa Rd. Contact the park's surf center at ☎637-5051. Gates closed daily 10pm-6am.)*

HALEIWA BEACH PARK. Although the beach is unremarkable, Haleiwa Beach Park is a local gathering place in the summer. **Haleiwa Surf & Sea,** 62-595 Kamehameha Hwy., launches **canoes** from this harbor, and arranges **scuba dives** and lessons, **sport fishing trips, surf lessons,** as well as **snorkel** tours and gear rental. (☎637-9887; www.surfnsea.com.) There are two surf breaks off the point to the right: **Pua'ena** and the experts-only **Pua'ena Point** on the outside. The beach has restrooms, showers, basketball courts, and picnic tables. *(Just past Anahulu Bridge on the left when heading toward Waimea Bay.)*

KAIAKA BEACH PARK. The 53-acre Kaiaka park is more of a draw than the beach itself, as the in-town beaches are less muddy and better for swimming in the summer. But the pleasant picnic grove, free campsites, and clean showers make the park a great family destination for the afternoon. *(About 1 mi. west of town, past the fire station on Haleiwa Rd. See Accommodations above for camping information. Gates close daily 6:45pm-7am.)*

KAWAILOA BEACH. Kawailoa Beach is the general name for this stretch of sometimes sandy, sometimes rocky coastline edged by private homes. **Chun's Reef** is the most popular surf break in this stretch, and has beachfront parking across from it, at the intersection of Plantation Rd. and Kamehameha Hwy. One of the largest pull-outs for cars (about 2 mi. southeast of Waimea Beach Park) is opposite a moss-covered rocky formation popularly known as **Alligator Rock.** If you park at Alligator Rock, there is a surf spot directly in front of you and, if you walk south (left) over the rock to the sandy beach, you'll come to two more surf spots: **Left Overs** and **Right Overs.** The swimming here is decent in the summer (the beach is rarely crowded), although there can be a bit of a riptide between the two surf breaks. Large **sea turtles** are commonly spotted swimming close to shore; look, but don't touch lest you incur a fine of $1000 from the turtle protectors who patrol the beach. *(Kawailoa stretches from Waimea to Pue'ena Point.)*

ACTIVITIES

In addition to Haleiwa Surf & Sea (see p. 166), Haleiwa is home to a generous number of outfitters that offer equipment rentals, surf lessons, scuba trips, and whale watches. If it happens in the water, you can do it in Haleiwa.

North Shore Diving Headquarters, 66-456 Kamehameha Hwy. (☎737-2822), next to Cafe Haleiwa, offers snorkel tours, scuba certification courses, and year-round diving. Owner/activist Ken Nichols has been featured on Real T.V. and Animal Planet. Open M-Tu and Th-F 9am-4pm, Sa-Su 8am-4pm.

Deep Ecology, 66-456 Kamehameha Hwy. (☎637-7946; www.deepecologyhawaii.com), in the same building as North Shore Diving Headquarters, coordinates 3hr. whale, turtle, and dolphin tours starting at $39. Trips typically go out daily, though rough seas in winter sometimes prevent tours. Open M-Tu and Th-F 9am-4pm, Sa-Su 8am-4pm.

Surf Hawaii Surf School (☎637-2622) in the North Shore Marketplace provides jet ski, surfboard, kayak, and bike rentals. Also offers internet access (see Practical Information, above).

SIGHTS

While Haleiwa's major draws are its unique businesses and world famous surf breaks, the town has a few cultural sights worth a quick visit.

NORTH SHORE SURF AND CULTURAL MUSEUM. No shirt? No shoes? No problem! Opened in August of 2002, North Shore Surf is quite possibly the world's most laid-back museum. Take a peek at their collection of surf memorabilia including posters, album covers, monochrome photos by legendary surf photographer LeRoy Grannis, vintage surfboards, and a very cool 1950 Ford Woody. Browse the museum's selection of jewelry and bottles collected from the ocean floor. *(66-250 Kamehameha Hwy., behind Patagonia in the North Shore*

Marketplace. ☎ 637-8888. Usually open M-Sa 9am-6pm, Su 10am-6pm. Free admission, though donations are greatly appreciated.)

LILIUOKALANI PROTESTANT CHURCH. Founded by Protestant missionaries in 1832, the church takes it name from Queen Liliuokalani, who spent her summers in Haleiwa and attended services here. Services were conducted entirely in Hawaiian until the early 1940s. Look closely at the seven-dial clock; the numerals on the face are replaced with the letters of the queen's 12-letter name. *(66-090 Kamehameha Hwy., across the street from Matsumoto's Shave Ice. ☎ 637-9364. Daily service at 10am. Open whenever the minister is in, generally mornings.)*

▣ SHOPPING

In addition to its surf boutiques, indistinguishable tourist haunts, and Patagonia and Quiksilver chain stores, Haleiwa has a great number of unique shops and galleries worth perusing.

▨ **Black Pearl Source,** 66-220 Kamehameha Hwy. (☎ 637-7776). The store and everything in it was designed and built by architect and jeweler Ben Thompson. Many of Thompson's rings, pendants, and earrings are designed to cradle the high quality, natural-color Tahitian black pearls (which are not black but green, blue, golden, apricot, and even purple) without drilling them, retaining the integrity of the pearl. The pearls are rarer and more expensive than white *akoya* pearls, but the store carries pieces to fit any budget. The pearls are worth a look, even if you're not going to buy. The star-struck should take note, as celebrity clients have included Gary Sinise, Justin Timberlake, and the margarita man himself, Jimmy Buffet. Open daily 10am-6:30pm.

▨ **Oceans in Glass,** 66-250 Kamehameha Hwy. (☎ 637-3366; www.oceansinglass.com), in the North Shore Marketplace behind Patagonia. Get a first-hand look at Krista Woodward as she hand-crafts intricate glass sculptures of graceful dolphins, sea turtles, humpback whales, and colorful reef fish. The unique pieces, created with a 2,000-year-old technique called lampworking, are all inspired by Krista's diving and snorkeling excursions in local coral reefs. The pieces, which begin at $25, can all be packaged and shipped to prevent damage in travel. Open daily 10am-6pm. D/MC/V.

Haleiwa Surf & Sea, 62-595 Kamehameha Hwy. (☎ 800-899-SURF or 637-9887; www.surfnsea.com), just past the Anahulu Bridge on the left. Of the town's several surf shops, Haleiwa Surf & Sea is the most well-known and has the best selection. Since 1965, they've supplied the North Shore surf community with affordable boards and accessories, as well as men's and women's clothing. Open daily 9am-7pm.

WAIALUA AND MOKULE'IA

Located at the base of the Waianae Range on the western stretch of the North Shore, Waialua was originally a port for the sandalwood trade. Until recently, Waialua's economy was fueled by the sugar cane industry, but the town has lacked stable agricultural production since its sugar mill closed in 1996. Though Waialua still bills itself as the "Home of the World's Best Sugar," the town is now trying its hand at banana and asparagus production. Primarily a residential and agricultural community, sleepy Waialua is of little interest to travelers. The ambitious waves and unpopulated beaches of Mokule'ia to the west, however, draw adventurous travelers and promise hours of thrills for kitesurfers (see **Kiteboarding to Extremes,** p. 448), skydivers, and hang-gliders.

■⧗ **ORIENTATION AND PRACTICAL INFO.** The small commercial center of **Waialua** sits at the crossroads of **Kealohanui** and **Goodale Road.** To reach **Mokule'ia** from Waialua, drive *mauka* (toward the mountains) on Goodale Rd. and turn right onto **Farrington Highway,** which ends 2½ mi. before Ka'ena Point, the northwest corner of Oahu. TheBus **#76** connects Haleiwa and Waialua.

The Waialua Public **Library** is located at 67-068 Kealohanui St. The library has handy schedules for TheBus, offers self-serve photocopying for $0.15 per page, and has five relatively new computers with quick and free **internet access** with 15min. time limit when all terminals are busy. (☎637-8286. Open Tu-Th 9am-6pm, F 9am-5pm, Sa 9am-2pm.) Between the library and the Aloha Gas Station is the **Waialua Shopping Center** at 67-208 Goodale Ave. For basic needs, visit the **Waialua General Store** (☎637-3131; open M-Th 9am-9pm, F-Su 8am-10pm) or **The Brown Bottle**. (Open daily 7am-10:30pm. Also sells liquor, beer, and wine.) Be sure to stock up if you plan on heading west for the night, as there are no convenience stores to speak of in Mokule'ia. If you're in the mood to strengthen your body, mind, and soul, you're in luck; **Bikram's Yoga Center** offers daily drop-in classes for only $12. (☎637-5700; www.bikramyoga.com.) For a bite to eat, try **Waialua's Chinese Kitchen ❶**, where traditional Chinese entrees run $5.50-8.50. (☎637-1688. Open daily 10:30am-7:30pm.) Wash your duds at **M and C Washerette.** (Wash and dry $1 each. Open daily 9am-10pm.) **ATM** machines are located at the Waialua Federal Credit Union and The Brown Bottle convenience store (see above), both inside the plaza. A public **pay phone** is located in the shopping center's parking lot. The Waialua **post office,** 67-079 Nauahi St., is open M-F 8:30am-4pm. **Postal Code:** 96791.

🏕️ 🏕️ ACCOMMODATIONS AND CAMPING. There are no hotels in Waialua, so travelers must continue on to Mokule'ia to find a place to sleep. Even in Mokule'ia, there are only two choices for camping and budget accommodations. The first and least expensive option is **Camp Mokule'ia ❶**, 68-729 Farrington Hwy. The site, owned by an Episcopal Church, is frequently booked by groups for conferences, but it's open to the public at all other times. Its small, windswept beach is too rough for swimming, but it's ideal for **kite surfing** (see p. 171). The tent area is in a wooded grove near the beach and has hot water showers and toilet facilities. There are cabins that contain 14-22 beds with two shared bathrooms in each. The camp lodge has eight private rooms with bath, eight shared bath doubles, and two shared bath triples available for nightly rental. For cheap, hearty meals, visit Camp Mokule'ia's dining hall, where $7 can buy you a substantial lunch and $8.50 gets you a hefty dinner. Facilities include a ropes course, volleyball court, climbing tower, swimming pool, and archery targets. Kayaks are also available to rent for $12 per hour. (☎637-6241; www.campmokuleia.com. Office open M-Sa 8am-5pm. Check-in 4pm. Check-out 1pm. Reservations required. Tent camping $6 with own tent; lodge rooms $60-70; $150 for a 14-person cabin. AmEx/D/MC/V.)

The second lodging option is **YMCA Camp Erdman ❷,** 69-385 Farrington Hwy., which sits about 2 mi. before Camp Mokule'ia, on a nicer (though still rough) beach. The camp is frequently rented to large groups, especially in the summer and on weekends; call for availability. Facilities on the property include a ropes course, swimming pool, climbing wall, basketball and tennis courts. No independent tent camping is allowed. There are tent sites available for a maximum of 10 people, as well as eight-person cabins with or without kitchens. Individuals can stay in shared cabins, and the friendly staff will make you feel like you're back at summer camp. Check out the nightly campfire at 8:30pm for songs, skits, and laughter. (☎637-4615; www.camperdman.net. Including meals, tent site $50; cabin $160; shared cabin Su-Th $43, F-Sa $51. **Short-term work** can be arranged for room and board; contact Bridget (ext. 30) for details. Reserve tent sites 7 days in advance and cabins 24hr. in advance. AmEx/MC/V.)

O A H U

HE BIG SPLURGE

KITEBOARDING TO EXTREMES

So you've stayed in a surf shack for a month and you have a bit of extra cash floating around in the pockets of your board shorts. If you're looking for something active, fun, and worth the splurge, look no further than **KiteHigh,** above the Coffee Gallery in Haliewa's North Shore Marketplace. They rent kayaks, surfboards, and snorkeling gear, but they specialize in kiteboarding, the fastest growing watersport on the planet. What other sport lets you jump 30 ft. in the air and come down with a butter-soft landing? Better yet, kiteboarding lessons leave you with an actual skill that you can do anywhere once you have the gear. If you've never tried it, this is a great place to learn, as KiteHigh is the only kiteboarding school on the North Shore. The beaches they use for lessons are absolutely empty, making for much safer conditions than at crowded Kailua. Basic lessons with instructors certified in CPR, first aid, and kiteboarding instruction cost $99, but a more substantial lesson that will take you from zero to kiteboarder in an afternoon runs around $250 (mention *Let's Go* for a discount). KiteHigh provides free snorkel gear and cold drinks for friends and family who want to watch you fly. Advanced lessons also available. (☎ 250-5483; www.kitehigh.com.)

For longer (and more expensive) vacation rentals, contact **Owen's Retreat**, 68-945 Farrington Hwy. Located between Camp Mokule'ia and Camp Erdman, Owen's provides a bit more luxury for those prepared to pay the price. (☎ 988-3369.)

BEACHES. Mokule'ia's unpopulated beaches are not great for swimming since the water and ocean bottom are usually quite rough. **Mokule'ia Beach Park,** across from Dillingham Airfield, has restrooms and showers but a reef, rather than a sandy bottom (other stretches to the left and right have sandy areas). Camping is allowed in the park by permit only; about a dozen sites are available, though camping is restricted between 8am on Wednesday and 8am on Friday.

ACTIVITIES. For travelers hoping to add a touch of thrill to their vacation, several companies operate adventure sports out of **Dillingham Airfield,** on the inland side of Farrington Hwy. Aspiring skydivers should enter the airfield at the east entrance (the first of three entrances to Dillingham Airfield as you drive out of town). Three major companies at 68-760 Farrington Hwy. offer safe, tandem skydiving with licensed instructors: **Skydive Hawaii** (☎ 637-9700; reservations recommended; Waikiki hotel pickup available; open daily 8am-sunset; all major credit cards accepted); **Drop Zone** (☎ 637-7007; www.dropzonehawaii.com; D/MC/V); **Pacific International Skydiving Center** (☎ 637-7472; open M-F 8:30am-4pm, Sa-Su 8:30am-sunset). Give yourself about 2hr. to complete the skydive, allowing time to sign a safety waiver and watch an instructional video. Though dives average about $150, be on the lookout for discount flyers and coupons.

At Glider Point, the second entrance to Dillingham Airfield, **Soar Hawaii Sailplanes, Inc.** (☎ 637-3147; www.soarhawaii.com) offers flying lessons as well as scenic and acrobatic rides of varying lengths; call for rates and free hotel pick-up. **Mr. Bill's** offers 20-40min. glider and sailplane rides from $35, as well as sky-surfing and aerobatic flying. Look for discount flyers and coupons to give your budget a break. (☎ 677-3404; www.honolulu-soaring.com; open daily 10am-5:30pm.)

HIKING. Where Farrington Hwy. ends, you can continue on foot or mountain bike to **Ka'ena Point** (see p. 177), tracing the former sugar cane railroad route. Local legend says that Ka'ena Point, the westernmost point on Oahu, is a "leaping place of souls" where the spirits of the recently dead can reunite with their ancestors. Whether or not you believe in spirits, you can enjoy Ka'ena's unique ecosystem, with its many plant and animal species seen nowhere else in the world. If you opt to do the 2½ mile trek on foot, park your rental car where the paved road ends, 1 mile past Camp Erdman. Be sure to lock your car and take valuables with you. Allow 1-3 hr. (one way) for the walk, depending on your pace. You can also take mountain bikes out this route. For rentals, check out Drop Zone (see above; rentals $15 a day) or **Island Bike Rentals,** 66-199 Kamehameha Hwy., in Haleiwa. (☎637-9991. $30-40 per day, $100-150 per week. Open Tu-Su 9am-5pm.)

For travelers seeking a more ambitious hike, consider the graded ridge of **Kealia,** a 7 mi. round trip trek with a climb of 2,000 ft. Though the hike is long, hot, and steep, it's a low danger route that's appropriate for intermediate level hikers. To reach the trailhead, traveling west, take the third and final entrance to Dillingham Airfield. Look for an access gate marked by a warning sign for low-flying aircraft. Go around the end of the runway, pass a low concrete building on the left, and park in the paved lot in front of the air control tower. The Kealia trail ascends a steep *pali* (cliff) en route to the summit of the Wai'anae Range. At the peak, hikers can enjoy a scenic overlook of an undeveloped leeward valley. As always, use caution when hiking; don't over-exert yourself, bring water, and travel with others.

LEEWARD COAST

Driving from Honolulu to Oahu's Leeward Coast is, geographically, like leaving Hawaii and entering New Mexico. Lush green mountains are replaced by arid brown ones, covered only by thick tangles of dry undergrowth. The land's stark beauty is complemented by some of the nicest and least-crowded beaches on Oahu. On calm days, the Pacific resembles a mirror, with only the occasional abrupt wave; on rough winter days, the surf can surge up to 20 ft. in height. Depending on the swells, visitors can enjoy the spectrum of water activities on the Leeward Coast, including surfing, snorkeling, diving, swimming, canoeing, and body boarding.

The Leeward Coast is also home to a large population of Native Hawaiians, many of whom have suffered low social and economic standing for centuries. When King Kamehameha surged through Oahu and forced the island's surrender at the Battle of the Nu'uanu Pali (see **Nu'uanu Pali Lookout,** p. 155), the inhabitants of Oahu were banished to the barren side of the Waianae mountains, unprotected from the blazing sun. The advent of agricultural advances and successful drilling for water brought powerful business interests, such as the sugar cane industry, to the Leeward Coast. With the help of the state government, they snatched up the majority of the water rights and the best land. Today, the region still lacks political and economic clout, but very recently small pockets of affluent housing have begun to pop up along the pristine beaches, creating a new socio-economic mix.

Despite the foreign development in the Leeward area, many Hawaiians here are wary of outsiders and visitors should be aware of the high incidence of theft in the area. Avoiding trouble requires common courtesy and sensitivity to the attitudes of locals, as well as common sense—*don't get caught in the Leeward area alone late at night.* While there are plentiful campgrounds, locals joke that if you plan to camp, you'd better bring at least three friends along. It's sometimes impossible to avoid confrontations; the best advice is to attempt to diffuse the situation, offer up your best *aloha* spirit, and, if that fails, leave the area.

⚡ ORIENTATION

The **Leeward Coast** encompasses the land that lies between the Koolau and Waianae Mountains. To get there, take H-1 west from Honolulu for 40min.; H-1 will end at **Highway 93 (Farrington Highway).** Traveling west on Hwy. 93 past Ewa, the road goes by **Kapolei,** just north of **Campbell Industrial Park,** an industrial community in the shadow of Honolulu that has a few spruced-up amenities. From here, the two-lane highway marches directly up the sun-baked Leeward Coast, past the rural communities of **Nanakuli, Maili, Waianae,** and **Makaha** and finally peters out before the wilderness of the westernmost tip of Oahu, **Ka'ena Point.** Be aware that the paved road ends before Ka'ena Point, and it is virtually impossible to drive around the western tip of the island, even with a 4WD vehicle.

⧉ TRANSPORTATION

By Bus: TheBus Country Express C and the 93 Express both serve the Leeward Coast as far as **Lawaia Street,** just south of Keau Beach park. The Country Express C starts at the Ala Moana Shopping Center and runs frequently with fewer stops; the 93 brings commuters from Downtown in the evenings only, running from the Leeward side to Downtown in the morning. $1.75, seniors and students 18 and under $0.75.

By Car: Driving is by far the easiest way to get around the Leeward Coast. Car rentals are available at the airport (p. 92) and Waikiki (p. 117). Waianae is a 40min. drive from Waikiki. Parking is plentiful on the Leeward Coast, but do not leave valuables in your car, as there is a high incidence of theft in the area.

⁊ PRACTICAL INFORMATION

City Hall: Waianae satellite, 85-670 Farrington Hwy. (☎696-6371), at the Neighborhood Community Center, north of where the Kaupuni Channel meets Pokai Bay, before Waianae Intermediate School. Has bus schedules and passes. Open M-F 8am-4pm.

Banks: In the **Waianae Mall Shopping Center,** 86-120 Farrington Hwy., there is a **Bank of Hawaii** (☎696-4227; open M-Th 8:30am-4pm, F 8:30am-6pm), and an **American Savings Bank** (☎673-2606; open M-Th 8:30am-4pm, F 8:30am-6pm). There are also a number of **ATMs** in the area.

Library: Waianae Public Library, 85-625 Farrington Hwy. (☎697-7868). **Internet access** available with card ($10 for 3 mo.). Open Tu, Th, F-Sa 9am-5pm, W 1-8pm.

Equipment rentals:

Hale Nalu, 85-876 Farrington Hwy. (☎696-5897), across from The Waianae Store on the right side of the highway heading north. Rents everything you need to make the most of your Leeward visit, even **beach chairs** ($4 per day) and **umbrellas** ($6 per day). **Snorkeling** gear ($6 per 24hr., $20 per week), **body boards** ($11/$36), **short boards** ($18/$66), **long boards** ($21/$76), **bicycles** ($21/$70), and **fins** ($4/$12). Open daily 10am-7pm. AmEx/D/MC/V.

Gravity Hawaii (☎942-2582; sky phone ☎381-7696). **Kite boarding** and **paragliding** from island expert Marc "Nalu" Hill, who operates from a mobile office. Boards and gear also available.

Emergency: ☎911.

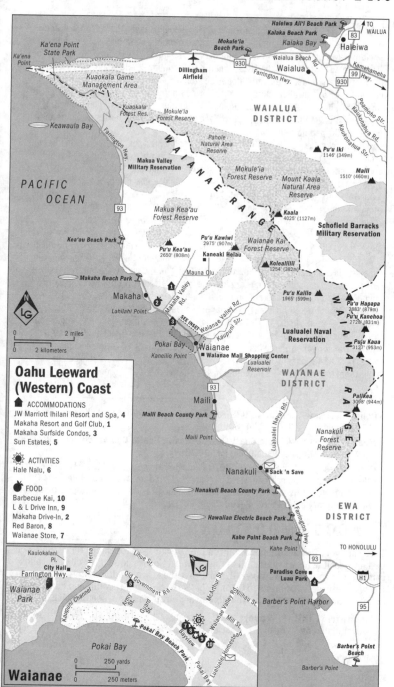

OAHU

**Oahu Leeward
(Western) Coast**

🏠 ACCOMMODATIONS
JW Marriott Ihilani Resort and Spa, **4**
Makaha Resort and Golf Club, **1**
Makaha Surfside Condos, **3**
Sun Estates, **5**

☀️ ACTIVITIES
Hale Nalu, **6**

🍎 FOOD
Barbecue Kai, **10**
L & L Drive Inn, **9**
Makaha Drive-In, **2**
Red Baron, **8**
Waianae Store, **7**

LUAUS Modern-day *luaus* are typically sunset feasts that celebrate auspicious occasions with food, music, dancing, and games. The tradition stems from the ancient Hawaiians' ritualistic food offerings to the gods. It was *kapu*, or taboo, for women to eat with men until 1819, when Kamehameha II abolished the system by holding a grand feast and sitting alongside women. From then on, *luaus* became an integral part of Hawaiian culture. The 19th century was the great era of the *luau*, when Hawaiian royalty lavished guests with feasts of epic grandeur. King David Kalakaua, the "Merrie Monarch," was especially fond of large parties and reportedly invited 1500 people to his 50th birthday *luau*.

The *luau* takes its name from the young *taro (poi)* leaves that are used in the preparation of many feast dishes. These leaves were used to wrap the food that went into the *imu*, or underground earthen oven. Other *luau* cuisine includes *poi*, chicken long rice, *lomi* salmon, *haupia* (coconut pudding), sweet potato, *kalua* pig, fish, and rice.

On Oahu, the **Polynesian Cultural Center's** (p. 155) Ali'i Luau is considered the most authentic. The Leeward, southwestern corner of Oahu is home to the other two main *luaus* on the island, both of which are quite expensive. Look for coupons in tourist publications to save on this must-see Hawaiian tradition. The *luau* at **Paradise Cove**, in Ko Olina, starts off on the right foot with a Mai Tai greeting and live Hawaiian music. There is also a Hawaiian village with shops, spear-throwing, *lei*-making, and hula lessons, and an amphitheater to explain just how the *imu* works. Many packages are available, including dinner, drinks, and transportation from Waikiki. (Take Farrington Hwy. to the Ko Olina exit and continue to Ali'inui Dr. Call ☎842-5911 to make reservations, or do so online at www.paradisecove.com. $60, ages 13-18 $50, ages 6-12 $40. 5-9pm. AmEx/MC/V.) Watch the Hawaiian court, enjoy dinner, and take in a Polynesian extravaganza at **Germaine's Luau**, at Barber's point in Waianae. Free shuttle transportation from Waikiki included. (Call ☎949-6626 for reservations. $53, ages 14-20 $43, ages 6-13 $31. Daily 6-9pm. Closed M from the 2nd week of Sept. until June. MC/V.) For more information, see **Luaus**, p. 24.

Police: Waianae Station, 85-939 Farrington Hwy. (☎696-4221). **Kapolei Station,** 1100 Kamokila Blvd. (☎692-4260).

Medical Services: Waianae Coast Comprehensive Health Center, 86-260 Farrington Hwy. 24hr. Emergency Department (☎696-7081).

Post Offices: Nanakuli Station, 87-2070 Farrington Hwy. (☎696-0161). Last collection M-F 4pm, Sa 2:30pm. Open M-F 10am-noon, 1-4:15pm. **Waianae Main Office,** 86-014 Farrington Hwy. (☎696-0161). Last collection M-F 5pm, Sa 4:30pm. Open M-F 8am-4:30pm, Sa 9am-noon. **Postal Code:** 96792.

▚ ACCOMMODATIONS

There are very few accommodations on the Leeward side of Oahu, and even fewer that are feasible for travelers. All of the Leeward Coast's county beach parks allow **camping** with a permit; however, the fact that these are predominantly local spots makes it unwise for tourists to intrude. *Let's Go* does not recommend camping at any Leeward beaches. For information on acquiring a permit, see **Camping**, p. 86.

JW Marriot Ihilani Resort and Spa, 92-1001 Olani St. (☎679-0079; www.ihilani.com). Take H-1 West and exit at Ko Olina onto Aliinu Dr. Continue through the security station and turn right onto Olani. The white facade of the imposing Ihilani Resort is visible from afar and nestled on the circuitous fairways of Ko Olina Golf Club. The lobby's ceiling rises all 17 floors to skylights at the pinnacle of the hotel and the sounds of footfalls on marble and the trickle of fountains filled with *koi* fish echo through the open space. Guests rave about the award-winning spa's full arsenal of treatments and other top-shelf amenities, which include swimming and lap pools, fine and casual dining (including the **Naupaka Restaurant,** p. 175), pool side bar, excellent tennis courts, and premier golfing. The rooms are tastefully appointed in beige and white, with deep European tubs in the grandiose bathrooms. 24hr. reception. Check-in 3pm. Check-out noon. Rooms $354-434. AmEx/D/DC/MC/V. ❺

Makaha Resort and Golf Club, 84-626 Makaha Valley Rd. (☎695-9544; fax 695-7558). From Farrington Hwy., make a right on Makaha Valley Rd. and follow the signs. All of the spacious and comfortable rooms have 2 doubles or 1 king-sized bed. Full bath, TV, A/C, and mini fridge in every room, and a much-appreciated pool. And of course, there's a golf course. Stop by the bar at sunset for a drink and one of the best views on the island. Reception 7am-10pm. Check-in 3pm. Check-out noon. Rooms $109. AmEx/D/MC/V. ❸

Makaha Surfside Condos, 85-175 Farrington Hwy., 1 mi. south of Makaha Beach Park. This 4-story cinder-block condominium sits on the beach and has 1-bedroom, 1-bath condos in addition to 2 pools and a covered parking garage. Various owners of the different units rent them to visitors; however, as they are not centrally organized, conditions, rates, and taxes may vary. 2 coin-op. laundry facilities, private phone. Don and Pat Maxwell (☎395-5960 or 554-8282) rent out condos for $325 per week. Inquire about taxes, parking, and cleaning fees. A bulletin board inside the complex lists additional owners who rent out rooms. ❸

Sun Estates, 85-786 Farrington Hwy. (☎696-6500), in Waianae. This office rents out 1- and 2-bedroom condos in Waianae. No A/C or parking. Princess HP condos high-season $110, low-season $95; Makaha Beach Cabanas $65/$55; Plantation 2-bedroom condos $95/$80. 1-time cleaning fee $55 for 1 bedroom, $65 for 2 bedrooms. Prices are higher and advance reservations essential during high season. AmEx/MC/V. ❷

◪ FOOD

Most of the dining options on the Leeward side are in Waianae, as business does not support a great deal of eateries in this sparsely populated area of Oahu. The **Waianae Store,** 85-863 Farrington Hwy., is a basic market. (☎696-3131. Open M-F 7am-9pm, Sa-Su 7am-8pm. D/MC/V.) There is a **Sack N' Save,** 87-2070 Farrington Hwy., in **Nanakuli.** (☎668-1277. Open daily 5am-11pm. AmEx/D/MC/V.)

   The Red Baron ❷, 85-915 Farrington Hwy., is a cozy restaurant known for its pizza ($3.50-26), "authentic" spaghetti plate lunch ($6.50, served until 5pm), and daily dinner specials like the prime rib (Tu and Th $13). They also serve beer and wine. (☎697-1383. Open M-Th 11am-9pm, F-Sa 11am-10pm. AmEx/MC/V.) Fine dining is virtually nonexistent on the Leeward Coast. If you are looking for a nice sit-down dinner, head back to the Marriott Ihilani's **Naupaka Restaurant ❺.** The elegant restaurant features pink snapper caught on the islands ($30) and a succulent rack of lamb ($34). The delicious creme brulee ($6) is a supremely divine way to finish your meal. (☎679-0079. Open daily 6:30am-2pm and 5:30-10pm.)

OAHU

LADY KILLER

A number of legends revolve around the Leeward Coast. The Kaneana Cave, a place of great ritualism and magic until relatively modern times, has several legends associated with it. In particular, the shark god and notorious shape-shifter Kamahoalii (known today as Makua Charley) is a regular feature in most of the tales, with the most popular myth alleging that he sired a son with a Hawaiian woman. The resulting half-man, half-shark was christened Nanaue and supposedly lived in the vicinity of what is now Kaneana Cave. Nanaue was a bloodthirsty soul and would catch unsuspecting victims, lure them to the cave, and eventually eat them. Some legends elaborate on this tale, saying that Nanaue was the lover of a beautiful girl whose parents turned her into a *mo'o* (lizard) to keep her away from him. Despite their efforts, the girl-lizard traveled down Kalena Stream, through Ko'iahi Gulch, and met her love near his cave.

Ka'ena Point is another area prominent in Hawaiian lore. As the westernmost point on the island, and the closest to the setting sun, it was thought to be the jumping-off point, or *leina*, into *Po*, the Hawaiian spiritual underworld, or "sea of eternity." The souls of the dead were tested before they could jump off; those who had led an honest life could continue to *Po*, but those who did not were doomed to wander the island.

A duo of drive-in eateries offer similar plate lunch, sandwich, and burger fare at the intersection of Waianae Valley Rd. and Farrington Hwy. **Barbecue Kai ❶**, 85-973 Farrington Hwy., has a mean BBQ Mix Plate ($5) that comes with chicken, teriyaki steak, and BBQ short ribs. (☎ 696-7122. Open daily 8am-11pm.) **L and L Drive Inn ❶**, 85-080 Waianae Rd., has found its way to the Leeward Coast and locals flock to $1.50 cheeseburgers and $5.15 chicken *katsu* plates. (☎ 696-7989. Open daily 6:30am-11pm. D/MC/V only on orders $10+.) Two miles north of this fast-food mecca, just past the intersection of Makaha Valley Rd., **Makaha Drive-In ❶**, 84-1150 Farrington Hwy., has comparable offerings (plate lunches $4-6) at competitive prices. (☎ 696-4811. Open M-Th 6am-8pm, F-Sa 6am-9pm.)

◪ BEACHES

There are a number of beaches on the Leeward Coast, all located off Farrington Hwy. The following beaches are listed from south to north, along the highway.

KAHE POINT BEACH PARK. More a stretch of rocky ground extending into the water than an actual beach, the park is located a few hundred yards up the highway, opposite the rusted Hawaiian Electric Kahe Power Plant. The beach does have a nice area of covered picnic tables and one outstanding feature: the view. Don't forget to tear your eyes away from the horizon every so often to make sure your car is still there. Camping is allowed with a permit. *(Kahe Point is the first beach north of Ko Olina on Farrington Hwy.)*

HAWAIIAN ELECTRIC BEACH PARK. More popularly known as "Tracks," for the old railroad tracks that run through it, Hawaiian Electric Beach has little to brag about. Though the bottom is rocky in places, it is safe for swimming during the summer (though there is no guard) and there are picnic tables, a pavilion, and restrooms. The beach is best known for its gentle waves that are perfect for beginning **body surfing**. *(Off Farrington Hwy., north of Kahe Point.)*

NANAKULI BEACH COUNTY PARK. This popular local beach is located within the Native Hawaiian stronghold of Nanakuli. The park is actually divided into northern and southern sections by a housing community. There are basketball courts, a baseball diamond, and a playground. Nanakuli beach is known for the diversity of activities available there: depending on the conditions, surfing, body boarding, body surfing, snorkeling, diving, and canoeing are possible. Although the northern section (also known as **Kalanianaole**) tends to be less agitated than the southern part, visitors should avoid swimming in the heavier winter surf. *(86-269 Farrington Hwy.)*

MAILI BEACH COUNTY PARK. Maili's long stretch of sand has been sectioned off into three parts by housing developments. Body boarding and body surfing are decent here and locals advise swimmers that the best spot is near the lifeguard stands. There are picnic tables and restrooms and, across Farrington Hwy. at the northern edge of the park, the **Maili Market** has a snack bar and tackle shop. *(87-021 Farrington Hwy., at the southern end of the town of Maili.)*

POKAI BAY BEACH PARK. Named after famed Hawaiian chief Pokai, this is reputed to be the safest swimming on the Leeward Coast, thanks to its protective coral reef. Locals do warn that the boat traffic here can leave the water oily and unpleasant, however. The southern end of the bay, which has picnic tables, restrooms, and lifeguard stands also has the ruins of **Kuilioloa Heiau.** The once-sacred site was damaged by army training during WWII and has since been eroded by the sea. *(85-037 Waianae Valley Rd., off Farrington Hwy. in Waianae.)*

MAKAHA BEACH PARK. Makaha is famous for its ferocious winter surf (averaging 15 ft. in height), as well as the annual **Makaha International Surfing Competition.** However, the beach is popular even during waveless days, when the flat waters make for safe swimming and superior **diving** in the myriad coral caves offshore, where white-tipped reef sharks and turtles have been spotted. Makaha is also reputed to have the best **snorkeling** on the Leeward Coast, along its active reef in front of the lifeguard stand on the northern part of the beach. The view from the wide, white beach south to **Mauna Lahilahi,** a small mountain that sits right on the water, is one of the coast's most picturesque. Grab a **shave ice** from the Granny Goose ice cream trucks that are often parked in the lot during the day and enjoy the view. The beach has plenty of picnic tables, restrooms, showers, and lifeguard towers. *(84-369 Farrington Hwy.)*

KEA'AU BEACH PARK. Though Kea'au isn't particularly good for swimming, the beach is known as a choice snorkeling and offshore diving spot. The park has very little sand and is edged by rocks that make entry difficult. *(Off Farrington Hwy., north of Makaha Beach Park around Kepuhi Point.)*

KEAWAULA BAY. Located within **Ka'ena State Park** (p. 177), on the tip of the island, Keawaula Bay catches the North, South, and West swells, which means that it draws experienced surfers, body boarders, and body surfers year-round. There is a small area that is safe for swimming close to the lifeguard stand. Snorkeling and diving are popular in calmer surf, and local fishermen crowd the point at the end of the beach, where Hwy. 93 turns into an unpaved road. There are lifeguards on duty during the summer, but there is very little in the way of other amenities. Do not drink the water! The lead content makes the water highly toxic. *(At the end of Farrington Hwy.)*

◉ SIGHTS

▨ **KA'ENA POINT STATE PARK.** The northwestern most point on Oahu, Ka'ena Point lies within the 853-acre Ka'ena Point State Park. *Ka'ena* translates to "the heat" and the point truly is one of the hottest and driest spots on Oahu. The park itself is almost completely undeveloped, though home to beautiful

Keawaula Bay (p. 177). In 1983, Ka'ena Point and its surroundings were designated the **Ka'ena Point Natural Area Reserve,** due to the region's exemplary coastal lowland dune ecosystem. Among the animals that frequent Ka'ena Point are laysan albatross, Hawaiian monk seals, green sea turtles, dolphins, and various seabirds. Good snorkeling and good surfing round out the gorgeous park's offerings.

Within the park, the **Ka'ena Point Trail** (2½ mi. one-way. Trailhead: the northern end of Farrington Hwy. Level: easy.) is a great family hike. The trail was originally built for the Oahu Railroad and Land, and runs between the ocean and the Waianae Mountains. Tiptoeing along the water's edge, the trail allows hikers to get intimate views of the ocean, tide pools, and natural stone formations. On calm days, myriads of secluded coves appear for the taking. Although the footing can be unsteady, the path is generally undemanding and you'll be able to take plenty of time to enjoy the tremendous scenery. This hike can be made more difficult by beginning from the north, in Mokoleia. *(At the end of Farrington Hwy.)*

KANEAKI HEIAU. Though it is located within a ritzy residential district, this 17th century sacred site is Oahu's most authentically restored *heiau* (temple). Visitors can catch a glimpse of ancient Hawaii, embodied in traditional prayer towers and altars. Originally for agricultural worship, the *heiau* was later converted to a temple for the god of war. It is possible that human sacrifice took place here. *(Take H-1 west to Farrington Hwy. Take the highway to Makaha Valley Rd. and turn right. Pass the Makaha Golf Resort and make a right onto Mauna Olu St. Follow the signs to the heiau, which is located on private property, within the Mauna Olu Estates. Open Tu-Su 10am-2pm. Free.)*

KANEANA CAVE. This 100 yd. deep grotto, also known as **Makua Cave,** was carved out many years ago when the seas were higher. The cave is the subject of a colorful legend involving **Nanue,** the shark man (see **Lady Killer,** p.176). Many centuries ago, the cave was regarded as sacred and *kahunas* (priests) performed religious ceremonies there. Nowadays, the cavern's visitors tend to be teenagers, and broken glass and graffiti decorate the interior. *(Off Farrington Hwy., about 2 mi. south of Ka'ena State Park. The cave is marked by a concrete barrier in front and a marker on the opposite side of the road, where visitors can park.)*

MAKUA VALLEY. Though it looks beautiful from the highway, Makua Valley has seen much violence in its life span. As one of the three valleys that make up the **Makua Military Reservation,** Makua was the site of tactical maneuvers and ammunitions practice during WWII. Undetonated training munitions supposedly remain in the valley and the area is presently closed to the public. A contract (set to expire in 2029) between the US Army and the State of Hawaii gives the Army complete control of 4190 acres of land in the area. *(Off Farrington Hwy., south of Ka'ena Point State Park.)*

MAUI

The second oldest, second largest, and second most developed island in the Hawaiian chain, Maui is far from second best. Maui strikes an appealing balance between a vacation paradise and a real place, complete with a thriving culture and economy. Not nearly as developed as Oahu, and with plenty more to do and see than Kauai, Maui makes a solid claim for the motto that locals hold to be true: *Maui no ka 'oi!* (Maui is the best!). Visiting families delight in the activities available on the buzzing beaches of Ka'anapali and Kihei and honeymooning couples discover romance on secluded coasts and waterfall hikes. This is only the beginning—travelers will be surprised at how much Maui has to offer.

Most visitors first become familiar with the dry, leeward side of the island where the resorts have turned *kiawe* deserts into golf courses. However, Maui's landscape is incredibly diverse. The less developed windward side of the West Maui mountains has acres of dense rainforest alive with native ferns and ripe fruits. At the high altitudes of Haleakala Crater, rainforest gives way to forests of towering pines, redwoods, and eucalyptus. The central valley, located in the narrow isthmus between Haleakala and the West Maui mountains, is carpeted from end to end with stalks of sugarcane. Fringed with pineapple fields, this area forms the heart of Maui's agricultural economy. Maui is the only island that maintains a significant sugarcane crop (43,000 acres), which staves off residential and commercial development in the valley.

Offshore, Maui's waters are teeming with marine life, including hundreds of species endemic to the island's reef—a veritable paradise for divers and snorkelers. Winter is Maui's high season. December through April, humpback whales gather off the southern coast, and their antics are visible from any beach. Big wave surfing on the North Shore coincides with whale watching and attracts its own onlookers. Surfing, body boarding, windsurfing, and kite surfing are popular sports year-round and form the center of both tourism and island life. Countless young people move to Maui to work and surf, cultivating a connection between their bodies and the natural environment. It's easy to see why the land remains such an integral part of native Hawaiian culture, as well as a highly relevant topic as Maui's land is increasingly threatened by over-development.

As commercialized as Maui seems to have become, the Hawaiian community's sense of identity remains strong and is constantly evolving to face contemporary challenges. Grassroots movements have sprung up to reclaim sacred lands, to educate visitors about Hawaiian history and culture, and to deal with internal community issues. The lively debates in the editorial pages of *Maui News* provide a glimpse of the most current concerns, and there a growing number of opportunities for visitors to learn actively from locals about native traditions. Maui's rich local culture is the essence of what makes the island so special—a fusion of ethnic groups whose love of the island is contagious.

✈ INTERISLAND TRANSPORTATION

Flights to Maui from the neighboring islands start at around $100 round-trip, although some cost as much as $175. Maui's major airport is **Kahului International Airport (OGG)**, in Kahului on the northern coast of Central Maui. It is served by international and national airlines, as well as interisland carriers. Flight sched-

HIGHLIGHTS OF MAUI

BE THE FIRST TO SEE DAY BREAK as the rising sun illuminates the horizon on Haleakala (p. 239).

SHED YOUR INHIBITIONS at clothing-optional Little Beach in Makena (p. 202).

ADMIRE the majestic grace of hundreds of humpback whales as they frolic off of Maui's shores from December to April (p. 198).

SNORKEL IN A SECRET COVE in the Ahihi-Kinau Natural Area Reserve (p. 202).

ules in and out of Maui change constantly. Be sure to check the latest flight times before you plan your trip. **Aloha Air** (☎ 800-367-5250; www.alohaair.com) flies to: Honolulu, Oahu (30min., 17-21 per day 6:55am-7:30pm); Hilo, The Big Island via Honolulu (1¼-1½hr., 8-10 per day 5:25am-7:00pm); Kona, The Big Island (30min., daily 2:00pm); Lihue, Kauai (1¾hr., 11-16 per day 5:55am-5:30pm). **Hawaiian Airlines** (☎ 800-367-5320; www.hawaiianair.com) flies to: Honolulu, Oahu (30min., 19-27 per day 6:27am-8:12pm); Hilo, The Big Island via Honolulu (1¾hr., 5-6 per day 5:20am-6:12pm); Kona, The Big Island (30min., daily 2:29pm); Lihue, Kauai (40min., daily 9:17am). **Pacific Wings** (☎ 888-575-4546 or 873-0877; www.pacificwings.com) offers daily service to: Hana, Maui; Hilo, The Big Island; Honolulu, Oahu; Kamuela-Waimea, The Big Island; Kaunakakai, Molokai; Kona, The Big Island; Lanai City, Lanai; Lihue, Kauai. In addition, they have scheduled flights to the Kalaupapa Peninsula on Molokai. There are two other airports on Maui: **Hana Airport (HNM),** on Maui's east coast, which sees mostly commuter flights and unscheduled air traffic; and **Kapalua Airport (JHM),** which facilitates only propeller airlines and commuter flights.

Speedishuttle runs from the airport to various locations on the island. (☎ 875-8070; www.speedishuttle.com. Make reservations 1 day prior to arrival. As you add people to your party, the fares get progressively cheaper.) **Akina Aloha Tours** (☎ 879-2828) runs shuttles between South and West Maui. For schedule and rates, see www.akinatours.com/maui_shuttle.htm.

The **Molokai Princess** (☎ 800-275-6969 or 667-6165; www.molokaiferry.com) makes daily trips between Maui, Molokai, and Lanai. It leaves from Lahaina Harbor (1½hr, daily 5:15pm; M, W, F-Sa 6:30am. One-way $40, children $20).

The easiest and most convenient way to get around Maui is to rent a car. For **inter-city** and **local transportation,** consult the **Transportation** section for each town.

⛫ ACCOMMODATIONS

In Maui, travelers can stay in budget hostels in Wailuku, Pa'ia, or Lahaina for less than $20 per night, in condominiums in Kihei for $65 and up per night, in B&Bs anywhere for $55-150 per night, or in hotels for $100 and up. For **long-term accommodations,** check the *Maui News*, in print or online at www.mauinews.com, for notices advertising rooms and cottages for rent. A studio cottage, depending on the location, costs $500-1000 per month.

Whatever your accommodations, make reservations as soon as you know the dates of your trip. High season generally runs December 15-April 15, and rates are usually highest during December and January. During high season, accommodations are booked 3-4 months in advance (even longer for some popular B&Bs). The low season (Apr. 15-Dec.15) is a good time to visit if you're looking to save some cash, as rates are generally lower and space is more readily available.

Maui

PACIFIC OCEAN

Au'au Channel

Alalakeki Channel

Alen...

Kahoolawe

Paiolo Channel

LAHAINA DISTRICT

WAILUKU DISTRICT

MAKAWAO DISTRICT

HANA DISTRICT

WEST MAUI MOUNTAINS

West Maui Natural Area Reserve

KAHAKULOA SECTION

HONOKOWAI SECTION

PANAEWA SECTION

OIHAU SECTION

Haleakala National Park

Hanawi Natural Area Reserve

Makawao Forest Reserve

Kanaio Natural Area Reserve

Ahihi-Kinau Natural Area Reserve

Towns and places

West Maui Airport
Honokowai
Kapalua
Napili
Kahana
Ka'anapali
Lahaina
Olowalu
Ma'alaea
Wailuku
Kahului
Kihei
Wailea
Makena
Keokea
Kula
Paia
Makawao
Pukalani
Pu'unene
Haiku
Kokomo
Huelo
Honomanu Bay
Ke'anae
Wailua
Nahiku
Hana
Kaupo
Kipahulu

Beaches and points

Honokohau Bay
Nakalele Point
D.T. Fleming Beach
Honokahua Bay
Ka'anapali/Dig Me Beach
Hanaka'o'o Beach Park/Canoe Beach
Ho'okipa Beach
H.A. Baldwin Beach
Kanaha Beach Park
Kalama Beach
Big Beach
Red Sand Beach
Hamoa Beach

Sites and parks

Kanaha Pond State Wildlife Sanctuary
Twin Falls
Puohokamoa Falls
Pu'u Ula'ula Summit 10023 (3055m)
Polipoli State Park
Ulupalakua Ranch
Waianapanapa State Park
Wailua Falls
Kanahuali Falls
Waihumala Falls
Waimoku Falls
Oheʻo Gulch

Roads

30, 340, 36, 398, 365, 360, 390, 37, 377, 378, 311, 380, 31

Uaoa Bay
Ma'alaea Bay

Honoapiʻilani Hwy
Kahekili Hwy
Kahului Beach Rd
Iao Valley Rd
Mokulele Hwy
Kuihelani Hwy
Upper Kihei Rd
N. Kihei Rd
S. Kihei Rd
Piʻilani Hwy
Mokulele Hwy
Olinda Rd
Kaupakalua Rd
Haleakala Hwy
Kula Hwy
Pulehu Rd
Baldwin Ave
Hana Hwy
Waipoli Rd
Kekaulike Rd
Kahekili Hwy
Crater Rd
Sliding Sands Tr.
Halemauʻu Tr.
Kaupo Tr.
weaiili Tr.

Kahului Airport
Hana Airport

0 5 miles
0 5 kilometers

AMPING

mping in Maui is possible with a little advance planning. Beaches and parks where you can pitch a tent all require **permits,** and some have maximum stays. There are a few **cabins** in state and national parks that are cozy, but they book months in advance (see individual site coverage for details). If you plan on camping in Maui, make sure you rent a car with a lockable compartment (not a soft top Jeep) for your gear. Prepare for mosquitoes, sun, rain, and if you are camping on Haleakala, cold and wind. Building a fire, where permitted, can be difficult due to lack of wood, so bring a **stove** for cooking and boiling water. Each type of park—county, state, and national—issues its own permits:

County parks (☎270-7389; www.co.maui.hi.us), including Kanaha Beach and Papalaoa near Lahaina, require a permit ($3 per person per night; $0.50 per child), good for a max. of 3 consecutive nights. Mail a money order in the appropriate denomination to: **Dept. of Parks and Recreation,** 1580-C Ka'ahumanu Ave., Wailuku 96793. Permits can be picked up at the War Memorial Gym next to Baldwin High School on Rte. 32 in Wailuku.

State parks (☎984-8109), including Polipoli and Waianapanapa, require permits, good for a max. of 5 days. Tenting fees are $5 per permit per night, with a max. of 10 people per permit. Cabin permits are $45 per night. Write to: **Division of State Parks,** 54 South High St., Rm. 101, Wailuku 96793. Specify the dates and the park at which you wish to camp, and give the names and ID numbers (driver's license, social security, or passport) of all campers. You can also call to make reservations M-F 8am-3:30pm.

Haleakala National Park issues its own permits at the Park Headquarters. They are free and available on a first-come, first-served basis. Apply 3 months in advance for the cabin lottery; see park coverage (p. 239) for details.

CENTRAL MAUI

The term "Central Maui" refers to the valley that stretches between the West Maui mountains on one side and the Haleakala volcano on the other. Aside from the county seat Wailuku and the commercial center of Kahului along the northern coast, there isn't much in the valley but vast fields of sugar cane. **Ka'ahumanu Avenue** and **Route 32 (Main Street)** run along the northern part of the valley all the way to the spectacular Iao Valley (p. 189) in the West Maui mountains. **Routes 36** and **37** connect the valley with the North Shore and Upcountry towns in the east (p. 219), and **Route 350/311 (Pu'unene Avenue/Mokulele Highway)** cuts through the cane fields to Lahaina (p. 203) and the towns and beaches of South Maui (p. 190).

KAHULUI AND WAILUKU

On the northern coast of the Central Maui Valley, these two towns merit little notice for their charms, but both offer several options for budget accommodations, including two inexpensive hostels. Kahului, the major airport gateway to Maui, is not a town so much as a chain of shopping centers, most of which sprawl along the main road, **Ka'ahumanu Avenue,** and along **Dairy Road,** which runs from Ka'ahumanu Ave. south to Lahaina and Kihei. West of Kahului, Wailuku is more of a cohesive town, centered around **West Main Street,** the continuation of Ka'ahumanu Ave. Clusters of mom-and-pop stores and restaurants give Wailuku more character than its larger eastern neighbor, though there's not much draw for tourists other than its central location and friendly accommodations. There are no attractions of note in Wailuku itself, but it is the gateway to the **Iao Valley.**

MAUI

Kahului & Wailuku

▲ ACCOMMODATIONS
Banana Bungalow, 9
Kanaha Beach Park, 1
Maui Beach Hotel, 3
Maui Seaside, 2
Northwind Hostel, 11
Old Wailuku Inn, 20

🍴 FOOD
Cafe Marc Aurel, 14
Cafe O'Lei, 18
Da Kitchen Cafe, 7
Down to Earth Natural
Foods, 8
Mañana Garage, 4
Open Air Produce
Market, 13
Ooka Supermarket, 16
Pizza in Paradise, 6
A Saigon Café, 17
Saeng's Thai Cuisine, 12
Tasty Crust
Restaurant, 10

🛍 SHOPPING
Maui Swap Meet, 5
Paperbacks Plus, 19
Request, 15

WISE WORDS When immersed in a bilingual culture, visitors can learn much about local values and beliefs by taking note of the words that are never translated. In Hawaiian newspapers, which are written primarily in American English, you'll often see the word *ohana* used to refer to anything from a lost-and-found classified ad ("Dogs lost—they are *ohana*—please return") to a story on political favoritism ("Pols take care of *ohana* first"). Although the word can be translated easily enough into "family," the concept of *ohana* has no counterpart in Anglo-American culture. Family means something to Hawaiians that is difficult to explain - something larger and all-encompassing. A similar translation difficulty is seen when driving in rural places with signs marked *kapu* or forbidden. The word *kapu* carries the connotation of being cursed, and implies a respect for the power of the land that "forbidden" does not. So if you want to understand how to think like the *kama'aina* (locals), there's no better way than learning the language of the land.

■ TRANSPORTATION

Flights: Kahului International Airport (OGG), on the northern coast of Central Maui, in Kahului. Kahului is the main airport for Maui, served by international carriers as well as **Hawaiian Airlines** (☎800-367-5320; www.hawaiianair.com; see p. 179 for more info), **Aloha Air** (☎800-367-5250; www.alohaair.com; see p. 179 for more info), and **Pacific Wings** (☎888-575-4546; www.pacificwings.com; see p. 179 for more info).

Buses: From the airport, **Speedishuttle** (☎800-977-2605 or 276-5014; www.speedishuttle.com) will take you where you need to go. Reserve a day in advance, either by phone or online. The **MEO (Maui Economic Opportunity) Public Shuttle** (☎877-7651; www.meoinc.om) runs free buses between Kahului and Wailuku. Routes #1 and 2 operate M-Sa approx. every 2hr. with multiple stops between the Wailuku town center and the shopping plazas in Kahului. Routes #1 and 2 also meet up with **Akina Aloha's** bus route #5 (10 per day 7:08am-5:45pm, $1) with express service to Ma'alaea and Lahaina at 7 stops including the Iao Theater in Wailuku, the Queen Ka'ahumanu Center, and the Maui Mall. Bus schedules are available at the Maui Visitors Bureau (see below) and the public libraries in Wailuku and Kahului. For more information, contact MEO Transportation and Akina Aloha Tours (☎879-2828; www.akinatours.com).

Car Rental: National car rental chains operate out of Kahului airport; see **Essentials,** p. 54. Alternatively, local car rental companies may have a more limited selection of vehicles, but they often offer better rates and less conspicuous cars. **Maui Cruisers Car Rental** (☎877-749-7889 or 249-2319; www.mauicruisers.net) has cars for $31 per day and $155 per week with no surcharge for under-25 drivers. **Aloha Rent-a-Car** (☎877-45-ALOHA/451-5641 or 877-4477; www.aloharentacar.com) also offers reasonably priced rentals with no under-25 surcharge.

■ PRACTICAL INFORMATION

Tourist Office: Maui Visitors Bureau, 1727 Wili Pa Loop (☎244-3530; www.visitmaui.com), off Imi Kala St., across from the Post Office in Wailuku. Although in a slightly obscure location, the staff is friendly and knowledgeable. It may, however, be easier to call with questions. Open M-F 8am-4:30pm.

Banks: Major bank branches line Kahului's highways. **24hr. ATMs** are located at all of the banks and in most shopping centers and malls. In Wailuku, there's a **Bank of Hawaii** at 2105 W. Main St. (☎871-8200), a First Hawaiian Bank at 27 N. Market St. (☎877-2377), and an **American Savings Bank** at 69 N. Market St. (☎244-9148). These branches all have 24hr. ATM machines, and are generally open M-Th 8:30am-4pm, F 8:30am-6pm.

Library: Kahului Public Library and Internet Access, 90 School St. (☎873-3097), off Kamehameha Ave. Open M and Th-Sa 10am-5pm, Tu-W 10am-8pm. **Wailuku Public Library and Internet Access,** 251 High St. (☎243-5766). Open M and Th 11:30am-8pm, Tu-W and F 10am-5pm. Both libraries also offer $0.15 copies. Internet access is unlimited with the purchase of a $10 visitor library card, valid for 3 months.

Laundromats: There are several laundry centers scattered throughout Kahului, including **W & F Washerette,** 125 S. Wakea Rd. (☎877-0353). Wash $1.75, dry $1. Open daily 6am-10pm. In Wailuku, **Happy Valley Laundry,** 340 N. Market St. (☎244-4677), is a few doors up from the Banana Bungalow. Wash $1.50 ($2 double load), dry $0.75. Open daily 6am-9pm. Both laundromats have coin machines and detergent available.

Emergency: ☎911.

Pharmacy: In Wailuku, try **Wailuku Professional Pharmacy,** 1900 Main St. (☎244-9099), is open M-F 8:30am-5:30pm, Sa 9am-1pm. In Kahului, head to **Long's Drugs** (☎877-0041), in the Maui Mall. Open M-F 8am-10pm (pharmacy closes at 9pm), Sa-Su 8am-9pm (pharmacy closes at 7pm).

Medical Services: In Wailuku, **Maui Memorial Hospital,** 221 Mahalani St. (☎244-9056) has 24hr. emergency service. The hospital is actually closer to Kahului and serves both areas.

Copy/fax services: In Kahului, **Kinko's** (see **Internet Access,** below) can meet all of your copying needs. In Wailuku, try **Copy Services,** 1975 Vineyard St. (☎242-7651; fax 242-7650), just south of Market St. Open M-F 9am-5pm.

Internet Access: Kinko's, 395 Dairy Rd., Kahului (☎871-2000), in the Dairy Center. In addition to their printing and copying services, Kinko's offers Internet access for $0.20 per minute. Open 24hr.

Post Office: 138 S. Pu'unene Ave., Kahului (open M-F 8:30am-5pm, Sa 9am-noon) or 250 Imi Kala St., Wailuku, off Mill St. (open M-F 8am-4:30pm, Sa 9am-noon).

Postal Code: Kahului 96732; Wailuku 96793.

ACCOMMODATIONS AND CAMPING

Accommodations in Kahului and Wailuku lean toward the budget end of the spectrum. Wailuku's hostels attract backpackers, windsurfers, and hangabouts, while Kahului's functional hotels draw business travelers and over-nighters looking for a bed near the airport. Lodgings in these towns provide a convenient base for exploring the natural beauty of the Iao Valley, but are a bit of a drive to Lahaina nightlife or Upcountry vistas.

Banana Bungalow, 310 N. Market St. (☎800-8HOSTEL/846-7835 or 244-5090; www.mauihostel.com), a few blocks from central Wailuku. The free tours offered by this well-maintained and energetically-run hostel take you places no other tour does. Inside the communal hostel, the receptionist's surfboard art decorates every wall, the hallways are carpeted, and the dorms are cozy and clean. Stay a week, and you'll feel like family. Linens, luggage storage, and safe available. Free Internet. Coin-op laundry. Communal kitchen and TV lounge with foosball table. **Short-term work** opportunities are available; see **Alternatives to Tourism,** p. 82 or email for information. Reception 8am-11pm. Quiet time after 10pm. Check-out 10am. Reservations recommended. 4- and 6-bed dorms $20; singles $38; doubles $52; triples $64. MC/V. ❶

Old Wailuku Inn at Ulupono, 2199 Kaho'okele St. (☎800-305-4899 or 244-5897; www.mauiinn.com). Follow Main St. (Rte. 32W) through central Wailuku and turn left on High St. (Rte. 30). The 3rd left is Kaho'okele; the inn is immediately on the right. Each of the 7 rooms in this B&B is decorated with native woods and locally handmade quilts. The owner cooks gourmet breakfasts each morning. All rooms have their own bathrooms, some with whirlpool tubs. 2-night min. stay. Reception 9am-5pm. Check-in 2pm. Check-out 11:30am. Reserve at least 3 mo. in advance with a $50 non-refundable deposit. Rooms $120-180 for double occupancy; each additional person $20. AAA and seniors 10% discount. MC/V. ❷

MAUI

Maui Beach Hotel, 170 Ka'ahumanu Ave. (☎888-649-3222 or 877-0051; www.mauibeachhotel.com), between Lono and Kane, near the Kahului airport. There's no beach at this hotel, although some rooms do overlook Kahului Bay. Convenience and price are what attract travelers here. All rooms have TVs, refrigerators, and A/C. The restaurant on the second floor offers a breakfast buffet ($6-8) and dinner menu (Tu-W 5:30-8pm all-you-can-eat sushi buffet). Free shuttle to and from airport runs hourly 7am-10pm. Internet available in the lobby ($3 for 10min.). Reception 24hr. Check-in 3pm. Check-out noon. 1-night deposit required for reservations; 72hr. notice required for cancellation refund. Standard room $98; superior $120; ocean view $145; oceanfront $185. Group rates available. MC/V. Wheelchair-accessible. ❷

Maui Seaside, 100 Ka'ahumanu Ave. (☎800-560-5552 or 877-3311; www.mauiseasidehotel.com), next to Maui Beach Hotel, near the Kahului airport. This family-owned hotel on Kahului Bay is well kept and has a nice inner courtyard, outdoor pool, and ocean view. All 200 rooms have A/C, cable TV, fridge, and private lanai. Breakfast included with some rooms. You can also rent cars through the hotel for $29-54 per day. Reception 24hr. Check-in 3pm. Check-out noon. Reservations with credit card recommended. Standard ground floor $118; with pool view and breakfast $126; with bay view and breakfast $140. AAA discount 10%. AmEx/MC/V. Wheelchair accessible. ❷

Northwind Hostel, 2080 Vineyard St. (☎800-9HOSTEL/946-7835 or 242-1448; fax 242-0905), with the entrance down an alley between Market St. and Church St. in downtown Wailuku; look for the international flags hanging from the 2nd-story porch. This laid-back hostel is not the tidiest, but the price is right for the surfers and backpackers who stay here. The breezy private rooms have a bed and a fridge. Free Internet. Shared kitchen and TV lounge. Luggage storage available. Laundry $1.75. Reception open 8:30am-10pm. Check-out 10am. Reservations accepted, but not required. Credit card surcharge. Weekly rates available. Dorms $18; singles $32; doubles $45. ❶

Kanaha Beach Park, off Amala Pl. near the airport car rental ports. From central Kahului, take Hobron Ave. off of Ka'ahumanu Ave. The first right is Amala Pl.; follow this coastal road and look for the park entrance on your left. With restrooms, outdoor showers and picnic tables on site, Kanaha Beach Park is a convenient and centrally located camping site. Set up your tent either in the shaded park grounds or right on the beach. Permits required. (See **Camping,** p. 182.) Campsite closed Tu-W for maintenance. Permits $3 per adult per night, $0.50 per child. ❶

🗘 FOOD

In Kahului, food options and supermarkets are located in the shopping centers along **Ka'ahumanu Avenue** For organic produce and packaged foods, **Down to Earth Natural Foods,** 305 Dairy Rd. in Kahului, has an impressive variety as well as a popular salad and hot bar. (☎877-2661. Open M-Sa 7am-9pm, Su 8am-8pm.) In Wailuku, **Ooka Supermarket,** 1870 Main St. (☎244-3931), is open M-Sa 6:30am-9pm and Su 6:30am-7pm. There's also an **open market** that sells fresh local produce and homemade baked goods right on **Market Street.** (☎276-4966. Open M-F 8am-6pm.) For a small town, Wailuku offers an impressive selection of international cuisine; **Vineyard Street** offers the most variety, and there are a few cafes and lunch counters along **West Main Street.**

🔳 Mañana Garage, 33 Lono St. (☎873-0220), off Ka'ahumanu Ave. in Kahului. Sandwiched into an office building between car dealerships and gas stations, the Mañana Garage is a pleasant surprise. Bright purple walls and the namesake metal garage door in the back create an inviting atmosphere that complements the creative Latin American cuisine. The entrees are a bit pricey (*paella* $25; guava tamarind salmon $18.50), but on *La Familia* Su and *Aloha* M they come at half-price! Tempting desserts (chocolate *dulce de leche* cake $5) round out the menu, while martinis and margaritas complement everything (cocktails $5-7; margaritas $22 per pitcher). Live music Tu-Sa, ranging from Brazilian lounge to homegrown rock. Dancing after dinner Sa. Happy Hour M-F 3-6pm. Open M-Tu 11am-9pm, W-F 11am-10:30pm, Sa 5-10:30pm, Su 5-9pm. ❷

A Saigon Cafe, 1792 W. Main St. (☎243-9560). From Wailuku, take Central Ave. to Nani St. and then turn right onto Kaniela St.; A Saigon will be on your left, though there's no sign. The no-frills tables of this unassuming Vietnamese restaurant are constantly filled with hungry tourists and locals. The 8-page menu is filled with endless options, including an entire page of vegetarian entrees. The house specialty *banh hoi* (vegetables, meat, and noodles that you roll yourself in rice paper; $9.25-10) is especially popular. The crispy noodles are an excellent choice as well, served hot with shrimp, calamari, and vegetables in a garlic sauce ($9.25). Open M-Sa 10am-9:30pm, Su 10am-8:30pm. MC/V. ❷

Cafe Marc Aurel, 28 N. Market St. (☎244-0852), in Wailuku center. The walls of this espresso bar are covered with coffee-themed prints and posters. Patrons sip lattes at glass-topped tables. Rich roasts, gypsy teas, light fare (quiches, muffins, and scones), and Häagen-Dazs ice cream all go down well with the soothing classical music in the background. Single espresso drinks $2-3. Open M-F 7am-6pm, Sa 7am-1pm. ❶

Cafe O'Lei, 2051 Main St. (☎244-6816), in downtown Wailuku. A gourmet bargain, this popular lunch joint showcases fresh local ingredients. Daily specials (blackened mahi mahi with fresh papaya salsa and rice $6) complement the standby menu of salads (Asian ginger chicken $7) and sandwiches (crab salad club on foccacia $7). Mostly a take-out lunch counter, but an airy dining room featuring colorful local paintings accommodates dine-in customers as well. Open M-F 10:30am-2:30pm. MC/V. ❶

Da Kitchen Cafe, 425 Koloa St. (☎871-7782), in Triangle Sq. off of Hana Hwy. in Kahului. For great local grinds, Da Kitchen is da best, brah. When this Hawaiian-style eatery threatened to close its doors, thousands of appreciative locals signed a petition to keep Da Kitchen alive. The petition worked, and now you'll have to compete with the locals for a seat at one of Da Kitchen's spacious booths or beach umbrella tables. This fun cafe serves heaping plates of *loco moco, kalua* pork, and teriyaki chicken ($8-9). Take-out available. Open M-F 11am-8pm, Sa 11am-3pm. AmEx/D/MC/V. ❷

Pizza in Paradise, 60 E. Wakea Ave. (☎871-8188). Every town needs its stellar pizza place, and in Kahului it's Pizza in Paradise. In a surfer-themed atmosphere, diners chow on incredible gourmet pizzas ($13-16), oven-baked subs ($6.50), and filling pasta dishes ($6.50). Be sure to take advantage of Family Feast Night: all you can eat and drink for only $8 (W 5:30-8:30pm). Free delivery in the Kahului/Wailuku area. Open M-Th and Su 11am-9pm, F-Sa 11am-10pm. MC/V. ❷

Tasty Crust Restaurant, 1770 Mill St. (☎244-0845), off of N. Market St. in Wailuku. The kind of place "where everybody knows your name," Tasty Crust is as local and cheap as they come; if you eat here twice in the same week, the gracious staff will remember your order. Locals crowd this 50-year-old Wailuku staple in the early morning for big, fluffy pancakes ($1.50 each) and cups of fresh-brewed joe ($1). Lunch and dinner entrees are likewise cheap and filling; enjoy sesame chicken with steamed rice and macaroni salad for a wallet-friendly $6.25. Open daily 6am-9pm. ❶

Saeng's, 2119 Vineyard St. (☎244-1567), at N. Church St. in downtown Wailuku. Saeng's stands out for its elegant atmosphere, both in the dimly-lit dining room and the open-air, garden lanai. The extensive Thai menu features 3 colors of curry (Pineapple Red Shrimp Curry $10) and highlights local seafood (mahi mahi ginger $12). Saeng's also offers a large selection of creative vegetarian options (Evil Prince Tofu $7.50). Lunch served M-F 11am-2:30pm; dinner nightly 5-9:30pm. MC/V. ❷

MAUI

MAUI

◀ BEACHES

KANAHA BEACH PARK. In the immediate Kahului area, Kanaha Beach Park is the most convenient beach option. Although the beach itself is windy and narrow, and the murky water and choppy waves make swimming unappealing, it's a great place to watch colored sails jump through the surf as adventurous kite surfers catch air. The park also has large grassy areas, grills, and picnic tables, making it a nice destination for a packed lunch or barbecue. Parking spaces are abundant in the park, but be sure not to leave any valuables in your vehicle. *(Off Amala Pl., behind the airport.)* If spectating isn't enough for you, **Action Sports** offers **kite surfing lessons** and will deliver the equipment to the beach. *(☎ 871-5857. $210 for 3hr. group lesson; $280 for 3hr. private lesson.)*

◉ SIGHTS

SUGAR MILL AND MUSEUM. Across the street from the still-operating sugar mill in Pu'unene (just south of Kahului), the ◙**Alexander & Baldwin Sugar Museum** offers a self-guided sampling of the sights, sounds, and tastes of the Maui sugar industry. Photographs, clothing, models, and artifacts document the history of the industry, with a focus on both the white plantation owners and the immigrants who worked the fields and mills. Sounds of old Hawaii accompany the different exhibits; in an informative 10min. video, you can hear the chants of the Polynesians who introduced sugar cane to Hawaii 1000 years ago and the simulated sound of water running through the irrigation ditches when Europeans began cultivating the plant The museum invites visitors to sample raw Maui sugar on the way out. *(3957 Hansen Rd., at Pu'unene Ave. From Kahului, take Pu'unene Ave. south; there will be signs for the sugar museum before Hansen meets Pu'unene. ☎ 871-8058; www.sugarmuseum.com. Open M-Sa 9:30am-4:30pm; Feb.-Mar. and July-Aug. also open Su 9:30am-4:30pm. $5, ages 6-17 $2.)*

BAILEY HOUSE MUSEUM. This 1833 mission house, now run by the Maui Historical Society, contains a small museum with artifacts that chronicle early Hawaiian history. The front room displays portraits of the Baileys, the family of sugar moguls who constructed the house and operated a female seminary here. The Hawaiian Room to the left displays the tools and ornaments of the early Hawaiians, and the two rooms to the right showcase the Maui-inspired paintings of Renaissance man and self-taught artist Edward Bailey, former headmaster of the girls' school. Also scattered throughout these rooms are utensils and other artifacts to illustrate the style that resulted from the fusion of European and Hawaiian culture. The upstairs bedrooms hold period furniture, handmade quilts, and items that belonged to Hawaiian royalty. *(2375 Main St., just outside Wailuku center on the road to Iao Valley. ☎ 244-3326; www.mauimuseum.org. Open M-Sa 10am-4pm. $5, ages 7-12 $1.)*

TROPICAL GARDENS OF MAUI. This four-acre garden and nursery showcases tropical trees and flowers from all over the world, including many rare plants endemic to Hawaii. If you're on the way to the Iao Valley, you might consider stopping here for a picnic and a leisurely stroll *(20-40min., depending on your pace).* Orchids, hibiscus, and the rare *nanu* (Hawaiian gardenia), are just some of the blossoms that line the garden paths. In the adjacent greenhouse, travel-safe plants are for sale. *(200 Iao Valley Rd. ☎ 244-3085; www.tropicalgardensofmaui.com. Open M-Sa 9am-5pm; last entrance at 3:15pm. Ages 8 and up $3, under 8 free.)*

KEPANIWAI PARK AND HAWAII NATURE CENTER. Farther up the road to Iao, Kepaniwai Park and Heritage Gardens commemorate the various immigrant groups that have settled in Hawaii. The numerous sheltered tables and restroom facilities make the park a decent stop for a picnic lunch. Next to the park, Hawaii

SUGAR'S LABOUR'S LOST
During the century between the US Civil War and the 1960s, sugar ruled supreme in Hawaii. While harvest months still bring the acrid smell of burning sugar to Maui's central valley, the Hawaiian sugar industry has shrunk considerably. Both the industry's development and decline are linked to the larger economic trend to move labor-intensive industries to places where labor is cheap, assuring industry leaders of higher profit margins.

In 1863, the end of slavery in the US spelled disaster for the South's sugar growers. The industry that had previously flourished in the deep South suddenly faced fierce competition from Hawaii's climate, soil, and relatively cheap labor supply. With the US-Hawaii Free Trade Agreement in 1875, the tariffs on Hawaiian sugar were removed, and Hawaii became the leader in US sugar production. The sugar industry built much of the infrastructure on the islands, and the immigrant laborers from Japan, the Philippines, Portugal, and elsewhere helped create the syncretic culture that exists today.

With the incorporation of Hawaii as a state in 1959 and the subsequent enforcement of US labor laws, Big Sugar (for the most part) abandoned Hawaii for cheaper labor in the Philippines and Indonesia. Today, sugar is still a $400 million industry in Hawaii and the state's leading agricultural export, but tourism has far surpassed sugar to become Hawaii's main source of income. (See **History**, p. 11.)

Nature Center, 875 Iao Valley Rd., offers pricey guided tours of the rainforest valley ($25, ages 8-12 $23; 1½hr. tours M-F 11:30am and 1:30pm, Sa-Su 11am and 2pm; call ☎244-6500 for reservations), and houses an all-ages interactive nature museum. (Iao Valley Rd. Park open daily until 7pm; free. Museum open daily 10am-3:15pm; $6, children $4.)

PROFILE. Half a mile past Kepaniwai Park and the Hawaii Nature Center, a sign on the right side of the road indicates the viewing point for a profile in the rock formations of Pali Ele'ele gorge. While local Hawaiians claim the profile to be that of a powerful ancient *kahuna* (priest), many visitors see the face of President John F. Kennedy; pull over at the bend in road and be your own judge.

IAO VALLEY STATE PARK AND THE IAO NEEDLE. The result of thousands of years of water pressure eroding the volcanic rock, the Iao Needle rises 2250 ft. above the Iao Valley. The Hawaiians affectionately called the structure *Kuku'emoku*, named after the phallus of the sea god Kanaloa. They considered the valley a sacred space, burying their *ali'i* (royalty) here and using the valley to fight their most important battles. In 1790, this was the site of the bloody victory of Kamehameha I over the rival chief of Oahu, which ultimately led to his coronation as the first king of Hawaii. The beauty of the natural forms is still awe inspiring. Walk up the 133 steps to the top of the path for a more intimate view of the formation. The paved path (which can be slippery when wet) meanders down to the fast-moving Iao Stream, where native kids blatantly ignore the "no swimming" signs, frolicking in the water that once irrigated the *taro* crops cultivated on the lush valley floor. The valley can be windy and chilly even when it's sunny in downtown Wailuku, so bring along a light jacket just in case. (Take Main St. through Wailuku and continue for 3 mi. The road ends at Iao Valley Park. Although it seems like a hike through the valley would be "gorge-ous," there is **no off-trail hiking** in Iao Valley; allow 30-35min. to see the entire park via the paved paths and steps. Restrooms available. Open daily 7am-7pm. Free.)

🎵 ENTERTAINMENT

For evening entertainment, **Mañana Garage** (see p. 186) offers occasional **live music.** The **Iao Theater** at 68 N. Market St. in Wailuku (☎242-6969; www.mauionstage.com) and the **Maui Arts and Cultural Center (MACC)** at 1 Cameron Place off Kahului Beach Rd. (☎242-7469; www.mauiarts.org) both hold live performances, the latter attracting international stars as well as local artists. The two **movie theaters** in Kahului are both located off Ka'ahumanu Ave.: the **Maui Mall Megaplex Cinemas** (☎871-6684) in the Maui Mall and the **Ka'ahumanu 6 Theaters** (☎873-3137) in the Queen Ka'ahumanu Center. The ⬛Maui **Film Festival** screens art films every Wednesday at the Castle Theater at the MACC, with live music and food served before and after the first screening. (☎572-FILM; www.mauifilmfestival.com. Shows 5, 7:30pm; $10 for single ticket.)

In lieu of shelling out the big bucks for a complete *luau*, enjoy a **free luau show** by the Old Lahaina Luau dancers every Saturday at 11:30am on Center Stage at the **Queen Ka'ahumanu Center.** The mall also offers a **Hot Hawaiian Music** presentation at 7pm on Fridays and 1pm on Saturdays. Call ☎877-4325 for more information.

Candlepin fans are in luck; Wailuku is home to the **Maui Bowling Center,** 1976 Vineyard St., just south of Market St. Get your roll on at just $2 a string. (☎244-4596. Open M and W-Th 10am-10pm, Tu 9am-10pm, F-Sa 10am-midnight, Su 10am-9pm.) For some fast-track action, **Maui Go Karts,** 191 Vevau St., can speed up your lazy Hawaiian afternoon or evening. (☎871-7619. Across the street from the Kahului Foodland. Open Su-Th 10am-8pm, F-Sa 10am-11pm. 5min. ride $6; 5 rides $20. MC/V.)

■ SHOPPING

Just about every major shopping chain has a store in Kahului. The town's highways are more like strip malls, and within a few miles' radius shoppers can locate just about anything they forgot to bring from home. On Saturday mornings, the **Maui Swap Meet,** on Pu'unene Ave. next to the Kahului post office, is *the* place to get amazing local produce, buy Hawaiiana clothing and jewelry, and peruse the giant junk sale. (☎877-3100. 7am-noon. Admission $0.50.)

North Main St. and Market St. in Wailuku are lined with antique stores, galleries, pawn shops, and bookstores. For music lovers, a trip to ⬛**Request,** 10 N. Market St. could easily fill a rainy afternoon. This second-hand music store has an impressive selection of new and used CDs ($8 and up), from hard-to-find indie labels to rows and rows of reggae. The vinyl is mostly pop and rock. (☎244-9315. Open M-Sa 10am-6pm.) For light beach reading, peruse the shelves of **Paperbacks Plus,** 1977 Main St. Used books are sold at half off the list price, and they'll even hunt down out-of-print and hard-to-find books. (☎242-7135; www.thehawaiianbookstore.com. Open M-F 8:30am-5:30pm, Sa 9am-5pm.)

SOUTH MAUI

Stretching from the port of Ma'alaea to Kihei, Wailea, and Makena on the southwestern shores of the Haleakala volcano, South Maui encompasses a vastly varied region. Kihei is the Miami Beach of Maui, a 6 mi. strip of condos, and touristy restaurants. Past Kihei, the swanky resorts of Wailea occupy the best beachfront property. Farther down, less developed Makena boasts the most impressive beaches of all, with dramatic cliffs, sandy shores, and views of Kaho'olawe and Molokini across the water. Beyond Makena, the paved road becomes an ancient path, winding past lava fields and bays teeming with fish. South Maui is hotter and drier than the rest of the island—December through April is the best time to visit. In addition to the pleasant weather, this is the only time to view the hundreds of **humpback whales** that migrate to Hawaii's coastal waters each year to breed.

MA'ALAEA

Ma'alaea isn't much of a town—what there is to see is concentrated in the commercial complex of **Ma'alaea Harbor Village,** 300 Ma'alaea Rd., off **Route 30** between Lahaina and Kihei. Tour companies use the harbor as the departure point for many boating and fishing trips.

◖ **FOOD.** There is a **restaurant** and **snack bar** in the Ocean Center, as well as several dining options in Maʻalaea Harbor Village. The **Maʻalaea Grill ❹** matches upscale seafood cuisine like sauteed mahi mahi in ginger butter with papaya salsa ($16), with an equally posh location overlooking the ocean. (☎243-2206. Open M 10:30am-3pm, Tu-Su 10:30am-9pm.) Sate your sweet-tooth with a snack from **Hula Homemade Cookies and Ice Cream ❶.** (Chocolate chip macadamia cookie $1.20. Open M-Sa 10am-6pm, Su 10am-5pm.)

◪ **BEACHES.** A narrow strip of sandy beach lines Rte. 30, but the current here is quite rough, and better swimming can be found farther south beyond Kihei. When the surf is up, experienced surfers and body boarders rip the southern swells that roll unobstructed into Maʻalaea Harbor; you can watch them from the seawall next to Buzz's Wharf restaurant, behind the Harbor Village. Public restrooms are located to the right of the restaurant.

▨ **OUTDOORS.** In the port behind the Harbor Village, there are a number of boats that run **snorkel** trips to Molokini, as well as **sunset cruises, fishing expeditions,** and **seasonal dolphin- and whale-watching trips.** Several different companies run boats, all of which are represented in the activities kiosk in Maʻalaea Harbor Village. Prices vary based on the length of the trip, number of passengers on the boat, and the food and drink served. Note that boats with an open bar tend to adopt a fraternity-party feel; if you don't intend to drink, your money may be better spent elsewhere. Known for their eco-friendly and educational tours, the ▧**Pacific Whale Foundation** (☎879-2615; www.pacificwhale.org), a non-profit international organization dedicated to marine research and conservation, runs several kinds of trips, led by certified naturalists. In addition to their location in the Maʻalaea Harbor Village, the foundation has several other branches throughout Maui. Pacific Whale also offers internships and volunteer programs; for more information, see **Alternatives to Tourism,** p. 78.

◔ **SIGHTS.** The other main attraction in Maʻalaea is the ▧**Maui Ocean Center,** an indoor/outdoor aquarium that showcases the mind-boggling diversity of Hawaii's marine life. The admission price is a bit steep, but the fish don't disappoint—many of the beautiful and bizarre species displayed can only be found in local waters, and even experienced snorkelers and scuba divers will be impressed by the range of creatures here. Tactile displays like the Touch Pool will entertain small children, while the placards beside the visual displays aim to educate visitors of all ages. Allow about 2hr. for the self-paced tour through the aquarium. *(192 Maʻalaea Rd., off Hwy. 30 in Maʻalaea Harbor Village. ☎270-7000; www.mauioceancenter.com. Open daily 9am-5pm; July-Aug. daily until 6pm. $19, seniors $17, ages 3-12 $13. Wheelchair accessible.)*

KIHEI

While cruising the congested Kihei strip, it's hard to believe that fifty years ago Kihei was just a small town on an unpaved road. In the last few decades, development in the area has exploded, and for several years, Kihei was ranked among the fastest-growing towns in America. Today, it must strike a balance between the consequences of overbuilding and the continued local demands for more affordable housing. While some consider Kihei, with its traffic and noise, the least attractive of Maui's charms, others enjoy an affordable vacation thanks to the town's condos, tasty take-out tacos, and cheap drink deals at local Happy Hours. If you do choose to stay in Kihei, make sure you find time to leave the strip—the best South Maui beaches lie beyond Kihei in Wailea and Makena.

✦ ⚡ ORIENTATION AND PRACTICAL INFORMATION

Kihei sprawls along the southwestern shore of the Haleakala volcano, which gradually rises above the condos and hotels on the *mauka* (mountain) side. **South Kihei Road** runs along the coast, and is studded with traffic lights and shopping centers. Cars move slowly here any time of day; the inland **Route 31 (Pi'ilani Highway)** that runs above Kihei all the way to Makena is a good alternate route.

Tourist Information and Services: The **Maui Information and Visitors Center** (☎874-4919) offers a personalized concierge service, making reservations for car rental, accommodations, activities, etc. free of charge. **Activity World** books activities like snorkel trips and helicopter rides at wholesale prices. Several Kihei locations include Kihei-Kalama Village (☎874-9500) and 2531 S. Kihei Rd. (☎874-9507).

Banks: Banks and **ATMs** dot both S. Kihei Rd. and Pi'ilani Hwy. There's an **American Savings Bank** at 1215 S. Kihei Rd. in the Kihei Town Center (☎879-1977), a **Bank of Hawaii** in Azeka Plaza II (☎879-5844), and a **First Hawaiian Bank** in the Lipoa Center (☎875-0055).

Library: Kihei Public Library, 35 Waimahaihai St. (☎875-6833), across from the Kukui Mall and behind the fire station. Unlimited **Internet access** with the purchase of a $10 visitor library card. Open Tu noon-8pm, W and F 10am-6pm, Th and Sa 10am-5pm.

Laundromat: Lipoa Laundry Center, 41 E. Lipoa St. (☎875-9266), next to Hapa's Night Club. Wash $1.50, dry $0.75. Change machine available. Open M-Sa 8am-9pm, Su 8am-5pm.

Emergency: ☎911.

Police: Non-emergency ☎244-6400. The station is next to the Foodland in the Kihei Town Center.

Pharmacy: There are no 24hr. pharmacies in Kihei. **Long's Drugs,** 1215 S. Kihei Rd. (☎879-2259), in Kihei Plaza, is open M-F 8am-10pm (pharmacy closes at 9pm) and Sa-Su 8am-9pm (pharmacy closes at 7pm).

Medical Services: The **Kihei-Wailea Medical Center,** 221 Pi'ikea Ave. (☎874-8100), in the Pi'ilani Village Shopping Center, caters to travelers. The center is open M-F 8am-8pm, Sa-Su 8am-5pm.

Fax Services: Mail Boxes Etc., 1215 S. Kihei Rd. (☎874-5556), in Kihei Plaza.

Internet Access:

Cyber Surf Lounge, in Azeka Plaza (☎276-6260), charges $0.15 per min. with a $3 minimum. Print-outs $0.25 per page. Open daily 9am-10pm.

Cyberbean Internet Cafe, 1881 S. Kihei Rd. (☎879-4799), in the Kihei Town Center near Foodland. After $2 for the first 10min., they charge $0.20 for each additional min. Smoothies ($4) and sandwiches ($6). Open M-F 6:30am-9pm, Sa 7am-9pm, Su 8am-8pm. AmEx/MC/V.

Hale Imua Internet Stop & Shop, 2463 S. Kihei Rd. (☎891-9219; www.haleimua.com), in the Denny's Plaza, charges $2 for the first 10min. and $0.10 for each additional min.

Post Office: 1254 S. Kihei Rd. (☎879-1987), next to Azeka Plaza. Open M-F 8:30am-4:30pm, Sa 9am-1pm.

Postal Code: 96753.

🏠 ACCOMMODATIONS

The majority of Kihei accommodations are unremarkable, though reasonably priced, condominiums. Many places have a 3- or 4-day minimum stay, and a price break for stays of more than 7 days. A stay at a **B&B** (see p. 195) is a good alternative to the condo scene. B&Bs are generally located in quiet residential neighborhoods with proximity to Kihei restaurants and beaches, but a world away from the noisy strip. The ones listed below are some of the few licensed B&Bs in Kihei; if these are booked, the hosts may be able to recommend one of many unlicensed B&Bs nearby.

CONDOS

Several companies specialize in Kihei condo and vacation rentals, including **AA Oceanfront Condo Rentals,** 1279 S. Kihei Rd. (☎800-488-6004; www.makena.com; books properties starting at $70 per night; reservation fee $25); **Affordable Accommodations Maui** (☎888-333-9747; www.affordablemaui.com; properties start at $55 per night; no fee); **Condominium Rentals Hawaii,** 362 Huku Li'i Place (☎800-367-5242; www.crhmaui.com; properties start at $71 per night; reservation fee $25); **Maui Condominium and Home,** 2511 S. Kihei Rd. (☎800-822-4409; www.resortquest-maui.com; properties start at $95 per night; reservation fee $25); and **Kihei Maui Vacations,** 2395 S. Kihei Rd. (☎879-7581; properties start at $64 per night; 10% commission charge). In addition to the rates quoted below, be prepared to pay an almost 12% accommodations tax, a reservation fee or commission charged by the reservation services (see above), and around $50 for a cleaning fee when you check out. Keep in mind that the beaches get nicer as you head south along Kihei Rd. Condos with addresses in the mid- to high-2000s along S. Kihei Rd. typically have the best access to one of the Kamaole parks or Keawakapu Beach. Those listed here are only a few of the dozens of condos available.

Mana Kai Maui, 2960 S. Kihei Rd. (available through Condominium Rentals Hawaii). This high-rise on Keawakapu Beach offers hotel rooms

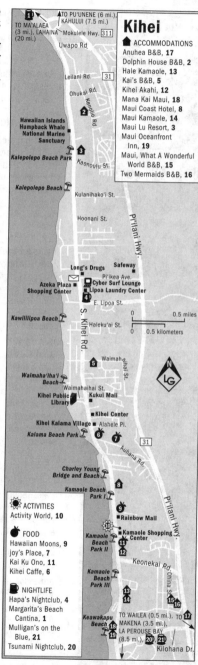

Kihei

♦ ACCOMMODATIONS
Anuhea B&B, **17**
Dolphin House B&B, **2**
Hale Kamaole, **13**
Kai's B&B, **5**
Kihei Akahi, **12**
Mana Kai Maui, **18**
Maui Coast Hotel, **8**
Maui Kamaole, **14**
Maui Lu Resort, **3**
Maui Oceanfront
  Inn, **19**
Maui, What A Wonderful
  World B&B, **15**
Two Mermaids B&B, **16**

☼ ACTIVITIES
Activity World, **10**

🍴 FOOD
Hawaiian Moons, **9**
joy's Place, **7**
Kai Ku Ono, **11**
Kihei Caffe, **6**

📓 NIGHTLIFE
Hapa's Nightclub, **4**
Margarita's Beach
  Cantina, **1**
Mulligan's on the
  Blue, **21**
Tsunami Nightclub, **20**

MAUI

HE BIG SPLURGE

MOLOKINI CALLING

When traveling on a limited budget, it's difficult to convince yourself to shell out the extra cash for a nice dinner or a tropical frozen drink, and as much as you want those *aloha* print car seat covers, you just can't have 'em. However, here's one big Maui splurge.

As soon as you set foot on Maui, activity centers barrage you with glossy brochures advertising un-filled snorkeling excursions to the small crater-shaped island of Molokini, situated midway between Maui and Kaho'olawe. No matter how much snorkeling you've done at various beaches and coves around the island, Molokini still calls.

With snorkel gear and mask de-fogger in hand, board the boat and enjoy the leisurely ride to "Molo," as locals call it. When you get in the water, you'll understand what all the fuss is about. Molokini and Makena (on Maui's southern coast) brings you face-to-face with turtles, gorgeous humpback whales spouting and breaching, and more fish and coral than you can imagine.

Several activity centers book snorkel trips to Molokini: **Maui Dive Shop** runs trips from Kihei Boat Harbor (☎879-3388; $44), **Pacific Whale Foundation** runs out of Ma'alaea Harbor (☎249-3811; $52), and **Boss Frog's** runs out of Kihei (☎875-4477; $60).

with A/C as well as 1- and 2-bedroom condo units both with or without A/C. All units have ceiling fans, cable TV, and access to the pool; condos have full kitchens and private lanais. Daily cleaning service included. Check-in 3pm. Check-out 11am. Reserve with $250 deposit. Full pre-payment due 30 days before arrival or Nov. 1 for any booking Dec. 15-Jan. 5. Car and condo packages available. Dec. 16-Jan. 5 and Feb. 1-28 $125-280; Jan. 6-Jan. 31 and Mar. 1-Apr. 15 $116-247; Apr. 16-Dec. 15 $95-217. AmEx/MC/V. ❹

Maui Kamaole, 2777 S. Kihei Rd. (available through Maui Condominium and Home), next to the Hale Kamaole and across from Kamaole Park III. Bright pink flowers line the property of Maui Kamaole, one of Kihei's newer resort complexes, which features a heated pool, jacuzzi, 2 tennis courts, BBQ, and an activities desk. The 1- and 2-bedroom units are more modern and spacious than those next door. All units have 2 bathrooms, A/C, cable TV and VCR, washer/dryer, and full kitchen. 4-night min. stay. Check-in 2pm. Check-out 10am. Cleaning fee included. Reserve with 3 nights deposit; full pre-payment due 30 days before arrival, or Sept. 1 for any booking Dec. 15-Jan. 5. For more than 7 nights, rates are $15-20 less per night. High-season $170-250. Low-season $140-205. MC/V. ❺

Kihei Akahi, 2531 S. Kihei Rd. (available through Maui Condominium and Home), across the street from Kamaole Park II. Studio, 1- and 2-bedroom units all have a ceiling fan, lanai, cable TV, washer/dryer, full kitchen, and access to 2 pools, tennis, and BBQ. 4-night min. stay. Check-in 2pm. Check-out 10am. Check-out cleaning included. Reserve with 3 nights deposit; full pre-payment due 30 days before arrival or Sept. 1 for any booking Dec. 15-Jan. 5. For more than 7 nights, rates are $10-15 less per night. Dec. 15-Apr. 15 $115-165; Apr. 16-Dec. 14 $90-135. ❹

Hale Kamaole, 2737 S. Kihei Rd. (available through Hale Kamaole Homeowners Cooperative, ☎800-367-2970), next to the Maui Kamaole and across from Kamaole Park III. 1- and 2-bedroom condos each have a lanai, A/C, cable TV, full kitchen, and access to 2 pools, tennis courts, BBQ, and laundry. 3-night min. stay. Check-in 3pm. Check-out 11am. Reserve with $100 deposit; full pre-payment due 30 days before arrival for any booking Apr. 1-Dec.15 and 60 days prior for Dec. 16-Mar. 31. 1 time cleaning fee for stays of less than 6 nights. Discounts for stays longer than 7 nights. Dec. 16-Mar. 31 $110-164; Apr. 1-Oct. 31 $85-121; Nov. 1-Dec. 15 $88-125. MC/V. ❹

BED & BREAKFASTS

Kai's Bed & Breakfast/Vacation Rentals, 80 E. Welakahao Rd. (☎800-905-8424, ext. 24 or 874-6431; www.mauibb.com). E. Welakahao Rd. is off the *mauka* (mountain) side of S. Kihei Rd. between the Foodland and Star Market; #80 is about 2 blocks from the beach. Each of the 3 rooms has a different arrangement and theme, and all feature elegant stone floors, TV, microwave, and fridge. Continental breakfast with seasonal fruit from the garden is served every morning in a basket on your porch. Beach towels, coolers, boogie boards, snorkels, bicycles, garden jacuzzi, and washer/dryer are available for guest use. 4-night min. stay, negotiable depending on season. Check-in 2pm. Check-out 10am. Reserve with 50% deposit at least 2 mo. ahead in low season (Apr. 15-Dec. 15), earlier for high season (Dec. 16-Apr. 14); balance due 30 days prior to arrival. $50-95 per night, $400-650 per week; slightly less in low season. MC/V. ❸

Dolphin House B&B, 69 Kalola Pl. (☎800-419-2521 or 874-0126; www.dolphin-house.com). From S. Kihei Rd., turn onto Ohukai Rd., then right on Kenolio Rd., and right on Kalola Pl. Its central location, comfortable accommodations, and reasonable rates make Dolphin House a great deal. The spacious garden rooms have king-sized beds, private lanais, and bathrooms; some have A/C. Non-garden rooms are smaller but still very comfortable. A studio cottage, separate from the house, has a kitchenette and luxurious tiled bathroom. Continental breakfast with fruit straight from the garden. 2- to 3-night min. stay. Check-in 2pm. Check-out 11am. Reserve with $100 deposit; 30-day cancellation policy. Rooms $55-90; studio cottage a steal at $90. MC/V. ❷

Maui, What a Wonderful World B&B, 2828 Umalu Pl. (☎800-943-5804 or 879-9103; http://amauibedandbreakfast.com), a 10min. walk from the beach. From S. Kihei Rd., turn left onto Keonekai Rd. at the Haleakala Shores sign. Go almost all the way up the hill before turning right onto Ohina St. Go over 3 speed bumps, turn left onto Alaume St., and then right onto Umalu Pl. Each of the 4 suites in this welcoming B&B has been freshly painted and thoughtfully decorated by hosts Eva and Jim Tantillo. All have private entrances and bathrooms, TV, and A/C; 2 have kitchenettes and 1 has a full kitchen. Extended continental breakfast served on the breezy lanai. Free laundry. No min. stay. Check-in 4pm. Check-out noon. Reserve 2-3 mo. ahead with 50% deposit; balance due 60 days before arrival. Studios $75-89, 1-bedroom $99. AmEx/MC/V. ❸

Two Mermaids on the Sunny Side of Maui Bed & Breakfast, 2840 Umalu Pl. (☎800-598-9550 or 874-8687; www.twomermaids.com). Follow directions for Wonderful World, p. 195. Located in a quiet residential neighborhood, this B&B is still close to the action. The hospitable mermaid hosts advise visitors on the best scuba diving spots and other local secrets. The 2 suites are colorful and homey, both with kitchens, cable TV, private bathrooms, and access to a well-kept pool. Continental breakfast features fresh fruit and local breads. Check-in 3pm. Check-out noon. Reserve at least 3 mo. in advance with 50% deposit; balance due 60 days prior to arrival. Suites $110-190. ❸

Anuhea Bed & Breakfast/Health Retreat, 3164 Mapu Pl. (☎800-206-4441 or 874-1490; www.anuheamaui.com), in the Maui Meadows neighborhood off Pi'ilani Hwy., just before Wailea. Host and Reiki Master Cherie Kolbo greets her guests with a warm *aloha,* welcoming them to her peaceful B&B and health spa. The secluded location of the house—a drive from the nearest beach—allows guests to enjoy a quiet escape, especially on the elevated lanai. Anuhea features 5 guest rooms, 3 of which have A/C. The central garden area features a jacuzzi, gazebo, and hammock for your relaxation pleasure. Full sit-down breakfast. 3-night min. stay negotiable depending on availability. Check-in 2pm. Check-out 10am. Reserve with 50% deposit; balance paid on arrival. All rooms July-Sept. $105, Oct.-June $115. AmEx/MC/V. ❹

MAUI

HE HIDDEN DEAL

SUSHI AT SANSEI

Much to the delight of South Shore seafood lovers, the success of Sansei's Kapalua location has ed to a second **Sansei** opening in Kihei. Sansei's popularity is well deserved—the ambience is swank and the sushi is first-rate. The *nigiri* is made with fresh, sweet ish and just the right amount of seasoned rice. The stars of the menu, though, are the *maki* rolls, creatively assembled into caterpillars and pink cadillacs. The sushi doesn't come cheap (*nigiri* $4.25-9.50, rolls $4-16), but early-bird and late-night specials make things slightly more affordable. The menu also includes cooked entrees and noodle dishes ($16-24) that infuse local produce with a Japanese flair. The descriptive sake and wine list will help you pair your meal with the perfect cool or dry beverage. If you take advantage of the early-bird food specials, know that the line starts orming well before 5pm, and by 5:29 it's wrapped around the plaza.

(1881 S. Kihei Rd. (☎879-0004), in the Kihei Town Center near Foodland. Open Su-W 5:30-.0pm, Th-Sa 5:30pm-2am. 25% off all food Tu-Sa 5:30-6pm; 50% off all food Su-M 5:30-6pm; 50% off all food, $1 off draft beverages, and free karaoke until closing (21+ only) Th-Sa 10pm-1am. mEx/MC/V.)

HOTELS

There are only three hotels in Kihei, all of which offer an alternative to the minimum stay and cleaning fees that condominiums require.

Maui Oceanfront Inn, 2980 S. Kihei Rd. (☎800-263-3387 or 879-7744; www.mauioceanfrontinn.com), on Keawakapu Beach. With the best beach location in Kihei and reasonable prices, the Maui Oceanfront is a great value. Each unit has a queen-sized bed, A/C, TV, microwave, coffee-maker, fridge, and telephone with data port. Paintings of local Hawaiian artists adorn the walls. Reception 24hr. Check-in 3pm. Check-out noon. Reserve with credit card; 3-day cancellation policy. Feb.-Mar. and June 20-Aug. 22 rooms $159-215; Apr. 1-June 19 and Aug. 23-Dec. 19 $127-199. Internet special 20% discount, AARP 25%, AAA 50%. AmEx/D/DC/MC/V. ❺

Maui Coast Hotel, 2259 S. Kihei Rd. (☎800-895-6284 or 874-6284; www.westcoasthotels.com/mauicoast), across the street from Kamaole Park I. This newly renovated hotel has little charm and unimpressive views, but offers good value for standard hotel comfort. Fitness center, pool, tennis courts, 2 outdoor jacuzzis, and activity desk. The 265 rooms all have A/C, lanais, cable TV, mini fridges, and in-room safes. Free laundry on-site. No min. stay. Reception 24hr. Check-in 3pm. Check-out noon. Reserve with 1-night deposit; 72hr. cancellation policy. Standard double $165-205; suites $235-350. Discount for seniors and AAA members. AmEx/D/DC/MC/V. Wheelchair accessible. ❺

Maui Lu Resort, 575 S. Kihei Rd. (☎879-5881; www.astonhotels.com). This low-rise hotel sits on 28 acres on the northern Kihei coastline. While the resort grounds are well-maintained, Maui Lu is a bit of a trek from any of Kihei's better golden-sand beaches. In lieu of the salt water, swimmers can instead enjoy the resort's Maui-shaped pool. All rooms have A/C, fridge, cable TV, and private balconies. Check-in 3pm. Check-out noon. Reserve with 1 night's deposit. Jan.-Mar., June 13-Aug. 17, and Dec. 24-31 rooms $108-180; Apr. 1-June 12 and Aug. 18-Dec. 23 $131-215. MC/V. ❺

🍴 FOOD

Kihei restaurants run the gamut from fast food to fine cuisine. Practically every place on the strip caters to tourists, so it can be hard to find a good value. For do-it-yourself cuisine, there are several supermarkets in the shopping centers on S. Kihei Rd., including **Foodland,** in the Kihei Town Center (open 24hr.), and **Safeway,** off Pi'ilani Hwy. in the Pi'ilani Village Center (open M-F 9am-8pm, Sa-Su 9am-5:30pm). The hot bar at **Hawaiian Moons Natural Foods** store, 2411 S. Kihei Rd., has healthy take-out meals and organic salads that you can enjoy at the beach across the street. (☎875-4356. Open M-Sa 8am-9pm, Su 8am-7pm. AmEx/DC/MC/V.) **Aloha Discount Liquors,** 2439 S. Kihei Rd., in the Rainbow Mall, is the best bet for cheap beer, wine, and alcohol. (☎874-8822. Open M-Sa 9am-11pm.)

Kihei Caffe, 1945 S. Kihei Rd. (☎879-2230), across from Kalama Park. Banana macadamia nut pancakes, mushroom avocado omelettes, and fresh Kona coffee make this the busiest breakfast joint on the Kihei strip. Order inside at the counter, and cross your fingers that an outdoor table will be open by the time you're done; this place fills up fast, and paper-reading locals are in no hurry to leave. Breakfast selections are $5-7; lunch salads, sandwiches, and burgers for $6-7. Open daily 5am-8:30pm. ❶

Da Kitchen Express, 2439 S. Kihei Rd. (☎875-7782), in the Rainbow Mall. This no-frills restaurant sells cheap, freshly prepared local and Hawaiian style food. For a smattering of everything, try the Hawaiian Plate (pork *lau lau, kalua* pork, chicken long rice, and *lomi* salmon $8.50), served with rice and macaroni salad. Breakfast (served 9-11am) features hearty omelettes ($5.75), plate lunches, and Maui-style sweetbread french toast ($5.25). Limited indoor seating, or take your meal to go. Open daily 9am-9pm. ❶

Thai Chef, 2439 S. Kihei Rd. (☎874-5605), in the Rainbow Mall. With as many plants as tables in its moderately-sized dining room, Thai Chef's romantic ambience makes it an appealing refuge amidst Kihei's strip-mall eateries. The extensive menu, numerous vegetarian options, and friendly service make Thai Chef (and its sister restaurant in Lahaina) a consistently solid dining option. Entrees $9-14. Open M-F 11am-2pm and 5-10pm, Sa-Su 5-10pm. D/MC/V. ❸

joy's place, 1993 S. Kihei Rd. (☎879-9258; www.joysplace.org), in the Island Surf Building at Auhana Rd. Health food fans flock to joy's, where organic, wholesome eating is a way of life. With lots of vegan and vegetarian options including organic sandwiches, salads, and wraps ($5.25-7.50), joy's menu emphasizes smart eating. Mostly take-out, but a few pleasant tables are available for sit-down dining. If you like what you taste, join joy for her drop-in cooking classes. Open M-Sa 10am-5pm. ❷

Pita Paradise, 1913 S. Kihei Rd. (☎875-7679), in the Kihei Kalama Village across from Kalama Park. Gyros, kabobs, and (of course) pitas ($8-15) are staples at this cafe; lunch and dinner entrees can be enjoyed either inside or on Paradise's deck. Authentic Mediterranean salad is heaped with cucumbers, tomatoes, olives, and feta ($8), but it's not complete without a luscious slice of baklava ice cream cake ($6). Take-out and vegetarian options available. Open M-Sa 11am-9:30pm, Su 5-9:30pm. MC/V. ❸

KKO (Kai Ku Ono), 2511 S. Kihei Rd. (☎875-1007). With its pleasant ocean view, gentle Tiki torch lighting, and occasional live Hawaiian music, KKO can be considered amongst Kihei's more posh dining options. Yet, with entrees ranging from $10-18, Kai Ku Ono is affordable enough not to exclude the budget traveler. Start the meal with tasty Thai grilled calamari ($9), and continue on with mango barbecue ribs or macadamia nut chicken. The varied menu also offers sandwiches, sushi, and pasta. Open daily 8am-11pm. AmEx/MC/V. ❸

⌒ BEACHES

The sandy expanse between Ma'alaea and Makena is basically one long beach broken up by lava formations. The North Kihei beaches are popular for windsurfing and sailing; the beaches farther south are better suited for swimming. Many of the beach parks have recreational facilities. **Kalama Park** is popular with skaters, and features tennis courts and sports fields. Just south of Kalama, **Charley Young Bridge and Beach** is full of sunbathers. All the **Kamaole Beach Parks (I, II, and III)** have showers, lifeguards on duty, and beautiful golden sand; Kamaole II and III are set

MAUI

back farther from the road than Kam. I and have some nice shady spots in addition to plenty of sun. **Keawakapu Beach,** past Kam. III, is usually uncrowded, so it may be worth the walk to check it out (parking is past Sarrento's Restaurant and the Maui Oceanfront Inn, in a lot at the entrance of Wailea on the left). For more beaches farther south, see **Wailea** (p. 200) and **Makena** (p. 201).

🔖 ACTIVITIES

SNORKELING. With over 450 different species of fish, 25% of which are found only in Hawaii (and 20% of those only in Molokini!), Maui is a can't-miss snorkeling experience. Nearly every beach has a formation of lava rocks jutting into the sea where fish congregate. **Kamaole I, II, and III** are great for novices. In Wailea, **Ulua Beach,** just past the Renaissance Wailea Hotel, has a rocky point that divides it from Mokapu Beach, and a reef that extends farther out. **Ahihi Bay,** 2 mi. past the Maui Prince Hotel in Makena (see p. 201), is a marine life preserve where fishing is prohibited, making it a spectacular spot for snorkeling. Two miles past Ahihi Bay, the fish preserve at **La Perouse Bay** is suited for advanced snorkelers who can handle the difficult entrances and exits along the rocky coast. Several companies run snorkel trips to **Molokini** and **Turtle Arches,** including the eco-friendly **Pacific Whale Foundation** (see p. 191), and the **Maui Dive Shop** (see below), both of which include gear in the cost of excursions. Kihei has plenty of purveyors of snorkel gear to rent daily or weekly; two of the most visible are **Boss Frog's,** 2395 S. Kihei Rd. (☎875-4477. $1.50-8 per day; weekly rates available) and **Snorkel Bob's,** 2411 S. Kihei Rd. (☎879-7449. $2.50-8.50 per day; weekly rates available.)

SCUBA DIVING. As sea conditions change daily, so do the best diving spots. The several diving shops on Kihei Rd. are more than happy to give advice on where to go; most shops that offer excursions plan their itineraries from day to day. Many companies rent gear, offer certification classes, and lead guided trips. **Dive and Sea Maui,** 1975 S. Kihei Rd. (☎874-1952; www.diveandseamaui.com), offers a 4-day basic open water certification class (private $350, group $250) as well as advanced classes. They also charter boats (gear included), and rent gear separately for those with certification ($20 per day). **Maui Dive Shop** (☎879-3388; www.mauidive-shop.com) has three locations in Kihei, and offers basic certification (private $450, group $300) and advanced classes, combination packages for gear and charters, and other discounted activities (helicopter trips, Haleakala bike rides, etc.).

SURFING AND BODY BOARDING. Summer is the season for south shore surfing, but even then the big waves don't come every day—ask a local surfer or call **High Tech Surf Report** (☎877-3611) for daily surf conditions. Various places along the strip rent **surf boards** (approx. $25 per day) and **boogie boards** (approx. $10 per week). Most **surf schools** operate out of Lahaina (see p. 203).

KAYAKING. These lightweight crafts are becoming an increasingly popular way to see some of Maui's more secluded coves. The **Ahihi Bay** fish preserve, between Makena and La Perouse Bay, is a popular kayak/snorkel destination. **Kayak Eco-Adventures** (☎891-2223) rents single kayaks for $25 per day, double kayaks for $40 per day, and gives guided tours starting at $49. **South Pacific Kayaks and Outfitters** (☎875-4848) leads tours starting at $59 per person and rents kayaks from $30.

WHALE-WATCHING. From December to April, anywhere you can see the ocean in South Maui, you can see whales, and anywhere you stick your head underwater, you can hear them. This unparalleled natural spectacle is truly incredible. The **Ocean Center** in Ma'alaea, the **Whale Observatory** near Kaleolepo Park off S. Kihei

Rd. (just south of Ohukai), and any of the hotels in Wailea make especially good whale-watching perches. To get up close, **whale-watching cruises** can be fun and educational (see **Pacific Whale Foundation** for our eco-friendly favorite, p. 191).

To learn more about these magnificent sea mammals from the perspective of both modern science and Hawaiian culture, stop by the ☀**Hawaiian Islands Humpback Whale National Marine Sanctuary**, 726 S. Kihei Rd. (☎800-831-4888 or 879-2818; www.hihwnms.nos.noaa.gov), just south of Ohukai St. on the *makai* (ocean) side of the road. This free educational center is managed through a partnership between the State of Hawaii and the National Oceanic Atmospheric Administration (NOAA), with the purpose of protecting humpback whales and their habitat within the islands. At the sanctuary, you'll find friendly volunteers, colorful displays, and free brochures and materials. Open M-F 10am-3pm. Free admission and parking.

🎵 NIGHTLIFE

Kihei is generally known as the hotbed for nightlife in Maui. Be sure to pick up a free copy of *Maui Time Weekly*, with a new issue every Thursday; its nightly entertainment listings will surely lead fun-seekers in the right direction.

Hapa's Nightclub, 41 E. Lipoa St. (☎879-9001), in the Lipoa Center. The best known nightspot in Kihei, Hapa's draws a sizeable crowd every night. Hapa's M, when the legendary Uncle Willie K. plays, is a local favorite; W is Aloha Nite with $2 drinks 'til midnight; Th is Ladies' Night with hip-hop DJs; F feature local bands; and Sa "Flava Zone" means drink specials all night. 21+ every night except Sundays, when doors open at 6:30pm for an all-ages dance party. Cover $5-10. Open every night until 1:30am.

Lulu's, 1945 S. Kihei Rd. (☎879-9944), at Alahele Pl. in Kihei Kalama Village. Lulu's is Kihei's newest and most up-and-coming nightlife spot; the decor is fun, the bartenders are friendly, and the drinks are free-flowing. The large 2nd-story room is fronted by an open patio, and couches and a pool table line the back wall. Priding itself on its "red carpet service at shag rug prices," Lulu's also offers food, live music, and logo gear. Happy Hour daily 4-7pm with $2 domestic drafts and $3 Mai Tais and well drinks. Open daily 11am-2am, with kitchen serving until midnight. MC/V.

Tsunami Nightclub, 3850 Wailea Alanui Dr. (☎875-1234), in the Grand Wailea Resort. Take the second entrance to park. This 10,000 sq. ft., $4 million club draws a flashy crowd for hot DJs and dancing on weekends. Dress to impress: no tank tops, flip-flops, or beachwear; no worn or torn clothing. 21+. Cover $10. Open F-Sa 9:30pm-2am.

Life's A Beach, 1913 S. Kihei Rd. (☎891-8010), next to Foodland in Kihei Kalama Village. Home of the $1 Mai Tai, this laid-back watering hole features karaoke and the occasional live band. Happy Hour daily 4-7pm. 21+ after 10pm. Open daily until 1:30am.

Mulligan's on the Blue, 100 Kaukahi St. (☎874-1131; www.mulligansontheblue.com), at the Wailea Golf Club. Take the first left after the Fairmont Kea Lani Hotel; Mulligan's is up the hill on the right. Priding itself as the only Irish Pub in Maui, Mulligan's is the perfect spot to savor a Guinness or Harp ($3.50 drafts). The building itself used to be a clubhouse, but is now as authentic Irish as any pub in Dublin, except with a gorgeous view of the ocean and surrounding islands. Mulligan's features live entertainment nightly: Su night features a toe-tapping Irish band; Tu is open mic night; and W is karaoke night. Happy Hour 5-7pm with $1 off drinks and 2 for 1 *pupus*. Open daily 8am-1:30am. D/MC/V.

Margarita's Beach Cantina, 101 N. Kihei Rd. (☎879-5275), in Kealia Beach Plaza on the northern edge of town (toward Ma'alaea). The tequila flows like water at this Mexican-inspired bar with a great ocean-front view. $2 margarita on the rocks from 2:30-5pm daily. Double shot of alcohol at any time of day for $1 more. Live music F 5-7pm. Open daily until 11:30pm.

FROM THE ROAD

NAKED AND PROUD

It was Sunday afternoon, and I was enjoying a relaxing day in Makena at Big Beach. I had already savored a fresh fish taco from a stand across the street, tried my hand at beach volleyball only to find out that I was playing against a team of semi-professionals from the Czech Republic, and meandered up and down Makena's ½ mi. stretch of golden sand. As the day dwindled, I noticed a steady stream of drum-wielding, dreadlock-wearing hippie types making their way to the north end of the beach. I watched as, drums in hand, they shimmied up the steep cliff and disappeared over the top. As the stream of people evolved into a flood, my curiosity got the better of me. I arose from my slumber and wandered over to the other side. And what to my wondering eyes should appear, but scads of naked hippies in a circle of cheer! They were drumming and dancing and praising the sky, and thought not of a single observing eye. Not everyone was naked, so I didn't feel *completely* out of place, but a good percentage of the beach was frolicking in their birthday suits. Apparently Sunday sunset is a busy time for Little Beach, the secluded bit of sand I had happened upon. They are a celebration of sorts, with a bonfire, a drum circle, dances, and chants. Not a soul was embarrassed and the spirit was free.

-Lucy Ebersold, 2003

WAILEA

"Affordable paradise" is not the first phrase that comes to mind as one drives along the impeccably landscaped **Wailea Alanui Drive,** Wailea's main drag, which is edged on one side with world-class golf courses and on the other with five-star resorts. Even if you can't afford the $200+ pricetag, don't be shy about taking advantage of Wailea's beautiful beaches. All Maui beaches are public, and those who own beachfront property (including the most exclusive resorts) are required to provide public access to the shore.

⚑ FOOD. If you want to splurge on a gourmet beach picnic, head to **Caffe Ciao ❷**, behind the adult pool in the Fairmont Kea Lani hotel. This boutique grocer sells sandwiches ($8.50), as well as high-end wine, cheeses, pastries, and other sundry items. Be sure to catch the occasional free samples. (☎875-4100. Open daily 6:30am-10pm. AmEx/MC/V.) **The Lobster Cove** and **Harry's Sushi ❹**, 100 Wailea Ike Dr., sells pricey but amazing sushi. Don't miss the melt-in-your-mouth Baked California Roll for Two. (☎879-7677. Reservations suggested. Open daily 5pm-midnight.) There are also a number of fine dining options within the **Shops at Wailea**, 3750 Wailea Alanui Dr. (☎891-6770; www.shopsatwailea.com), a collection of specialty (read: expensive) boutiques and restaurants in the middle of Wailea's resort strip.

⚑ BEACHES. There are five main beaches in Wailea, each occupying a crescent of soft sand bordered with outcroppings of volcanic rock. The first beach, **Keawakapu,** stretches for ½ mi. along the border between Kihei and Wailea. Less of a "scene" than other Kihei beach parks, Keawakapu offers great swimming and snorkeling on its artificial reef about 400 yd. offshore, which was installed in 1962 by sinking old cars 80 ft. down. Parking is available in the lot at the entrance to Wailea, on the *mauka* (mountain) side of S. Kihei Rd. **Mokapu** and **Ulua** are both pretty, but they are generally crowded with resort guests from the nearby Renaissance Wailea Hotel. The rocky point between the beaches makes for excellent snorkeling. **Wailea Beach** is the widest of the Wailea beaches, sandwiched between the Grand Wailea Resort and the Four Seasons Hotel. A pleasant walkway leads from Wailea to **Polo Beach,** a narrower beach fringed by an immaculate park with picnic tables, BBQ grills, showers, and restrooms. While the northern part of Polo Beach can be packed with Fairmont Kea Lani vacationers, the southern cove is generally less crowded. (Parking for Polo Beach is down a marked road just past the entrance of the Fairmont Kea Lani, about ½ mi. south of the Shops at Wailea.)

MAKENA AND BEYOND

Until very recently, Makena, south of Wailea, was entirely undeveloped. There is still only one hotel in Makena, the Maui Prince Resort, but the golf courses and tennis clubs on the *mauka* (mountain) side of **Makena Alanui** (the main and only road) stretch ever farther south. After you pass the Maui Prince and the last golf course, the *kiawe* desert resumes, and dirt roads on the *makai* (ocean) side lead to the best (and still gloriously undeveloped) beaches in Maui. Past the last sandy beach, a number of mansions have sprouted up in recent years, but even big houses don't detract from the rugged natural beauty at the end of the road.

⬛ BEACHES

PO'OLENALENA BEACH. After you pass the Fairmont Kea Lani, but before you reach the Maui Prince Resort, about 1¾ mi. south of the Shops at Wailea, there is a small sign for Po'olenalena Beach. A small parking lot marks the entrance to the beach. Also known as Chang's or Paipu Beach, this is the least crowded of Makena's beaches, and a real find at any time of day. The reddish sand of this isolated coastline can be a bit windswept and the currents are often very strong, but it is still a favorite among locals. You can see the Maui Prince down at the far southern end, but otherwise, the beach is undeveloped. People sometimes camp illegally under the shade trees, but if police see cars in the lot they will come inspect the beach, confiscate your tent, and possibly arrest you.

MAKENA LANDING. Heading south on Makena Rd., the next cove (a quick right after the Makena Surf condos) is **Makena Landing**, which was Maui's busiest port for sugar and cattle throughout the 1920s. The Beach Park at Makena Landing has showers, restrooms, a boat-launching ramp, and good snorkeling at the south side of the landing. Next to Makena Landing, the quaint and beautiful **Keawalai Church** (built in 1832 from offshore reef coral) still holds Hawaiian-Anglo church services on Sundays at 9:30am; all are welcome. After Keawalai Church, Makena Rd. comes to an end at a cul-de-sac at the edge of the Maui Prince Hotel. To reach the next beaches, you'll have to return to Makena Alanui Rd. and head south.

MALUAKA BEACH. If you continue south on Makena Alahui Rd. and take your first right after the Maui Prince Hotel, you'll reach the public parking area for golden Maluaka Beach, the best all-around beach for swimming and a favorite with families. The beach winds beneath 360 ft. Pu'u Olai, the visual landmark for Makena. Due to erosion and steep slopes, hiking is discouraged.

BIG BEACH. Big Beach, also called **Oneloa**, is part of **Makena State Park.** There are portable restrooms and picnic tables by the first (northernmost) entrance. There is no sanctioned camping on the beach, and the area becomes dangerous after dark, making camping unsafe as well as illegal. The last sandy beach for 43 mi., Big Beach stretches stunningly along the coast for a half-mile. Although the clear aqua water here may look tempting, the calm is deceptive; powerful waves break right on the shore, sweeping swimmers and body boarders off their feet and onto the sand at forces strong enough to break necks and backs. **Swimming and body surfing is not recommended at Big Beach.** The surf at adjacent Little Beach (see below) may look choppier but is generally safer, since the waves break farther out on the reef. Still, the strong riptide and currents merit precautions.

MAUI

LITTLE BEACH. Along the northern end of Big Beach, beneath Pu'u Olai, an out-cropping of volcanic rock hides a short, steep trail that leads to Little Beach on the other side. From its sandy shores, there are unobstructed views of Kaho'olawe, Molokini, and Lanai offshore. A lingering hippie hangout, Little Beach is unofficially **"clothing optional."** If you're used to the discretion exercised on most nude beaches, be prepared for the somewhat hormone-laden scene of Little Beach. On Sunday afternoons, the hippie contingent holds a drum and dance circle that can be quite a spectacle for the uninitiated observer (see **Naked and Proud,** p.72). While swimming or body boarding may be safer here than at Big Beach, the riptide and currents are incredibly strong—make sure someone is watching you and signal if you feel yourself being pulled out.

▟ OUTDOORS

AHIHI-KINAU NATURAL AREA RESERVE. Past the last entrance to Big Beach, the road narrows down to one lane and winds through the **Ahihi-Kinau Natural Area Reserve,** a 2000-acre conservation area. As you enter the reserve, several protected coves of **Ahihi Bay** are visible from the road. Since there is no fishing allowed in the reserve, any calm spot along the coast makes for excellent **snorkeling.** Continuing past Ahihi Cove, the road winds inland through a lava field—the path of the lava flow during the last eruption of Haleakala volcano around 1790. The area formed by the lava path is **Cape Kina'u,** and all the waters surrounding it are part of a protected natural reserve. No longer a well-kept secret, but still an adventure off the beaten path, a 45min. **hike** through the lava field ends in a more secluded spot for snorkeling. If you plan to hike, bring your snorkel gear and wear sturdy shoes. To find the trailhead, look at the numbers posted on the telephone poles. Around pole #18, there is a pull-out where you can park (don't leave valuables in your car). On the *makai* (ocean) side, there is a spray-painted marking on the roadside metal pipe. This marks the beginning of the trail. False starts to the left and right lead to huge precipices; the actual trail is a continuous path. With views of the ocean ahead and the rolling pastures of Haleakala behind, the walk is worthwhile for the unusual surroundings alone. The path terminates in a protected cove, and the narrow black sand and pebble beach on the left is the easiest entrance for snorkeling. Underwater growth has accumulated on the volcanic rock, and the area—aptly nicknamed "The Fishbowl"—is populated by a diverse array of colorful fish.

WEST MAUI

West Maui's mountains are older than Haleakala, and have been scarred over the years with deep rifts from stream erosion. The huge forms rise out of the cane fields in velvety folds before disappearing into the cloud cover. Unlike the valleys northwest of Wailuku (Iao and Waihee), which get almost 400 in. of rainfall per year, the *pali* on the leeward side are extremely arid.

It's a wonder how the region—especially the bustling port city of Lahaina—has managed to thrive without rain. Despite the apparent lack of water, West Maui has continued to grow, and resorts now stretch for ten miles north of Lahaina from Ka'anapali to Kapalua. The popularity of the area's real estate is well warranted, for the western coast is lined with gorgeous beaches and few sunbathers would trade the leeward coast's dry heat for the windward side's rain showers.

There is only one road in and out of West Maui, **Highway 30,** or **Honoapi'ilani Highway,** which becomes **Route 340 (Kahekili Highway)** north of Kapalua. Hwy. 30 is a two-lane road that hugs the scenic coastline from Ma'alaea north. Near Ma'alaea, Hwy. 30 intersects with **Route 380 (Dairy Road),** which goes northeast to Kahului and **Route 310/31,** which heads southeast to Kihei. Although on maps the northern route (Rte. 340) appears to be the quickest between Kapalua and Wailuku, it isn't. The road narrows down to one lane, which in many places is barely the width of a car, and hugs the cliffs with no guardrail protection from the water below. This route can be done as a **scenic drive** at a leisurely pace, but for everyday travel, stick to Hwy. 30. However, accidents occur frequently on Hwy. 30, and when they do, the road is closed for as long as it takes to investigate. Rte. 340 will be closed during accidents as well, just so no one will be tempted to take the hazardous back route. If this happens, just be prepared to sit and wait for a few hours, or turn around and go to the beach!

LAHAINA

Lahaina means "cruel" or "merciless sun" and visitors will quickly find that the city is aptly named—in any season, Lahaina is *hot*. Though it may be difficult to visualize, Lahaina was once prized by the Hawaiian royalty for its abundance of fresh water. The water and local hospitality also attracted commoners—Lahaina became a great whaling center during the first half of the 19th century. Whalers who came searching for humpbacks would often wreak havoc on the town, raping, pillaging, and starting drunken riots. The missionaries who set up homes to care for the unwanted offspring of sailors and local women were constantly at odds with the rowdy crews—they were even the target of cannonfire after laws were passed prohibiting women from swimming out to meet the ships.

Remnants of Lahaina's colorful history are still visible in the restored buildings and sites of the downtown historic district, although they are overpowered in many places by t-shirt shops, activities booths, and theme restaurants. Lahaina has become a tourist trap, but that doesn't keep people from enjoying it. Sitting on the seawall on Front St. provides never-ending people-watching entertainment (and the sunset over the water is pretty sweet too). Just keep in mind that if you tire of Mai Tais and timeshare proposals, there *is* another Lahaina to discover.

MAUI

◼ LOCAL TRANSPORTATION

Bus: In Aug. 2002, Maui welcomed its first public transportation system, **Holo Ka'a Public Transit.** Bus service is now available between Central, South, and West Maui. On West Maui, the buses make the following stops: Ma'alaea Harbor, Lahaina Center, Ka'anapali, Kahana, Napili, and Kapalua. In Lahaina, route **#2** (to and from Ka'anapali; $1 one-way fare) stops at the Lahaina Cannery Mall, The Wharf Cinema Center, and the Lahaina Harbor (at the flagpole). Buses leave once every hr., but since the system is fairly new, route schedules are constantly changing. Call the Holo Ka'a Public Transit office (☎879-2828) for the most up-to-date information.

Ferry: An easy and inexpensive way to reach Maui's neighboring islands is by the ferries out of Lahaina Harbor. The **Molokai Princess** makes daily trips to **Molokai.** For more information, call ☎800-275-6969 or 667-6165, or see p. 179. The **Expeditions** ferry sails to **Manele Harbor** in Lanai (45min.; one-way $25, 5 per day 6:45am-5:45pm; children $20) and back (5 per day 8am-6:45pm). The ride takes about 45min. To make a reservation, call Expeditions (☎800-695-2624 or 661-3756), or just show up at the pier; there are usually seats available.

Taxis: Though the town of Lahaina is completely walkable on foot, cabs might come in handy for those travelers staying slightly north or south of town. You'll have to call in advance to get a taxi; cabs rarely search for passengers. Several taxi companies operate right out of Lahaina, including **Ali'i Cab Co.** (☎661-3688), **Island Taxi** (☎667-5656), **La-Taxi** (☎661-4545), and **Rainbow Taxi** (☎661-0881).

Train: 975 Limahana Pl. (☎800-499-2307 or 667-6851. www.sugarcanetrain.com.) Off of Honopiilani Hwy., turn right onto Hinau St. and another right onto LImahana Pl. The Lahaina Ka'anapali & Pacific Railroad runs the Sugar Cane Train up and down Maui's northwest coast. Though more of a novelty attraction than an efficient means of transportation, the train is an entertaining way to get from Lahaina to the **Puukolii Station** in Ka'anapali. The historic steam engine replicates the way islanders traveled back in the days of Maui's booming sugar cane era; today, the panoramic views of the island make a ride on the train a fun afternoon diversion. Daily departures from Lahaina at 11:05am, 1, 2:30, 4pm. $16, ages 3-12 $10. Free parking available for train riders.)

Car Rentals: Most national chains operate near the airport out of Kahului (see p. 182), but local agencies can accommodate car renters within Lahaina. These agencies are convenient for those arriving to Lahaina by ferry, eliminating the need for an expensive cab or shuttle ride to Kahului. Although everything in town is within walking distance, having a car is useful to access the best beaches, hikes, and sights of the area.

Wheels USA, 578 Front St. (☎667-7751), just south of Banyan Tree Sq., with 2 other Maui locations in Kahului (☎871-6858) and Kihei (☎875-1221). Compact cars $25 per day or $130 per wk., with only a $6 per day surcharge for drivers under 25. Office open M-Sa 8am-5pm. MC/V.

✈ ORIENTATION

Lahaina is mid-way up Maui's western coast, leeward of the West Maui mountains. **Highway 30 (Honoapi'ilani Highway)** is the major two-lane bypass highway, running inland of the town center all the way north past Ka'anapali and Napili. In light traffic, it takes about 15min. to drive the 10 mi. from Lahaina north to Kapalua. Lahaina's main drag, **Front Street**, parallels the highway along the waterfront and is connected to it by five cross streets (from south to north: **Shaw Street, Dickenson Street, Lahainaluna Road, Papalaua Street,** and **Kenui Street**). **Waine'e Street** runs the length of Lahaina, between the highway and Front St.

⚑ PRACTICAL INFORMATION

TOURIST AND FINANCIAL SERVICES

Tourist Office: In the Old Lahaina Courthouse in Banyan Tree Sq. at 648 Wharf St. (☎667-9193; www.visitlahaina.com). A free walking tour map of historic sites is available, in addition to numerous other maps and brochures on attractions and activities. Gift shop, museum, art gallery, and restrooms. Open daily 9am-5pm.

Tours: See **Sights,** p. 213.

Banks: American Savings Bank, 154 Papalaua St. (☎667-9561; open M-F 9am-6pm, Sa 9am-1pm), **Bank of Hawaii,** (☎661-8781; open M-Th 8:30am-4pm, F 8:30am-6pm) and **First Hawaiian Bank,** 215 Papalaua St. (☎661-3655; open M-Th 8:30am-4pm, F 8:30am-6pm) are all located near the Old Lahaina Center and have **24hr. ATMs.** There are also ATMs in nearly every shopping center and plaza.

LOCAL SERVICES

Library: 680 Wharf St. (☎662-3950), across Papelekane St. from the Pioneer Inn. Self-service **copies** $0.15. Free **Internet access** with $10 visitor library card. Open Tu noon-8pm, W-Th 9am-5pm, F-Sa 10:30am-4:30pm.

Laundromats: Surprisingly, there are no laundromats in the immediate Lahaina area; to wash your duds, you'll have to trek north. In Napili, **Kahana Koin-Op Laundromat,** 4465 Honoapi'ilani Hwy. (☎669-1581), and in Honokawai, **One Hour Martinizing Dry Cleaning,** 3350 L. Honoapi'ilani Hwy. (☎661-6768) are two self-serve laundry options.

EMERGENCY AND COMMUNICATIONS

Emergency: ☎911.

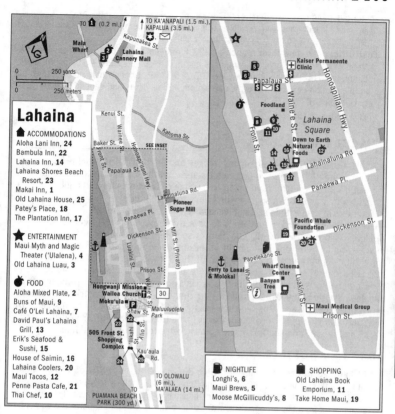

Lahaina

🏠 ACCOMMODATIONS
Aloha Lani Inn, **24**
Bambula Inn, **22**
Lahaina Inn, **14**
Lahaina Shores Beach
    Resort, **23**
Makai Inn, **1**
Old Lahaina House, **25**
Patey's Place, **18**
The Plantation Inn, **17**

⭐ ENTERTAINMENT
Maui Myth and Magic
    Theater ('Ulalena), **4**
Old Lahaina Luau, **3**

🍎 FOOD
Aloha Mixed Plate, **2**
Buns of Maui, **9**
Café O'Lei Lahaina, **7**
David Paul's Lahaina
    Grill, **13**
Erik's Seafood &
    Sushi, **15**
House of Saimin, **16**
Lahaina Coolers, **20**
Maui Tacos, **12**
Penne Pasta Cafe, **21**
Thai Chef, **10**

🍸 NIGHTLIFE
Longhi's, **6**
Maui Brews, **5**
Moose McGillicuddy's, **8**

🛍 SHOPPING
Old Lahaina Book
    Emporium, **11**
Take Home Maui, **19**

MAUI

Police: ☎ 244-6400, located north of Lahaina on Honoapiʻilani Hwy. above Wahikuli Wayside Park.

Pharmacies: There are no 24hr. pharmacies in Lahaina. **Long's Drugs** (☎ 667-4384), in the Lahaina Cannery Mall, is a kind of Wal-mart on speed, selling everything from pharmaceuticals to film to fine wine. Open M-F 8am-10pm and Sa-Su 8am-9pm. **Lahaina Pharmacy** (☎ 661-3119), in the Old Lahaina Center, is open M-F 9am-5:30pm, Sa 9am-2pm.

Medical Services: Kaiser Permanente Clinic, 910 Waineʻe St. (☎ 661-7400), and **Maui Medical Group,** 130 Prison St. (☎ 661-0051), are both open M-F 8am-5pm, Sa 8am-noon.

Internet Access: Travelers can go online at the Lahaina Public Library (see **Practical Information,** p. 204) and at **Buns of Maui** (see **Food,** p. 207), as well as at the following locations:

Down to Earth Natural Foods Store, 193 Lahainaluna St. (☎ 667-2855), is a very comfortable place to check your email ($4 per 15min.) with A/C, fresh veggie juices and smoothies, and a salad bar. Open M-Sa 7:30am-9pm, Su 8:30am-8pm. AmEx/MC/V.

Aliʻi Mocha Espresso Cafe, 505 Front St. (☎ 661-7800), has 4 DSL terminals and serves teas, coffees, and a few sandwiches on their gorgeous outdoor garden patio. $2 for the first 10min., $0.20 for each additional min. Open daily 7am-1pm and 4-9pm. AmEx/D/MC/V.

Swiss Cafe, 640 Front St. (☎661-6776), diagonally across from the Banyan Tree, serves Italian espressos, sandwiches, and smoothies, and charges $0.15 per min. with a $2 minimum. 12 computer stations; print-outs $0.50. Open daily 9am-6pm. No credit cards.

Post Office: The downtown branch at 123 Papalaua St. (☎661-0904), in the Old Lahaina Center, tends to have long lines and is open M-F 8:15am-4:15pm. The main branch, at 1760 Honoapi'ilani Hwy. (☎800-275-8777), about a mile north of town at the intersection of Leiali'i Parkway, offers more flexible hours and general delivery pick-up. Open M-F 8:30am-5pm, Sa 9am-1pm.

Postal Code: 96761.

ACCOMMODATIONS

Staying in Lahaina is possible on any budget, and most of the affordable accommodations in the old town have more character than the chain hotels and condos in the resorts farther north. If you plan to partake of Lahaina's limited nightlife, it's a good idea to stay in town so you won't have to drive home.

The nearest **campsite** is at **Camp Pecusa ❶**, 800 Olawalu Village Rd. (☎661-4303; www.maui.net/~norm/pecusa.html), a private campground on the coast run by the Episcopal Church of Hawaii. The camp's secluded sites and colorful cabins are located ½ mi. south of Lahaina right off of Rte. 30 (Honoapi'ilani Hwy.); look for a small blue sign about a half-mile south of the Olawalu General Store. Tent camping costs $6 per person; no reservations are accepted. The six-person cabins, however, can be booked ahead of time. There is also a county-maintained campsite at **Papalaua Wayside Park ❶**, just north of the tunnel between mile markers 11 and 12 on Honoapi'ilani Hwy. This beachfront site can be dangerous, since it's close to the road and frequently crowded. For information, call ☎270-7389 or check the Parks and Recreation section of the county web site, www.co.maui.hi.us.

B&BS AND HOSTELS

Old Lahaina House, 407 'Ilikahi St. (☎800-847-0761 or 667-4663; www.oldlahaina.com), on the corner of 'Ilikahi and Kaua'ula Rd., 1 block south of Shaw St. Nestled in the residential end of Lahaina, the house is only 1 block from a sandy beach and a brief walk from the historic district. Gracious owner sees that all rooms are equipped with beach towels and picnic cooler. All rooms have A/C, TV, phone, microwave, fridge, coffee maker, and private bath. Guests can enjoy the private pool in the house's tropical courtyard. Owner also manages a gorgeous 1-bedroom cottage across the street, complete with 4-poster bamboo bed, A/C, washer/dryer, and full bath. 3-night min. stay somewhat flexible. Reserve with 50% deposit; balance due 30 days prior to arrival. Rooms Dec.-Apr. $89-125; May-Nov. $69-115; cottage $150. AmEx/MC/V. ❸

Bambula Inn, 518 'Ilikahi St. (☎800-544-5524 or 667-6753; www.bambula.com). Around the bend from Old Lahaina House, Bambula is another comfortable guesthouse that offers privacy with 2 free-standing studio cottages and 1 additional room in the main house (with a private entrance). Each cottage has a full kitchen and bath, TV, BBQ, patio and outdoor shower. With a 3-night stay, guests are treated to a free sunset sail on host Pierre Chasle's boat, *Bambula*. Snorkel gear and body boards available for use. Reserve with 50% deposit. Room $79; cottages $100-110. AmEx/MC/V. ❸

Aloha Lani Inn, 13 Kauaula Rd. (☎800-572-5642 or 661-8040; www.maui-vacations.com/aloha), off of Front St. in the same private neighborhood as Old Lahaina House and Bambula Inn. This guest home offers 2 tropical-themed bedrooms that share a lanai, full kitchen, and living room complete with TV, VCR, stereo, and mini library. The house has no A/C, but ceiling fans keep the rooms pleasant. Owner makes guests feel at home with fresh-brewed coffee in the morning. Coin-op laundry. Free parking. 3-night min. stay. 50% deposit required. Rooms $69-79. MC/V. ❸

Patey's Place, 761 Waine'e St. (☎667-0999; www.hawaiian-hostels.com). There's no sign on the door; just look for the street number. Patey's is a basic hostel, offering the cheapest beds in West Maui and little else. It's not as well supervised as other hostels on the island, but the 10pm quiet rule tries to keep partying to a minimum. Mostly young people stay here, but there are several long-term guests. Guests share a kitchen, laundry, TV room, and back porch for lounging. 2 of the private rooms have private bathrooms; other guests share 4 bathrooms. Reception 8:30am-noon and 5-10pm. Checkout 10am. 4-bed dorms $20; singles $50; doubles $60. AmEx/D/MC/V. ❶

HOTELS AND INNS

Lahaina Inn, 127 Lahainaluna Rd. (☎800-669-3444 or 661-0577; www.lahainainn.com). Perfect for a romantic stay in old Lahaina, the Inn offers 9 rooms and 3 suites uniquely decorated with turn-of-the-century period furnishings and oriental carpets, all stocked with *yukata* robes for guests. Modern comforts include in-room classical music, A/C, and phones (but no TV). Guests can enjoy people-watching from the rocking chairs on the street-facing lanais. Continental breakfast (delivered to your room) included. Check-in 3pm. Check-out 11am. Reserve with 50% deposit. Rooms $109-169, depending on size, season, and view. AmEx/MC/V. ❹

Makai Inn, 1415 Front St. (☎662-3200; www.makaiinn.net), on the quieter northern end of Front St. An all-around excellent value for a budget inn. All suites have a bedroom, small sitting area, private lanai, full kitchen, and new bathrooms, but no TV or phone. No A/C, but rooms are comfortable with ceiling fans and the ocean breeze. All suites face the inner courtyard garden, and the pricier rooms have ocean views (the inn is right on the harbor). On-site parking and coin-op laundry. Check-out 11am. Reserve with credit card; no deposit required. Rooms $70-105. AmEx/MC/V. ❸

The Plantation Inn, 174 Lahainaluna Rd. (☎800-433-6815 or 667-9225; www.theplantation-inn.com). Footsteps from Front St., this peaceful inn offers 19 rooms and all the comforts of home. Each room has A/C, private bath, mini fridge, and TV, and is decorated with antique furniture and specialty beds. Views from guests' lanais range from the private inner courtyard and pool area to an aerial view of Lahaina. The Plantation Inn's cordial staff will treat you like royalty, and all guests receive a nightly $50 discount at the prestigious Gerard's restaurant (☎661-8939; www.gerardsmaui.com). Reception open daily 8am-9pm. 2-night deposit at time of booking. Rooms $157-197; suites $220-240. AmEx/D/MC/V. ❺

Lahaina Shores Beach Resort, 475 Front St. (☎800-642-6284 or 661-3339; www.lahain-ashores.com). The reason to stay here is the outside, not the inside—it's the only hotel in Lahaina located on a sandy beach, and it has a well-maintained pool and jacuzzi to boot. Rooms are nothing special, but they all have a full kitchen and private bath. The oceanfront rooms feature a very nice beach view; mountainside rooms glimpse the *pali* over the parking lot. Complimentary continental breakfast. Activity booth conveniently located in the lobby. Check-in 3pm. Check-out 11am. Reserve with $150 deposit. Studios $180-215; 1-bedroom $250-280. AmEx/MC/V. Not fully wheelchair accessible. ❺

▐ FOOD

It's hard to find a restaurant in Lahaina without a Hollywood theme and logo merchandise. Almost every place in town caters exclusively to tourists, which means inflated prices, but also variety—you can satisfy any food craving in Lahaina, from burgers to *bok choy*. With only a few exceptions, Lahaina restaurants stop serving by 9pm, so plan accordingly.

For a do-it-yourself meal, there is a 24hr. **Safeway** at 1221 Honoapi'ilani Hwy. (☎667-4392), in the Lahaina Cannery Mall and a **Foodland** in the Old Lahaina Center. (☎661-0975. Open daily until 11:30pm.) **Down to Earth Natural Foods Store,** 193 Lahainaluna Rd. (open M-Sa 7:30am-9pm, Su 8:30am-8pm; ☎667-

2855), on the corner of Waine'e St., has organic and local produce and packaged foods, as well as a salad and hot food bar.

CAFES AND TAKE-OUT

Penne Pasta Cafe, 180 Dickenson St. (☎661-6633; eatmaui@maui.net). Good-sized portions of pasta with homemade sauce (bolognese fettucine; $8) are served in a casual but classy atmosphere slightly removed from the busy, commercial Front St. Vegetarian options, like whole wheat spaghetti with roasted eggplant, tomatoes, oregano, and basil ($9) are big on flavor. Save room for dessert (tiramisu; $6). Beer and wine $3.50-5.50. Open M-Th 11am-9:30pm, F 11am-10pm, Sa 5-10pm, Su 5-9pm. Take-out and delivery available. MC/V. ❷

Aloha Mixed Plate, 1285 Front St. (☎661-3322; www.alohamixedplate.com), right on the harbor next to the Old Lahaina Luau. A great place to sample Hawaiian food. *Kalua* pig and other meats are served plate lunch-style (with 2 scoops of rice and 1 scoop of macaroni salad). Everything is served on paper plates, but the ocean view is first-class. During dinner, the drumbeats of the *luau* next door provide unexpected ambience. Plate lunches $5-10. Sandwiches $4.50-8. Outdoor seating only. Cocktails $4. Happy hour 2-6pm with $2.50 Mai Tais. Open daily 10:30am-10pm. AmEx/MC/V. ❶

Maui Tacos, 840 Waine'e St. (☎661-8883; www.mauitacos.com), in Lahaina Sq. Fresh corn tortillas, 5 kinds of homemade salsa, and a more-than-filling meal for under $6: it's either heaven or it's Maui Tacos. Open for breakfast too (egg burritos or *huevos rancheros;* $5). Additional locations in Napili Plaza and Kihei (see p. 197). Mostly a take-out joint, but feel free to enjoy your island spices in the small outdoor seating area. Open M-Sa 9am-9pm, Su 9am-8pm. AmEx/D/MC/V. ❶

Buns of Maui, 878 Front St. (☎661-5407), in the Old Lahaina Shopping Center, tucked into the strip of stores next to the Maui Myth and Magic Theater. The smell of sweet, gooey, cinnamon rolls lures locals from all over Lahaina; these buns are legendary. Topped with caramel, macadamia nuts, or pecans, the rolls ($3.50) are served nice and warm with a fork and knife. Buns of Maui also offers Internet access ($0.25 per min.), blended ice coffees, and a small gift shop. Open M-F 7:30am-6pm, Sa 7:30am-5pm, Su 8am-3pm. AmEx/D/MC/V accepted, with a $10 min. on charge cards. ❶

N THE MENU

FIT FOR A KING

Let your inner royalty shine at he **Feast at Lele,** a delight for all he senses. Brought to you by the producers of the Old Lahaina Luau, it's less a traditional *luau* han a phenomenal meal served oceanfront at sunset with a hula performance. Chef James McDonald, of Pacific'O and I'o ame, has designed a 5-course meal that takes your tastebuds on a Polynesian tour. The courses are served in a leisurely manner so hat you can enjoy the dance that goes along with each country. Guests begin in Hawaii with steamed *moi* fit for a king, then travel to Tonga for robust flavors and powerful dancing. Most guests claim Tahiti as their favorte, with sophisticated French influences melding in the creamy scallops, but Samoa makes a strong showing in the fire-dancing finale. The Feast of Lele contradicts everything you've heard about *luaus*—the food comes first and it's served at your table. The Feast of Lele is absolutely worth he splurge—it costs about the same as dinner for two at Maui's best restaurants, and it's a truly unique culinary experience. *(Held on the beach behind I'o. 505 Front St. ☎866-244-LELE; www.feastatlele.com. M-Sa evenings. Reserve 1-3 weeks in advance; the farther in advance you reserve, the better seats you'll enjoy. $95 ages 12 and under $65. Gratuity not included.)*

House of Saimin (☎667-7572), in the Old Lahaina Center next to the Lahaina Pharmacy. Steaming bowls of *saimin* (homemade fish broth with ramen noodles and other accompaniments) are served on a red U-shaped counter, beneath photos of the local Little League teams. This is the only place in town that serves food late at night. Open M 5-10pm, Tu-Th 5pm-2am, F-Sa 5pm-3am. ❶

RESTAURANTS

▨ **Cafe O'Lei Lahaina,** 839 Front St. (☎661-9491), through the entrance of the Ocean Front Marketplace. Cafe O'Lei is a real find. The ocean breeze and the sunset view from the restaurant's 2-tiered dining room are delightful; nightly live music on the upper deck puts the dining experience over the top. The food emphasizes fresh local ingredients, (*taro* salad with okinawan sweet potatoes $9; sauteed mahi mahi with ginger butter and papaya salsa $16), and all entrees come with a creative dinner salad. The lunch menu features salads and foccacia sandwiches in the $7-8 range. Open daily for lunch 10:30am-4:30pm, dinner 5-9pm. Reservations recommended. AmEx/MC/V. ❸

Erik's Seafood & Sushi, 843 Waine'e St. (☎662-8780), in the Old Lahaina Shopping Center. Newly-opened Erik's prepares fresh sushi you can write home about. The eager-to-please staff also serves up tasty oyster appetizers ($6-10) and fresh island fish entrees ($18-22). For the price-conscious, Erik's early bird specials knock off about a third of the price (daily 5-6pm). Also budget-friendly is the lunch menu with fish-focused sandwiches, salads, and pastas ($4-10). Take-out and delivery available. Open daily 11am-10pm. AmEx/MC/V. ❸

David Paul's Lahaina Grill, 127 Lahainaluna Rd. (☎667-5117; www.lahainagrill.com), is a consistently stellar, sophisticated restaurant, serving innovative New American food in a stylish environment. Renowned chef David Paul Johnson changes his world-class menu offerings frequently, drawing inspiration from local ingredients. Entrees $28-38. Reservations required. Open nightly from 6pm. AmEx/D/MC/V. ❺

Lahaina Coolers, 180 Dickenson St. (☎661-7082; www.lahainacoolers.com), ½ block off Front St. Serves up reliably good food at decent prices in a relaxed, open-air atmosphere. Varied menu with everything from tasty fish tacos marinated in fresh garlic and tomatoes to Evil Jungle Pasta in a Thai-style peanut sauce to burgers and steak. Egg and griddle breakfasts $6-11. Lunch $8-11. Dinner entrees $9-20. Happy Hour twice daily 3-6pm and 10pm-2am features $3 well drinks and microbrews. Open daily 8am-2am, full menu until midnight. ❸

Thai Chef (☎667-2814; www.thaichefmaui.com), in the Old Lahaina Shopping Center, next to Buns of Maui (see above). This cozy Thai restaurant has a solid reputation, with an extensive menu of curries, seafood dishes, and vegetarian options ($8-13). Open for lunch M-F 11am-2:30pm, dinner nightly 5pm-close. D/DC/MC/V. ❸

 BEACHES

Lahaina itself is not the place for sunbathing and swimming—the few sandy beaches have somewhat murky water, and are really only good for watching the sunset. There is a sandy beach behind the Lahaina Shores resort (with public access a few blocks south of the resort on Front St.) and a good local surf spot at the break a block south of the hotel, but other than those, the beaches north and south of town are much more appealing. **Puamana Beach County Park,** the first beach south of Lahaina, is a nice spot for a beachside picnic. **Launiopoko Wayside Park,** a mile farther south at mile marker 18, has restrooms and showers and a surf break popular with beginners. There is no camping allowed at

MAUI

O WORK, ALL PLAY

ANNUAL EVENTS IN LAHAINA

Can't decide when to go to Lahaina? You may want to schedule your visit around one of the many annual celebrations there.

In late January-early February, Lahaina ushers in the **Chinese New Year** with exciting lion dances and a street festival including Chinese martial arts, firecrackers, and food.

Mid-March welcomes the **Ocean Arts Festival** to Lahaina, a -day celebration of the annual migration of **Pacific Humpback Whales.** The festival showcases ocean arts, crafts, live music, and a "creature feature" exhibit for the kids.

Sing Happy Birthday to the famous **Banyan Tree** in mid-April. Lahaina honors its precious tree with a nature artworks fair and historical exhibits.

Maui's signature cultural event s the 2 wk. **In Celebration of Canoes** festival in May in honor of the voyaging canoe. Master carvers from the Pacific islands come together in Lahaina to create Polynesian canoes from wood logs. Events include an 'awa ceremony, parade, and ceremonial canoe launch.

It's **King Kamehameha Day** in June, and a colorful floral parade through town features traditional Pa'u riders on horses. The parade ends with an awards ceremony and festival in Banyan Tree Park.

Launiopoko. Both of these parks, however, are unimpressive when compared to the beaches north of Lahaina; for details see **Ka'anapali** (p. 215), **Napili** (p. 216), and **Kapalua** (p. 218).

ACTIVITIES

The activity booths that line Front St. offer an overwhelming number of choices. This is a big business; between helicopter rides, biking, and parasailing, companies market thrills from air, land, and sea. Most of these activities can be quite costly, and the brokers take a hefty cut as commission; sometimes booking with the company directly can be cheaper. Watch out for false advertising; many of the superlow rates you'll see on activity boards are only for visitors with timeshares. There are also activities (body boarding, coastal snorkeling, hiking) that cost little or nothing and don't require a middleman. If you do opt to go with an activities booker, *Let's Go* recommends **Tom Barefoot's Cashback Tours,** 834 Front St. (☎888-222-3601; www.tombarefoot.com) which doesn't require a timeshare, but offers a wide selection of well-organized activities at a discounted rate.

SNORKELING. Before you splurge on a boat excursion, know that there is excellent snorkeling at beaches all along the West Maui coast. A self-guided adventure will cost you only a few bucks for the mask and fins. Many companies in Lahaina rent equipment for $2-10 per day. **Maui Dive Shop** (☎661-6166) is courteous and professional, with several locations including one at the Lahaina Cannery Mall.

The best West Maui snorkel spots are north of Lahaina; see **Honolua Bay** (p. 218), **Kapalua Beach** (p. 218), **Kahekili Beach Park** (p. 216), and **Black Rock/Ka'anapali Beach** (p. 216) for details. If you want to take a boat excursion, head to the submerged crater of **Molokini.** On a good day, visibility at Molokini is over 100 ft. Plan on spending anywhere from $45-95; excursions typically take a few hours, and include equipment (mask, snorkel, fins, and sometimes a wetsuit), demonstration, drinks, and deli or BBQ lunch. Conditions can be variable at any time of year, and many a snorkeler set on going to Molokini has ended up at "Turtle Town" or "Coral Gardens," less glamorous spots just offshore that have decent snorkeling, but are not measurably better than what you can see from beaches for free.

SCUBA DIVING. The two most popular places for offshore dives near Lahaina are the neighboring island of **Lanai** and the **back wall of Molokini.** There are

multiple companies competing for boat dive business in Lahaina. **Extended Horizons** (☎667-0611) is known for good service on boat dives; **Maui Dive Shop** (☎661-6166; www.mauidiveshop.com) is larger and more impersonal, though still reliable. For shore dives, **Kahekili Beach Park** is a good place for beginners (most certification classes start here); **Black Rock,** below the Ka'anapali Sheraton, and the right side of **Honolua Bay** (in summer) are also popular West Maui dive spots. For shore dives, **Pacific Dive** (☎667-5331) is reputable and reasonably priced. Numerous companies give introductory classes, starting around $50.

SURFING. Ah, surfing, the sport of kings and bums alike. Driving into Lahaina from the south, you'll see surfers from the road—**Olowalu** and **Launiopoko** usually have reliable breaks, though conditions change daily so your best bet is to ask the locals. There is a local surf spot about a block south of the Lahaina Shores hotel that is usually uncrowded and good for beginners, but watch out for waves breaking in the shallow water over the coral. **Honolua Bay** is famous for its winter surf, but beginners should stick to watching from the sand. Board rentals start at about $20 per day with price breaks for weekly rentals. Expect to pay about $55 for a 2hr. surf group lesson and twice that for a private lesson. For mid-priced, reliable surf lessons, contact **Goofy Foot Surf School,** in the 505 Front St. Shopping Center. Beginners are guaranteed to stand and ride at least one wave in their first lesson, or it's free of charge. Intermediate lessons also available. (☎244-9283; www.goofyfootsurf-school.com. Beginner lessons daily at 8, 11am, 2pm. Shop hours M-Sa 7:30am-9pm, Su 9am-5pm. $55 group lesson, $125 private.)

BODY BOARDING. Catching waves on a body board is a lot easier than surfing. Driving toward Lahaina from the south, just look for spots with good conditions and other boarders, pull over, and jump in. **Puamana Beach,** just south of Lahaina, is usually a quality spot. Some of the beaches in Ka'anapali are also excellent for body boarding, especially the south end of **Ka'anapali Beach** and the blissfully deserted **Oneloa Beach** (see p. 218). All the surf shops in Lahaina also rent body boards for $5-8 per day or about $20 per week. For a great deal on rentals, hit up **West Maui Sports** on 1287 Front St. (☎661-6252), which offers boards for $2.50 per day. (Open daily 8am-8pm. AmEx/D/MC/V.)

SAILING. Lahaina looks even better from offshore than on land. The **Hyatt** (☎661-1234 ext. 3290.) in Ka'anapali rents Hobie Cats you can sail yourself

Sample some good eats and tasty treats in September with the **Taste of Lahaina** culinary festival. This fest of fine foods, beer, and wines includes cooking demonstrations and concerts by legendary Hawaiian musicians. Honor Maui's most innovative chefs at a dinner and cocktail party under the stars.

Halloween in Lahaina is something to write home about. Front St. is closed to traffic for a Costume Parade, and food and music in the streets makes Halloween in Lahaina resemble Mardi Gras New Orleans, minus the beads and nudity, of course.

Close out the year with the **Holiday Banyan Tree lighting** in December. thousands of colored lights decorate Lahaina's landmark tree, and songs and dancing happen in the park.

For updated information on Lahaina's events and festivals, visit www.visitlahaina.com, a web site sponsored by the Hawaii Tourism Authority.

IN RECENT NEWS

THEY PAVED PARADISE AND PUT UP A PARKING LOT

In 1992, Maui's Bishop Museum conducted archaeological work and discovered that buried beneath Malu'uluolelele Park, a baseball field and parking lot in modern-day Lahaina, lies Moku'ula. One of Hawaii's most significant and historical sites, Moku'ula is both a residence and a mausoleum to generations of Hawaiian rulers. The Bishop Museum confirmed the location of the Royal Mausoleum, a burial place that contained the remains of King Kamehameha III's mother, sister, and children.

Organizations like The Friends of Moku'ula and Maui Nei are making it their mission to restore what was once a place of righteousness and compassion into a spiritual center for Native Hawaiians and all who desire to learn about the sacred traditions of ancient Hawaii. With financial support from the County of Maui and the Office of Hawaiian Affairs, among others, the current restoration project will remove the fences and pavement that currently desecrate the area. Plans are in the works for the construction Hawaiian cultural center so that a new generation of Hawaiians will come to learn about and appreciate their spiritual past.

To learn more about Moku'ula and the progress of its restoration project, visit www.mokuula.com or www.mauinei.com.

for $45 per hr. Many companies have sunset and daytime sailing trips (some include dinner, others just snacks and drinks) on schooners or catamarans. **Trilogy** is by far the biggest operator, with numerous boats running all kinds of excursions. In addition to its beautiful boats, Trilogy's real advantage is its Lanai excursions—it is the only company that owns property on the island where they can land and do a nice BBQ lunch (or dinner, for sunset sails) overlooking Manele Bay. (☎ 888-638-4800; www.sailtrilogy.com. $79-229.)

PARASAILING. Parasailing looks scarier than it is—the ride is a gentle glide that lasts for about 10 minutes. Companies only operate May-December so they don't interfere with the whales during their breeding season. **Parasail Ka'anapali** has the best deal for singles and tandems and leaves from Mala Wharf on the northern end of town. (☎ 669-6555. $24-40 depending on season.) Another option is **UFO Parasail;** their rates are a bit higher, but they offer an optional simulated free fall at no extra charge. (☎ 325-5836; www.ufoparasail.com. $42-52.)

BIKING. Lahaina is more than manageable on two wheels. Although the coastal scenery may be appealing, biking along Honoapi'ilani Hwy. north or south of Lahaina isn't the safest due to heavy traffic and narrow shoulders in some areas. **West Maui Cycles** (☎ 661-9005) rents road and mountain bikes with daily and weekly rates. Many companies offer bike tours down the volcano. (For more information, see **Haleakala National Park,** p. 239.)

MOTORCYCLES AND SCOOTERS. Cruising the coast north and south of Lahaina on a motorcycle or scooter is an efficient (and fun!) way to reach some of the best beaches in West Maui. **Big Wave, Inc.** is the only Lahaina-based company to rent Vespas and state of the art mopeds. (☎ 866-303-9283 or 662-4600. 156 Lahainaluna Rd. Mopeds $30 for 2hr., $70 for 24hr. Vespas $50 for 2hr., $90 for 24hr.)

HELICOPTERS. While beautiful from the ground, West Maui and Molokai are spectacular from the air. Most companies tour both West Maui and Molokai during a 1hr. trip, peeking at the waterfalls hidden in the West Maui mountains, zipping across to the sea cliffs of Molokai, circling Molokai and returning to Iao Valley on Maui. Most companies list this ride at around $200 per person, but the activity booths cut that price almost in half; there's definitely flexibility for last minute bookings as well. Of all the companies that offer trips, **Alexair**

(☎877-4354) is the only one that has two-way headsets so you can talk to the pilots. **Blue Hawaiian** (☎871-8844) also has an excellent reputation, but there are several other companies that charge comparable rates.

WHALE-WATCHING. From mid-December to mid-April (peaking in February and March), hundreds of humpback whales come to Maui to breed before continuing up to Alaska for the summer. All along the southern and western coasts, the whales put on quite a show, and you don't need to leave shore to see them breaching and spouting. If you do want a closer look, the best company by far is **Pacific Whale Foundation,** 143 Dickenson St. (☎667-7447 or 249-8811; www.pacificwhale.org), a non-profit organization that contributes to whale research and conservation. They run a number of different trips; the basic two-hour whale watch runs $24-34.

◎ SIGHTS

The **Lahaina Restoration Foundation,** a non-profit agency that manages and maintains many of Lahaina's historic sites, publishes a brochure entitled *Lahaina: A Walking Tour of Historic and Cultural Sites,* available for free at the **Old Lahaina Courthouse Museum** and at their headquarters in the **Masters' Reading Room** on Dickenson and Luakini St. The walking tour describes 31 sites in Lahaina's historic district, reconstructing the town's history through its whaling and missionary days and also detailing the churches and cultural centers of Lahaina's various immigrant groups who were brought to the island to work the sugar plantations. For those with interests in Hawaiian history, but without the budget to take the guided tour of the town (see below), this is a better option.

The best money you can spend in Lahaina is the $37 it costs to take a guided tour with **▨Maui Nei,** an award-winning grassroots organization devoted to relating the history of Lahaina from the Hawaiians' point of view. Local guides, working from oral histories and traditional chants as well as archival research, lead small groups along a 2hr. walking tour of Lahaina's harbor and backstreets. In addition to breathing life into the historical sites, Maui Nei offers insight into what visitors can't see (and provides tasty refreshments along the way). The tour ends on what was once the sacred island of **Moku'ula,** the home and burial site of Hawaiian royalty. (☎661-9494. www.mauinei.com. Tours are conducted several times per week. Reservations required with 48 hr. notice. Tours meet on the front steps of the Old Lahaina Courthouse and finish at Maui Nei headquarters at 505 Front St.)

◪ HIKING

LAHAINA PALI TRAIL. (5½ mi. Trailhead: Ma'alaea, off Hwy. 30's 5-mi. marker. Elevation change: 1600 ft. Level: challenging.) This trail is most rewarding during whale season, when the view from the top of the ridge can include hundreds of whales frolicking in the channel (bring binoculars!). This hike works best if you have two cars, or can be dropped off in Ma'alaea and picked up in Olowalu. Starting from the eastern trailhead in Ma'alaea allows you to get the steep part over with first and finish at the beach. The path begins with a steep climb up to Kealaloloa Ridge; once there, hikers are treated to views of the central valley, Haleakala, and Kaho'olawe, Molokini, and Lanai offshore. The trail descends more gradually from the ridge, and *kiawe* trees provide some shade along the way. The end of the hike is in Olowalu, across the highway from the beach. Hikers should be equipped with

HE KAMEHAMEHA ONE

Outrage swept the Native Hawaiian community in 2002, when the trustees of Kamehameha Schools announced their decision to admit a non-Hawaiian student to their Maui campus.

Admitting the non-Hawaiian created such an uproar (combining historical grievances, cultural differences, and protests that mainland courts are inadequate for the multiracial Hawaiian population), that trustees reaffirmed their commitment to admitting only students with Hawaiian blood.

Since then, in June of 2003, a student who did not gain admission sued in Federal District Court for race discrimination. He claims the admissions decision was due to the fractional racial mix of each of the student's four biological grandparents, information requested on the admissions application.

The schools were established in 1884 by Princess Bernice Pauahi Bishop's will, expressing her wish for a school to meet the needs of Native Hawaiians. Today, the $6 billion private trust sponsors Kamehameha campuses on Maui, Big Island, and Oahu and enrollment has historically been limited to blood-Hawaiians.

Many Kamehameha families feel the school is the last great legacy of the Hawaiian monarchy, and should be preserved for Native Hawaiians.

sturdy hiking boots, plenty of water, and sunscreen. *(To reach the Ma'alaea trailhead from Lahaina, turn left at the 5 mi. marker on Hwy. 30, just south of the junction with Rte. 380. The trailhead and parking lot are clearly marked. Parking is available for a second car or pickup at the shaded lot at the 11 mi. marker on the mauka (mountain) side of Hwy. 30.)*

🎵 ENTERTAINMENT

Lahaina has a number of entertainment options. If your visit to Maui won't be complete without a **luau**, Lahaina is definitely the best place to attend one. To get a free dose of **hula**, head to the **Center Stage** at the Lahaina Cannery Mall; see **Polynesian Hula** Tuesdays and Thursdays at 7pm, and come back on Saturdays and Sundays at 1pm for your weekend fix of **Keiki** (children's) **Hula**. These presentations aren't anything elaborate, but you can't beat free hip-shaking.

LUAUS

Many of the hotels in Ka'anapali and Wailea offer their own versions of this traditional Hawaiian feast, but the most authentic is the **Old Lahaina Luau**, 1251 Front St., held nightly on the waterfront near Mala Wharf, across from the Cannery Mall. Guests are greeted with fresh orchid *leis* and a Mai Tai from the open bar. Along the water, local craftspeople display their wares and demonstrate *lei*-making and *poi*-pounding. Just before sunset, the *kalua* pig is unearthed from the *imu* in an intimate ceremony, and the feast begins, served buffet-style from thatched huts. Everything is well laid-out and organized to avoid lines and backups, and the food is traditional and tasty. Guests sit either on cushions and straw mats or in chairs at tables arranged in a large semi-circle around the grassy hula stage. The hula performance takes a historical approach, narrating the Polynesians' arrival to Hawaii and progressing through the missionary and plantation periods to modern times. The evening is definitely worth the price for the upgrade in food, service, and atmosphere from the average hotel *luau*. (☎800-248-5828 or 667-1998; www.oldlahainaluau.com. Reserve 2-4 weeks in advance, but last-minute cancellations may accommodate those who don't plan ahead. $75, ages 12 and under $45.)

SHOWS

Lahaina has two performances that do not include dinner, although both can be arranged with dinner packages at nearby restaurants. **'Ulalena** is a modern interpretation of ancient Hawaiian myths and recent Hawaiian history, communicated through dance, song, chant, and projected text and images. A live percussion group provides a pounding rhythm for the performers on stage. The show is colorful, engaging, and complex, impressing mainland visitors and attracting locals for return performances. (**Maui Myth and Magic Theater,** 878 Front St. ☎877-688-4800 or 661-9913; www.mauitheatre.com. 2 shows nightly Tu-Sa. $45-55, ages 3-10 $25-35.)

🖼 SHOPPING

Lahaina is a shopper's delight; countless small stores and boutiques line **Front St.,** and there are a number of large **shopping centers** in town. At the northern edge of town is the **Lahaina Cannery Mall.** (☎661-5304. Open daily 9:30am-9pm.) For crafts, clothing, and keepsakes that are actually made in Hawaii (rather than the Philippines or Taiwan), there's no better place than ■Na Mea Hawaii (☎667-5345), inside the mall. Everything in the store is handmade, from the carved fishhooks to the belts made of the bright feathers once used for the cloaks of *ali'i.*

For light beach reading, head to the **Old Lahaina Book Emporium,** at its new location at 843 Front St. Selling new and used books, the Emporium has an extensive Hawaiiana section as well as fiction, mysteries, poetry and more lining its dusty shelves. (☎661-1399. Open daily 10am-9pm.) Less than a block off of Front St. is **Take Home Maui, Inc.,** 121 Dickenson St., where you can break out the markers, decorate your very own coconut, and mail it home to that someone special for $22. They also ship pineapples, papayas, and macadamia nuts for those that just can't get enough Hawaiian produce during their stay. (☎800-545-6284 or 661-8067. Open daily 7:30am-6:30pm.)

🎵 NIGHTLIFE

As active as Lahaina is during the day and early evening, it is disappointingly short on nightlife. Pick up a copy of **Maui Time Weekly,** a free publication available at many restaurants and stores; the local mag publishes weekly nightlife and entertainment info. Most of the restaurants along Front St. have bars with cheesy live bands. **Moose McGillycuddy's,** 844 Front St., is reliably lively, especially on Tuesday when drinks are $1 after a $5 cover. Moose's prides itself as the home of the $3 Mai Tai. (☎667-7758. Happy hour 3-6pm. Open daily 7:30am-2am, kitchen open until 10pm.) The crowd moves to **Maui Brews,** 900 Front St., in the new Lahaina Center behind the Hard Rock Cafe, for $1 drinks on Wednesdays after a $5 cover. (☎667-7794. Restaurant open daily 8am-10pm, nightclub 9pm-2am, happy hour 3-6pm.) Both bars have live music nightly with dance clubs in the back and can be fun if you go with the right attitude. The locals head to **Gaby's Pizzeria & Deli,** 505 Front St., for nightly Happy Hour specials; from 9-11pm, well drinks are $2.50 and domestic drafts are $2. (☎661-8112. Open daily 11am-midnight) **Longhi's,** 888 Front St., with live music every Friday, is a classier venue for cocktails and dancing. (☎667-2288; www.longhi-maui.com; open daily 7:30am-10pm; complimentary valet parking nightly 5-11pm. 21+ after 9:30pm.)

KA'ANAPALI

Ka'anapali has long been a resort community. Hawaiian chiefs once prized its beaches for surfing; now tourists use them for every kind of beach activity imaginable. All the major hotel chains own properties on Ka'anapali Beach, a 3 mi. stretch of golden sand punctuated by the volcanic Black Rock that makes for spectacular snorkeling, scuba diving, and (for the brave) cliff jumping. This is one of the most prized places to stay in all of Maui; hotels here run at least $250 per night. Travelers on a budget may have more luck staying in Lahaina or renting a condo in Napili or Honokowai (see p. 216).

ACCOMMODATIONS AND FOOD. Of the major chain hotels on Ka'anapali Beach, the **Hyatt Regency Maui ❾**, 200 Nohea Kai Dr., is the biggest and most luxurious, with an incredible tropical lobby and waterslides in the swimming pool. (☎800-233-1234; www.maui.hyatt.com. Rooms $285-525; suites $600-3000.) **The Sheraton Maui ❾**, 2605 Ka'anapali Pkwy., has the best location, right on the cliff at Black Rock. (☎800-782-9488; www.sheraton-maui.com; rooms $280-470; suites from $850.) The best deal on the beach is the **Ka'anapali Beach Hotel ❾**, 2525 Kaanapali Parkway, which is definitely less over-the-top than its neighbors, and relatively affordable considering its posh oceanfront location. (☎800-262-8450; www.kbhmaui.com. Rooms $185-285; suites $225-600.) A paved beach walk runs between the Hyatt and the Sheraton; even if you're not staying at one of the fancy resorts, a stroll along this path will give you a wonderful glimpse of how the other half lives. The walk is particularly rewarding at sunset, when hotel *luaus* and live music concerts fill the strip. Most of the restaurants in Ka'anapali are expensive (entrees $25-40) and located in the hotels, but locals eat at **Jonny's Burger Joint ❶**, 2395 Honoapi'ilani Hwy., at the entrance to Ka'anapali, a hole-in-the-wall that serves the best burgers on the coast and cheap drafts. Enjoy cheap grub (burgers $5-7), a full bar, pool table, and juke box. (☎661-4500. Open daily 11:30am-2am.) **Hula Grill ❺**, on the waterfront in Whalers Village, is a bit over-rated and overpriced, but still one of Ka'anapali's more reasonable dining options, serving salads, sandwiches and pizzas for lunch ($8-10) and seafood specialties ($17-29) for dinner. (☎667-6636. Hula show and live Hawaiian music daily. Open daily 11am-11pm, dinner 5-9:30pm.) For family-style dining and super-cheap Happy Hour drinks, stop by **Rusty Harpoon Restaurant & Tavern**, also in Whalers Village. The "Daiquiri Capital of the World" blends up about a dozen fruity flavors of the frozen concoction ($3) 2-6pm and 10pm-close. (☎661-3123. Open daily until 2am.)

BEACHES. Ka'anapali's southernmost beach, **Hanake'o'o**, or **Canoe Beach**, is the launch site for canoe races, jet skiing, and other activities (park in the lot between mi. markers 24 and 25). Canoe Beach has decent snorkeling, full facilities, and lifeguards on duty daily. It is technically part of the same stretch of sand as **Ka'anapali Beach**, a popular beach fronted by the major hotels (parking is free in the lot next to the Sheraton). The section of shoreline between the Ka'anapali Beach Hotel and The Whaler is known as **Dig Me Beach**, for obvious reasons. People-watching here is great any time of day, and sunset is particularly beautiful. Ka'anapali Beach is marked by **Pu'u Keka'a** or **Black Rock**, an ideal place for **snorkeling** and beginner **scuba** lessons. King Kahekili's warriors used to demonstrate their bravery by jumping off the rock; today the brave/crazy do it voluntarily.

On the northern end of Ka'anapali, **Kahekili Beach Park**, on Kai Ala Pl. off of Honoapi'ilani Hwy., stretches for ½ mi. to Black Rock to the left, and quite a bit farther to the right, where it is much less crowded. Though edged by a few hotels, this long, narrow stretch of sand is surprisingly quiet and uncrowded; its grassy park with shaded picnic tables, BBQ grills, restrooms, showers, and lots of parking make Kahekili an ideal beach-day destination. Its clear, calm waters are popular with families, and are frequently used for introductory scuba classes.

HONOKOWAI, KAHANA, AND NAPILI

These three communities consist of one condominium development after another built along **Lower Honoapi'ilani Road,** and it's difficult to distinguish where one "town" ends and the next begins. **Honokowai** is the first development north of Ka'anapali, on a sandy beach that can't quite rival Ka'anapali Beach farther south. The next town, **Kahana**, has 1970s-style condos lining its rocky beaches. Finally, **Napili** is wedged between Kahana and Kapalua, with all of its condos either on or across from the sandy crescent of **Napili Bay,** an ever-popular family beach.

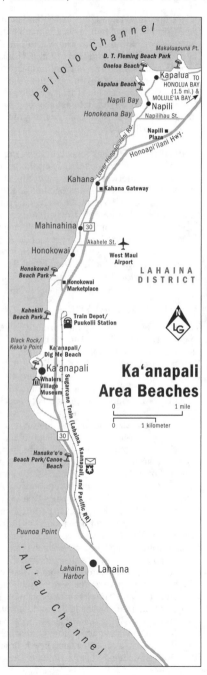

ACCOMMODATIONS. The condos in this area are, in general, more moderately priced than the Ka'anapali hotels to the south and the Kapalua resorts to the north. It's a good place to base your vacation for easy access to West Maui beaches and activities. Staying in a condo is especially convenient for families who want more than one bedroom, as well as access to a pool and recreational facilities. *Let's Go* recommends **Accommodations Hawaii** ❸❹❺, a vacation rental company based in Lahaina that handles 160 properties in Ka'anapali, Honokowai, Kahana, and Napili. All units are privately owned, and the prices are reasonable for every category. Pictures, rates, and details of the properties are on the web site. (☎800-847-0761; www.accommodations-hawaii.com. Rentals around $75-350 per night, with weekly and monthly rates available.)

FOOD. On Lower Honoapi'ilani Rd. the **Honokowai Marketplace** hosts a Star Market **grocery store** (open daily 5am-2am) and several take-out joints. Seemingly out of place in the marketplace is **Soup Nutz & Java Jazz,** a funky coffee and sandwich shop by day ($8-10 meals) and classy bistro by night (entrees $18-24). With a fountain in the dining room, Java Jazz is a pleasant relief from the standard strip-mall fare. (☎667-0787. Open M-Sa 6am-9pm, Su 6am-5pm. MC/V.) In AAAAA Rent-A-Space mall, just north of Honokowai Beach, **Honokowai Okazuya and Deli** ❶, 3600D L. Honoapi'ilani Rd., is a quality take-out joint and a local staple in West Maui. From deli sandwiches and pasta to spicy Chinese eggplant and chicken *katsu* plates, there is something for everyone. There are only a few stools inside, so everything is made-to-order and boxed to go. (☎ 665-0512. Plates $6-9. Open M-Sa 10am-2:30pm and 4:30-9pm. Cash only.) In Napili Plaza, 5095 Napilihau Rd., the Napili Market **grocery store** (☎ 669-1600), is open daily 6:30am-11pm, and there's an **ATM** machine inside. Also in the plaza, **Maui Tacos ❶** makes their own corn chips and tortillas, 5 kinds of salsa, and serves a filling meal for under $6—you can't beat that. (☎ 665-0222. Open M-Sa 9am-9pm, Su 9am-8pm.) Between Maui Tacos and the grocery store, **The Coffee Store** is blissfully air-conditioned and has **Internet access** ($2.50 per 15min.), delicious roasts (try the Vanilla Macadamia Nut), and soothing music. (☎ 669-4170; www.mauicoffee.com. Open daily 6:30am-8pm.)

◪ **BEACHES.** The best beach in these parts is **Napili Bay,** a crowded crescent of sand. Though the condos that front the beach do not allow public access to their parking lots, there is a limited amount of street parking. Public access to the shoreline is off Lower Honoapi'ilani Rd. on Hui Dr. and Napili Pl.

Kahana Beach, a pleasant little cove in front of the Kahana Sunset condos, has a sandy bottom, but lots of seaweed. Access to the beach is a bit difficult since the Sunset condos are private, and public access to Kahana Beach dumps you in a rocky cove a bit south of the actual beach. Stay away from **Ka'opala Beach** and **S-Turns Park,** which have been polluted by a dirty creek that empties into the ocean just south of the beaches. **Honokowai Beach Park** is a good place for a picnic (Okuzaya is just down the street) with easy parking access right off Lower Honoapi'ilani Rd., but better beaching can be had in Ka'anapali or Kapalua.

KAPALUA AND BEYOND

Towering Cook pines line the carefully planned roads of Kapalua, the most exclusive resort area in Maui. There's none of the glitz of Wailea, just the understated elegance of the **Ritz Carlton Kapalua** (☎ 800-241-3333 or 669-6200) and the **Kapalua Bay Hotel** (☎ 800-367-8000 or 669-5656), both of which have rooms from around $350 per night and (way) up. There are also a few expensive shops and galleries next to the Kapalua Bay Hotel (open daily 9am-6pm). There is really nothing in Kapalua for the budget traveler except **beaches,** which are free.

◪ **BEACHES. Kapalua Beach** is a gorgeous white-sand spot with clear and calm waters, making for great **snorkeling** off to the far left and right. A safe swimming spot year-round, Kapalua is highly popular among families and condominium renters in the area. The beach can get very crowded, and the small parking area is often chaotic. To reach the beach from Lower Honoapi'ilani Rd., look for a blue shoreline access sign immediately north of Napili Kai Beach Club.

North of Kapalua Beach, ◪**Oneloa Beach** is a gem of a beach located below the Ritz Carlton. Usually nearly empty, it's perfect for secluded sunbathing. It's better suited to body boarding than swimming though, as the sand gives way to reef and the waves are rather large. To reach public parking and beach access, take Office Rd. (the main road leading from the highway into Kapalua) and turn left at the end, then right on Ironwood Ln. Parking is before the gate, and the access path is opposite the parking lot. North of Oneloa, the better-known **D.T. Fleming Beach Park** has full facilities, lifeguards on duty, a large parking area, shade, and a mighty riptide, great for surfing and body boarding in winter. Turn left off the highway just after mi. marker 31; the beach is at the end of the road. **Molule'ia Bay** and **Honolua Bay,** between mi. markers 32 and 33, offer some of the best **snorkeling** on the island when it's calm (huge swells roll into Honolua Bay in winter, and only experienced surfers should take them on). Molule'ia Bay, also known as **Slaughterhouse Beach,** has a sandy entrance to the water at the end of a series of manicured steps down to the cove. Honolua Bay is rocky (no sand in sight!) but has an easy entrance into the water via an old boat ramp in the center of the bay. Many tour companies bring their snorkeling trips here. Parking is available in pull-outs around a hairpin turn along the road. To Honolua Bay, walk down off the *makai* (ocean) side of the highway, around the gate on the dirt road, and continue for 5min. through lush forest and across a dry riverbed; the road leads you right to the ramp.

◙ SIGHTS. One of the most beautiful, and certainly the most heart-pounding, drives on Maui, **Route 340 (Kahekili Highway)** winds its way along the coast for 20 mi. between Kapalua and Wailuku. In many places, the one-lane road narrows to the width of your car (seriously), with a cliff on one side and no guardrail between the road and the ocean a hundred feet below. The road is paved, so no 4WD is necessary, just alertness and a resignation to the 10mph speed limit. You'll be glad for your slow speed if you encounter a car coming from the other direction, and have to back up around hairpin turns. Allow at least 90 min. for the drive, more if you plan to stop along the way.

Traveling from Kapalua to Wailuku, the road continues as part of Hwy. 30 in two lanes past **Honolua Bay** (see **Beaches,** above). Between mi. markers 34 and 35, there is a beach called **Punalau.** You can see the beach from the road—look for the dirt road leading down to the left once you round the bay. The road may be blocked with boulders; park at the top and walk down. The beach is edged by cliffs and lava arches, making it truly spectacular for walking or picnicking, but it is too rough for swimming and snorkeling.

At the second major pullout between mi. markers 38 and 39 is the **Nakalele Blowhole.** The height of the spray depends on the tide; it can be the size of a building or nothing at all. At high tide, the blowhole is visible just paces from the pullout, but there's also a dirt trail that leads down for a closer look (about a 30min. walk each way). Use extreme caution—visitors have been killed when they venture too close and the spray catches them with surprising force.

Past mi. marker 41, the road narrows. There are a few stands selling shave ice and banana bread in the tiny village of **Kahakuloa.** Just past Kahakuloa, a rock formation known as **Kahakuloa Head** towers 636 ft. above the water; together with **Kahuli'anapa** behind it, the two hills form a distinctive silhouette identifiable from beaches on the North Shore. There's not much between Kahakuloa and Wailuku besides some gift shops, sculpture gardens, and galleries. As you near Wailuku, you enter the lush **Waihe'e Valley,** which receives almost 400 in. of rain per year. (To access this drive coming from the other direction, take Market St. straight out of Wailuku, or go along the coast from Kahului Beach Rd. to Waiehu Beach Rd. and turn right at the end onto Rte. 330.)

NORTH SHORE

Hana Highway begins just outside Kahului, but most travelers feel the road to Hana really starts in **Pa'ia,** a former sugar plantation town that now epitomizes Maui's laid-back surfer lifestyle. Past Pa'ia, the sleepy town of **Haiku** lies a few miles inland off the highway, and most travelers bound for Hana don't even realize it's there. The **Twin Falls,** on the eastern end of Haiku near **Huelo,** are just a few of the many waterfalls along Hana Hwy. Unfortunately, most of these falls are on privately-owned land, and hiking to them is technically trespassing. Beyond Huelo settlements are sparse, and the road winds around hairpin switchbacks, hugging the spectacular coastline all the way to Hana. A few small villages lie between Huelo and Hana, including the *taro (poi)* farming village of **Ke'anae,** but for the most part the road is surrounded only by lush tropical forest. **Hana** itself is a beautifully peaceful town with beaches and parks that warrant more than just a harried glance from the car. If time allows, it's worth continuing past Hana to **Ohe'o Gulch,** where you can hike to waterfalls and swim in freshwater pools. Those who haven't promised their rental car companies otherwise can continue around the southern coast of Haleakala on **Highway 31,** returning to Kahului via the arid **Kaupo Valley.**

PA'IA

Pa'ia is the center of healthy living on Maui. Organic food stores and yoga studios abound, existing amidst the surf culture that some of the North Shore's biggest waves bring to the area. During summer, its beaches are world-famous for wind-surfing; winter brings waves of staggering heights and the most daring of surfers. The town is also home to a great mix of restaurants and beach bars. Any time of year, Pa'ia makes for great people-watching—with bikini-clad Maui chicks, aging hippies, and salt-covered surfer dudes, Pa'ia attracts all kinds.

■ ⁊ ORIENTATION AND PRACTICAL INFORMATION

Pa'ia is essentially a crossroads town, located at the intersection of **Highway 36 (Hana Highway)** and **Baldwin Avenue,** which runs between Pa'ia and **Makawao** (see p. 244). Just west of Pa'ia and to the *makai* (ocean) side of Hana Hwy., there is a small residential community called **Spreckelsville,** which has a beach of its own but is within easy walking distance of Pa'ia's town center and beaches.

The **Nagata General Store** on Hana Hwy. sells basic necessities. (Open M-F 6am-7pm, Sa 6am-6pm, Su 6am-1pm.) There are three **gas stations** in Pa'ia along Hana Hwy. It's a good idea to gas up here if you're on the road to Hana; the only other gas station after Pa'ia is in Hana itself, and prices there are generally $0.30 per gallon higher. There's a **Bank of Hawaii** branch at 35 Baldwin Ave. with a **24hr. ATM.** (☎579-9511. Open M-Th 8:30am-4pm, F 8:30am-6pm.) Pa'ia's **laundromat** is at 129 Baldwin Ave. **Internet access** is available at **LiveWire C@fe,** 137 Hana Hwy., which also serves hot and cold coffee drinks and often hosts live music on its outdoor patio. (☎579-6009; www.livewirecafe.com. Internet $3 for 20min.) The Pa'ia outpost of the Makawao **post office** is located on Baldwin Ave., just south of town. (Open M-F 8am-4:30pm, Sa 10:30am-12:30pm.) **Postal Code:** 96779.

⁊ ACCOMMODATIONS

Pa'ia is one of the few places on Maui where good beaches, restaurants, and bars are all within walking distance of one another. It's easy to find a cheap place to stay here; many places even offer long-term rates. Travelers interested in private vacation rentals can look for postings on bulletin boards around town or head to **Ho'okipa Haven,** 62 Baldwin Ave., a booking agent for a wide range of studios, apartments and cottages in Pa'ia and Upcountry Maui. (☎800-398-6284 or 579-8282; www.hookipahaven.com. Rentals $70-250 per night, often with additional cleaning fees for stays shorter than a wk.) For additional budget accommodations nearby, see **Peace of Maui** (p. 226) in Hali'imaile, about a 10min. drive from Pa'ia.

IN-TOWN

▧ **Rainbow's End Surf Hostel,** 221 Baldwin Ave. (☎579-9057; www.mauigateway.com/
~riki/). Clean and friendly, this hostel is within walking distance of both Pa'ia and the
beach. Free Internet, a safe for valuables, board and bike storage, coin-op laundry, and

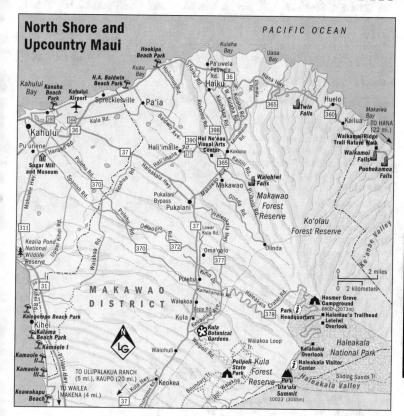

North Shore and Upcountry Maui

parking. Linens included. Common living room with TV/VCR. 2 kitchens and 3 bathrooms shared among 4 dorms and 3 private doubles. No curfew; quiet time after 10pm. Reserve as far in advance as possible with $50 deposit. Dorms $110 per week, $335 per mo.; doubles $200 per wk., $675 per mo. Shorter stays also available. ❶

The Inn at Mama's Fish House, 799 Poho Pl. (☎800-860-4852 or 579-9764; www.mamasfishhouse.com), 1½ mi. east of Pa'ia on Hana Hwy., off Kaiholo Pl. Located behind Mama's Fish House restaurant (guests get a discount), on Ku'au Cove, Mama's cottages are quite nice, but may not be as quiet or private as other vacation rentals in the area. All units have terra cotta tiled floors and patios, A/C, full kitchen, TV, VCR, stereo, grill, and beach access. Daily maid service included. 3-night min. stay; 7-night min. stay over Christmas. Check-in 3pm. Reserve a few mo. in advance with 1-night credit card deposit. Cottages $140-350. AmEx/MC/V. ❺

Pa'ia Gardens, 19 Luna Pl. (☎800-948-2877 or 579-8728), off Hana Hwy. next to Charley's Restaurant and Saloon. Basic rooms and apartments in a residential neighborhood, 2 blocks from Pa'ia center and the beach. The helpful owner can also serve as an agent for a wide range of accommodations in the area. Laundry, parking, and equipment storage on premises. 5-night min. stay, somewhat flexible. Reserve with $50 deposit. Rooms $35-55; apartments $45-75. ❷

Time: 1-2hr.	
Distance: 30 mi.	
Season: Any	

1 PAIA. Begin in this former plantation town, now the haven of health-conscious New Agers and devoted surfers. Take Baldwin Avenue southeast, past the old sugar mill, through the rustling cane fields.

2 MAKAWAO. After 7 mi., Baldwin Ave. ends in the town of Makawao. At the end, cross Makawao Ave. (between Polli's and Casanova's restaurants) to **Olinda Road.** The farther you go on Olinda, the prettier it gets—ranches and country pastures yield to eucalyptus groves (roll down the window and breathe deeply). As the road climbs to 4000 ft. in elevation, the switchbacks get steeper, the shoulder narrows, and the corners become more difficult to see around, so take your time and drive carefully.

3 PI'IHOLO RD. Just before the 12 mi. marker, turn left on Pi'iholo Rd. to loop back down. The turns here are tighter still; switch to a lower gear to save your brakes. Eucalyptus trees lines the way as the rural homesteads grow more eccentric—look for the house with the teepee. In the last mile or so before town, the landscape opens up to fields of pineapples. A left takes you back to Makawao, where you can easily backtrack to Pa'ia.

4 KAUPAKULUA RD. You can also continue the scenic drive by turning right at the end of Pi'iholo. This takes you to **Kaupakulua Road,** where dramatic cliffs hug the road's twists and turns. Kaupakulua Rd. ends 6 mi. later when it meets Hana Hwy. See **Hana Highway** scenic drive, p. 233.

This drive can also be reversed, starting from Hana Hwy. in Haiku, taking Kaupakalua to the Pi'iholo-Olinda loop, and going back through Makawao on Baldwin Ave. to Paia. The advantage of this direction is that you have an ocean view along Baldwin heading toward Paia; the disadvantage is that it's a bit harder to find the streets. If you have a good map and are attentive, you should have no problem.

Upcountry Maui Scenic Drive

222

OUT-OF-TOWN

▨**YMCA Camp Ke'anae,** 13375 Hana Hwy. (☎248-8355; www.mauiymca.org), about halfway between Pa'ia and Hana, on the edge of the Ke'anae Peninsula. Pitch a tent on the gorgeous property or stay in one of the co-ed dorms or cabins. Dorms share toilets and single-sex shower rooms, BBQ pit, industrial-sized kitchen, and gym. There are 2 4-person oceanview cottages, each with 1 queen-sized and 2 twin beds, full bathroom, kitchenette, lanai and grill. Coin-op laundry available. Bring bedding for dorm. The entire camp is frequently rented to large groups for weeks in the summer; call ahead for availability. Check-in 3pm. Check-out noon. Camping and dorms $15; cottage $100. ❶

▨**Aloha Maui Bed & Breakfast,** 101 Loomis Rd. (☎572-0298), off Hana Hwy. near Twin Falls. In its beautiful rainforest setting, Aloha Maui provides a relaxing getaway far from crowds. Tropical flowers loom over the 3 simple cottages of this B&B, all of which use solar energy and run filtered rainwater through their pipes. Continental breakfast includes homegrown fruit and flowers. All cottages have full kitchens and either indoor or outdoor bathrooms. 3-night min. stay. Reserve with 50% deposit. Guest room with kitchen $65, cottages $75-100. Weekly rates available. AmEx/MC/V. ❸

Kailua Maui Gardens, on Rte. 360 (☎572-9726; www.kailuamauigardens.com), a 25min. drive east of Pa'ia town. After Hana Hwy. becomes Rte. 360, look for the 5 mi. marker; ½ mi. past it, turn left across from the large red post box (#9). Enjoy private tropical paradise in one of Kailua Maui Gardens' secluded units. The Aloha Cottage, Jungle Bungalow, and Love Shack are all distinct, private cottages equipped with TV, VCR, full kitchen, and shared access to a large outdoor swimming pool, 2 spas, and 2 BBQ areas. There's also a 1-bedroom apartment available. 2-night min. stay. $20 surcharge if stay is fewer than 3 nights. Units $75-110. Weekly rates also available. ❸

🛝🍴 FOOD AND NIGHTLIFE

As befits a town whose inhabitants enjoy life to the fullest, there are plenty of choices for excellent eating in Pa'ia. A mecca for the health-conscious, **Mana Foods** sells bulk whole foods, organic and local produce, and packaged groceries. (49 Baldwin Ave. ☎579-8078. Open daily 8:30am-8:30pm. MC/V.) There are several bakeries in town, including **Moana Bakery and Cafe** (see below) and the exceptional **Cakewalk Pa'ia Bakery** on Baldwin Ave. next to the Pa'ia Fishmarket. (☎579-8770. Open M-Sa 8:30am-5pm and Su 8:30am-2pm.) For the best **fish tacos** in town, check out the stand in the alley off Baldwin Ave. (tacos $3; open daily 11am-4pm).

▨**Cafe des Amis,** 42 Baldwin Ave. (☎579-6323). The scrumptious crepes at this intimate and funky cafe are just as popular with the morning latte crowd as with the evening diners toting their own Merlot. Savory crepes ($6-9) are substantial enough for a full meal, while sweet crepes ($2-4) finish things off nicely (try the sugar and lime juice). The curries pack a tasty punch. Huge salads ($8) can easily be shared. Table service and take-out. BYOB. Open daily 8:30am-8:30pm. MC/V. ❷

▨**Pa'ia Fishmarket,** 100 Hana Hwy. (☎579-8030), at the corner of Baldwin Ave. The Fishmarket is a Pa'ia landmark, filled with happy people sitting at long wooden tables, eating good food, and sipping their favorite beers (Hefeweizen $4). The mahi mahi burgers ($6.50) are the best on the island. Fries, fish tacos, salads, seafood entrees ($12-17), and sushi also available. Counter service. Open daily 11am-9:30pm. D/MC/V. ❷

Moana Bakery and Cafe, 71 Baldwin Ave. (☎579-9999; www.moanacafe.com). Relax at a mosaic-topped table or in a deep booth. Breakfasts are a treat with homemade pastries, Belgian waffles, and hearty omelettes, but dinner is an adventure in decadent cuisine. Entrees include island pesto pasta with basil, cilantro, macadamia nuts and ginger ($10) and chili-seared *ahi* with mango salsa ($20). On weekends, brunch is a Moana specialty (Sa-Su 8am-3pm), with dishes like crabcake eggs benedict ($12). Open daily 8am-9pm. MC/V. ❹

Jacques Northshore, 120 Hana Hwy. (☎579-8844) is a windsurfers' hangout with (loud) live local music. Surf paraphernalia adorns the walls, colored lights line the bar, and brightly colored canopies and umbrellas substitute for a roof. Jacques offers expensive but creative appetizers (including sushi; spicy *ahi* roll $8), and while many entrees are a bit on the pricey side (up to $25 for some fish dishes), the menu's curries, salads, and pastas are more budget-friendly ($11-16). Most locals skip the entrees and head straight for the beer and music. Open daily for dinner from 5pm. MC/V. ❸

Hokus Pokus, 115 Baldwin Ave. (☎579-9144), across from the post office. This small and modest vegetarian/vegan restaurant isn't much on atmosphere, but magically serves up inexpensive meals for Pa'ia's health-conscious consumers. The eatery's 10 tables fill up quickly; if you can't get a seat (or make one appear out of your hat), take your tempeh burger ($6) or polenta au gratin ($10) to go. BYOB. Open daily 3-9pm. ❷

Charley's Restaurant and Saloon, 142 Hana Hwy. (☎579-9453), has 2 pool tables, occasional live music and dancing, and serves 3 meals a day. Hearty breakfasts feature pancakes so huge they literally spill off the plate ($3-6) and *ono* (delicious) eggs benedict ($10). The dinner menu features standard pub fare, including everything from burgers and ribs to pastas and pizza. The late-night scene here is hit-or-miss, but Charley's is one of the few spots in town that stays open past dinnertime. Live music Sa, M, W 10:30pm-1am. Open daily 7am-1am, food served until midnight. AmEx/MC/V. ❸

MIND-BODY MAUI

Maui is a mecca for those who seek health and youth through mind-body practices. Makawao and Pa'ia have a number of places where you can get in touch with that inner *om*.

Beyond Heaven, 3660 Baldwin Ave. (☎573-8828), in Makawao. Offers Kundalini, Iyengar, prenatal, and Hatha yoga classes, Tai Chi, massage therapy, and Nia Dance, in addition to a chemical-free hair salon. Classes $10-12. For schedules and information, call or check www.beyondheaven.com.

Maui Yoga Shala, 120 Hana Hwy. (☎579-6257), in Pa'ia. Offers some of the best yoga classes on Maui in a light-filled, hardwood-floored, and mirrored studio. Kriya Hatha, Ashtanga, and owner Nadia Toraman's special "Maui Yoga" technique all work your body and release your mind. Kathak dance, *capoeira*, hula, prenatal and kids yoga, Tai Chi, and Pilates mat classes available as well. Classes $10-15. For schedules and information, call, stop by, or check www.maui-yoga.com.

🏖 BEACHES

Pa'ia is surrounded by first-rate beaches. A few minutes west of town, **Pa'ia Bay** is great for swimming during the summer and is usually uncrowded, especially later in the day. In winter the surf and winds picks up, and the beach is popular among body boarders. Parking for Pa'ia Bay Beach is available either at the Youth and Cultural Center or at the Pa'ia Town Public Parking Lot, across from the Aloha Bead Company (see below). To the left of Pa'ia Bay, there is a trail that leads to a small, generally unpopulated, unofficial **nude beach.** A ½ mi. west of town, **H.A. Baldwin Beach Park** is a long, wide beach with playful surf (though it sometimes has a dangerous shorebreak). There are changing rooms and showers, as well as picnic tables, a big picnic shelter, and a large recreational field separating the beach from busy Hana Hwy. Just under a mile west of H.A. Baldwin Beach Park, the beach turns into **Sprecklesville Town Beach (Baby Beach)**, which can be accessed separately by heading onto Nonohe Pl. off Hana Hwy., veering right onto Nonohe Rd., and then turning left onto Kealakai Pl. to reach the shore. Parking is available in the red sand lot at the end of Kealakai Pl.; leave nothing of value in your vehicle—there have been recent reports of minor theft in the area. Baby Beach is so named for the protected swimming area to the right of the parking lot whose calm waters are perfect for *keiki* (children). Both Baby and Baldwin beaches are subject to strong winds that can kick up brutal sandstorms. A small and rarely populated stretch of sand can be found at **Ku'au Bay Beach;** look for the blue shoreline access sign ½ mi. east of the intersection with Baldwin Ave. About 2 mi. east of town along Hana Hwy., following the large sign for Ho'okipa Lookout, **Ho'okipa Beach** is world-famous for windsurfing. In summer, the relatively small waves attract beginners and longboard surfers to the break along the eastern end of the beach, while windsurfers race along the western end. The entrance is fairly rocky, making the beach poorly-suited for swimming. In winter, the entire bay is rocked with giant swells; only experienced surfers should venture out.

SHOPPING

■ **Maui Tropix,** 90 Hana Hwy. (☎579-9816). For over 25 years, Tropix surf shops have provided Maui with quality surf gear. Maui Tropix is the exclusive purveyor of the Maui Built brand (the surf company whose logo is displayed on local truck bumpers). Surfboards, t-shirts, stickers, and sunglasses all sold here. 2 additional locations at 261 Dairy Rd. in Kahului, and 715 Front St. in Lahaina. Open M-Sa 9am-6pm, Su 10am-6pm.

■ **Maui Girl,** 12 Baldwin Ave. (☎579-9266). Burn up the beaches in one of Maui Girl's original bikinis. In the center racks are the bikinis you'll lust after, with the silkiest fabrics and funkiest styles (not to mention $100 price tags). Around the perimeter are the mix-and-match tops and bottoms, perfect for any bronzed body. Open daily 9am-6pm.

■ **Aloha Bead Company,** 43 Hana Hwy. (☎579-9709), tucked behind the Maui Crafts Guild. Beads, beads, and more beads. In 2 small showcase rooms, the Aloha Bead Company boasts a wider variety than you'll find in most major craft stores. There's also a limited selection of unique, pre-made jewelry. Open daily 11am-6pm.

NEAR PA'IA

HALI'IMAILE

About halfway between Pa'ia and Makawao on Baldwin Ave., **Hali'imaile Road** branches off and runs through the pineapple fields to the tiny plantation town of Hali'imaile. The road continues past Hali'imaile to **Highway 37,** meeting it just south of the Pukalani Exit. In addition to a cluster of homes, Hali'imaile also has the **Maui Fresh Fruit Store and Pineapple Museum,** which sells pineapples, mango, and other local produce at an adjacent farmers' market. (☎573-5129. Open M-F 10am-6pm, Sa 9am-5pm.) On the first and second Saturdays of the month, there's also a modest **craft fair** next to the farmers' market featuring the works of local artists. The **Hali'imaile General Store ❺,** 900 Hali'imaile Rd., features the inspired "fusion" cuisine of Cordon Bleu-trained chef Beverly Gannon. The General Store is an experience in rustic elegance; enjoy culinary creations in an old country home complete with a wrap-around porch. On Monday nights, each diner who brings a can of food to donate to the local food pantry receives 50% off his or her entree (regularly $20-32), making the scallop risotto with truffles or the rack of lamb *hunan*-style delightfully affordable. (☎572-2666. Open for lunch M-F 11am-2:30pm, dinner served nightly 5:30-9:30pm. AmEx/MC/V.)

ACCOMMODATIONS. Peace of Maui ❷, 1290 Hali'imaile Rd., is surrounded by pineapple fields and boasts great views of Haleakala on clear days. The six hostel-style rooms on the ground floor of the main house share two bathrooms, a common living room, and a kitchen. Four rooms have queen-sized beds; two have bunk beds. All have TVs, fans, and access to free Internet and laundry. One cottage that sleeps two to four people, with full bath, kitchen, and lanai. The owner is happy to suggest other private accommodations in the area if there are no vacancies at Peace of Maui. (☎888-475-5045 or 572-5045; www.peaceof-maui.com. 7-night min. stay for cottage. Reserve with 50% deposit. Singles $40, doubles $45; cottage $85 for 2 people, $5 each additional person. AmEx/MC/V.)

HANA

Since the Hana Hwy. was paved in 1984, the town has undergone a considerable tourist boom. While not exactly "the last of old Hawaii," as it is sometimes called, Hana is relaxed enough to allow visitors to stop and smell the plumeria. Activities like exploring ancient *heiaus* (temples), watching the sun rise, strolling along secluded beaches, and joining the entire town in cheering on the local ball team are the little things that make time in Hana feel like a vacation from your vacation.

ORIENTATION AND PRACTICAL INFORMATION

Approaching Hana from the north, **Hana Highway** splits at the **police station** (☎248-8311), **fire station** (☎248-7525), and **Hana Medical Center** (☎248-8294). Hana Hwy. continues to the right, past the Hotel Hana-Maui. To the left of the police station, **Ua Kea Road** leads to **Hana Beach Park** and the accommodations along **Hana Bay.** Ua Kea ends after the community center and **Hana Ball Park;** turn right on **Hauoli Street** to return to Hana Hwy. Hauoli St. crosses Hana Hwy. by the Wananalua Congregational Church, just north of Hana's business district.

A **Bank of Hawaii** (☎248-8015) and the **post office** (☎248-8258) are located in the center of town at the Hana Ranch Center. (Bank open M-Th 3-4:30pm, F 3-6pm. Post office open M-F 8am-4:30pm.) The only **ATM** in Hana is located in the **Hasagawa General Store** at 5165 Hana Hwy. (☎248-8231. Open M-Sa 7am-7pm, Su 8am-6pm.) **Postal Code:** 96713.

TRANSPORTATION

Hana Airport is located 4 mi. north of town off Hana Hwy. on Alalele Rd. **Pacific Wings** (☎888-575-4546) offers regular nonstop service to and from Honolulu and Kahului; other airlines run less frequent flights. The only rental car company in Hana is **Dollar Rent-a-Car,** at the airport. (☎800-800-4000. Open M-Sa 8am-5pm; Su 9am-5pm.)

There is a **gas station** at 5200 Hana Hwy., in the southern end of town on the right-hand side of the highway; gas costs about $0.30 more per gallon here than elsewhere in Maui. For **24hr. emergency road service** and repair anywhere between Ke'anae and Kaupo, call **East Maui Mechanics** (☎248-8085 or 264-2446).

ACCOMMODATIONS

There are a number of accommodations in rural Hana that offer solitude, but the area is humid and thick with mosquitoes. Staying in **Hana Town** is peaceful, especially if you have views of Hana Bay at sunrise. Vacation rentals in **Hamoa Bay,** 2 mi. south of Hana, have prime locations along Hana's best beaches. For a complete listing of accommodations in Hana, check out the local web site, www.hanamaui.com, under Lodging.

Hana Bay Hale, 4950 Ua Kea Rd. (☎800-327-8097 or 248-8980; www.hanamaui.net/hanabayhale), on the right just before Hana Beach Park. Spacious 1- and 2-bedroom units overlooking Hana Bay. Hardwood floors, high ceilings, and huge windows invite relaxation. Lanai with outdoor furniture and electric grill, full bath, kitchenette (full kitchen in 2-bedroom unit), TV, VCR, stereo, laundry. Up to 4 people per unit. 2-night min. stay. Payment due in full before arrival. Rates $135-210. AmEx/MC/V. ❹

Hana Ali'i Holidays (☎800-548-0478 or 248-7742; www.hanaalii.com), on lower Keawa Pl. at Hana Bay Beach Park. Hana Ali'i manages 14 properties of varying quality and price ranges, but all with excellent locations within a 10 mi. radius of Hana town. Properties range from older budget studios that face the secluded black sand beach next to Hana Beach Park ($80), to a luxury 3-bedroom house on spectacular Hamoa Bay ($300). Look at the pictures and details of the properties on the web site, then call for availability. Check-in 2pm. Check-out 11am. ❸/❺

Joe's Place, 4870 Ua Kea Rd. (☎248-7033; www.joesrentals.com). Offering the cheapest beds in Hana, Joe's is a decent budget option. The rooms are simple, with aging carpets and bedspreads, but are kept quite clean. Guests share a common kitchen, living room with cable TV, and recreation room with picnic table. Check-in 3pm. Check-out 10am. Quiet time after 10pm. Reserve with credit card about 2 mo. ahead during high season. Rooms with shared bath $45, with private bath $55. MC/V. ❷

Aloha Cottages, 73-79 Keawa Pl. (☎248-8420), on a connecting road between Hana Hwy. and Ua Kea Rd. Clean studio apartment and 2-bedroom cottages in Hana town. Each cottage is equipped with a full kitchen and sleeps up to 4 people. Within walking distance of Hana Beach Park, the Aloha Cottages are simple, but are a great value for lodging in Hana town. Studio apartment $65, cottages $85. ❸

Waianapanapa State Park (☎248-4843), 4 mi. north of Hana town off Hana Hwy., on Honokalani Rd. Waianapanapa has campsites located only a few steps from the park's lava tube caves and coastal hiking trails. Facilities include restrooms, picnic tables, outdoor showers, and BBQ pits. A limited number of 6-person **cabins** are available ($45 per night for 4 people, $5 for each additional person), but they are generally booked at

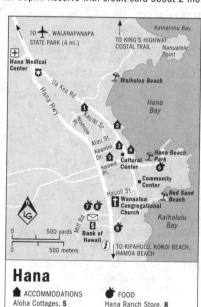

Hana

🏠 ACCOMMODATIONS
Aloha Cottages, **5**
Hana Ali'i Holidays, **4**
Hana Bay Hale, **3**
Hana Kai-Maui Resort, **2**
Joe's Place, **1**

🍎 FOOD
Hana Ranch Store, **8**
Hasagawa General Store, **9**
Hana Ranch Restaurant, **7**
Tutu's Snack Shop, **6**

MAUI

The 52 mi. trip from Kahului to Hana is one of the world's most impressive coastal drives; with over 600 curves and more than 50 single-lane bridges, the "Road to Heaven" offers incredible views of Maui's rainforests and waterfalls. While it takes about 2hr. to drive the route, the experience is much more rewarding if you stop along the way. Highlights of the journey are outlined below, but there's always more to explore. Fill up on gas in Pa'ia (there are no gas stations along the way), pack a cooler with snacks, and go!

1 HO'OKIPA LOOKOUT. About 2 mi. east of Pa'ia on the *makai* (ocean) side of Hana Hwy., Ho'okipa Lookout offers a killer view of Ho'okipa Beach. In summer, windsurfers fly over the choppy waves at lightning speed while longboard surfers wait patiently for a wave. In winter, the surf changes entirely, and swells over 10 ft. high (some over 25 ft.) fill the bay.

2 TWIN FALLS. If you want to make this a worthwhile excursion, go at 7am or take your chances, because by 8:15 the parking lot is typically full and the narrow trail to the falls is packed with Hana-bound tourists. As with most waterfall hikes, don't stop at the first fall—keep going! Usually where you see one fall, there is a bigger one above, and another above that—Twin Falls is no exception. If you beat the crowds, you may enjoy a lovely secluded swim beneath the falls, sharing them with nobody but the mosquitoes (don't forget your bug spray!). To get to the falls, pull over when you see the fruit stand after the 2 mi. marker, after Hana Hwy. turns into Rte. 360. Everyone ignores the "Private Property-No Tresspassing" signs, and passes through the gate onto the dirt road. After 2min., a few small trails branch off to the left to a rope swing and small pool. While many stop here for a quick cliff-jump, keep in mind that this is not the main attraction. After 10min., the trail forks at a small, hand-painted rock. As the arrow on the rock indicates, take the left fork and follow the path for another 10 yd. along the irrigation canals. After 3min., you'll reach the fall. Keep going and look for the steep path around to the right that leads up to the 2nd fall, about 5min. farther.

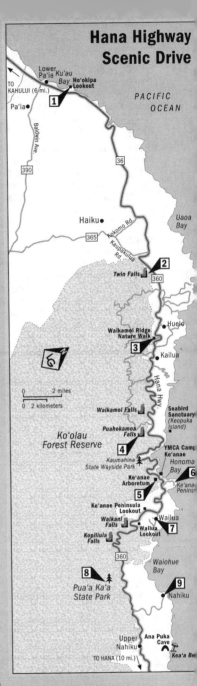

Hana Highway Scenic Drive

ROAD TRIP

3 WAIKAMOI RIDGE NATURE WALK. *Mauka* (on the mountain side), between mi. markers 9 and 10, this is an excellent short hike among native ferns, bamboo, eucalyptus, mango, and strawberry guava. Picnic tables are at the start of the trail above the parking area, and a more scenic and less crowded picnic area is at the top of the trail. Just above the parking area, the trail forks into 2 nested loop trails. To take the longer one (about 1 mi. total), bear left, then left again past the second bench. The trail climbs a bit past strawberry guava and *hala* trees, before leveling out and making a switchback to another bench. To the right, the trail continues through a stand of bamboo. It ends under mango trees in a quiet, grassy clearing, with a picnic shelter overlooking the ocean. To loop back down to the parking lot, either backtrack down the trail or walk down the old road. The end of the road is fenced off, but you can cut to the right and go around the wire.

Time: 2-4hr.

Distance: 52 mi.

Season: Any

4 PUAHOKAMOA FALLS. At the 11 mi. marker, a few parking spaces indicate the pull-off for Puahokamoa Falls. This stop draws a lot of visitors, many of whom enjoy lunch at the picnic tables. However, the deep swimming hole at the bottom of the falls makes Puahokamoa a great cliff-jumping spot for the brave ones in the car. If you do decide to take the plunge, exercise extreme caution; you may encounter some slippery rocks at the jump-off point.

5 KE'ANAE ARBORETUM. Less than 1 mi. past the YMCA Camp Ke'anae, just before mi. marker 17, the Ke'anae Arboretum offers another chance to stretch your legs. A corridor of impatiens leads to the main park, a garden of labelled trees and flowers that includes *taro*, breadfruit, and sugar cane. The 6-acre park is pleasant, but extremely damp, and the mosquitoes can be worse here than in other areas, which may discourage you from staying long.

6 KE'ANAE PENINSULA. The *taro*-farming village of **Ke'anae** lies on a wave-thrashed coast, a left turn off Hana Hwy. shortly after the arboretum. Here you'll find a peaceful Hawaiian town, centered on the **Ke'anae Congregational Church,** built in 1860 at the tip of the peninsula. The floor of the church is covered with mats traditionally woven from *hala* leaves. There is a picnic spot on the seawall overlooking the rocky beach, and a fruit stand just beyond, but not much else—please respect the locals who live here by coming and going quietly.

7 WAILUA. Just past mi. marker 19, the **Wailua Lookout** offers views of the tiny village of Wailua. The pride of the town is the **Our Lady of Fatima Shrine,** built in 1860, and the bougainvillea gardens maintained by many of Wailua's residents.

8 PUA'A KA'A. Between mi. markers 22 and 23, the freshwater pools of **Pua'a Ka'a State Park** are visible from the road. The 2 swimmable pools connected by a small waterfall make for a refreshing dip, but because they are less than a 2min. walk from the car, they are frequently crowded. The park also has shaded picnic tables, restrooms, and a pay phone. Parking is available on the *makai* (ocean) side of the highway.

9 NAHIKU. Between mi. markers 25 and 26, a road leads seaward to **Nahiku,** a small fishing village that is home to historic Christian church, built in 1867. Nahiku is East Maui's wettest town, getting more than 300 in. of rain per year. From Nahiku, it's another 10 mi. to Hana town.

HANA HIGHWAY DRIVING TIPS. Please keep in mind that many residents commute several times a day on this road. Use your **rearview mirror,** and use the pull-outs along the road to let cars pass you. **Do not stop on the road** to look at scenery or take pictures; this is dangerous and inconsiderate. On **one-lane bridges,** obey the yield signs but do not stop if you can see that the road ahead of you is clear. On steep downhill passages, **switch to a lower gear** rather than riding your breaks.

least 1 mo. in advance. Cabins are equipped with
bedding, towels, electricity, hot water, bathroom,
kitchen area, and miscellaneous cooking and eating
utensils. Campsites $5 per night. See **Camping**, p.
182 for permit information. ❶

Hana Kai-Maui Resort, 1533 Ua Kea Rd. (☎800-346-
2772 or 248-8426; www.hanakaimaui.com), across
from Joe's Place. The only AAA-approved accommodation in Maui, Hana Kai's standard condo-style units
may not be a "resort," but are comfortable neverthe-
less. The 18 studio and 1-bedroom units are located
on the black sand beach next to Hana Beach Park, but
not all units have ocean views. Full kitchens and private lanais in each unit. Check-in 2-5pm. Check-out
11am. Quiet time after 10pm. Reserve with full payment for 1-5 nights or ½ of the total for 6 nights or
more. Studios $125-145; 1-bedroom units $145-195.
Weekly and monthly rates available. AmEx/MC/V. ❹

🍴 FOOD

Bring groceries with you to Hana if you are staying
for more than a day or two. There are two general
stores where you can buy some necessities, the
Hasagawa General Store and the **Hana Ranch Store**
(☎248-8261; open daily 7am-7pm), both of which
are in the center of town. However, their selections of fresh produce, meat, and fish are very limited, and the prices of other items are high. There
are numerous **fruit stands** on the road north and
south of Hana. If you want fresh **fish,** try your luck
fishing off the pier in Hana Bay (Hasagawa's sells
fishing tackle and Hana Ranch Store sells bait
shrimp and frozen squid), or if you see a boat
trailer parked at the pier, wait until the fishermen
return and ask if they will sell to you.

At Hana Beach Park, **Tutu's Snack Shop** ❶ sells
burgers ($4.25), ice cream, cold drinks, and a very
handy map of Hana town. (☎248-8224. Open daily
8am-3:45pm.) The **Hana Ranch Restaurant** ❷, to the
left of Hana Ranch Store, is open for breakfast,
lunch, and dinner, but it's a bit overpriced for the
mediocre food it serves. (☎248-8255. Open daily for
breakfast 7:30-10:30am and lunch 11am-3pm. Dinner is served W and F-Sa only from 5:30-8:30pm.)
For a better deal, try Hana Ranch's **take-out window**
for plate lunches, burgers, and *saimin,* all under
$7. (Window open daily 7am-7pm.) The only other
prepared food option in Hana is the astronomically
priced restaurant at the **Hana-Maui Hotel.**

BEACHES AND OUTDOORS

WAIANAPANAPA STATE PARK. Four miles north of Hana, Honokalani Rd. is a marked road to the *makai* (ocean) side that leads to Waianapanapa State Park. In addition to the campsite and cabins (see **Accommodations and Camping,** above), the park encompasses several miles of shoreline along the rocky lava coast. **King's Highway Coastal Trail** is a well-defined path that parallels the coast all the way to Hana town, past ancient Hawaiian burial sites and *heiaus* (temples). Any part of the trail is worth walking for the gorgeous views and lava rock formations; the section from the park headquarters to the **Ohala Heiau** and back is only 1½ mi., and is surrounded by *hala* tree groves on one side and the violent sea crashing through lava arches and blowholes on the other. To the left of the campsite, there is a short loop trail that leads through the **lava tube caves.** Though the caves are steeped in poetic myth about a murdered princess, the crowds, stagnant water, and mosquitoes may disappoint. Below and to the right of the caves is a **black sand beach.** The shore area is small, and though the beach is in a somewhat protected cove, the surf can still be strong; watch out for rip currents. There is a more substantial black sand beach close to Hana town called **Popolana Beach,** in the cove just north of Hana Beach Park. (*☎ 248-4843. Pick up park maps and camping information at the park office, located in the caretaker's cottage. Office open M-F 7am-6pm, Sa-Su 8am-4pm.*)

 DENGUE FEVER WARNING. There were a few confirmed cases of **dengue fever** in Hana in early 2002, and although the disease is reported to be gone, the mosquitoes along all of the hikes are copious and hungry. Make sure you bring and wear plenty of **insect repellent.** Dengue fever can only be contracted from a bite from a mosquito who has previously bitten an infected person. Symptoms appear in 3-14 days, and may include headache, fever, and nausea. If you think you may be infected, seek medical help immediately.

HANA BEACH PARK. Just off Ua Kea Rd., past the Hana Cultural Center, Hana Beach Park occupies a stretch of dark sand along **Hana Bay.** The bay is protected and calm, making it a popular place for families with small children. Facilities include picnic tables, restrooms, and a snack bar. The beach is set against the red cliffs of **Kauiki Head.** The cliffs served as a fortress and battleground in 1775, when Kahekili, the king of Maui, attempted to recapture East Maui from the king of Hawaii who had conquered it several years before. Because of the steep grade and exotic plant life, hiking on Kauiki Head is not recommended. Hana-Maui Sea Sports runs **kayak and snorkel trips** from Hana Bay at 9:30am and 2pm daily. A representative may be set up in the park, or make reservations at the Hotel Hana-Maui Social Desk. (*☎ 248-7711 or 264-9566. Hana Beach Park gates open daily 6am-10pm.*)

KAIHALULU (RED SAND) BEACH. On the south side of Kauiki Head, a crescent of red sand beach has been carved from the cliffs above. The deep turquoise water that abuts the beach is incredibly clear, so bring your snorkel mask. Although an outcropping of rocks forms a barrier to keep the larger waves out, there is still a surprisingly swift current. The beach is beautiful and feels secluded. Nude bathing is a relatively common practice here. Follow Ua Kea Rd. to the end, and park on the left side before the lot designated for Hotel Hana-Maui guests (parking in the lot or on the other side of the street may get you ticketed or towed). Just after the

MAUI

Hana Community Center, cut left through the small grassy park; the trailhead is to the right. Marked with signs that warn you of the dangers you may encounter along the way, the path is difficult, but not impassable—just watch your footing very carefully. The grade is steep and becomes particularly hazardous in the rain; a fall off the cliff to the rocky shore below could result in injury or death.

KOKI AND HAMOA BEACH. Two miles south of Hana toward Kipahulu, turn left off Hana Hwy. onto Haneoo Rd., where a sign points the way to Koki Beach and Hamoa Beach, Hana's two best spots for swimming and surfing. **Koki Beach** is the first beach on the left. Red cliffs rise above the rocky sand to the left, while offshore to the right lies **'A-lau Island,** a seabird sanctuary. The sand stretches far into the water before the ocean gets too deep, making for a dangerous shorebreak. Although the beach is popular for surfing and body boarding, visitors should ask locals about currents and underwater hazards. Because of the potentially hazardous conditions, do not swim alone. Farther down the road, **Hamoa Beach** is a beautiful stretch of soft sand maintained by the Hotel Hana-Maui, though it is open to the public. Surfing and body boarding are popular here, and though swimming is generally safe, the occasional strong current can make for rough waters. Public restrooms and outdoor showers are available. Both Koki and Hamoa Beach get crowded in the afternoons but are virtually empty in the mornings and evenings.

👁 SIGHTS

HANA CULTURAL CENTER. Perched on a small hill overlooking Hana Bay, the Hana Cultural Center features a small museum, some authentically thatched *hales*, and a selection of native Hawaiian plants and trees, all of which attempt to preserve and teach the history and culture of tradition-steeped Hana town. The community-run center displays unique Hawaiian quilts, *kapa* (barkcloth) tapestries, and a selection of woodcarvings and artifacts. The grounds are also home to two buildings on the National Register of Historic Places: the old Hana police station and courthouse (still in use to this day), and the old jail building that was used until 1987. (*4974 Ua Kea Rd.* ☎ *248-8622; www.planet-hawaii.com/hana. Open daily 10am-4pm. Free tours of the grounds available by request. Suggested donation $3.*)

FAGAN MEMORIAL. High atop the large hill overlooking Hotel Hana-Maui and Hana Bay, this giant cross stands out as a dominant Hana landmark. The memorial was built in 1960 in honor of Paul Fagan, founder of Hana's first hotel, for his contributions to the town. An impressive view of the coastline rewards those who make the trek up to the cross. From the memorial, there's a beautiful jogging trail that cuts across the hillside. (*To reach the memorial, take the trail that begins in the guest parking lot across from Hotel Hana-Maui. At a brisk pace, it takes 15min. to make the ascent to the cross.*)

KA'ELEKU CAVERNS. Descend into immense lava tubes formed by ancient volcano flows in the caves at Ka'eleku, which are 250,000 times bigger than the lava caves at Waianapanapa State Park. Though pricey, tours of the caves are pretty cool, showing off the impressive stalactites and stalagmites within the lava tube. (*Ulaino Rd. Located 3 mi. before Hana town, near the 31 mi. marker on Hana Hwy.; the caverns are ½ mi. down Ulaino on the left.* ☎ *248-7308; www.mauicave.com. Scenic walking tour departs M-Sa at 11am (1hr. $29). The "Wild" Adventure Tour departs M-Sa at 1pm (2-2½hr., $69). A shorter version of the walking tour departs M-Sa at 4:30pm (½hr., $15). Reservations highly recommended.*)

NEAR HANA

KIPAHULU AND OHE'O GULCH

*Kipahulu is located 10 mi. south of Hana on Hana Hwy. The road to Kipahulu is narrow, but paved and easily negotiated by any vehicle. For practical information on the park, see **Haleakala National Park**, p. 239. Maps and information about the park can be obtained at the Kipahulu rangers' station (☎ 248-7375; open daily 9am-5pm), located in the main parking lot. The rangers' station also offers free 15min. natural and cultural history talks daily at 12:30, 1:30, 2:30, 3:30pm. The admission fee of $10 per vehicle is good for 7 days at both entrances to the park. Camping in the park does not require a permit. Campground facilities include chemical toilets, picnic tables, and BBQs, but **no potable water;** visitors must bring their own water to the park. Mosquitoes plague the area, so bring and wear plenty of **insect repellent.** Sturdy shoes are recommended for the waterfall hikes, and a guided 1hr. hike departs Su-F at 9:30am.*

Continuing 10 mi. south of Hana on Hana Hwy., a swath of **Haleakala National Park** stretches down to the coast through **Kipahulu Valley** and **Ohe'o Gulch,** home to the famed **Pools of Ohe'o.** This portion of the park is not connected to the crater by trails—beyond the hikes listed here are hundreds of acres of preserved forest that are not open to the public. The park is definitely worth a stop if you have time to spare.

POOLS OF OHE'O. (½ mi. Trailhead: northeast edge of parking lot. Elevation change: 100 ft. Level: easy.) *Ohe'o* is the Hawaiian name for what are referred to as the **Seven Sacred Pools,** quite a misnomer considering there are many more than seven pools and there is no evidence that they were ever considered sacred. From the bluff above the pools, you can usually get a clear view of the Big Island across the channel. Many choose to swim in the pools, although if you plan to hike to the ☒waterfalls, you'll find less crowded pools at **Makahiku Falls.** Under no circumstances should you swim in the ocean beyond the pools; the hazards include sharks that gather around the mouth of the Ohe'o Stream.

MAKAHIKU FALLS. (1 mi. Trailhead: across the street from the parking lot. Elevation change: 200 ft. Level: easy.) Pipiwai Trail approaches the falls from above, skirting the ridge of the gulch. At the top of the falls are two shallow pools where you can swim. To reach them, cut off the main trail to the right on a worn path just before the gated fence. A peek over the lip of the 2nd pool reveals the falls thundering 185 ft. to the churning stream below.

WAIMOKU FALLS. (4 mi. Trailhead: across the street from the parking lot. Elevation change: 1600 ft. Level: moderate.) Those who continue on the trail for another 1½ mi. above Makahiku Falls will enjoy a hike through a guava orchard, under the boughs of a banyan tree, across two bridges, and through a bamboo forest, finally ending at the base of the towering falls. The valley beneath the falls makes for a lovely picnic spot. Many choose to brave the icy water for a photo under the falls. The trail to the upper falls can often be slippery; sneakers or sturdy footwear are recommended.

THE ROAD FROM HANA

The road from Hana along **Highway 31 (Pi'ilani Highway)** from Kipahulu to Kula, couldn't be more different from Hana Hwy. Gone are the lush rainforests and roadside waterfalls. The southern route around Haleakala gives some sense of the vastness of the volcano; its arid plains and valleys are stark and desolate,

HANA TODAY

Leinaala Pula is the Managing Director of the Hana Cultural Center and Museum. In March 2003, she discussed Hana's importance to Maui, and the balance of locals and tourists that exists there.

LG: What is the overarching purpose of the Hana Cultural Center?
A: We're here to teach and preserve the history and culture of Hana town and to share them with the tourists.
LG: What to do you think is so special about Hana?
A: I think it's the people. They make Hana precious and memorable. People come to Hana for the scenery and sights, but when they actually interact with the local people, *that*'s when it becomes a special and memorable trip. It's so important to interact with the locals.
LG: What do you think is the locals' reaction to all the tourists?
A: There are mixed feelings. We have a lot of locals who depend on tourism for their livelihood. For example, there's only one hotel in Hana, and more than half of the people in Hana work there. But there are others who don't want Hana to change. I think tourists will always be a part of Hana because we're so far away and we're a destination.
LG: Do you foresee the town changing any time soon?
A: No, not at all... and that's a good thing.

meeting the sea in spurts of hardened black lava. In many ways, this route is even more spectacular than that of the Hana Hwy., and it is certainly the road less traveled. From the 30 mi. marker to the 25 mi. marker, the one-lane road is paved in patches, and hugs a cliff with no guardrail. Most car rental companies do not permit their cars to be driven on this route. Four wheel drive may be helpful in places, but it is not essential. Falling rocks and unseen hazards make traveling on the road especially unsafe after dark.

A mile south of Ohe'o Gulch, a dirt road to the *makai* (ocean) side just past the 41 mi. marker leads down to Palapala Hoomau Church, the site of **Charles Lindbergh's grave.** Lindbergh retired to Maui in 1971 (42 yr. after his nonstop solo flight across the Atlantic), but if you are paying homage to Lindbergh, please also respect the graves of the other Hawaiians buried here.

Eight bumpy miles past Kipahulu, the quiet town of **Kaupo** sits at the base of the Kaupo Valley. The **Kaupo Store** sells cold drinks and snacks, and merits a stop merely to peruse its collection of antique cameras, pocket watches, and miscellaneous relics left on the shelves since the early 20th century. (☎248-8054. Open M-Sa 9:30am-5pm.) The 3-day hike from the Haleakala crater (see **Haleakala National Park,** p. 239) ends in Kaupo; the store is a good place to have a car meet you if you plan on doing the hike.

Past Kaupo, there's nothing but ranch land for twenty miles. As the road winds northward above Makena, the **Ulupalakua Ranch** and **Tedeschi Vineyards** appear as a welcome oasis. If you arrive during business hours, stop in for wine tasting and refreshment (see p. 238 for details). Past Ulupalakua, the road meets **Highway 37 (Kula Highway),** which leads through **Upcountry** to Kahului and central Maui.

UPCOUNTRY MAUI

Upcountry Maui loosely encompasses the rural townships built on the slopes of the majestic Haleakala volcano. Though the region is only minutes from the bustling commercial center of Kahului, you'll feel a world away in Upcountry's quaint villages, rolling landscapes, and cooler temperatures. In the heart of Upcountry's pastoral hills lies **Kula,** where much of the island's produce is grown. In addition to sweet corn, greens, tomatoes, avocados, papayas, and other foodstuffs, Kula is home to magnificent floral gardens, many of which include the strange and hearty protea flower. South of Kula along **Highway 37 (Kula Highway),** the tiny hamlet of

Keokea boasts a coffee shop, general store, gas station, and art gallery, as well as thousands of acres of ranch land grazed by cattle and horses. The ranches' *paniolos* (cowboys) strut their stuff every year at the Fourth of July rodeo in **Makawao,** the only town in Upcountry with a sizeable main street. The old cowboy town is also home to a string of charming shops and galleries. North of Makawao, peaceful **Haiku** connects Upcountry and the North Shore and spills down to the coast from **Route 365 (Kaupakulua Road)** to **Route 36/360 (Hana Highway).**

KULA

Kula is full of surprises. The countryside is patched with rural pastures, eucalyptus forests, fields of exotic protea flowers, and at each turn there are spectacular views of the Central Maui Valley that spreads 4000 ft. below. Driving through Kula is a treat—every side road you venture down reveals something unexpected. Roaming herds of cattle share roads shaded by the clouds that hug the rolling slopes of the volcano. And of course, there is **Haleakala** itself (see p. 239), rising to a majestic 10,023 ft. above sea level and occupying an entire range of climate zones from cloud forest to crater moonscape.

ORIENTATION AND PRACTICAL INFORMATION

The main road that runs north-south through Kula is **Route 37 (Kula Highway).** Taking Rte. 36 east out of Kahului, you can pick up Rte. 37 at its junction near **Pukalani.** Kula Hwy. runs south through Kula and **Keokea** all the way to the **Ulupalakua Ranch** and **Tedeschi Vineyards** where it becomes Hwy. 31 and runs along the southern coast all the way to Hana (see **The Road From Hana,** p. 233). **Route 377 (Kekaulike Avenue)** makes a loop detour from Rte. 37, which makes for a very scenic drive past flowering jacaranda trees; **Route 378 (Haleakala Crater Road)** spurs out from Rte. 377. A good shortcut to Kihei or Kahului from Kula is **Route 370 (Pulehu Road),** which cuts down the hill and then west through the sugar cane fields from Rte. 37 just north of the **post office,** intersecting with Hansen Rd. by the sugar mill in Pu'unene. If you miss the turn, Holopini Rd. to the north also meets up with Pulehu. **Postal Code:** 96790.

ACCOMMODATIONS

There are no big hotels in Kula, but several cottages and B&Bs provide Upcountry peace and solitude. Nights are a bit cooler at these higher altitudes, so pack a few sweaters and long pants. Staying in Kula means at least a 30min. drive to get to the beach, but you'll have Haleakala hikes in your backyard.

Star Lookout, 622 Thompson Rd. (☎907-346-8028; www.starlookout.com). Drive up Rte. 37 past the 16 mi. marker in Keokea. Turn left at the fork across from Grandma's Coffee House and make an immediate right onto the 1 lane Thompson Rd. The glass front of Star Lookout's cottage looks down onto the Central Maui Valley below, which is framed by the ocean on both sides. The West Maui mountains loom in front and majestic Haleakala rises behind—the perfect setting for a peaceful retreat. The cottage has a full kitchen and sleeps 4-8 in 2 queen-sized beds, a loft, and a bunk room below. Tended by a couple from Alaska, the property features landscaped gardens, a bonfire pit, gas BBQ, and celestial telescope. The cottage has a wrap-around deck, cable, VCR, and a wood-burning stove. Laundry access available. 2-night min. stay. Reserve 6 mo. to a yr. in advance. $150 per night for 4 people, each additional person $15. ❺

Silver Cloud Ranch, 1373 Thompson Rd. (☎800-532-1111 or 878-6101; www.silvercloudranch.com). Follow directions for Star Lookout (above); Silver Cloud is ¾ mi. past it on the left. Chirping birds and grazing farm animals greet visitors to the property, which includes 6 rooms in the main house, 5 self-contained studios, and 1 private cottage. The lawn and gardens sprawl in front of the plantation-style house and guest cottages, affording an unobstructed view of the West Maui mountains, the ocean, and the valley between. An elegant living room in the main house—furnished with an antique piano, writing desk, spinning wheel, and comfortable sofas—opens through glass doors to a patio and garden. Full breakfast included. $15 surcharge for 1-night stays. Studios $136-188 depending on size and season. Plantation house rooms $110-162; all have private bath, 2 have lanais and ocean views. Private cottage $195. AmEx/MC/V. ❹/❺

Kula Lodge and Restaurant (☎800-233-1535 or 878-1535; www.kulalodge.com), on Rte. 377 (Kekaulike) just before the intersection of Rte. 378 (Haleakala Crater Rd.). This chalet-style lodge is as close to Haleakala National Park as you can get without camping there. Popular with older guests, the larger chalets have lofts that could accommodate a group of 4, as well as fireplaces and private lanais. On-site restaurant with impressive views (lunch entrees $10-17, dinner $18-28). Check-in 3pm. Check-out 11am. Reserve with full payment; cancel 30 days in advance for $25 fee. Chalets $110-165 for 2 people, each additional person $10. AmEx/MC/V. ❹

🗒 FOOD

Kula has surprisingly few eateries, considering the amount of produce grown in the area. ■**Grandma's Coffee House** ❶, 153 Kula Hwy., in the settlement of Keokea, is an Upcountry institution that serves excellent coffee (grown and roasted on the premises) and decadent cakes and pastries, as well as sandwiches ($5.50-7.25) and a daily hot special. (☎878-2140. Open daily 7am-5pm.) **Cafe 808** ❶, just up the road from the Holy Ghost Church on Lower Kula Rd., is a local joint that serves hearty breakfasts, deli sandwiches, and plate lunches (teriyaki chicken $5) in a no-frills, cafeteria-like space. (☎878-6874. Open daily 6am-8pm.) With a view similar to the one from the restaurant at Kula Lodge, **Kula Sandalwoods Cafe** ❷, on the *mauka* (mountain) side of Rte. 377, is a country club-style restaurant serving fancier sandwiches and salads ($7-10) and espresso drinks. (☎878-3523. Open M-Sa 6:30am-2pm, Su 6:30am-noon, though hours are flexible.) Across the street from Cafe 808, **Morihara Store** is a small market and the closest thing to a grocery store in Kula, also selling beer and wine. (☎878-2578. Open M-Sa 7am-8pm, Su 8am-8pm.)

🏔 OUTDOORS

TRAIL RIDES AND OFF-ROAD TOURS. To explore the Kula countryside on horseback just like the *paniolos* (cowboys), **Thompson Ranch Riding Stables** offers 2hr. trail rides from their Thompson Rd. location. *(Follow directions for Star Lookout (see **Accommodations**, p. 235). Rides start just past Silver Cloud Ranch on the left.* ☎878-1910. 2hr. ride $60.) For a more high-powered look at Maui's countryside, **Maui ATV Tours** offers 2 and 4hr. tours of Upcountry Ranchland. *(Maui ATV is located on the left just before the Ulupalakua Store & Deli and the Tedeschi Vineyards.* ☎878-2889; www.mauiatv-tours.com. 2hr. tour $90; 4hr. tour $125.)

POLIPOLI STATE PARK. Polipoli is a secluded recreational area high above Kula. The park's remote location deters many travelers from ever making it to Polipoli, which lies 6200 ft. above sea level on the western slopes of Haleakala. The park is a damp forest of non-native trees, including redwoods and eucalyptus, and is used by locals for pig-hunting and camping. Impressive views from the park look down across the Kula hills and to the neighboring islands of Kahoʻolawe and Lanai. Time spent at Polipoli is quiet; you might not see another person during your visit.

Visitors can access the park via **Waipoli Road** off of Rte. 377 (not via Polipoli Rd. as would be expected). Follow a series of steep switchbacks on the narrow one-lane road for 5 mi. (about 30-40min.), and you'll reach a hunter check-in station that also serves as a trailhead for many of Polipoli's hikes. To reach the campground in the park, continue on Waipoli Rd. The road becomes unpaved and hazardous after the cattle guard at mi. 6, and it's only accessible to travel in a 4WD vehicle. After another grueling 3½ mi. of dirt, mud, and potholes, the road forks; bear right and continue ½ mi. to the parking, picnic, and camping area. Without the proper vehicle, attempting this last stretch of road is just not worth it; satisfy yourself with the trailheads earlier on, or bring a mountain bike to pedal your way to the campground. In such a remote location, you're too far from the nearest phone to give the road a try.

Polipoli's trails are excellent for **hiking** or mountain biking. The trails have been recently reconstructed by Na Ala Hele, a group committed to preserving and maintaining Hawaii's state and county parks. Their work is evident, as trails are clean and well-marked with easy-to-follow signs.

WAIAKOA LOOP TRAIL. (4½ mi., 1½-2hr. Trailhead: Hunter check-in station at mi. 5 on Waipoli Rd. Level: moderate.) To reach the start of the loop trail, head ¾ mi. down the grassy road at the hunters' station to a gate and large sign marking the start of the trail. Remember to shut the gate behind you. The loop itself is a 2¾ mi. trek through pine forests and open hills. The pine trees provide a comfy blanket of needles on the ground, so watch your footing since it can get slippery. After about ½ mi. up the right side of the loop, the Waiakoa Trail connects with the Upper Waiakoa Trail; stay on the loop unless you are up for a much longer and more strenuous hike.

UPPER WAIAKOA TO WAIOHULI TRAIL. (10 mi. Trailhead: Hunter check-in station or Waiohuli Trailhead farther up Waipoli Rd. Level: challenging.) A hard trek with over 3000 ft. of elevation change. Follow the directions for the Waiakoa Loop Trail until you get to the fork for the Upper Waiakoa Trail. From here it's 2½ mi. until the trail merges into the Upper Waiohuli Trail. After the merge, it's another 3¾ mi. back to Waipoli Rd. If you parked at the hunters' station, remember that it's several miles down Waipoli Rd. to get to your car; try to arrange a second vehicle at the Waiohuli Trailhead. On the way down the Waiohuli Trail, you'll notice a shelter where the path connects with the Mamane Trail. Mamane continues another 1¼ mi. before it connects with the Skyline Trail from Haleakala National Park. This combination of trails can take several nights; check with the Visitor Center at Haleakala before starting on this lengthier trek.

Camping in the park is recommended because hikes are long and it takes a while to get to Polipoli in the first place. Camping permits cost $5 per night and can be obtained from the Division of State Parks. (☎ 984-8109, Make checks payable to the Department of Land & Natural Resources and mail them to the Division of State Parks, 54 S. High St., Rm. 101, Wailuku, 96793) The campground at Polipoli is very basic, with restrooms and picnic tables but not showers or drinking water. The temperatures here can drop below freezing at night, and the grounds are a damp place to pitch a tent. Other than a few pig-hunters, you might be the only person at the campground; think twice if you're camping by yourself. Another option is to reserve a rustic cabin in advance from the Division of State Parks. (☎ 984-8109. See instructions above for obtaining a camping permit. $45 for 4 people, each additional person $5. 10-person max.) Polipoli's cabin doesn't have supply cooking utensils and dishes. However, there are gas lanterns and a wood-burning stove. Remember, there is **no drinking water** in the park.

MAUI

◉ SIGHTS

BOTANICAL GARDENS. Unusual flowers and plants love Kula's rich soil, and there are several botanical gardens and flower farms that are open to the public. The University of Hawaii operates the 35-acre ⬛**Maui Agricultural Research Center** in Kula as a breeding ground for proteas and other Southern Hemisphere flora. Visitors are invited to stroll the center's grounds for free, observing the colorful spectrum of unique protea hybrids and impressive demonstration garden of All-American roses. With advance notice, the center's station manager David Oka conducts private tours of the grounds. Visitors need to check in at the main office before entering the gardens. *(209 Mauna Pl. To reach the Research Center from Rte. 37, take a left onto Copp Rd. between the 12 and 13 mi. markers. After a ½ mi. on Copp, turn left onto Mauna Pl. ☎878-1213; www2.ctahr.hawaii.edu. Open M-Th 7am-3:30pm. Free.)* For more touristed flower-viewing just off Kula Hwy., the **Enchanting Floral Gardens** slightly dispels the pleasure of discovering plants from around the world with tacky yellow arrows painted on a paved path, pointing visitors in a firm direction. *(2505 Kula Hwy. ☎878-2531. Open daily 9am-5pm. $5, children 6-12 $1.)* **Kula Botanical Garden** is removed from the main road on a 6-acre site. Established in 1968, the garden is a family-run operation showcasing native Hawaiian plants as well as unique specimens from around the world. *(638 Kekaulike Ave., almost 1 mi. from the intersection of Kula Hwy. and Rte. 377 (Kekaulike). ☎878-1715. Open daily 9am-4pm. $5, children 6-12 $1. MC/V.)* To purchase or ship tropical bouquets, try **Sunrise Protea Farm,** on Rte. 378 (Haleakala Crater Rd.), not far from the intersection of Rte. 377. Sunrise offers a free tour of its garden, a boutique that ships dry and fresh protea arrangements, and a small shop that sells coffee and snacks. *(☎800-222-2797; www.sunriseprotea.com. Open daily Sept.-May 7:30am-4pm; June-Aug. 7am-4:30pm. Free.)*

ART GALLERIES. Artists seem to flock to the lush countryside of Upcountry Maui; the surroundings ooze creative inspiration. As a result, Kula is home to a few small art galleries. The **Keokea Gallery** is an intimate space featuring the bright and colorful works of a four-member art cooperative. *(The Keokea Gallery is located on Rte. 37 next to Grandma's Coffee House. ☎878-3555. Open daily 9am-5pm, or by appointment. Free.)* Inside the Kula Lodge, on Rte. 377, the Curtis Wilson Cost Gallery showcases the works of Cost, an accomplished painter whose realist paintings gracefully capture the Maui landscapes. *(☎878-6544; www.costgallery.com. Open daily 8:30am-5pm.)*

ULUPALAKUA RANCH AND MAUI'S WINERY. On the site of a former sugar plantation and rose garden owned by mid-19th century whaling captain James Makee, Ulupalakua is now a 25,000-acre working ranch. The gem of the ranch, ⬛**Tedeschi Vineyards,** is an operational winery that produces local vintages from grapes, pineapples, and raspberries. The ride down to the ranch and winery is stunning, with undeveloped pastures on both sides and views of the Kihei coast far below. It's definitely worth the trip for the **free wine tasting** and a stroll around the grounds. The wines ($8-35) make great gifts—who would expect champagne from Maui? A one-room exhibit on the history of the *paniolo* (cowboy) tradition on Maui provides interesting food for thought as you decide between the Ulupalakua red or passionfruit-sweetened Maui Blush. There's a *paniolo*-themed gift shop across the street at the **Ulupalakua Ranch Store & Deli ❶,** where you can get fresh ranch burgers for $6. *(Take Hwy. 37 south from Kula for 5 mi. past Grandma's Coffee in Keokea. The vineyards also make a refreshing stop on the way back from Hana via Hwy. 31. ☎878-6058; www.mauiwine.com. Open daily 9am-5pm. Free guided tours (30-40min.) at 10:30am, 1:30pm. Deli open 11am-1:30pm.)*

HALEAKALA NATIONAL PARK

The gradually sloping shield volcano of Haleakala ("house of the sun") dominates the island of Maui. Haleakala National Park encompasses the upper slopes of the volcano and stretches down to Kipahulu, on the southeast coast near Hana (see p. 233 for **Kipahulu** coverage). The extreme landscape of Haleakala is an incomparable sight that offers striking diversity; from the Kipahulu coast to Haleakala's 10,023 ft. summit, there are as many climate zones as there are between Central Mexico and Alaska. The National Park was originally established to preserve the unique and fragile ecosystems and species of the Haleakala summit area, and park rangers and resource managers today are still actively involved in the protection of the rare native Hawaiian species that live here. Perhaps the most impressive geological feature of Haleakala is the "crater" at the summit; geologists have since determined that the gigantic depression was actually formed by erosion instead of a volcanic explosion. Sunrise atop the volcano summit is a stunning event that has become a pilgrimage for visitors to the island. Above the cloud line, you can see the sun rise out of the ocean, illuminating the horizon with every color in the spectrum; it's the best free light show you'll ever see. The hikes from the top traverse varied terrain, and can be modified to suit both the casual day-hiker and the camping trekker. The switchback road that runs from the crater moonscapes down through subalpine shrubland, cloud forest, rolling pasturelands, and intensely fragrant eucalyptus groves provides the most spectacular of all scenic drives, and leaves visitors humbled by the lonely majesty of the mountain.

AT A GLANCE: HALEAKALA NATIONAL PARK

AREA: 30,183 acres.

FEATURES: Haleakala Volcano, Kipahulu Valley, Ohe'o Gulch (p. 233).

HIGHLIGHTS: Hiking the huge crater at Haleakala's summit; observing endangered wildlife such as the silversword plant and nene goose in their natural habitat.

GATEWAY TOWNS: Kipahulu, p. 233; Kahului, p. 182; Kihei, p. 191; Kula, p. 235.

CAMPING: Camping is available at 2 drive-in campgrounds, 2 wilderness campgrounds, and 3 wilderness cabins. Camping is free but requires a permit, which is issued at Park Headquarters on a first-come, first-served basis. Permits are good for a max. of 3 nights per month, with no more than 2 nights at any given site.

FEES: Entrance fee $10 per vehicle, good for 7 days. No reservations required.

MAUI

🔢 PRACTICAL INFORMATION

Information: Haleakala National Park, P.O. Box 369, Makawao, 96768. ☎572-4400; www.nps.gov/hale.

Open: The park is open 24hr. daily. The road may be closed in extreme weather.

Fees, Permits, and Regulations: The entrance fee is $10 per vehicle, good for 7 days at both entrances to the park (the other entrance is in Kipahulu, south of Hana). There is a $5 fee for walkers, cyclists, or motorcyclists. Permits are required for camping at wilderness sites (not accessible by road), and can be picked up at Park Headquarters. Camping permits, good for a max. of 3 nights per month, with no more than 2 nights at any site, are free and issued on a 1st come, 1st served basis. Hunting, firearms, in-line skates, and skateboards are prohibited in the park. Pets and bikes are not allowed on trails. Do not pick flora or feed fauna in the park. Hikers must stay on marked trails to prevent erosion and preserve the fragile ecosystem.

Driving: From Kahului, take Rte. 37 to Rte. 377 to Rte. 378 (Haleakala Crater Rd.). Allow at least 2hr. from Kihei and 2½hr. from Ka'anapali and Napili to reach the summit. It takes a good ¾-1hr. to ascend the final 22 mi. once you turn onto Rte. 378. Plan appropriately if you want to see the **sunrise;** check sunrise times and weather conditions by calling ☎877-5111 before driving up, and remember that the first light hits about 30min. before the actual sunrise. Once you enter the park, the road is a series of steep **switchbacks;** take your time and watch for bikers, cattle, and other hazards. Stop at overlooks instead of trying to see everything from behind the wheel. On the way down, **switch to a lower gear** instead of riding your brakes to prevent brake overheating and failure. Slower vehicles must use pull-outs to let cars by; **do not attempt to pass cars.**

Weather: Weather conditions at the summit are extreme and can change rapidly. Strong winds, intense sunlight, and variable clouds make forecasts impossible; remember that current weather conditions are no guarantee for the next hour. If you are going for the sunrise, be prepared for cold (30-50°F); wear layers and bring blankets. If you are hiking, prepare for hot, cold, wet, and windy conditions. Sunscreen and water are essential. Call ☎877-5111 for current weather conditions and time of sunrise and sunset, or check http://banana.ifa.hawaii.edu/crater/.

Emergency: Visitors are responsible for their own safety in the park. There is a public phone in front of Park Headquarters at 7000 ft. The nearest hospital is 2hr. away, and in bad weather, helicopter rescues can be difficult or impossible.

Facilities: There are three **Visitor Centers** in the park. **Park Headquarters** at 7000 ft. issues camping and cabin permits and has phones, restrooms, maps, books, and information on the park. (Open daily 8am-4pm.) The **Haleakala Visitor Center** at 9740 ft. has portable restrooms, geological and environmental displays, a glassed-in overlook of the crater, and a helpful staff that dispenses hiking maps and information about the park. (Open daily in summer 6am-3pm, in winter 6:30am-3pm.) **Kipahulu** also has a Visitor Center and public phones. (Open daily 9am-5pm.) There is **no food or gas** in the park, so come prepared. There is **no water** in Kipahulu, and water from the sources in the Wilderness Area must be boiled or treated before drinking.

Guided hikes and events: 10-20min. talks on natural and cultural history are held at the Summit building daily at 9:30, 10:30, 11:30am. Park rangers lead 2 guided hikes. The Waikamoi Cloud Forest Hike meets M and Th at 9am at the Hosmer Grove shelter. The 3hr., 3 mi. hike is moderately strenuous, with a 500 ft. ascent/descent. The Sliding Sands Cinder Desert Hike meets Tu and F at 9am at the trailhead in the Visitor Center parking lot. The 2hr., 2 mi. hike is moderately strenuous with a 420 ft. descent/ascent.

Activities: Dozens of independent companies offer activities in the park, including biking down the volcano and horseback-riding in the crater. Rangers in the park report numerous serious injuries associated with the bike tours and do not endorse any of the companies. Bike tours range from about $50-80 per person, depending on the company and the time of day. Companies that run tours include: **Cruiser Phil's** (☎893-2332); **Maui Downhill** (☎877-8787); **Maui Mountain Cruisers** (☎871-6014); **Mountain Riders** (☎877-4944); **Maui Sunriders** (☎579-8970); and **Upcountry Cycles** (☎573-2888). Tours generally include hotel pick-up, breakfast, thermal suits, helmets, and equipment.

⛺ CAMPING AND CABINS

Overnight facilities in the park include two drive-in campgrounds, two wilderness campgrounds, and three wilderness cabins. The two drive-in campgrounds do not require permits; permits are required at the wilderness campgrounds and cabins and are issued on the day of the hike (8am-3pm) at **Park Headquarters.**

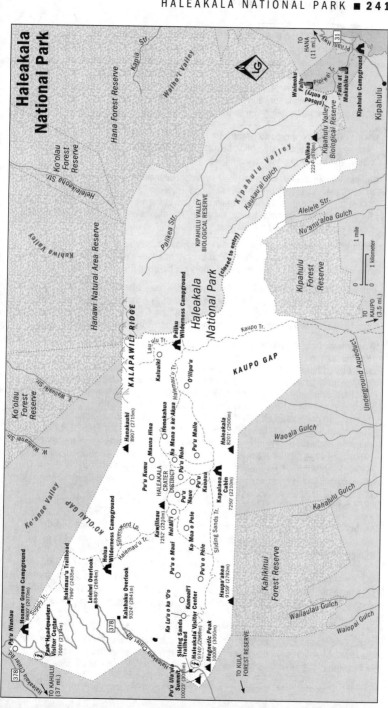

MAUI

Haleakala
National Park

Hana Forest Reserve

Ko'olau Forest Reserve

Waihou Str.

Kapia Str.

Waiho'i Valley

TO HANA (11 mi.) Hana Hwy 31

Waimoku Falls

Pipiwai Tr. (closed to entry)

Falls at Makahiku

Kipahulu Campground

Kipahulu

Kipahulu Valley Biological Reserve

Palikea 2224' (678m)

Kipahulu Valley

Keukau'ai Gulch

Alelele Str.

Nu'anu'aloa Gulch

Kipahulu Forest Reserve

Heleikeacha Str.

Kuhiwa Valley

Hanawi Natural Area Reserve

Palikea Str.

KIPAHULU VALLEY BIOLOGICAL RESERVE

(closed to entry)

Haleakala National Park

Paliku Wilderness Campground

TO KAUPO (3.5 mi.)

Underground Aqueduct

1 mile
1 kilometer
0

KALAPAWILI RIDGE

Lau'ulu Tr.

Kaluaiki

Kaupo Tr.

KAUPO GAP

Waoala Gulch

Ko'olau Forest Reserve

E. Wailuku Str.

W. Wailuku Str.

Ke'anae Valley

KO'OLAU GAP

Hanakauhi 8907' (2715m)

O'ili pu'u

Hana'u Tr.

Honokahua

Na Mana o ke'Akua

Pu'u Malie

Haleakala 8201' (2500m)

Mauna Hina

Pu'u Kumu

HALEAKALA CRATER DISTRICT

Pu'u Nole

Kahahulu Gulch

Holua Wilderness Campground

Halemau'u Tr.

Silversword Lp.

Kawilinau 7252' (2210m)

Halali'i

Pu'u Naue

Pu'u Kauaua

Kapalaoa Cabin 7250' (2210m)

Sliding Sands Tr.

Pu'u Nianiau

Hosmer Grove Campground 6800' (2073m)

Park Headquarters Visitor Center 7000' (2134m)

Supply Tr.

Halemau'u Trailhead 7990' (2435m)

Leleiwi Overlook 8840' (2694m)

Kalahaku Overlook 9324' (2841m)

Pu'u o Maui

Ka Moa o Pele

Pu'u o Pele

Ka Lu'u o ka 'O'o

Kamoali'i

Magnetic Peak 10008' (3050m)

Haupa'akea 9159' (2792m)

Kahikinui Forest Reserve

Wailaulau Gulch

Waiopai Gulch

TO KAHULUI (37 mi.)

378

Pu'u Ula'ula Summit 10023' (3055m)

Sliding Sands Trailhead

Haleakala Visitor Center

Haleakala Crater Rd.

378

TO KULA FOREST RESERVE

ALTITUDE SICKNESS. The summit of Haleakala is over 10,000 ft. in elevation. Hiking at high altitudes can cause shortness of breath, headaches, dizziness, nausea, and dehydration. Take it slow, drink plenty of water, and go back down if you have serious symptoms. Pregnant women, young children, and those with respiratory and heart conditions should consult with a doctor before traveling to high altitudes.

Hosmer Grove Campground. Near Park Headquarters at 6800 ft. Accessible to cars. Tables, grills, potable water, and chemical toilets available. Conditions are often cool, windy, and rainy. No permit required.

Kipahulu Campground. A 40min. drive south of Hana on the coast, Kipahulu is located at 20 ft. elevation, 15 mi. beyond Waianapanapa State Park, Kipahulu is not connected to the rest of the park by hiking trails or roads through the park. Accessible to cars. Tables, grills, and chemical toilets. No water. Conditions are often warm and wet with lots of mosquitoes. No permit required.

Holua Wilderness Campground. Holua is the most accessible of the wilderness sites, a 4 mi. hike down the Halemau'u Trail, at the top of Ko'olau Gap. Pit toilets and limited non-potable water (boil or treat before drinking). No open fires. Permit required.

Paliku Wilderness Campground. Located at the base of a rainforest cliff, Paliku is accessible via a strenuous 10 mi. hike up either Sliding Sands or Halemau'u Trail. It is the last campsite before the descent into the Kaupo Gap. Pit toilets and limited non-potable water (boil or treat before drinking). No open fires. Permit required.

Wilderness Cabins. There are primitive cabins at Holua and Paliku, as well as at Kapalaoa, 6 mi. down the Sliding Sands Trail in the cindercone desert. Each cabin has a wood burning stove, cooking utensils and dishes, 12 padded bunks, pit toilets, limited non-potable water and firewood. No electricity. Cabin reservations are awarded by monthly lottery. Applications must be submitted in writing 3-12 mo. prior to requested date. No phone or fax requests accepted. A waiting list is not maintained; you are contacted only if you have been awarded a reservation. Calls regarding vacancies and cancellations are accepted daily 1-3pm (☎572-9306). Full payment must be received 3 wk. prior to stay or your reservation will be cancelled. Cabins $40 per night for groups of 1-6; $80 per night for groups of 7-12. Mail applications to: Haleakala National Park, P.O. Box 369, Makawao 96768.

HALEAKALA FLORA AND FAUNA

The extreme conditions on Haleakala make the diversity of life there even more incredible. The rare **ahinahina,** or silversword plant, is endemic to the volcanic uplands of Maui and the Big Island of Hawaii. Its silvery spines grow for 30-50 yr., then blossom once with hundreds of purplish blooms, after which the plants shrivel and die. If you don't want to hike 10 mi. to the **Silversword Loop** on the valley floor, just stop at the **Kalahaku Overlook,** off the main road at 9324 ft., where the plants grow near the paved path. **Silver geraniums** are easy to identify along the Halemau'u Trail, with five-petaled white flowers blossoming in summer and early fall. Not too many creatures live in the summit lava fields, so the inch-long **black wolf spider** is at the top of the food chain. This spider carries its young on its back and hunts for food on the ground instead of building a web. The **nene** (the Hawaiian goose, and the State Bird), is nearly extinct, but occasionally makes an appearance in the park. Never feed a wild nene, or any fauna in the park. It is illegal to pick flowers or disturb plants in the park. So look, but don't touch!

HIKES

The drive to the summit, the overlooks along the road, and the summit itself give visitors a sense of the range of landscapes the park has to offer. However, to experience these landscapes more intimately, you must hike them. The park can challenge hikers of any level with trails of various lengths; some can be completed in an hour or two, while others take multiple days. There are two main trails from the summit area—**Halemau'u** and **Sliding Sands**—which connect on the crater floor.

HOSMER GROVE NATURE LOOP. (½ mi., 30min. Trailhead: Hosmer Grove Campground. Elevation change: 240 ft. Level: easy.) To reach this easy self-guided nature loop, which travels through 20th-century alien cloud forest and native Hawaiian subalpine shrubland, park at Hosmer Grove Campground (6880 ft.), near Park Headquarters. Brochures describing the flora and fauna on this ½ mi. nature walk are available at the trailhead.

HALEMAU'U TO VALLEY RIM. (2¼ mi. Trailhead: Halemau'u. Elevation change: 800 ft. Level: easy.) The first leg of the Halemau'u trail, to the valley rim and back, is a fairly level short hike. Follow the signs off Haleakala Crater Rd. for the Halemau'u trailhead (8000 ft.), 3½ mi. above Park Headquarters. The trail begins with a clearly defined path paved with rocks and gravel, and winds through an aeolian meadow, before suddenly opening to a mist-filled valley. About one mile in, you reach the rim of the vast crater, with its 300 ft. high reddish cindercones looking like mounds of sand. You can turn back here, or continue down the switchbacks to the valley floor (another 2 mi. and 1200 ft. elevation change).

SLIDING SANDS TO THE FIRST CINDERCONE. (5 mi. Trailhead: Haleakala Visitor Center. Elevation change: 2800 ft. Level: moderate/challenging.) Sliding Sands is a steep and windswept descent through the dramatic moonscape of the crater. The trailhead is at the bulletin board in the Visitor Center parking lot (9740 ft.). After the winding descent, the trail forks; the left fork leads to **Ka Lu'u O Ka 'O'O**, the first cindercone. Because of the altitude and steep grade, going out takes twice as long as going in, so pay attention to the time as you hike.

HALEMAU'U TO SILVERSWORD LOOP. (10 mi. Trailhead: Valley Rim. Elevation change: 2800 ft. Level: moderate/challenging.) Follow the directions for the first leg of the Halemau'u trail. After reaching the valley rim, continue down the series of switchbacks to the valley floor. About 4½ mi. past the Holua cabin, a spur trail loops around past a field of the rare *ahinahina* (silversword) plant. Again, plan on spending twice as long ascending the switchback trail as it took on the way down.

SLIDING SANDS TO HALEMAU'U TRAILHEAD. (11¼ mi. Trailhead: Haleakala Visitor's Center. Elevation change: 6000 ft. Level: moderate/challenging.) This combination allows you to experience the radically different terrain that both trails have to offer. After the steep descent to the crater floor (a little over 4 mi. from the Sliding Sands trailhead), you'll see the intersection with Halemau'u Trail, which leads off to the left. After another 2½ mi., you'll reach Holua cabin; from the cabin, it's a challenging 4mi. of switchbacks to the Halemau'u parking lot. The trailheads are 6 mi. apart on the steep Haleakala Crater Rd., so before hiking into the crater, stop at Park Headquarters and arrange a car drop or ride with other visitors.

KAUPO GAP. (18 mi. one-way. Trailhead: Haleakala Visitor Center. Level: challenging.) This 3-day hike traverses the crater floor and descends through the rainforest in the southern valley of the park. To do the Kaupo hike, request a brochure at the Visitor Center or Park Headquarters; you'll need to arrange a ride back unless you want to do the whole trek twice.

MAUI

PUKALANI

Pukalani is the most populated town in Maui's Upcountry, but it is primarily a residential community, and the interest it offers to travelers are the conveniences of its grocery stores, banks, and commercial plazas. For tourists staying in Kula or Makawao, Pukalani is a short drive to pick up basic necessities.

■ ⓲ **ORIENTATION AND PRACTICAL INFORMATION.** Pukalani rests along **Route 365** about 2 mi. south of Makawao and 6 mi. north of Kula on Rte. 37. From Kahului, take Rte. 37 (Haleakala Hwy.) for about 6 mi. If you're headed directly to Haleakala or Kula, take the Pukalani Bypass, which avoids the town center and offers a more direct route to these more popular destinations. **Pukalani Square** is located just north of the intersection of Rte. 365 and Rte. 37 on Makawao Ave. In this square, **Upcountry Medical Center,** 81 Makawao Ave. offers drop-in medical care. (☎572-9888. Open M-F 8am-5pm, Sa 9am-3pm.) Next door is **Paradise Pharmacy,** which also has a self-serve copy machine. (☎572-1266. Copies $0.15. Open M-F 9am-6pm, Sa 9am-4pm.) The square is also home to a **First Hawaiian Bank** (☎572-7238) with a 24hr. **ATM.** The **Pukalani Terrace Shopping Center** is located just south of the intersection of Rte. 365 and Rte. 37. Here you'll find a branch of **American Savings Bank** (☎572-7263; open M-F 9am-6pm, Sa 9am-1pm), **Upcountry Laundry & Dry Cleaning** (☎573-1818; open M-Sa 8am-9pm, Su 8am-5pm; wash $2, dry $0.25 per 5min.), and the **post office** (open M-F 9am-4pm, Sa 10am-noon). **Postal code:** 96768 or 96788 (P.O. boxes only).

▟ **FOOD.** Since dining options in Kula and the surrounding area are quite limited, a trip down to Pukalani might be a good idea. Pukalani is also a good food stop for hungry hikers heading down Haleakala Crater Rd. after a long day in the volcano. The aptly named **Cow Country Cafe ❷** 7 Aewa Pl., off Old Haleakala Hwy., is a cozy stop for a hearty breakfast or light lunch. Enjoy a traditional plate lunch ($8-12), burger ($7-8), or salad ($9) amidst the cow wallpaper, cow curtains, and flying cows hung from the ceiling fans. (☎572-2395. Open M-Sa 7am-2pm, Su 7am-1pm.) For cheap, filling plate lunches ($6-7), join hungry locals at **Mixed Plate ❶** in the Pukalani Terrace Shopping Center. (☎572-8258. Open daily 6am-1pm and F 4-8pm for dinner.) Also in the Terrace Shopping Center is a 24hr. **Foodland.** (☎572-0674.)

MAKAWAO

Makawao is the only real "town" in Upcountry, with shops, restaurants, and a discernible main street. The Western-style storefronts hint at Makawao's *paniolo* (cowboy) past, but aside from the annual Fourth of July rodeo, Makawao spends most of the year catering to tourists. In addition to store after store of "*aloha* wear," you'll find a plethora of galleries displaying locally-made arts and crafts. As one would expect from the heart of cow country, the steak here is prime. Casanova's is the only real nightclub around, featuring live music and nightly DJs.

■ ⓲ **ORIENTATION AND PRACTICAL INFORMATION**

The central district of historic Makawao is located where **Makawao Avenue** (which runs from **Pukalani** and Hwy. 37) intersects with **Baldwin Avenue** (which continues 7 mi. northwest to **Paia**). **Olinda Road** meanders upcountry from the end of Baldwin Ave. **Kaupakulua Road** continues north to **Haiku** from the end of Makawao Ave. and eventually connects with Hana Hwy. There's a **public parking lot** on Makawao Ave.; park here, and you'll be close enough to walk to all of Makawao's shops, galleries, and restaurants.

The public **library** is located at 1159 Makawao Ave., next to Down to Earth Natural Foods. (☎573-8785. Open M and W noon-8pm, Tu, Th, and Sa 9:30am-5pm.) For **Internet access** and **copy services**, head to **1 Stop Postal Shop** on Makawao Ave. between the post office and the library. (☎572-3088; fax 572-3671. Internet $0.15 per min. with a $2 min. Copies $0.10. Open M-F 8am-6pm, Sa 9:30am-3:30pm.) The **post office** is just south of town at 15 Makawao Ave. (Open M-F 8:30am-4:30pm, Sa 8:30-11am.) **Postal Code:** 96768.

▶ ACCOMMODATIONS

Makawao makes a convenient base for exploring Upcountry and the North Shore, although the charms of the town itself are limited to a good place to wake up with a cup of coffee, and perhaps an afternoon of shopping. The nearest beach is about a 15min. drive from town. There are no hotels in Makawao, but there are several B&Bs of varying quality just outside of town.

Hale Hoʻokipa Inn Makawao, 32 Pakani Pl. (☎877-572-6698 or 572-6698; www.maui-bed-and-breakfast.com), off Makawao Ave. a few blocks south of town. The host is an expert on local hikes and outdoor adventures. The bedrooms all have antique beds, painted wood floors, and private bathrooms with shower. Buffet breakfast. Check-in 3pm. Check-out 11:30am. Reserve with 50% deposit; balance due on arrival. Rooms $95-125; 2-room suite $145-155. $15 surcharge for 1-night stay. MC/V. ❸/❹

Wild Ginger Cottage, 355 Kaluanui Rd. (☎573-1173). Take Baldwin Ave. out of Makawao center toward Paʻia; ¼ mi. past the Hui Noʻeau Visual Arts Center, turn right onto Kaluanui Rd. Continue on Kaluanui for ¾ mi.; just over the bridge, turn left through the iron gates. Descend into the tropical jungle of Maliko Gulch to find this cozy studio cottage nestled among banyan trees and kahili ginger. Queen-sized bed, ceiling fan, TV, VCR, gas grill, private screened porch. 2-night min. Reserve with 50% deposit, balance due on arrival. Check-in 3pm. Check-out noon. $115 per night. ❹

Banyan Tree Vacation Rentals, 3265 Baldwin Ave. (☎572-9021; www.hawaii-mauirentals.com), ¾ mi. from Makawao town. The grounds of Banyan Tree Rentals are lush and luxurious, featuring a large outdoor swimming pool. Guests can also enjoy the hammocks and old-fashioned rope swings scattered on the property. The bungalows offer "a taste of Old Hawaii," and a bit of peeling paint only adds to the rustic quality of the place. Studio cottages $85-110; 3-bedroom, 3-bath plantation house with living room and full kitchen $300. No credit cards. ❸/❺

▶ FOOD

There are several good places for a light lunch on Baldwin Ave., in addition to heavier Mexican and steakhouse options for dinner. For more culinary selection, **Paʻia** (p. 220) is only a 10-15min. drive down Baldwin Ave. Natural foods store **Down to Earth** at 1169 Makawao Ave. (☎572-1488), next to the library, is open daily 8am-8pm for healthy groceries and salad. The modest **Komoda Store and Bakery ❶**, 3674 Baldwin Ave., is famous for their *malasadas* (Portuguese donuts), cream puffs, and freshly baked donuts. The bakery's large brown building is unmarked, so just follow the scent of fresh pastries. (☎572-7261. Open M-Tu and Th-F 7am-5pm, Sa 7am-2pm.) The **Rodeo General Store,** at 3661 Baldwin Ave., is an old-fashioned market stocked with basic groceries and super-cheap pre-packaged salads, sushi, and sandwiches. (☎572-1868. Open daily 6:30am-10pm.)

MAUI

CAFES AND RESTAURANTS

Cafe O'Lei, 3679 Baldwin Ave. (☎573-9065), tucked in the Paniolo Courtyard. With locations also in Wailuku, Lahaina, and Ma'alaea, the Cafe O'Lei restaurants have a highly favorable reputation among locals. Makawao's branch serves light lunch on a quaint outdoor patio, and uses the freshest local ingredients in the Foccaccia sandwiches (snowcrab and avocado $8) salads (taro (poi) and Molokai sweet potato on Kula greens $8). The daily specials are reliably delicious. Open M-Sa 11am-4pm. ❷

Casanova's Italian Deli, 1188 Makawao Ave. (☎572-0220), at the intersection of Baldwin Ave. Casanova's Deli has more reasonable prices than the full-scale Italian restaurant of the same name next door, but a similarly funky atmosphere. Mirror mosaics bedeck the walls, and there are a few wooden tables in the rear alcove where you can take your reasonably-priced counter-service sandwiches (baked eggplant and smoked mozzarella $5). Open M-Sa 7:30am-6pm, Su 8:30am-6pm. AmEx/MC/V. ❶

Polli's, 1202 Makawao Ave. (☎572-7808), at the intersection of Baldwin Ave. Polli's motto is "Come in and eat or we'll both starve." Polli's serves up heaping portions of Mexican dishes, all under $12. The setting is intimate, the staff is spunky, and the margaritas are free-flowing. Entrees are hearty, and homemade chips and salsa come with every meal. Anything on the menu can be modified for vegetarians. The bar in back is a local hangout, especially for Happy Hour (M-F 4-5:30pm) when domestic beers are $2.50 and margaritas are $3.50. Open daily 10am-10pm. D/MC/V. ❷

Duncan's Coffee Company & Rockin' Sushi, 3647 Baldwin Ave. (☎573-9075). Though the sushi bar is tiny, the fish is fresh and the rolls are reasonably priced ($5-6). Fresh brewed and bulk coffee, Lappert's ice cream, pastries, salads and sandwiches (grilled panini $6) are all available. Try a "Larry," "Curley," or "Moe" for breakfast. Open M-Th 6:30am-9pm, F-Sa 6:30am-10pm, Su 8:30am-9pm. AmEx/DC/MC/V. ❶

Cafe del Sol, 3620 Baldwin Ave. (☎572-4877), tucked in the plaza behind Maui Hands, next to Hot Island Glass. Creative egg breakfasts (Mediterranean frittata $7), fresh baked muffins and pastries, local greens, and sandwiches are served at the counter. Sandwiches are a bit pricey (roasted chicken salad on a croissant $8), but the atmosphere is relaxed and playful, with brightly painted walls bedecked with fanciful artwork. Shaded outdoor patio dining is removed from busy Baldwin Ave. Breakfast M-Sa 8-11am, Su 8am-1pm; lunch M-Sa 11am-5pm. DC/MC/V. ❶

Kitada's Kau Kau Corner (☎572-7241), on Baldwin Ave. in an older building across from Maui Hands gallery. Cheap local food for breakfast (M-Sa 6-11am) and lunch (until 1:30pm). Saimin $3.25. Sandwiches $2-4. Plates $4.25-5.50. ❶

Stopwatch Sports Bar & Grill, 1127 Makawao Ave. (☎572-1380). The "sport" in the name is due to their 3 TVs, but paintings of brightly-colored Hawaiian flora decorate the walls. A decent stop for a burger ($6-7) and a beer ($3.50-4.50), Stopwatch is a local favorite for its 2-for-1 dinner specials (W-Th 5-8:45pm) and large selection of homemade fruit and cream pies. Sample Maui-brewed beers on tap, like Kona Longboard and Firerock Pale Ale. Happy Hour daily 4-7pm. Open daily 11am-midnight. MC/V. ❶

🗂 SHOPPING

Crafts stores and artists' galleries line Baldwin Ave. Handmade wooden bowls, jewelry, paintings, and prints are well represented in the galleries; although they aren't cheap, you may find that unique souvenir you've been looking for.

Hui No'eau Visual Arts Center, 2841 Baldwin Ave. (☎572-6560; www.huinoeau.com), 1 mi. from Makawao center. This beautiful estate, a bit further out of town than the other galleries, eschews the ubiquitous "island art," offering 6 exhibits per yr. of work by contemporary local artists. Hui No'eau also sponsors visiting artists in residence, and offers classes and workshops in painting, photography, printmaking, and ceramics. The 1917 house and landscaped grounds, once part of the Baldwin estate, are worth a stroll. Open M-Sa 10am-4pm. Grounds and house free; donations accepted.

Randy Jay Braun Gallery, 1156 Makawao Ave. (☎573-1176; www.randyjaybraun.com). Braun's black and white photographs are subtly hand-colored, and his collection captures the *aloha* spirit of the island's faces and spaces. The gallery offers prints, cards, and posters that make good Maui souvenirs. Open M 11am-6pm, Tu-F 9am-6pm, Sa 10am-6pm, Su 10am-3pm. MC/V.

Maui Hands, 3620 Baldwin Ave. (☎572-5194; www.mauihands.com), in The Courtyard. Representing over 200 local artists, this gallery displays hand-crafted ceramics, glass, wood, and prints. Open M-Sa 10am-6pm, Su 10am-4pm. AmEx/MC/V.

Hot Island Glass, 3620 Baldwin Ave. (☎572-4527; www.hotislandglass.com), behind Maui Hands. Visitors come in droves to marvel as artist-owners Chris Lowry and Chris Richards blow their glass pieces at Maui's only hand-blown glass gallery (glass-blowing most days 10:30am-4pm). The artwork is reasonably priced, with bowls starting at around $60 and their trademark jellyfish for $300. Open daily 9am-5pm. AmEx/MC/V.

David Warren Gallery, 3625 Baldwin Ave. (☎572-1288; www.davidwarrengallery.com). This family-owned artistic showcase was Makawao's trend-setting first art gallery. It has since evolved into a family co-op that displays the works of the talented Warrens, including unusual and reasonably priced woodworking (Maui driftwood vase $25) and other crafts. Open M-Sa 10am-6pm, Su 10am-4pm. AmEx/D/MC/V.

⬛ NIGHTLIFE

Both **Polli's** and the **Stopwatch Sports Bar and Grill** (see above) have bars that attract a local crowd of devotees, but upscale Italian restaurant **▧Casanova's,** 1188 Makawao Ave., is the real pulse of Upcountry nightlife. Wednesday is ladies' night ("Wild Wahine Wednesday"), billed as the best late-night entertainment in Maui, and the place is packed by 10:30pm. By 11:30pm, people start dancing to the DJ-spun mainstream hip-hop. Fridays and Saturdays also attract a crowd for live bands starting at 10pm. Check the free local publication *Maui Time Weekly* for Casanova's entertainment schedule. (☎572-0220. $5 cover and 21+ after 10pm.)

HAIKU

The sleepy town of Haiku is as poetic as its name, and consists of little more than a few stores, small restaurants, and a post office. The sprawling lands around the town occupy a sizable chunk of land on the north side of Upcountry, spilling down to the North Shore along Hana Hwy. Frequent rain showers result in lush land, cool and humid air, and strikingly vivid rainbows. Torch ginger speckles the verdant landscape with flaming color, while plumeria and soft orange *puakenikeni* flowers infuse the air with heavy floral perfume. Staying in Haiku is a peaceful experience close to North Shore windsurfing beaches and on the road to Hana.

⬛ ORIENTATION. Hana Highway defines the northern edge of Haiku with Pa'ia to the west and Huelo to the east. **Haiku Road** loops inland from Hana Hwy., intersecting with **Kokomo Road, West Kuiaha Road,** and **East Kuiaha Road** before reconnecting with Hana Hwy. Kokomo, W. and E. Kuiaha Rd., and **Ulumalu Road** all run northwest to southeast from the Hwy. to **Kaupakulua Road,** which is the main road connecting **Makawao** to residential Haiku. Kaupakulua ends at Hana Hwy. just before **Twin Falls.** The Haiku town center is the intersection of Haiku Rd. and Kokomo Rd., where Haiku Rd. turns east. The only other orientation you might need to find your way around Haiku is to recognize **Five Corners,** the awkward intersection where Kaupakulua intersects with Ulumalu Rd. and several smaller roads.

⚐ PRACTICAL INFORMATION. Almost everything you'll need in Haiku is located in the Haiku Marketplace, 810 Haiku Rd., in the old cannery building, including the **medical clinic** (☎575-7531; open M-F 8am-noon and 2-6pm, Sa 8am-noon), **pharmacy** (☎575-7522; open M-F 9am-6:30pm, Sa 9am-noon) and **laundromat** (☎575-9274; wash $1.75). Even in the small town of Haiku, you can still get **Internet access; 1 Stop Postal Shop** in the Haiku Marketplace at 810 Haiku Rd. has four high-speed computers as well as self-serve copy machines. (☎572-2049. Internet $0.15 per min. with a $2 min. Copies $0.10. Open M-F 8am-6pm, Sa 9:30am-3:30pm.) The **post office** is located on Haiku Rd. in the town center. (Open M-F 8:30am-4:30pm, Sa 9-11am.) **Postal Code:** 96708.

TOW-IN SURFING AT JAWS Every year in late December or early January, there is a grand *Pohai na keiki nalu* ("gathering of the surf kids") to witness one of the greatest spectacles in the islands: tow-in big wave surfing at Jaws. When the waves are breaking just right off of a certain coastline below a pineapple field in Haiku, surfers have jet skis tow them into waves that can reach heights of 100 ft. from crest to trough (the average Jaws wave height measures 25-40 ft.). Surfers are strapped into their boards (a controversial technological shift that has changed the sport of surfing), allowing them to rip nasty tricks on their way down the wave—comparable to skiing down a mountain that is about to eat you. After the ride, the surfer holds his breath and waits for the jet ski to tow him to safety before the next wave breaks. Surfers train for years to do this, practicing holding onto heavy rocks below the surface to increase their lung capacity, which they'll need to survive the wave breaking above them. Lifeguards wait just outside the impact zone should they be needed—even though only the best of the best pros surf Jaws, it's still a death-defying act. News of when and where Jaws occurs spreads by word of mouth, so keep your ears open for a chance to see this crazy event. You can monitor the waves yourself at **www.mauiweathertoday.com,** which uses unclassified US Navy charts to monitor ocean activity.

⚐ ACCOMMODATIONS. There are a number of private homes that rent out cottages on their property. The cottages vary enormously in price and quality. Two of the finest cottages are found at ▧**Eagle's Nest ❷**, 2360 Umi Pl., perched at the top of Haiku Hill, with killer views of Ho'okipa and the North Shore below. The cottages themselves are private and impeccably crafted, with tiled floors, 18 ft. open beam ceilings, and full kitchens with granite countertops. Each has a work of art for a front door, sculpted by the artist-owner. (☎575-9041. 7-night min. stay or $65 cleaning fee for shorter stays. Reserve with $300 deposit; balance 30 days prior. two-bedroom cottage $135 per night, $15 each additional person. Studio cottage $75 per night. Monthly rates available.) Less dramatic, but a decent value, is the **Haiku Getaway Maui ❸**, 1765 Haiku Rd., located at the intersection of Haiku Rd. and W. Kuiaha in the low-lying (wet and humid) area of Haiku. The two studios and the two-bedroom cottage have full baths; the larger studio and the cottage both have a screened-in lanai and washer/dryer. All units have a full kitchen, gas grill, TV, VCR, and ceiling fan. (☎575-9362. 3-day min. for studios and 5-day min. for the cottage. Reserve with credit card. Studios $65-85, 2-bedroom cottage $99.)

The bright pink country home of **Ho'okipa Hale ❸** greets guests to its secluded location at 1350 Kauhikoa Rd., ¾ mi. from the intersection of Haiku Rd. The accommodations are basic and the location is a bit remote, but the price is right; guests have everything they need in either the private cottage, luxury suite, or standard rooms. Ho'okipa Hale's gracious hosts even provide beach chairs, boogie boards, and snorkel gear. Singles, couples, and families are all welcome, and there's no minimum stay. (☎575-9357; www.hookipa-hale.com. 50% deposit due 30 days before arrival. Dec.-Apr. standard single $40, luxury suite single $50, double $50; luxury double $60; cottage $90. May-Nov. standard single $35; luxury suite single $45, double $45; luxury double $55; cottage $90. MC/V.)

◨ **FOOD.** On the Kokomo Rd. side of the Haiku Marketplace, ▨**Colleen's Bake Shoppe and Cannery Pizza ❷**, 810 Haiku Rd., offers flaky pastries, hearty sandwiches ($6.50 with a fresh chocolate chip cookie), salads, and gourmet pizza ($9-19) like the Sweet Pea with ricotta cheese, roasted red peppers, green peas, and pesto. Hungry young locals flock here for the tasty food and casual atmosphere. (☎575-9211. Open daily 6am-9pm.) Another local favorite is **Pauwela Cafe ❶**, 375 W. Kuiaha Rd., off of Hana Hwy. in the Pauwela Cannery. Known for its fresh-brewed coffee and all-day breakfasts, Pauwela also serves tasty sandwiches and salads ($4-7). Combine a stop at the cafe with a showroom tour of ▨**Da Kine Hawaii,** the famous surfboard manufacturer next door. (☎575-2495. Open M-F 9am-1pm.) Tucked into the Haiku Town Center (the plaza next to the post office and across the street from the Haiku Marketplace), **Veg Out ❶**, 810 Kokomo Rd., caters to vegetarians and vegans with healthy, wholesome, and tasty stir-frys ($7), sandwiches ($3-5), tacos ($5), smoothies ($2.75), and juices ($3-4) served at the counter. The tiny restaurant has only six tables, usually filled. (☎575-5320; open M-F 10:30am-7:30pm, Sa 11:30am-6pm. MC/V.) **Hana Hou Cafe ❶**, at the Haiku Marketplace in a separate building from the main cannery, offers traditional Hawaiian plate lunches like pork *lau lau* or chicken long rice ($6.50-7.50) and a pleasant courtyard where diners can ignore the fact that they're really in the middle of a parking lot. (☎575-2661. Open daily 10am-10pm.) For a quick fish or chicken taco on the go ($3), hit up **Island Tacos ❶**, a makeshift food stand at the edge of the Haiku Marketplace parking lot. (Open daily 11am-4pm.) For grocery staples, visit the **Haiku Grocery Store** in the Haiku Cannery Marketplace (☎575-9291. Open daily 7am-9pm), or **Fukushima General Store** across the street. (☎575-2762. Open daily 6:30am-8pm.)

M A U I

MOLOKAI

If Oahu is heading toward the future, Molokai is proudly tied to the past. Amid Hawaii's many resorts and tourist traps, Molokai is the closest you can get to old Hawaii. Fishponds dating from the 17th century, several of which are still operational today, line the southern coast, and some residents choose to spend a portion of the year living in true Hawaiian fashion—at beach campsites. The island's population is over half Native Hawaiians, a percentage that is second only to Ni'ihau. Molokai is fighting to preserve its current state of non-modernization; there has been recent controversy over development plans and private residences that encroach upon traditional hunting grounds.

At one time, Molokai was respected and revered for its many powerful *kahunas* (priests), and visitors from all over made pilgrimages to the island to seek the priests' counsel. For a time, the island was free from armed conflict because it was considered sacred. Now Molokai retains little of its former influence, however, and the island is struggling. Jobs are scarce and unemployment, sometimes as high as 15%, rivals even the mainland's most depressed counties. Most recently, a drug problem and ongoing debate over whether to allow cruise ships to stop on Molokai have dominated local headlines (see **Cracking Down on Ice,** p.270).

Molokai's laid-back residents nonetheless maintain a positive outlook on life. The birthplace of both the *aloha* spirit and the hula, Molokai is known as "The Friendly Isle" for a reason. Drivers often smile and wave amiably at passersby, and you won't find a single stoplight here. The two-lane highway that stretches from one end of the island to the other is always traffic-free, although the slow pace of some of the island's 7000 inhabitants sometimes causes a bit of a backup. Nobody seems to mind, however, since there's no reason to be in a hurry. A sign that greets visitors at the airport says it all: "*Aloha!* Slow down: this is Molokai."

HIGHLIGHTS OF MOLOKAI

SET FOOT ON SACRED GROUND at the 'Ili'ili'opae Heiau, the second-largest traditional Hawaiian temple in the islands (p. 269).

GET BACK TO NATURE at the rugged Kamakou Preserve, home to 219 endemic plant and animal species (p. 262).

SOJOURN to the sobering former leper colony at Kalaupapa Peninsula (p. 259).

ROPE A STEER in *paniolo* lessons at the Molokai Ranch in Maunaloa (p. 274).

✈ INTERISLAND TRANSPORTATION

Molokai is most easily accessible by plane, though there is also a ferry service from Maui. All take major credit cards except Molokai Air Shuttle.

- **Molokai Air Shuttle,** 99 Mokuea Pl. in Honolulu (☎545-4988), along Lagoon Dr., just behind the airport. There is also an office at the Molokai airport (☎567-6847). By far the cheapest way to get to Molokai. From Honolulu, 6-10 flights daily ($40 each way). Also flies to the **Kalaupapa Peninsula** ($25 each way to and from the Molokai Airport; one-way $55, round-trip $90 from Honolulu). Offices open M-Sa 8am-5pm.

Molokai

PACIFIC OCEAN

Kalaupapa Airfield

Kalaupapa

Kalaupapa National Historical Park

Pali Tr.

Pala'au State Park

Molokai Museum

Ironwood Hills Golf Course

Burdy's Macadamia Nut Farm

Kualapu'u

Hoolehua

Kala'e

Kalae Hwy.

Maunaloa Hwy.

470

480

465

460

Farrington Ave.

Moomomi Ave.

Pu'u Peelua Ave.

Manunapu'u Rd.

Maunaloa Hwy.

Mo'omomi Beach

Kawaaloa Bay

Mo'omomi Preserve

460

Maunaloa Hwy.

Kamakou Rd.

Maunaloa

Kaluakoi Rd.

Kaunala Rd.

Kawakiu Beach

Make Horse Beach

Kepuhi Beach

Papohaku Beach

Dixie Maru Beach

Hale O Lono Harbor

Kalohi Channel

Molokai Forestry Reserve

Kamakou 4970' (1515m)

Pelekunu Valley

Pelekunu Valley Overlook

Waikolu Valley

Waikolu Lookout

Kamakou Preserve

Kaunakakai

Kaunakakai Wharf

450

One Ali'i Beach Park

Kawela

Kamehameha V Hwy.

Kakahai'a Beach Park

Kamalo

Kamalo Wharf

Uaalapue

Kalua'aha

Ili'ili'opae Heiau

Puko'o Harbor

450

Waialua Beach

Murphy's Beach

Rock Point

Moku Ho'oniki Island

Halawa

Halawa Bay

Pu'u O Hoku Ranch

Mo'oula Falls

Hipuapua Falls

Halawa Valley

Papalaua Valley

Kahiwa Falls

Pailolo Channel

MOLOKAI

4 miles

4 kilometers

0

0

Pacific Wings (☎888-575-4546; fax 873-7920). 3 flights daily from Honolulu and 1 from Kahului ($77 each way). Also flies to the **Kalaupapa Peninsula** for same rates.

Island Air, 99 Kapalulu Pl., on Lagoon Drive behind the airport in Honolulu (☎800-323-3345; www.islandair.com). From Honolulu (8 flights daily) or Maui (2 flights daily) from one-way $82, round-trip $184. 5% discount for Internet bookings.

Paragon Air (☎800-428-1231 or 244-3356), a charter-only company that flies to **Molokai** and **Kalaupapa** from Honolulu and Maui (one-way $65-72, round-trip $98-110), and also offers **air tours** of Molokai. Rates vary, depending on duration of flight.

The Molokai Princess (☎661-8397 or 667-6165; www.molokaiferry.com) runs between the **Molokai Wharf** and **Lahaina,** Maui. (90min.; departs Maui 5:15pm daily, and 6:30am M, W, F, Sa. Departs Molokai M-Sa 5:45am; M, W, F, Sa 2:30pm; Su 3:30pm. one-way $40, children $20.)

⨍ LOCAL TRANSPORTATION

Once on the island, renting a car is an absolute necessity, as there is no public transportation. There is a single highway that stretches east-west from one side of the island to the other, making Molokai easy to navigate.

Budget has an office in the Molokai Airport (☎800-527-0700 or 567-6877; www.budget.com), as does **Dollar** (☎567-6156). Both offices are open daily 6am-7pm. Check for Internet specials. **Island Kine Auto Rental** (☎553-5242; www.molo-kai-car-rental.com), a local outfit if ever there was one, rents cars, trucks, vans, and 4x4s from their lot on Ala Malama Ave., east of town. Telephone and web rentals $40-66 per day. **Molokai Rentals and Tours** (☎800-553-9071 or 553-5663) rents cars, jeeps, and 4x4s ($30-150). All rental agencies accept AmEx/D/MC/V. Also try **Molokai Outdoors** for car and moped rentals, as well as **shuttle** service from the airport (☎553-4477). **Taxis** are astronomically expensive but available when flights are running—usually early morning to 9pm—from **Molokai Off-Road Tours & Taxi** (☎553-3369 or 552-2218), just outside of Kaunakakai, or in the Kaluakoi area.

No rental cars, including 4x4s, are technically permitted off paved roads by any rental car companies, but the rule is rarely enforced (or announced, for that matter). Even in a 4x4, never drive off-road in the rain; you *will* get stuck.

Gas prices in Molokai are often substantially higher than on Oahu or Maui. Always drive with your fuel level in mind, as there are only 3 gas stations on the island, none of which are east of Kaunakakai or near the airport. If you need assistance, call one of the full-service stations in Kaunakakai. Shirley Rawlins's Chevron, 20 Maunaola Hwy. (☎553-5580), is open daily from 6:30am-8:30pm. Kalama's Gas Station, 53 Ala Malama Ave. (☎553-5586), is usually a few cents cheaper. Open M-Th 6:30am-8pm, F-Sa 6am-9pm, Su 7am-6pm.

⌘ ACCOMMODATIONS AND CAMPING

Molokai isn't an easy place to find budget accommodations, especially if you're traveling solo. There is no hostel, and most of the less expensive options are condos or beach houses better suited for couples and large groups. Couples can find great deals at the various **B&Bs** on the island; try them before staying at a hotel or renting a condo. For a list of nearly all the accommodations available, including a large number of properties leased directly by their owners, pick up an **Accommodations Directory** at the **Molokai Visitors' Association,** 28 Kamoi St. in Kaunakakai.

Also consider paying a visit to the web site of **Swenson Real Estate,** located at the intersection of Hwy. 460 and 470, which rents houses, condos, and cottages for $75-600 per night. Most two- or three-bedroom houses go for $100-125. (☎800-553-3648; www.island-realestate.com. Open M-F 9am-4:30pm. AmEx/MC/V.) **Friendly Island Realty** leases dozens of properties all over the island, from studio apart-

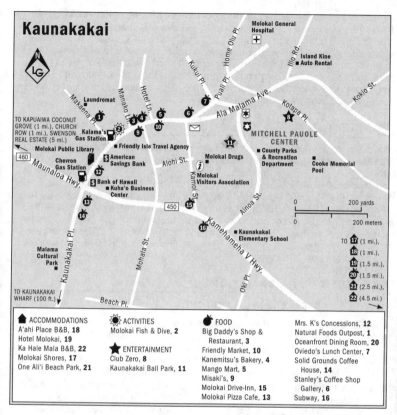

Kaunakakai

TO KAPUAIWA COCONUT GROVE (1 mi.), CHURCH ROW (1 mi.), SWENSON REAL ESTATE (5 mi.)

Molokai Public Library

Chevron Gas Station

Maunaloa Hwy.

460

Malama Cultural Park

Kaunakakai Pl.

TO KAUNAKAKAI WHARF (100 ft.)

Beach Pl.

Makaena Pl.

Manako Ln.

Hotel Ln.

Laundromat

Kalama's Gas Station

Friendly Isle Travel Agency

American Savings Bank

Bank of Hawaii
Kuha'o Business Center

Alohi St.

Mohala St.

Kukui Pl.

Puali Pl.

Home Olu Pl.

Molokai General Hospital

Ala Malama Ave.

Molokai Drugs

Kamoi St.

Molokai Visitors Association

450

Kamehameha V Hwy.

Ilio Rd.

Island Kine Auto Rental

Kolapa Pl.

Kokio St.

MITCHELL PAULE CENTER

County Parks & Recreation Department

Cooke Memorial Pool

Ainoa St.

■ Kaunakakai Elementary School

Oki Pl.

0   200 yards
0   200 meters

TO 17 (1 mi.),
18 (1 mi.),
19 (1.5 mi.),
20 (1.5 mi.),
21 (2.5 mi.),
22 (4.5 mi.)

🏠 ACCOMMODATIONS
A'ahi Place B&B, **18**
Hotel Molokai, **19**
Ka Hale Mala B&B, **22**
Molokai Shores, **17**
One Ali'i Beach Park, **21**

☀ ACTIVITIES
Molokai Fish & Dive, **2**

⭐ ENTERTAINMENT
Club Zero, **8**
Kaunakakai Ball Park, **11**

🍴 FOOD
Big Daddy's Shop & Restaurant, **3**
Friendly Market, **10**
Kanemitsu's Bakery, **4**
Mango Mart, **5**
Misaki's, **9**
Molokai Drive-Inn, **15**
Molokai Pizza Cafe, **13**

Mrs. K's Concessions, **12**
Natural Foods Outpost, **1**
Oceanfront Dining Room, **20**
Oviedo's Lunch Center, **7**
Solid Grounds Coffee House, **14**
Stanley's Coffee Shop Gallery, **6**
Subway, **16**

MOLOKAI

ments ($65-90) to one-bedroom condos ($75-125) to full beach houses ($75-125). Check the web site for photos and more information. (☎800-600-4158 or 553-3666; www.molokairesorts.com. Office open M-F 8am-5:30pm, Sa 8am-3pm.)

In addition, Molokai has several excellent campgrounds. Four campgrounds require permits. For county campgrounds One Ali'i and Papohaku Beach, contact the **Department of Parks and Recreation,** 90 Aiona St., in the Mitchell Pauole Center in Kaunakakai. (☎553-3204. Office open M-F 8am-4pm.) For Pala'au State Park, call the **State Parks Office** (☎984-8109; open M-F 8am-4:30pm) or drop by the caretaker's office at the entrance to the park. (Open daily 9am-3pm.) Permits are $5 per group per night, up to 10 in a group, five-night max. stay. To camp at the Waikolu Lookout in the Molokai Forest Reserve, contact the **Division of Forestry and Wildlife** (☎984-8100; office open M-F 8am-4:30pm; 2 night max. stay. 1 week advance noticed required), or write to them at 54 South High St., Room 101, Wailuku, HI, 96793. It's best to check with individual landowners to make sure camping is permitted in any place other than the four listed above.

KAUNAKAKAI

Kaunakakai is truly the center of Molokai, both geographically and culturally. Located on the south shore about halfway between the east and west end of the island, Kaunakakai is home to almost all of Molokai's grocery stores, shops, and nightlife, as well as its government offices, police, hospital, and banks. The slow pace of traffic along Ala Malama Ave., the main drag, might at first frustrate travelers in a rush, but after adjusting to Molokai's laid-back lifestyle, those same travelers will appreciate the rustic charm of this old-fashioned town. It takes less than an hour to walk all of Kaunakakai's paved roads, and after 9pm on any given night, you may have them all to yourself. Almost every visitor to the island is sure to stop in Kaunakakai at least once; don't rush—there's more here than meets the eye.

ORIENTATION

The heart of Kaunakakai is the intersection of **Route 460 (Maunaloa Highway)** and **Ala Malama Avenue.** There's a **Chevron** station in the northwest corner of the intersection, and both of the town's banks are located on the northeast side in the **Molokai Center,** a business complex that stretches north along the first block of Ala Malama. At the end of the block, Ala Malama turns east for another three blocks, the area where most of the town's businesses are located. The highway continues east about a block below Ala Malama, but its name changes to **Route 450 (Kamehameha V)** as it leaves town. The easiest way to navigate is by the highway mi. markers, which begin at mi. 0 in Kaunakakai, and ascend in both directions.

PRACTICAL INFORMATION

TOURIST AND FINANCIAL SERVICES

Tourist Office: The **Molokai Visitors' Association,** 28 Kamoi St. (☎808-553-5221 or 800-800-6367, www.molokai-hawaii.com), in the Kamoi Professional Center (½ block north of the highway), dispenses useful information on private accommodations, but offers little firsthand knowledge of the island. Also the place to pick up brochures for the majority of the island's accommodations and attractions. Open M-F 8am-4:30pm.

Banks and ATMs: Bank of Hawaii, 20B Ala Malama Ave. (☎888-643-3888), and **American Savings Bank,** 40 Ala Malama Ave. (☎553-8391), in the Molokai Center on the right side of the street as you turn onto it from the main highway. Both banks open M-Th 8:30am-4pm, F 8:30am-6pm. **24 hr. ATMs** are out front.

LOCAL SERVICES

Library: The small **Molokai Public Library,** 15 Ala Malama Ave. (☎553-1765), in the Civic Center has knowledgeable staff, plenty of books about Molokai and Hawaii, and 3 computers with **Internet access.** $10 for a 3 mo. pass to all of Hawaii's public libraries. Open M and W 12:30-8pm, Tu, Th, F 10am-5pm.

Internet: In addition to the library and the island's only Internet cafe (slated to open in late summer 2003, see p. 257), a few of the local schools have computer labs with Internet connections and scheduled time for public use. Schedules fluctuate, but in general, the **Kaunakakai Elementary School** (☎553-1730), located in town, and the **Kilohana Elementary School** (☎558-2200), located past mi. marker 13 on Kamehameha Hwy., have afternoon and evening hours during which their computer labs are available for public use. Furthermore, the **Kuha'o Business Center,** located in the green building on the north side of Kamehameha Hwy. just east of Ala Malama, has a pair of computers with Internet connections that are available M-F 9am-4pm.

Laundry: A public laundromat is located just off Ala Malama on Makaena Pl., behind the Natural Foods Outpost. Wash $1, dry $0.25. Quarters only, change and detergent sold at the gas station 2 stores down. Open daily 7am-9pm.

Recreation Center: The **Mitchell Pauole Center,** on Ainoa St., next to the police station, ½ block south of Ala Malama, is home to most of the town's recreation facilities, all of which are open to the public free of charge. The Cooke Memorial Pool (☎553-5775 or 553-3204) is open in the summer M-W and F-Sa approximately 8am-4:30pm, and Th and Su 1-4:30pm. Winter hours vary. The gymnasium (☎553-5141) is open for basketball M-F 11am-3pm, Sa 10am-3pm, and has a weight room open M-F 8am-9pm. Tennis courts, a skateboarding park, and baseball fields are also available for use.

EMERGENCY AND COMMUNICATIONS

Emergency: ☎911.

Police: 110 Ainoa St. (☎553-5355), between the Mitchell Pauole Center and the fire department, just off Ala Malama.

Pharmacy: Molokai Drugs, 28 Kamoi St. #100 (☎553-5790), in the Kamoi Professional Center. **Wheelchair rental** $9 per day. $10-14 to process 35mm **film.** Souvenirs, toiletries, and even a few office supplies. Open M-Sa 8:45am-5:45pm.

Hospital: Molokai General Hospital, 205A Puali Pl. (☎553-5331). Located at the end of Puali Place, just 3-4 blocks north of Ala Malama; blue signs indicate the way from Ala Malama on the eastern end of downtown. 24hr. emergency room.

Post Office: 120 Ala Malama Ave. Open M-F 9am-4:30pm, Sa 9-11am.

Postal Code: 96748.

▌ ACCOMMODATIONS AND CAMPING

Although there are few, if any, accommodations within a walk of downtown Kaunakakai, the first 5 mi. to the east of town along Hwy. 450 host a wide range of quality accommodations, including hotels, condos, B&Bs, and campgrounds.

▨ **Ka Hale Mala Bed & Breakfast,** 7 Kamakana Pl. (☎553-9009; www.molokai-bnb.com), about 5 mi. east of town along Hwy. 450, and then left on Kamakana Pl., near the end of the small cul-de-sac. One of Molokai's nicest B&Bs, occupying the 1st floor of a beautiful private residence. Spacious suite has a master bedroom, a dining room with a full kitchen, a living room that can sleep 2, and a lanai. Amiable owners are knowledgeable about the island and are happy to share their expertise with you over breakfast. Beach and outdoor equipment are free for guests to borrow. Breakfast additional $5 per guest. Suite $70 (1-2 guests); each additional person (including children) $15. ❸

Hotel Molokai (☎553-5347; fax 553-5047), just before the 2 mi. marker east of town. Hotel Molokai's status as a center of community nightlife is what sets it apart from other area lodgings. The hotel's "Polynesian-style accommodations" are tucked away among a handful of separate 2-story buildings that feature lots of bamboo architecture. The rooms all have phones, lanais, TV, and laundry access, and the higher-end rooms have ceiling fans, cable TV, refrigerators, and kitchenettes. The restaurant and bar (see p. 258) is located poolside, just steps from the ocean. Frequent live entertainment at the bar and the presence of **Molokai Outdoors,** one of the island's biggest outdoor activities centers (see p. 257), in the hotel. Rooms $85-140. AmEx/D/MC/V. ❸

Molokai Shores (☎553-5954 or 800-535-0085; www.marcresorts.com), about 1½ mi. east of town on Kamehameha Hwy. These roomy condos, most with ocean views, are a good value when the expensive rack rates are discounted; all have full kitchens, patios, cable TV, ceiling fans, and access to swimming pool and laundry facilities. Some rooms have phones; local calls are free. Frequent discounts can even give walk-in guests 1-bedroom rates in the $90-100 range. Office open M-F 8am-4pm, weekends 8am-1pm. 1-bedroom (1-4 people) $155; 2-bedroom (up to 6) $199. AmEx/D/MC/V. ❺

MOLOKAI

A'ahi Place Bed & Breakfast, 215 A'ahi Place (☎553-8033, www.molokai.com/aahi), located about 1½ mi. east of town, 1 block east of Molokai Shores, at the very end of A'ahi Place, which branches steeply uphill off the main highway to the north for about ½ mi. before it ends. A'ahi Place B&B boasts 3 separate, unique accommodations. The main cottage is a beautiful, 1-bedroom building, with living room, full kitchen, 2 double beds, laundry, and A/C. No TV or phone. A'ahi Place also offers about the cheapest room on the island: a trailer with a bed, 2 chairs, a small table, bathroom, and perhaps a cockroach or two. The trailer can be a decent place for the solo traveler to sleep and get a hot shower. Occasionally a room in the main house, is available to rent. All guests have access to the kitchenette, washing machine, BBQ, and TV on the porch, and are free to borrow outdoor equipment. Owner offers discounts for longer stays and advice about island activities. Breakfast available for extra fee. Reserve cottage online, months in advance; call for other availability. Trailer $35; cottage $75; main house $125. ❷

One Ali'i Beach Park, just past the 3 mi. marker on the *makai* (ocean) side of Kamehameha Hwy. There are actually 2 parks located here, One Ali'i I and One Ali'i II (pronounced oh-neh ah-lee-ee), located adjacent to each other (the eastern lot is I, the western lot is II). One Ali'i I is the best place to camp, featuring a large concrete pavilion equipped with picnic tables, working lights, electrical outlets, restrooms, and showers. One Ali'i II is slightly smaller, and only has a small building with restrooms, but also features a sand volleyball court (bring your own net). The ocean is unappealing for swimming along the shoreline of both parks. Friendly locals often rent out the pavilions on weekends for parties and *luaus*. 3-night max. stay. Camping permits required. $3 per night per camper. See **Accommodations and Camping,** p. 252. ❶

FOOD

GROCERY STORES AND MARKETS

Friendly Market, 90 Ala Malama Ave. (☎553-5821 or 553-5595). The largest grocery store on the island is well-stocked and lives up to its name. Open M-F 8:30am-8:30pm, Sa 8:30am-6:30pm. AmEx/MC/V.

Misaki's (☎553-5505), on the corner of Ala Malama and Mohala St. Slightly smaller than Friendly Market, but has a better selection of wine, and specials on beer. Deer heads and antlers on display. Open M-Sa 8:30am-8:30pm, Su 9am-noon. AmEx/MC/V.

Natural Foods Outpost, 70 Makaena Pl., (☎553-3377), just ½ block off Ala Malama, where it turns east. An organic grocery store with 100% local produce. Vegetables ($1) on sale inside, as well as burritos, burgers, and sandwiches ($3-6). Open M-Th 9am-6pm, F 9am-4pm, Su 10am-5pm. Sandwich shop open M-F 10am-3pm. AmEx/MC/V.

Mango Mart, 93 Ala Malama Ave. (☎553-8232). The closest thing to 1-stop shopping on Molokai. One side stocks health and beauty items, office supplies, electronics, housewares, souvenirs, and camping equipment. The other side carries food (including good bulk items like granola bars for camping) and rents DVDs. A renovated deli is expected to open in fall 2003. Open M-Sa 8am-8pm, Su 8am-6pm. MC/V.

RESTAURANTS

🖾 **Kanemitsu's Bakery,** (☎553-5855) in the center of Ala Malama Ave. A buzzing breakfast hang-out for locals who gather around the tables to gossip, Kanemitsu's sells Molokai French Bread, famous throughout the islands for its distinctive flavor and texture ($2.15 per loaf). Loaves of the next day's bread ($4.75) are sold fresh and hot out of the oven Tu-Su 10pm-2am, from the kitchen accessible via the alley to the right of the store, at a window marked "knock here." Open M and W-Su 5:30am-6:30pm. ❶

▨ **Oviedo's Lunch Corner** (☎553-5014), just past Sundown Deli on Puali Pl. 1 block from Ala Malama. Authentic Filipino food like crunchy roast pork and chicken papaya, or even pigs feet and tripe stew for the more adventurous. Lunch ($8) comes with rice and a main dish. Ice cream $2. Open daily 10:30am-5:30pm. ❷

Oceanfront Dining Room (☎553-5347, ext. 6103), is the restaurant at Hotel Molokai, about 2 mi. east of town. One of Molokai's nicest and most expensive restaurants. Casual during the day when breakfast and lunch are served; dinner is only a slightly fancier affair (slippahs are fine!), with steak and seafood entrees from $15-20. The highlight of the restaurant is the atmosphere; the dining room is a few feet from the ocean, offering spectacular views. F night is the time to go, when live poolside entertainment brings a healthy crowd of tourists and locals. Open daily 7:30am-9pm. AmEx/MC/V. ❹

Molokai Pizza Cafe (☎553-3288), on Kaunakakai Pl. (the wharf road) on the right end of the small shopping strip 1 block south of the hwy. Kaunakakai's family restaurant, serving a variety of foods in its diner-style interior, complete with $0.25 miniature rides. Medium-thick pizza, S/M/L cheese $8.50/11/13.30. Personal 6 in. pizza (the "Molo-kini") $5. Also serves subs ($8), burgers ($7-9), pasta ($7.60-10), BBQ ribs, fresh fish, and, on W, burritos and fajitas ($9). Free delivery to Hotel Molokai and Molokai Shores. Open M-Th 10am-10pm, F-Sa 10am-11pm, Su 11am-10pm. MC/V. ❷

Molokai Drive-Inn (☎553-5655), 15 Kamoi St., on the corner of the highway and Kamoi St. Fast-food island-style—no franchise, greasy, good, and dirt cheap. 2 eggs, meat, hash browns, and a drink $5. Waffles $3. Plate lunches $6.25-7. Hamburgers and tacos $2. Takeout is popular. Open Su-Th 6am-10pm, F-Sa 6:30am-10:30pm. ❶

Solid Grounds Coffee House, (☎553-9929) located on Kaunakakai Pl. (the wharf road) on the left end of the small shopping strip 1 block south of the highway (in the same building as Molokai Pizza Cafe). A small coffee shop attached to a Christian Bookstore, the recently-moved Solid Grounds Coffee House is a comfortable place to sip a coffee ($1) or a smoothie ($3.75). They also serve waffles ($1.25) and bagels ($2). Open M- F 5:30am-5pm, Sa 6am-2pm. ❶

Stanley's Coffee Shop Gallery (☎553-9966), 125 Puali Pl., just north of Ala Malama on the eastern end of town. Expected to open in late summer of 2003, Stanley's will lure customers with 3 attractions: coffee, art, and Internet access for a small fee. The coffee shop will also serve baked goods, hot dogs, and *saimin*. Local artists' work will be available for viewing and sale. Expected to be open M-Sa 6am-2pm. ❶

Mrs. K's Concessions (☎553-3201), in the Molokai Center, across from the library on Ala Malama Ave. A small burger joint that serves plate lunches ($6-7) and sandwiches ($3). Open M-F 5:30am-5:30pm, Sa 5:30am-2pm. ❶

Big Daddy's Shop and Restaurant (☎553-5841), in the middle of Ala Malama Ave. Part convenience store, part plate lunch dispensary ($6.50 for 2 choices), also selling shave ice ($2) and fresh *poke, shoyu,* and *limu ogo* sashimi salads by the pound. Store open M-Th 8am-10:30pm, F-Sa 8am-11pm, Su 8am-10pm. Food served daily 10am-4pm. ❶

Subway, 230 Kamehameha Hwy. (☎553-4432), on the east end of town, across the highway and slightly east of Kamoi St. The only chain restaurant on the island, notable because it's open late and on Su. Open Su-Th 8am-8pm, F-Sa 8am-9pm. ❶

🏊 ACTIVITIES

Molokai offers a range of outdoor activities—some of the most popular are hiking, kayaking, and snorkeling. There is surfing and golf on the island, too, but not as much as other Hawaiian islands. A few outfits near Kaunakakai offer rentals and guided trips of all kinds. **Molokai Outdoors,** located across from the front desk at Hotel Molokai (☎553-4477), is the island's best resource for information about everything outdoors, including trips to the Kalaupapa Peninsula (see p. 259), and hiking in Halawa Valley and the rainforest. Most rental equipment can be taken out for same-day, 24hr., and weekly rentals. 24hr. rentals include snorkeling gear ($10), kayaks ($30, $40 for 2), surfboards ($25-30), body boards ($8), and mopeds ($25). They also offer a few ½-day and full-day guided tours of the island ($80-141), if you want to see everything and you only have a short period of time. If there's something you want to do that they don't offer, they'll send you in the right direction. Open M-Sa 8am-5pm, Su 8am-4pm. Another place that offers tours and rentals is **Molokai Fish and Dive** (☎ 552-0184), who have a shop in town at 61 Ala Malama Ave. They rent snorkel gear, body and surf boards, kayaks, and offer tours and surfing lessons. For scuba diving, call **Bill Kapuni's Snorkel and Dive** (☎ 553-9867), for Molokai's divemaster, who leads multiple tours each day over the barrier reef.

👁 SIGHTS

About a mile or two west of town lies the **Kapuaiwa Coconut Grove**. The coconut grove, an 11-acre expanse of coconut trees gone wild on the south side of the highway, is the original stomping grounds of King Kamehameha V; he planted the trees in the 1860s to provide shade for visiting royalty as they bathed in the sea. It is one of the few remaining royal coconut groves in the state, and is currently being renovated as a campground by the Hawaiian Home Lands Department. A drive past the grounds will probably satisfy most avid coconut sightseers, but there is also room on the highway to pull over if one wishes to stroll the grounds. Please respect this historically significant site.

The Hawaiian Home Lands Department also grants land across the street from the coconut grove to any religious organization that has a sufficient percentage of Native Hawaiians in its congregation. The result is **Church Row,** a row of over half a dozen places of worship. Some are small, one-room operations, and others are larger and more modern. Locals from all over the island swarm to services on Sunday mornings, creating the island's only noticeable traffic.

Across the highway from Ala Malama Ave., the road becomes Kaunakakai Pl. and leads out to **Kaunakakai Wharf,** about ¼ mi. from the highway. The wharf offers great views along the shore and toward the mountains. About three quarters of the way out the wharf on the west side is a small area, with showers, where locals swim. The main activity on the wharf is still fishing; the **Molokai Ice House,** a fishermen's cooperative established in 1988, makes its home at the end of the wharf on the east side. The cooperative no longer acts as a restaurant and fish market, but sometimes fisherman sell their catch at the end of the wharf early in the morning or late in the afternoon, and plans are in the works to organize monthly fish fries.

During June and July, every other Saturday morning a raucous crowd gathers to watch **outrigger canoe races** and sip cold drinks from concession stands run by local canoe clubs. Molokai's four canoe clubs, each with members from ages 10 and older, begin training in the spring for their summer races.

Just before the wharf on the west side of Kaunakakai Place, a stone platform is all that remains of King Kamehameha V's vacation home. The area is designated **Malama Cultural Park,** and archaeologists believe it was once a *heiau* (temple).

🎵 ENTERTAINMENT

The best of Molokai nightlife is found Fridays at the **Kuhio Lounge,** the bar at Hotel Molokai. From 4 to 6pm, locals gather to play ukuleles and drums at the weekly jam, and there is informal singing and hula dancing as well. A live band usually comes on after the jam session and plays until the bar closes (around 10:30pm). If you're lucky, they might be serving complimentary *pupus*. The other six nights of the week, the Kuhio Lounge is usually open until 10pm, depending on the number of customers. The bar opens daily at 11:30am.

Next to the **Mitchell Pauole Center** at the intersection of Ala Malama Ave. and Ainoa St. is the **Kaunakakai Ball Park,** where the Molokai Farmers have a substantial home field advantage over all the competition (who fly in from Maui or Lanai). The locals take their Little League very seriously. Softball players can be seen taking batting practice many weeknights, and you can inquire about league schedules at the Mitchell Pauole Center. Basketball leagues also run in the nearby gym, where stands afford visitors a chance to catch a game.

For the under-21 crowd, **Club Zero,** a youth center in the Mitchell Pauole Center next to the pool, has pool tables, super couches, a 64 in. TV, video games, and cable. The club is part of a larger youth center which runs other area youth programs. Super-friendly staff welcome youth of all ages. (☎553-3675. Open M-Th 2-10pm, F 2-11:30pm, Sa 9am-midnight.)

On Saturday mornings, starting around 6am and lasting past noon, local merchants set up a **market** on the sidewalk in front of the Molokai Center on Ala Malama Ave. Originally fresh produce was the main draw, but recently many merchants have brought arts and crafts. Arrive early to get the fresh produce!

CENTRAL MOLOKAI

KALAUPAPA PENINSULA

Kalaupapa is a flat, leaf-shaped land formation on Molokai's northern shore. It is separated from "topside" (the rest of Molokai) by a 1000 ft. wall of mountains, and is accessible solely by air or a steep trail. The peninsula was created by a separate volcanic eruption (hence its geographic isolation from the rest of the island), and measures about 2½ mi. long (from the cliff to the point), and about 2 mi. wide. In the middle of the peninsula is Kauhako Crater, the center of the ancient eruption, and today an 800 ft. deep lake. Kalaupapa's beauty is rivaled only by its infamy— the area is home to a former leper colony that ceased operations in 1969. Many ex-patients still inhabit the peninsula. Kalaupapa's story is one of tragedy and selfless heroism, and a visit is deservedly among the most popular activities on the island.

KALAUPAPA'S STORY

The first documented case of **leprosy** in the Hawaiian Islands was in 1835. At the time little was known about the disease, apart from the fact that it was introduced by westerners. King Kamehameha V, however, knew enough to fear that leprosy could infect his people and destroy his kingdom. To prevent this, he chose the most isolated spot in all the islands, a cove called **Kalawao** on the southeastern part of the Kalaupapa peninsula, and starting in 1866, persons with any type of skin condition were banished there. Patients would be "diagnosed," rounded up with little or no notice, put on a ship, and literally dumped in the water near Kalawao, sometimes hundreds of yards offshore. Some drowned, others succumbed to hunger or exposure, but none returned. Until around 1890, when the main settlement moved from Kalawao to the drier and more hospitable village of Kalaupapa, death was so common that the colony was described by some as a "living cemetery."

By 1870, a few Christian missionaries had arrived to tend to the sick. The missionaries built grass huts for themselves, but most patients lived outdoors. Few missionaries remained on the peninsula for more than a few months until **Father**

Damien, or Joseph De Veuster, a Catholic priest from Belgium, arrived in 1873. In the same year, **Gerhard Hansen** isolated the bacteria that causes leprosy, and the disease came to be known as **Hansen's disease.**

Damien, originally sent to Kalaupapa for his carpentry skill, was scheduled to fix the roof of **St. Philomena Church** in one week, and then leave. When he saw the suffering of Kalaupapa's residents, he knew how badly he was needed, and decided to stay. Devoted to improving the lives of the residents, he built houses and dug graves by day, and at night he worked to finish and build an addition to the church. Though he never finished the church, he did build nearly 300 box-like houses, and, on average, dug about one grave per day. Until Damien arrived, residents hid themselves from outsiders and were ashamed to enter the church, as many had lost portions of their cheeks or mouth and feared they would desecrate the building with their saliva. Damien cut holes in the floor for these poor souls to discreetly spit through, and welcomed them into the church.

Damien was diagnosed with leprosy in 1883 and died in 1889, at the age of 49. Even without treatment, leprosy is among the least contagious of diseases. Of the over 1000 workers on the peninsula since 1870, Damien is the only documented case of infection. In 1995, Damien was beatified by Pope John Paul II and is now a candidate for sainthood. His native Belgium acquired Damien's remains in 1936, but his right hand was re-interred at St. Philomena Church in 1995.

Mother Marianne Cope, a Franciscan nun from New York, arrived during the last year of Damien's life and remained on the peninsula for nearly 30 more years. She acquired more supplies for the residents than any other missionary, and is known as the founder of the hospice movement. **Brother Dutton,** who came in 1886, carried on Damien's work for 44 years, building homes and finishing St. Philomena.

HULL HOUSE In the early 1800s, expanded international trade presented the *ali'i* (royalty) with tantalizing goods imported from lands as far away as Turkey. Merchant salesmen from the West, aware of the great demand for aromatic sandalwood in Asia, tempted the *ali'i* with offers of jewelry, firearms, and alcohol in exchange for the precious trees. The members of Hawaiian royalty couldn't resist, and they forced the *maka'ainana* (commoners) to cease their work in the *taro (poi)* fields and instead, to uproot the sandalwood forests. In order to measure the amount of wood that could be moved in any one voyage, a pit was dug in the approximate size and shape of the hull of a merchant vessel. The blood and sweat of the common folk furnished the royalty with expensive trinkets and toys, and allowed exploitative merchants to reap staggering profits from Asian sales of sandalwood. The *maka'ainana*, in turn, destroyed all new sandalwood saplings to prevent future generations from suffering a similar fate; but the island had already been forever robbed of its beautiful sandalwood trees.

In the 1940s, sulfa antibiotics were discovered to be an effective treatment for leprosy, and by the 1960s the disease was no longer considered contagious. However, the quarantine on Kalaupapa was not lifted until 1969. Until then, children born to residents were taken by the state and put up for adoption. After 1969, no new patients were admitted, and residents were free to leave, but many opted to stay rather than try to reintegrate themselves into families or start a new life.

During its years of operation, over 7000 people were sent to the Kalaupapa colony. From its peak of 1800 residents in 1970, there are fewer than 38 left today, and they range in age from 61-90. Residents get the mail and the newspaper daily; groceries and supplies are airlifted in twice each week, and larger items such as furniture and automobiles are brought in once a year on a barge. All the homes on the peninsula are owned by the state. The grounds, officially a National Historical Park, are maintained by Hawaii Parks Services.

 The only way to travel through the Kalaupapa Peninsula is as part of an organized tour. It is against state law to explore the peninsula on your own, and it is disrespectful to the area's residents.

TRANSPORTATION

There are three ways to get to Kalaupapa. You can hike down the strenuous but magnificent trail, you can fly to an airstrip on the far side of the peninsula, or you can ride a mule down the trail. All three require advance reservations.

BY FOOT. Hiking the 2¾ mi. **Pali trail** is by far the cheapest and most rewarding option, though the trail is hard on the knees and may be difficult for those not in decent physical condition. It descends over 1600 ft. along 26 numbered switchbacks until it finally reaches sea level and leads east for the final ¼ mi. to the end of the road, where tours begin. The trail begins just inside the Pala'au State Park. From town, take Hwy. 460 west, then turn right at Hwy. 470. The trail entrance is 15min. down the highway, just past the mule stables, on the right at a metal gate with a sign warning not to enter without a permit. Though the laws requiring permits are now defunct, you must have an advance reservation with **Damien Tours** (see p. 262), or else you will be turned away at the bottom of the trail.

If you plan to **hike,** be absolutely certain to start out *before* the mules depart at 8:30am to avoid the worst of their excrement on the way down (it is unavoidable on the way up, and make no mistake about it: droppings from previous days are a part of the trail). Bring plenty of **water.** The hike takes about 1¼hr., and allows for fabulous views of Kalaupapa. At the base of the trail, walk toward the settlement. You'll pass a black sand beach—one of the island's most dangerous—and as you enter an open area, notice the bleachers on the right that read, "wait here for tour."

BY AIR. If you prefer to **fly,** you will need to arrange both a flight and a tour reservation with Damien Tours (see p. 262), unless your airline explicitly states that they will handle the tour reservation. The prices listed here are for the flight only and do not include the tour. Consider hiking down and flying back, or vice versa, as the hike can be very enjoyable. **Molokai Air Shuttle** is the cheapest option. (☎545-4988. $25 each way to and from the Molokai Airport in Hoolehua; one-way $55, round-trip $90 from Honolulu. Offices open M-Sa 8am-5pm.) Other options include **Pacific Wings,** which flies from Honolulu (☎888-575-4546 or 873-0877; fax 873-7920; $65 each way), or **Paragon Air,** a charter-only company that services Kalaupapa from Honolulu and Maui and can combine the trip with an air tour of Molokai for an extra fee. (☎800-428-1231 or 244-3356; one-way $50-70, round-trip $89-110.)

BY MULE. The final option, the **mule ride,** differs from the preceding two in that the **Molokai Mule Ride** company (☎800-567-7550 or 567-6088; www.muleride.com.) includes both lunch and a tour in the price ($150 per person). Up to 18 people can join the mule caravan down the trail each day. The trip begins at the stables across the street from the Pali Trailhead, at the entrance to Pala'au State Park, 5 mi. up Hwy. 470 from Hwy. 460. Though many participants enjoy the ride immensely, there are two potential drawbacks: first, mule riders are sometimes part of a tour led by someone other than Richard Marks (see **Tour** p. 262); second, on the chance that Richard includes mule riders on his tour, he sometimes affectionately refers

MOLOKAI

to them as the "jackass patrol," giving hikers and fliers a sense of camaraderie at the expense of mule-folk. Still, mule riders avoid the mule droppings on the trail, and can buy T-shirts that say, "I'd rather be riding a mule on Molokai," always sure to be a great conversation starter. Try to book at least a week in advance.

◥ TOUR

Damien Tours (☎ 567-6171) operates all of the tours of Kalaupapa. You must have advance reservations to visit the settlement, and tours cost $30 (cash or personal check only, payable at the start of the tour) and take place every day except Sunday. Bring your own lunch, since it is not provided as part of the tour. Try calling early in the morning or late in the afternoon to reach someone in the office.

Once you arrive at the bleachers near the mule corral, wait for the charismatic ◪**Richard Marks** to arrive in his big blue bus, cat food in tow. Richard is both the tour guide and the sheriff of Kalaupapa, as well as a former patient. Nearly 40 years ago, he became the third member of his family to live at Kalaupapa. He's quite a character, and his tours are heartfelt as well as entertaining. Try to get a seat near the front of the tour bus to hear him well. The tour begins around 9:45am and ends around 2pm.

The tour stops at the **docks,** where residents gather once a year to gossip about everybody's new cars and furniture when the barge delivers supplies, **St. Francis Church,** the walls of which are adorned with images of **Father Damien,** and the grave of **Mother Marianne.** Richard also makes a stop at the **Visitor Center,** which is filled with a large array of books about Damien and Kalaupapa. Richard can advise you as to which are worthwhile, but *Yesterday at Kalaupapa* is an excellent choice for its photography, and *Separating Sickness* contains some of the better narratives about residents' lives. The latter portion of the tour takes place around the old Kalawao settlement site. From the park, you can see dome-shaped **Okala Rock,** the only place in the world where the Okala Palm grows wild.

The most poignant part of the tour is the history of Father Damien's life, recounted at **St. Philomena Church.** His grave, though not his body, is located outside. While the tour bus passes through the settlement, no stops are made at places where residents might congregate, such as the post office, the hospital, or the parks services office. This is to protect the privacy of the residents. Also be aware that **photography of residents is strictly prohibited.**

KAMAKOU PRESERVE

The 22,774-acre Kamakou Preserve is like no other place in the islands. The peak is the highest point of the island, just under 5000 ft. above sea level. The preserve is home to more than 250 different species of Hawaiian plants, 219 of which can only be found in Hawaii. The plants feed indigenous insects, which in turn support the local bird population. Among the rarities of the area are the Molokai thrush and creeper. If you camp, you may even see a *pueo* (Hawaiian owl) in the twilight.

The preserve owes its existence to the generosity of the Molokai Ranch, which sold the land rights to the Nature Conservancy in 1982, along with the rights to the Mo'omomi Preserve (see p. 266). The ranch maintains control of the water rights, however, as the area provides 60% of the island's water via a tunnel to the Kualapu'u Reservoir (see p. 266). The **Nature Conservancy** (☎ 553-5236; www.nature.org/hawaii; open M-F 7:30am-3pm) encourages visitors to stop by their office or at least call them before visiting the preserve. Their office is located at 23 Pueo Pl., in the second cul-de-sac on the right in the Molokai Industrial Park, down a road that leads south from Hwy. 460 a little over 3 mi. west of Kaunakakai. At the office they have maps of Kamakou Preserve as well as staff that can answer any questions and update you on current preserve conditions.

GETTING THERE To reach the preserve safely, a **4WD vehicle** is essential. If driving a 2WD vehicle, **turn around at the first sign of rain.** In the event you get stuck, you'll have to hike all the way back down to call your rental agency or one of the gas stations in Kaunakakai (and suffer the embarrassment and expense of car retrieval). Keep in mind that the last few miles of the road are at high elevation; they can be rainy even when it is sunny at the bottom. Use first gear and go slowly, driving around (not over) the manhole covers that appear at odd intervals along the road, as they can damage your axles. Try not to drive in ruts; instead, straddle them with the wheels of your vehicle, or drive up on the shoulder to avoid them. If you lose traction and start to slide, ease up on the gas and turn into the skid. Lastly, avoid stopping if your vehicle is on an upward incline, as many parts of the road are passable only with momentum.

ORIENTATION AND PRACTICAL INFORMATION. The road that leads to the preserve begins west of Kaunakakai on **Highway 460.** Turn north just east of the Manawainui Bridge, which precedes the 4 mi. marker. The pavement ends and the dirt road begins almost immediately at the Homelani Cemetery. The first 5 mi. or so of this road are fairly easy-going until you pass the entrance sign for the **Molokai Forestry Reserve** after about 5¾ mi. Though the massive trees may be beautiful, the road is not. Even a 4WD vehicle may encounter traction problems while trying to climb up the steep grades after this point. If you see a trickle of water running down the ruts of the road, do not continue unless you are in a 4WD; this indicates that the ground is saturated and almost guarantees that you will get stuck.

This part of the island was a popular place to live back in the days of Kamehameha the Great, but the only people you'll see today are hikers, locals checking on remote *pakalolo* gardens, and Robin, the resident woodcutter, who sells carvings from his business just past the forest reserve entrance. He has painted a sign outside instructing visitors to honk their car horns or ring the bell by the gate if they want a tour of the woodshop. There's a restroom just outside his gate, too.

After around 10 mi. total, you will just be able to make out **Lua Moku ʻIliahi,** or the Sandalwood Measuring Pit, on the left (see **Hull House,** p. 260). After another mile and a bit, you will reach the entrance to the Kamakou Preserve and the **Waikolu Lookout.** Waikolu, or "three waters" refers to the many waterfalls that run over the mountains and into the region's streams. At 3700 ft., the lookout has stunning views of the surrounding valleys. Though Waikolu's frequent rain and clouds can obstruct the view, early morning is often clear. There are squat toilets and a spare **campground,** but no potable water. The lookout makes a great base camp for exploring the preserve, though it can be a bit chilly and wet. Camping permits are available through the **State Division of Forestry and Wildlife.** They cost nothing, but you must notify the state of your stay (2-night max.) and have your permit in hand when you camp. For permit information, see **Accommodations and Camping,** p. 252. After the Waikolu Lookout is the western boundary of the Kamakou Preserve. Camping is only permitted in the state forest reserve, not the Kamakou Preserve.

GUIDED TOURS. If you are concerned about getting to and hiking through the preserve yourself, or if you'd simply like to avoid the long walk from the Waikolu Lookout, consider arranging a guided hike with the **Nature Conservancy.**

MOLOKAI

LEND A HAND TO THE LAND

Two of Molokai's most beautiful natural wonders, the **Kamakou Preserve** and the **Mo'omomi Preserve**, are managed by the local branch of the **Nature Conservancy**, an international, private, nonprofit organization dedicated to the preservation of native plants and animals all over the world. Some of the most recent efforts have concentrated on organizing agreements between public and private landowners to protect Hawaiian forests and watersheds, as well as continuing work to rid Hawaiian lands and waters of invasive alien species.

The Conservancy is always looking for volunteers. A recent series of projects on Oahu helped clean alien algae from Waikiki Beach. On Oahu and Maui, Saturday work trips are scheduled monthly.

Some recent Molokai volunteers spent time removing weeds, cleaning beaches, and maintaining fences, roads, and trails in both of Molokai's preserves. The Nature Conservancy's web site, www.nature.org/hawaii, includes a form to indicate how long you'll be in the area and what kind of work you're interested in doing.

To get in touch with the Molokai office of the Nature Conservancy, call ☎ 552-5236, or visit their office in the Molokai Industrial Park, about 3 mi. west of Kaunakakai. Open M-F 7:30am-3pm.

Guided hikes are generally less time-consuming, since you are driven directly to the trailheads, and the tour leaders often have worthwhile background knowledge about the region. The Nature Conservancy runs an eight-person trip usually on the first Saturday of the month. Hikers meet at the airport at 8:30am and return by about 3:30pm. A $25 donation is suggested, and advance reservations (with a $25 refundable deposit; ☎ 553-5236; www.nature.org/hawaii) are required.

🔲 HIKING. The Nature Conservancy asks that you stay on the roads and marked trails to avoid damaging the surrounding vegetation. From the Waikolu Lookout, the road is impassable in anything but a 4WD, and you'll have trouble even in a 4WD. The safest course of action is to park here and walk to the trailheads, unless you have extensive off-road driving experience—or a bunch of people to help you push. Before you leave the lookout, sign in on the Nature Conservancy's log sheet, which often has information about road conditions. In addition, be sure to bring lots of water, as well as rain gear and sturdy shoes or hiking boots that you won't mind getting (very) muddy.

The main trail in Kamakou Preserve is the **Pepeopae Trail.** Its trailhead is about 3 mi. past the Waikolu Lookout, down the main road, and is clearly marked with a sign. Many side roads branch off the main road here, but lead only to private property. The trail itself is a 6-8 in. boardwalk, covered in chickenwire for better footing, that winds its way for slightly over a mile through one of Hawaii's wettest regions. The substantial rainfall (over 170 in. annually) has miniaturized the plant population of the area, creating the Pepeopae Bog. Stay on the boardwalk; it gives hikers a chance to experience the remarkable vegetation and topography of the preserve without jeopardizing the environment.

At the end of the boardwalk is a tiny strip of grassy lawn on the edge of a cliff, also known as the 🔲**Pelekunu Valley Overlook.** The overlook offers truly spectacular views of high grassy cliffs towering over the Pelekunu River, as well as the turquoise waters of the Pacific to the left. On a good day, wispy clouds just barely obscure the tops of the cliffs from view. The 5760-acre valley is under the care of the Nature Conservancy and closed to the public, as it is one of the few remaining spawning grounds for several species of marine life.

A few other trails crisscross the Kamakou Preserve, although none are regularly maintained, and the Nature Conservancy does not recommend visitors attempting to hike them. That being said, they do exist, and the staff at the Nature Conservancy may be able to help you find them if you're a very experienced hiker. The **Hanalilolilo Trail** branches off the main road about 200 yd. past the Waikolu Lookout and eventually merges with the Pepeopae Trail (although it is poorly maintained and very difficult to navigate successfully). Another trail at the end of the road past the Pepeopae trailhead leads through a **tunnel to Cymoh Falls**, a small waterfall. Be sure to ask the staff at the Conservancy about the condition of these trails before you attempt them.

KALA'E AND KUALAPU'U

The area toward the end of Hwy. 470, about 4-5 mi. up the road from Hwy. 460, is called **Kala'e**, and is high enough in elevation to get a lot of sun and a little rain on most days. A choice spot for agriculture, the tiny town of **Kualapu'u**, located at Farrington Ave. at Hwy. 470 (just 2 mi. up Hwy. 470 from Hwy. 460), was once the island headquarters of the Del Monte Company. When they closed shop in the 1980s, the town suffered and shrank. In recent years, the coffee bean has replaced the pineapple, and the town's main attraction is now a small coffee plantation.

🖪 FOOD

🖪**Coffees of Hawaii, Inc. ❶**, at the corner of Farrington and Hwy. 470, serves local brew any way you like it. At the very least, drop by and enjoy free samples of their many flavors of coffee on the covered lanai. Better yet, try a cup of the shop's signature frozen drink, the Mocha Mama ($3.75). The shop also serves sandwiches and other light fare ($3-5). A 45min. plantation walking tour takes visitors through all the steps of coffee production, and the on-site gift shop sells plenty of souvenirs and, of course, coffee (8 oz. bag $7). If you time your vacation right, you might catch the annual early-November Molokai Coffee and Cultural Festival, complete with entertainment and rides. (☎567-9241; www.coffeehawaii.com. Open M-F 7am-4pm, Sa 8am-4pm, Su 10am-4pm. Tours M-F 9:30, 11:30am. $7, children $3.50. Call ahead to ensure that a tour will be running.) **Kamuela's Cookhouse ❶**, a few doors down, is one of the older family-run businesses on the island, and just about the only restaurant between Kaunakakai and Maunaloa. The lemon chicken plate lunch ($7.50) is superb, and the hamburgers ($3.50) are large and juicy. (☎567-9655. Open M-F 8am-6pm, Sa-Su 8am-2pm.) Next door on Farrington is the **Kualapu'u Market**, a well-stocked grocery store that also rents VHS tapes and DVDs ($4.50). (☎567-6243. Open M-Sa 8:30am-6pm. Video store open M-W and F-Sa.)

🖸 🖪 SIGHTS AND CAMPING

PALA'AU STATE PARK. Pala'au is a peaceful state park in an often-clouded forest of ironwood trees. It would make an ideal camping spot, if not for the frequent drizzles and lack of potable drinking water. If you don't mind getting a little wet, however, bring your own water and pitch a tent on the soft needles that cover the ground—chances are, you'll have the park to yourself. **Camping permits** are an absolute necessity, or your car will be ticketed by the police. See **Accommodations and Camping,** p. 252, for permit information. The park has restrooms and outdoor showers. Be aware that local youths frequently drag race on the highway on weekend nights and can be quite noisy.

For daytime visitors, there's a large pavilion and lawn on the left side of the road and a smaller picnic area with tables and trash cans on the right. At the end of the road a map and informative display describe the park's two main attractions. A visit to **Phallic Rock,** 5min. from the end of the highway by foot along a marked trail, will be rewarding whether you're a woman seeking fertility or just a phalli fan. Legend has it that a woman who brings offerings to the rock and sleeps a night next to it will wake up pregnant. A sign declares that the rock is a natural formation, which has only been carved "to some extent" by humans. Judge for yourself. Two minutes down a trail in the opposite direction is the **Kalaupapa Lookout,** which has stunning views of the peninsula of the same name, and five placards that recount the history of the peninsula and the leprosy victims cast away there. If you don't hike down to the leper colony (see p. 259), at least check out the view, as it is one of Molokai's best. The unofficial trail that leads to the left into the forest from the lookout offers is a pleasant hike through ironwood forest, but little else, and peters out after ¼ mi. *(At the very end of Hwy. 470, about 5 mi. from Hwy. 460.)*

■ **PURDY'S MACADAMIA NUT FARM.** Purdy may very well run the most hospitable macadamia nut farm in the world, making it one of Molokai's best-known tourist attractions. Visitors are welcomed by the man himself and given a full tour of the working farm. Unlike commercial operations on Oahu, Purdy does not use any irrigation, pesticides, or chemicals of any kind, and visitors have the privilege of wandering freely throughout the property. The trees on his 5-acre farm are about 80 yr. old, and they produce nuts year-round. Purdy will insist you crack your own nut before you help yourself to nuts and samples of macadamia honey on slices of fresh coconut. *(On Lihi Pali Ave., ½ mi. from the intersection with Farrington Ave., on the right. From Hwy. 470, turn left on Farrington Ave., then right on Lihi Pali after 1 mi. ☎567-6601. Open Tu-F 9:30am-3:30pm, Sa 10am-2pm, weather permitting. Free.)*

IRONWOOD HILLS GOLF COURSE. Not to be mistaken for a championship resort course, Ironwood Hills is still a pleasant nine-hole layout set in a beautiful, upcountry venue. The unpretentious pro shop is in a trailer, and run by a good-natured caretaker. *(About 3¾ mi. from the intersection with Hwy. 460 on Hwy. 470 on the left down a dirt road, just before the sugar mill. ☎567-6000. Open daily 7:30am-5pm. $18 for 9 holes, $23 for 18. Cart rental $10 per 9 holes. Club rental $7 for 9 holes, $12 for 18.)*

HOOLEHUA

This large, dry area west of Kala'e divides eastern and western Molokai. Most of the land in the area is under the auspices of the department of Hawaiian Home Lands, which provides homesteads to ethnic Hawaiians.

◪ **PRACTICAL INFORMATION.** The ▨**post office** (☎567-6144), located on Puupeelua Ave. (Hwy. 480) at its intersection with Farrington Ave., has a **Post-A-Nut** service—you can send a genuine Molokai coconut to your friends back home for the price of postage ($3-7). Peggy, the smiling postmaster, collects and provides the nuts and even keeps a few felt pens around to write on the husks. (Open M-F 7:30-11:30am and 12:45-4:30pm.) **Postal Code:** 96729.

◪ **SIGHTS.** One of the only coastal sand dune ecosystems left in Hawaii, the ▨**Mo'omomi Preserve** is home to a half-dozen endangered plant species that cannot be found anywhere else on the planet. Its pristine coast is a breeding ground for green sea turtles, a rarity in the populated portions of the islands, and the terrain is colorful and rugged. The many white-sand beaches located along this portion of the coast are expansive and perpetually empty, but not very good for swimming or other aquatic activities. Most beaches are rocky, and in some cases, inaccessible because they are surrounded by sensitive preserve land. Still, they are some of the most beautiful beaches on the island, even if you only view them from afar.

The Mo'omomi Preserve is one of two Molokai preserves that are managed by the **Nature Conservancy** (☎553-5236; www.nature.org/hawaii) and open to the public, the other being Kamakou Preserve (see p. 262). The Nature Conservancy's office is located at 23 Pueo Pl., in the second cul-de-sac on the right in the Molokai Industrial Park, down a road that leads south from Hwy. 460 a little over 3 mi. west of Kaunakakai (open M-F 7:30am-3pm). Maps and information about Moʻomomi Preserve are available at the office, and the staff encourages visitors to stop in before they visit the preserve to get up-to-date information and to ask questions. The preserve is private property, so respect the efforts of the Conservancy to keep it in shape and protect the wildlife.

There are three ways to access the preserve. The first is by hiking a trail about ¾ mi. from the Moʻomomi Pavilion to the east. To get to the trail, take Hwy. 460 from Kaunakakai to Hwy. 480. Turn left at Farrington Ave., and continue straight until the asphalt ends. The dirt road straight ahead is smooth most of the way, although a few ruts can be monsters and may tilt your vehicle at odd angles. After about ½ mi., a sign points visitors down a dirt road to the right (Anahaki Rd.). The road runs for about 2 mi., passing through a gate about halfway down, before it reaches a pavilion on the eastern edge of Moʻomomi Bay. The pavilion is owned and maintained by the Hawaiian Home Lands Dept. (as is all the land in the area), and has restrooms, an outdoor shower, and picnic tables, as well as room to park cars. The road may be passed with a 2WD in good weather, if you drive slowly and watch out for rocks. To be safe, though, go with a truck or 4x4. From the parking area, the trail leads to the left along the shore of Moʻomomi Bay and then Kawaaloa Bay until it reaches the preserve. Within the preserve are a number of endangered plants, so once you leave the bay, be absolutely certain that you **hike only on trails or roads,** or you might step on an endangered plant or squash a rare sea bird's underground nesting area. The trail leads for about a mile along the coast, and offers some of the most magnificent views of untouched beaches and sand dunes you can imagine. A road also leads through the preserve from the edge of Kawaaloa Bay, and makes for a nice hike, too. Always keep in mind that it is illegal to remove any part of the preserve, be it animal, vegetable, or mineral.

The two other ways to enter the preserve are by car and on a guided tour. The Nature Conservancy can sometimes grant permission to visitors to use the 4WD roads through the preserve with advance notice. Guests must contact the Conservancy and ask for a key to the gates to the preserve. Lastly, the Nature Conservancy leads guided monthly hikes through the preserve on the third or fourth Saturday of each month for a suggested donation of $25. Hikers are picked up at the airport at 8:30am, and returned by 2pm. Visitors with their own 4x4 can join the guided tour group with permission—the limit is one additional vehicle with each group. To reserve a spot, a $25 refundable deposit is required. Contact the Nature Conservancy for more info.

The land directly to the east of Moʻomomi Preserve is also a worthwhile area to visit. It is all private land owned by the Hawaiian Home Lands Dept., so again, treat it with the utmost respect. The rocky beach directly below and to the left of the parking area is not good for either swimming or sunbathing, but the purple volcanic tide pools are worth checking out. Continue on the foot trail to the left along the coast for 5min. or so to reach **Moʻomomi Beach,** an idyllic spot to let the hustle and bustle of the populated world soak away into the sands. The surf can be dangerous, so stay alert; there are no lifeguards on the beach. The rocky shoreline makes swimming here less than ideal, but it is an ideal sunbathing spot.

Beyond Moʻomomi Bay along the same trail is **Kawaaloa Bay,** a similar (but much longer) stretch of beach. Again, the surf is strong, and some rocks make for tough and dangerous swimming, but the beach is long and beautiful, and is another secluded spot just to hang out. At the western edge of Kawaaloa Bay is the eastern edge of the **Moʻomomi Preserve.**

MOLOKAI

THE FIGHTING COCKS OF KALA'E AND

HOOLEHUA. As you drive along the highways of Molokai, keep your eyes open for A-frame huts or wire cages about a foot high, located in front yards or fields. The chickens raised inside are intended neither for eggs nor for food. Rather, these structures are pseudo-barracks where fighting cocks are trained. Originally brought to the islands by Filipinos, cockfighting has become a popular pastime on Molokai. The animals are generally kept close together in order to encourage aggressiveness, but they are tethered far enough apart so that they cannot actually fight one another. Although cockfighting is illegal, raising fighting cocks is not. Despite the grisly end which most of these creatures face, their long feather plumes and bright colors are quite beautiful, and are worth a closer look. The farther reaches of Farrington Ave. are the best place to hunt for fighting cocks, though you might encounter a few along Hwy. 470 east of Kaunakakai, past mi. marker 5.

EAST OF KAUNAKAKAI

The drive east from Kaunakakai becomes progressively more beautiful the farther you go, as the road becomes narrower and less-traveled. The "towns" listed here are really nothing more than clusters of houses along the road. Other than the 'Ili'ili'opae Heiau, most sights are visible from the road, making this a great place to roll down the windows and sightsee from the car.

◤ ACCOMMODATIONS

▨**Kamalo Plantation Cottage ❸**, through the gate next to mailbox 300 on the mountainside of the highway, is just across from St. Joseph's Church before the 11 mi. marker. A stay on this lush 5-acre property is truly an island-style experience. The guest cottage is a lovely, well-furnished studio with a king-sized bed, kitchen, bird-watching deck, indoor and outdoor showers, tons of privacy, and access to the nearby *luau* hut complete with a gas grill for BBQs. (☎558-8236; www.molokai.com/kamalo. 2-night min. stay. Cottage $85 single/double occupancy.)

The owners also rent the A-frame **Moanui Beach House ❹**, at mi. marker 20, near the golden sands of Murphy's Beach. Both the cottage and the beach house are stocked with fruit from the family's plantation and home-baked bread. The residence has two airy bedrooms with king-sized beds, one-and-a-half baths, a large kitchen, as well as living and dining rooms. (3-night min. House $140 single/double occupancy; each additional guest $20.)

The **Wavecrest Resort ❸** is located at mi. 13. A laid-back condo complex, the resort sits on an attractive (though not swimmable) lagoon with a good view of Maui. There are two lighted tennis courts, as well as shuffleboard facilities and a putting green. All rooms have a kitchen, patio, TV, and ceiling fans; other furnishings vary. There's no A/C or telephones. (Wavecrest management office ☎558-8101. Open M-F 8am-2pm, Sa 11:30am-12:30pm. For reservations, call Friendly Island Realty ☎553-3666, or Swenson Realty ☎553-3648. 1-bedroom $70-80; 2-bedroom $135; 1-time cleaning fee $40/$50 for stays under 1 wk.)

◖ FOOD

Just about the only place to grab groceries or some lunch on the east side of the island is the **Neighborhood Store and Counter ❶** (☎558-8498), just short of mi. marker 16. In addition to the small but well-stocked market (meats, cheeses, snacks, drinks, alcohol, ingredients), the food order window serves up egg sandwiches ($4), mahi mahi burgers ($4) and other treats (honey dip chicken plate lunches $7; milkshakes $4). Video rental (VHS or DVD $3.50) is available for a rainy day. (Open daily 8am-6pm. Food counter closed W.)

👁 SIGHTS

🔲 'ILI'ILI'OPAE HEIAU

To reach the heiau (temple), watch for the Hawaiian Home Lands marker on the right just after the small Mapulehu bridge, about ½ mi. past mi. 15. It is difficult to find a place to park, since all the shoulders are narrow (and privately owned). It is easiest to turn around once you've passed the bridge and park on the mauka (mountain) side of the road just west of the bridge, where there is a small expanse of grass to the right of a mailbox and dirt road. Immediately across the street from the Home Lands marker (mauka) is mailbox #488 and yet another dirt road with a gate that reads, "No Hunting, Private Property, Keep Out, Keep Gate Closed."

Located within the tiny village of Puko'o, the colossal 'Ili'ili'opae Heiau is not to be missed. Fortunately, in recent years, the site has been opened to the public. At one time advance permission was required to access the *heiau* (temple); however, the property owners became so frustrated by the number of telephone calls requesting access that they now allow visitors to stop by unannounced, provided that they stay on the road and don't make their presence known. To visit, walk *around* the gate along the path on the left side (opening the gate is a bad idea, since the gate holds up the fence). Continue walking up the dirt road for almost ½ mi., until you see a wall of stones near a house on your right. These stones are a *heiau*, but they are not the *heiau*. A narrow path leads into the forest just a bit farther up on the left, underneath a handpainted sign that reads *"heiau"* and has an arrow.

This is an awesome and holy place. Legend has it that this *heiau* was built in one marathon night by a massive human chain that snaked its way inland over the mountain to the north shore's Wailau Valley. To view the entirety of this feat of human engineering, continue walking along the trail up the hill. A 2min. hike reveals a great view of the flat surface of the *heiau*, which rivals a football field in size. The surface is remarkably level, and it is commonly believed that the *heiau* was more than twice its present size while it was in use.

'Ili'ili'opae is the second-largest *heiau* in Hawaii, and was used as a temple for human sacrifice, as well as a training ground for *kahunas* (priests) from all the islands. It is holy to the Hawaiian people, as the work of a mighty civilization that has all but disappeared. Treat it with respect by not touching any of it.

KAWELA. A small residential development between mi. markers 4 and 6, Kawela is notable for its views and its bloody history. Kawela is the battleground where Kamehameha I defeated Molokai's warriors on his way to uniting all the islands. It is said that in the hills above Kawela is a *pu'uhonua*, an ancient place of refuge. To get a great view of the ocean, shoreline fishponds, the barrier reef, or Lanai, drive up any of the streets on the mountain side of the road. Especially good are the views from the Kawela Plantation II Rd., at about mi. 4.7. At about mi. 5.5, **Kakahai'a Beach Park** stretches for ¼ mi. on the narrow strip of land between the highway and the ocean, and has picnic tables and a few grassy patches suitable for a picnic, though it is close to the highway. Across the street from the park is the **Kakahai'a National Wildlife Refuge**, a wetland area that has been set aside as a bird sanctuary. It is closed to the public, but **Nene O Molokai**, a non-profit facility for the endangered Hawaiian state bird, is near mi. marker 4. Here, you can see the birds and get information about other birding spots. The

CRACKING DOWN ON ICE

One of Hawaii's most recent domestic problems has been a surge in the use of the drug Crystal Methamphetamine, also known as Ice." The addictive stimulant is dangerous because of the irrational behavior it provokes in its users, which has resulted in cases of domestic abuse, property crime, violent crime, and several murders in recent years.

Ice has been known to Hawaii or over a decade, but politicians and law enforcement have been slow to combat it. Reports from the first half of 2003 show that Ice use is still increasing in the islands. The good news is that Governor Linda Lingle's administration and state law enforcers have recently made the fight against Ice one of their primary initiatives, forming a joint state house-senate committee to hold hearings and investigate, and organizing a state-wide summit for September 2003.

Molokai has not been able to resist the Ice epidemic. Clandestine labs are suspected to exist on the island, and abuse has sparked a community outcry. An anti-Ice rally was held in July of 2003, along with a series of anti-drug forums. Visitors to the island are made aware of the Ice epidemic by handmade signs, calling for a crackdown on Ice, and an end to the abuse that is tearing apart amilies island-wide.

facility can't handle heavy traffic, so call ☎ 553-5992 about visiting, or check the web site, http://aloha.net/~nene. Plans are in the works to set up a scheduled time for general visitation.

KAMALO. Between mi. markers 10 and 11, Kamalo was once the economic and civic center of the island. The **Kamalo Wharf** can be accessed via the dirt road on the right at the major bend in the highway about 100 yd. after the 10 mi. marker. Once the island's main unloading docks, the wharf, now reduced to stones, is home to a few semi-permanent campers and the occasional outrigger race. If you walk out on the wharf, you'll have spectacular views of the inland mountains, which go from being very dry to very lush at about this point along the highway. About ½ mi. farther down the road is **St. Joseph's Church,** one of two remaining churches built by Father Damien outside the Kalaupapa peninsula. The church is simple, and no longer holds weekly services, but still gets its share of visitors, who often sign the logbook inside. About 1 mi. farther, a poorly-visible wooden sign on the right denotes the **Smith-Bronte Landing Site,** where the first civilian flight from the mainland to Hawaii ended in a safe crash-landing in 1927. The flight took 25hr., and Honolulu was the original destination. The sign is located at the eastern end of a long guardrail that runs along the ocean side of the highway around mi. 11.8.

UALAPUE AND KALUA'AHA. The village of Ualapue is clustered just past the 13 mi. marker, and about 1 mi. later, on the *mauka* (mountain) side of the highway in Kalua'aha, are the remnants of the **Kalua'aha Church,** built in 1844 by the first missionary to the island. What remains of the church is its 3 ft. thick concrete outer wall. Monthly services are still held under a tarp inside the great walls of the old church. The building is set about 100 yd. off the highway, at the end of a big lawn. Just ¼ mi. past it is the well-known **Our Lady of Sorrows Church.** Today's building is the 1966 reconstruction of the original, which was built by Father Damien in 1874. Services are held Sundays at 7am. Across the street from the church is the **Niaupala fishpond,** one of the most easily viewed of the ancient fishponds of the south shore.

EAST TO HALAWA BAY

From roughly mi. marker 20 onward, the road is basically one lane and has a fair number of cliff's-edge hairpin turns. The view is well-earned by braving the ride. Sea cliffs, secluded beach coves, and expansive pastures await.

The road is paved and smooth all the way to Halawa Bay, but use caution nonetheless, especially the first time you make the trip or in the rain. Don't hesitate to honk your horn as a warning when you approach tight corners, and drive slowly. Be certain your first time driving beyond mi. marker 20 is not at night—it's dangerous to do so, and you'd miss the view, which is half the reason to go to Halawa.

WAIALUA BEACH. Just before the 19 mi. marker, Waialua Beach is popular place among locals who gather here to sunbathe, snorkel, and socialize. The beach stretches from the confluence of Waialua Stream and the ocean a couple hundred yards to the west, and is a good spot for swimming. In the summer, children jump from the highway bridge into the stream to rinse off the salt before heading home. Limited parking is available on the side of the road, and to access the beach without trespassing through private property, enter near the western end of the beach, where the highway runs along the beach.

■MURPHY'S BEACH. Also known simply as 20 mi. beach, Murphy's Beach is the east shore's most popular swimming and snorkeling spot. The strip of sand isn't wide, but the waters here are especially interesting because Murphy's Beach is the eastern end of the 28 mi. barrier reef that extends along the south shore of Molokai. Plenty of parking is available in the grassy lawn on the south side of the highway just beyond the 20 mi. marker. Like Waialua, Murphy's Beach is distinctly Molokaian: no shower or restroom facilities, but still a fabulous place to relax and enjoy the day, provided you aren't in a hurry to get anywhere.

ROCK POINT. Just past Murphy's Beach, around a bend in the road before the 21 mi. marker, is a rocky area called (appropriately enough) Rock Point. The area is one of the island's most popular surf spots, especially in winter, but can be dangerous. The rocks are sharp and the water is shallow in places, so know what you're doing before you charge into the spray. Right at the 21 mi. marker, at a low point in the road, is a small strip of sand across from a couple of houses. This unnamed beach has a protected shoreline and makes for decent swimming. A better spot to swim and sunbathe is located about ½ mi. farther down the road. This unnamed cove is similar, but larger and sandier. *(To access the break at Rock Point, there is room to park 2-3 cars on the side of the highway right next to the lone 10 ft. tall boulder immediately on the makai (ocean) side of the road.)*

PU'U O HOKU RANCH. After mi. marker 21, the road winds its way upward into the cattle pastures of the Pu'u O Hoku Ranch. Around mi. 24, the road levels and widens a bit, and you should be able to glimpse **Moku Ho'oniki Island,** recently named a bird sanctuary but originally used for target practice by WWII bombers. Located at the 25 mi. marker, the main offices of the ranch double as the **Last Chance Store,** where you can pick up cold drinks and candy.

The ranch has a lodge that sleeps 22, which it rents out to large groups for conferences, as well as two tremendous vacation cottages. The **Sunrise Cottage** is a two-bedroom, two-bath house with a kitchen and a covered lanai. The **■Grove Cottage ●** is a 2100 sq. ft., four-bedroom, three-bath house with spectacular views of Maui and a sunny master bedroom. Both are set in bucolic pastures, far enough even from the ranch offices to have complete privacy.

Those not staying at the ranch can still take advantage of the unique horseback riding options they offer. A one hour guided trail ride is $55, with the second hr. for $20, and $15 for each additional hour. The ranch also offers three specialty rides. The ½ day beach ride ($120), early morning sunrise ride ($80), and full-day waterfall ride ($145) all traverse secluded countryside ranch land, and are sure not to disappoint. *(Last Chance Store, ☎ 558-8109; www.puuohoku.com. Open daily approximately 9am-4pm. Both guest cottages are $125 for 1 or 2 people; each additional person $20. Weekly stays $750.)*

NO WORK, ALL PLAY

HULA BABY

The goddess Laka is said to have given birth to the hula in Ka'ana, on Western Molokai. Originally a religious practice, the ritualized dance had eight dancers accompanied by the sounds of a sharkskin log drum called a *pahu*. Both dancers and drummer made regular offerings to Laka. However, after Christian missionaries converted local chiefs in the early 1800s, the hula was deemed heathen and forced underground.

During the late 1800s, King Kalakaua again encouraged the teaching and open practice of the hula. A new incarnation, known as *hula ku'i*, used an *ipu* gourd as a drum rather than the *pahu*, out of respect for the holiness of the older ritual. By the mid-1900s, Hollywood had sensationalized the dance. Tourists were more interested in the sexually suggestive moves of coconut bra-clad dancers than the cultural and religious significance of the hula, and the traditional chant was abandoned in favor of a more catchy song-based accompaniment.

The birth of the hula is celebrated the 3rd weekend in May at Papohaku Beach on Molokai. The festival is called **Ka hula Piko,** and the dancing begins late at night. The dancers are only visible at first as shadows against the stars, and as the sky brightens, a traditional chant begins. The dancing continues throughout the day, with workshops every evening by renowned *kumu hula* (hula teachers).

■ **HALAWA VALLEY AND BAY.** About ½ mi. past the 26 mi. marker, a mesmerizing lookout over Halawa Valley has views of Moa'ula and Hipuapua Falls (Moa'ula to the left, Hipuapua to the right), as well as the beach below. As you descend into the valley, be mindful of the stone wall on the edge of the highway, especially while passing oncoming traffic (if you encounter any).

Believed to be the site of Molokai's first settlement in AD 700, Halawa Bay epitomizes the essence of Molokai: primal and untouched. Though the area had quite a few residents at one time, tsunamis in 1946 and 1957 left so much salt behind that the farmland went bad and all but a half-dozen of the residents moved out. The bay is a fabulous (and free) place to camp, and is popular among locals, who usually pitch semi-permanent tents on the far side of the beach.

At the bottom of the highway, there's a small green church on the left and a campground restroom with an outdoor shower on the right. Do not drink the water; it does not meet health standards. The paved road ends, and a short dirt road leads around a corner to a good place to park and access the beach. The main beach is accessible by wading across a small stream next to the parking area, and is a great place for swimming, body boarding, and surfing. To the right, a smaller beach, separated from the main beach by a rocky point, is also a nice place to sunbathe or swim. The grass lawn between the two stretches is ideal for a picnic, or a campsite—close enough to make use of the campground facilities, but far enough to have an ocean view. It is also a considerable distance from the far side of the beach, which is more crowded. Lock your car, keep a close eye on your valuables, and remember the nearest payphone is back at the 13 mi. marker, and the nearest grocery store is at the 16 mi. marker.

■ **MOA'ULA AND HIPUAPUA FALLS.** Halawa's real attraction, aside from the overall grandeur of the place, is the hike to the magnificent pair of waterfalls up Halawa Stream, **Moa'ula Falls** and **Hipuapua Falls.** The hike crosses private property and for some time was closed to visitors except as part of a guided tour. After a squabble between local landowners and the state parks department, people have relaxed for the most part—be confident about making the hike, but be respectful; try not to make your presence a nuisance to the people who are allowing you the privilege of crossing their land, and of course, stay on the trail and pack out everything you pack in.

Depending on the weather and recent rainfall, the hike to Moa'ula Falls takes at least 1hr., and you'll need another ½hr. to get up to Hipuapua Falls. The

Moaʻula Falls hike is gentle the whole way, with just one river crossing. Getting to Hipuapua Falls involves scrambling over river rocks and through some muddy patches—it might be difficult for those unaccustomed to hiking through the woods. The rewards of reaching the falls, though, are well worth the trouble. The pool below Moaʻula Falls is wide, deep, and swimmable (beware of falling rocks). The waterfall itself is two-tiered, and carries an impressive volume of water down the mountain. Hipuapua Falls is narrower, but single-tiered, so from the pool at its base, one can see the top of the falls as water cascades down the cliff face. The pool below Hipuapua is shallower, but still a great place to relax and enjoy the solitude. *(Getting to either falls along the trail requires good directions. As you enter the Halawa Valley from the highway, park your car in the open area next to the stream, just beyond the end of the paved road. Walk back along the dirt road past the church, and then bear right along the dirt road for ¼ mi. until you cross the bridge over Halawa Stream. Immediately after you cross the bridge, turn left onto the tire-track dirt road with a "no parking" sign on a fencepost on the left of the entrance to the road. The road leads to a house about 100 yd. away; the trail to the falls branches off the road to the left where a 6 ft. plank crosses a narrow canal. From here the trail runs through a taro (poi) farm and past a wooden fence on the left decorated with art. The trail continues on for about 1 mi. through woods, and runs along a white pipe on the ground for most of its length. At one point the trail crosses from the left side to the right side of a 3-4 ft. high rock wall.)*

NEAR HALAWA

NORTH SHORE SEA CLIFFS AND WAILAU VALLEY

The north shore of Molokai is home to the world's tallest sea cliffs. The cliffs were formed when the Makanalua Peninsula, a large chunk of the island created by the Kauhako Caldera, fell off and sank into the sea after thousands of years of pounding surf eroded its foundation. As recently as 5 yr. ago, chunks of the cliffs were still breaking off and sliding down into the ocean. The stunning masses of rock and earth are spotted with swaths of bright green grass and the occasional herd of mountain goats, grazing high above the ocean's surface. In wet weather, dozens of waterfalls spill over the cliffs into the ocean, above a shoreline dotted with hidden coves and sea caves. The north shore sea cliffs are indeed a remote part of an already remote island.

Four major valleys span the 12 mi. of coastline from Halawa to the Kalaupapa Peninsula: from east to west they are Papalaua, Wailau, Pelekunu, and Waikolu. Papalaua Valley is the smallest of the four, but home to one of the most impressive waterfalls visible from the sea, Papalaua Falls. The cliffs just beyond Papalaua Valley are home to Kahiwa Falls, the highest ocean-terminating falls in the world, and the longest waterfall in the state. This thin stream of water spills down the face of the cliffs from an elevation of 1750 ft. and eventually plunges into the sea.

Wailau Valley, about an hour's boat ride from Halawa Bay, is where local Molokaians go for their vacations, to escape the "hustle and bustle" of Kaunakakai. The largest of the north shore valleys, Wailau was once accessible via the dangerous Wailau Trail, which stretched from the ʻIliʻiliʻopae Heiau over the mountains. Today the trail is in disrepair, and opinion varies as to whether or not it's passable.

Pelekunu and Waikolu Valleys cover the rest of the north shore all the way to the Kalaupapa Peninsula. They are as remote, uninhabited, and untouched by man as anywhere on Molokai. Both can be viewed from lookouts in the Kamakou Preserve (see p. 262), or from the sea, but are virtually impossible to visit on foot.

The sea cliffs are only accessible by boat. The ocean below the cliffs can be quite rough but is a popular spot for advanced sea kayaking. The current flows swiftly away from Halawa, and kayakers must arrange in advance for a boat to retrieve them. Boat tours of the north shore are an easier way to get a look at Molokai's sea cliffs, and are offered by a few boat owners in town. **Molokai Action**

MOLOKAI

Adventures (☎558-8184), goes out from Halawa from 2-5 times per wk., for sightseeing, fishing, whale-watching (in winter), or snorkeling. Sightseeing trips sometimes include an hour-long stop in Wailau Valley, and are sure to come with plenty of stories. Try calling early in the morning or late at night, and be flexible—the weather and the owner's (Walter's) schedule can make it hard to pin down an exact date for a tour. Depending on what you want to do, boat rides run 3-4 hr. and cost $50-100 per person, but prices are negotiable and family rates are offered.

WESTERN MOLOKAI

Western Molokai is vast and for the most part uninhabited. The Molokai Ranch owns most of the land in this region, and apart from the small town of Maunaloa and the condo developments around the now-defunct Kaluakoi Hotel, it is mostly empty pasture land. Dry and dusty, the west gets 12 in. of rain or less each year, and water has to be piped in from the wetter east side to support human habitation. The beaches on this side of Molokai are by far the best on the island and, with the area's remoteness, you can find at least one all to yourself.

On your way out, be sure to stop at the ■**Beach Boy Ranch** in Hoolehua, past the back of the airport on Rte. 460 (Maunaloa Hwy.) You can't miss it—it's the only kooky organic produce farm (and the only building) on the highway. If you ask, the foreman John will give you a tour. All produce grown on-site ($1 per lb.).

MAUNALOA

The only real reason to visit Maunaloa, a one-block town dominated by the Molokai Ranch, is to buy a kite, take in a movie, or see the ranch. The town's 374 residents are nearly all employed by either the ranch or the condo developments down the road, and the newness of most of the buildings is a striking contrast to the older false fronts of the stores in Kaunakakai. The ■**Big Wind Kite Factory,** 120 Maunaloa Hwy., is well worth a trip to Maunaloa. Kites of all colors and styles adorn the walls ($25-95). The store also has an eclectic mix of knick-knacks from around the globe, as well as a collection of books about Molokai, Hawaiian music CDs, marionettes, extreme kite-boarding magazines, and a line of Hawaiian shirts. (☎552-2364. Open M-Sa 8:30am-5pm, Su 10am-2pm.)

Molokai Fish and Dive (see p. 257), in cooperation with the Sheraton, runs an **outfitters center** (☎552-0184) that rents every kind of equipment imaginable and offers activities to hotel guests and the general public for relatively steep prices. Options include hikes of various difficulties ($30-85), sea kayaking ($55-85), learn-how-to-lariat-a-steer *paniolo* lessons ($80), mountain biking ($30-85), snorkel gear ($11 for 24hr.), body boards ($8-11 for 24hr.), and surf boards ($25-40 for 24hr.).

To reach Maunaloa, take Hwy. 460 west, which becomes the main road of the town. The **post office** is located across from the general store. (☎522-2852. Open M-F 8am-4:30pm. **Postal Code:** 96770.) Once there, the only place to stay is the **Molokai Ranch ●**, a 54,000-acre working ranch with 7000+ head of cattle that moonlights as a first-class luxury resort. The facilities are superb but expensive. Though the ranch is privately owned, Sheraton assumed management in 2002. Accommodations are split between the ranch's lodge and the Kaupoa Campground, located 9 mi. from Maunaloa, on a pleasant beach. Three years young, the lodge has rooms equipped with A/C and footed bathtubs, a zero-horizon pool, a fitness center, restaurant and bar. (Restaurant and bar open to the public daily 7am-9pm.) The upscale campground is populated by 40 "tentalows," solar-powered, steel-and-canvas structures on a raised platform, each with two bedrooms, a lanai, restroom, shower, fan, and beds. **Kaupoa Beach House,** the lone building at the campground, serves three meals a day to guests (open Sa night to the public) and other amenities like electrical outlets and an Internet connection. The beach campground is only accessible to guests, or to the public on Saturday night if you check in with the Sheraton desk first. (☎660-2710 or 552-2741; www.sheraton.com/hawaii. Lodge rooms $360-425 for 1-2 people; tentalows $275-320 for 1-2 people; $50 for each extra adult in lodge or tentalow. All rooms and tentalows sleep up to 4.)

With the recent closing of the Village Grill, the only place to eat other than the ranch's dining room is **Paniolo Cafe ❶** (which recently replaced a KFC itself) on N. Wai'eli St. next to the cinema. (☎552-2625. Plate lunches $5.50, 2 for $8, burgers and sandwiches $3-5. Open daily 11am-7:30pm. AmEx/D/MC/V.) There's snack food at **Lucky's Gas and Oil** convenience store, next to the general store and across from Paniolo Cafe, which happens to be the only gas station east of Kaunakakai. (☎552-2627. Open M-F 7am-1pm, Sa 10am-2pm.) For groceries, try the well-stocked **Maunaloa General Store,** 200 Maunaloa Hwy. (☎552-2346. Open M-Sa 8am-6pm.) The **Maunaloa Town Cinema** is the only movie theater on Molokai. Located on the same street corner as the rest of the places in town, it has three screens, and shows two movies on each screen per day. (☎552-2616 or 552-2707. Showings at about 4, 7pm. $6.50, ages 3-11 and 62+ $4; matinee (before 6pm) $4.75.)

KALUAKOI

About 1½ mi. before Maunaloa, a turnoff from the highway on the right leads about 4 mi. down Kaluakoi Rd. to several condo developments, as well as most of the west side's beaches. A block down Lio Pl., you'll find **Paniolo Hale ❹,** a beautiful 77-unit condominium complex. Eighteen of the units are in the rental pool, and many of the rest are available through Friendly Isle Real Estate or the directory at the Molokai Visitors' Association. Most are well-furnished condos that feel like houses, all with full kitchens, living rooms, and some with screened lanais. This is, by far, the best value on the West End. (☎800-367-2984 or 552-2731; www.paniolo-haleresort.com. Dec. 15-Mar. 31 studio (sleeps 1-2) $135-155; 1-bedroom (sleeps 1-4) $210-230; 2-bedroom (sleeps 1-6) $245-265. Low season studios $95-115; 1-bedroom $115-135; 2-bedroom $145-165. $10 per extra person.)

Across the street from the Kaluakoi Villas, on Kepuhi Beach Rd., sits **Ke Nani Kai ❸,** another condo complex with slightly smaller rooms than Paniolo Hale. It's a nice place to stay if you can take advantage of one of the many deals offered online. (☎800-535-0085 or 552-2731; www.marcresorts.com. Office open M-F 8am-3pm, Sa 8am-1pm. 1-bedroom starts at $93. 20% discount for AAA members.)

The Kaluakoi Hotel closed in 2000 due to a lack of investor confidence and a decline in tourism. The units that have not been subsumed by Kaluakoi Villas are in a state of disrepair and give a depressed feeling to the area. The **Kaluakoi Villas ❹** are fairly well-maintained, however, located just down Kaluakoi Road from Ke Nani Kai and Paniolo Hale. They're a bit pricey for what you get, but frequent Internet specials can save you 20% or more, and AAA rates are also available. (☎800-367-5004 or 552-2721; www.castleresorts.com. 1-bedroom studio with kitchenette $135-155; 2-bedroom with kitchenette $160-240.)

WEST END BEACHES AND CAMPING

PAPOHAKU BEACH. About 2½ mi. long, Papohaku Beach is the king of West End beaches. It has the most surface area of any beach in Hawaii; it can measure up to 60 yd. in width, depending on the time of year and the tide. The beach has so much sand, in fact, that some of it was sent to Oahu during the mid-1950s to create Waikiki Beach. Papohaku is backed by a number of small dunes, and the wind frequently picks up the sand. The water is no good for snorkeling, although perfect

MOLOKAI

for a dip between sunbathing sessions. Although you may see an occasional body surfer, the water is known for a strong undertow; even locals exercise caution.

Papohaku Beach has three main access points from **Kaluakoi Road,** all with showers and signs reading "Beach Access, Public Right of Way" displayed prominently. From north to south, the first is **Papohaku Beach Park,** which is also the only campground on the West End. It is usually uninhabited and peaceful. The site has showers, restrooms, picnic tables, and BBQ grills. Camping permits are required and can be purchased at the Department of Parks and Recreation (see p. 252).

The second access point, **Lauhue,** has the most pleasing setting. Located about ½ mi. from Papohaku Beach Park, it's surrounded by taller dunes and sits farther away from the condo developments. It also has more beach area than the third access point, **Papapa.** The site of **Ka Hula Piko,** a hula festival held every May, the Papapa Beach is a little rocky. However, it does boast a good view of the entire expanse of Papohaku. The other access points are far too rocky for swimming, and neither has enough sand to satisfy the serious sunbather.

■ **DIXIE MARU.** At the end of Kaluakoi Rd. The beach on the right, Dixie Maru, is a protected cove that is almost circular in shape. The surrounding rocks and vegetation give the place an air of seclusion and the water is calm and good for swimming. Boarders should look elsewhere for surf, however.

KEPUHI BEACH. At the opposite (north) end of Papohaku Beach, this beach is accessible by turning off Kaluakoi Rd. onto Lio Pl. and walking through the Paniolo Hale complex. Kepuhi Beach is the most crowded of all the beaches on the west side due its proximity to the condos.

■ **MAKE HORSE.** For a far better sand and sun experience, walk down the dirt road at the Paniolo Hale parking lot to Make Horse Beach, which may very well be one of the best beaches in Hawaii. The beach is actually a series of three crescent-shaped bays of white sand, separated by high volcanic rock that obscures each from view. If you have too much company at the first beach, just try the others to the right. A favorite fishing spot among locals, with good surf in the winter, but Make Horse isn't the place to snorkel. "Make" (mah-kay) means "dead," and the beach is so named because during the 1800s, locals would slaughter horses by running them off the high plateau to the right of the beach.

KAWAKIU BEACH. The most isolated of the West End beaches, Kawakiu Beach takes a little work to find. To get there, continue straight on Lio Pl. instead of turning left towards the Paniolo Hale parking lot. The road ends after about 100 yd. Park here and walk down the red dirt road immediately ahead for about 35min. The road is in poor condition; even a 4WD is likely to get stuck. Keep on the main road, as there are several smaller roads that veer off. The pristine beach that awaits is sure to be devoid of tourists (though there may be a couple locals).

HALE O LONO HARBOR. The only part of the southern portion of the western shore that is open to the public, the harbor is accessible via a dirt road just beyond the Molokai Ranch Lodge in Maunaloa down Mokio St. A quiet beach lies just east. If the gate is locked, you can get the key from the Molokai Ranch front desk.

LANAI

Travelers in search of peaceful serenity, friendly locals, and outdoor adventure should head to Lanai. A quiet, slow-paced paradise, with just one small town and only a few paved roads, Lanai isn't for those looking for touristy Hawaiian glitz and glamour. Though its industry now centers around its two secluded luxury resorts, the island was once home to the world's largest **pineapple plantation.** Its 15,000 acres accounted for over 90% of total US pineapple production, and many of the island's older residents are former field laborers. The community is small and close-knit, and people are genuinely amiable and polite—it is considered common courtesy to wave at all oncoming drivers and pedestrians, especially outside of town. Prices on Lanai are a bit higher than on other islands, but if you want to escape the dense tourism of Oahu and Maui, you'll get what you pay for here.

Lanai has been under the control of nearby **Maui** since before recorded history. It is still part of Maui County, but has too few voters (with only 3000 residents) to hold much sway in local politics. While about 80% of Lanai's working population is employed in resort operations by the **Lanai Company,** control of the island is mostly in the hands of **Castle and Cooke,** a private company that owns 98% of the island. Lanai, however, hasn't always enjoyed such a peaceful and simple existence. For generations, Maui chiefs believed that evil spirits inhabited the island. Prince Kaulula'au, the unruly son of King Kaka'alaneo, is said to have used trickery to rid Lanai of its spirits during his exile there in 1400. As a reward, Kaulula'au was given control of the island and he encouraged immigration from other islands. Life on Lanai remained relatively calm until King Kalaniopuu of the Big Island, after a humiliating defeat by King Kahekili in Maui, took his frustration out on Lanai by unleashing King Kamehameha. Kamehameha and his troops were brutal, slaughtering people on every part of the island. His wrath was so fierce that when Captain George Vancouver sailed past the island in 1792, he didn't bother to land because of Lanai's apparent lack of villages and population.

Deterred by shipwreck-causing ocean swells, travelers to Lanai were scarce until 1861, when a group of Mormon missionaries, led by **Walter Murray Gibson,** arrived and began to build a holy city in the Palawai Basin. In 1864, it was discovered that Gibson had been using church funds to acquire land for himself, and he was excommunicated. This didn't faze him; he befriended King Kalakaua, who eventually appointed him Prime Minister. As such, Gibson effectively controlled the entire kingdom. After Gibson's death, his daughter and her husband started the Maunalei Sugar Company at Keomuku, but were forced to cease operations in 1901 when their wells turned brackish. In 1910, the couple acquired more land to form the Lanai Company, and tried their hands at cattle ranching. New Zealander **George Munro** was hired as foreman, and he is credited with planting the tall pine trees that still shade the central portion of the island. In 1917, the Baldwin Brothers bought the Lanai Company, and five years later, sold it to **James Dole.**

Dole had studied agriculture, with a specialization in canning, at Harvard. He built Kamalapau Harbor and Lanai City and connected them with highways, and is responsible for much of the island's infrastructure. Thanks to his business savvy, the exotic pineapple became a household staple for millions of Americans. By the late 1930s, the Great Depression and the availability of cheap land and labor in Southeast Asia lured Dole overseas, and the Castle and Cook Company bought out his interest in the island. David Murdoch is the current CEO of Castle & Cook, and the two resorts that now comprise Lanai's primary industry are his brainchildren.

Though the introduction of the resorts to Lanai has yet to have a major effect on daily island life, the hotels have experienced a steady rate of growth in recent years, due in part to the increase in wealthy and celebrity guests. With rumors of the Lanai Company's plans to build luxury vacation homes on the island, Lanai's population could soon skyrocket, jeopardizing the island's quaint charm and hospitality. Locals, however, have great pride in their island, and visitors to Lanai might not observe any changes for quite some time.

HIGHLIGHTS OF LANAI

GO OFF-ROAD on the rugged Munro Trail and experience untamed Lanai (p. 283).

TRAVEL BACK IN TIME in the Garden of the Gods, with its ancient stone formations and mythical history (p. 284).

LET YOUR IMAGINATION WANDER at Shipwreck Beach, where many a doomed sea vessel has run aground (p. 285).

◤ INTERISLAND TRANSPORTATION

The easiest and least expensive way to reach Lanai is by **ferry,** which runs from **Lahaina, Maui** to **Manele Harbor** (45min., 5 per day 6:45am-5:45pm; $25 one-way, children $20) and back (5 per day 8am-6:45pm). The ride takes about 45min. To make a reservation, call Expeditions (☎800-695-2624 or 661-3756), or just show up at the pier; there are usually seats available.

If you aren't coming from Maui, you'll have to fly. Schedules change frequently, so check airline web sites or call for current departure cities and times. **Hawaiian Air** (☎800-367-5320 or 838-1555 on Oahu, 800-882-8811 on neighboring islands; www.hawaiianair.com) flies from Honolulu (30min., 1 per day 4:28pm, $82 one-way) as well as many other cities (even Las Vegas and Juneau), depending on the season. **Island Air** (☎800-323-3345, Oahu ☎484-2222, neighboring islands 800-652-6541; www.islandair.com) flies from Honolulu (30min., 7 per day, approx. $80 one-way). **Pacific Wings** (☎888-575-4548 or 873-0877, www.pacificwings.com), flies from Honolulu (30min., 1-2 per day 9:30am-5:30pm, approx. $65 one-way) and Kahului, Maui (15min., 2 per day 8:15am-4:20pm, approx. $65 one-way).

◤ LOCAL TRANSPORTATION

Once on the island, you'll need to rent a car, as there is no local transportation other than **Rabaca's Limousine Service.** (☎565-6670. Open 24hr. $5 per person between town and the airport, $10 to Manele Bay. 2-person min.) The island's many dirt roads are suitable only for 4WD—a necessary luxury if you want to get anywhere on the island. None of the rental companies on Lanai offer supplemental insurance. The island is covered in loose red dirt, so get a hard top and close your windows unless you want to end up coated in dust and mud.

 Adventure Lanai Ecocentre, 338 8th St., is a laid-back operation run by Kayak John, aka "Mikey," a relaxed and helpful islander with an uncanny knowledge of Lanai and all it has to offer. The gang at Adventure Lanai rents safari-style 4WD Jeep Wranglers with big off-road mud tires, roof racks, A/C, snorkel gear, body boards, and an ice chest for $104 per day. Nine-passenger 4WD Suburbans with all the gear are also available for $139 per day. Unlike the competition, they let you take their vehicles anywhere. Reservations are highly recommended. Adventure Lanai also rents rooms (see **Accommodations and**

Lanai

Kalohi Channel

Au'au Channel

Polihua Beach

Ka'ena Point

Shipwreck Beach

Awalua Tr.

Lapaiki Tr.

Polihua Tr.

Federation Camp

Maunalei

Kahokunui

430

Ka'ena Tr.

Kanepu'u Preserve

Garden of the Gods

Keomuku Beach

Lanai Sporting Clays

Polihua Rd.

Keomuku Rd.

Keomuku

Cemetary Rd.

Ka Malamalama Church and Maunelei Sugar Mill

Honopu Bay

Nanahoa Tr.

Lanai City

Lana'ihale
3386' (1032m)

Munro Tr.

Ka'halepalaoa

Lopa

PACIFIC OCEAN

Awalua Ave.

Kaumalapau Hwy.

Luahiwa Petroglyphs

Manele Rd.

Hoike Rd.

Awehi Tr.

440

Airport Rd.

Miki Rd.

Palawai Basin

Kaumalapau Harbor

Kaupili Rd.

Lanai Airport

Manele Rd.

Naha

N
LG

Kolokolo Cave

Kaunolu Bay

Manele Tr.

Kaunolu

Hulopo'e Beach

Manele Bay/ Manele Harbor

0   4 miles

Halulu Heiau

Pu'u Pehe Cove

Sweetheart Rock

0   4 kilometers

Kealaikahiki Channel

Camping, p. 280) and every kind of outdoor equipment you can imagine. They run several **tours,** including a 4x4 adventure along the Munro Trail, the Garden of the Gods, and Shipwreck Beach ($99), a kayak/snorkel trip ($99), a downhill road bike trek ($99), and surfing and scuba diving trips ($99-129). All tours are catered to the traveler's request. Adventure Lanai also offers **bike rentals** at the cheapest rates on the island ($25 per day). Ask John and his crew any questions about Lanai and the current quality of its roads. Free pick-up available at Manele Bay Harbor for renters. Mention *Let's Go* for discounts. (☎565-7373; www.adventurelanai.com. Open M-Sa 8am-5:30pm.)

If you prefer to rent from a national company, **Dollar,** 1036 Lanai Ave., south of Dole Park, has a fleet of red and yellow Jeep Wranglers ($129 per day) and Jeep Cherokees ($145 per day) that are usually available without a reservation. Cars, which are restricted to paved roads by both the rental agreement and the terrain, range from $60-129 per day. Reserve well in advance. Dollar also has useful daily updates on road conditions. Beware of hidden rental fees and high towing rates. (☎800-533-7808 or 565-7227. Open daily 7am-7pm.)

The only **gas station** on the island is **Lanai City Service,** on the Dollar property. Gas is pricey, often pushing $2.75 per gallon. (Open daily 7am-7pm. AmEx/D/MC/V.)

LANAI CITY

Though the "city" is actually more of a quaint town, Lanai City is the social and cultural center of the island, providing Lanai's residents with their basic needs. Built by Jim Dole in 1922 to house plantation workers and their families, Lanai City was the first planned community in the islands. Almost all of Lanai's inhabitants live in the brightly painted houses here. At an elevation of nearly 1600 ft., Lanai City is usually cool and misty, and clouds frequently obscure the tops of Munro pines that appear throughout the town, giving it the feel of a forest park. Visitors won't see a single stoplight or fast-food joint in Lanai City, but they'll find a lovely community of restaurants, shops, and art galleries.

ORIENTATION

Lanai City surrounds **Dole Park,** a large, rectangular grassy area that runs basically east-west. Its longer borders are **7th Street** to the north and **8th Street** to the south. The area is designated as the **Lanai City Commercial Park,** and most of the town's stores and eateries are located along these streets. The town is bordered by the two largest streets—**Fraser Avenue** to the west, and **Lanai Avenue** to the east. All streets are at right angles, and those running east-west are numbered 3rd-13th, with 3rd St. the farthest north. Those running north-south run alphabetically, starting with Fraser in the west and ending with Queens in the east.

PRACTICAL INFORMATION

Banks: Bank of Hawaii, 460 8th St., at Lanai Ave. (☎565-6246). **First Hawaiian Bank,** 644 Lanai Ave. at 7th St. (☎565-6969). Both are open M-Th 8:30am-4pm, F 8:30am-6pm and have 24hr. **ATMs** in front, though Bank of Hawaii closes daily from 1-2pm.

Laundromat: Launderette Lanai, on 7th St. and Houston. Wash $1.25, dry $0.75. Detergent $0.75. No change machine. Open daily 5am-8:30pm.

Emergency: ☎911.

Police: 312 8th St., at Fraser Ave. (☎565-6428). Open 24hr.

Hospital: 628 7th St., east of Lanai Ave. (☎565-6411). **Emergency room open 24hr.,** administrative office open M-F 8am-4:30pm.

Copy services: At the Lanai **Education Center** of Maui Community College, on 7th St. and Houston. Copies 5¢. Open daily 9am-5pm.

Internet Access: Also at the **Education Center** (see above). Though the center's 12 computers are restricted to educational use only from 1-4pm, they are free and open to the public daily 9am-noon and 4-5pm. Internet is also available at the **public library,** 555 Fraser Ave., (☎565-7920). $10 temporary library membership required. Open Tu, Th-F 8am-4pm, W 1-8pm, Sa 11am-4pm.

Video Rental: Lanai Family Store, 443 7th St. (☎565-6485). Wide but dated selection of VHS tapes ($3 per day). Open M-Sa 10am-noon and 3-6:30pm, Su 4-6:30pm.

Post Office: 620 Jacaranda, just north of Dole Park (☎565-6517). Open M-F 9am-4pm, Sa 10am-noon. Self-service stamps and shipping open 24hr.

Postal Code: 96763.

ACCOMMODATIONS AND CAMPING

Lanai is famous for its five-star resorts, due in large part to the **Lodge At Koele** (☎800-565-3868 or 565-7300), located just north of town, and its sister resort the **Manele Bay Hotel** (☎565-7700). Though a room at either of these legendary spots

Lanai City

ACCOMMODATIONS
Dreams Come True, 13
Hotel Lanai, 11
Rasta House, 7

FOOD
Blue Ginger Cafe, 4
Canoes, 5
Coffee Works, 1
Henry Clay's Rotisserie, 12
Pele's Other Garden, 8
Pine Isle Market, Ltd., 9
Richard's Shopping Center, 10

SHOPPING
Gifts with Aloha, 3
Lanai Family Store, 6
Mike Carroll Gallery, 2

($325-2200) might break the bank, a walk through their grounds is free. **Okamoto Realty,** 730 Lanai Ave. (☎565-7519; www.lanairealestate.com), has several vacation rentals, mostly upscale three-bedroom cottages ($150-175). Check online for details and photos. Several **B&Bs** in town offer a range of good, affordable options.

Dreams Come True, 547 12th St., at Lanai Ave. (☎800-566-6961 or 565-6961; www.dreamscometruelanai.com). Each room in this bright, cheery 3-bedroom B&B has private marble bath, whirlpool tub, and bathroom skylight. Rooms share access to a full kitchen and backyard garden deck. Jeep Cherokees available for guests to rent ($100 per day). Also ask about massage therapy ($50). Singles/doubles $99, additional person $25. Entire house (fits 10) $380. Owners also rent out other homes nearby; check the web site for constantly-changing information. AmEx/MC/V. ❸

Rasta House, rented through Adventure Lanai Ecocentre at 338 8th St. (☎565-7373; www.adventurelanai.com. See **Interisland Transportation,** p. 278). Painted in a distinctly Jamaican color scheme, Rasta House has character to spare. 3 bedrooms, 6 beds (1 is a double), 1 sunken bathroom, and a tile counter with stools in the kitchen. Approx. $60 per person, but prices decrease dramatically if you rent as a group. Mention *Let's Go* for a substantial discount. Reservations required. AmEx/MC/V. ❷

Hotel Lanai, on Lanai Ave., above 8th St. (☎800-795-7211 or 565-7211; fax 565-6450; www.hotellanai.com). Hotel Lanai is a fantastic value for the service you'll receive. The staff is warm and friendly, and the 10 welcoming rooms all come with quilted bedspreads, pine dressers, immaculate modern bathrooms, large rugs, and ceil-

LANAI

ing fans. Local art adorns the walls. Complimentary continental breakfast and shuttle service to the public beach. Check-in 1pm. Check-out 11am. Spacious rooms for 1-3 people $105-135. Private cottage $175. AmEx/MC/V. ❸

Hulopo'e Beach Park camping, near Manele Bay (see p. 287). There are 6 official campsites, each with a grill and access to restrooms. The showers that line the beach have pipes that catch the sun, heating the water. There are often groups of locals in semi-permanent campsites on the beach. If you find that the campsites are all booked (a frequent occurrence on weekends), try to find a local to sponsor you, which may allow you to camp for free. You can't beat the location or the price; Hulopo'e Beach is simply gorgeous. One-time $10 registration fee, plus an additional $5 per group per night. For reservations contact Castle & Cook (☎565-7700) or call the park ranger at the beach office (☎565-2345; office open daily 8am-5:30pm). ❶

☕ FOOD

The hotel restaurants on Lanai are all exorbitantly expensive. The only exception is **Henry Clay's Rotisserie ❺**, at Hotel Lanai, which serves superb cajun-fusion cuisine and is only marginally out of reach for budget travelers. (Appetizers $10-15, entrees $18-36. Open daily 5:30-9pm.) On Saturday mornings, there's a **swap meet** in Dole Park where locals serve homemade ethnic dishes and socialize.

GROCERY STORES AND MARKETS

Pine Isle Market, Ltd., 356 8th St. (☎565-6488). Equal parts grocery store, hardware store, and drug store, Pine Isle is the closest thing to a supermarket on the island. Also carries beer and wine. Open M-Sa 8am-7pm.

Richard's Shopping Center, 434 8th St. (☎565-6488). Another grocery store *cum* hardware store, with a decent selection of produce and the cheapest ice and coolers in town. Also sells beer, wine, and liquor. Open M-Sa 8:30am-6:30pm.

RESTAURANTS

▨ **Pele's Other Garden,** on 8th St. and Houston St. (☎565-9628). By day, Pele's is a genuine New York deli-style eatery that serves quality sandwiches ($6-8) on fresh homemade bread. Enjoy lunch on the outdoor patio overlooking Dole Park. By night, the staff changes the lighting, tablecloths, music, and menu to create a romantic Italian bistro. Try the bruschetta ($5). Pasta dishes (available in half or full portions, $12-19) go well with a glass of wine. Reservations recommended. Open M-Sa 9:30am-3pm for lunch, 5-9pm for dinner. AmEx/D/MC/V. ❸

Canoes, 419 7th St. (☎565-6537). Though this local favorite recently underwent a change in management and name (formerly Tanigawa's), Canoes has maintained its quality food and friendly atmosphere. Open for breakfast and lunch, it attracts locals who gather early in the morning to *talk story*. The pancakes ($3.75) are not to be missed, and the daily lunch specials are a guaranteed hit (burgers and sandwiches $2.50-6). Dine-in or take-out. Open M-T and Th-Su 6:30am-1pm. ❶

Coffee Works, 604 Ilima St., north of Dole Park (☎565-6962). Coffee Works has recently come to Lanai after 29 years in business on Oahu. They ship coffee across the country, but you can enjoy yours on the large deck out front. The house special espresso milkshake ($4.50) is worth every penny. Pizza bagels, deli sandwiches, cinnamon buns, and other light fare $3-5. Look for $1 off coupons at Adventure Lanai Ecocentre (see p. 278). Open M-F 5am-4pm, Sa 6am-4pm, Su 6am-1pm. ❶

Blue Ginger Cafe, 409 7th St. (☎565-6363). Blue Ginger is Lanai's all-purpose eatery and the best bargain on the island. (Two eggs, choice of meat, rice, and toast $5. Plate lunches $6-9. Dinner specials $13-15.) Known for its fresh fish, usually *ono* or mahi mahi; if you don't want yours lightly fried, ask the chef to broil it. Mexican food on Tu. Open daily 6am-8pm. ❷

🛍 🎨 SHOPPING AND ART

The quiet and calm pace of life in Lanai City provides an inspiring and creative forum for the arts on the island. The few art galleries and shops that have recently opened around Dole Park easily allow visitors to spend an afternoon perusing the work of local artists and craftspeople.

🖼 **Mike Carroll Gallery,** Jacaranda St. (☎ 565-7122; www.studiomike.com), just behind Okamoto Realty on 7th St. This cozy gallery features island-inspired paintings, photography, and prints created by local artists and complemented by the Chinese furniture on display. While original works sell for anywhere from $500-2500, decent-sized prints are reasonable ($25-75). Shipping available. Open Tu-Sa 11am-5pm, or by appointment.

Gifts with Aloha, 363 7th St. (☎ 565-6589; fax 565-9129; www.giftswithaloha.com). Local artwork, handcrafted jewelry, and aloha-inspired clothing and keepsakes. This aptly-named shop also provides shipping services. Open M-Sa 9:30am-6pm.

🎵 ENTERTAINMENT

There isn't much to do on Lanai after dark other than sleep or see a first-run movie at the **Lanai Playhouse,** 465 7th Ave. (☎ 565-7500. $7, ages 3-12 and seniors $4.50, under 3 free.) The only bar in town is at Henry Clay's Rotisserie in Hotel Lanai (well drinks $5-6). A good way to spend the evening is to wander the streets just before sunset, when locals tend their gardens and children play in the streets.

For some daytime excitement, head north of town on Keomuku Rd. toward Shipwreck Beach and turn left after 1½ mi. at the **Lanai Pine Sporting Clays** sign, where you can blast compressed fertilizer discs with a 12-gauge shotgun on a gorgeous sporting clay range. Both car rental agencies provide a voucher for ten free shots, and it's worth taking advantage of the offer if you have time. (☎ 563-4600; reservations@lanai-resorts.com. Reservations highly recommended. $75 for 25 clays, $105 for 50. Open daily 9am-2:30pm.) If clays aren't your bag, try archery. ($45 for a 45-minute introductory session, $35 for experienced shooters.)

For Tiger Woods aspirants, the Lodge at Koele maintains the nine-hole, par three **Cavendish Golf Course** (on Keomuku Rd., just north of town), a public course free to residents and visitors. Take advantage of the well-maintained grounds for a complimentary round if you bring your own clubs. (Donations appreciated.)

CENTRAL LANAI

MUNRO TRAIL

To reach the trail from town, take the highway (Keomuku Rd.) toward Shipwreck Beach. Past the Lodge at Koele, take a right onto Cemetery Rd. With the cemetery on your right, veer left after the pavement ends and look for a sign that marks the trailhead. The trail is about 8½ mi. long and can take anywhere from 1¼-3hr. to complete, depending on road conditions. Also expect to spend about 30min. making your way from the end of the trail back to the highway.

If you only have time to do one off-road trek while you're on Lanai, this is by far your best bet. The Munro Trail is named for the New Zealand naturalist who planted Lanai's magnificent pines. Much of the trail passes five-alarm views of Maui, Molokai, and Oahu, as well as the former pineapple fields of Lanai far below.

Be certain to stay on the main road. Side roads are often very muddy because they only exist for water drainage purposes; it should be clear which is the most-traveled road. The only potentially confusing point is after 2 mi. where the road to the left stops after only 50 yards, leading visitors to a **lookout** over the gigantic Maunalei Gulch, the source of the island's drinking water.

ROM THE ROAD

STUCK IN THE MUD

After reading *Let's Go: Hawaii 2003*s coverage of Lanai, I was a bit skeptical of my ability to hop in a 4x4 Jeep and cruise around the island's unmapped miles of dirt roads. Though my New England lead foot was accustomed to driving in the snow, my off-roading skills weren't exactly up to snuff. Much to my relief, I received an offer to tour Lanai's lesser-known sites with Benjamin, a friendly local who was born and raised on the island. My mother would be relieved: I had an experienced tour guide to take me around Lanai, and I wouldn't have to put myself behind the wheel of a Jeep.

Settled in Benjamin's pick-up truck, we hit the road. Our first stop was Shipwreck Beach, a peaceful spot on the northeast corner of the island. Shipwreck was relatively easy to get to, and I was feeling much more confident about my afternoon trek, and wondering why it was that last year's *Let's Go* was so adamant about the dangers of Lanai's unpaved roads. I mentioned this to Benjamin, and he assured me that in all his years on the island, not once had he been stuck.

Never count your chickens before they hatch. Our next destination, the ancient town of Keomuku, was on a more obscure stretch of Lanai's coast. But I felt confident with Benjamin behind the wheel, so we started our journey south. As there were large ruts in the road, Benjamin decided to

> Munro Trail is generally in good condition, but it can only be navigated in a 4WD vehicle. Be absolutely certain not to attempt the trail if it has rained in the last 24hr.—there are several places where an inopportune skid could send your vehicle over the edge of the road and into a deep ravine. Check with a car rental agency for an update on road conditions before you go. Drive slowly, use first gear, and keep your eyes on the road.

The main road bears right instead, and it takes you as close as you can get to **Lana'ihale**, Lanai's highest point (3,368 ft.). After another mile or two, just past the communications tower on the left, is a good view of Ho'okio Gulch, the site of the defeat of Native Lanaian warriors by King Kamehameha.

At the end of the trail, there are three options. The road to the far right heads back toward the mountain, but it stops at a gated fence after about 1½ mi. The road to the left is the shortest route back to the highway; veer right at the first major fork, proceed through a cattle gate, and continue onto Ho'ike Rd., which connects to the highway at a stop sign and six large pine trees. Turn right to head back into town. The road straight ahead eventually meets up with the road on the right, but before it does, make a sharp left onto a red dirt road, just before some large boulders on the left, where the road you've been traveling on curves right. This red dirt road eventually becomes Ho'ike Rd. If you get lost, backtrack, and aim for the pine trees that line the highway.

THE NORTH SIDE

■ GARDEN OF THE GODS

Half a mile beyond the Kanepu'u Preserve; see directions below. The Garden is approximately 20min. from town. The drive requires a 4WD vehicle, but the road is usually in decent condition if it hasn't been raining. There are a few places where a careless driver might tip his vehicle, but the drive is less challenging than most others on the island.

Keahi Kawelo, or Garden of the Gods, is a vast, desert-like expanse of red earth populated by thousands upon thousands of rock towers. Though some of these are only three stones tall, others are large, intricate structures that have impressively withstood the elements for ages. These more complex towers were supposedly created by the gods, inspiring locals to follow suit with their own man-made versions. The winding topography of the wind-swept terrain and sheer magnitude of the towers are both surreal and awe-inspiring. The towers are concentrated at the beginning of the garden, but to fully appreciate the splendor of the place, drive all the way through. Late afternoon is the best time to visit the garden, when the towers cast long shadows in the early evening and the warm tones of the setting sun complement the colors of the lunar landscape.

KANEPU'U PRESERVE

To reach the Kanepu'u Preserve, take Keomoku Rd. north from town. Just past the Lodge at Koele, turn left onto the dirt road between the tennis courts and the stables. Past the stables, turn right at the intersection with the rock that reads "Garden of the Gods."

A road leading over three sets of cattle grates enters the silvery ironwood and pine forest that comprises the beginning of the 460-acre preserve. After a short mile on this road, you'll see a sign for a self-guided trail on the right. The hike is very short, and provides information about the rare vegetation in the preserve, including the largest collection of **native Hawaiian dry forest** on the island. Some 48 native species can be found here, including endangered Lanai sandalwood and rare Hawaiian gardenia. The preserve is maintained by the **Nature Conservancy,** 730 Lanai Ave. (☎565-7430), and free tours can be arranged upon request.

SHIPWRECK BEACH

To get to Shipwreck Beach, take Keomoku Rd. until it ends; turn left onto a sandy dirt road at the end of the highway. Be careful not to drive into any of the large ruts in the road. The road is usually decent, but do not attempt it in a 2WD vehicle or in the rain. Under no circumstances should you drive on the beach itself; doing so is illegal and risks becoming stuck.

The drive to Shipwreck Beach is simply beautiful. The short dune grass along Keomuku Rd., the highway north of town, flows along and around hills, winding to the sea. The narrow road offers arresting views of both Molokai and Maui as well as the abandoned, rusting hulls of two large ships that give the 4 mi. stretch of white sand beach its name. This part of the island gets less than a dozen inches of rain per year, and the vegetation is just sparse enough that the bright red dirt of the region peeks through, creating a rough-hewn patchwork of contrasting colors.

The first of the nearby sights is **Federation Camp,** a cluster of deserted fishing shacks built in the early 20th century by the island's pineapple plantation

take a short-cut via the beach. I remembered reading somewhere that driving on the beach was illegal, but I thought nothing of it, since Benjamin was a *local.* He knew what he was doing. As we cruised down the beach, I marveled at how fun it was to drive right on the shore. And then it happened. I felt the front wheels just sink into the wet beach sand, and I knew it was over. Cursing in pidgin, Benjamin fruitlessly tried to back the truck out of the sand. It was no use; we weren't going *anywhere.*

After an hour of digging, Benjamin and I locked up the truck and walked 4 mi. before we were able to hitch a ride back to town. I didn't mind the walk; I was on a gorgeous island hiking in the warm sun. But Benjamin didn't feel so honored. After a few miles of frustrated cursing, Benjamin turned to me and said, "I guess we should have listened to your guidebook." I couldn't help smiling.

-Lucy Ebersold, 2003

workers as vacation homes. A few minutes beyond the houses is a turnaround area with picnic tables. Park here and continue walking in the direction you've been driving to reach a cement foundation that once supported a lighthouse. With your back to the sea, walk down the small ramp of the lighthouse foundation and continue for about 100 yards (past a boulder that warns "Do Not Deface") to reach some well-preserved **petroglyphs.** Look carefully to see these ancient drawings of warriors and animals, believed to date back to AD 500-900. To reach the beach from the petroglyphs, either continue to the right through a dry creek bed or back-track and walk down from the lighthouse. Though the beach can at times be appropriate for snorkeling or swimming, it's more enjoyable for beachcombing and strolling.

Once on the beach, walk along the coast toward the shipwreck, which becomes visible almost immediately. You'll pass a sign for the **Kaiolohia-Kahue Trail,** which was built in the 19th century by the territorial government to link several small coastal settlements. It has been designated a "demonstration trail" by the Na Ala Hele Trails Access Program, and is scheduled to be ready for hiking by 2004.

As you continue, keep your eyes open for dozens of piles of sand scattered around holes in the ground. These crab homes, combined with the bizarre array of colors and textures in the surrounding vegetation, give an unearthly feel to the beach. **Sea turtles** have been known to lay eggs on this beach at night. After about 15min. you'll reach the closest point to the **Liberty Ship,** a WWII-era frigate that became stuck on the reef due to navigational error. There are nearly a half-dozen other shipwrecks along the beach, and bits of them frequently wash up on shore. Most of the wrecks are no longer visible, except the one at **Awula,** 6 mi. beyond the Liberty Ship and accessible via a rough dirt road beyond the Garden of the Gods.

KEOMUKU BEACH AND ENVIRONS

To get to Keomuku Beach from the end of the highway, veer right on a dirt road that runs parallel to the beach. The village is about 5½ mi. down. At the time of writing, the road was in good condition for 3 mi. After that, the road was completely washed out and impassable, forcing traffic to drive along the beach itself. This is neither safe nor legal, since the beach is passable only at low tide, and even then you run a sizeable risk of getting stuck in the deep sand. Also, you will have no way of knowing where to stop to see the sights if you drive on the beach. Check with your rental agency to see if the road has been re-graded before heading out.

The narrow strip of dark sand that runs from the end of Keomuku Rd. southeast to Kahalepalaoa Landing is fit for neither swimming nor sunbathing. The water is shallow and rocky, and the beach is often marred by trash. Until 1900, this part of the island was the most densely populated; now it's empty, save for the occasional fisherman or campsite.

After about 5½ mi. you will reach **Keomuku Village,** a former sugar plantation. The plantation was operated by the Maunalei Sugar Company, which failed in 1901. The only noteworthy sight is the **Ka Malamalama Church,** which was built by the inhabitants of surrounding villages after the collapse of the island's sugar industry.

Drive slowly as you leave the village; after about a mile, a walking trail on the right leads inland to **Kahe'a Heiau,** once the site of human sacrifices, which was partially dismantled by the Maunalei Company to build a railroad. The railroad moved sugar to the **Halepalaoa Landing** south of the *heiau.* The landing has a decent view of Maui and the best beach for sunbathing on this side of the island.

Another 4½ mi. down the road lies **Lopa Beach,** noteworthy only because you must pass it on the way to **Naha,** the site of an ancient fishpond. Naha is nearly 12 mi. from the end of the highway, and probably not worth the trek, though Maui residents sometimes charter boats that drop them at the beach there for the day.

THE SOUTH SIDE

MANELE BAY AND HULOPO'E BEACH

Dominated by the luxurious Manele Bay Hotel, Manele Bay is home to Lanai's most popular **beach,** only **campground,** and a small harbor where you can catch the ferry to Maui (see **Interisland Transportation,** p. 278). From town, take the highway (Manele Rd.) south. As the road straightens out, you'll be driving through the caldera of an extinct volcano. This tree-lined **Palawai Basin** was once the center of the Dole Plantation.

At the very end of the highway, after a series of sloping switchbacks down to shore, the road forks. To the left is **Manele Harbor,** the ferry landing. The harbor was the site of a Hawaiian fishing village during the 18th century, and was the island's principal port until the construction of the commercial harbor at Kaumalapa'u. To the right is **Hulopo'e Beach Park,** the island's best beach for **swimming, snorkeling,** and **sunbathing.** The surf is nothing special in the summer, but picks up in the winter. The white-sand beach is large enough to never be crowded. Both the beach and the harbor are part of a conservation district which prohibits boat fishing and the removal of any objects, including rocks. Hulopo'e also holds the island's only **campsite,** and the facilities are fabulous, complete with picnic tables, BBQ grills, showers, and restrooms (See **Accommodations and Camping,** p. 280).

From the beach, walk along the bay to the left to reach **Pu'u Pehe Cove,** full of multi-colored volcanic rock formations. At low tide, take the steps down to the cove's tide pools teeming with young marine life. Continue along the bay to reach Pu'u Pehe Rock, also known as **Sweetheart Rock** (see **Sepulchre by the Sea,** below). This southeastern lookout is a romantic spot to watch the morning sunrise or catch stunning views of nearby Maui.

SEPULCHRE BY THE SEA According to Hawaiian legend, a local fisherman decided to build his home in a cave to prevent other men from laying eyes on his beautiful wife, **Pehe,** for fear that they would covet her. One day, while he was working on the other side of the island, a sudden storm swept his home into the sea, taking his wife with it. Her family recovered the body and brought it back to town. Late that night, the fisherman stole her body and buried it on top of an offshore island (Pu'u Pehe or "Sweetheart Rock"). Then, overcome with grief, he jumped off the rock to his death. The villagers buried him next to his wife, and if you stand close to the island, you can just make out two grave-like rock formations on its surface.

While at the beach, stroll around the grounds of the Manele Bay Hotel; there's a distinct path off to the right when facing the water that takes you up to the resort. You'll pass the *luau* grounds on your right and will soon arrive at Manele Bay's pool area. The facilities are only for the use of registered guests, but the view of the beach from the hotel is worth the quick walk.

LUAHIWA PETROGLYPHS

From town, take Manele Rd. toward Manele Bay. After the 7mi. marker, look for the back of a stop sign to the left of the once-paved Ho'ike Rd. After a short mile on this road, make a sharp left at a fencepost where the road rises. Continue along this road until you see a large pipe in the ground, and cross over the pipe and onto the high road. Follow both the road and the pipe about ½ mi. to a turnaround; the petroglyphs are on the right.

Lanai's largest collection of petroglyphs is scattered throughout a four-acre area. The ancient etchings of bird heads, circle patterns, people on horseback, and even the occasional dog are still visible centuries after their initial inscription, though some are unfortunately quite weathered. Be careful as you scramble around the hill; the footing can be tricky. You don't need a 4WD to get to there, but you do need lots of clearance; a regular car won't cut it.

KAUNOLU

Reaching Kaunolu is a bit tricky; you'll definitely need a 4WD vehicle. From town, take Kaumalapau Hwy. toward Kaumalapau Harbor. Past the 3 mi. marker on the left, you'll see the back of a stop sign and 2 dirt roads, 1 high and 1 low. Take the low road and reset your odometer just as you leave the highway. After ½ mi., take the red dirt road on the left, which runs parallel to the formerly-paved road that you've been on thus far. 2 mi. from the highway, keep your eyes open for a hydrant-like pipe on the left. The pipe sticks vertically out of the ground about 4 ft., and has a wheel-shaped handle at the top. You'll notice a smaller pipe on the right side of the road, also hydrant-like, which may be hidden in some brush. Turn right with the fence on the right side of the road, which stops just before the hydrants and makes a 90° turn. Do not go farther if it has rained in the last 24hr. Park and walk the rest of the way if the road becomes impassable. After 2.8 mi., veer right toward the lighthouse. After 4.4 mi., note (and ignore) the sign which claims that you can park to the right of the road. At the end of the road, take the right fork and park near the picnic table underneath a kiawe tree.

Despite the grueling drive to Kaunolu, the town is well worth a visit for its historical interest. The site of a small fishing village, Lanai's best-preserved *heiau*, and the vacation home of Kamehameha the Great, Kaunolu also boasts the most ruins and artifacts on the island; archaeologists are frequently seen prowling the lands. **Kaunolu Bay** is the southwestern-most point of the island, where currents from the north and east converge.

In Kamehameha's day, Kaunolu villagers lived on the right side of the bay and were plagued by flash floods during periods of heavy rain. You can just make out the ruins of Kamehameha's house past the picnic table on the hill on the left. Hike down to the beach and walk across it. At the far side you can walk inland, past the remains of a canoe shed that served as the village shrine to the fishing god, and climb up to the **Halulu Heiau.** Note the square fire pit in the center of the *heiau*, as well as the well-preserved north and west walls. The site is considered holy by the Hawaiian people; do not climb on the walls, and don't move or remove any rocks.

Walk toward the ocean for a good view of **Kane'apua Rock,** a large island about 100 yards from shore. With your back to the rock, proceed inland about 25 yards to see some faded **petroglyphs** on a group of large rocks in a quarter-circle. To the left is **Kahekili's Leap,** a 5 ft. opening in the cliff wall where Kamehameha's warriors would prove their valor by jumping into the shallow water below. The opening creates a dramatic frame for Shark Island, which resembles the dorsal fin of a shark. Peer to the right for a view of Kolokolo Cave, where a now-dormant lava tube is believed to have run through the cliffs into the Kaunolu village ravine.

KAUMALAPA'U HARBOR

Though there isn't much there, the quick trip to Kaumalapa'u Harbor is worthwhile simply because it is connected to town by a paved road. At one time, over a million pineapples a day were sent to canning plants on Oahu via the harbor, but today it is a drab commercial facility operated by an oil company. It is also the landing site for the weekly barge that supplies the island with goods such as cars, furniture, industrial equipment, and wholesale products retailed at grocery and hardware stores. The area is rarely populated after 5pm, and the stone wall that borders the road is a great perch from which to watch the sunset.

Surfing in Hawaii

Known as the "sport of kings," surfing was born and bred in Hawaii. *Ali'i*, or Hawaiian royalty, perfected the sport in the 1700s, and King Kamehameha could often be seen riding waves alongside his favorite wife, Queen Ka'ahumanu. In the early 1900s, Duke Kahanamoku reigned the surf scene. He and his group of Waikiki Beachboys helped turn the sport into a national trend with their surfing skill and striking looks.

As surfing's popularity swelled, so did its associated adrenaline levels. The popular slogan "Eddie Would Go," often seen on t-shirts and bumper stickers, refers to the legendary moves of Eddie Aikau on Oahu's North Shore in the early 1970s. Eddie would go where no other big-wave rider dared, swimming out in 60-foot surf, risking life and limb for the thrill of the tube. The extreme sport of tow-in surfing, though no less dangerous, has since replaced the perils of paddling through pounding waves. Jet skis tow surfers from calm, onshore harbors to beyond the break, just in time for the intrepid individual to drop in for a monster set. Maui's world-renowned Peahi Bay—also nicknamed "Jaws" for its all-consuming waves—was home to the first annual Tow-In World Championship, held in January 2002, as well as the site of the unforgettable sequence in the latest Bond movie, *Die Another Day*, in which three camouflaged stunt men (all from Hawaii) are dropped from a helicopter into the surf below.

Today, surfing is one of the world's most popular sports and has developed into a thriving industry. Movies, fashion, and music have cemented surfing's place in pop culture. New technology now allows designers to tailor boards to unique surf conditions, so that surfers own not just one but an entire fleet of different models. Shapers such as Dick Brewer of Kauai and Maui's Rod Ole and Jeff Timpone are the elite artists of the surfing design world.

Surfing is also the second-fastest growing sport among women. While Queen Ka'ahumanu may have paved the way for her gender, the past 50 years have witnessed the most rapid rise in the number of surfing kahunesses. Changes in board construction have made surfboards easier for women to carry and maneuver. In 1959, the first Gidget movie was released, promoting the image of female surfers. Women finally made their way into the professional circuit with the founding of the Women's Pro Surfing Association in 1979 (though their winnings are still less than half that of professional male surfers). The best evidence for the growing popularity among women comes from *Surfer Magazine*; world pro Lisa Andersen was featured on its cover in 1995 with the line, "Lisa Andersen surfs better than you." Now, surf schools such as Surf Diva in California and Maui Surfer Girls in Maui cater primarily to women, while retailers like Girl in the Curl and Chicks with Sticks have also gained popularity. Movies have become the latest focal point for the rapidly spreading craze among *wahine* of all ages. The movie *Blue Crush*, shot on location in Oahu and released in 2002, re-introduced surfer girls to the big screen for the first time in a half-century. On any given day, women make up a solid percentage of those catching waves, dropping in, carving out their own place in this colorful pastime. *Imua!*

Maren Lau was a Researcher-Writer in Hawaii for Let's Go: California & Hawaii 1997. *She now lives in Maui and attends business school.*

KAHO‘OLAWE

LAND

At about 45 sq. mi., Kaho‘olawe, located 6 mi. south-west of Maui, is the smallest of Hawaii's eight major islands. At its widest and longest points it measures 11 mi. by 7 mi. The highest point on Kaho‘olawe is **Moa‘ulanui** (1477 ft.), the caldera of the volcano that created the island. Kaho‘olawe's sloping northern and western coasts were heavily populated by feral goats and sheep until 1988; overgrazing by these animals destroyed the region's plant cover, causing massive soil erosion. The silt that washed into the ocean as a result of this erosion killed much of the coral that originally grew there.

HISTORY

Early Hawaiians first inhabited Kaho‘olawe 1000 yr. ago, fishing and farming from settlements that spanned the width of the island. Originally named **Kanaloa** or **Kohemalamalama,** after the god of the ocean, Kaho‘olawe was also a renowned training ground for *kahunas* (priests), and the island is still home to hundreds of *heiaus* (temples) and shrines.

After the arrival of Westerners to the Hawaiian islands in 1778, Kaho‘olawe was inhabited by criminals who had been exiled from Maui. They managed to subsist by raiding settlements on Maui and Lanai. The island's population dwindled until 1858, when R.C. Wyllie, a Scottish resident of Kauai, unsuccessfully tried to start a sheep ranch on Kaho‘olawe. A second attempt during the early 1870s also failed, due to over-grazing. In 1917, a cattle rancher named **Angus MacPhee** signed a 37-year lease giving him Kahoolawe's land rights for $200 per annum, provided that he improve the island. An investor named Harry Baldwin bought a large interest in the **Kaho‘olawe Ranch** in 1922, and MacPhee began selling his cattle on Maui for a profit. During his years on the island, MacPhee decreased the goat population to manageable levels and reduced erosion by planting eucalyptus and Australian range grass.

As part of the war effort during WWII, Baldwin and MacPhee gave a small portion of Kaho‘olawe to the US Army, who turned it into an artillery range, despite the island's fragile archaeological and cultural inheritance. On December 8, 1941, the day after the Japanese attack on Pearl Harbor, the US Navy appropriated the entire island, citing a national emergency, and began using it for bombing practice. After the war, the Navy was supposed to return the island to Baldwin and MacPhee, but no action was taken until the lease ran out in 1954. To maintain control of Kaho‘olawe, President Eisenhower signed an executive order placing the island under the authority of the Secretary of the Navy. The order stipulated that the island must be restored to habitable condition once it was no longer needed by the military. Nearly every instrument of war used by the US military and its allies since WWII has been dropped, fired, or detonated on Kaho‘olawe, and the island holds the dubious distinction of being the most bombed island in the Pacific both during and after WWII. Due to the dangers posed by unexploded ammunition on the island and in its surrounding coastal waters, Kaho‘olawe has been uninhabited since it fell into the hands of the military.

In 1976, Hawaiian residents formed the **Protect Kaho'olawe 'Ohana,** a group dedicated to voicing public opposition to the bombing of Kaho'olawe and demanding the return of the island to the Hawaiian people. The 'Ohana staged several occupations of the island, leading to the arrest and conviction of a number of protestors. During the early 1980s, the US offered Kaho'olawe to foreign allies for use in bombing exercises, prompting objections from environmental groups in Great Britain, Australia, New Zealand, and Japan. The international media attention generated by the protests eventually led to cancellation of the bombing.

The 'Ohana also filed a lawsuit demanding the return of the island on environmental and religious grounds. The suit was partially settled in 1980, when the federal government signed a consent decree allowing visitors access to the island for cultural, educational, religious, scientific, or archaeological purposes. Under the decree, the 'Ohana have brought over 5000 visitors to Kaho'olawe. Several hiking trails have been cleared, and a few religious sites have been rededicated.

In October 1990, President George Bush, Sr. ceased all bombing on the island, and in November of the same year Congress established the **Kaho'olawe Island Conveyance Commission** to draft terms for the return of the island to the State of Hawaii. From December 1990 until July 1993, the commission held public hearings and conducted research, eventually outlining some general clean-up measures that would be necessary to make Kaho'olawe habitable.

In November 1993, Congress passed a law prohibiting any future military activity on Kaho'olawe. The law also appropriated $400 million in federal funds for a 10 yr. cleanup operation under a special Memorandum of Understanding between the US Navy and the State of Hawaii. That same year, the Hawaii State Legislature established the **Kaho'olawe Island Reserve,** declaring the island and the waters within two miles of its coast closed to public access. On May 7, 1994, the island was officially returned to the State of Hawaii, and the governor established a seven-member **Kaho'olawe Island Reserve Commission,** which is dedicated to preserving the island's archaeological, historical, and environmental resources for future generations.

In 2002, the Smithsonian Institution in Washington, D.C. held an exhibit on Kaho'olawe entitled *"Ke Aloha Kupa'a I Ka 'Aina"*—"Steadfast Love for the Land." The exhibit provided an historical journey through Hawaiian history on the island.

TODAY

The goals of the 10 yr. clean-up plan scheduled to expire November 11, 2003, proved a bit too lofty for the federal government. The Navy had originally intended to clear all surface debris, make the land reasonably safe for human access, re-vegetate the island with native species, clear hiking trails, and construct camping and educational facilities. Unfortunately, the contractors hired by the Navy were held to extremely low standards—only 85% of a particular job had to be completed to qualify the contractor for full payment. As a result, the clean-up has been woefully unsuccessful. As of October 2002, 15,953 acres of Kaho'olawe had been cleared. As of 2002, the Navy estimated that almost 5 million pounds of scrap metal had been collected.

Though much of the island is now reasonably safe for closely controlled visits by the 'Ohana and their guests, visions of true public access remain far-fetched. Access to the still-contaminated waters around the island is still restricted.

If you are set on visiting Kaho'olawe, contact the Protect Kaho'olawe 'Ohana (www.kaho'olawe.org) to inquire about joining one of their monthly trips. The trips have a religious and cultural focus and are primarily for Hawaiian residents, so don't expect a tour. Oahu's access coordinators are Kim Birnie (☎383-1651) and Davianna McGregor (☎956-7068).

KAHO'OLAWE

FURTHER INFORMATION

For general information about the island, contact the **Kahoʻolawe Island Reserve Commission,** 811 Kolu St. Suite 201. (On Oahu ☎ 243-5020, neighbor islands ☎ 468-4644; www.hawaii.gov/kirc.) Also try the **US Navy's web site** (www.efdpac.nav-fac.navy.mil/news/kaho/hp1.htm), which has updates about the clean-up process and pictures of bombs being detonated on the island. The various sections about Kahoʻolawe on the website of the **Bishop Museum,** 1525 Bernice St., Honolulu, may also prove informative. (☎ 847-3511; www.bishopmuseum.org.) The museum also stocks older books about Kahoʻolawe in its store.

Most **books** about Kahoʻolawe are out of print and hard to find. Your best bet is *Kahoʻolawe Na Leo o Kanaloa: Chants and Stories of Kahoʻolawe.* The book contains stories and chants about the island as well as a collection of photographs. **Inez MacPhee Ashdown,** the daughter of Angus MacPhee, recorded the history of her father's ranch, as well as some stories told to her by local Hawaiians, in a book called *Kahoʻolawe,* which has been out of print since 1970. Jay Hartwell's book, *Na Mamo: The Hawaiian People Today,* contains an insightful chapter about Kahoʻolawe. The more scientifically minded will appreciate J. Gilbert McAllister and Bernice P. Bishop's "Archaeology of Kahoʻolawe," a paper published in Vol. 115 of *The Museum Bulletin* in 1933, which was reprinted by the B. Kraus Reprint Company in 1971. The article, also available at the Bishop Museum, includes original accounts of Kahoʻolawe from before the bombing started.

KAHOʻOLAWE

NORTHWESTERN HAWAIIAN ISLANDS

LAND

The Northwestern Hawaiian Islands are an archipelago of reefs, small islands, and coral atolls that stretch for 1000 mi. across the Pacific from 150 mi. northwest of Kauai. The land areas of the expanse constitute a federal wildlife refuge which is administered by the US Fish and Wildlife Service. The islands and their surrounding waters constitute the **Northwest Hawaiian Islands Coral Reef Ecosystem Reserve,** which is the largest protected area in the US, covering 131,800 sq. mi. (3½ million acres). The unique and fragile **ecosystems** of the Northwest Hawaiian Islands contain over 70% of the coral reefs located in US waters, as well as 7000 marine species, half of which are endemic (unique to the island chain). Among the threatened and **endangered species** that reside there are: the Hawaiian monk seal, the loggerhead turtle, the hawkbill turtle, the leatherback sea turtle, and the green sea turtle.

About 1400 monk seals reside in the islands, with the largest breeding colony located on **French Frigate Shoals,** an atoll in the chain. **Nihoa Island** is the first island in the chain, as well as the largest, at 170 acres in area. Next is **Necker Island** (Mokumanamana Island), the top of a giant shield volcano that is also the oldest-known active volcano in the chain. Numerous *heiaus* (temples) on the island indicate that it was once inhabited, or at least frequented, by ancient mariners. French Frigate Shoals (Mokupapapa Island), **Gardner Pinnacles** (Puhahonu, named for their resemblance to turtles coming up for air), and **Marco Reef** (Nakukakala, meaning "surf that arrives in combers") follow in the chain. Nearby **Laysan Island** (Kauo, meaning either the yolk or white of an egg) is a large atoll which somewhat resembles a cracked egg, and is notable for the salty lagoon at its center, as well as the large number of birds that nest on the island. Beyond it lies **Pearl and Hermes Atoll,** called Holoikauaua by the ancient Hawaiians. The name means "dog-like animal that swims in the water." **Kure Atoll** (Kanemiloha'i, named for Pele's brother) is the most distant island, but before it lie the **Midway Islands** (Pihemnau, meaning "the loud din of birds"), the best-known group in the island chain. Midway includes an atoll and a few small islands, including Sand Island and Green Island.

HISTORY OF THE ISLANDS

There exists evidence of human presence on the islands from ancient times, and it is known that King Kalakaua had a wooden house built on distant Kure Atoll in 1885 and stocked it with provisions for anyone who became stranded on the island. US acquisition of the islands in 1867 led to more permanent activity, at Midway in particular. In 1903, part of the trans-Pacific cable was laid on the island and residents came to Midway to manage the station. **Midway** was made a national defense area in 1941 and served as a US Naval Base through WWII. One of the most decisive battles of WWII's Pacific Theater occurred at Midway Islands in June of 1942. The **Battle of Midway** was a victory for US forces which turned the tide of war in their favor against the Japanese. (See **History: World War II,** p. 17.) Midway continued to serve as a naval base until 1996 when the area was deemed a **National Wildlife Refuge** by the US Fish and Wildlife Service and was opened for ecotourism.

TODAY

Over the past decade, federal officials have hemmed and hawed over the fate of the Northwestern Hawaiian Islands. There are a number of administrative organizations for the islands and their surroundings, some of which overlap in jurisdiction. In 1992, the Midway Islands officially relinquished their military role when the Department of Defense shut down the Midway Naval Air Facility. It is now a federal refuge under the management of Midway Phoenix Corp. Most of the dry land within the Northwestern Hawaiian region is part of a **national wildlife refuge,** while the state controls everything within three miles from the beaches.

The **National Oceanic and Atmospheric Administration's National Ocean Service** manages the **Coral Reef Reserve** of the islands, conducting scientific research for fisheries and protected species, as well as documenting and removing marine debris from the islands and reefs. Meanwhile, the **US Fish and Wildlife Service** manages and protects the two wildlife refuges of the islands. These organizations, together with the **State of Hawaii Department of Land and Natural Resources, US National Park Service, University of Hawaii, Bishop Museum,** and the **Hawaii Maritime Center,** among others, have participated in multiple and diverse research projects on and around the islands. Learn all about their projects at www.hawaiianatolls.org.

Until 2002, the Midway Islands housed a resort for **ecotourism.** However, the Midway Phoenix Corp. shut down all operations in March 2002, citing a lack of profit. For more information on the Midway Islands and possible travel there, contact the **Midway Atoll National Wildlife Refuge,** P.O. Box 29460, Honolulu, 96820-1860. (☎ 674-8237; http://midway.fws.gov.)

FURTHER INFORMATION

Isles of Refuge: Wildlife and History of the Northwestern Hawaiian Islands, by Mark J. Rauzon. An account of the biology and history of the islands, complete with high-quality photographs and artwork.

Midway, by Hugh Bicheno. Complete with illustrations and maps, this account focuses on why the Japanese strategy failed during the battle of Midway.

Midway: The Battle That Doomed Japan, by Mitsuo Fuchida, Masatake Okumiya, Thomas B. Buell, and Kenji Kawakami. Told from the Japanese perspective, this version of the battle presents first-hand accounts from 2 naval aviators who give their insights as to why Japan lost at Midway.

Miracle at Midway, by Gordon William Prange, Donald M. Goldstein, and Katherine V. Dillon. Featuring eyewitness accounts from both sides, this narrative describes the battle of Midway in vivid detail, and how American military strategy led to a turning point in the Pacific War.

Northwestern Hawaiian Islands

PACIFIC OCEAN

200 miles
200 kilometers

Kure Atoll
Midway Atoll
Pearl and Hermes Atoll
Lisianski Island
Laysan Island
Marco Reef
Gardner Pinnacles
French Frigate Shoals
Necker
Nihoa
Kauai
Oahu
Maui
Hawaii

Tropic of Cancer

Kure Atoll
Sand Island
Green Island

Midway Atoll
Sand Island
Gooney Spit Is.
Eastern Island

Gardner Pinnacles
100 yds
100 m

Pearl and Hermes Atoll
North Is.
Little North Is.
Sand Is.
Bird Is.
Southeast Is.
Grass Is.
Kittery Is.
Seal Is.

Marco Reef

French Frigate Shoals
Trig Is.
Skate Is.
Tern Is.
Round Is.
Whale Is.
Mullet Is.
Shark Is.
Nea Is.
East Is.
Gin Is.
Le Pérouse Pinnacle
Little Gin Is.
Disappearing Is.

Laysan Island

PACIFIC OCEAN

Nihoa Island
Necker Island
Gardner Pinnacles
French Frigate Shoals

Tropic of Cancer

Kauai
Niihau

Scale for all detail maps except Gardner Pinnacles:
1 mile
1 kilometer

Lisianski Island

Necker Island
Shark Bay

Nihoa Island
Adams Bay

NW ISLANDS

THE BIG ISLAND

Let your love affair with the state of Hawaii grow here on its namesake island, but expect no whirlwind romance—Hawaii, better known as The Big Island, is vast and varied, and commands both time and attention. The island is about 4040 sq. mi. in area and is ever-expanding, thanks to Kilauea's constant eruptions. Geologically the youngest of all her sisters, The Big Island is nonetheless the largest and one of the most environmentally diverse. Within the island's borders 11 out of 13 climate ecosystems are represented, from the subarctic summits of Mauna Loa and Mauna Kea, to the rainforests of the Hamakua Coast, to the lava fields of the Ka'u desert. To journey through The Big Island is to brush with the rawest forces of nature—earth, sea, and sky. Here, you can almost touch the stars at the planetariums on Saddle Rd., see land birthed at the lava flows of Kilauea, and ride the waves of the mighty Pacific Ocean. The essence of Hawaii thrives in its hidden valleys and striking vistas. The effort required to discover its hidden side only amplifies an appreciation for the many facets of the island, as though you were able to see them as the Native Hawaiians who first settled here once did.

The spirit of Hawaiian pioneers is still strong in The Big Island, the birthplace of the islands' greatest king, Kamehameha I. The archaeological ruins on the island serve as a reminder of the accomplishments of this culture, and the respect with which the ancients treated the land. Places with significance to Native Hawaiians, like Ka Lae and Mo'okini Luakini Heiau, have undeniable *mana* (spiritual power).

Today, the first Hawaiians' spirit of *aloha* is maintained alongside the island's unique blend of practicality and idealism. Yet, as is always the case in a place with so much to offer, development has reared its ugly head, and seems to contest the values and ideals held by much of the local population. While big resorts and their incumbent infrastructure of golf courses and shopping malls has thus far been limited to the South Kohala Coast, vacation homes and Wal-marts are spreading at an alarming rate. Some development is inevitable on this island, but it remains to be seen whether Hawaii will be able to grow sustainably.

HIGHLIGHTS OF THE BIG ISLAND

SNORKEL among a rainbow of colorful fish in Kealakekua Bay's coral reefs (p. 341).

HIKE to the floor of Waipi'o Valley (p. 352) to a secluded, mile-long beach.

TRAVERSE the Kilauea Iki Crater, which was a lake of lava just 40 years ago, in Hawaii Volcanoes National Park (p. 312).

LIVE YOUR DREAM OF PARADISE at the stunning, 400 ft. Akaka Falls (p. 307).

SEEK INNER PEACE at the Buddhist temple of Nechung Dorje Drayang Ling (p. 347).

✈ INTERISLAND TRANSPORTATION

Flights from the Big Island to neighboring islands start at around $90 each way. Flight coupons are the cheapest option, and the mini kiosks of **Cut Rate Tickets** are their most convenient source. The kiosk in **Kailua-Kona** is located on downtown Palani Rd., next to Tesoro gas station. (☎326-2300. Open M-F 8:30am-6pm, Sa 9am-5pm.) The kiosk in **Hilo** sits next door to the Minit Stop on Rte. 11. (☎969-1944. Open daily 9am-5pm.) All coupons have expiration dates, and all seats must be booked directly through the airlines after purchase.

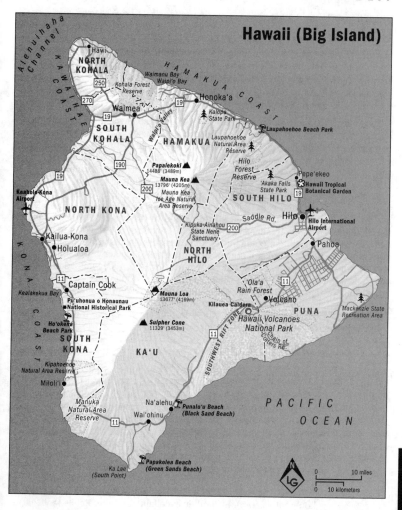

Hawaii (Big Island)

The Big Island has two major airports. **Keahole-Kona International Airport,** Keahole Airport Rd. (☎329-2484), 7 mi. north downtown **Kailua-Kona** off Rte. 19, is closest to South Kohala's crescent of resorts and thus sees the majority of international traffic. It is also served by inter-island carriers. **Aloha Airlines** (☎800-367-5250 or 935-5771; www.alohaairlines.com) flies to: Honolulu (14 per day 6:55am-8:20pm); Kahului, Maui (1 per day 10:55am-2:50pm); Lihue, Kauai (5 per day 8:55am-3:15pm). **Hawaiian Airlines** (☎800-882-8810; www.hawaiianair.com) flies to: Honolulu (14 per day 6:20am-8pm); Kahului, Maui (1:30pm); Lanai City, Lanai (3:30pm); Lihue, Kauai (10 per day via Honolulu 6:20am-6pm).

One half-mile south of the intersection of Rte. 11 and Rte. 19, **Hilo International Airport,** Airport Access Rd. (☎934-5801), sees mostly interisland flights, but is also served by **United Airlines** (☎800-241-6522). **Aloha Airlines** flies to: Honolulu (45min., 9-11 per day 6:25am-8pm); Kahului, Maui (7 per day via Honolulu 6:34am-5:05pm);

Lihue, Kauai (1¾hr., 4:10pm direct; 7 per day via Honolulu 6:30am-5:05pm). **Hawaiian Airlines** flies to: Honolulu (45min., 6 per day, 6:30am-6:15pm), Kahului, Maui (30min., 3 per day 6:30am-3:20pm); Lihue, Kauai (2hr., 6 per day 6:30am-6:15pm); Lanai (1 per day via Honolulu, 3:20pm). The **visitors' booth** by the baggage claim provides helpful maps and brochures. (Open daily 6am-8pm.) An $8-10 **taxi** ride is the only available transport from the airport to downtown Hilo.

⌷ TRANSPORTATION

Based in Hilo, the **Hele-On Bus** (☎961-8744; www.co.hawaii.hi.us) is The Big Island's only island-wide system of public transport. Buses are clean, modern, and comfortable, and fares are cheap. Unfortunately, catching a bus from anywhere *other* than downtown Hilo can be a challenge. This can prove problematic for budget travelers as most inexpensive flights (especially those via Honolulu) now arrive in Kona, where the only bus out of town departs daily at 6:45am.

Renting a car is the best and most convenient way to see the Big Island. Many beaches, volcanoes, and waterfalls are otherwise inaccessible. Although 4WD is not an absolute necessity, it does afford access to **Waipi'o Valley, Green Sands Beach,** and the summit of **Mauna Kea.** Strangely enough, such vehicles are hard to come by. Because most car companies prohibit travel on all but paved roads, even normally 4WD vehicles are sometimes stripped of 4WD capacity. Reasoning that visitors who abide by contract shouldn't technically *need* 4WD, only a handful—**Alamo, Dollar,** and **Harpers** among them—guarantee 4WD upon reservation. **AAA** (☎800-736-2886) provides roadside assistance to card holders throughout The Big Island, with the exception of the western-most half of Saddle Road. If you're in question about coverage area, call ahead. For inter-city and local transportation, consult the **Transportation** section for each town.

⌂ ACCOMMODATIONS

Budget travelers do best on the Hilo side, where a handful of **hostels** offer beds for $20 per night and public transportation to Volcanoes National Park and the Waipi'o Valley area is feasible. **B&Bs** have been popping up all over The Big Island (especially in South Kona and along the Hamakua Coast), offering the best mid-range accommodations. The **Hawaii Island B&B Association, Inc.** is a collection of over 50 B&B owners, and their web site (www.stayhawaii.com) lists accommodations by region. **B&Bs Online** (www.bbonline.com/hi/region4.html) is another good resource, with links to B&B web sites throughout The Big Island. For those planning a longer stay, **vacation rentals** are another affordable alternative. In addition to the booking agencies listed in the accommodations section for Kailua-Kona (see p. 331), **West Hawaii Property Services,** 78-6831 Ali'i Dr., Ste. 234A (☎800-799-5662 or 322-6696; www.konarentals.com), is another excellent resource. **Hotels** ($50-200) are ubiquitous in downtown Hilo and Kona, and **mega-resorts** ($250-to the moon) line the beaches of South Kohala. Low season (Apr. 15-Dec. 15) can offer deep discounts of up to 40% at even the swankiest of establishments.

⛺ CAMPING

Camping on the Big Island is possible with a bit of advance planning. Beaches and parks where you can pitch a **tent** all require permits, and most have maximum stays. On some more secluded beaches, travelers can get away with rolling out a sleeping bag, but this is discouraged. Some of the best camping on the island is found beach-front in **Waipi'o Valley,** in Volcanoes National Park at **Namakani Paio** or **Halape,** or in upcountry **Kalopa State Park,** on the northern side of the Kohala range. Building a fire can be difficult without a pre-bought supply of fire wood. Be sure to bring bug repellent, water bottles, and a **stove** for cooking and boiling water.

State, county, national, and private parks issue their own **permits**. See **Hawaii Volcanoes National Park,** p. 307, for more information on camping within that park.

Bishop Estate (☎322-5300), issues permits for camping in Waipi'o Valley. At press, the future of formalized camping within the valley was uncertain. Tents, however, appear to remain on the far side of the river regardless of regulation. Call ahead to inquire.

County Parks (☎961-8311; www.hawaii-county.com) require a permit (adults $6, ages 13-17 $2, ages 12 and under $1), good for a max. of 7 consecutive nights in winter, 14 in summer. Permits can be purchased online with a printer and major credit card, or write: Department of Parks and Recreation, 101 Pauahi St., Ste 6, Hilo 96720.

State Parks (☎974-6200.) require permits. Apply over the phone or write: Division of State Parks, Department of Land and Natural Resources, 75 Aupuni St., PO Box 936 Hilo 96720. Rates vary. Open M-F 8am-3:30pm.

HILO

The devastating tsunamis that struck Hilo in 1946 and 1960 have had a lasting impact here. Businesses seeking higher ground abandoned the old-fashioned downtown, which was ravaged twice. Hilo's buildings thus remain unchanged from its heyday in the first half of the 20th century. Hilo is the Big Island's metropolis, but despite housing more than a quarter of the island's population, it has a small-town feel. Hardly a tourist hotspot, and featuring a culture of alternative lifestyles, pan-Pacific shops and eateries, a colorful farmer's market, and botanical gardens and rainforest, it's an ideal place to get a taste of the real Hawaii.

◆ ORIENTATION

Hilo lies on the Big Island's east coast, at the intersection of **Route 19,** from the Hamakua Coast and Waimea, and **Route 11,** from Hawaii Volcanoes National Park. Kailua-Kona is 87 mi. away, across Saddle Rd. There are two distinct portions of Hilo: downtown and the neighborhoods of Waiakea and Pu'ainako. Downtown has Hawaii County seat and a number of museums and restaurants. **Bayfront Highway** (Rte. 19) and **Kamehameha Avenue** run parallel along Hilo Bay; Kamehameha serves as downtown's de facto Main St. Farther back from the water **Kilauea Avenue** and **Kino'ole Avenue** are the main arteries that run roughly parallel to the bay. **Waianuenue Avenue** is the major cross street, and becomes Saddle Rd. **Kanoelehua Avenue** (Rte. 11) runs through Waiakea and Pu'ainako, southeast of downtown.

◆ TRANSPORTATION

INTERCITY TRANSPORTATION

Buses: Hilo is the hub of the **Hele-On bus** (☎961-8744; www.co.hawaii.hi.us for schedules), and it is easier to get around the island from here than from anywhere else. Buses depart from the green-roofed **Mooheau Bus Terminal**, across from the farmers' market at the corner of Mamo St. and Kamehameha Ave. (Open M-F 7:05am-4:30pm. Tickets 10 for $5.) The office sells tickets in packets of 10; each bus trip requires a certain number. Paying in tickets instead of cash grants a 10-20% discount. Travelers relying on Hele-On should purchase their tickets in bulk in Hilo, as small town sellers are often inconspicuous and not all drivers accept cash. Hele-On runs to: **Kailua-Kona** (3¼hr., M-Sa 1:10pm, $6) via **Honoka'a** (1½hr., $3.75); **Waimea** (2hr. 10min., $4.50); **Ka'u** via **Hawaii Volcanoes National Park** (1hr. 5min., 2:40pm, $2.25); **Pahala** (1¾hr., $3.75); **Na'alehu/Wai'ohinu** (2¼hr., $4.50); **Ocean View** (2hr. 35min., $5.25); **Pahoa** (1hr., M-F 2:40 and 4:45pm, $2.25). See **Interisland Transportation** (p. 296) for more transportation and **Hilo International Airport** information.

LOCAL TRANSPORTATION

Buses: Hele-On (☎961-8744), also runs an intra-Hilo bus system that makes stops throughout town, including **Banyan Drive, Prince Kuhio Plaza, Hilo Library,** and **Hilo Medical Center** via **Mooheau Bus Terminal** (M-F 7:05am-4:30pm, $0.75).

Taxis: Ace One Taxi (☎935-8303. Open 24hr.) serves Hilo and its environs. **A-1 Bob's Taxi** (☎959-4800 or 963-5470; runs 5am-10pm) serves Hilo, Puna, Volcano, and Hamakua. Both companies charge a $2 initial pick-up fee, then $2 per additional mi. Airport to downtown Hilo $8-10.

Car Rental: All national chains have offices at the airport (☎934-5801), on Airport Access Rd., off of Rte. 11 about ½ mi. south of the intersection of Rte. 11 and Rte. 19. **Alamo** (☎800-327-9633 or 961-3343). 21+. Under-25 surcharge $25 per day. Open daily 6am-8pm. **Budget** (☎800-527-7000 or 935-6878, ext. 25 or 26). 21+. Under-25 surcharge $20 per day. Open daily 6am-8:30pm. **Dollar** (☎800-800-4000 or 866-434-2226). 21+. Under-25 surcharge $20 per day. Open daily 6am-8:30pm. **Thrifty** (☎800-367-2277 or 961-6698). 21+. Under-25 surcharge $15 per day. **Harper Car & Truck Rentals of Hawaii,** 456 Kalanianaole Ave. (☎969-1478), rents 4WD vehicles as well as economy cars and, unlike other companies, does not restrict travel to the island's major roads. Open M-Th 6:30am-5pm, F-Su 6:30am-6pm.

Bike Rental: Da Kine Bike Shop, 12 Furneaux Ln., (☎934-9861), next to Canoes sandwich shop, off Kamehameha Ave. Hilo's self-defined 'rent-a-wreck' bike shop. Solid bikes from hybrids to antique cruisers. $10-20 per day, negotiable long-term rentals. Helmet and lock provided for short-term rentals. Open M-F noon-6pm, Sa 9am-3pm.

⏱ PRACTICAL INFORMATION

TOURIST AND FINANCIAL SERVICES

Tourist Office: The Hawaii Visitor's Bureau, 250 Keawe St. (☎800-648-2441 or 961-5797; www.bigisland.org), at the corner of Keawe and Haili St., is primarily a marketing agency for the island, but provides a decent map, a slew of brochures, and helpful directions. Open M-F 8am-4:30pm.

Budget Travel: Cut Rate Tickets, 688 Kanoelehua Ave. (☎969-1944), at the corner of Kanoelehua and Leilani St., adjacent to the Minit Stop gas station, offers discount rates on interisland flight coupons. Open M-F 7am-7pm, Sa 9am-5pm.

Banks: Bank of Hawaii, 417 E. Kawili St. (☎935-9701), at the corner of E. Kawili St. and Kanoelehua Ave. Open M-Th 8:30am-4pm, F 8:30am-6pm. **First Hawaiian Bank,** 1205 Kilauea Ave. (☎969-2211), at the corner of Kilauea and Kekuanaoa. Open M-Th 8:30am-4pm, F 8:30am-6pm, Sa 9am-1pm. **24hr. ATMS** and other banks also in town.

LOCAL SERVICES

Bookstores: Otherwise known as "The Map Shop," **Basically Books,** 160 Kamehameha Ave. (☎961-0144), on the bayfront, stocks ▓ **Nell's Maps** and shelves of Hawaiiana. Open M-Sa 9am-5pm, Su 10am-3pm. **Borders,** 301 Makaala St. (☎933-1410), off Rte. 11 in the Waiakea Center, with Wal-mart and Island Naturals. Open Su-Th 9am-9pm, F-Sa 9am-10pm.

Library: ▓ **Hilo Public Library,** 300 Waianuenue Ave. (☎933-8888), is blessed with a dynamic and welcoming staff. Centered around a grassy courtyard, a good half of this library is open air. Excellent children's section. **Internet access** on 6 monitors with high-speed connections. 3 mo. visitor card ($10) affords free internet at any of the Big Island's 13 public libraries. Open T and W 11am-7pm, Th, Sa 9am-5pm, F 10am-5pm.

Public Swimming Pools: The Kawamoto Swim Stadium, 214 Kanoelehua St. (☎961-8698), in Ho'olulu Sports Complex. Facing the waterfront in downtown Hilo, take Kamehameha Ave. south toward Volcano-bound Rte. 11, and hang a right onto Kanoelehua

1 mile

1 kilometer

TO RICHARDSON BEACH PARK (2.5 mi.)

Onekahakaha Beach Park

Leahi St.

Kionakapahu Pond

Keokea Point

Hilo Tropical Gardens

Andrew's Ave.

Brown Ave.

Baker Ave.

Pua Ave.

Desha Ave.

Kauhane Ave.

King Todd Ave.

Krensz Ave.

Lokoaka St.

Carlsmith Beach Park

Puhi Bay

Hilo International Airport

Blonde Reef

Kuhio Wharf

Silva St.

19

Reed's Bay Beach Park

Harper Car & Truck Rentals

Hilo Post Office

Blonde Reef

Kuhio Bay

Kawamoto Swim Stadium

Suisan Fish Auction

Kanoelehua Ave.

Bank of Hawaii

'Ohu'ohu St.

Pohaku St.

Makaala St.

Liliuokalani Gardens

Banyan Dr.

Waiakea Peninsula

Ho'olulu Park

Hualani St.

Kekuanaoa St.

Island Naturals

Hilo Bay

Uhane

Kaulainaiwi Island

Coconut Island

Lihiwai

P'ilani St.

Lelani St.

E Lanikaula St.

Hilo Bike Hub

Kilauea Ave.

Longs Drugs

Hilo Shopping Center

Cut Rate Tickets

Hilo Arboretum

Lokahi Park

TO HAWAII VOLCANOES NATIONAL PARK

Walloa R. State Rec. Area

Kamehameha Ave.

Waiakea Pond

Walloa Area Visitor Center (i)

Hilo Quality Washerette

Kino'ole St.

Ululani St.

Kapiolani St.

University of Hawaii at Hilo

Mohouli St.

University Park UH Hilo

Komohana Rd.

TO WAIMEA (25 mi.) HONOKAA (38 mi.)

19

Bayfront Hwy.

Bayfront Beach Park

SEE DOWNTOWN INSET

Keawe St.

Walnaku R.

Ma'ulua St.

Walainuenue Ave.

Ponahawai St.

Wilanoa St.

Lanikaula St.

Walakea St.

Kumuloa St.

Aupuni St.

Walnaku 2 Ave.

Kaiwike Rd.

Pukihae Strt.

Polakuanaka Strt.

Alealea Point

3

TO RAINBOW FALLS (0.25 mi.)

Downtown Hilo

200 yards

200 meters

Bayfront Beach Park

Bayfront Hwy.

Mooheau Bus Terminal

Hilo Farmer's Market

Mamo St.

Pacific Tsunami Museum

Kamehameha Ave.

Keawe St.

Hawaii Visitor's Bureau (i)

Kino'ole St.

Sack N Save

Ululani St.

Waianuenue Ave.

Maui's Canoe

Beach Dog Rentals & Sales

Laundromat

Shipman St.

Kilauea Ave.

East Hawaii Cultural Center

Big Island Massage

Hilo Public Library

Lyman Museum & Mission House

Haili Church

Kapiolani St.

Waiuku

BIG ISLAND

St. just after the bridge. Olympic-size pool. Public rec. swim M-F 9-11am, 1:30-3:45pm, 6-7:15pm, Sa-Su 9-11:45am and 1-3:45pm. Adult lap swim M-F 11am-12:15pm (short), 12:15-1:30pm (long).

Laundromats: Hole-in-the-wall and unnamed, Hilo's cheapest laundromat is just around the corner from Hilo Bay Hostel, at the intersection of Keawe and Shipman St. Wash $1, magma-temperature dry $0.25 per 5min. Open daily 6am-10pm. **Hilo Quality Washerette,** 210 Hoku St. (☎961-6490), near the corner of Kino'ole, behind 7-Eleven. Wash $1.50-4, Dry $0.25 per 5min. Open daily 6am-10pm. Last wash 8:45pm.

Equipment Rental: Hilo Surplus Store, 148 Mamo St. (☎935-6398). Open M-Sa 8am-5pm. **Pacific Rent-All,** 1080 Kilauea Ave. (☎935-2974). Open M-Sa 7am-5pm, Su 9am-11am. Both supply tents, sleeping bags, and other camping gear.

Weather Conditions: ☎935-8555. The Internet-connected touch-screen outside of **Mokupapapa Discovery Center** on bay-front Kamehameha Ave. also provides detailed weather and surf conditions. 24hr. Free.

EMERGENCY AND COMMUNICATIONS

Emergency: ☎911.

Police: Hilo Police Station, 349 Kapiolani St. (☎961-2213), at the corner of Kapiolani Ave. and Kukuau St.

Rape Crisis Hotline: ☎935-0677. 24hr.

Pharmacy: Long's Drugs, 111 E. Pu'ainako St. (☎959-5881), in Prince Kuhio Plaza. Open M-F 8am-10pm, Sa 8am-9pm, Su 8am-7pm.

Medical Services: Hilo Medical Center, 1190 Waianuenue Ave. (☎974-4700). 24hr. emergency room.

Internet Access: When the library is closed, try **Beach Dog Rentals and Sales,** 62 Kino'ole St. (☎961-5207), at the corner of Kino'ole and Waianuenue. Internet access $2.50 per 20min., $7.50 per hr. Open M-F 8am-7pm, Sa-Su 10am-2pm.

Post Office: Hilo Main Post Office, 1299 Kekuanaoa St. (☎800-275-8777), on the road to the airport. Open M-F 8am-4:30pm, Sa 8:30am-12:30pm.

Postal Code: 96720.

LOCAL MEDIA AND PUBLICATIONS

Local newspapers are: **West Hawaii Today,** 75-5580 Kuakini Hwy. (☎329-9311), in Kona, which covers the Kona coast; and the **Hawaii Tribune-Herald,** 355 Kino'ole St. (☎935-6621), in Hilo. Both are published M-F and Su. Smaller, less overtly commercial magazines include **Big Island Beach & Activity Guide** and **Coffee Times,** available at most visitor information centers.

There are a number of **radio stations** on the island, but the undisputed king is KAPA (99.1 FM Kona, 100.3 FM Hilo & Ka'u), which plays all Hawaiian, all the time. **National Public Radio (NPR)** broadcasts out of Hilo at 91.1 FM and can be picked up on the Kona side at 90.7 FM. The Big Island has no television station of its own; Hawaiian news comes from the national affiliates out of Honolulu.

ACCOMMODATIONS

Hilo Bay Hostel, 101 Waianuenue Ave. (☎933-2771), just across from Kaikodo Restaurant in downtown Hilo. This venerable old building used to be a plush hotel, and its memory hasn't faded. Male and female "dorms" are actually sun-filled rooms with double beds. Crisp cotton linens provided. Diner-style kitchen available for use. $10 key deposit. Check-out 11am. Dorms $20; single with shared bath $42; double with shared bath $54; 2 double beds (up to 4) with private bath $65. V/MC. ❷

▓ **Shipman House Bed & Breakfast,** 131 Ka'iulani St. (☎800-627-8447 or 934-8002; www.hilo-hawaii.com). From Rte. 19, take Waianuenue Ave. 5 blocks, turn right on Ka'iulani St., and continue over the rumbling bridge. Victorian-style house with 5 spacious rooms, porches and towering ceilings for a classy ambience. All with private bath, room 184 with claw-footed tub. Robes and kimonos provided. Talented neighbors are invited to play on the Steinway grand. Check-in 3-6pm. Check-out 10am. Reservations recommended. Doubles $169-189; each additional guest $25. AmEx/D/MC/V. ❺

Dolphin Bay Hotel, 333 Iliahi St. (☎935-1466; www.dolphinbayhilo.com). Take Keawe St. over the Wailuku River north of town and make your 2nd left onto Iliahi. Just a short walk from downtown, this meticulously maintained hotel is one of the best values in Hilo. All 18 of the large, fanned rooms have full kitchens, and some have their own lanai. Coffee, fresh papaya, and bananas are available in the lobby, and warm cinnamon rolls are shipped from the local O'Keefe bakery each morning. Check-in 1pm. Check-out 11am. Reservations essential. Standard doubles can accommodate 2-4 ($66-76). 1 room can accommodate up to 6 ($99). MC/V. ❸

Arnott's Lodge, 98 Apapane Rd. (☎969-7097; www.arnottslodge.com). From the end of Rte. 11 by the Hilo waterfront, take a right onto Kalanianaole St. and continue for over 1 mi. to a left on Apapane Rd. This well-run hostel has plenty of dorm beds, private rooms, Internet access, full laundry and kitchen facilities. Also rents bicycles and snorkeling equipment and runs tours to Hawaii Volcanoes National Park, Mauna Kea, North Kohala and Hamakua, and South Point and Green Sands Beach ($43-48). There's lots of info on **short-term work** opportunities nearby. Check-out 10am. **Camping ❶** $9 per person. Bunks $17; single rooms with shared bath $37; doubles $47; rooms with bath $57; with A/C $62; 2-bedroom suite with kitchen (fits 6) $120. DC/MC/V.❷

Wild Ginger Inn, 100 Pu'ueo St. (☎800-882-1887 or 935-5556; www.wildginger-inn.com). From downtown Hilo, take Keawe St. over the river; the street becomes Pu'ueo St. You can't miss this loud, peachy-pink establishment. 'Bamboo' doubles have hardwood floors and old school character, but cramped private baths. Lower tier rooms are still being renovated. Quaint tropical garden and outdoor BBQ facility, but be sure to bathe in mosquito repellent before use. 2 well-placed hammocks hang in the lobby. Breakfast of breads and fruits included. Self-service laundry; wash $1.25, dry $1. Check-out 11am. Rooms $45-99. AmEx/D/MC/V. ❷

Hilo Seaside Hotel, 126 Banyan Dr. (☎800-560-5557 or 935-0821; www.hiloseaside.com). On Banyan Dr., near the intersection with Kalanianaole Ave. Overlooking a finger of Hilo Bay, but away from the hustle and bustle, this low-key hotel is a no-hassle place for a night. Clean and simple rooms with A/C, ceiling fans, refrigerators, lanais, and a swimming pool. Check-in 3pm. Check-out noon. Rooms $69. AmEx/D/MC/V. ❸

◪ FOOD

The colorful **Hilo Farmers' Market,** on Mamo St. between Kamehameha and Kilauea, runs all day, every day, with special 7am starts on Wednesday and Saturday. **Island Naturals,** 303 Makaala St., in the Waiakea Center, is Hilo's best natural food store. Their gourmet take-out buffet has a ▓vegetarian lasagna to rival any Italian grandmother's. (☎935-5533. Hot dish and salad buffet with vegan options $7 per lb. Open M-Sa 8am-8pm, Su 9am-7pm. AmEx/D/MC/V.) The **Suisan Fish Auction,** 85 Lihiwai St., near the intersection of Lihiwai and Banyan Dr., is a spectacle worth seeing. Those alarmed by the sight of 4 ft. *ahi* can stop by the retail store next door. (☎935-9349. M-F, bidding starts 7:30am. Store open M-F 8am-5pm, Sa 8am-4pm.)

▓ **Naung Mai Thai Kitchen,** 86 Kilauea Ave. (☎934-7540). Near the corner of Kilauea and Mamo St. Everything at this authentic Thai restaurant is done with an unassuming grace, from the arrangement of the tables to the exquisite food. Spring rolls $7-8. Curries $8-11. BYOB. Open for lunch M-Th 11am-2pm. Open daily for dinner 5-8:30pm. ❷

■ **Kaikodo Restaurant,** 60 Keawe St. (☎961-2558). Across from the Hilo Bay Hotel at the corner of Keawe and Wainuenue Ave. NYC-born owners have imported big city flare to downtown Hilo, delighting the local cosmopolitan underground. Owners specialize in 16th- and 17th-century Ming China. Live jazz common Sa-Su nights. Definite romantic possibility. Affordable appetizers: seared tofu with ginger and seaweed salad ($6). Pricier plates: Miso glazed seared salmon ($21). International tap: Guinness, Newcastle, Sierra, Steinlager, and Kona Pacific. Open daily 11am-2:30pm and 5-9:30pm. ❹

Bears' Coffee, 106 Keawe St. (☎935-0708), between Waianuenue and Kalakaua, just around the corner from Hilo Bay Hostel. Locals convene between 7-9am for a little morning conversation. With country home stenciling, throw-back prices, and a mantle of childhood friends, patrons are reassured that all is well in the world. Enjoy hot or iced coffee ($1.50-2.25); granola, fruit, and yogurt ($4); waffles ($3.50) or eggs ($3-4). Sandwiches $4.50. Open M-F 6:30am-4pm, Sa 7am-1pm, Su 7:30am-noon. ❶

Canoes Cafe, 14 Furneaux Ln. (☎935-4070), near the corner of Furneaux and Kamehameha. The 1920s walls of this hole-in-the-wall cafe are plastered with canoeing memorabilia. Known for generous salads and sandwiches ($6.25) like *ahi* with Maui onions on foccacia. Open M-Sa 8am-3pm, Su 10am-2:30pm. AmEx/D/MC/V. ❷

Seaside Restaurant, 1790 Kalanianaole Ave. (☎935-8825), east of downtown Hilo, 4 mi. out of town on Kalanianaole from its intersection with Rte. 11. Zero ambience, but the fish is fresh from the ponds below and every entree comes with salad and hot apple pie. Seaside greens ($9), steamed mullet wrapped in *ti* leaves ($20). Vegetarian pasta ($10.50). Wheelchair accessible. Open Tu-Th and Su 5-8:30pm, F-Sa 5-9pm. ❹

Ocean Sushi Deli, 239 Keawe St. (☎961-6625), near the corner of Keawe and Haili St. A bustling joint that rolls up lunch for pretty much all of downtown Hilo. The friendly staff is glad to assist sushi novices in navigating the giant selection of fresh fish. *Nigiri* $2.50-4. *Hosomaki* and *temaki* $1.40-4.50. Specialty rolls $2.50-7.50. BYOB. Open M-Sa 10am-2pm and 4:30-9pm. AmEx/D/MC/V. ❶

Cafe Pesto, 308 Kamehameha Ave. (☎969-6640), near the corner of Kamehameha Ave. and Mamo St. Enormous bayfront windows cause passersby to halt not for the stylish ambience (checkerboard floor, lofty ceilings, and candlelight), but for the designer thin-crust pizzas dripping with olive oil. Pizzas available all day ($8-19). Lunchtime sandwiches $9-11. Salads $5-11. Dinner pasta dishes $15-18. Open Su-Th 11am-9pm, F-Sa 11am-10pm. AmEx/D/MC/V. ❸

Hawaiian Jungle, 110 Kalakaua St. (☎934-0700), adjacent to Kalakaua Park between Keawe and Kino'ole St. The Mexican and Peruvian menu is known for its *tamales* ($8) and plates of *enchiladas,* beans and rice ($9). Green salad in tortilla basket $9. Service has a mellow pace. Mid-week live music and Peruvian puppet show schedules hang on the front door. Open Su-Th 11am-9pm, F-Sa 11am-10pm. D/MC/V. ❷

Cafe 100, 969 Kilauea Ave (☎935-8683), near the corner of Kilauea and Kekuanao'a St. The birthplace of the *loco moco,* and still home to the cheapest eats in town, this roadside drive-in has met the onslaught of fast food chains and healthy diets, and emerged unscathed. Most meals $2-4, all items under $7. Open Sa-Th 6:45am-8:30pm, F 6:45am-9pm. ❶

Hilo Homemade Ice Cream, 41 Wainuenue St., in a tiny nook just downhill from the Hilo Bay Hostel and the intersection of Keawe and Wainuenue. In addition to the traditional flavors are ginger, macadamia nut, and blueberry cheesecake. Single scoop $2, double $3. Kona mocha-almond hot fudge sundae $3.45. Open M-Sa 10:30am-5pm.

◖ BEACHES

Hilo is not known for its beaches, but this has less to do with its weather than with its topography, which is dominated by rocky coastline. The best spots to go are east of downtown Hilo along Kalanianaole Ave. **Onekahakaha Beach Park,** a little less than 2 mi. northeast of the intersection of Rte. 11 and Kalanianaole Ave., has a sandy-floored pool for swimming and lawn for picnicking, with basic facilities. **Richardson Ocean Park,** at the end of Kalanianaole Ave. about 4 mi. east of Hilo, has a bit of black sand masquerading as a beach, and is a popular spot for body boarding and snorkeling, with lifeguards, picnic tables, rest rooms, and showers.

🏔 OUTDOORS

BANYAN DRIVE & LILIUOKALANI GARDENS. The drive runs around the Waiakea Peninsula in a towering, leafy tunnel. While the Banyan trees that form this vaulted ceiling are by no means rare on this side of the island, these trees are noteworthy because many of them were planted in the 1930s by celebrities from all over the world, like Babe Ruth and Franklin Roosevelt. The drive also passes the lovely **Liliuokalani Gardens,** a 30-acre Japanese-style park created to honor Hawaii's Japanese population. The oceanfront park, with fishponds, pagodas, and arched bridges, is beautifully maintained. *(Banyan Dr. is east of downtown Hilo.)*

WAILOA RIVER STATE RECREATION AREA. Driving between downtown Hilo and the strip malls and developments near Rte. 11, it's a welcome oddity that such a prime piece of realty on the shores of Hilo Bay would be spared simply to give the citizens fields and beaches on which to play. The area had been developed until the 1946 tsunami, which destroyed everything in its path. Residents rebuilt their homes and businesses in the years that followed, only to have them devastated again in 1960. After that time, the land was set aside as a park in a concession to the power of the sea, with a memorial dedicated to the victims. *(The park is along Kamehameha Ave. and Bayfront Hwy., between downtown Hilo and Banyan Dr.)*

KALAKAUA PARK. A statue of Hawaii's merrie monarch, David Kalakaua, sits with a hula drum and *taro (poi)* leaf in hand beneath the park's immense Banyan tree. The park is a splendid bit of green in the midst of sidewalks and streets, and makes for a good resting place on a tour of Hilo. Bordering one edge of the park is the **East Hawaii Cultural Center,** which promotes the arts on the Big Island through many different forums. The exhibition gallery houses the work of many local artists for public enjoyment. *(Park is in downtown Hilo at the corner of Waianuenue Ave. and Kino'ole St. Cultural Center open M-Sa 10am-4pm. Free.)*

WAILUKU RIVER AND RAINBOW FALLS. Just west of downtown Hilo, the Wailuku River runs to meet the ocean from the slopes of Mauna Kea. From Keawe and Ka'iulani St. bridges, **Maui's Canoe** is visible in the middle of the current. Legend has it that this unique rock formation was created when the great warrior ran aground as he rushed to save his mother from a watery grave underneath **Rainbow Falls.** The falls are nice enough, but the **rope swing** is where the action is. From the parking lot, take the left hand trail through the trees, passing to the right of the enormous Banyan. Continuing along the path toward the roar brings you to a calm swimming hole, protected from the dangerous middle current. Local kids may be swinging from the Banyan ledge above, more than happy to initiate newcomers on the appropriate technique. A word of caution: after hauling the rope up with the throw-down lasso, be sure that the two are detached before swinging. Swing at your own risk. *(From downtown, follow Waianuenue Ave 2 mi. uphill. Watch for the green sign.)*

🏛 📷 MUSEUMS AND FESTIVALS

LYMAN MUSEUM. Hawaiian history occupies center stage at this fascinating museum. The **Lyman Mission House,** which was built in 1839, is the oldest frame building on the Big Island, and has been restored to represent the lifestyle of mis-

BIG ISLAND

sionaries to Hawaii during the mid-19th century. A guided tour takes you through the home, which includes many original furnishings, tools, and household items. Next door is the **Lyman Museum** itself, the galleries of which explore topics such as the formation of the islands, Hawaiian culture from the arrival of the first Polynesian settlers through the waves of international immigrants, and the astronomical observations on the summit of Mauna Kea. It also features changing exhibitions of modern Hawaiian art. *(276 Haili St.* ☎ *935-5021. Open M-Sa 9am-4:30pm. $10, seniors $8, students $3, family rate $21.)*

PACIFIC TSUNAMI MUSEUM. In a city ravaged by tsunamis twice in 15 years, the diagrams and charts that explain how these enormous walls of water are created become all the more profound. Knowledgeable tour guides provide insightful introductions, and exhibits shed light on recorded tsunamis from around the world. There's also an illuminating video that features the recollections of Hilo tsunami survivors. *(130 Kamehameha Ave., at the corner of Kamehameha and Kalakaua St.* ☎ *935-0926; www.tsunami.org. Open M-Sa 9am-4pm. $5, seniors $4, students $2.)*

PANAEWA RAINFOREST ZOO. Panaewa is the only tropical rainforest zoo in the US, and home to over 75 animal species, including a white Bengal Tiger, Water Buffalo, Aldabra Tortoise, and Pygmy Hippo. *(A few mi. south of Hilo on Mamaki St., off of Rte. 11. www.hilozoo.com. Open daily 9am-4pm. Free.)*

▩**MERRIE MONARCH FESTIVAL.** When **King David Kalakaua** ascended the throne in 1883, he took great measures to reassert Hawaiian culture following half a century of missionary influence. Kalakaua (also known as the **Merrie Monarch** because of his support of dance and music) brought **hula** back into the public sphere by including it in his coronation ceremony. One hundred and sixty years later, the memory of this last Hawaiian king is celebrated in Hilo the week after Easter. The celebration, which includes a giant parade and other festivities, culminates in a hula competition among dancers from across the islands and both sides of the Pacific. Take a look at any of the photo books by Kim Taylor Reece; nearly half of his shots are from Hilo's Merrie Monarch. Tickets go on sale on New Year's Day and sell out quickly. *(For ticket information, call the Hawaii Naniloa Resort at* ☎ *935-9168.)*

▣ ♫ NIGHTLIFE AND ENTERTAINMENT

Despite being the largest city on the island and a college town, Hilo's more traditional nightlife can be lackluster. There are, however, films aplenty, from the artsy and foreign at **Palace Theatre** to $1 Hollywood flicks at **Kress**. If you're up for some adventure, take Saddle Rd. up to Mauna Kea for a free nightly stargazing session.

Shooters, 121 Banyan Dr. (☎969-7069). A boisterous crowd of all ages turns up to take in the weekend live music (often Hawaiian-Country fusion) and clouds of smoke. Happy Hour daily 3-8pm, drafts $2. Open M-Th 3pm-2am, F-Sa 3pm-3am, Su 6:30pm-2am.

Cronies, (☎935-5158), on the corner of Kamehameha St. and Waianuenue Ave. Under fluorescent lights, 2 corner pool tables attract the most attention in an otherwise bare space. Computer dart boards and a big screen TV provide the auditory ambiance. Cronies is known for the best crab cakes ($7.50) and *sashimi* ($8) in town. Food served M-Sa 11am-11pm. Bar fills up Th for pitcher specials (Bud or Coors $1; Imports $4; Guiness $9). 8pm-1:30am. Karaoke M-W, F, Sa 10:30pm-1:30am. Open M-W 11am-midnight, Th-Sa 11am-1:30am.

Palace Theatre, 38 Haili St. (☎934-7777), between Kamehameha Ave. and Keawe St. A striking relic from Hilo's glory days, the theater plays host to a single art-house (often foreign) film each week, as well as local and visiting musicians and live theater performances. Most film showings M, Tu, Th-Sa 7:30pm, Su 2pm. $6. Palace also shows children's films F-Sa mornings 9-11am. $2.

Kress Cinemas, 174 Kamehameha Ave. (☎961-3456), on the corner of Kamehameha and Kalakaua St. Mainstream Hollywood films for back-in-the-day fares. Reels generally arrive a few wk. after mainland release. Shows M-Th 4-9pm, F-Su 2-9pm. $1. Matinees F, S, Su $0.50. All day Tu $0.50.

Prince Kuhio Stadium Cinemas, 111 E. Pu'ainako St. (☎959-4595), in Prince Kuhio Plaza. First-run Hollywood flicks, $7.75, children $4.75. Matinees before 6pm M-F, before 3pm Sa-Su $4.75.

◢◣ DAYTRIPS FROM HILO

■ PEPE'EKEO SCENIC DRIVE

About 5 mi. north of Hilo. Watch for the broad green sign leading left off the highway.

The well-marked Pepe'ekeo Scenic Drive branches off Rte. 19 on a journey through rainforest and above the pounding surf of the Hamakua Coast before returning to the highway 4 mi. later. The serpentine road crosses over streams on tiny one-lane bridges and winds in and out of ravines lined with passion fruit vines.

About 1½ mi. in, the road leads to the **Hawaii Tropical Botanical Garden,** overlooking **Onomea Bay.** The garden, which follows the slope of the road down to the sea, is home to over 2000 different species of tropical plant life from around the globe. A trail leads visitors through scenery rich with bromeliads, gingers, and orchids. Banyan and palm trees tower overhead. The combined effect is of a pristine natural paradise. The only drawbacks to this mesmerizing locale are the mosquitoes and the price. Bug repellent is provided. (☎964-5233; www.hawaiigarden.com. Open daily 9am-4pm. $15, under 17 $5, under 5 free. 1 yr. family pass $35.)

Before returning to the highway, the drive passes ■**What's Shakin' ❶,** 27-999 Mamalahoa Hwy., a stand that blends superior smoothies ($4-4.50). Their concoctions—with names like Mango Tango, and Peanut Bruddah—use no added sugars or ice, only fresh fruit and juice. (☎964-3080. Open daily 10am-5pm.)

AKAKA FALLS STATE PARK

15 mi. north of Hilo, about 4 mi. up the side of Mauna Kea. From Rte. 19, a marked turn-off between the 13 and 14 mi. markers leads to Rte. 220 and the falls. Restrooms and picnic tables are adjacent to the parking lot.

The towering Kahuna Falls (400 ft.) and Akaka Falls (442 ft.) make Akaka Falls State Park one of the highlights of the Hamakua Coast. The tiny park is packed with delights, including the awe-inspiring falls and a well-kept walking path. The half-mile paved loop begins at the parking lot, and travels between the two falls, then turns back for a short trek through a vibrant rainforest of orchids and redhead ginger, filled with mossy Banyan trees, gigantic ferns, and stands of bamboo.

HAWAII VOLCANOES NATIONAL PARK

Home to the world's most active oceanic hotspot and the only two active volcanoes on the Hawaiian Islands (Mauna Loa and Kilauea), Volcanoes National Park is never the same place twice. Along the park's southeastern coast, 2000°F lava flows boil into the Pacific Ocean, constantly redefining the boundaries of the island. At press, the current eruption from the Pu'u O'o vent along Kilauea's east rift zone had added 544 acres of new land since 1983, and that number grows daily.

Both Mauna Loa and Kilauea are shield volcanoes with gentle slopes that rise gradually over many miles. Although they can't boast the dramatic steep-angle peaks formed by more violent volcanoes, their slow, continuous activity makes them much more accessible for scientific study and general viewing.

BIG ISLAND

The Kilauea Caldera is often jokingly referred to by rangers as "the drive-in volcano." On any given day, visitors can witness lava flows oozing and dripping from the east rift zone near the end of Chain of Craters Road. One of the most unforgettable experiences in the park is the hike that many visitors take after sunset to watch lava flows light up the night sky.

Whereas the Western imagination has long been obsessed with the volcano for its hell-fire destructive powers, Native Hawaiians worship **Pele,** the goddess of the volcano, as goddess of both creation and destruction. Visiting the park is a power-

---

AT A GLANCE: HAWAII VOLCANOES NATIONAL PARK

AREA: 218,000 acres.

FEATURES: Kilauea, Mauna Loa, Ka'u Desert, Puna Coast, Pu'u Loa Petroglyphs.

HIGHLIGHTS: Hiking over a'a and pahoehoe lava rocks, steam vents, cinder cones, pit craters, ancient petroglyphs, and (if lucky) active lava flows along the East Rift Zone of the Kilauea Caldera.

QUICK FACT: NASA astronauts have trained for lunar landings in the Ka'u Desert, because of the terrain's similarity to the moon's surface.

GATEWAY TOWNS: Volcano, 1 mi. (see p. 317). Hilo, 30 mi. (see p. 299).

CAMPING: Camping available free of charge and without reservations at designated campsites (p. 310). Stays limited to 7 days per mo. and no more than 30 days per yr. Registration required for backcountry camping.

FEES & RESERVATIONS: $10 per vehicle; $5 per pedestrian, bicyclist or motorcyclist.

---

ful reminder of how inseparable these two forces must be. Perhaps nowhere else in the world can one witness so intimately the feeling that life and space are still very much in genesis on Planet Earth.

✳ ORIENTATION

Currently, the only entrance to the park is from **Route 11 (Hawaii Belt Road),** 30 mi. southwest of Hilo and 96 mi. southeast of Kona. There used to be another entrance from Hwy. 130 (Kalapana Rd.) in the southeast, but this route has been closed since 1989 when lava flows took out more than 8 mi. of highway. Within the park there are two main roads: the 11 mi. **Crater Rim Drive** circles Kilauea Caldera, and the 20 mi. **Chain of Craters Road** descends the eastern flank of Kilauea toward the coast and abruptly ends where the road meets a bank of lava from an ongoing flow. This area is known as 'End of Chain of Craters Rd.' Note that because you must turn around here, Chain of Craters Rd. is technically 40 mi. long. **Hilina Pali Road** accesses the more remote western portion of the park, while **Mauna Loa Road** ascends the mountain and ends at the trailhead of a route to the summit.

▣ TRANSPORTATION

Volcano (p. 317) is the nearest gateway town, and can satisfy all visitors' basic needs. While a car isn't essential to travel in the park, it is significantly more difficult to see all of the attractions without one. If renting a car is an impossibility, the **Hele-On bus** runs between the park's Visitor Center and Mooheau Bus Terminal in Hilo. (☎961-8744. M-F leaves Volcanoes National Park 8:10am, arrives Hilo 9:20am; leaves Hilo 2:40pm, arrives Volcanoes National Park 3:45pm. $2.25 or 3 Hele tickets.) **Parking** is in the park is plentiful.

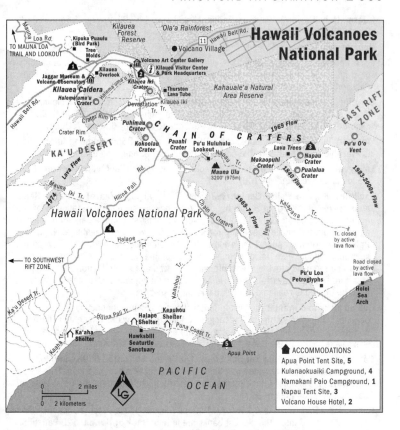

Hawaii Volcanoes National Park

ACCOMMODATIONS
Apua Point Tent Site, 5
Kulanaokuaiki Campground, 4
Namakani Paio Campground, 1
Napau Tent Site, 3
Volcano House Hotel, 2

PRACTICAL INFORMATION

Much of the park is **wheelchair-accessible,** including the Kilauea Visitor Center, Jaggar Museum, Volcano House Hotel, Volcano Art Center, Devastation Trail, and the pathways to the Steam Vents, Keanakako'i, Pauahi Crater, and Muliwai a Pele.

CLIMATE HOPPING. Volcanoes National Park is hospitable at any time of year. However, visitors should come prepared for extremes of hot and cold, as well as wet and dry, often within the same day. Covering elevations from sea level to 13,677 ft., the park cannot be defined as any one climate. All told, the range of ecosystems in such a small space is nothing short of sublime. Visiting the rock moonscapes of the Ka'u Desert, the sandy beaches of Halape, the tidepools of the Puna Coast, the ancient 'ohi'a rainforests that surround the caldera, the grasslands of the Hilina Pali, the fields of lava flows along the east rift zone, the ravines of the southwest rift zone, the groves of eucalyptus and koa trees at Namakani, and the alpine summit of Mauna Loa all within less than 400 sq. mi., likens to a cross-continental experience that took Ibn Batutta a lifetime.

Information: Hawaii Volcanoes National Park, P.O. Box 52, Hawaii National Park, 96718-0052. ☎985-6017. www.nps.gov/havo.

Hours: Open 24hr.

Fees, Permits, and Regulations: $10 per car or $5 per pedestrian, bicyclist, or motorcyclist; good for 7 days. Year-long Hawaii Volcanoes Pass $20. Year-long Golden Eagle Passport, good for entrance at parks nationwide, $50.

Gas: The archaic pumps of the Volcano Store (☎967-7210), next to the Volcano post office, still function daily 5:30am-7pm. There is an Aloha gas station, 19-3972 Old Volcano Rd. (☎967-7555), at Kilauea General Store (open daily 6:30am-7:15pm).

Weather: For weather conditions, call ☎961-5532 or 935-8555. **Eruption Information** is available at ☎985-6000. The park also broadcasts a radio bulletin on AM 530.

Emergency: ☎911. The nearest major medical facility is the **Hilo Medical Center,** 1190 Waianuenue Ave. (☎974-4700).

Facilities: Kilauea Visitor Center (☎985-6017; www.nps.gov/havo) and **Park Headquarters** (☎985-6000), a couple hundred yards beyond the entrance station along the northern arc of Crater Rim Dr. should be everyone's first stop in the park for maps and eruption updates. Office open daily 7:45am-5pm. **Showers** are available at **Namakani Paio Campground,** about 3 mi. west of the park entrance along Rte. 11. Keys to the showers available from Volcano House for $3. Potable water is scarce in the park, so it's a good idea to stock up. **Potable water** is available at the Visitor Center, Jaggar Museum, Thurston Lava Tube, and Namakani Paio Campground. Catchment water that must be treated is available at most backcountry shelters.

Guided hikes and events: The Visitor Center shows a 25min. introductory film about the park daily 9am-4pm on the hr. The ranger-led **lectures** and **walks** offer a good introduction to the natural history and geology of the region. Daily schedule for lectures and walks varies; consult the Ranger Activity bulletin board at the visitor center.

Camping Equipment: Hilo Surplus Store, 148 Mamo St. (☎935-6398), in Hilo, sells tents, backpacks, stoves, sleeping bags, and raingear at discount prices. **True Value Hardware** in Volcano Village also sells basic supplies including Iodine tablets for water purification (see p. 317).

Banks and ATMs: There is a **24hr. ATM** in the Volcano House Hotel, across the street from the Visitor Center. The nearest banks are in Hilo: **Bank of Hawaii,** 120 Pauahi St. (☎935-9701), and **First Hawaiian Bank,** 1205 Kilauea Ave. (☎969-2211).

▐ ACCOMMODATIONS AND CAMPING

Backcountry camping is allowed at designated cabins, shelters, and campgrounds and is allowed by permit only. Permits are free and can be easily obtained at the Visitor Center on a first-come, first-served basis no earlier than one day before you begin your trek. Tent sites, a small shelter, pit toilets, and water catchments are available on the coast at **Ka'aha, Halape,** and **Keauhou Shelters. Apua Point** on the coast has tent sites, but no shelter or water. The **Pepeiao Cabin** in the Ka'u desert has three bunks and water catchment. **Napau Crater** only has tent sites and pit toilets. There are two cabins en route to the summit of Mauna Loa, one at Red Hill (7½ mi. from the trailhead) and the second at the summit caldera (11½ mi. from Red Hill). Both have bunks and mattresses. Stays are limited to three nights per site and to groups of no more than 12 people. Be aware that the water catchments at all of these sites are *not potable* and must be treated before drinking. Backcountry campers are encouraged to follow "leave no trace" ethics. No fires are allowed. Instead, ask the ranger about camp stoves when you pick up your permit. Other than these sites, camping in the park is strictly prohibited.

Volcano House Hotel (☎967-7321), along Crater Rim Dr., across from the Visitor Center. Perched on a ledge overlooking the Kilauea Caldera, Volcano House was 1st built in 1877 to lodge pilgrims who flocked to the great lava lake that filled the Halemaʻumaʻu Crater. Unfortunately, the 'pit of boiling fire' has since drained and along with it much of the charm. Clean, simple rooms are comfortable, but with crater views starting at $165, you might expect a bit more. Restaurant serves buffet-style breakfast, lunch, and a la carte dinners ($9.50-22). Reception 24hr. Check-in 3pm. Check-out noon. Reservations required. Singles and doubles $85-185; each additional person (up to 2) $15. Park entrance fees apply. AmEx/D/MC/V. ❸

Namakani Paio Cabins (☎967-7321), in the Namakani Paio Campground. All cabins have 1 double bed and 1 bunk bed, linens, a sheltered picnic bench, and fire pit. There is 1 light in the cabin, but no electrical outlet. Check-in 3pm. Check-out noon. Reservations are required well in advance through the Volcano House reception desk. Singles and doubles $40; each additional person (up to 2) $8. Park entrance fees apply. ❷

Namakani Paio Campground (☎967-7321), 3 mi. west of the park entrance on Rte. 11. Sheltered in a cove of giant eucalyptus and *koa* tees, Namakani provides a tranquil escape after a day exploring the volcanoes. Campsites are free and available on a first-come, first-served basis. The 2 large fields and pavilion area are often crowded, but campers can usually find enough room to set up a tent. Restrooms and fire pits. Keys to the cabin showers can be obtained from the Volcano House reception desk for $3 per 24hr. Stays limited to 7 days per yr. For those without a car, there is a path directly across from the entrance on Hwy 11. that leads to the Jaggar Museum (½ mi). ❶

Kulanaokuaiki Campground (☎967-7321), off of Hilina Pali Rd., 4 mi. southwest of Chain of Craters Rd. Situated in the midst of the Kaʻu Desert, this secluded spot gives a sense of the backcountry without the trek. There's no shade or water and you'll be sleeping on lava, but you can rejoice in the fact that there's probably not another person for miles around. 3 sites with more on the way. Pit toilets and fireplaces but no drinking water. Stays limited to 7 days per yr. Free. ❶

🔊 ⚠ SIGHTS AND OUTDOORS

Many of the park's major attractions can be accessed by car along **Crater Rim Drive, Chain of Craters Road,** and **Mauna Loa Road.** All three roads are biker-friendly.

CRATER RIM DRIVE

Beginning at the Visitor Center, Crater Rim Drive is an 11 mi. loop that circles the Kilauea Caldera, passing through a cross-section of recent and historic lava landscapes. There is a lot that one can miss from the car, so if you have time, consider walking at least part of the 11 mi. **Crater Rim Trail** that circles the crater. From the Jaggar Museum to Kilauea Iki Overlook is especially interesting to see on foot.

Overlooks and points of interest are all marked by road signs and are clearly labeled on the maps distributed at the Visitor Center. Traveling counter-clockwise from the Visitor Center (as most cars seem to do, though you don't have to), you will pass sulfur banks, steam vents (also known as Pele's Sauna), crater pits, cinder cones, lava tubes, and deep fissures along the southwest rift zone. Placards at each sight offer information on the geology, history, and legends surrounding each sight. The following are a few highlights from Crater Rim Drive. For more slightly off-the-beaten-path experiences, see **Hikes,** p. 314.

KILAUEA CALDERA. Don't be fooled by the barren summit crater that you will be circling for the next 11 mi. is currently one of the most active volcanoes in the world. From the 1800s until 1954, the caldera was the site of Kilauea's most dramatic eruptions, including boiling lava lakes and fountains up to 2000 ft. high.

BIG ISLAND

However, since 1955, most of the action has shifted to Kilauea's southwest and east rift zones (a rift zone describes a weak spot in the mountain side where underground magma can more easily break to the surface). Nonetheless, evidence of volcanic activity, past and present, is still visible around the caldera.

HALEMA'UMA'U CRATER. Hawaiian legend tells that the volcano goddess Pele moved south along the Hawaiian chain, fleeing successive islands as her sister Namakaokaha'i (goddess of the sea) tried to destroy them. Pele finally settled in the immense Halema'uma'u crater atop Kilauea, where she still lives today. From the early 1800s until 1924, Halema'uma'u was the site of a dramatic lava lake that captivated the world. The crater visible today was formed in 1924 when the lava lake suddenly drained and the ground dropped several hundred feet. In Hawaiian, Halema'uma'u means 'house surrounded by the *ama'uma'u* fern.' The reference is to a longstanding battle between Pele and Kamapua'a, the god of cloud, rain, and forest, over a personal insult. Eventually, Kamapua'a saved himself from the last bit of Pele's rage by surrounding Kilauea with the rugged *ama'uma'u* fern. True to legend, *ama'uma'u* is usually the first plant to grow in lava fields, often within months after an eruption. Although Pele's home is visible from all of Crater Rim Dr., it is best viewed from the Jaggar Museum or the Steaming Bluff Lookout.

> Halema'uma'u emits strong sulfur fumes—children, pregnant women, and those with heart and/or respiratory problems should avoid the crater.

KILAUEA IKI CRATER AND PU'U PUA'I CINDERCONE. In November 1959, the cliff walls of Kilauea Iki ("Kilauea the little") burst open, flooding the crater with a pit of liquid fire 400 ft. deep. Lava soon started blasting vertically in dramatic fountains nearly 2000 ft. high—the highest ever recorded on Kilauea. When it was over, one massive volcano was left: 1 mi. long, 3000 ft. across, and 380 ft. deep.

During the eruption, lava spatter from the fountain oxidized, forming the reddish-brown Pu'u Pua'i ("gushing hill") cindercone. The cindercone formed on the southwest side of the crater rather than uniformly around its edges because the spatter and ash were carried by the prevailing Pacific trade winds. If you would like to get closer to Kilauea Iki, check out the Kilauea Iki Trail, p. 314.

DEVASTATION TRAIL. This self-guided plank trail stretches through a portion of rainforest buried in pumice cinders during the 1959 eruption of Kilauea Iki. The rain of volcanic debris left only a skeleton of what was once a densely forested area. (An easy 1 mi. hike round-trip; wheelchair-accessible.)

THURSTON LAVA TUBE. Lava tubes are formed when a river of hot lava cools enough so that the outer edges of the flow crust over, but the molten interior continues to move, leaving a tunnel behind. In 1913, Lorrin Thurston, a local newspaper man, was the first non-native to discover this tube; it has been a popular park attraction ever since. The first portion of the Thurston Tube is lighted, and you can walk down and investigate. Although stairs lead back to the surface after a couple hundred yards, the tube extends another 300 ft. This stretch is far more exciting than the short, guided part. You will, of course, need a flashlight. Much of the tube is overrun with a living canopy of roots that have penetrated the rock revealing the density of 'ohi'a and fern rainforest above. The experience is wet and magical.

CHAIN OF CRATERS ROAD

The drive along Chain of Craters Rd. is about 40 mi. round-trip, and there is neither gas nor water available below the Visitor Center, so make the necessary preparations before leaving. Chain of Craters is also the park road most likely to be closed due to lava flow or fires; check with the Visitor Center about current conditions.

HILINA PALI ROAD. This road intersects with Chain of Craters Rd. at the 2.2 mi. marker. Heading into the heart of the Ka'u Desert, this 9 mi. road is an escape into barren solitude, one missed by most visitors. It ends at the Hilina Pali Overlook, where a vast horizon of ocean and sky meets the edge of this 2280 ft. cliff. Apart from numerous scenic overlooks, the two main attractions are the petroglyphs and, somewhat ironically, the point where the road finally ends, cut short by massive lava flows from the Pu'u O'o vent.

PU'U LOA PETROGLYPHS. While the terrain of Hawaii Volcanoes National Park is in its geological infancy, the land is ancient by human standards and boasts Hawaiian rock art from before the arrival of Western settlers. Some of the most striking examples of these works can be found on the slopes of Pu'u Loa, home to the largest gallery of petroglyphs in Hawaii, with over 15,000 carvings. From the parking lot along Chain of Craters Road, a 2 mi. round-trip trail leads to a boardwalk that allows for close examination of the symbols and figures that tattoo the rock.

HOLEI SEA ARCH AND END OF CHAIN OF CRATERS ROAD. The Pu'u O'o-Kupaianaha rift zone of Kilauea has been in a continuous state of eruption since January 3, 1983 when P'u O'o first blew her top. The early years of the eruption had lava fountains as high as 1500 ft. By 1986, the eruption had shifted character to its present state of more gentle *pahoehoe* flows and lava tubes. Because tubes insulate lava from heat loss, these flows are able to travel across the long *palis* (cliffs) all the way to the ocean where they continue to add substantial land mass to Hawaii's youngest island. In 1988, lava flows first blocked sections of Hwy. 130. In 1989, the park's southeastern Visitor Center was leveled by another surge. In 1990, the entire town of Kalapana was destroyed. In total, more than 8 mi. of highway have been swallowed by the current eruption. If you hike northeast along the costal lava rocks from the end of the road, you'll come upon a series of road signs buried by lava flow that make ironic photographs ('reduce speed ahead,' 'stop.') and even an old, partially buried car. Although sea arches are common on the coasts of Hawaii where large ocean swells provide the raw power for erosion, at more than 90 ft., the Holei Arch is exceptional. Hawaiian legend tells that this is the site of a great battle between Pele and her sister Namakaokaha'i, goddess of the sea. To explore the current eruption further, see **Going to the Flow,** p. 314.

MAUNA LOA ROAD

This scenic drive starts about 2 mi. west of the park entrance off of Rte. 11. The road climbs 3000 ft. through rainforest to the ◪**Mauna Loa Lookout** (13½ mi. from Rte. 11), a secluded spot perfect for a quiet moment of reflection.

Mauna Loa is the world's most massive mountain. Rising 18,000 ft. from the ocean floor below the surface of the Pacific, and climbing another 13,677 ft. above sea level, Mauna Loa towers over Mt. Everest. In sheer bulk, it is 100 times the size of Washington's Mt. Rainier. Stop for a moment and consider the sheer enormity of what rests beneath your feet.

Near the start of the road there is a turn-off to see the lava trees. These phantoms of the old forest were formed when *pahoehoe* lava flows engulfed an especially moist tree (usually 'ohi'a) and hardened around it before the tree burned away. Just over 1 mi. on Mauna Loa Rd. after the turnoff from Hwy. 11, is **Kipuka Puaulu,** an enclave of native forest that has managed to avoid the torrents of lava that have ravaged Mauna Loa over the centuries. This oasis of upland forest is full of *koa* and 'ohi'a trees, as well as many other native plants, insects, and birds that have been partially sheltered from invasive foreign species by the surrounding fields of lava. An easy 1¼ mi. trail offers a good view of this treasure.

🏹 HIKING

GOING TO THE FLOW Exploring lava flows past the end of Chain of Craters Rd. requires vigilance and care—the newly formed land is unstable and lava flows are unpredictable. The experience is unparalleled, though, and with proper precautions, should not be missed.

Evening is the best time to venture out into this sea of liquid rock. Cracks and holes sometimes form in the upper crust of a lava tube forming "skylights," which provide a window into the molten landscape of fire below. Before you set out, be aware of the dangers of lava. Whether the flow is 3hr. or 30min. from the end of the road, it pays to heed warnings. Consult the ranger station or national park service for more information and be sure to watch the safety video at the Visitor Center (every hour on the hour daily 9am-4pm). The Visitor Center provides daily updates on eruptions and will be able to inform you about any present activity. It is important to remember that this is a *real* volcano and volcanoes are not easily tamed for a live viewing audience. Thus, what you actually see at the end of the road will depend wholly on Pele's temperament at your time of visit. Flows are variable, and there is always the possibility that conditions may be too dangerous to allow hikers onto the flow. Here are a few precautions to keep in mind:

Stay off of "benches" created by lava flowing into the sea, and don't go near the water! Benches collapse easily, and waves splashing onto molten lava can cause "tephra jets," which are small "explosions" that can scald unsuspecting onlookers.

Stay alert and prepare an escape route when walking down a moving lava flow.

Watch for Fires! Lava can easily set grasslands on fire. With a bit of wind, this can be very dangerous. Also, burning organic material causes the buildup of methane gas underground which can ignite in powerful methane explosions.

Get ready! Bring water, heavy boots or shoes, a flashlight, a first-aid kit, sunscreen, long pants, a hat, and gloves. It is also a good idea to bring extra batteries as the high heat can rapidly drain their energy. Temperatures on a flow can exceed 120°F, and many of the injuries that occur in the park—dehydration, heat exhaustion, and sunstroke—can be avoided by being informed and prepared.

The hiking in Hawaii Volcanoes National Park is some of the best on the island, since there are over 150 mi. of trail to choose from. There is a list of suggested hikes at the Visitor Center that includes routes for all skill levels. Whatever the adventure, some level of preparedness is always required—lots of water, appropriate clothing (including rain gear), and sturdy footwear are essential. Many of the hikes cover long stretches of black lava rock fields which can get exceptionally hot. Keep in mind that drinking lots of water is not enough to avoid heat stroke and heat exhaustion under these circumstances. If you are planning to try one of the more challenging hikes, be sure to bring a source of salt (like a sports drink powder) to replace valuable electrolytes as you sweat. Trails over lava flows are loosely designated by piles of neatly arranged rocks known as *ahu* (cairns). Strong winds can sometimes knock down even the best of *ahu*. If this happens, don't worry. Most of the trails are fairly well trafficked, making it possible to guess at the direction of the next *ahu* while keeping the last *ahu* in sight.

🏹 **KILAUEA IKI TRAIL.** (4 mi., 2-3hr. round-trip. Trailhead: Lava Tube parking lot along Crater Rim Dr. Level: moderate.) If you only have time for one hike in the park, this may be it. Just over 40 yr. ago, the surface of Kilauea Iki Crater was a boiling lake of molten lava. Today, hikers revel in the experience of walking on what could be termed hell frozen over. The hike itself is not very long, but give yourself plenty of time to enjoy the view from the crater floor. The first part of the hike descends 400 ft. through *ʻohiʻa* and *hamuʻu* rainforest. Once in the crater, a barren moonscape is before you. The hike also provides a rare opportunity to witness the first stages of volcanic succession following an eruption. Just 40 yr. after the lava drained in Kilauea Iki, the signs of life are everywhere apparent as fern fiddles break through cracks and *ʻohiʻa* trees plant their first roots.

HALEMAʻUMAʻU TRAIL. (3 mi. one-way, many trail combinations possible. Trailhead: Volcano House Hotel. Level: moderate.) This trail traverses the smooth *pahoehoe* cover of Kilauea Caldera floor to Halemaʻumaʻu Crater. It is perhaps the best way to experience the massive scale of the caldera as it takes you directly to the center. The ground is often so hot over the black lava floor of the crater that thermal updrafts can create their own system of wind currents. If you are lucky, you may also spot the *ʻio*, a small reddish-brown hawk native to Hawaii on a late afternoon glide. Bring lots of water.

PUʻU HULUHULU TRAIL. (2 mi. round-trip. Trailhead: Mauna Ulu Overlook. Level: moderate.) This short 1 mi. hike takes you to the summit of Puʻu Huluhulu ("shaggy hill"), a 150 ft. cinder cone formed by buildup from the eruption of Mauna Ulu in 1974. From here, you can see the dramatic course of 1969 and 1974 lava flows from Mauna Ulu as they seared the forest. *Kipukas* (islands of forest left untouched) can also be seen. On a clear day, the steaming Puʻu Oʻo vent is visible on the horizon. Hiking beyond this point requires a permit, so most visitors turn back. To go farther into the heart of the current eruption, see the next hike.

■ **NAPAU TRAIL.** (14 mi., 6-9hr. round-trip. Trailhead: Mauna Ulu parking lot along Chain of Craters Rd. Level: challenging.) Continuing past the Puʻu Huluhulu summit, the Napau trail is the only dayhike in the park that requires hikers to register at the Visitors Center. Napau is also the only trail in the park that brings you face to face with the breathing heart of the current eruption at the Puʻu Oʻo vent. If you walked to the rim of Pʻu Oʻo, you would peer into a giant, bubbling lava lake. Unfortunately, the land around Puʻu Oʻo is too unstable to hike, so you can only go as far as Napau Crater to catch a glimpse of Pele venting her rage in clouds of volcanic gas. On a clear day, the sight is utterly humbling. Just before Napau Crater, you will pass a series of old mud brick walls that mark the remains of a massive *pulu* industry. *Pulu* is the feathery protective coating that surrounds the fiddlehead of budding *hapuʻu* tree ferns. From 1867 until 1881, a series of factories sprung up near Napau to harvest this valuable fuzz for use as pillow stuffing. During this brief window, 4 million lb. of *pulu* were harvested, nearly wiping out the ancient *hapuʻu* from the region. When customers realized that the down-like *pulu* quickly turns to dust as it ages, business seems to have done the same. Be prepared to hike over long stretches of *aʻa* and *pahoehoe* flows. Bring lots of water, the trail is hot and there is no water at Napau, only a pit toilet and tent sites.

KEAUHOU AND PUNA COAST TRAILS. (16½ mi. through Keauhou or 19 mi. through Halape. Trailhead: Mau Loa o Mauna Ulu on Chain of Craters Rd. End: Puʻu Loa Petroglyphs. Level: challenging.) This trek descends the Hilina and Puʻuʻeu *palis* through ever-changing landscapes of black barren lava, *ʻohiʻa* forest, and grasslands. Throughout this hike, you will notice thin slivers of golden lava rock known as Pele's hair and small drops of shiny black lava rock known as Pele's tears. These are both formed as airborn lava drops cool during an eruption. At the end of Keauhou trail (5 mi.) you can head straight to the rocky tidepools of Keauhou Shelter (2 mi.) or continue on to ■**Halape Shelter** (3 mi.).

If you have time, don't skip Halape. After hours of hiking, Halape appears on the horizon like a palm tree oasis in the desert. The white sand beaches here are a popular nesting site for Hawksbill and Green Sea Turtles and chances are you may get to see them. There are fewer than 30 Hawksbill Turtles known to nest in Hawaii between March and October, so follow the signs to preserve this endangered ecosystem. There are two spots at Halape not to miss. The first is Kumu Niu, popularly called Halape Iki ("Halape the little"), a cove of white sand and palm trees that might very well seem to be your own personal paradise. To get there, hike southwest along the coast for about 20min.; you can't miss it. The sheltered cove of Halape Iki is an ideal place to snorkel if you don't mind packing in the equipment. The second spot is a freshwater swimming hole. To get there, stand with your back to the ocean, facing the pit toilet at Halape. You will notice a cliff that drops off into a ravine. Head toward the cliff and follow the ravine to your left until you see the pool. Don't drink this water without purification; it may contain runoff from cattle ground uphill. It is also slightly brackish. You may want to plan at least a one day layover to fully enjoy Halape. Although not quite as magical as Halape, Keauhou and Apua Point are also great places to camp. Beware of high surf at all sites and check weather forecasts before leaving. In 1975, an earthquake in the Pacific generated a massive tsunami that struck very near Halape.

KAʻU DESERT AND HILINA PALI TRAIL. (21 mi. Trailhead: Kaʻu Desert Trailhead, along Rte. 11, 10 mi. west of the main park entrance. Varying levels.) Treks in this area of the park can be as long as you make them. In total there are more than 21 mi. of terrain between Crater Rim Drive and Hilina Pali Overlook, but hiking any portion of the desert provides a good sense of the intense heat and solitude that characterize this region of sun and rock. From the trailhead, it's an easy 1 mi. walk to see the Footprints Trail left in the desert rock after the 1790 eruption of Kilauea. As the story goes, a band of warriors were traveling across the desert back to Kaʻu when the volcano erupted, discharging clouds of gas and ash that suffocated the men and immortalized their path.

MAUNA LOA TRAIL. (36½ mi., 3-4 days round-trip. Trailhead: Mauna Loa Strip Road. Level: challenging.) The steep 7000 ft. route changes elevation on an average of 388 ft. per mi. The ascent to the summit of Mauna Loa passes through a moonscape of barren *aʻa* and *pahoehoe*. Most hikers spend a night in the cabin at Red Hill in order to pace themselves and acclimatize before topping out at Mauna Loa Cabin (13,250 ft.). If you're not blown away by the sheer immensity of Mokuʻaweoweo Caldera, the year-round flash-snow storms may do the job. The ascent is recommended only for experienced and well-equipped backpackers. Altitude sickness is a frequent problem even among the extremely fit, causing dizziness, headaches, nausea, and fatigue. Those interested should consult the rangers at the Visitors Center. Mauna Loa can also be summitted by less rigorous means by starting at the Mauna Loa Weather Observatory, accessible via Saddle Rd. (see p. 319).

🏛 ● MUSEUMS AND FESTIVALS

JAGGAR MUSEUM AND HAWAIIAN VOLCANO OBSERVATORY. Exhibits at the Jaggar Museum combine information on current scientific research related to geology and natural history of the area with traditional Hawaiian perspectives on myth and legend. The museum can be a useful tool to understanding the area, so stop here early in your trip to the park. The Observatory is closed to the public, but the museum offers bits and pieces of their current research. *(On Crater Rim Dr. Open daily 8:30am-5pm. Admission included in park entrance fee.)*

VOLCANO ART CENTER GALLERY. Volcano Art Center Gallery, adjacent to the Kilauea Visitor Center, houses an extensive collection of visual and literary works by more than 200 local artists all inspired by the spiritual and cultural presence of

DESERT RAINS A quick trip around Kilauea Caldera reveals a strange anomaly: within minutes the barren landscape of the Ka'u Desert in the southwest suddenly becomes a region of lush rainforest. The transition is so abrupt it seems impossible. So, what's the secret behind this natural paradox? The fact is, the Ka'u Desert is not your average desert. This 'desert' receives about as much rain as its neighboring tropical rainforest to the east. But this is no ordinary rain. High levels of sulphur dioxide released during volcanic eruptions combine with atmospheric gases to form a potent acid rain. According to rangers, the acidity level of rainfall on any given day in the desert can be as low as 3.4, putting it on a par with vinegar! Pacific trade currents guide winds to the southwest, determining where rain falls, and thus, where plants can grow. As shown around the caldera, the difference between the two regions can be as abrupt as night and day. Sulphur dioxide is also responsible for volcanic air pollution, or smog, popularly known as "vog." When inhaled, this thick haze may cause or aggravate respiratory problems. For more information, contact the US Geological Survey, Hawaii Volcano Observatory. (☎967-7328; http://volcanoes.usgs.gov.)

the volcanoes. Don't miss the collection of photographs by *National Geographic*-featured artist G. Brad Lewis, or the handmade *koa* and *'ohi'a* furniture. (☎967-7565. Open daily 9am-5pm. AmEx/D/MC/V.)

SPECIAL EVENTS. On most Tuesday evenings, the park holds lectures and slide presentations by guest speakers on topics ranging from water catchment to vent creation, an event known as **After Dark in the Park.** (In the Kilauea Visitor Center Auditorium; ask at the Visitor Center for details. Tu 7pm. Free.) In mid-July, the park plays host to Hawaiian artists and musicians from across the islands during the **Kilauea Cultural Festival.** Hawaiian music and hula, instruction in native crafts and games as well as demonstrations of island traditions are all part of the festivities. There is also a hula *kahiko* (ancient style hula) performance in late May or early June and a royal court procession to Halema'uma'u Crater at the end of August. (On the grounds of the Kilauea Military Camp, less than 1 mi. west of the Visitors Center on Crater Rim Dr. Admission included in the park entrance fee. Check at the park information desk or at www.nps.gov/havo for updated information on park activities.)

VOLCANO

Nestled in the thick of an ancient *hamu'u* (tree fern) and *'ohi'a* rainforest, Volcano Village remains pleasantly cool at an elevation of nearly 4000 feet. During the 19th century, the fertile volcanic soils of the village attracted workers from around the world to labor in local sugar cane plantations. Coming in waves from many continents, these immigrants brought fragments of life from their ancestral homes to this new, yet ancient, land. Today, the native rainforest is interlaced with groves of bamboo, wild orchid, ginger, Portuguese fire trees, and the purple lasiandra—a visual testament to the rich patchwork of cultural history in Volcano. Located just over 1 mi. northeast of Volcanoes National Park, Volcano Village has two historic general stores and a series of beautiful B&Bs that accommodate the high rate of traffic without losing the distinct feeling of homes established long ago.

ORIENTATION AND PRACTICAL INFORMATION

Life in Volcano centers on **Old Volcano Highway (Volcano Road),** which runs parallel to **Route 11** for just over 1 mi. before coming to a dead end on the northeast end of the village. **Haunani Road** and **Wright Road** run perpendicular to Volcano

Rd., connecting the village to Rte. 11. A car is the best option for getting to and from Volcano. Alternatively, the **Hele-On** bus runs from Hilo to the Visitor Center in Volcanoes National Park (p. 307), 1½ mi. away, and will sometimes detour onto Volcano Rd. by request.

The **Volcano Visitor Center,** 19-4084 Volcano Rd., in the Volcano Village Center, is usually unmanned, but full of brochures as well as updates on vacancies at local B&Bs. (☎967-8662. Open daily 9am-5pm.) Many stores (including Kilauea General Store) have **cash machines,** although there is no 24hr. ATM in town. **Volcano Wash and Dry** is located in Volcano Village behind Volcano True Value. (Wash $1.75; dry $1.50. Open daily 8am-7pm.) One of the few places in town to stock up on camping and hiking supplies, **Volcano True Value,** in the Volcano Village Center, carries batteries, flashlights, and water-purifying iodine tablets. (☎967-7969. Open M-F 8am-5:30pm, Sa-Su 8am-5pm. AmEx/D/MC/V.) The nearest **police station** is on Old Volcano Rd. in Kea'au, just outside of Hilo. **Internet** junkies can get their fix at the **Lava Rock Cafe,** on Old Volcano Hwy. (☎967-8526. $3 per 20min. Open M 7:30am-5pm, Tu-Sa 7:30am-9pm, Su 7:30am-4pm.) Head to the **Volcano Post Office,** 19-4030 Old Volcano Hwy., next to The Volcano Store, for snail mail. (☎800-275-8777. Open M-F 7:30am-3:30pm, Sa 11am-noon.) **Postal Code:** 96785.

ACCOMMODATIONS

Volcano Lodging (☎800-908-9764 or 967-8617) and the Volcano Village **web site** (www.hawaii-volcano.net/village) are helpful resources for finding local accommodations, as is the Volcano Visitor Center (see above).

▓ **Holo Holo Inn,** 19-4036 Kalani Honua Rd. (☎967-7950 or 967-8025; www.enable.org/holoholo). Coming from the park, make a left onto Volcano Rd. Turn left onto Haunani Rd. just past the Volcano Store and make another left onto Kalani Honua Rd. Built with the hope of creating an inviting spot for international travelers, the Holo Holo Inn is indeed a backpacker's dream with spotless rooms, laundry facilities, showers, spacious kitchen, and eclectic library collection. Check-in 4-9pm. Check-out 11am. Dorm beds $17 (HI-AYH members $15, but linens not included); doubles $40. ❶

▓ **My Island B&B Inn,** 19-3896 Volcano Rd. (☎967-7216 or 967-7110; www.myislandinnhawaii.com), on Old Volcano Hwy. between Wright Rd. and Pearl Ave. Gordon Morse, the father of this family-run B&B, has written several guides to exploring the Hawaiian Islands, all of which are available for use by guests. The house was originally built by the Lyman family (the Big Island's first missionaries) in 1886, and all of the rooms have maintained their historic charm. Full breakfast is creative and delicious. Look forward to the signature 'My Island Papaya.' Reservations recommended. Singles $50, with private bath $85; doubles $65/$100. MC/V. ❷

Kilauea Lodge, Old Volcano Hwy. (☎967-7366; www.kilauealodge.com), between Haunani Rd. and Wright Rd. The spirit of community is still evident around the 1938 'Fireplace of Friendship' at this converted YMCA summer camp. The rooms are nothing like your average camp, with fireplaces and foot massage tools. Full breakfast included. Check-in 3pm. Check-out noon. Reservations recommended. Rooms $135-175; each additional person $15. 10% AAA discount. AmEx/MC/V. ❹

Volcano Inn, 19-3820 Old Volcano Hwy. (☎800-997-2292 or 967-7293; www.volcanoinn.com). Surrounded by a cozy lanai, this custom-designed home is full of interesting niches to relax in and is replete with modern amenities and fresh flowers in its colorfully decorated rooms. Units feature private baths, phones, refrigerators, cable TV/VCRs, as well as stained-glass windows in some suites. Reservations recommended. Singles $75-90; doubles $90-130; additional guests $20. D/MC/V. ❸

Carson's Volcano Cottages, 6th St. (☎800-845-5282 or 967-7683; www.carsonsvolcanocottage.com). From the park toward Hilo on Rte. 11, after the 26 mi. marker, turn right onto Jade Ave., then take another right onto 6th St. If you're aching for some pampering, look no further than this B&B set in the heart of the rainforest. Many of the ornate rooms and cottages feature luxuries like wood-burning stoves, goose-down comforters, and private hot tubs. Check-in 3-5pm. Check-out 11am. Reservations recommended. Doubles $110-165; each additional person $15. AmEx/D/MC/V. ❸

Aloha Junction B&B, Old Volcano Hwy. (☎888-967-7286 or 967-7289; www.bbvolcano.com), next to the post office. The lifestyle of sophistication once enjoyed by plantation owners is hard to match. Aloha Junction comes close, with uniquely decorated rooms, stellar breakfasts, and a garden hot tub. There's even a tree house bedroom for the young at heart. Full kitchen. Rooms $60-99; each additional person $20. MC/V. ❷

🗋 FOOD

The **Volcano Farmers' Market** sets up shop on Sundays (8:15-10:30am) at the Cooper Center, near the corner of Volcano Rd. and Wright Rd.

MARKETS

Volcano Store (☎967-7210), at the corner of Haunani and Volcano Rd. This historic landmark has been a favorite stopping place for visitors en route to the National Park for several generations. Stock up on groceries and general supplies. If you haven't yet experienced the Hawaiian Spam obsession, check out the Spam sushi rolls (½ roll $1.75). Gas pump in front. AmEx/D/MC/V.

JP's Volcano Cafe (☎985-7456), behind the Volcano Store. Mega-sandwich combos and burgers for under $5. Great on the go. Open M-Sa 6:30am-5:30pm, Su 9am-5pm. AmEx/D/MC/V.

Kilauea General Store (☎967-7555), on Volcano Rd. between Haunani Rd. and Wright Rd. Groceries and general supplies; soup of the day ($3.75), pizza by the slice ($2.25), and microwave for customer use. Gas pump in front. Open M-Sa 7am-7:30pm, Su 7am-7pm. AmEx/D/MC/V.

RESTAURANTS

Volcano's Lava Rock Cafe, Old Volcano Hwy. (☎967-8526), next to Kilauea General Store. Favorites include sweetbread french toast ($4.50), grilled mahi mahi ($7), and Hawaiian Tsunami Salads ($6.50-7:50). **Internet** access (see **Practical Information,** p. 317). Open M 7:30am-5pm, Tu-Sa 7:30am-9pm, Su 7:30am-4pm. MC/V. ❶

Thai Thai Restaurant, 19-4084 Volcano Rd. (☎967-7969), in the Volcano Village Center next to True Value. Classic Thai cuisine reveals yet another dimension to Volcano's historic cultural diversity. Massaman Curry $11. Thai Basil Stir Fry $10. Open daily 5-9pm. AmEx/D/MC/V. ❷

Kilauea Lodge, Old Volcano Hwy. (☎967-7366), in the heart of Volcano between Haunani and Wright Rd. Enjoy island-influenced European classics while surrounded by photographs of the volcanoes by National Geographic-featured local artist G. Brad Lewis (most are for sale). Entrees $20-30. Open daily 5:30-9pm. AmEx/D/MC/V. ❺

SADDLE ROAD

Winding its way between the two highest points on the Big Island—**Mauna Kea** to the north and **Mauna Loa** to the south—Saddle Rd. (Rte. 200) is a journey through a topographical cross-section of Hawaii.

From the Kona Coast, the road first climbs the slopes of Mauna Kea. From the rolling grasslands of Parker Ranch, the vegetation becomes sparse. About 19 mi. from the intersection of Rte. 190 and Saddle Rd. lies **Mauna Kea State Recreation Area.** Unmarked **John A. Burns Way,** 7 mi. farther on the north side of the highway,

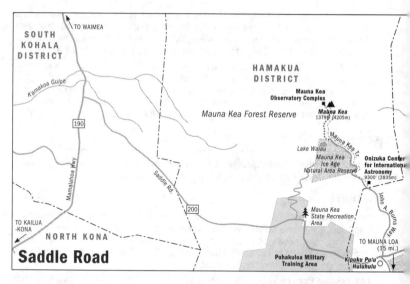

Saddle Road

leads up Mauna Kea to the **Onizuka Center for International Astronomy.** A graded track continues on to the mountain's summit. When the road reaches Mauna Loa, there is another abrupt change in landscape. The incline to the distant summit of Mauna Loa is a mishmash of lava fields, punctuated only by a few brave ʻohiʻa. A few hundred yards from the turn to the Mauna Kea summit, a rough track heads north to the **Mauna Loa Weather Observatory** on the upper slopes of the mountain. From here, Saddle Rd. begins to drop down toward Hilo in a series of twists and turns. The challenge of driving is increased by fog—it can be so thick that it's hard to see the road in front of you. As the road heads toward the Pacific, the flora becomes luxuriant, made a deep green by all the moisture in the air.

On the Kona side, Saddle Rd. leaves Rte. 190 about 6 mi. south of Waimea and 33 mi. northeast of Kailua-Kona. On the windward side, **Waianuenue Avenue** splits just above downtown Hilo and forms **Kaumana Drive,** which becomes Saddle Rd. in the foothills outside of town. Saddle Rd. stretches 54 mi. from end to end.

Be prepared for a rough ride; the highway gets heavy use from tanks and other military vehicles commuting between Kawaihae Harbor and Pohakuloa Military Training Area, located along the lower slopes of both mountains. The drive along Saddle Rd. is spectacular, but almost all rental car companies, except for local Harper Car and Truck Rentals (see p. 300), forbid you from driving their cars on it. Those who take this road should come well-prepared with plenty of gas, water, and warm clothes.

MAUNA KEA

At a towering 13,796 ft., Mauna Kea, or "White Mountain," is taller than many mainland mountains. Yet despite its size, Mauna Kea is known for a less readily apparent feature. The dry, stable air of the summit, as well as the extremely dark sky above it, makes for some of the world's best astronomical viewing conditions.

The Onizuka Center for International Astronomy, located on an unmarked turnoff at the 28 mi. marker, educates visitors about the high-tech telescopes located at the summit. John A. Burns Way leads just over 6 mi. to the Onizuka Center,

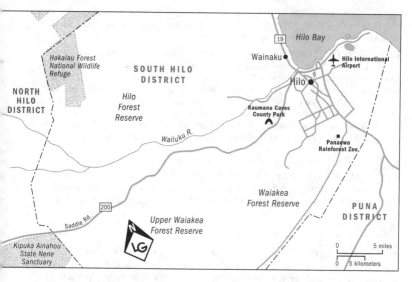

climbing almost 3000 ft. and yielding impressive views of the "saddle" between the mountains, Mauna Loa, and the smaller cinder cones on Mauna Kea's slopes. The only real hazard along this section of Saddle Rd. is the free-roaming cattle.

🔘 SIGHTS

MAUNA KEA STATE RECREATION AREA. Located near the 35 mi. marker, 25 mi. southeast of Waimea and 7 mi. west of the Mauna Kea summit road, this simple park is a good place to base Saddle Rd. explorations. The park has rest rooms, picnic tables, and a pay phone, in addition to a short hike that features great views of Mauna Kea, Hulalai, and Mauna Loa. There are also seven **cabins** with kitchens, bathrooms, and showers available for rent. (To reserve a cabin, call the Department of Land and Natural Resources, State Parks Division, 75 Apuni St. ☎974-6200. $45 per night.)

ONIZUKA CENTER FOR INTERNATIONAL ASTRONOMY. Perched on the slopes of Mauna Kea at 9200 ft., the **Visitor Information Center** for the summit telescopes is an invaluable resource. The center is named after **Ellison Onizuka,** an astronaut from The Big Island who died in the 1986 Challenger explosion. A number of exhibits detail the form and function of the summit's 13 telescopes, which range from the dual 390 in. Keck telescopes that allow for binocular-like focus, to Japan's Subaru, which, at 27 ft. in diameter, is the world's largest optical telescope. Displays provide introductions to astronomy and Mauna Kea's natural history.

The center also practices astronomy on a more grass-roots level, with nightly **stargazing** sessions. The program begins with an orientation video, which is followed by a discussion of astronomy and Mauna Kea. Then, using several small telescopes (11-16 in.), visitors are able to observe an array of stellar phenomena, including globular clusters, supernova remnants, and white dwarfs. It is crucial to dress warmly; temperatures range from 40-50° F during the summer and 25-50° F during the winter. If you have your own 4WD vehicle, consider going on one of the Center's **summit tours.** The 4hr. tour includes an orientation video and acclimatization period, caravan ride to the summit, overview of all the telescopes, as well as a guided visit to one or two of them. (From Saddle Rd., turn onto John A. Burns Wy. at the 28 mi. marker. The center is just over 6 mi. up the road. ☎961-2180; www.ifa.hawaii.edu. Center open M-F 9am-noon, 1-5pm, 6-10pm, Sa-

Su 9am-10pm. Free. Coffee, hot chocolate, tea and snacks available at the center. Stargazing daily 6-10pm. Free. Summit tours Sa-Su 1-5pm. Free. Children under 16 and pregnant women not allowed on tours due to high-altitude health hazards.)

DRIVING TO THE SUMMIT. If you have a 4WD vehicle, you can drive to the top yourself. Visitors are allowed on the summit only from sunrise to sunset, as car headlights interfere with the observations after dark. The road to the observatories is well-maintained but unpaved until the last few miles and, because of its fantastically steep grade, is suitable only for 4WD vehicles. The drive from the Onizuka Center to the summit is 6½ mi. and should take about 30min. Once there, the University of Hawaii telescope and the WM Keck Observatory both have **Visitor Centers.** For all the technological wizardry of the telescopes, however, the sky is amazing even to the naked eye.

> The air on the summit has only 60% of the oxygen available at sea level, causing many people to suffer from altitude sickness at the summit. Pregnant women, children, individuals who are overweight or in poor health, and those with a history of heart or respiratory problems are advised not to make the trip.

HIKING

MAUNA KEA TRAIL. (6 mi. Trailhead: Onizuka Center. Elevation change: 4500 ft. Level: challenging.) The Mauna Kea Trail climbs from the Onizuka Center to the summit and takes around 4hr. to complete. The path is itself is marked with posts and rock *ahus* (cairns) and essentially parallels the summit road. Given the altitude and elevation gain, this is an extremely difficult hike, but it provides an intimate view of the mountain's topography, as well as stunning views. Among the unique sights are the eerie landscapes of the Mauna Kea Ice Age Natural Area Reserve. In addition, the trail leads straight to magical Lake Waiau, the third-highest lake in the US, located at 13,020 ft. amidst Mauna Kea's lava fields.

TOURS

Paradise Safaris leads nightly tours to the summit for sunset viewing and stargazing. The trips include pick-up at various spots along the Kona and Kohala Coasts, hooded parkas, and a light supper. (☎322-2366. $150.) The knowledgeable guides from **Arnott's Lodge,** 98 Apapane Rd., in Hilo, lead trips from Hilo to Mauna Kea for sunsets and stargazing several times a week. (☎969-7097; www.arnottslodge.com. M, W, F departure time seasonally adjusted. $75 for non-lodge guests.) **Mauna Kea Mountain Bikes,** allows you to plunge off the top of Mauna Kea on a 7000 ft. descent to Saddle Rd. They drive you to the top, follow you down, and provide all the equipment you need. (☎888-682-8687 or 883-0130; www.bikehawaii.com. From $115 for 1 person to $85 per person for a group of 4.)

MAUNA LOA

Just east of the Mauna Kea turnoff, a serpentine road climbs the Mauna Loa shelf volcano 7 mi. to the **Mauna Loa Weather Observatory,** 11,000 ft. above sea level. The drive takes about 45min. and although the road is slowly crumbling, it is passable in any car. The observatory is purely scientific in its objectives and there is no Visitor Center of any kind, so be sure to arrive prepared.

HIKING

OBSERVATORY TRAIL. (5½ mi. one-way. Trailhead: Mauna Loa Weather Observatory. Elevation change: 2500 ft. Level: challenging.) The paved road ends at the observatory, meeting the beginning of the hike to the summit of Mauna Loa or the

Puna

ACCOMMODATIONS
Kalani Oceanside Retreat, **3**
Pineapple Park Hostel, **1**
Steam Vent Inn, **2**

cabin on the opposite rim of **Mokuʻaweoweo Caldera.** There is nothing easy about this hike; a good portion of your time is sure to be spent scrambling across the precariously loose rubble of *aʻa* (lava) fields and temperatures consistently drop below freezing on the summit. Inclement weather is common here, and picturesque skies are the exception rather than the rule on Mauna Loa. Still, for all the obstacles of the trail, the gaping expanse of the Mauna Loa summit is well worth any hardship suffered along the way. For more information about hiking Mauna Loa, see **Hawaii Volcanoes National Park,** p. 307.

PUNA

Tucked away on the southeast corner of the island, the Puna district is a lush botanical wonderland that thrives in the fertile backyard of the island's two active volcanoes, Mauna Loa and Kilauea. During the 1960s, vast stretches of undeveloped land made cheap by the constant threat of eruption attracted a wave of hippies from the mainland. Traveling Puna today is an unexpected blast from the past, where 60s culture is alive and kicking. Set on a landscape of dramatic lava flows, Puna also offers a diverse natural cross-section fun to explore. Puna is perhaps best seen as a roadtrip along the triangle from Rte.130, to Rte.

BIG ISLAND

132, to historic coastal Rte. 137, and back to Rte. 130. On weekends, pass through one of Pahoa's popular farmers' markets and assemble a fresh picnic lunch before hitting the long stretch of black-sand and lava-cliff beaches on Rte. 137.

PAHOA

The center of hippie culture in Puna, Pahoa is perhaps best known for its cheap farmers' markets and beach gatherings on the weekends. Pahoa is also home to a number of cultural and health retreat facilities where visitors come to rejuvenate their spirits with yoga, dance, and meditation. Based in the heartland of volcano country, Pahoa can be an exciting place to view lava flows and steam vents. The village gets its name from the two-headed dagger that enabled native tribes to successfully defend themselves against aggressors. Today Pahoa struggles against new aggressors; whether it be the constant threat of Pele's anger or the commercialization of one of Hawaii's most unspoiled regions.

◼ ⟦ ORIENTATION AND PRACTICAL INFORMATION

Pahoa is located off **Highway 130 (Pahoa-Kapoho Road)** near its intersection with **Highway 132** just under 20 mi. south of Hilo. From Hilo, take a right at the sign for Pahoa Village onto Government Main Rd.; all of Pahoa's main attractions can be found along this 1 mi. stretch through town.

Pahoa Natural Groceries doubles as the seat of Pahoa's sparse public transportation system; the **Hele-On** bus (☎961-8744) leaves from its doorstep for **Hilo** (1½hr., M-Sa 6:05am, $2.25).

While there is no official tourist office in Pahoa, **Pahoa Natural Emporium** on Government Main Rd. is a good resource for information and offers a free copy of their 'Puna Tour Guide.' (☎965-6634. Open daily 10am-6pm.) The **First Hawaiian Bank** on Government Main Rd. (☎965-8621; open M-Th 8:30am-4pm, F 8:30am-6pm) has **24hr. ATM** service. **N&P Mart** is the place to get gas before hitting the coastal roads. (Open daily 5am-9pm.) Free **Internet access** is available to Hawaii library card holders at **Pahoa Public Library,** 15-3070 Pahoa-Kalapana Rd., adjacent to the yellow school at the intersection of Hwy. 132 and Hwy. 130. (☎965-2171. Open M 1-8pm, T-F 9am-5pm.) At **Suds 'N Duds** in Pahoa Village Center, you can show off your vintage 60s wear while you wash it. (☎965-8881. Wash $1.25-2, dry $0.25 per 15min. Open daily 7:30am-7:30pm.) There is a **free public swimming pool** behind Pahoa Cash & Carry. (Open M-F at 9am-6pm, Sa-Su 9am-4:30 pm.)

Other local services include: a sporadically-manned **police satellite station** on Government Main Rd. across from Pahoa Hardware; **Pahoa Rx Pharmacy,** in the Pahoa Village Center (☎965-7535); and the **Pahoa Post Office,** 15-2859 Puna Rd. (☎800-275-8777; open M-F 8:30am-4pm, Sa 11am-2pm). **Postal Code:** 96778.

⟦ ACCOMMODATIONS

Pineapple Park Hostel, 11-3489 Pikake St. (☎877-865-2266 or 968-8933; www.pineapple-park.com). Heading west on Rte. 11, turn left onto South Kalani Rd. after mi. marker 13. At the T-junction, turn right on Pohala St., and follow it to the end of the pavement before turning left onto Pikake St. Though a bit out of the way, Pineapple Park is worth the trip, featuring a large kitchen with complimentary snacks, BBQ grill, laundry facilities, Internet access, and clean bunks. Converted sleeper buses are a popular option for groups. Private rooms also available, including a 4-room VIP suite. Ask about trading a bed for a few hours of housekeeping per wk. (See **Alternatives to Tourism,** p. 83.)Buses $15; bunks $20; private rooms $50; VIP suite $95. MC/V. ❶

Steam Vent Inn, between mi. markers 14 and 15 on Hwy. 130 just north of Kamaili Rd. (☎965-8800; www.steamventinn.com). A retired architect, the owner of this innovative B&B has managed to turn a natural volcanic steam vent into a 120° resort-style sauna.

Choose an ocean-view room, a garden-side room, or an old airstream mobile home, converted to a bamboo hide-away. Massage and reflexology are available for $45 per hr. Breakfast is often served fresh with homegrown fruits. Stay includes full access to kitchen, garden and the company of 2 resident peacocks. Ocean-view $85; garden-side $65; mobile home single $35, double $45. AmEx/D/MC/V. ❸

Kalani Oceanside Retreat, RR2 Box 4500 Pahoa-Beach Rd. or Hwy. 137 (☎800-800-6886 or 965-7828; www.kalani.com), This new-age oasis of creativity is a unique experience, with a little something for everyone. Spectacular oceanfront setting, sumptuous vegetarian cuisine ($10-$16.50) and a variety of classes including yoga, ecstatic dance, waterdance, and hula on Tu nights ($10 each). Clothing is optional after 6pm. Atmosphere is gay-friendly, though by no means exclusive. Their 1 or 3 mo. volunteer program provides a unique **short-term work** alternative (see **Alternatives to Tourism,** p. 82). Reservations recommended. Campsites $20; dorm rooms $60; rooms with shared bath $135, with private bath $135-240. AmEx/D/M/V. ❶/❹

🍴 FOOD

Weekends in Pahoa offer endless options to explore local farmers' markets and craft villages. The two biggest are the following: **Maku'u Farmers Association Cultural and Craft Village** on Sundays from 8am-1pm (located on Hwy. 130 just over 2 mi. north of Pahoa; look for the 'slow down' signs). Don't miss their signature Cane Juice Stand offering juices, sorbet, and hemp seed and cane ice cream ($2-3). **The Pahoa Farmers' Market,** Sundays from 8am-1pm on Government Main Rd. has great fresh fruit and produce.

Pahoa Natural Groceries, 15-1403 Government Main Rd. (☎965-6263), is next to the Pahoa Natural Emporium. If it isn't organic or all natural, you won't find it here. Products are pricey, but attract a cult-following. Hot plate of the day (often vegetarian) is $5.50 per lb. Sandwiches $2.75-3.50. There is also a 'waterman' in the parking lot where you can fill up for $0.50 per gallon. Open M-Sa 7:30am-8pm, Su 7:30am-6pm. MC/V. ❶

Paolo's Bistro, 333 Government Main Rd. (☎965-7033). Feels like home, but with an award-winning Italian chef. Garden gazebo seating available. Entrees $9-19. Open Tu-Su 5:30-9pm. MC/V. ❹

Jo Mama's, on Government Main Rd. next to Paolo's (☎965-0072). Open mic on W nights beginning at 6pm until 'whenever the music dies.' Drum set, keyboard, piano, bass, and karaoke machine all available for use, or bring your own instrument. Fresh *lilikoi* and other fruit smoothies, coffee, chowder ($3.50 a bowl) and sandwiches. No alcohol. At press, Jo Mama's was only open W nights; call for new hours. ❶

AK Pizza, across from Luquin's Cantina on Government Main Rd. (☎965-9395). Pictures of its sister establishment in Alaska's Denali region line the walls. Pizza by the slice ($2) or 12 in. for $11.50. Open M-Th 11am-9pm, F-Sa 11am-10pm. AmEx/D/MC/V. ❷

Pahoa Fresh Fish, 15-2925 Government Main Rd. (☎965-9898). An ideal stop to pick up fresh fish if you are planning a BBQ by the coast. Whole *ahi* $2.50 per lb. or cut $9 per lb. Open daily 9am-7pm. ❷

👁 SIGHTS

The triangle defined by Hwy. 130, 132 and 137 makes an exceptional day trip. The ocean is incredibly beautiful, but beware dangerous surf. Locals recommend swimming only at Champagne Pond and Alanuihaha.

LAVA TREE STATE PARK. Heading east on Hwy. 132, giant albizia trees arch over the road. Within 2 mi. lies Lava Tree State Park, where a 1790 eruption from Kilauea's East Rift Zone drowned the surrounding rainforest in *pahoehoe* lava flows. The 'lava trees' were formed as lava congealed around moist *'o'hia* trees. The trees eventually burned away, but the lava had already hardened, forming a forest of shells that still survives. Restrooms and picnic shelters are available.

KUMUKAHI LIGHTHOUSE. Continuing east, Hwy. 132 ends just short of the ocean on lava flows that lead to the old Kumukahi Lighthouse. Rather than turn right onto Hwy. 137, continue straight on the dirt road to the ocean. The old lighthouse has been replaced by a new one of steel, but you can still see where the flow from a 1960 broke into two, sparing the original structure. Though the new light tower is not that exciting, the site offers convenient access to **Champagne Pond**, one of Puna's legendary swimming havens. From the oceanpoint, you will see a gray lava road on the right that heads toward Kapoho Bay. It is just over 1 mi. to the bay where Champagne Pond awaits. This protected, freshwater cove is gently heated by volcanic activity deep below. The tidepools of **Kapoho Bay** provide endless snorkeling options, but they are more easily reached by Kapoho-Kai Rd. off Hwy. 137.

ALANUIHAHA PARK. Located just past the 10 mi. marker on Hwy. 137, Alanuihaha Park is an ocean- and spring-fed pool protected from strong tides by a manmade wall. The site is one of the few places on the southeast coast where swimming is safe, making it a popular weekend attraction for local families. *(Park open daily 7am-7pm, lifeguard on duty 9:30am-4:45pm.)*

ISAAC HALE BEACH PARK, A popular launching spot for local fisherman, and a favorite (and therefore often crowded) place for roadside camping, with toilets and picnic shelters. *(On Pohoiki Bay off of Hwy. 137 less than 1 mi. south of Alanuihaha.)*

MACKENZIE STATE RECREATION AREA. Set on elegant cliffs overlooking the Pacific under the shade of an old Ironwood grove, this area is quiet and secluded— perhaps the best place along the coast for visitors to camp. Permits are required. See **Camping**, p. 298 for permit information. *(Off Hwy. 137 between mi. markers 13 and 14. Note: This stretch of road between Isaac Hale and Mackenzie often floods during high tides.)*

KEHENA BEACH. Every Sunday, Kehena's black sand and palm paradise comes to life with a nude jam session. The action starts around noon and continues until sunset when the party transfers to free pizza dinner at the Hare Krishna Temple nearby. Clothes are always optional at Kehena, but if you come during the week it will likely be just you and the surf. *(The beach is located at mi. marker 19 on Hwy. 137. The path to the beach is marked by the 'Government Property' sign.)*

STAR OF THE SEA PAINTED CHURCH. Saved from the 1990 flow that wiped out Kalapana, the church stands as a tribute to Hawaiiana history. On Saturdays the parking lot is host to the **Kalapana Farmers' Market** from 8am to 1pm. *(Located on Hwy. 130 just north of its intersection with Hwy. 137. Open daily 9am-4pm.)*

KAILUA-KONA

Kailua-Kona, or Kona as it is most popularly known, is The Big Island's tourist capital. The town owes its popularity to one fact: it enjoys more sun day-in and day-out than anywhere else in the islands. Once the seat of Hawaii's royalty, Kailua-Kona is now a vacation hotbed, with condo after condo hovering over the narrow shoreline, and malls packing into the foothills.

⬛ ORIENTATION

Kailua-Kona lies on the western, leeward coast of The Big Island, in the shelter of cloud-covered Halualai (still considered active by the volcanologists down the road). From **Keahole-Kona Airport**, **Highway 19** runs south toward Kona town, becoming **Highway 11** after crossing **Palani Road**. This nondescript intersection of chameleon coastal highway (certain sections are alternately referred to as **Hawaii Belt Road, Mamalahoa Highway**, or **Queen Ka'ahumanu Highway**, to make matters more confusing), and Palani

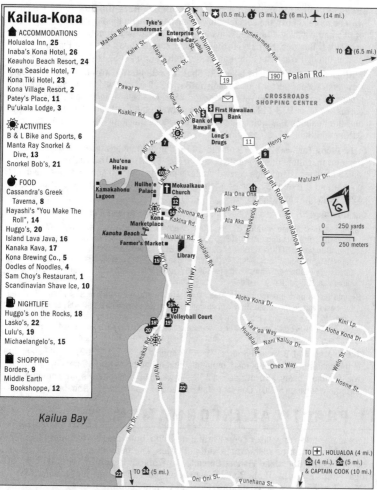

Kailua-Kona

🏠 ACCOMMODATIONS
Holualoa Inn, **25**
Inaba's Kona Hotel, **26**
Keauhou Beach Resort, **24**
Kona Seaside Hotel, **7**
Kona Tiki Hotel, **23**
Kona Village Resort, **2**
Patey's Place, **11**
Pu'ukala Lodge, **3**

☀️ ACTIVITIES
B & L Bike and Sports, **6**
Manta Ray Snorkel & Dive, **13**
Snorkel Bob's, **21**

🍴 FOOD
Cassandra's Greek Taverna, **8**
Hayashi's "You Make The Roll", **14**
Huggo's, **20**
Island Lava Java, **16**
Kanaka Kava, **17**
Kona Brewing Co., **5**
Oodles of Noodles, **4**
Sam Choy's Restaurant, **1**
Scandinavian Shave Ice, **10**

🍸 NIGHTLIFE
Huggo's on the Rocks, **18**
Lasko's, **22**
Lulu's, **19**
Michaelangelo's, **15**

🛍️ SHOPPING
Borders, **9**
Middle Earth Bookshoppe, **12**

Rd. is the directional *pico*, or navel, of Hawaii's west coast. From the intersection, Hwy. 19 cuts north through the lava fields of **South Kohala**, beyond whose banks hide fabulous beaches and a resort-lined coast. Heading south, Rte. 11 heads toward slow-paced coffee towns **Holualoa** and **Captain Cook**, and the dramatic **Kealakekua Bay**. Climbing uphill from this central intersection, Palani Rd. ascends inland to become **Route 190** on its way toward **Waimea** and **Saddle Road**, while descending into town, it crosses **Kuakini Highway** to become **Ali'i Drive**, Kona's seawall-hugging main drag.

🚗 TRANSPORTATION

Flights: Keahole-Kona International Airport, Keahole Airport Rd. (☎329-2484), is 7 mi. north of downtown Kailua-Kona, off Rte. 19. One of The Big Island's 2 major airports. Laid-back and open air, Keahole is served by international as well as inter-island carriers, among them **Aloha Air** (☎935-5771), **Hawaiian Airlines** (☎800-882-8811), and **Island Air** (☎329-8183).

Buses: Public transportation here is minimal. **Hele-On Bus** (☎961-8744; www.co.hawaii.hi.us), the sole inter-town transportation on the Big Island, is based out of Hilo and catching a bus from anywhere else can be quite a feat. Check web site for schedules. Bus departs daily at 6:45am from the Lanihau Center on Palani Rd. and passes through **Waimea** (1¼hr.) on its way to **Hilo** (3hr., M-Sa 6:45am, $5.25).

Shuttles: From the airport, try **Island RV Shuttle** (☎334-0464; www.island.com) for solo travelers ($8 per person), or **Speedishuttle** (☎329-5433), which can accommodate groups of up to 12. Reservations required 48hr. in advance. In the city, **Ali'i Shuttle** (☎775-7121 or 938-1112), runs a route between the Lanihau Center on Palani Rd. and the Keauhou Bay Hotel, stopping at bus stops along Ali'i Dr. (M-Sa every 1½hr. 9:20am-6:20pm; $2, $5 per day).

Taxis: Aloha Taxi, ☎329-7779 or 325-5448. Call 24hr. in advance to request their 6-person van. Other options are **C&C Taxi** (☎329-6388), and **D&E Taxi** (☎329-4279), which provides island-wide service. All taxis provide metered service with a $2 initial charge and a rate of $2 per additional mi. Fixed rate between the airport and town $20. Taxis run 6am-10pm.

Car Rental: 4WD vehicles are helpful, but hard to come by and often expensive.

Airport rentals: Alamo (☎800-327-9633 or 329-8896). 21+. Under-25 surcharge $25 per day. Open daily 5:30am-9pm. **Avis** (☎800-321-3712 or 327-3000., ext. 0). 25+. Open daily 5am-9pm. **Budget** (☎800-527-7000 or 329-8511). 21+. Under-25 surcharge $20 per day. Open 5am-9:30pm. **Dollar** (☎800-800-4000, automated line). 21+. Under-25 surcharge $20 per day. Open daily 5:30am-9:30pm. **Thrifty** (☎800-367-2277 or 877-283-0898, ext. 6). 21+. Under-25 surcharge $20 per day. Open daily 5:30am-10pm.

Beyond the airport: The folks at **AA Aloha Cars-R-Us** (☎800-655-7989 or 879-7989) often find the best deals in the island. They can guarantee 4WD. **Enterprise** (☎331-2509) operates out of a hard to find office on Luhia St., off Palani Rd. behind Gold's Gym. They handle mostly local rentals, so they *won't* pick you up. Often basement prices, though. **Harper's** (☎969-1478) is the only company without offroad restrictions, but they charge exorbitant rates. Slightly less in Hilo.

Bike Rental: B&L Bike and Sports, 75-5699 Kopiko Pl. (☎329-3309), off of Palani Rd. in the center of town, rents road, mountain, and hybrid bikes for $30 per day, $150 per wk. Triathlon bikes $50 per day, $200 per wk. B&L also offers a full shipping and assembly service ($190). Call for details. Open M-F 9am-6pm, Sa 9am-5pm.

⁊ PRACTICAL INFORMATION

There is no state-run visitor center in Kailua-Kona, but time-share centers line Ali'i Dr. and hawk various restaurants and activities. The nearest non-partisan visitor resource is the **Big Island Visitors Bureau,** 250 Waikola Beach Dr., Ste. B15, in the Kings' Shops in the Waikola Beach Resort Complex, 25 mi. north of town off Hwy. 19. (☎886-1655; www.bigisland.org. Open M-F 8am-4:30pm.)

TOURIST AND FINANCIAL SERVICES

Activity Booking: Eco-Adventures (☎800-949-3483 or 329-7116; www.eco-adventure.com) recently moved from the King Kamehameha Hotel to the lighthouse building, just past the "Welcome to Kailua-Kona sign," on Palani Rd. as it descends into town. They offer bookings for every imaginable activity, but specialize in **scuba dive** instruction and certification. See **Activities**, p. 334.

Equipment Rental: While **Snorkel Bob's** is the most visible of rental shops, **Manta Ray** affords the best weekly prices on top quality gear, hands down. If you're planning to snorkel for more than a wk., consider purchasing your own flippers at **Wal-mart,** on Henry St., above Rte. 11. (Full snorkel set: $35 adult, $15 junior.)

Manta Ray Snorkel and Dive, 75-5744 Ali'i Dr. (☎326-2682. www.mantaraysnorkeldive.com). A family enterprise, Manta Ray keeps things simple and streamlined with top quality gear at a single price. **Snorkel gear:** $6 per day, $13 per wk. **Rx lenses** $9 per day, $23 per wk. **Body boards** $5 per day, $15 per wk. For those wary of water, body boards with magnifying viewing lenses make underwater exploration a breeze. **Snorkel-friendly flotation devices** ($5 per wk.) also available. See **Activities,** p. 334, for Manta Ray-run underwater adventures.

Snorkel Bob's, 75-5831 Kahakai Rd. (☎329-0770), offers a broader budget spectrum, and thus the truest budget option of base quality gear. Snorkel gear hang suspended from fishing nets in colorful order. $2.50-7.50 per day, $9-30 per wk. Package with Rx masks ($10 per day, $40-45 per wk.). 24hr. rentals. Open daily 8am-5pm.

Banks: Next to the Lanihau Center, **Bank of Hawaii,** 75-5595 Palani Rd. (☎326-3900), **exchanges currency** and has a **24hr. ATM.** Open M-Th 8:30am-4pm, F 8:30am-6pm. There's also a branch with extended hours, but limited services in the **Safeway** (☎326-3966), above Wal-mart on Henry St. Open M-F 9am-6pm, Sa-Su 9am-2pm. Just up the road, **First Hawaiian Bank,** 74-5593 Palani Rd. (☎329-2461), offers similar services. Open M-Th 8:30am-4pm, F 8:30-6pm, Sa 9am-1pm.

LOCAL SERVICES

Bookstores: The ◪**Middle Earth Bookshoppe,** 75-5719 Ali'i Dr. (☎329-2123), in the Kona Plaza Shopping Arcade, stocks shelves with an eclectic general collection and the largest selection of Hawaiiana in the state. A friendly intellectual vibe. Open daily 9am-9pm. The familiar enormity of **Borders Books,** 75-1000 Henry St. (☎331-1668), is at the corner of Henry St. and Rte. 11. Open Su-Th 9am-9pm, F-Sa 9am-10pm.

Library: Kailua-Kona Public Library (☎327-4327), on Hualalai Rd., connecting Kuakini Hwy. to coastal Ali'i Dr., offers free **Internet access** with a 3 mo. visitor card ($10). Open Tu 11am-7pm, W-Th and Sa 9am-5pm, F 11am-5pm.

Laundromat: Tyke's Laundromat, 74-5483 Kaiwi St. (☎326-1515). Wash $1-3 per load, dry $0.25 per 6min. Open daily 6:30am-9:30pm. Last load 7:30pm.

Weather Conditions: ☎961-5582.

EMERGENCY AND COMMUNICATIONS

Emergency: ☎911.

Police: Kealakehe Station (☎326-4646), on Queen Ka'ahumanu Hwy. about 1 mi. north of town, next to the Kealakehe Transfer Station.

WHAT'S IN A NAME?
Kona or Kailua? The double name suits the dual nature of the Big Island's tourist capital. **Kailua,** as the town was originally called, has had a long history at the center of things. Hawaiian royalty ruled from this portion of the coast before the arrival of *haoles* (foreigners), and Kailua Bay was later chosen as the spot of the first Western settlement on the island. During the last half of the 19th century the town was the hub of trade for the windward coast.

Today, cruise ships replace the freighters in the bay, just as most of the family-run shops and wooden store fronts of the city's historic downtown have given way to chain stores hawking silk *leis* and helicopter rides. Like mom-and-pop shops have lost out to chain stores, so Kailua has lost out to Kona. The hyphenated name first came about when Kailua began to vie for inter-island and international limelight, and had to compete with another Kailua on Oahu. **Kona,** which literally means "windward," describes Hawaii's entire western coast, but over the last quarter of a century, as tourism has dwarfed all other industries, the name has come to be synonymous with the town itself.

Sexual Assault Crisis Line: ☎935-0677. Operators advise the lines may be busy; if no one picks up, keep trying. 24hr.

Pharmacy: Long's Drugs, (☎329-1632), downhill from the intersection of Rte. 11 and Palani Rd. in the Lanihau Shopping Center. Open M-Sa 8am-9pm, Su 8am-6pm.

Hospital: Kona Community Hospital, Rte. 11 (☎322-9311), 15 mi. south of Kailua-Kona in Kealakekua. 24hr. emergency room. The closest **Hyperbaric** (altitude sickness) **Treatment Center** (☎587-3425) is in Honolulu.

Internet Access: In addition to the Kailua-Kona Public Library, **Island Lava Java,** 75-5799 Ali'i Dr. (☎327-2161), in Ali'i Sunset Plaza, offers Internet access for $3 per 15min. Open daily 6am-10pm. Chill vibe, Kona coffee at hand. For those nursing more of a snowcone itch and unfazed by blaring hard rock, **Scandinavian Shave Ice,** 75-5699 Ali'i Dr. (☎331-1626), also has 3 terminals. In a blue-front building by the boat harbor on the northern end of Ali'i Dr. $2.50 per 15min. Open daily 10am-9pm.

Post Office: Kailua-Kona Post Office, 74-5577 Palani Rd. (☎800-275-8777 or ☎331-8307), next to the Lanihau Center. Open M-F 8:30am-4pm, Sa 9am-1:30pm.

Postal Code: 96740.

⌐ ACCOMMODATIONS

INNS AND B&BS

▓ **Kona Tiki Hotel,** 75-5968 Ali'i Dr. (☎329-1425), just over a mi. south on coastal Ali'i Dr. Kona Tiki maintains a 50s-60s tropical paradise feel, including fresh white paint with turquoise balconies. 15 ocean-view rooms are surrounded by a volcanic seawall. Comfortable mattresses. Though ground floor can be humid, 2nd and 3rd floors are breezy and sunlit. Reception 7am-7pm. Check-in 3pm. Check-out 11am. Reservations essential. Doubles with queen bed $59; queen and twin $72, with kitchenette $79; each additional guest $8, ages 2-12 $6. ❸

▓ **Holualoa Inn,** Mamalahoa Hwy (☎800-392-1812 or 324-1121; www.konaweb.com/hinn), 5 mi. from downtown Kailua-Kona in Holualoa Village (for directions to town, see **Near Kailua-Kona: Holualoa,** p. 336). Set back from the roadside, the Holualoa Inn feels peaceful. Built on a coffee estate at 1400 ft., the grounds are an ampitheater for the ocean view. Rooftop gazebo overlooks a pool, secluded hot tub, and the Pacific. Breakfast and afternoon fruit and cheese plate included. Pool-side day rooms equipped with bath, shower, and luggage storage for guests with late flights. Ages 13+. Doubles $175-225; $30 per additional person. 15% off for 7+ nights. MC/V. ❺

▓ **Inaba's Kona Hotel,** Mamalahoa Hwy. (☎324-1155), in Holualoa Village, 5 mi. from Kailua-Kona. 1 mi. past the turquoise-bordered 'Holualoa' sign, on the left (for directions to town, see **Near Kailua-Kona: Holualoa,** p. 336). The Inaba's old-fashioned (and very pink) residence has been a local fixture since 1926. The house's cheerful clutter is the collection of 3 generations. ▓ **Back rooms #10** (double and twin) and **#11** (double) are steals. High ceilings, wood floors, and sweeping ocean views. The view from the male toilet (also pink) is tremendous. Check-in, check-out flexible. Reservations recommended. Owners will rent any room as a single ($25), double ($30), or triple ($30), when vacant. ❶

Pu'ukala Lodge, Mamalahoa Hwy. (☎888-325-1729 or 325-1729; www.Puukala-lodge.com), 7 mi. from downtown off Palani Rd. Call for directions. An eclectic place where polished 'o'hia trunks brace the living room ceiling from koa floors, and french toast is served on silver platters. The additional $10-20 for upper rooms affords light-filled rooms with ocean views, plush green carpeting, and an enormous private bath; basement rooms just don't compare. 2-night min. stay. Reservations essential. Doubles $75-110; each additional guest $25. Travelers' checks accepted. MC/V. ❸

RESORTS, HOTELS, AND HOSTELS

Kona Village Resort, Ka'upulehu Dr. (☎825-5555 or 800-367-5290; www.konavillage.com). Watch for the night-lit "Haluali" sign to the *makai* (ocean) side of Rte. 19, just north of the Kona airport. One of Hawaii's 1st resorts, built on the site of an ancient Hawaiian fishing village, Kona Village exudes a "going native" feel. Guests stay in isolated, grass-roofed *hales* along the shorefront. The *luau* is considered one of the best on the island. Standard "American Plan" includes 3 meals per day. Ceiling fans, coffee makers, and mini fridges, but no TVs or phones. 1-room *hales* $515-910; 2-room $850-1125. AmEx/D/MC/V. ❺

Keauhou Beach Resort, 78-6740 Ali'i Dr. (☎322-2441), 5 mi. south of Kailua-Kona town in Keauhou. Architects built the front of this hotel *over* the water. Sea turtles visit the shallow reef below, and guests peer down at them from ground floor balconies. Keauhou offers typical hotel rooms, but atypically large reductions of inflated rack rates. By booking cheaper rooms first, then requesting an upgrade upon arrival, bargain-hunting guests can enjoy ocean-view rooms (upon availability) for comparative peanuts. 2 pools, 2 lit tennis courts, and a golf course. All rooms with A/C and mini fridge. Wheelchair-accessible. Doubles $189-309; when rooming with adults, children under 17 are free. "Super Saver" rates can drop prices to $119. ❻

Kona Seaside Hotel, 75-5646 Palani Rd. (☎329-2455; www.konaseasidehotel.com). Smack in the middle of downtown, on the busy corner of Palani and Ali'i Dr., rooms here are simple. Standard pool-side and garden-side wings are more tranquil.; the air is fresher, the noise is less, the beds are more comfortable, and rooms don't require a stuffy elevator ride. The best views are from Pool Wing #308-301 and #208-201. All rooms have A/C, cable TV, and mini fridges. Excellent rental car deals also available through the hotel. Economy $29 per day; midsize $39; Lincoln towncar $54. Reception 24hr. Check-in 3pm. Check-out noon. Standard doubles $77, deluxe doubles $87. Prices can rise or fall $10 in either direction. AmEx/D/MC/V. ❷

Patey's Place, 75-195 Ala Ona Ona St. (☎326-7018; www.hawaiian-hostels.com). Heading downhill on Palani Rd., turn left onto Kuakini Hwy. Take a left onto Kalani St., then turn left again onto Alahou St., followed by a left onto Ala Ona Ona St. A 2-building complex covered in colorful ocean murals, Patey's is Kona's only official hostel. Kitchen, TV room, washing machines, and Internet ($5 per hr.). Occasional opportunities for **short-term work** available (see **Alternatives to Tourism,** p. 82). Shared bathrooms. Bedding included. Airport shuttle $10. Reception 8:30am-1:30pm and 4:30-10pm. Check-out 10am. Dorms $20; singles $35; doubles $46, with TV $50. MC/V. ❶

CONDOS

Visitors who plan to stay for more than a few days can often find better deals with condos than with the line of beach hotels marching down Ali'i Dr.

Hawaii Resort Management, 75-5776 Kuakini Hwy. (☎800-622-5348 or 329-3333; www.konahawaii.com) in the Kona Islander Inn. Offers condos in a number of complexes, including the oceanfront Kona Magic Sands, Kona Billfisher, and Kona Islander Inn. 3-night min. stay. Dec. 15-Mar. 31 $69-125, weekly $345-665; Apr.1-Dec. 15 $59-95, weekly $245-495. ❸

Knutson & Associates, 75-6082 Ali'i Dr. (☎800-800-6202 or 329-6311; www.konahwaiirentals.com), in the Casa de Emdeko mall. Offers slightly more upscale options, including the Kona Riviera and Casa de Emdeko. 3-night min. stay. Dec. 15-Mar. 31. $90-210; Apr.1-Dec.15 $70-180. ❸

BIG ISLAND

🔃 FOOD

Groceries are extraordinarily expensive in Kona. Good sushi is often more cost-effective than a supermarket run. Do-it-yourselfers can still try **Kona Natural Foods,** 75-1027 Henry St., in Crossroads Shopping Center (☎329-2296; open M-Sa 9am-9pm, Su 9am-7pm) or the **Safeway** (☎329-2207; open 24hr.) next door. For a camping trip stock-up, consider tagging along with a friend and their membership card to **Costco Wholesalers** (☎334-0770). Home to charter boats that venture off the coast for deep sea fishing, **Honokohau Marina,** 3 mi. north of town off of Queen Ka'ahumanu Hwy. is still the best spot to buy fresh *ahi* steaks, charbroiled right there at the dock. At the end of each day (3:30-5pm), fishermen display their catches on Kailua Pier just like in the old days.

CAFES AND TAKE-OUT

▨ **Kanaka Kava,** 75-5803 Ali'i Dr. (☎866-327-1660 or 327-1660), down the sideway between Black Pearls and Sunglass Hut in the Sunset Plaza. Although first and foremost a kava (a black peppery brew) bar, Kanaka Kava has a reputation for the best Hawaiian food in Kona. Frequent kava drinkers stack their personalized shells behind the bar. Outstanding seafood salad of shrimp, scallops, *ahi* or mahi mahi steak, and organic greens with homemade miso dressing ($12). Greens, cucumber, and avocado salad with miso ($8), with delicious baked tofu or *ahi* steak only $2 more. Shell of kava $3. And for tender-palette first-timers, a *kavalada* of kava, coconut milk, and pineapple juice ($5). Open M-W and Su 11am-10pm, Th-Sa 11am-11pm. ❶

▨ **Hayashi's 'You Make the Roll,'** (☎326-1322), on the *mauka* (mountain) side of Ali'i Dr., at the uphill end of the Kona Marketplace Plaza. Mr. Hayashi dishes sizeable rolls into plastic to-go containers for unbelievable prices. Fill out a notecard to establish your own concoction. Outdoor seating includes umbrella-shaded patio furniture. 6-piece cucumber roll $2. 8-piece California roll $3.50. 8-piece combo of fresh spiced *ahi*, Maui onions, avocado, and watercress $3.25. For the (large) family: 50-piece platters available with 2hr. advance notice ($23-25). Open M-Sa 10:30am-7pm. MC/V. ❶

Island Lava Java, 75-5799 Ali'i Dr. (☎327-2161), just across from the sea, between the volleyball court and farmers' market lot. Look for the green umbrellas. Home to a local morning coffee-and-muffin crowd. Genial surfer-types serve a coffee, muffin, and piece of fruit combo ($4). They plunk whole raspberries into the oat-berry muffins (sold out by noon), make huge cinnamon buns ($3, sold out by 8:30am), and iced mochas ($4.25). Sandwiches with veg. options $5.25-7. Open daily 6am-10pm. MC/V. ❶

Scandinavian Shave Ice, 75-5699 Ali'i Dr. (☎331-1626). Shave ice is packed into neon blossom cups, then doused with crayola colored syrups (natural coloring does not prevail here). Kids love it. Hard rock blaring, the whirring of cast iron ice shavers, and swirling colors create an entertaining chaos. Internet access available. Small shave ice $2. Open M-Sa 10am-9pm, Su 11am-9pm. MC/V. ❶

RESTAURANTS

Cassandra's Greek Taverna, 75-669 Ali'i Dr. (☎334-1066), under blue and white striped awnings, across from the north harbor. Open-air setting with harbor views. Excellent skewered chicken *souvlaki*, marinated in wine and char-broiled, with sides of salad and garlic-heavy *tzatziki* $9. Greek salad with tomatoes, olives, cucumbers, and feta $8. Open daily 8am-10pm. MC/V. ❷

Huggo's, 75-5828 Kahakai Rd. (☎329-1493), at the southern end of Ali'i Dr. in Kona, across from the seawall. Come watch the sun set—the food is excellent, but you're paying half its price for the view. Classy, hard-wood interior overlooking the water, and open-air until the spray of winter surf adds too much salt to dinner. Live music is common. Lunch-time sandwiches like grilled portabello with red peppers on rye ($11). For dinner, try Huggo's best-selling *lilikoi miso ahi* ($30). Vegetarian wild mushroom pasta with ginger $20. Lunch M-F 11:30am-2:30pm, abbreviated lunch menu M-F 2:30pm-4:30pm, dinner daily 5:30pm-closing. AmEx/D/DC/MC/V. ❺

Oodles of Noodles, 75-1027 Henry St. (☎331-2572), in the Crossroads Shopping Center, makes the best of its supermarket plaza location. With its richly colored design and classy wooden furniture, owners pay almost as much detail to a hip presentation as to the food itself. Featuring noodle-based favorites like pad thai with chicken ($14) and fettucine alfredo, as well as a large vegan menu, this restaurant is likely to please most everyone. *Lilikoi* iced tea $3. BYOB. Open daily 11am-9pm. MC/V. ❹

Sam Choy's Restaurant, 73-5576 Kauhola St. (☎326-1545), in the Cal-Cam Centre of the new industrial park off of Queen Ka'ahumanu Hwy. north of town. A meal at Sam Choy's is like taking a bite of The Big Island itself—the menu is a compilation of local favorites from the Fried Poke Omelette ($8.50) to the Kaloko Steak ($13). Breakfast $3.50-13. Lunch $5-13. Open M-Sa 6am-2pm, Su 7am-2pm. ❸

Kona Brewing Co., 75-5629 Kuakini Hwy. (☎334-2739), in the North Kona Shopping Center. A happening restaurant and microbrewery with a patio perfect for enjoying a Captain Cook Pie (pizzas $8-23), Mauna Loa Spinach Salad (salads $7-10), or suds like the Lavaman Red Ale (pints $4). Open M-Th 11am-9pm, F-Sa 11am-10pm. ❸

LUAUS

Island Breeze Luau (☎326-4969) at King Kamehameha's Kona Beach Hotel, is held on the beach adjacent to Kamalahonu and Ahu'ena—Kamehameha the Great's capital at Kona. Shows Tu-Th and Su nights. $57 per person, children 6-12 $22, under 5 free.

Luau at Kona Village Resort, 14 mi. north of Kona, takes the experience to a another level. The F night *luau* has been a tradition at the resort for over 30 yr. It's also the oldest continuously-running *luau* on The Big Island, featuring Hawaiian foods prepared the traditional way and Polynesian dancing. Reservations are essential, as the show often sells out wks. in advance. $76 per person, ages 6-12 $46, under 6 $22.

◪ BEACHES

Kailua-Kona's beaches are hiding. Beyond the lava beds flanking Hwy. 19, distant oases of palms signal the presence of sandy stretches surrounding crescents of clear water. The most pristine beaches are usually accessible only on foot or via unmarked, unpaved, and often hole-pocked roads, left in disrepair to deter an overabundance of visitors. The more popular beaches of South Kohala front a string of resorts, but are still fully accesible to the public. The following beaches are listed in south-to-north order along Hwy. 19, the first just north of Kona and the last at the tip of South Kohala.

WAWALOLI. Wawaloli is well-known for its warm, protected tide pools, great for exploring and deep enough for a bird-bath splash. Explosions of surf crashing against the protective lava bench put on quite a show for sunning spectators. *(The beach is 5 mi. north of downtown Kona on Rte. 19, between mi. markers 95 and 94, accesible via the paved entrance to the Natural Energy Lab. Gates close 7pm.)*

KEKAHA KAI. Kekaha Kai is a slim strip of well-shaded white sand and usually calm waters. There is neither drinking water nor facilities here. *(10 mi. north of downtown Kona on Rte. 19, down a bumpy but passable road between mi. markers 90 and 91. Gates are open M-Tu and Th-Su 9am-8pm.)*

SPY A TRI

Every year, on the 3rd Saturday n October, the streets of Kailua-Kona overflow with chiseled men and women from around the globe. These throngs do not descend upon the town to work on their tans; they're here for the **Ironman Triathlon.** This famous race, the Triathlon World Championship, has almost single-handedly brought triathlons into the world consciousness. Competitors swim 2.4 mi., bike 112 mi., and run a full 26.2 mi. marathon. The drama and excitement of some of the world's greatest athletes pushing themselves to the utmost limits of human endurance are the highlights of each race.

Still, the Ironman is not solely about world-class specimens of the human physique—for many who compete in the Ironman, finishing the race before the cheering crowds on Ali'i Dr. is much more important than even approaching the course records. The event is said to bring out the best of Kona, and whether you're here to compete or just to enjoy yourself on a more low-key vacation, be sure to soak in the spirit of exploration and camaraderie that Ironman inspires.

■ MAKALAWENA. Isolated and unknown, Makalawea is a 20min. walk or a bumpy 4WD ride across baking lava fields. Fine sand cushions the bare bottoms of occasional nude sunbathers. There is neither drinking water nor facilities; bring extra water. *(North of downtown Kona on Rte. 19, between mi. markers 89 and 90.)*

■ KUA BAY (MANINI'OWALI). Also commmonly called Manini'owali, Kua Bay is a 15-20min. walk beyond the highway pull-off. The beach at Kua Bay features fine white sand and excellent swimming when waters are calm. The waves are powerful here, so when the surf's up, it's best to stay on the sand. No shade, drinking water, or facilities. *(Just north of mi. marker 88, off Rte. 19 north of downtown Kona.)*

'ANAEHO'OMALU BEACH (A-BEACH). See **South Kohala,** p. 367.

WAIALEA (69) BEACH. The only reason we've left this beach without a thumb is to prevent too many visitors. This is one of the most idyllic beaches on The Big Island, known only to *akami*, or savvy, residents. For this reason, it is especially deserving of respect and consideration—remember to pack out what you pack in. Facilities are often locked—bring plenty of water. *(Turn makai (toward the ocean) off of Hwy. 19 between mi. markers 70 and 71 onto Puako Rd. Take your 1st right at the dump gate onto a single lane road, then continue to telephone pole #71, where a clay dirt path passable by 2WD leads toward the beach.)*

■ HAPUNA BEACH. When the surf is up, Hapuna is a body boarder's heaven (see **Activities,** p. 334). Consistently named among America's top beaches, its ½ mi. long, 200 ft. breadth of sand is classic. Excellent swimming in calm seas, but when the surf kicks up, it can clobber the unsuspecting. Life-guards on duty every day, 9am-4pm. Full, but run-down facilities. *(Public entrance well-marked off Rte. 19, between mi. markers 69 and 70.)*

MAUNA KEA. Another perfect crescent of sand, accessible only through the Mauna Kea Hotel. Waves lap the shore, creating prime gentle swimming conditions. Public parking is limited, and when the daily alloted permits are out, that's it. See **South Kohala,** p. 365, for more information. Mauna Kea has full facilities. *(32 mi. north of downtown Kona on Rte. 19 between mi. markers 68 and 69.)*

🏊 ACTIVITIES

SNORKELING. Kona's most popular snorkeling spots are a 30min. drive to the south. The steep-cliffed crescent of **■ Kealakekua Bay** (see p. 341) was formed when many acres plunged into the sea. The best snorkeling is on the bay's far side, where a white obelisk marks the British monument to Captain Cook. Dolphins and sea turtles often frolic nearby. *(To Kealakekua, take Rte. 11 south from Kona, through Captain Cook to mi. marker 111. Take a left down winding Napo'opo'o Rd. (Rte. 160), then your 1st right (also Napo'opo'o Rd.), past the old coffee mill to the parking area.)*

SCUBA DIVING. Instructors at **Eco-Adventures** (☎329-7116 or 800-949-3483; see **Practical Information,** p. 328), offer scuba diving adventures for every skill level. Expect to pay around $125 for introductory dives. Open-water certification courses run between 3-4 days, plus text-book time ($425). Travelers with SCUBA instructor certification might start here if searching for **short-term work** in the area, as Eco-Adventures may be able to place divers with other local companies.

BODY BOARDING. **Hapuna Beach** is the undisputed favorite for medium-surf body boarding. The waves here are highly variable and deserving of respect, even though this is one of The Big Island's few lifeguarded beaches. **Manta Ray Snorkel and Dive** in Kona rents 'professional' quality body boards for $5 per day, $15 per wk. (see **Practical Information,** p. 328). **White Sands Beach Park,** on Rte. 11 south of Kailua-Kona and just north of the 4 mi. marker, is also a popular body boarding beach when a shallow, offshore sand bar is present. Amenities include restrooms, showers, and a volleyball court.

KAYAKING. The mile-long paddle across **Kealakekua Bay,** also one of The Big Island's top snorkeling destinations, offers some of the best kayaking in the Kona area. (See **Snorkeling,** above, for directions to the bay.) The best kayak-rental outfits aren't actually in Kona, but in Captain Cook. For those with some kayaking experience, **Aloha Kayak Company** (☎322-2868), *makai* (toward the ocean) at mi. marker 111 on Mamalahoa Hwy., can be the best deal. Rental prices are: ½ day single $20, tandem $30; 24hr. $25/$45; weekly $100/$150. Paddles, backrests, life vests, car rack, and dry bag included. They also offer **guided kayak tours** of the bay. (1½ hr. morning kayak $30 per person; 2hr. afternoon trip $45; 4hr. afternoon trip with lunch $65. Half price on all trips for children under 12.) For those with less-experienced kayakers, **Kona Boys,** 79-7539 Hawaii Belt Rd., on Mamalahoa Hwy. north of downtown Kealakekua, is a bit more expensive, but their guides are all excellent and fully lifeguard-certified. Their rental prices are: single $27, tandem $47. Their **private guided tours** are consistently ranked the best in the state. (9:30 am-2pm. Lunch, paddles, backrests, life vests, dry bag, cooler, and car rack included. $135 per person.)

◎ SIGHTS

HULIHE'E PALACE. One-time governor of Hawaii John Adams Kuakini built this home in 1838, and it later became a favorite retreat for royal families. Beneath a layer of plaster, inner walls of lava rock and coral lime mortar mirror the exposed exterior of Moku'aikaua Church across the way. The home's chandeliers and burgeoning closets testify to the royal family's passion for Western fashions. From 1874-1891, Hulihe'e was home to King Kalakaua, and as the venue for constant dances, parties, and festivals, helped earn him the title of Merrie Monarch. The palace lay abandoned in the early 20th century, serving as a playground for neighborhood children. The Historical Society even reports that an enthusiastic group of card players made good use of the palace front porch, often playing poker by the light of a kerosene lamp. Having gathered together the palace's once-dispersed collection of Hawaiian artifacts, including the javelins and spears of Kamehameha the Great, The Daughters of Hawaii now maintain the palace as a museum. *(75-5718 Ali'i Dr. ☎329-1877; www.huliheepalace.org. Open M-F 9am-4pm, Sa-Su 10am-4pm. $6, seniors $4, ages 18 and under $1.)*

BIG ISLAND

MOKUAIKAUA CHURCH. Constructed in 1837 of lava rock and coral lime mortar, this is the oldest church in the state. It's also the tallest structure in town; for years fishermen used the 112 ft. steeple for navigation purposes. If you look upward to the *koa* rafters, you can see where the heavy timbers were painstakingly connected with gnarly *'ohi'a* pegs. The church also features a model of the *Brig Thaddeus*, the Hawaiian equivalent of the Mayflower. *(At the northern end of Ali'i Dr. ☎ 329-1589. Open daily during daylight. Free.)*

AHU'ENA HEIAU. Ahu'ena Heiau was the centerpiece of Kamehameha the Great's government from 1813-1819. Kamehameha, the only man to unite the Hawaiian archipelago under one ruler, was born on the Kohala coast in the 16th century. After consolidating his authority over the other islands, he returned to Kona to rule (see **History**, p. 11 for more information). He built Ahu'ena Heiau at its present location and dedicated it to Lono, the god of agriculture and prosperity. At the top of the building is a golden plover, a slender little bird thought to have lead the first Polynesian settlers from the South Pacific to the Hawaiian islands, 5000 mi. away. *(At the northern end of Kailua Bay, adjacent to King Kamehameha's Kona Beach Hotel. Grounds are open to the public. Free.)*

■ NIGHTLIFE

Downtown's most happening half-acre surrounds the volleyball court on Ali'i Dr. Just around the corner from mellow Kanaka Kava and overlooked by the boisterous verandas of surrounding bars, the court sees a round of nightly pick-up games. Wander down to the green bench if you'd like to join in. Locals set up spectator chairs, and sandy-haired children complacently lick their cones from the adjacent **Dairy Queen** (open 10am-10pm).

Lulu's, 75-819 Ali'i Dr. (☎331-2633), next to the Coconut Grove Marketplace, is the best place to party in Kona. Pool tables, countless TVs, chili lights, and a vast upstairs lanai make Lulu's the closest thing to a nightclub you'll find on The Big Island. Ambitious plans to create the largest Twister board "ever" are currently in the works. F-Sa $5 cover. Open daily 11am-2am.

Huggo's on the Rocks, 75-5828 Kahakai Rd. (☎329-1493), at the southern end of Kailua Bay next to the Royal Kona Resort. The drinks aren't cheap (beer $4-7), but you're paying for the sky over your head, and the sand beneath your feet, with the ocean crashing just a few yards away. Open M-F 11:30am-11pm, Sa-Su 11:30am-12:30am.

Lasko's, 75-5819 Kuakini Hwy. (☎331-2558), up the hill from downtown near the intersection of Kuakini and Rte. 11. Out of most tourists' radar, this joint is a great spot to grab drinks and a simple meal, and relax Hawaiian-style with the locals til the wee hours of the morning. DJ on F-Sa. Open M-F 11am-2am, Sa-Su 2pm-2am.

Michaelangelo's, 75-5770 Ali'i Dr. (☎329-4436), in Waterfront Row. Michaelangelo's morphs from trendy restaurant to hopping dance party most nights after 10pm. The lavender walls and faux trellis are not exactly stylish, but the grooves can't be denied. $3 Mai Tai served daily 11am-4pm. Ladies' nights W and Sa. Retro nights M and Su. College night Th. Dancing nightly 10pm-2am.

NEAR KAILUA-KONA

HOLUALOA

After crossing Palani Rd., continue south on Rte. 11 past Borders for another 2 mi. At the green sign for Holualoa, turn left, up steep Halualai Rd. and keep right at the T junction. Continue winding uphill for 3 mi., making a near U-turn at the bright turquoise-bordered sign into Holualoa Village.

Holualoa is a good half-century away from nearby Kailua-Kona. Long one of Kona's coffee-growing centers, an influx of artists and craftspeople have changed the face of the main street, converting old pool halls and saloons into art galleries, yoga centers, and eclectic shops. The most striking example of this transformation is the **Kona Arts Center,** on Rte.180 (Mamalahoa Hwy.), housed in the old coffee mill. This non-profit organization is dedicated to cultural enrichment, offering classes in a number of disciplines, including painting, pottery, and fabric design. (Membership $35 per mo. Open Tu-Sa 9:30am-2pm.)

Just down the road at the intersection of Hualalai Rd. and Mamalahoa Hwy. is the wonderful **Kimura Lauhala Shop,** which has been weaving and selling *lauhala* hats, baskets, and carrying cases since the 1930s. The simple elegance of these pieces is made all the more appealing by their low prices. (☎324-0053. Open M-F 9am-5pm, Sa 9am-4pm.) The town's daily commercial life revolves around **Paul's Place,** a store that has been in the business of selling everything but the kitchen sink for decades. (☎324-4702. Open M-F 7am-8pm, Sa-Su 8am-8pm.)

Visitors who ascend to the hill-side greenery of Holualoa tend to return often. Stay awhile at ▨**The Holualoa Inn ➒,** or at hyacinth-pink ▨**Inaba's Kona Hotel** just up the street. For more information on either lodging, see **Accommodations,** p. 330.

KEAUHOU

Keauhou is 6 mi. south of Kailua-Kona along Ali'i Dr.

The laid-back beachside community of Keauhou sits on a picturesque strip of sand along the gently arcing curve of Kahaluu Bay. Kahaluu Beach is the site of some great **snorkeling** and some of the best **swimming** in Kona's immediate vicinity. Just north of Kahaluu Beach, tiny **St. Peter's Catholic Church** sits precariously on the water's edge, looking as though it might be swept out to sea by a strong gust. The small quarters and simple decoration focus the attention on its sole window, behind the altar, which frames an expanse of blue.

A number of companies sail **snorkel cruises** from the bay. Some trips provide lunch, and some only snacks; some boats are shaded, while others let the sun beat down. Be sure to bring extra water, sunglasses with a strap, and plenty of sunscreen. If you miss the boat, Kahaluu Bay Beach Rentals, 78-6685 Ali'i Dr., across the street from Kahaluu Beach, rents snorkel gear. (☎322-4338. Open daily 8:15am-5pm. $6 per day; $18 per wk.) **Fair Wind,** 78-7130 Kaleiopapa St. (☎800-677-9461 or 322-2788; www.fair-wind.com), is the granddaddy of Kona snorkel cruises, and has an exclusive permit to moor their catamaran in Kealakekua Bay. They offer an array of tours including the Deluxe Morning Cruise (9am-1:30pm; adults $90, children ages 4-12 $50), the Afternoon Snack Cruise (2-5:30pm; adults $58, children ages 4-12 $36), and the Afternoon Deluxe Cruise (M, W, Sa 2-6:30pm; adults $85, children 4-12 $47). **Dolphin Discoveries,** 77-116 Queen Kalama Ave., can offer a more personalized adventure. The husband-and-wife team are both certified naturalist guides, and can take guests to the best and most remote snorkeling and dolphin-sighting spots in the Kona area with their bouncy orca raft. (☎322-8000; www.dolphindiscoveries.com. Morning trip: 8am-noon. Adults $74, children 4-12 $59. Afternoon: 12:30-3:30pm. All ages $59. Snacks included, but bring your own lunch.)

If you're hankering for a meal after a day at the beach, look no farther than the **Royal Thai Cafe ➋,** in the Keauhou Shopping Center on Kamehameha III Rd. No wonder all the Buddhas are smiling in this refined restaurant—anyone surrounded by food this good would have to be happy. (☎322-8424. Curries $9-$14; veggie dishes $9. Open daily 11am-10pm. AmEx/D/MC/V.)

SOUTH KONA

On an island such as this, a few miles can make a world of difference. While the hustle and bustle of Kailua-Kona are just up the road, the sleepy coffee towns of Honalo, Kealakekua, Captain Cook, and Honaunau precariously straddle the Hawaii Belt Rd. (Rte. 11) on the slopes of Mauna Loa. This series of towns has a funky vibe all its own, and this stretch of coastline is one of the most culturally and ecologically rich on the island. Significant pieces of history are protected at Pu'uhonua o Honaunau and the Captain Cook Monument, and natural wonders are the main draws to Kealakekua Bay and Miloli'i. In this area, Hawaiians and *haoles* (foreigners) alike recognize the need for preservation, and take steps to ensure that the legacy of conservation continues.

✸ ORIENTATION

South Kona's main drag is **Route 11** (also known as the **Hawaii Belt Road** or **Mamalahoa Highway**). Off of this strip, there are a number of roads running east down to the coast, and west, up the mountain. The more significant ones for tourists descend the mountainside to the ocean. These are **Napo'opo'o Road,** which runs into **Middle Keei Road** and drops to the southern end of Kealakekua Bay and **Route 160.** Rte. 160 accesses Pu'uhonua o Honaunau and eventually leads to the Bay. Honalo and Honaunau are about 8 and 20 mi. south of Kailua-Kona, respectively.

⌨ TRANSPORTATION

Driving is the easiest way to get around South Kona. Some travelers hitchhike, but it can be dangerous and *Let's Go* does not recommend it. **Taxis** service the area, but they are generally expensive: **Paradise Taxi and Tours** (☎329-1234; open 24hr.; $2 per mi.) and **D&E Taxi** (☎329-4279; open 5am-10pm; $2 per mi.) are two options.

The **Hele-On bus** (☎961-8744) runs from Honaunau north to Kailua-Kona and west to Hilo. Buses from Honaunau Elementary School to: **Kailua-Kona** (50min.; M-Sa 5:55am; $2.25) via Yano Hall in **Captain Cook** (5min.; $0.75), Konawaena Schools in **Kealakekua** (15min.), and Ben Franklin in **Kainaliu** (20min.); and from Captain Cook to **Kailua-Kona** (50min.; M-Sa 10:45am, 2:15pm; $2.25). See www.hawaii-county.com for the most up-to-date fares and schedules.

One of the preferred methods of transportation in the area, especially in Kealakekua Bay, is **kayak.** A number of rental companies hawk the crafts along Mamalahoa Hwy. from Kealakekua to Captain Cook. (See **Activities,** p. 334.)

🛈 PRACTICAL INFORMATION

TOURIST AND FINANCIAL SERVICES

Tourist Office: The **H.N. Greenwell Store Museum,** 81-6551 Mamalahoa Hwy. (☎323-3222; www.konahistorical.org), home of the **Kona Historical Society,** just south of downtown Kealakekua, offers a good range of historical information about the area. Local stores also have knowledge for visitors looking to get off the beaten track. Open M-F 9am-3pm. Donations gratefully accepted.

Banks: Bank of Hawaii (☎322-9377), and **First Hawaiian Bank** (☎322-3484), next to each other on Mamalahoa Hwy. in downtown Kealakekua, are both open M-Th 8:30am-4pm, F 8:30am-6pm and have **24hr. ATMs.**

LOCAL SERVICES

Bookstore: Island Books, 79-7360 Mamalahoa Hwy. (☎322-2006), next to Sandy's Drive-in, in the Kainaliu Center, shelves an impressive collection of used and rare general titles. Open M-Sa 10am-7pm, Su 1-8pm.

Library: Kealakekua Public Library (☎323-7585), on Mamalahoa Hwy. in downtown Kealakekua, offers **Internet access** to Hawaii Public Library Card Holders. 3 mo. visitor card $10. With 4 computers, Internet appointments are recommended. Open M and Tu noon-6pm, W 1-7pm, F 11am-4pm, Sa 10am-4pm.

Laundromat: Hale Holoi Laundromat, next to Cap's Drive-In, just north of downtown Captain Cook. Open daily 6am-9pm.

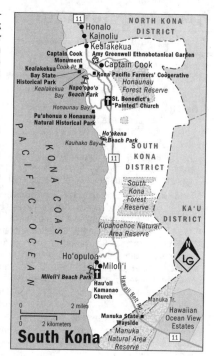

South Kona

Outdoor Equipment: Hawaii Forest and Trail, 74-5035B Queen Ka'ahumanu Hwy. (☎331-8505), next to GasPro, between downtown Kona and the airport. USGS topo. and trail maps, water filters, and solar shower contraptions. Open daily 7am-5:30pm.

Weather Conditions: ☎961-5582.

EMERGENCY AND COMMUNICATIONS

Emergency: ☎911.

Police: A **sub-station** on Mamalahoa Hwy. in the center of Captain Cook is sporadically manned. The nearest district station is just north of downtown Kailua-Kona on Rte. 19 (☎326-4646).

Pharmacy: Kealakekua Pharmacy, 79-7460 Mamalahoa Hwy. (☎322-1639), in Mango Court, south of downtown Kainaliu. Open M-Tu and Th-F 9am-5pm, W 9am-3pm.

Hospital: Kona Community Hospital (☎322-9311), on Haukapila St. in Kealakekua. 24hr. emergency room.

Internet access: Free at **Kealakekua Public Library. Kona Mountain Cafe,** 81-6637 Mamalahoa Hwy. (☎323-2700), in Kealakekua. $2 per 15min. Open M-F 6:30am-6pm, Sa 7am-5pm, Su 7am-4pm.

Post Office: Kealakekua Post Office, Mamalahoa Hwy. (☎800-275-8777), in the Central Kona Center. Open M-F 9am-4:30pm, Sa 9:30am-12:30pm.

Postal Code: 96750.

BIG ISLAND

🗗 ACCOMMODATIONS AND CAMPING

B&Bs are plentiful along the Kona Coast, where agro-tourism has become the norm and there's nary a resort in sight. Individual visitors and groups in search of a unique retreat may inquire into accommodations at **Paleaku Peace Gardens,** 83-5401 Painted Church Rd. (☎328-8084; www.paleaku.com) between Kealakekua Bay and Pu'uhonua o Honaunau. (See **Sights,** p. 341.)

🗟 Rainbow Plantation, Rte. 11 (☎800-494-2829 or 323-2393; www.aloha.net/~kon-abnb), between Pineapple Park and the Chevron Station, just north of the turn-off for Kealakekua Bay. Grounds are a jumble of coffee groves and tree ferns with peacocks and multicolored lights. The "Crow's Nest" is set in a former coffee shack, and the "Jungle Queen" refers to a suite within a restored fishing boat, now moored permanently in the backyard. Outdoor kitchen pavilion has midnight snacks. Full breakfast included. 2-night min. stay. Doubles $84-105; each additional person $15. V/MC. ❸

Cedar House B&B and Coffee Farm, Bamboo Rd. (☎328-8829; www.cedarhouse-hawaii.com). From downtown Captain Cook, turn uphill onto Kiloa Rd. at mi. marker 110, between the post office and Choicemart. Kiloa becomes a single lane; turn right at the T junction onto Kinue Rd. Take the next left onto Greenwell Mountain Rd., then left again onto Bamboo Rd., keeping an eye out for the small sign on the left. In the midst of a coffee farm high above Kealakekua Bay, in-house rooms have views of the South Kona Coast. The more secluded "Coffee Barn" cottage is perfect for families, with kitchen, bathroom, entertainment center, and stacks of games. Breakfast fairies leave trays of fresh bread and fruit early each morning. Full breakfast included for in-house guests. Rooms $70-95; cottage $110 (up to 3); each additional person $10. MC/V. ❸

Beautiful Edge of the World B&B, (☎800-660-8491 or 328-7424; www.bnb-choices.com/usa/hawaii/edge-of-the-world.bnb), off of Rte. 11 in Captain Cook. As the roads above Kealakekua Bay are unmarked, owner Kurt often meets guests at the Manago Hotel in order to caravan home. Edge-of-the World offers 3 rooms: a 2nd-story "Crow's Nest" with king-size bed, full bath, and stupendous view, the "Pacific Room" with king-size bed and bathroom like a bowling alley, and a cheery "Nut Room" with skylight and shared bath. Inquire after the treehouse perched in the mango tree. Owners speak multiple languages. Check-in noon. Check-out noon. Rooms $60-90. ❸

Affordable Hawaii at Pomaikai "Lucky" Farm B&B, 83-5465 Mamalahoa Hwy. (☎800-325-6427 or 328-2112; www.luckyfarm.com), south of Captain Cook between mi. markers 107 and 106. Working on her macadamia and coffee farm, in addition to her B&B, innkeeper Nita provides a 100% pure Kona taste of Big Island eco-tourism. With a green tin roof, bare plank construction, and high ceilings, the converted Coffee Barn recalls an era before jumbo jets and vacation packages. 2 spacious "greenhouse" rooms below (up to 4) and 1 "farmhouse" double off the living room. Full breakfast included. Rooms $60-75; additional guests ages 5 and up $10. MC/V. ❷

Pineapple Park B&B, 81-6363 Mamalahoa Hwy. (☎877-865-2266 or 323-2224; www.pineapple-park.com), north of downtown Captain Cook, is more of a hostel than a B&B, and sees a healthy amount of European traffic. While the 4 private rooms upstairs are light-filled and spacious, the 2 street-side bunk rooms have more galley-like proportions. Full kitchen, BBQ, high-speed Internet ($10 per hr.), kayaks for rent ($20-45 per day), and a shuttle to Kealakekua Bay. They occasionally trade a bed for a few hours of housekeeping a wk., or can arrange some other form of **short-term work** (See **Alternatives to Tourism,** p. 83). Dorm bunks $20; private rooms $55-65. MC/V. ❷

Hookena Beach County Park (☎808-961-8311; www.hawaii-county.com) is at a well-marked turn off Mamalahoa Hwy., about 2½ mi. south of its intersection with Rte. 160. The park offers the only legal camping in the area; pitch your tent under palms right on the beach—just watch for falling coconuts. The hassle of permit mailing is no more: reserve, pay for, and print out your permit in 5min. online. 7-day on-site limit June-Aug. 14-day limit all other mo. Adults $6, teens $2, children 12 and under $1. ❶

❐ FOOD

Kona Pacific Farmers Cooperative (☎328-2411; kpfc@gte.net; www.kpfc.com), hosts a **farmers' market** every Thursday from 8am to 4pm behind the old cooperative mill on Napoʻopoʻo/Middle Keei Rd., just uphill from Kealakekua Bay. From Captain Cook, continue south on Rte. 11 to mi. marker 111. Turn right down Napoʻopoʻo Rd. just after the Chevron, following the signs for Kealekekua Bay. Keep right on Napoʻopoʻo Rd. at its intersection with Middle Keei Rd. and the Cooperative will be ½ mi. down on the right. Follow the pink donkeys to the market out back.

▨ **Nasturtium Cafe,** 79-7491 Mamalahoa Hwy. (☎322-5083), north of Captain Cook next to Seven Senses. Offering an abundance of fresh foods from *ahi* to zucchini, this tiny cafe is the place for a sit-down lunch in South Kona. Salads ($8-11), and enticing sandwiches ($7-10). Open M-F 11am-6pm, last seating 5:30pm. ❷

▨ **Aloha Angel Cafe,** 79-7384 Mamalahoa Hwy. (☎322-3383), in downtown Kainaliu. This hip cafe is situated around the venerable Aloha Theater, and offers the best of outdoor dining on a breezy lanai with views down to the ocean. An eclectic menu features island ingredients. **Aloha Theater** film screenings nightly 7:30pm ($6). Breakfast and lunch $6-13. Dinner $14-24. Open daily 8am-2:30pm and 5-9pm. MC/V. ❹

The Coffee Shack, 83-5799 Mamalahoa Hwy. (☎328-9555), south of Captain Cook. Perched over the coastline hundreds of feet below, the breakfasts, sandwiches, pizzas ($6.50-12) and desserts are as amazing as view. Open daily 7am-5pm. D/MC/V. ❷

Billy Bob's Park 'N Pork, 81-6372 Mamalahoa Hwy. (☎323-3371), north of downtown Captain Cook, next to "Just Ukes," and across the street from Pineapple Park. Heaping helpings of meat and all the fixin's at the southernmost BBQ in the USA. The Bodacious Meal ($10) includes 2 meat sides, chuckwagon beans, and corn bread with honey butter. Chili and Rice $4. Open M-Tu and Th-Su 5-9pm. MC/V. ❷

Evie's Natural Food, 79-7460 Mamalahoa Hwy. (☎322-0739), next to Subway in Mango Court south of Kainaliu, is a good spot to stock up for a picnic, or to grab sandwiches at the deli. Evie's also posts a list of **short-term work** opportunities, including farm jobs that trade room and board for labor (see **Alternatives to Tourism,** p. 82). Open M-F 8am-7pm, Sa-Su 9am-5pm. AmEx/D/MC/V. ❶

Bong Brothers, 84-5229 Mamalahoa Hwy. (☎328-9289), in Honaunau. This little hole-in-the-mountain is the place to cure the munchies with fresh local fruits and vegetables or a scrumptious smoothie ($3.50). Open M-F 9am-6pm, Sa 10am-6pm. ❶

❻ ☈ SIGHTS AND ACTIVITIES

KEALAKEKUA BAY. The bay and its spectacular coral reef are much the same as they were at the time of Captain Cook's famous arrival over 200 years ago. The area is protected as a **Marine Life Conservation District,** a designation which severely limits fishing in the bay, and prohibits the anchoring of boats in order to preserve the myriad marine life that call the waters home. **Snorkeling** is excellent throughout the well-developed reef that has formed on the shelf between the sheer *palis* (cliffs) and the Kaʻawaloa Cove, at the northwestern end of the bay.

The only part of the bay accessible to automobiles and appropriate for the launching of watercraft is Napoʻopoʻo Beach at the southeastern end in **Kealakekua Bay State Historical Park.** In addition to a launching site, the park has restrooms, picnic tables, some big surf, and **Hikiau Heiau State Monument,** a significant Hawaiian temple. (*To reach the park from Rte. 11, take Napoʻopoʻo Rd., about 18 mi. south of Kailua-Kona between Kealakekua and Captain Cook. The road winds down the mountainside for a few mi. before joining Middle Keei Rd. and continuing on to the bay. The entire journey from highway to shoreline is about 4 mi. The distance from the southeastern to the northwestern shore is about ½ mi., making for an easy kayak or reasonable paddle for able swimmers.*)

BIG ISLAND

FLIPPER, IS THAT YOU? Kealakekua Bay is one of the best spots in Hawaii to see **spinner dolphins,** who make this crescent of water their personal playground. They are slender dolphins that generally do not exceed 7 ft. in length and have dark grey backs and white stomachs with long, slim snouts. Spinner dolphins travel in groups, or pods, and while they feed in the deep channels offshore, they spend much of their time resting and playing in shallow water. Leaping out of the water to mind-boggling heights and then spinning laterally before splashing down, Spinner dolphins seem to be natural circus performers. With their tremendous leaping ability they are able to rotate as many as 16 times during one flight. They are capable of even more amazing aerial maneuvers like head-over-tail spins when their leap is a series of mid-air somersaults. While there's no schedule for this circus, your best bet for catching a glimpse of these acrobats is in the early morning.

BAY TOURS. Many companies in the area offer **snorkel** cruises or **kayak** excursions to the Kealakekua reef. For more information on snorkeling, see **Near Kailua-Kona: Keauhou,** p. 337. For more information on kayaking, see **Activities,** p. 334.

CAPTAIN COOK TRAIL AND MONUMENT. At the northwestern end of the bay, is the Captain Cook Monument, a 27 ft. pillar erected in Cook's honor by fellow Brits in 1878, 100 yr. after he set foot on Hawaii. The monument stands near the site where Cook was killed, and has sparked much debate because it is viewed by some Native Hawaiians as a testament to cultural domination. (See **History,** p. 11 for more information on Cook's landing.) While a number of ships recreating Cook's voyage have anchored in the bay and left plaques commemorating his "discovery," the ruins of the village of Ka'awaloa, which was founded when Britain was still an uncivilized hinterland of the Roman Empire, are a good deal more interesting to explore. The ruins occupy the flats behind the monument.

To reach the monument, head to the **Captain Cook Monument Trail.** (4 mi., 2½hr. round-trip. Trailhead: Right-hand side of Napo'opo'o Rd., 200 yd. from the intersection of Rte. 11. Level: moderate.) The trail is the first unmarked dirt road on the downhill side of the road, and descends the slope to Ka'awaloa Cove, passing through overgrown sugar cane, exposed lava fields, and finally dense foliage along the shoreline. The hike loses elevation on the way down, which means a bit of a climb back up. Heading downhill, the trail follows a road for the first few hundred meters before branching off to the left through fields of gigantic grasses and wild brush. Farther down, the terrain opens up to *a'a* fields. The trail approaches the coast, with sweeping views of the surrounding countryside. On its final descent, the path drops into shaded coastal forest. Bring plenty of water, appropriate footwear and clothing, and, of course, snorkeling gear.

If you'd rather ride on horseback down the trail, go to **King's Trail Rides,** on Mamalahoa Hwy. between Kealakekua and Captain Cook. The excursions include lunch and snorkeling gear, and take about 4hr., with 2hr. of riding. (☎323-2388; www.konacowboy.com. $135 per person, over age 7 only. $50 advance deposit required by credit card or money order to Kings Trail Rides, P.O. Box 270, Kealaekua.)

FARMS AND GARDENS. The **Amy Greenwell Ethnobotanical Garden,** gives a sense of the close relationship the Hawaiians had with the land before Cook's arrival. Home to Native Hawaiian species as well as those brought by Polynesian settlers, this 15-acre garden provides a representative look at the plants and cultivation techniques perfected by the islanders before the arrival of Europeans. (☎323-3318. On Mamalahoa Hwy., uphill from Captain Cook Monument, just north of downtown Captain Cook. Open M-F 6:30am-5pm, but people are welcome to walk through the garden at any time. Tours W *and F 1pm, $5. Groups of 5 or more can arrange tours. Suggested donation $4.)* Tours at the **Kona Pacific Farmers Cooperative** provide insight into the ins and outs of coffee growing. The facility has been processing coffee since 1910 and now handles over 5 million pounds of beans a year. It is the oldest and largest coffee cooperative in the US, and one of the best places to buy 100% pure Kona coffee. They also host a **farmers' market** all day on Thursdays. *(☎ 328-2411; www.kpfc.com. 82-5810 Napo'opo'o/ Middle Keei Rd. toward the bay; follow the pink donkeys. Free tours.)*

ST. BENEDICT'S "PAINTED" CHURCH. John Berchman Velge, a Belgian Catholic priest, built **St. Benedict's "Painted" Church** between 1899 and 1904. Using ordinary house paints, and some divine inspiration, he created the closest there is to a Gothic cathedral in Hawaii. The vibrant colors of the interior are a blend of the islands and the Old World, with faux marble columns blossoming into palm trees and a vaulted ceiling complete with tropical sky. *(Just up the hill from Pu'uhonua o Honaunau. Take Rte. 160 north onto Painted Church Rd., just west of the 1 mi. marker, or take Napo'opo'o Rd. and turn onto Middle Keei Rd., then right onto Painted Church Rd.)*

PU'UHONUA O HONAUNAU NATIONAL HISTORICAL PARK

The park entrance is on Rte. 160, 4 mi. downhill from where Rte. 160 leaves Rte. 11 between mi. markers 103 and 104. The park can also be reached via a 4 mi., one-way road that runs from Napo'opo'o Beach. There is no public transportation to the park, but you can take the Hele-On Bus (☎ 961-8744) from Kailua-Kona to the Honaunau stop and walk down (see South Kona transportation, p. 327). The Pu'uhonua o Honaunau Visitor Center has helpful information about the park. Restrooms and water fountains as well. (☎ 328-2288 or 328-2326; www.nps.gov/puho. Open daily 7:30am-5:30pm.) An orientation talk given at the amphitheater every 30min. from 10-11am and 2-3pm provides a good introduction to the site and its offerings. Park open M-Th 6am-8pm, F-Su 6-11am. $5 per car.

Once the home of Kona's royal chiefs, the reconstructed thatched buildings, lava rock walls, and platforms of Pu'uhonua o Honaunau National Historic Park still evoke the spirit of the ancient Hawaiians. Honaunau Cove's sheltered beach was ideal for canoe landings, and fresh water was always available, making it the natural location for the *ali'i* (royalty) to establish one of their major residences. The royal residence had no single palace or other dominating structure, but was made up of a number of buildings within the coconut grove. This area, along with the canoe landing, was open only to *ali'i* and their attendants. All others were prohibited by the *kapu*, or sacred laws, to enter these grounds or in any way to mar the *mana*, or spiritual power, held by the *ali'i*. It was believed that the breaking of the *kapu* would cause the gods to react violently with lava flows, tsunamis, or earthquakes. (See **Give Me Shelter,** p. 344.) The area still holds a certain power, and the park provides insight into aspects of ancient Hawaiian life and culture.

There are actually two distinct parts of Pu'uhonua o Honaunau, the **Royal Grounds** and the *pu'uhonua*, or **Place of Refuge,** separated by a massive stone wall which was built in 1550 and still stands today. The walking tour of the royal grounds and place of refuge, which is laid out for visitors in the park brochure given out at the entrance station, covers the major points of interest within the park. These include: **Keone'ele,** the sandy beach that was the royal canoe landing; the **Great Wall,** a physical as well as spiritual demarcation between the royal grounds and the *pu'uhonua;* and **Hale o Keawe,** the reconstructed temple and mausoleum which imparted the place of refuge with great *mana*.

The well-maintained royal grounds and *pu'uhonua* are the park's primary attraction, but **Ki'ilae Village,** a ¾ mi. walk from the Visitor Center along the 1871 trail, is also worth exploring for anyone interested in the daily life of the early Hawaiians. You can pick up a guide booklet for the village at the Visitor Center. Highlights of the walk include the **Waiu-O-Hina Lava Tube,** which opens out in the

GIVE ME SHELTER The ancient Hawaiians lived under the rigid structure of a society based on the sacred laws, or **kapu**. The penalty for violating the *kapu* was always death. The *kapu* governed daily life, including everything from the interaction of men and women to the relationship between the *ali'i* (royalty) and the commoners. Those who broke the *kapu* were allowed a second chance only if they could make it to the **pu'uhonua** (place of refuge) adjacent to the royal grounds without being killed. To do so, one had to run the gauntlet of warriors who surrounded the *pu'uhonua*. If an outlaw were to reach the *pu'uhonua*, a ceremony of absolution was performed by the *kahuna*, after which the offender could return home safely. Non-combatants in war as well as defeated warriors also sought a haven in the *pu'uhonua*. Hawaiians conducted war in order to exterminate the enemy rather than simply to gain territory, but those unable to fight could find safety in the *pu'uhonua* until the battle was over, after which their allegiance was sworn to the victor. The *pu'uhonua* was deemed a sanctuary because it was the final resting place of the bones of the *ali'i*, and the seat of their *mana* (spiritual power). The newest *heiau* in Pu'uhonua o Honaunau was dedicated in honor of Keawe, the great-grandfather of Kamehameha I, who possessed such powerful *mana* that it protected the entire *pu'uhonua*.

middle of a cliff overlooking the ocean, and **Keokea Holua,** a slide constructed out of lava rock used by the Hawaiians for *holua*, or sledding. The coast on either side of the park is home to numerous fish as well as rare spinner dolphins. The snorkeling beneath the cliffs and in protective coves is excellent, and the reef just north of the park in Honaunau Cove is a renowned spot for underwater exploration.

KA'U

Tucked away in the southwest corner of the island, the Ka'u district is a mishmash of landscapes, people, and ideas. Full of macadamia nut farms, abandoned sugar cane fields, and pastures, Ka'u is ripe for exploration. From the Hawaiian Ocean View Estates in the lava fields of the west coast, to the windswept pastures of Ka Lae, to the towns of Na'alehu and Pahala and the volcanic playground of the Ka'u Desert and Hawaii Volcanoes National Park, there is plenty to see. Although Ka'u is not the place for travelers seeking gourmet dining or sizzling nightlife, those enticed by the region's wilderness will be right at home.

Southern Ka'u District

KA'U Ka'u Forest Reserve
Nechung Dorje Drayang Ling
Pahala
Hawaii Ocean View Estates
Ocean View
Hawaii Belt Rd.
Punalu'u
Punalu'u Beach (Black Sand Beach)
Wai'ohinu
TO MANUKA STATE NATURAL AREA RESERVE (1 mi.)
11
Honu'apo Bay
Na'alehu
Kama'oa Wind Farm
South Point Rd.
Ka'alu'alu Bay
0   10 miles
0   10 kilometers
Ka Lae National Historic District
Papakolea Beach (Green Sands Beach)
Ka Lae (South Point)
Ka Lae Beach

🖳 TRANSPORTATION

The only means of transportation to and from Ka'u is the **Hele-On bus** (☎961-8744), which runs M-F from Ocean View Center to **Hilo** (2hr. 40min.; 6:40am; $5.25) via the **Wai'ohinu/Na'alehu** gas station (20min.; 7am; $4.50), and **Pahala Shopping Cen-**

ter, adjacent to the bank (1hr.; 7:30am; $3.75). Furthest from Hilo, the stop at Ocean View center is serviced by request only. Travelers are required to phone in their request by 3pm of the afternoon prior to travel.

🧭 ORIENTATION

Whatever you want to call it, **Route 11, Hawaii Belt Road,** or **Mamalahoa Highway,** is the undisputed Ka'u thoroughfare. Ocean View, Wai'ohinu and Na'alehu, and Pahala are all located in close proximity to what is the district's only link to the outside world. The only other major route in the area is **South Point Road,** which runs the 11 mi. between Rte. 11 and Ka Lae.

🛈 PRACTICAL INFORMATION

TOURIST AND FINANCIAL SERVICES

Tourist Office: The **Punalu'u Bake Shop,** Hawaii Belt Rd. (☎929-7343), in downtown Na'alehu, is the closest thing to a tourist office in Ka'u. The affable staff offers more sweet bread samples than ready answers, but they would be happy to provide a few brochures with directions to the black- and green-sand beaches. Open daily 9am-5pm.

Tours: Down the road in Ocean View, **Kula Kai Caverns** (☎929-7539 or 929-9725; www.kula-kaicaverns.com), leads tours of some of the island's most spectacular lava tubes, which are over 1000 yr. old. Trips range from a 30min. introduction ($12) to a full-out spelunking adventure in Maelstrom Cave (3-4hr., $65). All tours are by reservation only; call for details.

Banks/ATM: Na'alehu's sole **ATM** is inside **Video Showplace,** on Hawaii Belt Rd. (☎929-8436), in Na'alehu Shopping Center. Open M-Sa 10am-7pm, Su 11am-7pm. A 2nd **ATM** in Ocean View (☎929-7516) is next to the Ocean View Market, up Prince Kuhio St. from Hawaii Belt Rd. Open M-Sa 10am-8pm, Su 11am-7pm. Nearest **bank** with a **24hr. ATM** is **Bank of Hawaii,** (☎928-8356) in the Pahala Shopping Center, at the corner of Kamani and Pikake St. in Pahala. Open M-F 8:30am-noon and 1-3pm.

LOCAL SERVICES

Library: **Na'alehu Public Library,** Hawaii Belt Rd. (☎939-2442), behind the post office, provides **Internet access** to Hawaii State Library card holders. 3 mo. visitor card ($10). As only 2 computers are available, it's best to call the librarian before opening hours (daily 9am-noon) to reserve a slot. Open M, W, F noon-5pm, T-Th 1-6pm.

Laundromat: The **Wash** (☎929-7072) sits with its back to Desert Rose Cafe (see **Food,** p. 346), making laundry in Ocean View a potentially delicious experience. Wash $1.50, dry $0.25 per 8min. Open M-Sa 6am-8pm, Su 7am-8pm. If you miss last load at 7pm head south to **Star Wash,** next to Video Showplace in the Na'alehu Shopping Center. No phone, but Star's customers are welcome to call the owner's home (☎929-7004). Wash $1.50, dry $0.25 per 7min. Last wash 8:30pm. Open daily 6:30am-10pm.

Weather: ☎961-5582.

EMERGENCY AND COMMUNICATIONS

Emergency: ☎911.

Police: **Ka'u District Police Station** (☎939-2520), is southeast of Na'alehu on Hawaii Belt Rd. at the 62½ mi. marker. Though the office is only open M-F 7:45am-4:30pm, **non-emergency dispatch** (☎935-3311) is 24hr. There's also a red **emergency phone** hanging in a white box outside the office door.

Hospital: Ka'u Hospital (☎928-8331), on Rte. 11 in Pahala, provides basic medical services and a 24hr. emergency room.

Pharmacy: The on-site community health clinic at Ka'u Hospital in Pahala doubles as the region's only pharmacy, **Ka'u Community Pharmacy** (☎928-6252). Open M, W, F 8am-5pm. Larger pharmacies are located along Rte. 11 in Captain Cook and Hilo.

Telephones: There's a **pay phone** across the street from the post office in downtown Na'alehu.

Post Office: Na'alehu Post Office, 95-5663 Mamalahoa Hwy. (☎800-275-8777). Open M-F 7:45am-4:15pm, Sa 10:15-11:15am.

Postal Code: 96772.

⛏ ACCOMMODATIONS

There aren't many options for accommodations in this region; the best are in the tiny town of Wai'ohinu.

◪ **Margo's Corner,** Wakea Ave. (☎929-9614). From Rte. 11, turn down South Point Rd. after the green sign between mi. markers 69 and 70. Heading toward the ocean, take a left onto Kama'oa Rd., then the 1st right down Wakea Ave. Keep an eye out for the rainbow flag. 2 beautifully crafted suites pamper guests with luxuries like a sauna and massage table. Guests on a budget may also set up a tent in the front garden. Delectable breakfast and dinner included. On-site natural food store. Reservations appreciated. Camping $25 per person; suites $75-115. ❶/❹

Macadamia Meadows, Kama'oa Rd. (☎929-8097; kaleena@aloha.net). Turn onto Kama'oa Rd. next to Wong Yuen Store and head up the hill. It'll be about ½ mi. up on the left. While the 8-acre working macadamia nut farm may be its most compelling attraction, there are plenty of amenities for guests at this lovely Japanese-style cedar home, including a tennis court, swimming pool, and BBQ. Many rooms include refrigerators, microwaves, and cable TV. Rooms $65-135. AmEx/MC/V. ❸

Shirakawa Motel, Mamalahoa Hwy. (☎929-7562), across from Wong Yuen Store in Wai'ohinu. The southernmost motel in the US is about as cheap as you can get on this island. The simple rooms are clean, and provide a good place to bed down en route between Kona and Hilo. Singles $30; doubles $35, with kitchenette $42, with full kitchen $50; roll-away beds $10, child-sized $8. ❷

🍴 FOOD

◪ **The Desert Rose Cafe,** Hawaii Belt Rd. (☎939-7673), in Pohue Plaza in Ocean View. This unassuming diner blends into the a'a (lava) desert that is Hawaii Ocean View Estates, but dishes out some of the best food in Ka'u ($5.75-11.25) with lots of daily specials. Not to be missed. Open daily 7am-8pm. ❷

Na'alehu Fruit Stand, Mamalahoa Hwy. (☎929-9009), just down the road from the 76 gas station in the eastern end of downtown Na'alehu. With everything from local fruit and vegetables to Haagen-Dazs ice cream and Nantucket Nectars, this local market can fuel South Point adventures. Hearty sandwiches in sand-proof wrap $3. Saucer-size cookies $3.75 per dozen. Open M-Th 8am-7pm, F-Sa 8am-8pm, Su 8am-6pm. ❶

Shaka Restaurant, 95-5763 Mamalahoa Hwy. (☎929-7404), in downtown Na'alehu near the post office. Na'alehu may not have much to offer when it comes to culinary delights, but this friendly restaurant with a relaxed island flair serves up a variety of home-cooked meals at reasonable prices. Open Tu-Su 10am-9pm. MC/V. ❷

Punalu'u Bake Shop, Mamalahoa Hwy. (☎929-7343), in Na'alehu center. Their famous sweetbread is baked here and shipped around the island, so get it while it's hot. They also serve plate lunches ($6-7) and ice cream on their lanai. Open daily 9am-5pm. ❶

◎ SIGHTS

MANUKA STATE WAYSIDE. This turn-off amid the forests and crumbling lava fields of **Manuka State Natural Area Reserve** is an ideal spot to cast off the chains of resort packages and rental car agreements in favor of natural calm. The 2 mi. **Manuka Loop Trail** runs through 8 acres of land that was set aside in the mid-1930s for 48 species of native Hawaiian flora and 150 other species from around the Pacific. The park is also a quiet locale for a lunch or rest stop with bathrooms and shaded picnic tables. *(Between the 81 and 82 mi. markers on the Hawaii Belt Rd.)*

NECHUNG DORJE DRAYANG LING. Once a Japanese *Nichiren* Mission, this Buddhist temple was established by Nechung Rinpoche in 1973 as a non-sectarian center for Buddhist teachings, and is worth even a short visit. The entire complex is colored in traditional Tibetan style and beautifully maintained. The Dalai Lama visited the temple in 1980 and again in 1994, giving a talk to several thousand people. Immaculate grounds, punctuated with towering eucalyptus, palm trees, and

> # MILOLI'I Tucked 5 mi. below Rte. 11, between the 88 and 89 mi. markers, in the no-man's-land of lava fields and dense forest between the Kona coast and the rolling pastures of Ka'u is Miloli'i—one of The Big Island's last true fishing villages and a vestige from another era. Although a traditional lifestyle based in and around the sea holds sway here, the town itself is anything but traditional, with 4X4s and SUVs parked in the shadow of satellite dishes atop newly constructed homes. The torturous drive down to the town provides panoramic views of the titanic lava flow that devastated the area in 1926, and there is still so little vegetation in the black fields that the lava seems freshly cooled. At the end of the road is **Miloli'i Beach Park** along with the tiny **Hau'oli Kamana'o Church.** The park offers restrooms and a sheltered picnic area as well as camping, and there is some good **snorkeling** along the rough shoreline.

bamboo, as well as a number of peacocks, add to the sense of serenity. Individual visitors interested in quiet introspection and rest are welcome to stay for a minimum of 2 nights. *(From Rte. 11 take the turn-off to Pahala, 12 mi. northeast of Na'alehu and 22 mi. southwest of Volcano. Take the first right onto Pikake St. and follow the paved road 4 mi. The temple will be on the right. ☎928-8539; www.nechung.org. Programs without spending the night $15. Dorms $35; singles $50; doubles $70.)*

KA LAE/SOUTH POINT

The 11 mi. road that goes from the Hawaii Belt Rd. (between the 69 and 70 mi. markers, 6 mi. west of Wai'ohinu) to South Point is like a runway to another world. Dense rainforest gives way to pastures full of cattle and the spectacle of the **Kama'oa Wind Farm.** Some of the enormous windmills have lost their blades and look like fallen soldiers, but others whip around at a considerable clip. Below these giants are fields that stretch down to the sea. Most rental companies don't permit their cars to drive this road.

BIG ISLAND

👁 SIGHTS

KA LAE NATIONAL HISTORIC LANDMARK DISTRICT. Near the coast, the road enters the 710-acre Ka Lae National Historic Landmark District. It eventually forks, and the right-hand route heads to a parking lot and 30 ft. cliffs. The left-hand track leads to the Ka Lae Information Center where there's parking for those setting out on the hike to Green Sands Beach. *(Office open daily 9am-6pm. Parking $5.)*

KA LAE BEACH. Ka Lae is a spectacular spot—the convergence of currents from the windward and leeward sides of the beach create some pretty intense surf. A number of ladders and platforms on the cliff's edge adjacent to the parking lot enable fishermen and their catches to get up from the boats moored below, and double as a common venue for cliff jumping.

SOUTH POINT. "The Point" itself is a couple of minutes beyond the parking lot at the extremity of the island. This piece of land is thought to be the spot of the Polynesians' first landing in the Hawaiian Islands, and has been an important location throughout Hawaiian history as both the site of Kalalea Heiau, which still stands today, and because of its abundance of fish.

🌊 BEACHES

GREEN SANDS BEACH. From the Ka Lae Visitor Information Center, Green Sands Beach, or **Papakolea,** is a 3 mi., hour-long jaunt along the coast. If you can handle the walk, Green Sands should not be missed. Be sure to get directions, as the trail is not marked. The beach is not the verdant green of the surrounding pasture, but more of a drab olive, thanks to the olivine. Regardless of its color, the solitude and stunning beauty of the spot will knock you over—if the ripping winds and crashing waves don't do it first. Surrounded by lava rock cliffs shaped by the ravages of wind and water, the narrow strip of sand resembles a vestige of Eden, somehow overlooked by all those who have explored this coast before. Come early enough in the day and you'll likely have the place to yourself. The surf here, which is generally bigger than at most other beaches on the island, makes for excellent body surfing. Be sure to bring plenty of water and appropriate footwear as the walk back may seem even longer after a couple of hours basking in the sun.

PUNALU'U BLACK SAND BEACH. Eight mi. northeast of Na'alehu and a little less than 5 mi. south of Pahala along Rte. 11 lies Punalu'u Beach, the island's largest black sand beach and home to a large population of hawksbill turtles. Unfortunately, this combination of attractions has made Punalu'u very popular, especially with the tour buses that perpetually circle the island. It's rare that the area is not packed with visitors. Still, Punalu'u is a nice place to take a dip or **snorkel** around the rocks that serve as the primary feeding grounds for the turtles. You can sometimes spot them from the shore or from underneath the coconut palms that shade the sparkling sand. Just south of the beach itself are county park facilities, including protected picnic areas, restrooms, showers, and campsites.

HAMAKUA COAST

The drive along Rte. 19 (Hawaii Belt Rd.), between Hilo and W
some of the most spectacular tropical scenery on the island.
around each bend in the highway, and rainbows of brilliant
mountainside. Although Hamakua was once the sugar cane
Big Island, not a single plantation remains today. Nothing h
left by the former sugar industry, and the region is one of the few places un un-
island where extensive expansion has not been the prevailing trend. Unlike
much of the Big Island, the Hamakua Coast still has stretches of land that are
inaccessible by car. Between Pololu Valley and Waipi'o Valley, a dozen miles
of virgin shoreline can only be reached via ocean-going vessels or legs strong
enough to hike up and down the *palis*. Small communities now occupy the
intriguing historic shells of what were once bigger, bustling towns, but no one
seems to mind the downsizing.

HONOKA'A

For much of the 19th and 20th centuries, Honoka'a occupied a lofty position in the
Big Island's sugar cane industry. The sugar industry eventually waned, however,
and Honoka'a's last mill closed in the 1990s. Honoka'a has rallied, forging a future
on its own terms. The circa-1920 store fronts of the town's main drag still house a
hardware store and a five-and-dime, but recently, funky art galleries, antique
shops, and restaurants have sprung up among them. The range of establishments
reveals the diverse nature of Honoka'a's residents as well.

ORIENTATION AND TRANSPORTATION

Honoka'a sits along **Route 240,** just off of Rte. 19, about 40 mi. northwest of Hilo
and 15 mi. east of Waimea. **Waipi'o Valley** is 9 mi. northwest of town, at the end of
Rte. 240. Life in Honoka'a centers on **Route 240 (Mamane Street),** which is home to
almost all of the town's businesses; a handful more lie along the highway up the
hill. From Waimea, **Plumeria Street** leaves Rte. 19 and drops down through
Honoka'a, meeting Mamane St. in the center of town.

Honoka'a is on the main route between Hilo and Kona, and receives more traffic
from the **Hele-On bus** than any other small town on the island. Buses run from the
high school to **Hilo** (1¼hr.; M-Sa 5:50, 8:30am, 3:15, 5:10, 5:25pm; $3.75) and **Kona**
(1¾hr., 2:40pm, $4.50) via **Waimea** (40min., $0.75) from the Dairy Queen on Rte. 19.

PRACTICAL INFORMATION

Despite the presence of two tourist information centers in Honoka'a, travelers will
be hard pressed to rustle up some useful information. The **Honoka'a Visitor Center,**
adjacent to Tex Drive-In along Rte. 19, is more of a gift shop than anything else.
However, it is staffed and there are a few brochures. (☎775-0598 or 966-5416;
www.hawaii-culture.com. Open daily 9am-5pm.) In town, the **Hamakua Heritage
Center and Visitor Information** is little more than a shack filled with flyers for local
(and not-so-local) tourist attractions. No one seems to man this office, which
means it has the one bonus of being open 24hr.

Honoka'a does have a few helpful services. Both **Bank of Hawaii** (☎775-7218) and
First Hawaiian Bank on Mamane St. (☎775-7276) have **24hr. ATMs.** Both banks are
open M-Th 8:30am-4pm and F 8:30am-6pm. The **Honoka'a Public Library,** 45-3380

.ane St., offers **Internet access** to those with a Hawaii Public Library card. No
.op use. (☎775-8881. Open M and Th 11am-7pm, Tu-W 9am-5pm, F 9am-3pm.)
.aundry facilities are available at **PJ Suds Washerette,** on Kike St., near the corner
of Kike and Mamane St. (☎987-7731. Wash $1.50, dry $0.25 per 5min. Last wash
8:30pm. Open daily 6am-9pm.) The **Honoka'a Swimming Pool,** on Mamane St., next
to the high school, is open to the public. (☎775-0650. Open mid-afternoons M-F.)
For **weather information,** call ☎961-5582. For **emergencies,** call ☎911 or the **police**
substation (☎775-7533) on Mamane St., across from Honoka'a Theater. **Liu's Pharmacy,** 45-3551A Mamane St., is hiding around back, across from the bank. (☎775-
0496 or 775-9974. Open M-F 8am-6pm, Sa 9am-1:30pm.) The **post office** is at 45-490
Lehua St., on the corner of Lehua and Mamane St. (☎800-275-8777. Open M-F 9am-
4pm, Sa 8:15-9:45am.) **Postal Code:** 96727.

▟ ACCOMMODATIONS AND CAMPING

Waipio Wayside, off of Hwy. 240 (☎800-833-8849 or 775-0275; wayside@bigis-
land.net), on the way toward Waipi'o Valley, a few mi. west of downtown Honoka'a. Formerly a plantation house, this secluded inn boasts incredible views of the Pacific
Ocean. Each bedroom is individually decorated and comfortable, but the gazebo and
various decks are the best places to soak up the soothing tropical atmosphere. Breakfast included. Rooms $95-155. AmEx/D/MC/V. ❸

Hotel Honoka'a Club, Mamane St. (☎800-808-0678 or 775-0678; www.hotel-
hono.com). You can't miss this rambling establishment, built in 1908 as a club for plantation managers. With the death of the sugar industry, the building was transformed into
a hotel, though the clean, eccentrically decorated rooms are reminiscent of an earlier
era. Breakfast included. Linens not provided. Reception 8am-1pm and 4-8pm. Check-
out noon. Standard dorms $15, semi-private $25; standard doubles $55, with bath
$65; 2-bedroom suites (up to 4) $85. V/MC. ❶

Kalopa Forest State Park and Recreation Area, located off of Rte. 19, about 1 mi.
south of the intersection of Rte. 19 and Rte. 240. Excellent grassy tent sites under an
'o'hia and eucalyptus canopy at a cool 2500 ft. Tent sites available on a first come, first
served basis. Reserve cabins in advance by calling ☎974-6200, or speak to the caretaker stationed at the park entrance, where you can get a permit. Cabins include access
to the recreation hall and kitchen. Bedding provided. Check-in 2pm. Check-out 10am.
Camping free. Cabins $55-175. ❷

◨ ♫ FOOD AND ENTERTAINMENT

Cafe Il Mondo, 45-3626A Mamane St. (☎775-7711). The folks behind the counter are
doing what they love here, and customers reap the benefit of their passion for pizza.
Slices $2.25-2.75, ▧ Antipasto $7.25. Pizzas $9-18.25. Open M-Sa 11am-8pm. ❶

Jolene's Kau Kau Korner Restaurant, (☎775-9498) at the corner of Mamane St. and
Plumeria St. A friendly local joint serving down-home grub, including mahi mahi and
teriyaki you-name-it. If you want authentic Hawaiian favorites, this is the place to stop.
Plate lunches and dinners $6.50-8. Open M, W, F 10am-8pm, Tu and Th 10am-3pm. ❶

Simply Natural, Mamane St. (☎775-0119). Unique dishes such as *taro*-banana pancakes ($3.50) augment a menu of reliable stand-bys, including tempeh sandwiches
and garden burgers ($6). The juxtaposition of rainbow ceiling fans and checkerboard
linoleum floors make for a fresh take on typical diner decor. Open M-Sa 9am-4pm. ❶

Mamane Street Bakery, Mamane St. (☎775-9478). Freshly baked bread and pastries
($0.75-$4), perfect for a picnic. Open M-Sa 6am-3pm. ❶

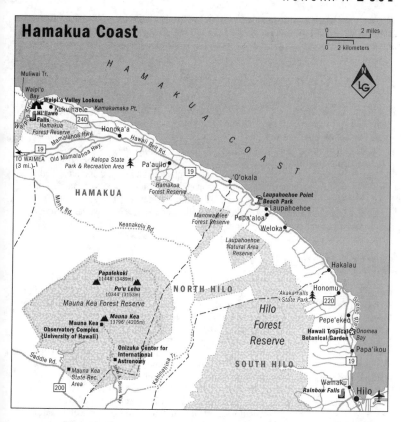

Hamakua Coast

0 — 2 miles
0 — 2 kilometers

Muliwai Tr.

H A M A K U A

C O A S T

Waipi'o Bay
Waipi'o Valley Lookout
Kukuihaele Kamakamaka Pt.
Hi'ilawe
Falls
Hamakua
Forest Reserve
240
Honoka'a
Mamalahoa Hwy. Hawaii Belt Rd.
19
TO WAIMEA Old Mamalahoa Hwy.
(3 mi.) Kalopa State Pa'auilo
Park & Recreation Area
19
'O'okala

HAMAKUA

Hamakua
Forest Reserve

Mana Rd.

Manowaialee Laupahoehoe Point
Forest Reserve Beach Park
Papa'aloa Laupahoehoe
Keanakolu Rd. Weloka

Laupahoehoe
Natural Area
Reserve

Hakalau

Papalekoki
11448' (3489m)
Pu'u Lehu NORTH HILO 'Akaka Falls Honomu
10344' (3153m) State Park 220
Mauna Kea Forest Reserve
Hilo
Mauna Kea Mauna Kea Forest Pepe'ekeo
Observatory Complex 13796' (4205m)
(University of Hawaii) Reserve Hawaii Tropical Onomea
Botanical Garden Bay
Onizuka Center for Papa'ikou
International
Astronomy 19
Saddle Rd. SOUTH HILO
Mauna Kea Wainaku
State Rec. Rainbow Falls Hilo
Area
200

Tex Drive-In, 45-690 Pakalana St. (☎ 775-0598), above downtown Honoka'a, just off of Rte. 19. Owner Ada has made *malasadas* (Portuguese donuts) famous on the Big Island ($.85). The beef for her excellent burgers ($3-5), comes from right up the street. Heaping mahi mahi salad $8.25. Open daily 6am-9pm. ❶

Honoka'a People's Theater, on Mamane St. (☎ 775-0000). The theater has been painstakingly restored over the last decade, and now shows a wide range of movies, from arthouse films to Hollywood blockbusters. $6, seniors $4, under 12 $3.

⚐ OUTDOORS

KALOPA FOREST STATE PARK AND RECREATION AREA. This 615-acre reserve has been protected since 1903, but much of the surrounding land has been all but destroyed by sugar cane production. The park includes 100 acres of virgin Hawaiian rainforest situated between heights of 2000 and 3500 ft. The land receives approximately 90 in. of precipitation a year. An easy ¾ mi. loop, the Native Forest Nature Trail, passes through the heart of the 'ohi'a forest. There are other trails within the greater forest reserve area, including the Gulch Rim Trail, which skirts Kalopa Gulch and Hanaipoe Gulch. Group cabins, a campground, and a picnic area (see **Accommodations and Camping**, p. 350) are all available for public use. *(Located off of Rte. 19, about 1 mi. south of the intersection of Rte. 19 and Rte. 240. Watch for the green sign turn-off just south of Honoka'a town. The park is 3½ mi. up a narrow winding road.)*

LAUPAHOEHOE POINT Early in the morning on April 1, 1946, the children of the village of Laupahoehoe ("leaf of smooth lava") were greeted at school by a peculiar sight. Their school, which was set at the tip of a finger of land jutting into the Pacific, normally overlooked turbulent waves crashing against the lava shoreline. That day, however, the nooks and crannies of the rough black headland, usually covered by water, were dry. Students and teachers ventured down to the shore to investigate the phenomenon. Minutes later, a massive tsunami crashed down upon them. The entire school was wiped away, and 20 children and 4 teachers were killed.

Today, the point is home to a well-maintained beach park with a monument dedicated to those lost in the disaster. Facilities include restrooms, showers, picnic tables, and campsites, as well as volleyball and basketball courts. The point is about halfway between Hilo and Honoka'a, 1 mi. off of Hwy. 19, at the end of a marked turn.

WAIPI'O VALLEY

The massive valley, which is a mile wide at its mouth and extends 6 mi. back from the coast, inspires awe in even the most jaded traveler. Walled in by 2000 ft. high *palis* (cliffs), Waipi'o Valley is a world unto itself. The wide, twisting **Waipi'o Stream** channels fresh water from the Kohala Mountains to the sea. This natural irrigation nourishes an abundance of fruit trees, which are ripe for the picking. Lush *taro (poi)* patches dot the landscape, and trees sink under the weight of avocados, coconuts, mango, guava, and passion fruit. With a stunning gray-sand beach that stretches between the warm surf of the Hamakua Coast, canopied rainforest, striking waterfalls, and myriad vistas, the valley has a little bit of everything.

Before the arrival of Captain Cook in 1778, between 4000 and 10,000 Native Hawaiians had established their own private Eden in the crevices of Waipi'o Valley. The largest of the seven valleys on the windward side of the Kohala Mountains, the Waipi'o Valley was once the political and religious center of Big Island. 'Umi, the first ruler to unite the people of the Big Island, systematically laid out *taro (poi)* fields in Waipi'o in the 16th century. The bounty from the valley's fields could feed the entire island during times of need. The valley began to attract non-Hawaiians a few hundred years later. The immigrants took advantage of the fertile climate to farm small plots, and by the end of the century, the valley boasted schools, churches, and restaurants, as well as a post office, jail, and hotel. The **tsunami** of 1946 wiped out almost all of the valley's homes and infrastructure, forcing inhabitants to move to higher ground. Today, the valley is home to no more than 100 residents, and much of the cultivated land has been reclaimed by the rainforest. For those willing to explore it, the spirit of the land remains untarnished.

▶ ORIENTATION

The road ends here. Civilized **Route 240** fittingly terminates at the parking area for **Waipi'o Valley lookout.** From here, an extraordinarily steep paved road winds its way 900 ft. to the valley floor. With grades of 20-35% and hairpin turns, it is passable only with a hearty 4WD, and in first gear at that. There's a reason why Honoka'a towing is busy. Descending vehicles must yield to ascending traffic. Visitors with 2WD may park at the lookout and hike the steep half mi. to the valley floor. Once there, it's another muddy quarter mi. to the right to reach the beach.

CAMPING

Camping is free for up to four nights at four sites, on the eastern side of Waipi‘o Stream. Permits are available from the **Bishop Estate,** 78-6831 Ali‘i Dr., in Keauhou Shopping Center, which owns 60% of the land in the valley and manages it with the intent of preserving Hawaiian heritage. (☎322-5300. Open M-F 7:30am-4:30pm.)

HIKING

The easiest way to explore the valley is with your eyes, from the **Waipi‘o Valley Lookout** at the end of Rte. 240, at the top of the eastern *pali* (cliff), 900 ft. above the valley floor. Across the valley, on the opposite *pali*, you can see the switchback trail that climbs over to **Waimanu Valley** on that side of the ridge. The views from the lookout are more expansive than any you'll see once you head down into the valley itself, but you're cheating yourself if you stop here. From the lookout, a steep (but relatively short) paved road plunges to the valley's floor. All rented 4WD vehicles are prohibited from traveling anywhere below the valley rim, so walking becomes the only option. The hike down is a brief 30min., but can be slippery when wet. The hike back up should take about 45min. and is somewhat easier because you're more in control. Bring plenty of water; there are no facilities.

At the base of the *pali*, the road forks and the left branch heads back into the interior of the valley while the right continues down to the beach. A left turn yields views of the shimmering **Hi‘ilawe Falls** (1200 ft.), Hawaii's highest single-drop waterfall. It's possible to hike to the base of Hi‘ilawe in about 1½hr., but it requires bushwhacking through rainforest thicket. Adventurers need also show sensitivity; "*kapu*" (forbidden) and "No Trespassing" signs line the way.

Turning right at the fork takes you on a muddy 10min. walk to the matchless **Waipi‘o Beach.** Looming *pali* border the sandy expanse, which is bombarded by the aggressive Pacific surf. Despite a strong riptide and rough waves, the beach is popular with surfers. Waipi‘o Stream cleaves the beach in two on its way to the ocean, and the western bank is much less popular than the more accessible eastern shore. Be careful when crossing the stream—the current is stronger than it looks and the stream is deeper in some places than in others.

From the beach, you can see the impressive **Kalauahine Falls** sparkling in the east. There's a rough trail going fairly loose lava rock that runs from the intersection of the cliffs and the ocean to the foot of the falls. At the western end of the beach, a switchback trail leads up the *pali* and over to Waimanu Valley. Waipio's neighboring valley is about 10 mi. away, but the trek up the valley wall to a series of secluded pools and a glittering waterfall makes a good day hike. If you plan on going any farther, make sure to come well-prepared with appropriate water, food, and rain gear, as well as a **backcountry camping permit** from the **Division of Forestry and Wildlife,** 19 E. Kawili (☎974-4221) in Hilo. Like Waipi‘o, Waimanu Valley once had a Hawaiian settlement, which has since been abandoned.

TOURS

If you've been down to the valley floor and want to see things from another perspective, there are several outfits that offer tours along the Waipi‘o rim including **Waipi‘o Ridge Stables** (☎775-1007), and **Kukui ATV & Adventures** (☎775-1701). While these tours, and those listed below, are an interesting way to see the valley, they are not the only options. Waipi‘o's waterfalls and beach are off-limits to tours.

BIG ISLAND

Waipi'o Valley Shuttle (☎ 775-7121), embellishes the natural beauty of the valley with educational tidbits. The tour features views of Hi'ilawe Falls and *taro* patches, and knowledgeable guides narrate tales of Hawaiian history and legends in the background. The 1½hr. tours leave from Waipi'o Valley Artworks in Kukuihaele. M-Sa 9, 11am, 1, 3pm. Reservations recommended. $40, ages 10 and under $20.

Waipi'o Na'alapa Stables (☎ 775-0419; naalapa@ilhawaii.net), offers 2½hr. horseback adventures in the valley. Experienced guides lead the rides through the rainforest to spectacular waterfalls and vistas. Trips begin at Waipi'o Valley Artworks in Kukuihaele. M-Sa 9:30am, 1pm. Reservations required. $75.

Waipi'o on Horseback (☎ 775-7291), has leisurely excursions that highlight waterfalls and one of Waipi'o's largest *taro* farms. Meet at the Last Chance Store in Kukuihaele for a drive to the valley floor. M-Sa 9:30am and 1:30pm. Reserve 24hr. in advance. $75.

Waipi'o Valley Wagon Tours (☎ 775-9518), explore the *taro* fields, lush tropical foliage, and majestic waterfalls of the valley from the cushioned seats of a mule-drawn covered wagon. The 1½hr. tours depart from the Last Chance Store in Kukuihaele. M-Sa 9:30, 11:30am, 1:30, 3:30pm. Reservations required. $40, children $20.

WAIMEA

A history of Waimea is a history of **Parker Ranch.** This is horse and cattle country, a cross in landscape between Colorado and Scotland. Though only 10 miles from balmy Kohala beaches, the air here is crisp and cool. The Parker story began in 1793, when Captain George Vancouver gave a herd of long-horned cattle to King Kamehameha. Kamehameha bade them go forth and multiply, declaring hunting them to be *kapu* (forbidden). This lasted for 10 years, during which the cattle became a ferocious lot, notorious for their rampages, even chasing Hawaiians from their homes. By the early 19th Century, King Kamehameha had hired Massachusetts-born marksman John Palmer Parker to round up the cows, shoot the wild ones and tame the rest. This Parker did, and so garnered royal favor—so much so that he was granted a small plot of land on the slopes of Mauna Kea, and in 1816, married the granddaughter of King Kamehameha, beginning a collection of acreage that would top out at 225,000 and become the vast Parker Ranch.

A benevolent giant, or a family dictatorship? As always, land spelled power. More than a decade after the death of Samuel Smart, the ranch's sole surviving heir, the multi-million dollar Parker Corporation's board of trustees still run this town. Waimea's private prep school and public hospital are both funded solely by the copious Parker cashflow. The presence of the Parker millions has distorted Waimea's trajectory as a small Hawaiian town—on one hand shaping its downtown into a suburb of the Kohala resorts, and on the other providing the community with economic resources and opportunity. Visitors and residents themselves seem to try to negotiate their position in relationship to this powerful name, all the while questioning whether Waimea owns Parker or Parker owns Waimea.

✈ ORIENTATION

40 mi. northeast of Kona and 54 mi. northwest of Hilo, Waimea is set smack dab in the middle of The Big Island's northern half, at the intersection of **Route 190 (Hawaii Belt Road)** and **Route 19 (Mamalahoa Highway or Kawaihae Road)** in the Kohala hills. Rte. 190 from Kona bisects Rte. 19 in the town center. From the Parker Ranch Plaza, the eastern half of Rte. 19 runs 15 mi. to Honoka'a and the Hamakua coast. The other half of Rte. 19 heads toward the port of Kawaihae, while **Route 250 (Kohala Mountain Road)** splits off toward Hawi.

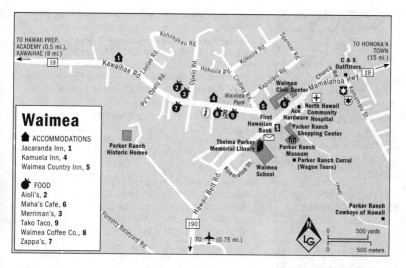

Waimea

ACCOMMODATIONS
Jacaranda Inn, **1**
Kamuela Inn, **4**
Waimea Country Inn, **5**

FOOD
Aioli's, **2**
Maha's Cafe, **6**
Merriman's, **3**
Tako Taco, **9**
Waimea Coffee Co., **8**
Zappa's, **7**

LOCAL TRANSPORTATION

Flights: Waimea-Kohala Airport is 1½ mi. south of Waimea Center, off of Rte. 190, heading toward Kailua-Kona. The primary carrier, **Pacific Wings Airlines** (☎888-575-4546 or 887-2104; www.pacificwings.com) runs flights to **Honolulu** (daily 11:40am, M and W-Su 10:10am) and **Kahului**, Maui (daily 11:40am, M and W-Su 5:55pm). All flights, regardless of destination, are $74 and may be reserved on the phone with credit card (☎888-575-4546). Cash payment requires tracking down an elusive agent at the understaffed airport office (open F-Su 8am-noon and 5-6pm).

Bus: The **Hele-On bus** (☎961-8744; www.co.hawaii.hi.us/mass_transit/transit_main.htm) passes through Waimea with some consistency. Daily trips to **Hilo** from both Ace Hardware (1¼hr.; 2:55, 4:55, 5pm; $4.50) and the Parker Ranch Center (1hr. 40min., M-Sa 8:05am, $4.50), as well as to **Kailua-Kona** from the Parker Ranch Center (1¾hr., M-Sa 3:20pm, $3).

Taxis: The sole surviving taxi company in the Waimea area is based 10 mi. out of town. Drivers from **Alpha Star Taxi** (☎885-4771) hesitant to make a 20 mi. run to the airport, but will always pick up customers in a bind. $2 base rate and $2 per additional mi.

Bike and Equipment Rentals: C&S Outfitters, 64-1066 Mamalahoa Hwy. (☎885-5005), at the corner of Hwy. 19 and Kamamalu St. Full suspension bikes $30 per day, $130 per wk. Kayaks (Nov.-Apr.) $30-45 per day, $120-160 per wk. Open M-Sa 9am-5pm. Grant at **Mauna Kea Mountain Bikes** (☎888-682-8687 or 883-0130; www.bike-hawaii.com), offers full-suspension rentals and off-road mountain bike excursions. Kona GT $25-30 per day, $130 per wk. See **Tours,** p. 358.

PRACTICAL INFORMATION

Tourist Office: Waimea Visitor Center, 65-1291 Kawaihae Rd. (☎885-6707; www.northhawaii.net or www.kamuela.com). Open M-F 8:30am-3:30pm.

Banks: Bank of Hawaii, 67-1191 Mamalahoa Hwy. (☎885-7995). Open M-Th 8:30am-4pm and F 8:30am-6pm. **First Hawaiian Bank** (☎885-7991), in front of the Parker Ranch Center at the corner of Mamalahoa Hwy. and Kawaihae Rd. Open M-Th 8:30am-

NO WORK, ALL PLAY

THE BOYS OF SUMMER

I arrived at the **Parker Ranch's Paniolo Park** for the 40th annual **July 4th Horse Races and Rodeo** to see the stands were packed, but the audience was as strange a rodeo crowd as I could imagine. Rather than seeing Stetsons and denim, I saw tie-dyed tees, plumeria *leis*, and *aloha* shirts. I found a spot in the colorful crowd and took my seat above the arena. All the riders were *paniolos* from the island's many ranches, but the wranglers from Parker Ranch really stood out. They cleaned up both in the races and rodeo competitions, showing poise their colleagues couldn't match. In the last event of the morning, the relay race, I placed my bet on the boys from Waimea—$10 on Parker Ranch. The riders took their positions, and with the wave of a flag, they were off. They were neck and neck at the first pass until the Parker Ranch rider pulled out. On the inside turn, the other rider clawed his way back. At the next pass, it was unclear who was ahead, and as the cowboys headed for home, the other rider edged in front. But with a burst of speed the Parker Ranch rider pulled out all the stops, winning by a nose. I went to collect my cash, and was sad to find that one of my boys had dropped the baton on the first leg, disqualifying the team. No worries—I'm sure the Parker *paniolos* will be back in the saddle shortly.

-Bryden Sweeney-Taylor

4pm, F 8:30am-6pm, Sa 9am-1pm. Both have **24hr. ATMs.**

Library: Thelma Parker Memorial Library, 67-1209 Mamalahoa Hwy. (☎887-6067), just behind the Waimea middle school gym, has **Internet access** for those with a Hawaii Public Library card (3 mo. visitor card purchased at the front desk; $10). Open M-Tu and Th-F 9am-4:30pm, W noon-7:30pm.

Swimming Pool: The pool at **Hawaii Preparatory Academy,** 65-1692 Kohala Mt. Rd. (☎881-4028), is open for public lap swim M-F 6-7am, noon-1pm; senior swim M-Th 11am-noon; public open swim Su 1-4pm. $2.

Emergency: ☎911.

Police: Waimea Police Station (☎887-3080 or dispatch 935-3311), located at the top of the hill in the Waimea Civic Center, at the corner of Kamamalu St. and Mamalahoa Hwy. Office open 7:45am-4:30pm. Emergency phone located just outside the office.

Pharmacy: Village Pharmacy, 65-1267 Kawaihae Rd. (☎885-4824), next to Tako Taco. Open M-F 8:30am-5:30pm, Sa 8:30am-1:30pm.

Hospital: North Hawaii Community Hospital, 67-1125 Mamalahoa Hwy. (☎885-4444), next to Ace Hardware. Look for the blue signs. 24hr. emergency room.

Post Office: Kamuela Post Office, 67-1197 Mamalahoa Hwy. (☎800-275-8777). Open M-F 8am-4:30pm, Sa 9am-noon. As there are 2 other Waimeas in the state, *be sure to address mail to **Kamuela**, not Waimea.* Your letter could otherwise end up in Kauai.

Postal Code: 96743.

■ ACCOMMODATIONS

■ **Jacaranda Inn,** 65-1444 Kawaihae Rd. (☎885-8813; www.jacarandainn.com), From the intersection of Rte. 19 and 190 in Waimea Center, continue west down Rte. 19 toward Kawaihae (Kawaihae Rd.) Jacaranda is set back to the right, just past the 85 mi. marker. Canopy beds and whirlpool baths are here for half the Kohala price. Built in 1897, Jacaranda retains an understated plantation feel: hardwood floors, chandeliers and wood-paneled library. Each room is unique. The "Vanda" is old-fashioned, with a king-size iron bed (our favorite), while the "Hibiscus" is whimsically Costa Rican. Check out the web site for previews. Custom breakfast included. Check-in 3-6pm. Check-out 11am. Reservations recommended. Room 6 is wheelchair-accessible (up to 4). Rooms $95-225; 3-bedroom cottage $350 (up to 6). MC/V. ❸

Kamuela Inn, 65-1300 Kawaihae Rd. (☎800-555-8968 or 885-4243; www.hawaii-bnb.com/

kamuela.html), just west of Waimea Center along Rte. 19 (Kawaihae Rd.), and past the ball field. More of a stylish motel than an inn, Kamuela is Waimea's best mid-range value. Spacious and clean rooms exhibit an upcountry motif. Complimentary muffin breakfast served in the enclosed lower level art gallery. Check-in 3pm. Check-out noon. Standard doubles with private bath and cable TV $59, queen bed upgrade $72; triples with kitchenette $89; quads with kitchenette $99. AmEx/D/MC/V. ❷

Waimea Country Inn, 65-1210 Lindsey Rd. (☎800-367-5004 or 885-6711; www.castleresorts.com), off Kawaihae Rd. just west of Waimea Center, before the Parker school. The spacious rooms on the 2nd floor have tall, exposed ceilings. Reception 7am-11pm. Check-in 3-11pm. Check-out noon. Rooms $95-118. AmEx/D/MC/V. ❸

🍴 FOOD

Pick up fresh produce and bouquets at the **Homestead Farmers' Market,** in the parking lot of the State of Hawaii Department of Home Lands, 2 mi. east of Waimea center at the 55 mi. marker on Rte. 19 (Sa 7am-noon).

Aioli's (☎885-6325), in Opelo Plaza on Kawaihae Rd., a little less than 1 mi. west of Waimea center. A bistro with both traditional and innovative offerings, including house special garlic soup, famous *lilikoi* cheesecake, and roasted rack of lamb and spinach, roquefort, and walnut-stuffed pasta (entrees $14-23). Open Su 8am-2pmTu 11am-4pm, W-Th 11am-8pm, F-Sa 11am-9pm. Reservations recommended. D/MC/V. ❹

Maha's Cafe, 1 Waimea Center (☎885-0693), off of Mamalahoa Hwy.(Rte. 19) in downtown Waimea. Set in the historic Spencer House, the restaurant is named after one of the queens of Hawaiian home cooking, Harriet-Ann Namahaokalani Schutte Kraan ("Maha"). Although best known for their sandwiches (lamb and mango chutney $9), Maha's also makes a killer smoked *ahi* quesadilla with *lilikoi* salsa ($11). Breakfast $2.75-5.25. Open M and Th-Su 8am-4:30pm. AmEx/D/MC/V. ❷

Tako Taco, 65-1271 Kawaihae Rd. (☎887-1717), on Rte.19 1 mi. west of the town center, across from Hawaii Preparatory School. Straight out of Baja beach, this cheerful tin-roofed taqueria is the place to pick up tasty Mexican eats for cheap. Indoor counter and stools, as well as umbrella-shaded outdoor seating. Burritos $4.25-8.50. Tacos $3.50-8.50. Salads $6.50-8.50. Open daily 11am-8pm D/MC/V. ❶

Merriman's (☎885-6822), on Kawaihae Rd. next to Aioli's. Specializing in cutting-edge Hawaiian regional cuisine, Merriman's uses fresh Big Island products to create inventive, delectable dishes. Lunch $6.50-12, dinner $19-33. Lunch M-F 11:30am-1:30pm, dinner nightly 5:30-9pm. Reservations recommended. AmEx/MC/V. ❺

Zappa's, 65-1210 Kawaihae Rd. (☎885-1511), behind the Opelo Corner gas station. Zappa's tosses up Waimea's best pizzas and dishes out solid grinders and pasta. Take-out available. Pizzas $9-22, grinders $7, pasta $8-9. Open M, W-F, Su 6:30am-1:30pm and 4:30-7:30pm, T and Sa 6:30am-1:30pm. D/MC/V. ❷

Waimea Coffee Co. (☎885-4472), in Parker Sq. on Kawaihae Rd. (Rte. 19). The best place to grab a cup of joe ($1.25-1.50). Open M-F 7am-5pm, Sa 8am-4pm. ❶

🐎 TOURS

The wide-open views of the rolling Kohala hills are best experienced by riding a horse into the wind. A number of quality outfits operate horseback tours both in Waimea and a few miles north toward North Kohala. Reservations should be made

48hr. ahead if possible. Calling ahead for a weather check is also never a bad idea. Be sure to bring warm clothes, long pants, and a slicker if you have one. The wind whips and misty rain and fog descends quickly.

Paniolo Riding Adventures (☎889-5354), located 14 mi. north of Waimea Ct. on Rte. 250, just past the 13 mi. marker in Kohala. Similar to Dahana's ride, but with 1 more hr. in the saddle. Guides lead riders across the open expanses of a working ranch, all the more exciting during calving season. (2½ hr. $89.)

Dahana Ranch (☎885-0057), 7mi. northeast of Waimea on Rte. 19. Call for directions. A great value, Dahana's open range rides are uniquely *outside* Parker estate. Guides lead riders up through rolling green pasture land into the hills of Mauna Kea. (1½hr.; 9, 11am, 1, 3pm. $55 per person. No experience necessary. Min. age 3!) Dahana also offers a round-up ride and cattle drive for more advanced riders. (2½hr.; $100.)

Parker Ranch Cowboys of Hawaii (☎885-5006), behind the Parker Ranch Center, following the succession of 2 fluorescent pink signs. A low-key outfit run by 2 amiable cowgirls (and some cowboys) with a desire to share their historical knowledge of early *paniolo* culture and its color. (2hr.; 8:15am, 12:15, 4pm. Min. age 7. $79 per person.)

Parker Ranch Wagon Tours (☎800-262-7290 or 885-7655), in Parker Ranch Corral, next to the Parker Ranch Visitor Center. This is certainly no open-range adventure, but a tame 45min. spin around a small section of Parker Ranch in a covered *paniolo* wagon. Minimal exertion. (Hourly Tu-Sa 10am-2pm. Tours $15, ages 12 and under $12.)

Mauna Kea Mountain Bikes (☎888-682-8687 or 883-0130; www.bikehawaii.com), offers on- and off-road mountain bike tours around Waimea. Cross-country trip up Mana Rd. onto Parker Ranch land is a gradual climb up the rolling foothills of Mauna Kea (9am-noon. $65). *Kamikaze* trip from Mauna Kea summit is not for the faint of heart (or the young, or the pregnant, or the sane. 8am-noon; $130). Bikes included. Reserve 24hr. in advance. See **Rentals,** p. 355.

◉ SIGHTS

PARKER RANCH HISTORIC HOMES These exquisitely maintained homes illustrate two different eras in the history of Parker Ranch. **Mana Hale** is the New England-style wooden saltbox that served as John Palmer Parker's home during his first years as a rancher. Palmer actually hauled this home gleaming *koa* board by gleaming *koa* board from Mauna Kea to its present location, 12 mi. away. **Pu'uopelu**, or "meeting place," was built in 1862 and was home to Richard Smart, 6th generation Parker, until his death in 1992. The home is an excellent showcase for his French Impressionist and Chinese art collection. *(On Rte. 190, 1 mi. south of town on the road to Kona. ☎885-5433. Open M-Sa 10am-5pm. Last admission 4pm. $8.50, seniors $7.50, children $6. Joint admission to museum and historic homes $12, children $9.50.)*

PARKER RANCH MUSEUM For all the Parker Ranch hype around Waimea, the museum dedicated to its history is surprisingly low-key. A small exhibit hall explores a bit of early Hawaiian history before focusing on the ranch's owners—from John Palmer Parker in the early 1800s to 6th-generation Parker, Richard Smart, who died in 1992. Most of the displays are visual and a 25min. video detailing the ranch's history provides useful background information. *(67-1185 Mamalahoa Hwy., in the Parker Ranch Center. ☎885-7655; www.parkerranch.com. Open daily 9am-5pm. Last admission 4pm. $6, seniors $5, children $4.50.)*

KAHILU THEATRE This state-of-the-art theater, founded by Richard Smart in 1981, is the Big Island's premier performance venue. From fall to spring, the theater plays host to a wide range of global artists, such as Bela Fleck and the Flecktones and the Aspen Santa Fe Ballet. It has local performers and productions regularly and screens art-house films throughout the year. *(67-1186 Lindsey Rd., behind the Parker Ranch Center. ☎885-6868 or 887-6368 for movie info.; www.kahilutheatre.org. Box office open M-F 9am-noon and 1-4pm. Tickets for major events $28-45.)*

NORTH KOHALA

Hawaiians are reputed to have over a hundred words for wind. The one that dominates North Kohala is *'apa'apa'a*, or "unforgiving." Funneling through the channel between Maui and the Big Island, the *'apa'apa'a* has joined force with the ocean, thrashing and sculpting the island's oldest volcanic mountain range over the course of nearly one million years. Too often overlooked by travelers making their way around the island, North Kohala is an ideal place to enjoy by horse or on foot.

It is on these rolling mountains that Kamehameha was born and would go on to successfully unify the Hawaiian Islands for the first time. Hawaiian unity has suffered a great deal in recent years as native factions remain polarized over whether and how Hawaii should fight for national sovereignty or if they should accept a proposal for status as a 'nation within a nation' (similar to Native Americans on the mainland). In the face of these struggles, many Hawaiians invoke the memory of Kamehameha and the unity he inspired from the mountains of North Kohala.

HAWI AND KAPA'AU

Small, and well off the beaten path now, Hawi and Kapa'au used to be major centers in Kohala during Hawaii's sugar era. In fact, Hawi was considered one of the island's largest sugar towns before the Kohala Sugar Company finally closed in the mid-1970s. Today, a row of stores (and empty storefronts) lines the sides of Akoni Pule Hwy. in a jungle of wild sugar cane. The beauty of North Kohala has inspired a set of art galleries, selling the works of local artists in Hawi and Kapa'au. Both towns can be a fun place to look for gifts and enjoy dinner or ice cream.

▗▛ ⌐ ORIENTATION AND TRANSPORTATION

Hawi is at the intersection of **Route 250 (Kohala Mountain Road)** and **Route 270,** 19 mi. north of Kawaihae and 20 mi. northwest of Waimea. This stretch of Rte. 270 is also known as **Akoni Pule Highway** and the town's main drag. It continues east from Hawi, through Kapa'au, and ends 7 mi. later at the Pololu Valley Lookout.

North Kohala is the one district that is not linked via the Hawaii Belt Rd. The **Hele-On** bus has daily routes from downtown Kapa'au to **Hawi** and the six resorts in **South Kohala,** the last of which is the Hilton Waikoloa. (☎961-8744. $2.25.)

▞ PRACTICAL INFORMATION

At one time the Kohala Courthouse, the **North Kohala Civic Center,** in downtown Kapa'au, serves as the area's Visitor Center, and is staffed by helpful senior citizens. (Open M-F 10am-4pm.) The **Bank of Hawaii,** on Akoni Pule Hwy. in downtown Kapa'au, has a **24hr. ATM.** (☎889-6217. Open M-Th 8:30am-4pm, F 8:30am-6pm.) Gas is available at the **Hawi Shell Station.** (☎889-5211. Open M-F 5:30am-

6:30pm, Sa 6am-6:30pm, Su 8am-4pm.) They also have an auto shop open M-F 7:30am-5pm, and on occasional weekends. The **Kohala Book Shop,** 54-3885 Akoni Pule Hwy., in downtown Kapa'au, is the largest used bookstore on the island,

---

THE ONCE AND FUTURE KING About 2 mi. east of Kapa'au, along Hwy. 270 to Pololu Valley, just above a narrow bridge, a huge boulder sits on the side of the road. The lump of lava rock would be indistinguishable from any other, if not for the "HVB Warrior" sign posted next to it.

Legend holds that Kamehameha demonstrated the potency of his *mana*—and validated his claim to rule over all the islands—by carrying this rock over his head up from the beach below. The impossibility of this feat is slightly tempered by other myths, which maintain that Kamehameha stood between 6 ft. 8 in. and 7 ft. 4 in. tall.

---

with an extensive collection of Hawaiiana. (☎889-6400. Open Tu-Sa 11am-5pm. Closed in Sept. MC/V.) The **Bond Memorial Public Library,** on Akoni Pule Hwy. in downtown Kapa'au, offers **Internet access** to Hawaii State Public Library card holders. (☎889-6729. Open M noon-8pm, Tu-Th 9am-5pm, F 10am-2pm.) **Kohala Computer Center,** on Akoni Pule Hwy. in downtown Hawi, also has **Internet access.** (☎889-1002. $3 per 15min., $10 per hr. Open M-F 8am-4:30pm.) The **North Kohala District Police Station** (☎889-6540) is in Kapa'au, behind the Kamehameha statue and North Kohala Civic Center. **Kamehameha Pharmacy** is at 54-3877 Akoni Pule Hwy., in downtown Kapa'au. (☎889-6161. Open M-F 9am-12:30pm and 1:30-5pm.) **Kohala Hospital** (☎889-6211), is east of downtown Kapa'au, off of Hwy. 270. **Hawi Post Office,** 55-515 Hawi Rd., sits near the corner of Rte. 250 and 270. (☎800-275-8777. Open M-F 8:30am-noon and 12:30-4pm, Sa 9am-10am.) **Postal Code:** 96719. **Kapa'au Post Office,** 54-396 Union Mill Rd., is a smaller office. (☎889-6766. Open M-F 7:30am-4pm, Sa 9-10:30am.) **Postal Code:** 96755.

ACCOMMODATIONS AND CAMPING

Kohala Country Adventures Guest House ❸, ¼ mi. above Kapa'au on the road between the Bank of Hawaii and the statue of Kamehameha, is a cozy B&B nestled within 11 acres of farmland, offering spectacular views of the North Kohala countryside from their sundeck room with sunset lanai porch ($150), garden room with jacuzzi ($99), and economy rooms ($70). More than two guests are $15 per person. Rooms include refrigerator and kitchen access, BBQ grill, rec. room, and piano. (☎866-892-2484 or 889-5663; www.kcadventures.com. Reservations recommended. Check-in 3pm. AmEx/D/MC/V.) **Kohola Village Inn** ❶, 55-514 Hawi Rd., is right in the middle of downtown Hawi, at the corner of Rte. 250 and 270. The rooms here are not spectacular, but convenient for a night. (☎889-0419. Check-in 4:30pm. Check-out noon. Doubles $58; triples $68; 2-room suites $88-98. MC/V.) If you need a bit more space, **Kohala's Guest House** ❷, about 3 mi. east of Kapa'au, offers a studio ($49) or either side of a fully furnished duplex house equipped with full kitchen, three bedrooms, TV, and laundry facilities. To get there turn *makai* (toward the ocean) from Hwy. 270 onto the road that leads to Keokea Beach. The Guest House is less than ¼ mi. in on your right. (☎889-5606; http://home1.gte.net/svendsen/index.htm. House up to $125 per night or $600 per week.) **Mahukona Beach Park** ❶ is the only place to camp on the North Kohala coast (less than 1 mi. north of Lapakahi Historical Park on Hwy. 270; before mi. marker 15). Although the camp sites have little shade relief, many locals come to snorkel in this unique 'industrial underwater.' The port just north of the campgrounds was the site of the Hawaii Railroad Co. until the early 1900s, when business derailed. The coast here is teeming with yellow tang and underwater debris. Adventurous snorkelers can follow an anchor chain from the port about 150 ft. to the remains of a sunken steamboat that rests largely intact in just 20 ft. of water. The campground has showers, a pavilion with electricity, and toilets, but bring your own water. County permits required, see p. 298 for permit information. (☎961-8311; www.hawaii-county.com.)

⚑ FOOD

Kohala Health Foods (☎889-0277) on Akoni Pule Hwy. in Hawi, is the perfect option for vegetarian travelers, serving Volcano sandwiches ($4-5), fruit smoothies ($3.25), and fresh fruit juice ($2). Open M-F 10am-6pm, Sa 10am-4pm. AmEx/D/MC/V. ●

Bamboo, Akoni Pule Hwy. (☎889-5555), in downtown Hawi. Quality Hawaiian-style local plates served in a restored historic building have become *the* reason many people come to Hawi. Favorites include *kalua* pork and cabbage, a Hawaiian staple ($9), *Pua'a A Opai* (pork tenderloin and black tiger shrimp on papaya salad), and their original house passion fruit margarita. Try the a bit of everything Hawaiian on the sampler plate ($14). Open Tu-Sa 11:30am-2:30pm and 6-9pm, Su 11am-2pm. DC/MC/V. ❸

Hula La's Mexican Kitchen (☎889-5668), in the Kohala Trade Center in Hawi. A basic walk-in *taqueria* with satisfying burritos ($6.50-7.50). 4 varieties of salsa are so popular, they sell by the pound ($10) or more reasonably sized bowls ($1.50). Open M-Su 11am-8pm, but hours are subject to change depending on business. ●

Sushi Rock (☎889-5900), on Akoni Pule Hwy. in Hawi, just east of the intersection with Hwy. 250. Sushi rolls with Hawaiian influences are a local favorite ($5.50-9). Additions include papaya, roasted Macadamia nuts, Hawaiian chili sauce, and Mexican *ceviche*. Open M-Tu and Th-Sa noon-2:30pm and 5:30-8pm, Su 5-7:30pm. AmEx/D/MC/V. ❷

Kohala Coffee Mill (☎889-5577), on Akoni Pule Hwy. in Hawi. Heaping scoops of Tropical Dreams Hawaiian Ice Cream ($2-4), as well as fruit smoothies ($3.75), and a wide selection of teas and coffees ($1.75-3). Flavors rotate daily, including banana-mango, jamocha-macadamia nut and white pineapple sorbet. ●

The Sugar Shack (☎889-5454), on Akoni Pule Hwy. in Hawi. Sugar plantations may have died in the 70s, but retro candy is alive and well here. Salt Water Taffy ($3.50 per lb.), Pixy Stix, red licorice in the jar, and Rainbow Hawaiian shave ice ($1.50-2.50). Open T-Th and Sa 10am-5pm, F 10am-6pm, Su noon-5pm. MC/V. ●

Jen's Kohala Cafe (☎889-0099), on Akoni Pule Hwy. in Kapa'au. With Hawaiian favorites and Thai spice (entrees $8.25-9.50), Jen's has *aloha* to spare. Snag a tasty salad ($7.50), sandwich ($5.50-6), or ice cream ($2). Open M-F 10am-5pm, Sa-Su 10am-3:30pm. Thai dinner Sa-Su 4:30-8:30pm. MC/V. ❷

🐎 TOURS

If you're looking to ride the range *paniolo*-style, there are a number of operations available to assist you. For listings see **Tours** in Waimea, p. 357. For self-guided driving adventures, roadtrip the 20 mi. along Mountain Hwy. 250 from Hawi to Waimea, and stop for a scenic afternoon picnic.

BIG ISLAND

Another unique option for seeing the North Kohala countryside is **Flumin' Da Ditch**, 55-519 Hawi Rd., above the intersection of Hwy. 250 and 270 in Hawi. Kids who grew up on sugar plantations were known to grab anything that floated and go 'flumin' in the ditches, tunnels, and flumes of Kohala's complex irrigation system. After the sugar industry died, a group of locals decided to revive the tradition on a larger scale by offering kayak rides on over 3½ mi. of the Kohala Ditch. The trip is a wet-adventure and a chance to learn about the design, construction, and history of the Kohala Ditch Project and the 600 Japanese laborers who made it possible (see **Building Da Ditch**, p. 362). The guides all grew up flumin' da ditches as children and have stories about life in North Kohala. (☎889-6922; www.fluminda-ditch.com. Trips daily 8:15am; 12:15pm. $89, children 5-18 $68. AmEx/D/MC/V.)

BUILDING DA DITCH
Sugar cane is an intensely demanding crop. Over the course of two years, it can take more than 2000 lb. of water to produce just one lb. of refined sugar. By the early 1900s, the rapid growth of North Kohala's sugar plantation economy had created a water crisis. Too many streams had been recklessly diverted to water the thirsty crops and a more sustainable solution was clearly in order. While the North Kohala's plains remained parched and sunny, the deep valleys along the area's coast were drenched with over 300 in. of rainfall per year. The solution to the water problem was therefore simple in theory: transport water from the streams and reservoirs of the east to the sun-drenched plains of the west, thereby doubling production. However, the actual construction of the Kohala Ditch would become one of the most ambitious and dangerous irrigation projects ever attempted: 22½ mi. worth of 57 tunnels, 19 flumes (closed aqueducts made of wood and concrete designed to carry water over ravines), and numerous collection ditches were built at an elevation of over 1000 ft. The engineering world stood astounded at its completion in 1906, after only 18 mo. of labor by 600 Japanese laborers (17 of whom died in the process). Accolades poured onto the desks of head engineer Michael O'Shaughnessy and plantation owner John Hind. The North Kohala sugar plantations ceased to operate in 1975, but until then the Ditch played an extremely important role in sugar production, allowing plantations to overcome drought more than once.

NORTH KOHALA SIGHTS

LAPAKAHI STATE HISTORICAL PARK

The park is located just off Hwy. 270, near the 14 mi. marker. Bring your own water and sunscreen. Open daily 8am-4pm. Free.

Polynesian sailors first discovered the sheltered coves of Lapakahi nearly 600 yr. ago, and decided it was the safest place to land their canoes and build a village. Eventually, some of the first villagers moved up into the wetter Kohala Mountains, where they could farm more extensively. For 500 yr., native life thrived on the bounty of land and sea with fresh fish from the coast and coconut, *kamani* nuts, *taro (poi)* root, and *ulu* (breadfruit) crops on shore. Upland farmers traded with the coastal fishermen in an arrangement called *ahupua'a*. Then, in 1918, the seven streams that fed Lapakahi from high in the Kohala Mountains were diverted by plantation owners struggling to sustain a growing sugar cane industry. The lush fields of the *ahupua'a* very quickly dried into the red-sand desert seen today. The fate of Lapakahi became a common tragedy for Native Hawaiians and by the mid-1900s there were no surviving *ahupua'a* on the island. Today, Lapakahi is the only native village that has been at least partially restored to reflect traditional ways of life. Its coastal waters are protected by the **Koai'e Cove Marine Conservation District**.

The Visitor Center at Lapakahi has maps of a 1 mi. trail, indicating canoe landings, houses, salt pans, fish shrines, burial grounds, and the fragments of a road that once connected the mountains to the coast allowing *ohana* (family) to trade *taro* for fish.

In its time, Lapakahi was considered to be a sacred healing ground because of the high number of medicinal roots and plants that grew on its coast. Today, many traditional healers still frequent the site for ceremonies and ask that visitors respect the sacredness of their historic home. Signs request that visitors not bring their picnics to the beach. **Snorkeling** here is exceptional (after all, this is a marine conservation district), but is permitted only in the cove accessed by a path directly *makai* (toward the ocean) from the Visitor Center. Ask before leaving, to be sure you are swimming in the right spot. The water is so clear here, you can see a rainbow of fish from the rocks without any snorkel equipment. The Visitor Center has a limited amount of drinking water, but be sure to bring your own.

MO'OKINI LUAKINI HEIAU AND KAMEHAMEHA'S BIRTHPLACE

To reach the heiau (temple), turn makai (toward the ocean) at the sign for Upolu Airport at mi. marker 20 on Rte. 270. Follow the road for 2 mi. to the airport runways. At the airport, turn left the rutted dirt road that runs parallel to the coast. This road is often swamped with large mud pools making it impassable by cars with low clearance or 2WD. Most people choose to walk at this point. After about 1½ mi. you will see the HVB warrior indicating the direction of each historic site; the heiau is on the hill to the left and Kamehameha's birthplace is another ¼ mi. down the right-hand fork, just up from the coast. For more information about visiting the heiau call ☎ 591-1170 or 591-1142.

Hawaiian chants and oral histories stress that the most important factor in building a sacred *heiau* (temple) is not the design of the building, but the choice of the site. Located on a windswept green *pali* (cliff) overlooking the Pacific the outline of Maui's Haleakala Mountain, the Mo'okini Heiau is undoubtedly a site of great *mana*, or spiritual power. Whereas most *heiaus* tend to be dedicated to Lono, the god of harvest, the *heiau* at Mo'okini is dedicated to Ku, the god of war. Known as *luakini heiaus*, temples dedicated to Ku were the only spiritual sites to offer human sacrifices.

Built in 480 BC, the Mo'okini Heiau has a simple rectangular design and stretches to nearly 250 ft. by 125 ft. According to legend, the 30 ft. walls are made of basalt stones passed from the Pololu Valley in one night along a 14 mi. human chain. For hundreds of years, the site was accessible only to *ali'i* (royalty) and high priests making sacrifices. However, in 1963, Mo'okini Luakini Heiau was designated the first **National Historic Landmark** in Hawaii and opened to the public.

A few hundred yards down the coast from the *heiau* there is a large, double-walled enclosure reputed to be the site of **Kamehameha's birth.** Although the exact date of Kamehameha's birth is still disputed, Maude Makemson, an astronomer at Vassar College, made the most convincing guess in 1942. According to Hawaiian oral tradition, Kamehameha was born on a stormy night in late fall. On the preceding night, an unusual celestial light was seen rising in the east and passing the zenith of North Kohala. The object moved west, north of two constellations recognized by the *kilo hoku* (Hawaiian astronomers). Makemson did some astronomical detective work and determined that it must have been the 1758 appearance of Halley's Comet that marked the great king's birth. Towering at a peak of 5480 ft., the North Kohala mountains would provide Kamehameha with a commanding view of Maui, allowing him strategic vision in his advance to unify the islands.

POLOLU VALLEY

Rte. 270 ends abruptly at the Pololu Valley Lookout on the western rim of Pololu Valley, about 6 mi. from Hawi.

The Pololu Valley is the first of seven valleys carved into the Kohala Mountains by thousands of years of Pacific erosion. A miracle of time, water, and circumstance, the lush valleys are found nowhere else on the island. From the east, Waipi'o is the only other valley accessible by car. The valley was once home to *taro (poi)* farmers, but now it is visited mainly by those seeking a moment of wonder.

The **Pololu Valley Trail** departs from the parking lot at the end of the road and drops quickly down the slope to the valley's gray-sand beach. From top to bottom, the gently sloping trail takes about 20min. Views from the trail are spectacular. At one point, it wraps around the cliff, bringing the tips of at least four valleys into view. Near the beach, the valley is densely vegetated, and farther back into the valley is all private land, indicated clearly by 'no trespassing' signs. In theory, there is a switchback trail that climbs the *pali* (cliff) at the far end of the valley into the adjacent **Honokanenui Valley** (similar to the trail that climbs from Waipi'o Valley to Waimanu). However, this path is wildly overgrown and almost impossible to find. The hike is attempted only by serious backpackers who come equipped for a serious backcountry adventure. Some especially determined explorers have been known to hike all seven valleys from Pololu to Waipi'o, venturing into some of the most remote landscapes on the island. This can be very dangerous as river crossings are quickly and dramatically affected by high tides.

SOUTH KOHALA

The most luxurious resorts of South Kohala are islands within an island, oases surrounded by seas of *a'a* lava. Hwy. 19 carves through these desolate lava flows on its way toward the weather-rounded Kohala range; it is along this formidable route that men and women run the grueling marathon leg of the annual Ironman Triathalon. From the comfort of airport shuttles, visitors bound for a week of beach-side pampering grimace at the sight of athletes training on the punishing asphalt.

There are no true towns—only resort endeavors backed by multi-million dollar budgets could roll out the miles of sprinkler lines and ready-made turf required to turn such a primordial landscape green. The resorts themselves are their own self-contained villages. The South Kohala coast annually enjoys a near-perfect 363 of 365 days of sun. The resorts take meticulous care of the beaches, combing the sand smooth for aerial photographs and providing beach chairs, cool showers, and hammocks along some stretches. Because every inch of Hawaiian shoreline is by law *public access*, even travelers on a shoestring budget can live it up on the sands of the most exclusive resort beach—just don't forget your bag lunch.

MAUNA LANI BAY HOTEL

19 mi. north of the Kona airport on Hwy. 19, between mi. markers 73 and 74. Continue around the 2nd right at the rotary.

The Mauna Lani Bay Hotel ❺, 68-1400 Mauna Lani Dr., is the most intimate and elegantly sophisticated of the South Kohala resorts. Guests searching for tranquility find it here, with an atrium of palm trees and ponds filled with goldfish and endangered sea turtles. Guests arrive and are placed in cushioned chairs to sip chilled juice while the staff handles the particulars. Rooms are simply and thoughtfully designed, each with a marble-floored bath and full tub. Rooms open out onto a sizable balcony, some overlooking the pool and two jacuzzi spas. On the beach, hammocks swing from coconut trees, and cabanas line an 'enhanced' length of sand.

The land surrounding Mauna Lani is redolent with historical and cultural significance, with ancient fishponds, settlement remains, and an extensive collection of petroglyphs. Inquire at the reception desk for personally tailored directions. Also the 'greenest' of the Kohala resorts, the Mauna Lani takes over 50% of its energy from rooftop solar panelling, and even employs two full-time biologists to watch over the endangered *honu* seaturtles in residence here.

The Mauna Lani's rack rates are fairly stiff; their deals don't usually dip below $300. The reservations desk concedes that the best available rates are not found by booking directly, but through www.expedia.com. (☎855-6622; www.maunalani.com. Doubles $385-710; 2-person ocean view suites $1200; 2-bedroom bungalows $4900-5500. AmEx/D/MC/V.)

Kohala Coast

■ ACCOMMODATIONS
Fairmont Orchid at Mauna Lani, **3**
Hapuna Beach Prince Hotel, **2**
Hilton Waikoloa Village, **6**
Mauna Kea Beach Hotel, **1**
Mauna Lani Bay Hotel, **4**
Waikola Beach Marriott, **5**

THE FAIRMONT ORCHID AT MAUNA LANI.

19 mi. north of the Kona airport, between mi. markers 73 and 74 on Hwy. 19. Take the 1st right to the Orchid at the rotary.

The Fairmont Orchid at Mauna Lani ❺, 68-1400 Mauna Lani Dr., exudes a European-style affluence. At one time the Ritz-Carlton, the spirit has yet to depart. Facing directly west, the mansion-like Sunset Terrace serves as a portal for the sun; there's a reason why all the chairs are not facing straight ahead. Grounds are grand and expansive, and the staff is hospitable and concerned. They even sneak into the bathrooms while you're away to fold the tissue into those little triangles. Now that's service. "Super Saver" promotional rates can sometimes knock off $100. (☎800-845-9905; www.fairmont.com/orchid. Rooms $349-699; suites $914-1804.)

MAUNA KEA BEACH HOTEL.

32 mi. north of Kona on Hwy. 19. between mi. markers 68 and 69. The hotel has set aside parking spaces for visitors to its Kauna'oa (Mauna Kea) Beach.

The opulent Mauna Kea Beach Hotel ❺, 62-100 Mauna Kea Beach Dr., sits on the northern end of **Kauna'oa (Mauna Kea) Beach,** a stunning crescent of sand sloping to the bay. Laurence Rockefeller welcomed his first Western guests here to paradise in 1965. At the time, the resort was unlike anything else in the world. Although it is approaching its 40th birthday, the entire complex recently underwent a multi-million dollar restoration and is just as swank as ever. Within the resort are six restaurants and lounges, including the swanky **Batik,** two 18-hole golf courses, and 13 tennis courts, as well as an incredible collection of artwork.

BIG ISLAND

Complete with song, dance, and *kalua* pig, the Mauna Kea's Tuesday night *luau* also benefits from the prime beach-front location. Discounts for rack rates sometimes bring prices to $225 per night. (☎800-882-6060 or 882-7222; www.maunakeabeachhotel.com. *Luau* Tu 5:45pm. $76, children 3-12 $38. Reservations recommended. Check-in 3pm. Check-out noon. Rooms $360-620. AmEx/D/MC/V.)

HAPUNA PRINCE HOTEL

From Kona airport take Rte. 19 north to mi. marker 70. The Hapuna entrance will be on the mauka (mountain) side of Rte. 19, just south of the Mauna Kea entrance. The access road curves beneath the highway and toward the ocean in a disorienting underpass loop. As a guard is present to inquire your business, visitors interested in access to Hapuna Beach only should head back to the public entrance between mi. markers 69 and 70.

Hapuna Beach Prince Hotel ❺, 62-100 Kauna'oa Dr., sits kitty-corner above the northern end of **Hapuna Beach.** (For more on Hapuna Beach, see **Beaches,** p. 333.) No garden views here—each of the hotel's 350 rooms feature a partial to full ocean view and private lanai. Discounts and "hot-deals" are usually better here than at Mauna Kea across the street. Partial ocean-view rooms can go for as low as $180 per night. (☎800-882-6060 or 880-1111; www.hapunabeachprincehotel.com. Check-in 3pm. Check-out noon. Reservations recommended. Rooms $360-610; suites $1200-7000. AmEx/D/MC/V.)

HILTON WAIKOLOA VILLAGE

From Kona airport take Rte. 19 north to Waikoloa Beach Dr., which is on the makai (ocean) side between mi. markers 76 and 77. Two brown terrace-roofed structures mark the entrance. Keep straight past the Waikoloa Beach Marriott on the left and the Kings' Shops on the right. All grounds open to the public.

Missed that trip to Disneyworld last winter? Everything in the Hilton Waikoloa Village ❺, 425 Waikoloa Beach Dr., is larger than life. Nine-foot vases tower above hotel guests and the lobby chandelier casts a shadow the size of an SUV. Its reputation as an over-the-top playground for the whole family is deserved. With 1200 rooms, seven restaurants, two golf courses, eight tennis courts, a multi-million dollar art collection, and a 4-acre lagoon linked by (breath) miles of pathways, an air-conditioned monorail, and slow-cruising transport boats navigating a network of waterways. Mild-mannered barracuda swim through the canals, and exotic birds appear moat-locked on their own islands. Children love it, but adults might be a bit overwhelmed. (☎900-221-2424 or 886-1234; www.hiltonwaikoloavillage.com. Legends of the Pacific Luau F $60, ages 5-12 $27. Check-in 3pm. Check-out noon. Rooms $199-549; suites $995-5800. AAA discounts on rack rates. AmEx/D/MC/V.)

Regardless, young and old are abuzz about **Dolphin Quest,** an educational program that allows guests to interact with Atlantic bottlenose dolphin's from Florida's Gulf Coast. Children join the dolphins in the sandy shallows, teens can learn about careers in marine science, and adults (16+) snorkel in a deep salt-water lagoon while dolphins frolic about. Despite the Disney association, this is not Seaworld; the dolphins choose to engage with or ignore those who are visiting their home. The majority of proceeds go toward marine research. Rates begin at $150 for 30min.-1hr. Reservations are essential, best made at original time of booking.

WAIKOLOA BEACH MARRIOTT

From Kona airport, take Rte. 19 north to Waikoloa Beach Dr., between mi. markers 76 and 77. Public parking for A-Beach is open sunrise to sunset.

The Waikoloa Beach Marriott ❺, 69-275 Waikoloa Beach Dr., sits on the northern end of **'Anaeho'omalu Beach,** a popular crescent of sand locally and less tongue-twistingly known as **"A-Beach"** (see below). Comfortable rooms provide all the amenities required of a mega-resort, but the floral patterns are predictable. There's much carousing in the jacuzzis late at night, when colored spotlights spread over the lawn and central pool. One of the Marriot's best deals is the $75 twilight rate at the **Beach Golf Course,** 18 dramatic seaside holes designed by famous golf course architect Robert Trent Jones (reservations ☎886-6060). Twilight rate begins at 2pm. (☎800-922-5533 or 866-6789; www.outrigger.com. Check-in 3pm. Check-out noon. Rooms $315-535; suites $965-3100. AmEx/D/MC/V.)

'ANAEHO'OMALU BEACH

To reach the beach, make the turn for the Waikoloa Beach Resort between mi. markers 76 and 77, 8 mi. south of Kawaihae and 25 mi. north of Kailua-Kona. The beach parking lot is the 1st left turn on the road across from the Kings' Shops.

Waikoloa Beach Resort sits on a white-sand beach that stretches south toward Kona along a picturesque bay. Known to locals as "A-Beach," or "A-Bay," 'Anaeho'omalu's consistently calm waters and sandy bottom make it one of the most popular swimming spots around. It also offers some of the island's best **windsurfing** and **snorkeling.** *'Anaeho'omalu* translates to "protected mullet" and descends from ancient Hawaii when the bodies of water between the large coconut grove and the beach were royal fishponds stocked with mullet.

At the northern end of A-Beach, the Waikoloa Beach Marriott provides a volleyball net, a circuit of workout stations, and rows of free beach chairs. **Ocean Sports,** the beach hut on the sand, arranges all sorts of aquatic activities in the area—from snorkeling ($6 per hr., $25 per wk.) to sunset cruises. (☎886-6666. Open daily 8am-5pm. Cruises M, W, F 4:30pm departure. $69, ages 3-12 $40.)

The beach is part of a state park, and has showers, toilets, and drinking water at its southern end. **Camping** is also allowed within the park with a permit. Heading south along the coast, there are a number of secluded spots where you can sleep right on the beach. (Contact the Department of Land and Natural Resources, State Parks Division, 75 Apuni St. ☎974-6200. Permits are $5 per day.)

PU'UKOHOLA HEIAU NATIONAL HISTORIC SITE

Located 10 mi. west of Waimea and 34 mi. north of Kailua-Kona along Rte. 270 near the intersection of Hwy. 19 and 270, the park and its Visitor Center (☎882-7218; www.nps.gov/puhe) are open daily 7:30am-4pm. Free admission. The self-guided walking tour of the sites begins at the Visitor Center, where an orientation film is shown.

With the construction of the highway and Kawaihae Harbor nearby, Pu'ukohola Heiau ("Temple on the Hill of the Whale") has been stripped of some of its original natural splendor. Still, it retains a commanding position on the coastline and holds immense historical and cultural significance. The *heiau* was one of the last sites constructed before outside influences encroached on traditional Hawaiian culture. According to legend, it also played a key role in Kamehameha's ascendancy.

The first site along the walking path is the sprawling Pu'ukohola Heiau, built by Kamehameha in the late 18th century. The temple measures 224 ft. by 100 ft. with 16-20 ft. walls. The temple platform is now bare, but during Kamehameha's time it was covered with ceremonial structures. Farther down the hillside, between Pu'ukohola Heiau and the ocean, is **Mailekini Heiau,** an older structure thought to have been built for war-like or agricultural purposes. This *heiau* is nearly the size of Pu'ukohola, but its construction is inferior. **Hale o Kapuni Heiau,** submerged just offshore, was dedicated to the shark gods. Although initially built above the high-water mark, it has been underwater since the 1950s. On the beach below Pu'ukohola and Mailekini lies **Pelekane,** the royal courtyard of Kawaihae. Kamehameha II prepared to take the throne here following his father's death. Across Rte. 270 and off the self-guided walking trail in the corner of the park, is the site of **John Young's homestead.** Young, a British sailor stranded here in 1790, became a trusted military adviser to Kamehameha as well as his trading agent. His European-style house was built using basalt and a mortar composed of sand, burnt coral, *poi,* and hair.

The park is one of the few places on the Big Island that officially celebrates **La Hae Hawaii,** or Hawaiian Flag Day, every July 31. In addition, **Establishment Day** (Aug. 17) is also honored with a Hawaiian cultural festival, held on the weekend in August closest to the 17th.

KAUAI

As the oldest and northernmost of the major islands, Kauai stands apart in the Hawaiian chain. Hawaiian spirit flourishes among the island's 58,000 residents, and locals are fiercely proud of both their heritage and Kauai's relative lack of commercial development. Aptly nicknamed "The Garden Isle," Kauai's plentiful rains nurse the verdant land and support local agriculture. Kauai's rainforest jungle is best described as primordial (*Jurassic Park* was filmed here, after all), but markers of the island's 6 million weathered years are apparent in its impressive geological features. Kauai's miles of sandy shoreline testify to the land's relative age, and they mark the border between the shimmering blue of the Pacific and the green land of the interior. The cliffs of the Na Pali Coast, the island's deep valleys, and the jagged Waimea Canyon were all carved by millennia of running rainfall—the northeast slope of Wai'ale'ale Mountain is the wettest spot on earth, receiving over 450 in. of rain annually.

Kauai's peaceful solitude, as well as the abundant opportunities to get back to nature that are readily available in the island's untamed landscape, once attracted a healthy hippie culture. Though their particular presence has since diminished somewhat, Kauai still draws a more rugged, individualistic type of traveler than Maui or Oahu. Of the visitors who come here to blaze their own paths through "real Hawaii," many are drawn to the hiker's paradise of the Na Pali Coast, and its spectacular Kalalau Trail. Opportunities for exploration are endless, whether you wish to lose yourself on the island's trails, bask on its beaches, or immerse yourself in the *aloha* spirit on Kauai, a paradise within Paradise.

HIGHLIGHTS OF KAUAI

INDUCE VERTIGO on the trails and overlooks of the Waimea Canyon, the Grand Canyon of the Pacific (p. 426).

GO ONE-ON-ONE WITH SEA TURTLES in the waters of PK's Beach, one of the many beautiful beaches near Po'ipu (p. 412).

SPY on rare birds, spinner dolphins, monk seals, and humpback whales at the Kilauea National Wildlife Refuge (p. 394).

TAME the Kalalau Trail, the hard-core hiker's mecca on the Na Pali Coast (p. 406).

◪ INTERISLAND TRANSPORTATION

All commercial flights fly into **Lihue Airport (LIH)**. Direct flights to Kauai from the mainland are rare, and most passengers connect in Honolulu. However, **American Airlines** (☎800-433-7300; www.aa.com) has daily non-stop service to Kauai from Los Angeles, and **United Airlines** (☎800-241-6522; www.united.com) flies daily from Los Angeles and San Francisco. **Aloha Airlines** (☎800-367-5250; www.alohaairlines.com) flies to: Hilo, The Big Island (2hr., 8 per day 6:30am-5pm); Honolulu, Oahu (30min., 17 per day 6:30am-8:30pm); and Kailua-Kona, The Big Island (2hr., 10-12 per day 6:30am-6pm). **Hawaiian Airlines** (☎800-367-5320; www.hawaiianair.com) flies to: Hilo, The Big Island (2hr., 10 per day 6:30am-4:30pm); Honolulu, Oahu (30min., 16-20 per day 6:30am-8:15pm); Kahului, Maui (1½hr., 26-32 per day 6:30am-6:45pm); Kona, The Big Island (2hr., 14-17 per day 6:30am-5pm); Lanai City, Lanai (3hr., 2-4 per day); Molokai (1½hr., 1-2 per day 2:37pm, 3:07pm). Flights to Kauai begin at around $100 round-trip, but schedules change frequently; be sure to check web sites or call for current information.

The Kauai Bus runs six routes around the island, but the easiest and most convenient way to get around Kauai is by **car.** For **inter-city** and **local transportation,** consult the **Transportation** section for each town.

⚑ CAMPING

Camping in Kauai can be an easy way to save on travel expenses, and oftentimes the view from the sand more than makes up for the lack of amenities. There are a number of state and county parks on the island that allow camping with a permit, though they require that campers have tents. The various county parks are closed on certain days of the week and, unless otherwise noted, campers are limited to seven nights at each campsite. Some state parks also have **cabins** available for rent. If you plan on camping in Kauai, it's a good idea to rent a **car** with a lockable compartment for your gear. Be prepared for **mosquitoes, sun,** and **rain.** You might want to bring a **stove** for cooking and boiling water. Each type of park in Kauai issues its own **permits.**

County parks (☎241-6660; www.kauaigov.org/parks.htm). There are 7 county parks that allow camping, and each campground is closed 1 night per week for maintenance; from west to east, they are closed: Lucy Wright (M), Salt Pond (Tu), Hanamaulu Beach (W), Anahola Beach (Th), 'Anini Beach (Tu), Haena Beach (M), and Hanalei Beach (Open only F, Sa and holidays). Each requires a permit, which is good for a maximum of 6 consecutive nights (due to above closings listed). Limit 60 days in a year-long period. Permits $3 per night, free for Hawaii residents and those under 18, if accompanied by an adult. Contact Dept. of Public Works, **Division of Parks and Recreation,** 4444 Rice St. (known as the Mo'ikeha Building), Ste. 150, Lihue, Kauai 96766. Office on the right side of the first floor as you enter the circular part of the building. Permits are issued M-F 8:15am-4pm.

State parks (☎274-3444; www.state.hi.us/dlnr/dsp/dsp.html). The 3 state parks on Kauai are Koke'e, Polihale, and Na Pali Coast. Koke'e and Polihale State Parks cost $5 per night per campsite, 10 people allowed per campsite, with a max. stay of 5 nights. 1 permit per park within a 30-day period. At Koke'e State Park, cabins are rented through **Koke'e Lodge** (see p. 426). Na Pali Coast State Park consists of 3 campsites along the 11 mi. Kalalau Trail, and one campsite beyond it, Miloli'i campsite, accessible only by boat. Permits cost $10 per night per person, with up to 5 people allowed per group (larger groups must apply for another permit); the max. stay at Na Pali Coast State Park is 5 days, with no more than 3 nights at Miloli'i. Applications must be filled out in person at the office of the **Division of State Parks,** 3060 Eiwa St., Room 306, Lihue, Kauai 96766. The **Forestry and Wildlife office,** where the Division of State Parks is located, is in the white building with narrow vertical windows behind the Big Save Market when viewed from Hwy. 56. Turn left out of the 3rd floor elevator, then right.

Forest reserves (☎274-3433), including Kawaikoi (3 night limit), Sugi Grove (3 night limit), Waimea Canyon (4 night limit), and Waialae (2 night limit) require permits. Permits can be obtained free of charge at the **Forestry and Wildlife office.** See directions above. Permits are issued M-F 7:45am-4:30pm.

Kauai

Kauai Channel

PACIFIC OCEAN

Papaa Bay
Moloa'a Bay
Anahola Bay
Anahola
Kuhio Hwy.
Koolau Rd.
Kilauea Bay
Kilauea
Kalihiwai
Kilihiwai Bay
Kalihiwai
Kilauea R.
Kapa'a
Wailua
56
581
Opaekaa Falls
580
Wailua Falls
Kealia Rd.
Kamalu Rd.
583
Maalo Rd.
Kohola Falls
Kuamoo Rd.
Wailua R.
ANAHOLA MTNS
MAKALEHA MTNS
KAWAIHAU DISTRICT
Hanamaulu Bay
Kuhio Hwy.
Lihue
51
50
58
Nawiliwili Bay
Nohiu Bay
Kawailoa Bay

Princeville Airport
Princeville
Kuhio Hwy.
Hanalei
Hanalei Bay
Hanalei R.
56
Kalika 4200' (1280m)
LIHUE DISTRICT
Waialeale 5148' (1568m)
Halenanahu Res.
Huleia National Wildlife Refuge
Waita Res.
Koloa
Last Eruption on Kauai
Po'ipu
Keoniloa Bay

Kenomene Bay
Waimha Bay
Waimha R.
Lumahai R.
Haena
HANALEI DISTRICT
NAMOLOKAMA MTNS
LA'AU RIDGE
Hinalele Falls
Puuaomui Falls
Kilohana 4022' (1226m)
WAINIHA RIDGE
Alakai Swamp
Waialae Falls
Kawaikini 5243' (1598m)
Kalalauanaheheehele 4240' (1292m)
Papaa 3059' (932m)
Kouaa R.
Hanapepe R.
Kanaele Swamp
Kalaheo
Halemai Rd.
Koloa Rd.
520
540
KOLOA DISTRICT
Lokoawa Bay
Kukuiula Bay

Hono onapali Natural Area Reserve
Na Pali Coast State Park
Nualolo Kai State Park
Miloli'i State Park
Kula Natural Area Reserve
Pihea 4284' (1306m)
Pu'u o Kila Lookout
Waipoo Falls
Koke'e State Park
550
Pu'u Lua 3476' (1059m)
Waimea Canyon Lookout
Waimea Canyon State Park
Waimea Canyon
Waimea Canyon Dr.
Koke'e Rd.
Olokele R.
Makaweli R.
Waimea R.
WAIMEA DISTRICT
550
Kekaha
Waimea
Kikiaola Harbor
Waimea Bay
Polihale State Park
Kaumualii Hwy.
50

Hanapepe
Port Allen
Hanapepe Airport
Hanapepe Bay
'Ele'ele
Wahiawa Bay
50

Kaulakahi Channel

4 miles
4 kilometers
0
0

KAUAI

EAST SHORE

Anchored by Lihue, Kauai's county seat, the eastern shore is the center of both government and commerce for the island. Most of Kauai's population is concentrated here, as evidenced by the multitude of restaurants and shopping centers. Drop your bags and buy your groceries here, but seek the true beauty and adventure of the island elsewhere. The area just north of Lihue, also known as the Coconut Coast, was once the home of *ali'i* (royalty), and now provides a cross-section of Kauai's offerings from *heiaus* (temples) to boating on the Wailua River.

LIHUE

Welcome to the Big City. Home to the island's only Wal-mart (off of Hwy. 56 on the north side of town), and the official headquarters of Kauai County, dusty Lihue sees plenty of tourist traffic. Everyone comes, but despite a number of notable historic attractions and a decent beach, few stay the night. Originally a plantation town that housed workers from the sprawling Grove Farm, Lihue has yet to grow into its important new role, and those expecting cosmopolitan sophistication will be gravely disappointed. For travelers on a budget, however, Lihue's central location and affordable hotels brighten up an otherwise dull town. The relatively high ratio of locals to tourists also means that the restaurants of Lihue typically feature some type of local cuisine (Japanese, Korean, Hawaiian, etc.), and serve good portions for a low price. Expect shopping, good food, and relatively inexpensive housing in Lihue, but not the posh resorts and sights found elsewhere on the island.

◼ ORIENTATION

Lihue is shaped roughly like a big "V" that opens to the west, with **Rice Street** and downtown forming the right side, **Nawiliwili Road** forming the left side, and **Nawiliwili Harbor** creating the base. Most budget accommodations are located downtown, while the central waterfront holds more luxurious hotels and Kalapaki Beach. From the beach, Nawiliwili Rd. runs northwest to Kauai's largest shopping center, **Kukui Grove,** and ends when it intersects **Highway 50,** which leads southwest out of Lihue towards Koloa and Po'ipu. **Highway 56 (Kuhio Highway)** begins in Lihue and leads out of town to the north, towards Wailua and Kapa'a.

◼ TRANSPORTATION

Flights: Lihue Airport, 3901 Mokulele Loop (☎246-1448), 2 mi. east of town. See **interisland Transportation,** p. 369)

Buses: The Kauai Bus (☎241-6410) runs 6 bus routes around the island, offering infrequent (every 1-3hr.) but affordable transportation between Kauai's communities, M-Sa. Route 700 runs M-F within the city of Lihue. The main routes run east-west along the south shore from Lihue to Kekaha, and north-south along the east shore from Lihue to Hanalei, and stop at every town along the route. Carry-ons are limited to 9x14x22 in., and oversized backpacks and suitcases are prohibited. Besides the regularly scheduled stops, riders can request on-call pickup at a number of locations. Schedules are avail-

KAUAI

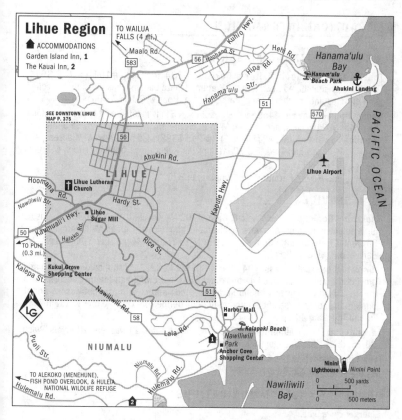

Lihue Region

♦ ACCOMMODATIONS
Garden Island Inn, 1
The Kauai Inn, 2

able at the Kauai Visitors Bureau and most of the big stores in town, like the Lihue Big Save and Wal-Mart. $1.50 per ride, seniors over 60 and ages 7-18 $0.75, children 6 and under free; frequent rider monthly pass $15.

Taxis: Cab rides are a costly luxury on Kauai. Fares begin with an initial $2 fee and $2 are added for each additional mi. Most companies tack on an additional $0.35 per bag and $5 per surfboard. Most will also provide vans upon request. The following companies offer service throughout the island: **Akiko's Taxi** (☎822-7588), **City Cab** (☎245-3227), **North Shore Cab** (☎ 828-6189), and **South Shore Cab** (☎742-1525).

Car Rental: For the less image-conscious traveler, ▨**Rent-a-Wreck,** 3501 Rice St. Ste. 112A (☎ 632-0741), in Harbor Mall (the turquoise building by Nawiliwili Bay), offers used cars and SUVs, as well as a few new rentals, at considerable savings. Rates vary with age of car and length of rental, and discounts may be negotiated with the very friendly management. Open M-F 8am-6pm, Sa 8am-5pm. In addition, **Alamo** (☎800-327-9633 or 246-0645), **Avis** (☎800-831-8000 or 245-3512), **Budget** (☎800-527-7000 or 245-1901), **Dollar** (☎800-800-4000 or 866-434-2226), **Hertz** (☎800-654-3131 or 245-3356), **National** (☎800-227-7368 or 245-5636), and **Thrifty** (☎800-847-4389 or 246-6252) are all located at the airport, and charge similar rates. Travel agents, package deals and AAA can usually get you a discount.

KAUAI

⚡ PRACTICAL INFORMATION

TOURIST AND FINANCIAL SERVICES

Tourist Office: Kauai Visitor's Bureau, 4334 Rice St. #101 (☎245-3971; www.kauaivisitorsbureau.com), in the Watamull Plaza building, has the standard collection of maps and brochures, and staff available. Open M-F 8am-4:30pm.

Banks: Bank of Hawaii, 4455 Rice St. (☎245-6761) is located next to the post office, has **24hr.** ATM access, and is open M-Th 8:30am-4pm, F 8:30am-6pm, Sa 9am-noon. **American Savings Bank,** 4318 Rice St. (☎245-3388) also has **24hr.** ATM access, and is open M-Th 8:30am-4pm, F 8:30am-6pm. Its Kukui Grove branch is open M-F until 6pm, Sa 9am-4pm.

Camping and Hiking Permits: see **Camping,** p. 370.

LOCAL SERVICES

Bookstore: Border's Books Music & Cafe, 4303 Nawiliwili Rd. (☎246-0862), carries a large selection of maps and other publications about Hawaii. Open M-Th 9am-10pm, F-Sa 9am-11pm, Su 9am-8pm. Cafe open M-Th 7:30am-10pm, F 7:30am-11pm, Sa 8am-11pm, Su 8am-8pm.

Library and Internet Access: 4344 Hardy St. (☎241-3222). Visitor cards cost $10 and provide full privileges, including book and video borrowing and Internet access, for 3 months at all of Hawaii's public libraries. 6 computers with internet access and 1 printer; also, only 1 use of the internet per day per person. Open M and W 11am-7pm, Tu and Th-F 9am-4:30pm.

Laundromat: Lihue Laundromat, in Rice Shopping Center. 24 washers, 28 dryers. Wash $0.25, dry $1.50, detergent $0.50. Open 24hr.

Weather Forecast: ☎245-6001.

Marine Forecast: ☎245-3564.

EMERGENCY AND COMMUNICATIONS

Emergency: ☎911.

Police: 3060 Umi St. (☎241-1711).

Hospital: Wilcox Memorial Hospital, 3420 Kuhio Hwy. (☎245-1100).

Internet Access: Wild Bill's, 4303 Nawiliwili Rd. (☎245-9085), next to Borders Books in the K-Mart Plaza, next to the Kukui Grove Shopping Center. 6 computers with DSL connection, a CD burner, and a printer. $5 for the first 30 min., $1 for each additional 10 min., printing $1 per page. Bill's also serves up pizzas (12 in. $10, 16 in. $15), sandwiches, and wraps ($6-10). Open early for breakfast, too. Open M-Sa 6:30am-11pm, Su 9am-11pm. AmEx/D/MC/V.

Post Office: 4441 Rice St. (☎800-275-8777). Open M-F 8am-4pm, Sa 9am-1pm.

Postal Code: 96766.

☗ ACCOMMODATIONS

Those looking for luxury and spectacular surroundings will likely accelerate their rental cars right out of Lihue, but the town's central location and the relative abundance of affordable accommodations make it a good choice for the budget traveler. Although the **Kauai Marriott,** fronting Kalapaki Beach, has two highly-regarded golf courses, pretty views, and all the usual luxuries of a major resort, its location within drab Lihue makes other resorts shine in comparison.

Downtown Lihue

🏠 ACCOMMODATIONS
Motel Lani, **2**

⭐ ENTERTAINMENT
Kukui Grove Cinemas, **4**

🍴 FOOD
Aromas, **7**
Hamura Saimin Stand and Halo Halo Shave Ice, **3**
Kalapaki Beach Hut, **9**
Nueva España, **10**
Okazu Hale, **5**
Oki Diner and Bakery, **1**

🍸 NIGHTLIFE
Duke's Canoe Club Barefoot Bar, **8**
Nawiliwili Tavern, **11**

🛍 SHOPPING
Borders, **6**

🦑 **The Kauai Inn,** 2430 Hulemalu Rd. (☎245-9000, www.kauai-inn.com), just past Nawiliwili Harbor on the left. Take Rice St. toward the harbor, turn left on Wilcox St. at Hale Kauai, follow Wilcox over the one lane bridge, turn right onto Hulemalu Rd., and the Inn is on the left. The family-owned Kauai Inn lacks the extravagance of the larger resorts on the island, but is nicely located off the beaten path, and offers a great value and plenty of luxury. Beautifully landscaped grounds, tropical flowers, and lush palm trees surround a small pool and pleasant courtyard. Their deluxe rooms—with soft carpeting, private lanais, king-size (or 2 double) beds, refrigerators, microwaves, and cable TV—are arguably Lihue's best deal. Continental breakfast served on the outdoor patio. Coin laundry on-site. Reception 8am-9pm. 48 units. Basic room without A/C $69, with A/C $79, deluxe suite $109. ❸

Garden Island Inn, 3445 Wilcox Rd. (☎245-7227 or 800-648-0154; www.gardenislandinn.com), across from Anchor Cove Shopping Center, easily visible from Rice St. All 21 units have cable TV, refrigerators, microwaves, wet bars, coffeemakers, and fresh flowers. Nicer rooms feature a private lanai and an ocean view. The cheerful staff provide frank opinions of local restaurants and attractions. Perhaps the best feature of the Inn, though, is its policy of lending guests snorkel gear, beach towels, chairs—even the single set of old golf clubs in the corner of the office—completely free; it's just one example of the individual attention paid to guests. The great location, across the stream from

KAUAI

the Harbor Mall and within walking distance of Kalapaki Beach, can become a little loud some nights. Reception 8am-9pm. Basic room with no A/C $65, 2nd floor with A/C and private lanai $85-95, suite $125. ❸

Motel Lani, 4240 Rice St. (☎245-2965). Lots of plants and a friendly staff brighten up the dull cinder block building. 6 basic, small rooms have beds, bathrooms, mini refrigerators, and A/C. 3 larger rooms feature TVs. Clean, functional, and centrally located in Lihue, Motel Lani is a great deal, especially for those who spend most of their day away from their hotel room. TV with cable in the lobby. Reception 6:30am-9:30pm. 1 night, 1-2 persons from $36; 3 persons from $54. 2+ nights (deposit required), 1-2 persons from $34; 3 persons from $52 per day. $14 per additional person. No credit cards, no phones in rooms. ❷

🍴 FOOD

Lihue plays host to an unbelievable assortment of restaurants, and a good meal awaits around every corner. A typical restaurant features Asian, Hawaiian, or American cuisine (or a mix of all three), at relatively low prices. The majority of customers are locals, which means that the quality and price of food matter more than the aesthetics of the restaurant. Those looking for something a little fancier are best off saving their dollars for a splurge in scenic Po'ipu or Princeville. There is a **Big Save Market** behind the Kauai Museum at the corner of Hardy and Eiwa. (☎245-6571. Open daily 7am-11pm.) **Star Market,** in Kukui Grove Shopping Center, also carries all the necessities. (☎245-7777. Open daily 6am-11pm.) Lihue holds two **Sunshine Markets,** which are outdoor, weekly sales of fresh Kauai grown fruit, vegetables, and flowers. One is held on Mondays at 3pm in Kukui Grove Shopping Center (a privately organized sale) and another on Fridays at 3pm in the lot behind Vidinha Stadium (a public sale). A schedule for the public sales is available by calling the Office of Economic Development (☎241-6390). **Vim 'n Vigor,** in Rice Shopping Center, is Lihue's only health food store, and carries grains, soy products, vitamins, and pre-packed sandwiches and salads. (☎245-9053. Open M-F 7:45am-5pm, Sa 7:45am-2pm.)

🍽 **Deli and Bread Connection** (☎245-7115), next to Macy's in Kukui Grove Shopping Center. A deli, bakery, and kitchenware store rolled into one, the Connection is a popular lunchtime stop for those who want to stay or take their meal to go. The "famous" Oriental sweet bread, endless variety, and reasonable prices make the wait worthwhile. A number of vegetarian selections (Veggie Burger served hot $5.50) and fresh daily soups compliment the menu of standard (B.L.T. $4.25) and unique ("crimp," or crab and shrimp $5) sandwich options. Outdoor seating available in the mall. Open M-Th and Sa 9:30am-7pm, F 9:30am-9pm, Sun 10am-6pm. MC/V. ❶

🍽 **Kauai Bakery and Cinnamons** (☎246-4765), in Kukui Grove Shopping Center, in the middle of the outdoor mall between Long's and Star Market. This hole in the wall is home to a staff of friendly, hard-working bakers, as well as a steady flow of eager customers. Simply put, they make some of the best freshly-baked goods around, including donuts ($0.60), pastries ($1-3), and custom birthday cakes ($22 and up). Don't miss the incredibly moist banana bread or the perfect apple turnovers ($1-3). Also delicious are the ham and cheese roll ($1.50) and the pig in a blanket ($1.50). Most of the good stuff sells out by noon. No indoor seating, but tables outside in the mall area. Open M-Th and Sa 7am-7pm, F 7am-9pm, Su 7am-6pm. ❶

Kalapaki Beach Hut, 3474 Rice St. (☎246-6330), across from Harbor Mall. Juicy, flame-broiled burgers ($4-6.50), tons of toppings (try the Aloha Classic—teriyaki glaze, pineapple and cheese; $5.60), and a prime location make the Beach Hut a popular lunchtime destination. Most people take their burgers to go, but seating is available—just don't expect much from the advertised "ocean view" upstairs. A better option might be to take your burger over to a picnic table at Nawiliwili Beach Park. The breakfast menu includes a range of omelettes ($5-7), as well as pancakes, french toast, and an egg sandwich ($3.75). Burgers are turkey or beef; *Keiki* (kids) meals with burger, fries and drink $4; garden burgers and Maui *taro* burgers $5. Open daily 7am-7pm, breakfast from 7-10:30am. AmEx/D/MC/V. ❶

Okazu Hale, 4100 Rice St. #6 (☎245-6554), in the turquoise strip mall behind Ace Hardware. Just steps off the tourist path, Okazu Hale serves yummy Japanese meals to a lively local clientele. Lunch and dinner served with *miso* soup, rice and tossed salad. Some good bets include teriyaki chicken ($6) and veggie tempura ($6.50). Vegetarians will rejoice over the stir-frys, rice bowls, and ramen. The small dining area, sterile decor, and parking lot view leave much to be desired aesthetically, but the quality food keeps customers coming back. *Saimin* $3-6. Daily specials, half orders, takeout, and catering services available. Open M-Sa 11am-2pm and 5-9pm. ❶

Aromas, 3501 Rice St. (☎245-9192), located on the second floor of Harbor Mall, serves delicious food all day long in a comfortable, laid-back atmosphere with indoor and outdoor seating. Omelettes served with potatoes or rice and toast ($6.50-8), and *Bajitos* (fish tacos—baja style; $9.50), are available among the wide selection of breakfast and lunch dishes, respectively. The dinner menu features vegetarian dishes (pasta primavera $16) as well as options for carnivores, like the grilled NY steak ($24). A decent view of the ocean from the patio and some of the best service around makes a meal at Aromas a thoroughly enjoyable event. Takeout available upon request. Open Tu-F 7am-9:30pm, Sa-Su 8am-9:30pm. ❸

Nueva España (☎632-0513), in Anchor Cove Shopping Center. All but a few tables line the spacious patio overlooking Nawiliwili Bay, and the pleasant setting makes the hearty Mexican breakfasts (*huevos rancheros* $7) even more delicious. Vegetarians will be pleased with the array of meatless dishes, ranging from taco salad to *chiles rellenos*. Lunch and dinner entrees $8-16. Open daily 8am-9pm. D/MC/V. ❷

Hamura Saimin Stand and **Halo Halo Shave Ice,** 2956 Kress St. (☎245-3271), at Halenani. Clearly Lihue's *saimin* headquarters, hordes of locals and a few savvy travelers slurp bowls of the noodle soup with a hint of seafood flavor at a winding, orange counter. Brusque service is only a result of Hamura's popularity—a stream of hungry customers keeps the waitress behind the counter busy. $1 BBQ chicken or beef sticks (shish kebab style) complement the bowls of *saimin* ($3.50-6.25). No vegetarian options, but one of the cheapest meals in town. Open M-Th 10am-11pm, F-Sa 10am-1am, Su 10am-9:30pm. Pretty good shave ice ($2-3) served M-F 10am-4pm. ❶

Oki Diner and Bakery, 3125 Kuhio Hwy. (☎245-5899), a yellow building just east of Rice St. on the *mauka* (mountain) side of the highway, next to the McDonalds. A comfortable diner complete with jukebox, covered patio, and picture menu, Oki serves "award-winning" hotcakes 21hr. a day. Burgers, sandwiches, and local cuisine round out the menu, with most entrees available in regular or "mini" sizes. The selection, service, and prices make Oki a simple and reliable destination for a bite to eat. Meals range from $5-8. An entree and the all-you-can-eat salad bar is only $9 M-F 11am-10pm. For a break from sandwiches, order an *Oki bento* box (a mid-sized lunch featuring teriyaki chicken, corned beef hash, an omelette, and rice, among other things) to go, complete with napkin and plastic knife and fork ($3.75; served 7am-midnight). Breakfast served all day; Oki is just about the only late night option in town. Open daily 6am-3am. ❶

BEACHES

KALAPAKI BEACH. A surprisingly pretty beach considering its overgrown commercial surroundings, Kalapaki entices beachgoers with ¼ mi. of fine white sand. The surrounding bay creates gentle waves perfect for swimming, sailing, body boarding and beginner surfing. You may, however, have to jostle with abandoned catamarans, volleyball nets, and Marriott guests with beach chairs for an empty spot of gradually sloping beach. To the west of the beach, **Nawiliwili Park** provides a site for recreation and picnicking with tables, grills, bathrooms, outdoor showers, and grass galore. (Public parking is available on the far east side of the Marriott, via the main entrance of the Marriott (follow the signs that say "beach access") or in the Nawiliwili Park lot behind Anchor Cove Shopping Center.)

HANAMA'ULU BEACH PARK. Two miles east of Lihue, in the dusty town of Hanama'ulu, there are prime beachfront campsites. Hanama'ulu Beach is narrow and crescent-shaped with fine sand but somewhat silty waters. Gentle swells, an all-sand bottom, and a few small breakers make it a great beach for swimming, body boarding, beginner surfing, and kids. Full facilities, although slightly run-down, including grills, picnic tables, trash cans, showers, a pavilion, a grassy park, and a prime oceanfront location, welcome mostly local campers. A county park camping permit is required. For more information, see **Camping,** p. 327. (2 mi. east of Lihue on Hwy. 56. Take a right onto Hanama'ulu Rd., then the third right onto Hehi Rd. for ample parking.)

SIGHTS

Well before the advent of Wal-Mart, Lihue was the center of commercial life on Kauai. The town's location alongside Nawiliwili Harbor, the island's main port, supported the grand old sugar plantations that shaped Kauai's history. Today, historic sights allow visitors to relive the island's golden age, as well as the time of its great kings.

GROVE FARM HOMESTEAD MUSEUM. Those who reserve well in advance (think 1 week or more) can enjoy an intimate and informative 2hr. walking tour of the residence of **George "G.N." Wilcox,** Kauai's first and greatest sugar baron. The tour, limited to six people, begins in G.N.'s office, with a brief biography of the hard-working man who funded his Yale education by gathering *guano*. Continuing through the estate, the tour stops in the spartan cottage G.N. called home, as well as the spectacular main house that he gave to his brother Sam and his family of seven. Gleaming *'ohi'a* wood floors, a grand *koa* staircase, beautiful paintings, and vast collections of books and Hawaiiana are just a few of the well-preserved furnishings. The tour also includes visits to the kitchen (where a tasty surprise awaits), a plantation cottage, and a very nicely furnished guest house that puts G.N.'s own humble cottage to shame. A devout Christian, G.N. preferred to spend his hard-earned dollars helping others, and, among other good deeds, he donated both the land and the finances for Nawiliwili Harbor. The grounds surrounding the house feature tropical gardens, lush orchards, and acres of pastures. (Northbound on Nawiliwili, turn right at the small sign onto a private dirt road about 1¼ mi. from the harbor. ☎ 245-3202. Tours M and W-Th at 10am, 1pm. Reservations required. $5 requested donation.)

KILOHANA. Built in 1935 by G.N. Wilcox's youngest nephew, **Gaylord Parke Wilcox,** and his wife, Ethel, Kilohana was once the grandest and most expensive home on Kauai. In fact, the word *kilohana* translates to "not to be surpassed," which was Gaylord's goal when he had it built. Today, the over 15,000 sq. ft. Tudor-style mansion's eight bedrooms and accompanying bathrooms have been converted into

KAUAI

retail shops featuring local art, jewelry, and collectibles. The living room, hallways, and other rooms of the house have been restored to their original condition, and are filled with furniture and artwork that dates to the 1930s, when the Wilcoxes ordered a house-full of furnishings from Gump's in San Francisco, a high-class specialty store. Unlike other historical homes, Kilohana welcomes guests to sit on the furniture and truly experience the house. Take a seat on the couch in the curtained nook at the rear of the living room—where Gaylord conducted his private business—and you'll feel almost as if you've stepped back into Kauai's golden age. Guests are also free to wander around the 35 acres of flowering gardens, historic cottages and the working farm that surround the main house, all of which provide a spectacular view of the inland mountains. The **galleries** within the Kilohana house are worth a look, if only for the innovative ways in which the owners have used their space. Housed in the Wilcoxes' library, the **Country Store** displays Hawaiian crafts on the original library shelves.

Those who would like to learn more about Kilohana's history can do so on a Clydesdale horse-drawn carriage tour of the grounds. **Gaylord's Restaurant ❹,** whose tables take the original lanai, provides a peaceful setting for an outdoor lunch. *(1½ mi. north of Lihue on the mauka (mountain) side of Hwy. 50. ☎245-5608. 20min. carriage rides daily 11am-6pm; $10, children 12 and under $5. 1hr. sugar cane wagon rides M-Tu and Th at 11am, 2pm; $24, children under 12 $12; reservations required. Restaurant open for lunch M-Sa 11am-3pm ($7-12), dinner daily 5-9pm (from $18), brunch Su 9:30am-3pm (from $9). Reservations requested (☎245-9593). Luau Kilohana Tu, Th 5pm. $58, over 60 and teenagers 13-18 $54, children 5-12 $30, under 5 free. House and galleries open M-Sa 9:30am-9:30pm, Su 9:30am-5pm. Free.)*

KAUAI MUSEUM. Small, but overflowing with information, the Kauai Museum provides an introduction to everything you ever wanted to know about the island—and a nice place to spend a rainy afternoon. A self-guided tour of the museum begins in the smaller Rice building (one of two buildings that comprise the museum) with an aerial video that shows an overview of the island. Comprehensive displays illustrating Kauai and Ni'ihau's geologic origins and ecology combine with others featuring the islands' history. *(4428 Rice St. at Eiwa. ☎245-6931. Guided 1½ hr. tours M-Th 10am. Open M-F 9am-4pm, Sa 10am-4pm. $5, over 65 $4, students age 13-17 $3, children 6-12 $1, under 6 free.)*

WAILUA FALLS. Ancient Hawaiian *ali'i* (royalty) dove from the cliffs overlooking the pool to prove their courage. Today, classic television fans may recognize the waterfalls from the opening scenes of *Fantasy Island.* The southern fork of the **Wailua River** creates this natural wonder, and the appearance of the falls varies with rain and the river's flow. Come early to avoid the crowds and enjoy the morning sunlight sparkling on the falls. Midday visitors will likely share the view with at least a dozen others, but there is plenty of room. The incredible convenience of the lookout doesn't detract from the quality of the sight—it's a must-see if you're spending a day near Lihue. *(From Lihue, drive 1 mi. east on Hwy. 56 and turn left at Hwy. 583 (Ma'alo Rd.). The road ends 4 mi. later at the falls.)*

ALEKOKO (MENEHUNE) FISHPOND OVERLOOK. According to legend, the *menehune* were a race of mischievous, pot-bellied elf-like creatures who lived in the forest and were famed for completing complicated building projects overnight. Many years ago, a Hawaiian king asked the *menehune* to build him a fishpond, and they happily complied. Thousands of *menehune* formed a long line stretching to the west and passed lava rock from Kalaheo all the way back to Lihue where others skillfully shaped the walls of the pond. Despite their efforts, the *menehune* were unable to complete the seaward wall, and, as the sun began to rise, they hurriedly washed their hands (scratched and bleeding from the rough lava rock) in

LEGENDS OF THE TALL

Nounou Mountain, better known as the **Sleeping Giant,** stretches from Wailua to Kapa'a. It is named for the legendary giant who once lived there. Loved by the townsfolk, when the giant sat down to rest, he flattened hilltops and made them fit for farming. Wherever he stepped, the villagers planted banana trees in his footprint. The giant, always sleepy, would sleep and wake for hundreds of years at a time, and while sleeping he became covered with dirt and plants. The people aptly named him *Kanaka-nunui-moe,* which means "the sleeping giant."

Once, the village chief ordered the people to build a great *heiau* (temple), using the finest natural resources available, to be completed in less than once cycle of the moon. Nunui (for short) noticed the townsfolk were sad, and asked them why. They explained their impossible task, and he told them he would build the *heiau.* When he was done, the whole town celebrated, and Nunui became especially sleepy. He lies asleep to this day, his head resting on a hill west of Kapa'a. The highest peak is his forehead, then the bump of his eyebrows, his long flat nose, slightly open mouth, and broad chest are visible. The best view is across the street from the Chevron station on the highway.

the pond before disappearing into the woods. *Alekoko* (rippling blood) provided the ancient Hawaiian royalty with fish—their primary source of protein. *'Ama'ama* (striped mullet) and *awa* (milk fish) continue to thrive in the pond today, laying their eggs amidst the tangled roots of mangroves that have taken hold along the walls. Unfortunately, although beneficial to the fish, the roots of the invasive mangroves are causing irreparable harm to the rock walls. The overlook itself is a small structure along the edge of the river valley, hundreds of feet above the pond, with a sign describing the history and mythology of the pond, as well as information about its present-day fish. The view is beautiful, although the fact that the walls of the pond can no longer be seen from the overlook (as a result of plant growth) is a bit disappointing.

The lush, undeveloped wetlands, fertile hills, and valleys to the west of the overlook form part of the **Huleia National Wildlife Refuge,** established in 1973 to protect the habitats of endangered endemic waterbirds, including Hawaii's largest population of *koloa* ducks. Movie buffs may recognize the river valley as the site of Indy's heart-pounding, rope-swinging escape in one of the opening scenes of *Raiders of the Lost Ark.* Unfortunately, the refuge is closed to the public, with the exception of a few guided boat and kayak adventures up the river. If you're at the fishpond overlook, it's worthwhile to drive a few minutes along the border of the wildlife refuge, to take in the beautiful scenery along the road. *(From Nawiliwili Rd., turn onto Wilcox Rd. at Hale Kauai or onto Niumalu Rd., farther to the northwest. Both eventually lead over a 1-lane bridge, after which you turn right onto Hulemalu Rd. Drive about 1mi. up to a small lookout on the left.)*

NININI LIGHTHOUSE. A good place from which to spot humpback whales, the 86 ft. Ninini Lighthouse also offers a fantastic, if incredibly windy, view of the ocean and Nawiliwili Bay. At Ninini Point (the site of the lighthouse), a few patches of grass and plenty of volcanic rocks can provide the setting for an unforgettable picnic. If you're lucky, an attendant may be on site to escort visitors to the top, and if you hang around for a half-hour or more, you have a good chance of seeing a jet soar directly over you only seconds before it lands at Lihue Airport. *(Entrance off Hwy. 51 between the airport and Rice St. About a ½ mi. north of Rice St., turn toward the sea at the blue "Shoreline Access" sign. Drive straight past the gatehouse and after ¼ mi., follow the road as it makes a sharp left at the stop sign. Here the road separates a golf course on the right and the airport on the left. Stay right at the fork in the road (the left fork says "private road no outlet"), and stay on the paved road. Past a "Shoreline*

Access - Ninini Point" sign, stay left at the "Running Path" sign, intersect the golf cart path and you'll see the 11th and 12th tees of the golf course—the 12th tee is marked by an alligator statue. The last stretch of the road is dirt, and roughly follows the fence of the airport on the left, until a dirt parking lot.)

LIHUE LUTHERAN CHURCH. Hawaii's oldest Lutheran church was founded by a congregation of German immigrants in 1883. Having suffered extensive damage from Hurricane Iwa in 1982, the church was rebuilt according to the original plans. The relatively small, cream-colored building conceals a beautiful interior, laid out in the "old upside-down ship style" that recalls the immigrants' 6 mo. sea voyage around Cape Horn to reach the islands. Just as the deck of a ship slopes to shed rainwater, the floor of the church bows upward in the center. The ceiling mimics the curvature of a hull, and the ships' original oil lamps have been wired with electricity. Where is the captain's bridge, you might ask? They've got that one covered, too—it's the balcony where the organist sits. But how is the forecastle of the ship represented? It's the pulpit, of course. Alright, but where are the sails of the ship? Naturally, they can also be seen in the... wait, a minute... churches don't have sails! The oft-visited church has an impressive guestbook that's worth a glance. *(4602 Hoomana Rd. About ¼ mi. up Hoomana Rd. from Hwy. 56 (across Hwy. 56 from the sugar mill, about 200 yards west of its intersection with Rice St.) and the church is on your right. ☎ 245-145; fax 246-8626; lihluth@hawaiian.net. Services Su 8, 10:30am.)*

📺 🎵 NIGHTLIFE AND ENTERTAINMENT

Unassuming as it may appear, Lihue is the place to be after dark; nightlife here is as thick as it gets in Kauai.

Rob's Good Times Grill (☎ 246-0311), in Rice Shopping Center. Happy Hour draws familiar *pau hana* (literally "quit work time") faces to this casual neighborhood bar. Rob and his wife, Lolly, pour drinks and mingle with customers who kick back in booths or battle it out on the foosball table. Pool tables, tons of TVs, and the only dance floor in town keep things going until closing time, although once the loud dance music starts, the club atmosphere dominates the bar as well as most attempts at conversation. Enjoy local *pupus* (sliced hot dog with onions $5) and typical bar food (jalapeño poppers $6) while bobbing to Top 40 hits. Karaoke M and Tu 6pm-2am, country line dancing W 8-11pm and dance party 11pm-close, dance music F-Su 9pm-2am. Happy Hour daily 2-6pm (draft and domestic beers $2.75). Open daily 2pm-2am.

Lihue Bowling Center (☎ 245-5263), in the Rice Shopping Center. 28 lanes, video games, and a diner (local *pupus* and meals $2-5.50) provide entertainment enough, but things get even more exciting with "Rock 'n Glow" bowling on weekends. A lounge offers cheap beer on tap (14oz. Bud $1.75), other drink specials for $5, and most interestingly, a view through a window across all 28 lanes from halfway down the lane—a unique perspective. $3.25 per game, students $2.60, children and seniors $2.35; shoe rental $1.50. "Rock 'n Glow" F-Sa 9-11:30pm, $10. Open M-Th 9am-11pm, F-Sa 9am-11:30pm, Su noon-10pm.

Kukui Grove Cinemas, 4368 Kukui Grove (☎ 245-5055). Across Nawiliwili Rd. from Kukui Grove Shopping Mall, and 1 block back on Kukui Grove Rd., Kauai's biggest movie theater has 4 screens showing current films. Adults $6.50, seniors over 60 $5, children 12 and under $3.50. Bargain matinees (first show on Sa and Su) $3.50. Shows M-Th 6-9pm, F 4-9pm, Sa-Su 1:30-10pm.

Duke's Canoe Club Barefoot Bar, 3610 Rice St. (☎ 246-9599), at the west end of Kalapaki Beach, with an entrance from the beach as well as from the Marriott Courtyard. Separated from the sand of Kalapaki Beach by only a sidewalk and a strip of neatly manicured lawn, Duke's serves island pupus (from $3) and drinks (Mai Tai $5.75, local

KAUAI

TRAFFIC JAM ON THE WAILUA RIVER

The Wailua River has always been a popular waterway for recreational boaters, but recently, there has been a struggle between commercial users of the river and the state over how to best manage the river to maintain the environment as well as the safety of all the river's users. Motorized tour boat operators, sailboats, kayakers, water skiers, swimmers, and others, all try to share the navigable part of the waterway that runs about 4 mi. from Mt. Wai'ale'ale to the east shore of the island.

In November of 2002, according to *The Kauai Garden Island* (www.kauaiworld.com), new administrative rules concerning the river were signed into effect by outgoing Governor Ben Cayetano. Under these rules, traffic on the river is regulated by times, locations, and numbers of commercial activities. The new rules, for example, limit the number of unguided, commercial kayaks allowed on the river to 48 per day, spread out among 4 different companies each allowed to rent to 12 people per day. As a result, the cost of renting a kayak has significantly increased.

Many river users are angry about these limitations and their effects. Since the new rules, Governor Linda Lingle has taken over, and the river users are trying to improve river management with her cooperation. For now, though, traffic on the river is still limited.

beer on tap $4.50) to sunburnt beachgoers. Although the ambience may seem a little contrived—wooden tables are shielded by grass umbrellas, an indoor waterfall cascades into the bar, and servers wear *aloha* shirts—the stunning view can't be beat. Patronized mostly by tourists, prices are a hair higher than other bars, but the picturesque setting makes it worthwhile. Taco Tu is a great deal from 4-6pm, with $2.50 draft beer and $2 fish tacos; Tropical F 4-6pm means $4 tropical drinks. Live music Th 4-6pm, F 4-6pm and 9-11pm. Open daily 11am-11:30pm.

Nawiliwili Tavern, 3488 Paena Loop (☎245-1781), in the old Hotel Kuboyama next to Kalapaki Beach Hut. Wall-to-wall neon beer signs and posters of bikini girls make the Tavern's decor a prototypical college fraternity boy's dorm room. Darts, billiards, shuffleboard, video games, and lots of beer welcome a mixed crowd, while TVs stay tuned in to ESPN. The back room boasts Kauai's largest karaoke collection, where you can practice before displaying your skills during the F night contests. Billiards contests Th 7pm, $10 entry fee. Locally brewed Keoki on tap ($3). Happy Hour daily 2-6pm (all drinks $0.50 off). Food 5pm-midnight. Open daily 2pm-2am.

WAILUA

The Tahitian pioneers who first settled Hawaii landed in Wailua, where "two waters become one." The spot, at the meeting of the north and south forks of the great Wailua River, became the center of the Tahitians' new society. Long the preferred home of the Hawaiian *ali'i* (royalty), Wailua and its surrounding lands have always been Kauai's most prestigious—and most popular—address. Nowadays Wailua is characterized by the recreational activities available on the Wailua River and the ocean, as well as the number of resorts that surround the town.

ACCOMMODATIONS

Wailua is home to a number of mid-range hotels, small B&Bs, and mid-level resorts (think suites and pools, but not golf courses), most of which advertise on the Internet. Both of the following are located on the oceanfront, and have all the usual features of resorts. **Aston Islander on the Beach ❹,** 4-484 Kuhio Hwy. (☎822-7417; www.islanderkauai.com), behind the Coconut Marketplace, between Wailua and Kapa'a, has rooms starting at $148, and **Aloha Beach Resort ❺,** 3-5920 Kuhio Hwy. (☎823-6000, www.abrkauai.com), just south of Wailua River on the east side of the highway, is a fancier resort whose rooms start at $239. A slightly less expensive, but still luxurious, option is the 200-room **Kauai Sands ❸,** 420

Papaloa Rd., part of a Hawaiian family-owned chain that also operates on Maui and the Big Island. The efficiently-run hotel features super-clean rooms with two double beds or one king-sized bed, fans, cable TVs, mini fridges, and private lanais. The oceanfront grounds also include two swimming pools, a laundry room, exercise facilities, and a restaurant. (☎822-4951 or 800-560-5553; fax 822-0978. Rooms $60-110, but promotional rates $55-99 often available.)

◖ FOOD

Wailua Shopping Plaza and Kinipopo Shopping Village are across Kuhio Highway from one another, immediately north of the Wailua River bridge, and both feature a number of shops and restaurants.

Caffe Coco, 4-369 Kuhio Hwy. (☎822-7990, fax 821-0066), at the back of a parking lot on the *makai* (ocean) side of the highway just past Kinipopo Shopping Village. With both indoor and garden seating, Caffe Coco features a variety of tasty dishes for vegetarians and carnivores alike. Platters combine salads, rice, and other sides with entrees such as black sesame *ahi* ($18), Pacific-rim tofu ($18), and slow-roasted pork ($16). BYOB with a $5 corkage fee. Live music nightly, including Hawaiian Th, Hula F, and Jazz Su. The open-air seating at the coffee shop is a quiet place to snack on homemade pastries and desserts (samosas $3.50, big cookies $2). Open for lunch Tu-F 11am-5pm, dinner Tu-Su 5-9pm. ❹

Kintaro, 4370 Kuhio Hwy. (☎822-3341), opposite Caffe Coco. Kintaro's upscale dining room serves Kauai's best Japanese cuisine. Most menu options are complete dinner combinations served with *miso* soup, rice, and tea (soba noodles, salmon, and beef teriyaki $17). There are also a few Western dishes, such as charbroiled filet mignon with fresh vegetables ($20). Extensive selection of sushi (*make* $3-14). Hibachi seating or regular tables. Reservations recommended. Open M-Sa 5:30-9:30pm. ❹

Aloha Kauai Pizza, 4-484 Kuhio Hwy. (☎822-4511), in Coconut Marketplace on the east side of the highway. One of only a few pizza joints around, this small stand in the middle of Coconut Marketplace serves a variety of delicious Italian dishes to hungry mallgoers. The juicy, flavor-filled, medium crust pizza comes in 7 in., 12 in., and 16 in. pies (cheese $5.50, $12, $15), but is not sold by the slice. The house specialty is the "Artichoke Eddie," ($6.50, $17, $23) that comes highly recommended by the staff. Calzones and lasagna ($5.50-6.50), as well as sandwiches ($6) round out the menu. Outdoor seating is available in the mall. Open daily 11am-9pm. MC/V. ❷

Korean Bar-B-Q Restaurant, 4-356 Kuhio Hwy. (☎823-6744), in Kinipopo Shopping Village. A local favorite, this small restaurant offers a tasty alternative for lunch on the go. For those unfamiliar with *katsu* and *bibim-bob* (mixed rice but not fried), the menus are complete with pictures. Plate lunches (teriyaki beef and BBQ chicken combo $7) include rice, miso soup, and *kimchee,* as well as veggies. Open M and W-Su 10am-9pm, Tu 4:30-9pm. ❶

Wailua Family Restaurant, 4361 Kuhio Hwy. (☎822-3325), offers breakfast, lunch, steak, and seafood to locals and travelers all through the day, and makes a good stop for families and large groups looking for variety. Customers choose from the menu on the wall on their way in and order and pay for their meal before seating themselves in the indoor dining room or the roomy patio. Steaks ranging from the 7 oz. sirloin ($10) to the "King Cut" prime rib ($23), grilled *ahi* ($16), and a variety of stir fry options, including veggie ($11), are complemented by a fully-equipped salad bar. Open Su-Th 6:30am-9:30pm, F-Sa 6:30am-10pm. MC/V. ❸

The Fish Hut, 4-484 Kuhio Hwy. (☎821-0033), in Coconut Marketplace, is a stand that serves fish almost any way you can imagine. Fish tacos, fish burgers, fish wraps, and fish salad are the standard fare ($7-8), or get the combo plate ($9) and combine oyster, scallop, or shrimp (choose 2), with fries on the side. The fresh-baked sourdough bread makes the sandwiches a treat, and a root beer float with ice cream ($3) is a nice way to top off a meal. Meals are served on paper plates and outdoor seating is available in the mall on picnic tables. Daily specials; takeout available. Open M-Sa 11am-9pm, Su 11am-8pm. ❷

⚠ OUTDOORS

WAILUA RIVER STATE PARK. The unifying link between all of the area's attractions is the majestic Wailua River, which flows 21 mi. from its source atop Mt. Wai'ale'ale to the northern end of Lydgate Park. Separated into two branches for much of its path, the river forms one dominating waterway as it descends to sea level, mixing with salty ocean water to form a brackish environment that supports healthy populations of fish.

During the time of the *ali'i* (royalty), the Wailua River basin was the home of the royal chiefs, who claimed this area for its sandy beaches, easy canoe landings, fertile fields, and fresh and salt water resources. Known as the King's Highway, in honor of Kauai's last king, Kamehameha, the river is accompanied by a line of *heiaus* (temples), paralleling the water's path from mountain to ocean. Six of the *heiaus* that form this sacred path can be seen today, while the seventh sits atop the wild summit of Wai'ale'ale. Nearly all of the sights listed below fall within the rather confusing boundaries of the thousand-acre Wailua River State Park, which encompasses the Wailua River, the town of Wailua (see p. 382), Opaeka'a Falls, Kuamo'o Rd., Fern Grotto, and Lydgate Park.

Although dominated by tourist-filled riverboats, the Wailua River is also a favorite of kayakers who put in on the north bank. Turn from Kuhio Hwy. onto Kuamo'o Rd. (just north of the bridge over the river) and take the 2nd left into Wailua River State Park. The river holds two main attractions for kayakers: **Fern Grotto,** a swimming hole and cliff jump, and **Secret Falls** (see listings below). The falls requires a short hike, whereas the other two are accessible by river. A round-trip to all three sites covers about 6 mi., and could take 3-4 hr., including stops. A convenient place to rent kayaks is **Wailua Kayak and Canoe,** located next to the Smith's Tropical Paradise shack on the north bank (also on Kuamo'o Rd.). From here, the river is a short walk away. All rentals come with a map, dry bag, cooler, and brief orientation for first-time kayakers. (☎821-1188. *Single kayak $35 per day; double $70 per day. Open M-Sa 8am-5pm.*)

LYDGATE STATE PARK. A popular beach park, Lydgate's long, grassy lawn is dotted with picnic tables. A few shade trees provide refuge along the modest sands that front two wonderful saltwater pools. Artificial lava rock walls enclose the large pools that shelter swimmers from the unpredictable surf and create a paradise for beginning snorkelers. The larger pool is deep enough for those looking to showcase their strokes, while the shallower adjoining pool is appropriate for younger *keiki* (children). Restrooms, showers, a lifeguard stand, and a large pictorial fish finder back the pool-front beach at the northern end of the park. On the other side of the parking lot, **Kamalani Playground** welcomes water-wary children.

Hikina A Ka La ("rising of the sun"), at the extreme northern end of the park, is the first of seven *heiaus* (temples) connecting ocean to mountain. The stacked rock walls form a large rectangle, within which the *kahunas* (priests) celebrated the dawning of each new day with prayers and chants. At one end of the *heiau* was **Hauola,** the City of Refuge, where criminals could go to find sanctuary from punishment. Untouchable within its boundaries, the criminals could stay until purified of their wrongdoings by a *kahuna*. A very short nature walk proceeds through a series of four or five signs with historical information about the *heiau*. Behind the sanctuary, near the mouth of the river, the sand hides boulders that bear etched petroglyphs. *(From Kuhio Hwy., turn toward the ocean onto Leho Dr. at the Lydgate State Park sign north of the 5mi. marker (a few hundred yards south of the bridge over Wailua River). About ½ mile down Leho Rd., a right turn on Nalu Rd. leads to the parking lot.)*

FERN GROTTO. Once a temple for the worship of Lono, the Hawaiian god of the harvest and fertility, the famed cave now welcomes tourists by the boat-load, and brides and grooms by the dozens. Although still an appealing example of natural beauty, the Fern Grotto of years past has recently become less than spectacular. In order to facilitate photo-happy tourists, the state cut down a large number of ancient trees; unable to adapt to the increased sunlight, the beautiful ferns that used to cover the entire cave have been reduced to sparse, dangling bits. The only way to reach the grotto is by river. Two companies, **Wai'ale'ale Boat Tours** (☎822-4908) and **Smith's** (see below), cruise the 2 mi. from the Wailua Marina, leaving every ½hr. on the ½hr. 9-11:30am and 12:30-3:30pm. The cruise takes about 1½hr. and costs $15 for adults and $7.50 for children with both companies. *(The marina is on the southern bank of the Wailua River, down a paved road just south of the bridge on Kuhio Hwy. over the river.)*

SMITH'S TROPICAL PARADISE. Descended from a whaler who came to Kauai on an early boat, the Smith family has helped to introduce visitors to the beauty and culture of the island for three generations. The 1½hr. covered **boat tours** to Fern Grotto include a 30min. stop at the cave, with a guided walk up the trail and some history. A group of musicians serenades each group from below, taking advantage of the grotto's perfect acoustics to sing the Hawaiian Wedding Song. Hula dancers and a Hawaiian band entertain passengers on the outbound cruise; the return trip features local stories and legends.

A 30-acre tropical garden, west of the marina, is divided into themed areas featuring rainforest plants, fruit trees, a fish-filled lagoon, a Polynesian village, and more. The gardens also play host to Kauai's most authentic *luau* (see **Entertainment,** p. 386) three nights a week. *(174 Wailua Rd., past the marina. ☎821-6895; fax 822-4520; smiths@aloha.net. 1½hr. boat cruise $15, children $7.50. Tours sail daily 9-11:30am and 12:30-3:30pm. Self-guided walking tour of gardens $5.25. Open daily 8:30am-4pm.)*

◎ SIGHTS

KUAMO'O ROAD (HIGHWAY 580). Running along the northern bank of the river from the famous Coco Palms Resort, where Elvis tied the knot in *Blue Hawaii*, past Opaeka'a Falls, the highway follows the course of the historic King's Path, along which the *ali'i* (royalty) walked from one religious site to another. The following sights all lie along the road.

POLIAHU HEIAU. Some believe Poliahu, a large *heiau* (temple) overlooking the river, was built by the mystical *menehune* who shaped the rock walls out of stones carried up from the river below. Religious ceremonies took place here until the abolition of the Hawaiian religion in 1819. The *heiau* ruins has walls about 3 ft. high now, and thicker than they are tall; there is a scenic lookout of the Wailua River from the same turnout that provides parking for the *heiau* visitors, and signs are up to explain the historical significance of the river. *(On the south, or river, side of the road, about 1¼ mi. up Kuamo'o Road road from Kuhio Hwy. right next to the dirt road that leads to the bellstone, ¼mi. downhill from the Opaeka'a Falls overlook.)*

OPAEKA'A FALLS. A tall waterfall flowing in a number of broad streams to a pretty pool below, Opaeka'a Falls is a popular scenic viewpoint. An unofficial trail leads to the top of the falls from a dirt turnout on the north side of the road about

KAUAI

200 yards past the parking lot, right where the guardrail ends. Other trails are known to lead to the pool below the falls, too. *(The viewpoint is located along a sidewalk that runs west from a parking lot 1½ mi. up Kuamo'o Rd. on the right.)*

🎵 🎬 ENTERTAINMENT AND NIGHTLIFE

Wailua rivals Lihue as the center of Kauai's modest nightlife. The small dance floor at patio-style **Tradewinds**, in the Coconut Marketplace, fills up with giddy locals and sunburned tourists on weekend nights. Arcade games, a jukebox, satellite sports, and dart boards entertain the less rhythmically-inclined. Although Tradewinds has no kitchen of its own, guests are welcome to order from the menu of any other restaurant in the shopping center. (☎822-1621. Happy Hour daily 2-7pm; Mai Tais $4, domestic beers $2.50. Karaoke Su-Tu, Th, Sa 8pm; DJ W night; local bands F 9:30pm; Karaoke contest Sa 10pm, darts tournament 8pm. Open daily 10am-2am.) The Coconut Marketplace also offers family-friendly entertainment with a **free hula show** certain nights of the week at 5pm on the main stage in the middle of the mall—stop by the mall to check on the schedule. The **Coconut Marketplace Cinema** shows new releases on two screens. (☎821-2324. Shows daily 1:30-9:30pm. $6.50, seniors and children under 12 $4, matinees $4.)

■**Smith's Tropical Paradise** (see **Wailua River State Park,** p. 384) hosts the island's most spectacular *luau*. Gates open at 5pm, and guests are welcome to take a self-guided tour of the gardens, or take a guided tour by tram ($1) instead. Following the *imu* ceremony (the unearthing of the pig which has been cooked for hours in an underground pit), cocktails and music accompany a buffet dinner, after which the festivities move to the lagoon amphitheater. A troupe of 25 dancers and entertainers performs in a fantastic show highlighting the many cultures of Hawaii. The multicultural aspect of the *luau* makes it unique among Kauai's *luaus*. (*Luau* M and W-F 5pm. $58, ages 7-13 $29, ages 3-6 $19, show only $15, ages 13 and under $7.50.)

WAIPOULI

Infamous for horrendous traffic, the short stretch of highway running north from Wailua to Kapa'a is lined with shopping centers that afford some of the island's best prices. The constant flow of cars provides ample customers for Waipouli's many restaurants, which rival the ritzier North and South Shore establishments.

🛈 **PRACTICAL INFORMATION.** The most affordable groceries on the island line the shelves of ■**Safeway Food and Drug,** 831 Kuhio Hwy., also in Kauai Village. Take a few extra minutes and apply for a "Safeway Club Card" to conserve a lot more cash. (☎822-2464. M-F 8am-8pm, Sa-Su 9am-6pm.) Those with piles of dirty clothes will love the triple-load washers and dryers at the **Kapa'a Laundry Center,** 1105J Kuhio Hwy., in Kapa'a Shopping Center. (☎823-3113. Wash $1.50, dry $0.25. Open daily 7:30am-9:30pm.) The Kapa'a **post office,** 1101 Kuhio Hwy., is tucked away at the back of Kapa'a Shopping Center behind the laundry. (☎800-275-8777. Open M-F 8am-4pm, Sa 9am-2pm.) **Postal Code:** 96746.

🍴 **FOOD.** Waipouli's extensive shopping centers house a wide variety of dining options. **Papaya's ❶,** 831 Kuhio Hwy., in Kauai Village Shopping Center, is a whole foods market selling fresh fruits and veggies. There is also a popular deli counter (veggie stir fry $6, sandwiches $5) that caters to a loyal lunchtime clientele. (☎823-0190. Open M-Sa 9am-8pm. Food served until 7pm.) **King and I Thai Cuisine ❷,** 901 Kuhio Hwy., in Waipouli Plaza, has a long menu of reasonably priced meals ($7-10) and a whole section of vegetarian dishes. (☎822-1642. Dinner served daily 4:30-9:30pm.) Just north of Waipouli Plaza, on the *mauka* (mountain) side of the road,

Coconuts ❸, 919 Kuhio Hwy., has a funky, modern dining room, pleasant patio seating area, and an affordable menu. The menu includes organic green salads (from $6.50), teriyaki dipped Atlantic salmon ($17), seafood paella ($20), and usually one vegetarian pasta dish. (☎ 823-8777. Dinner served M-Sa 4-10pm.)

🎵 **NIGHTLIFE.** Inflatable footballs and *papier-maché* Kahlua bottles dangle from the ceiling at **Lizard Lounge Bar & Grill ❸** in Waipouli Town Center. Talkative regulars down good draft beers in the cozy booths, along the bar, or hanging around the pool tables, dart boards, and juke box. The kitchen cooks up a number of entrees to satisfy late-night munchies. (☎ 821-2205. BBQ ribs $14, pesto sea scallops $18, Draft beer $3, domestic beers $2.25. Food served until 1am. Happy Hour daily 2-6pm. Open daily 10:30am-2am.)

KAPA'A

Settled as a plantation town in the late 1800s, Kapa'a followed sugar with rice, and a group of Chinese merchants and mill owners funded much of the town's development. While the rest of the country suffered during the Great Depression, Kapa'a became a center of commerce, thriving as a cannery for locally produced pineapple. Home to a large number of the island's residents, and conveniently located next to the shopping centers of Waipouli, Kapa'a continues to thrive today. A community of young, independent, free-spirited travelers supports the numerous health food stores in town, and it's no coincidence that the only two hostels on Kauai are located down the street from each other in Kapa'a. In fact, Kapa'a is probably one of very few towns in which it's easier to find a fresh fruit smoothie than a glass of beer. Affordable restaurants populate the historic wooden buildings that line Hwy. 56 in Downtown, and family-friendly beaches stretch nearly the whole length of the town, just blocks east of the highway. Kapa'a is also home to a number of surf shops that rent boards.

■✱🛈 ORIENTATION AND PRACTICAL INFORMATION

Downtown Kapa'a occupies a few blocks of **Kuhio Highway** just north of the 8 mi. marker. While tourists generally stick to the coast, the residents of Kauai's most populous town make their homes farther inland.

Bank of Hawaii, 1407 Kuhio Hwy. (☎ 822-3471), on the *mauka* (mountain) side of the highway at the northern end of downtown, and **First Hawaiian Bank,** 1366 Kuhio Hwy. (☎ 822-4966), on the *makai* (ocean) side in the center of town, are both open M-Th 8:30am-4pm, F 8:30am-6pm. Each bank also has a **24hr. ATM.** The well-stocked shelves of the **Kapa'a Public Library,** 1464 Kuhio Hwy. (☎ 821-4422, the red building on the ocean side of Hwy. 56 just south of the stream crossing) are available for browsing M, W, F 9am-5pm, Tu and Th noon-8pm. Four computers provide **Internet access** to library card holders (3 month pass $10). Cardless travelers can surf the web at **Aloha Dude Internet Hut,** 1387 Kuhio Hwy, next to Olympic Cafe. (☎ 822-3833. DSL connection $3 per 15min., $5 min. Printing $0.50 per page, faxes $2 for the 1st page, $1 each additional page. Open daily 9am-7pm.)

🛏 ACCOMMODATIONS

The lodgings listed below are located within a few blocks of downtown Kapa'a.

🏠 **Kapa'a Beach House,** 1552 Kuhio Hwy. (☎ 822-3313), on the *makai* (ocean) side of the road on the north side of town. To park here, drive 1 block north of the Beach House and turn toward the ocean from Hwy. 56 onto Kou St., then take an immediate right to head back south along the oceanfront access road where there are parking spots behind the hostel. A relaxed, family-run hostel, the rambling, 3-story Beach House features a shared outdoor kitchen, comfortable patio-style common area with TV, VCR, stereo, and comfy couches, washing machine and clotheslines, and a fantastic view of the Pacific from the signature rooftop shower. Spacious dorms, featuring extra-long full bunks with curtains and mirrored walls (a holdover from the building's days as a chiropractic gym), open up to oceanfront patios. Very friendly and accommodating management. Linens provided. Single bunks $23, doubles $35. Private rooms, with 4 beds and shared bath $50 for 2 people; each additional person $5. Cash only. ❶

Hotel Coral Reef, 1516 Kuhio Hwy. (☎800-843-4659 or 822-4481; www.hotelcoralreef.com), on the *makai* (ocean) side of the road past the library toward the northern end of town. Pretty tile floors, small refrigerators, fans, cable TVs, and ocean views make the phone-less, basic rooms a good value. Reception daily 7am-9pm. Ocean-view rooms $59, oceanfront rooms with sliding glass doors and private lanais $89, two-room suites $79; each additional person $10. MC/V. ❷

Kauai International Hostel, 4532 Lehua St. (☎823-6142; www.hostels.com/kauaihostel), 1 block to the *mauka* (mountain) side of downtown. Steps from downtown Kapa'a, the International Hostel hosts a predominantly European clientele of backpackers. Facilities include a shared kitchen and laundry room, cable TV, and 2an outdoor pool table. Whenever enough guests are interested, the staff enjoys leading sightseeing or hiking daytrips around the island. Dorms $20, $120 per week; private double $50. MC/V. ❶

FOOD

Hungry visitors will not be disappointed by downtown Kapa'a's numerous restaurants.

Mother of All Juice Bars, aka Killer Juice Bar, 1586 Kuhio Hwy. (☎821-1905), at Kou Rd., is an outdoor stand that sells fresh local produce and baked goods, including cold coconuts ($1.50) and freshly baked organic bread. Creative sandwich combinations include a chevre cucumber nori wrap ($5), and marinated tofu or chicken ($5 or $6)). Fresh juices, frozen fruit frosties, smoothies, cookies almost the size of your face ($1.50), trail mix, fig bars, and dried fruits ($2-4 per ½ lb.). In downtown Kapa'a, next to the ABC store, the **Full Moon Cafe** (☎822-0345) is owned by the same people and sells similar fare. Open daily 8:30am-6pm. $20 min. for credit cards. ❶

Olympic Cafe, 1387 Kuhio Hwy. (☎822-5825), on the *mauka* (mountain) side of the highway, in the center of town. Huge windows and open doors welcome the sun into the dining room, and provide diners with a view of the sidewalks of downtown Kapa'a for a meal of nonstop people-watching fun. The extensive menu will please a whole family of picky eaters from meat lovers (chili burger with seasoned waffle fries $8.25), to fish fans (*ahi* burrito $11), to staunch vegans (tofu salad $9.25). Open daily 6am-3pm. ❷

Java Kai, 1384 Kuhio Hwy. (☎823-6887), the big green building in the center of town. Good coffee drinks, including lots of cold, blended concoctions of caffeine sweetness. Cushy armchairs and popular magazines make it a pleasant place to sit, although the seating is limited. Free refills on mango iced tea and lemonade "for here." 16 or 20 oz. smoothies from $4.50; various baked goods including big muffins and yummy *aloha* bars $1-3. Open M-Sa 6am-5pm, Su 6am-1pm. MC/V. ❶

Ono Family Restaurant, 1292 Kuhio Hwy. (☎822-1710), on the *makai* (ocean) side at the southern end of downtown. Cozy wooden booths and super-nice waitresses welcome diners like family. Breakfast features lots of egg dishes, including a whole page of omelettes ($6-8.25), as well as fruit smoothies ($4), and tropical hotcakes with

Kapaʻa to Kilauea Scenic Drive

1 KEALIA BEACH. At the 10 mi. marker, the long, golden-sand beach, well-known as a surf spot, is visible from the highway. A dirt parking lot at the northern end, past a lifeguard stand and a port-a-potty, provides access to the most sheltered part of the beach. Swimmers and less experienced wave-riders are advised to stay within the protective breakwater and watch as seasoned body boarders and surfers battle the giant waves.

2 DONKEY BEACH. One half-mile past the 11 mi. marker, a short driveway leads to a small parking lot. From here, the beach is a 10min. walk down a well-marked path through picturesque privately owned fields. At the bottom, a long crescent of rock-edged golden sand awaits. Trees provide a bit of shade; for sunbathers, the chirping birds and the empty fields backing the secluded beach make for a pleasant tanning spot. The waves come fast here, and the incredibly strong breaks challenge even experienced surfers, who generally prefer the more accessible Kealia Beach.

3 ANAHOLA. A sleepy little community inhabited mostly by Native Hawaiians, Anahola's major tour-

TIME: 20min.

DISTANCE: 13 mi.

SEASON: Any

attraction is **Duane's Ono-Char Burger ❶**, on the *makai* (ocean) ...e of the highway just south of the 14 mi. marker. Concrete tables topped with umbrellas provide ...hady place to eat or to endure the sometimes frustratingly long wait. A huge variety of toppings ...nplement the famous ¼ lb. burgers (plain "*ono*" burger $4; "local boy" with teriyaki sauce, ched-...' cheese, and pineapple $5.65); wash it down with creamy milkshakes for $3. (☎822-9181. ...en daily 10am-6pm.) Immediately after the 14 mi. marker, the first Aliomanu Rd. (southern ...nch) leads to the northern half of **Anahola Beach Park.** Most residents favor the more protected ...ers of the southern end, accessible from Anahola Rd. between the 13 and 14 mi. markers, ...re the uncrowded beach and picnic tables set the stage for a tranquil afternoon.

...OʻOLAU RD. A narrow country road lined with flowering trees and wide green fields, Koʻolau ...forms a loop with ends connecting to Hwy. 56, and also leads to two of the area's prettiest ...ches. Crescent-shaped **Moloaʻa Beach** hides behind a wall of secluded homes and vacation ...tals. To get there, turn right on the first Koʻolau Rd., just before the 17 mi. marker, and take ...ther right onto Moloaʻa Rd. Park at the end of the road on the left, and walk down to the ...ch. Walk to the right, to the southern end, where the daunting waves that greeted you give ... to gentle aquamarine swells. This part of the beach also boasts fine sand that makes for a ...asant stroll along the shore. **Larsen's Beach** can be reached from a dirt road branching off ...*kai* (toward the ocean) about 1 mi. south of the point at which the northern end of Koʻolau Rd. ...rsects Hwy. 56, just south of its 20 mi. marker. A short trail leads from a parking area at the ...of the dirt road to the beach. **Snorkelers** will enjoy the exceptionally clear waters during the ...n summer months—at other times, a strong rip current can make the waters unsafe.

North Shore Kauai

bananas, macadamia nuts, and coconut ($7). The midday menu is packed with sandwiches, burgers (pineapple burger with teriyaki sauce, lettuce, and tomato $6.25; eat your chili burger with a fork and knife), veggie items, and local favorites (Portuguese style pork $8; *saimin* $4). Breakfast served daily 7am-1pm, lunch 11am-2pm. ❷

◢ BEACHES

Those tired of fighting traffic on the way to North Shore beaches happily swim and sunbathe along Kapaʻa's continuous stretch of sandy beach. Fronting the ocean just south of downtown, **Waipouli Beach Park** (better known as **Baby Beach**), on Moana Kai Rd., boasts fine golden sand and a long stone breakwater running north from the end of Makaha Rd., which forms a shallow pool at the southern end of the beach. A shower and good-sized parking lot lie farther north. On the other side of the canal, **Kapaʻa Beach Park** parallels downtown Kapaʻa. The long, very narrow beach is popular with kite surfers, who usually stick to the southern end. Restrooms, a soccer field, and a big parking lot back the sandy shore. Neither beach is as picturesque or secluded as any of the beaches to the north of Kapaʻa, on the way to Kilauea, but both are family-friendly and very accessible. Those who prefer chlorine to salt can get wet at **Smokey Louie Gonsalves Jr. Swimming Pool,** a public oceanfront pool at the end of Kou St., toward the ocean from the Mother of all Juice Bars. Although smaller than the adjacent Pacific Ocean, this pool is still a hit with kids, and you won't get sand down your shorts. (Summer hours M, T, Th-Su 1-4:30pm.)

◤ ACTIVITIES

Although the east shore of Kauai isn't as well-known for surfing as the north and south shores of the island, Kapaʻa, Wailua, and Waipouli are all home to a number of shops that rent surfboards, body boards, and other equipment, including

CAMPING
Hanakoa Campground, 1

SHOPPING
Ching Young Village, 2
Hanalei Center, 3
Kong Lung Center, 5
Princeville Shopping Center, 4

kayaks for trips up the Wailua River. **Surfboards** usually rent for $10-20 per day and $70-100 per week, depending on the type of board (short boards are generally cheaper than long boards). Roof racks (made soft, so they don't scratch the tops of cars) typically cost an additional $5/$15 per day/week. **Body boards** are much cheaper than surfboards, renting at about $5/30 per day/week. Snorkel gear usually costs $5/15 per day/week, and may or may not include fins.

Tamba Surf Company, 1543 Kuhio Hwy. (☎823-6942), located in Kapa'a on the west side of Kuhio Hwy., at the northern end of town across the street from the Kapa'a Beach House, focuses strictly on surfboards and body boards; very friendly management and competitive rates make it a solid choice for a rental. **The Wave Surf Company,** 1267 Zulu St. (☎821-1199), is located within sight of Kuhio Hwy., just to the west of the highway, across the street from the Pono Kai Resort, and rents snorkel gear in addition to surfboards and body boards. In Wailua, the **Kauai Water Ski and Surf Company,** 356 Kuhio Hwy. (☎822-3574), has a good selection of surfboards, body boards, and snorkel gear, and exceptionally low rates ($50 per week for short boards). In Waipouli, the **Activity Warehouse,** 788 Kuhio Hwy. (☎822-4000), can also meet your surf, kayak, bike, and golf rental needs.

■ NIGHTLIFE

Although Kapa'a doesn't have much in the way of traditional nightlife, you can grab a drink and party the night away at **The Shack,** 1639 Kuhio Hwy. (☎823-0200), on the west side of the street at the very northern end of town. A burger restaurant by day ($5-7), at night the Shack hosts a crowd of all ages in its roomy, rowdy interior, complete with two bars and two pool tables. Try the live jazz Wednesday 9-11pm, live local music Saturday 8-11pm, and daily Happy Hour 4-6pm.

KAUAI

NORTH SHORE

The northern, windward side of Kauai is the wettest and most lush part of an island already known for its heavy rainfall and verdant landscape. The region is a remote place on an already remote island; life for both locals and wealthy mainland refugees is slow and surrounded by beauty. In the winter, the surf is up on the North Shore, transforming its beaches from swimming and snorkeling beaches to a hardcore surfer's paradise.

KILAUEA

Sprawling pastures, organic farms, and grassy bluffs shape peaceful Kilauea. While many of the island's former plantation towns have moved away from farming and toward tourism, this small North Shore community shuns cheesy commercialism. Known for its picturesque lighthouse and seabird refuge, Kilauea is home to a motley collection of people including Hawaiian families, wandering surfers, and dreadlocked hippies, all of whom live in harmony in this eclectic town.

■✦ ⚡ ORIENTATION AND PRACTICAL INFORMATION

The town of Kilauea is centered along **Kilauea Road,** which does not actually intersect Hwy. 56, but instead begins about 100 yards to the northeast of the highway, where it branches off **Kolo Road.** Kolo Rd. meets Hwy. 56 about ½ mi. north of the 23 mi. marker; Kilauea Rd. runs for just 2-3 mi. to the northeast until it reaches **Kilauea Point,** the northernmost point of land in all the Hawaiian islands. **The Kong Lung Center,** on Kilauea Rd. at Keneke Rd., has restaurants, shops, and a movie theater. The town also boasts the only highway gas station between Kapa'a and Princeville—**Shell,** on the right as you turn off the highway into Kilauea from the south. (Open M-Sa 6am-8pm, Su 7am-4pm.) Next door to the Shell, the **Menehune Food Mart** has a Bankoh (Bank of Hawaii **ATM**) that is open daily 6am-9pm.

◗ FOOD

Kilauea's few restaurants feature fresh ingredients grown in the surrounding lush valleys. Those who prefer to cook for themselves can stock up on organic herbs and all sorts of good stuff at the weekly **Sunshine Market** (Th 4:30pm), in the parking lot next to Kilauea Farmers' Market.

■ **Lighthouse Bistro** (☎828-0480), located in Kong Lung Center. This high-ceilinged, open-air, bistro-style restaurant serves stylish gourmet food. Dinner entrees include fresh fish ($20), mango cherry chicken ($17) and cannelloni quatro formaggio ($16), and are complemented by an extensive list of wines and mixed drinks (Mai Tai $7). All-you-can-eat pasta is served nightly ($14); local legend holds that the record for the most plates of pasta eaten in a single sitting is 5. Impeccable service. Lunch M-F 11am-2pm, Sa noon-2pm. Dinner daily 5:30-9pm. MC/V. ❹

Banana Joe's (☎828-1092). Look for the yellow sign on the *mauka* (mountain) side of the highway, just north of town. Island produce, juices, and homemade granola line the counters of this friendly fruit stand. A pineapple frostie ($3), made from freshly frozen fruit, is perfect after a long, hot drive on the highway. Open daily 9am-6pm. ❶

Kilauea Bakery and Pau Hana Pizza (☎828-2020), in Kong Lung Center. Decadent cakes, cookies, and brownies will satisfy any sweet tooth, and a wide selection of coffees and teas wash down the tasty baked goods. For lunch, the ovens turn out delicious pizzas (16 in. cheese $16.25), topped with healthy extras such as tofurella, spinach and local fish, as well as traditional meats (Italian sausage, pepperoni, and smoked ham). The indoor seating area is small, but warmly lit and comfortable; outdoor seating also available. Bakery open daily 6:30am-9pm, pizza daily 11am-9pm (by the slice, 11am-4pm). ❶

Kilauea Farmers' Market (☎828-1512). A small grocery in Kong Lung Center next to the movie theater, this market sells local organic vegetables, gourmet foods, an extensive selection of wines, and basic ingredients. The deli counter in back whips up hearty sandwiches (avocado veggie $6.50, fresh island fish $7), homemade soups, and salads. Open daily 8:30am-8:30pm. Deli open M-Sa 10am-2pm; call in an order during deli business hours and pick it up from the refrigerator anytime later that day. ❶

◤ BEACHES

Other than **Kahili Quarry Beach,** most of the area's best beaches lie to the west of Kilauea in the rural town of Kalihiwai. The town's winding mountain roads hide spectacular beaches and towering waterfalls. **Kalihiwai Road,** once a U-shaped loop bridging the Kalihiwai River, was split by a tsunami that destroyed the bridge in the 1950s. The two branches of the road now meet at the base of **Kalihiwai Bay,** on the sandy shores of **Kalihiwai Beach.**

▧ SECRET BEACH. Officially Kauapea Beach, this formerly hidden spot has outgrown its mysterious nickname, and the small parking area can now barely accommodate the shiny rental cars lined up along the road. Despite its discovery, Secret Beach is still a true gem. A vast expanse of superfine golden sand sprinkled with lava rocks, the beach, one of the widest on the island, features big surfing waves, (especially in winter) and beautiful views of Kilauea Point and the surrounding bluffs. From the bottom of the trail, the sands stretch far to the right, where a sheltered cove and more gently sloping shore provide safer swimming. *(From Hwy. 56 northbound, turn right on the first Kalihiwai Rd., (what is now the "east branch" of the once-connected road) just before the 24 mi. marker, and then right again at the 1st dirt road. Park alongside all of the other cars and follow a steep, well-marked trail for 10min. down to the beach.)*

KAHILI QUARRY BEACH. Tucked away on a dirt road, Kahili Quarry Beach (aka Rock Quarry Beach) is perfect for a peaceful afternoon. The sands slope into a sharp foreshore toward the right. The left side of the beach has more protection and safer swimming, though the mouth of the Kilauea stream sometimes creates cloudy water and unpredictable currents. The quarry is usually pretty empty, save for a few surfers. In the summer, the frequent but modestly-sized waves and sandy bottom make these waters ideal for beginner and intermediate surfers. *(Accessible from Wailapa Rd., which runs seaward from the highway between the 21 and 22 mi. markers. After ½ mi., follow a dirt road downhill to the left, and park at the end. The beach is a very short stroll to the right or left. More parking is available to the left down the dirt road extension between the 2 metal posts; drive a 4WD in wet weather.)*

KALIHIWAI BEACH. Body boarders and surfers come to play in the waves off the shore, while local families favor Kalihiwai for weekend picnics. A wide crescent of sand, the beach continues to the west on the other side of the lava-rock lined river mouth, which can be tough to cross in high surf. The western portion of the beach, which is also known as Hanapai Beach, is also accessible from 'Anini Rd. where it reaches the ocean. It is more secluded than the main, eastern section of Kalihiwai Beach, and is less picturesque, smaller, and probably not worth the trouble except for the very curious. The sandy-bottomed river also provides a nice place to swim—a short rope swing will keep kids and Indiana Jones wannabes entertained.

(Take the 1st (east) Kalihiwai Rd. to the end and park under the trees facing the beach, or take the 2nd (west) Kalihiwai Rd. to its end and park in the small parking lot before you wade across the shallow river to get to the beach. The majority of people use the 1st Kalihiwai Rd.)

'ANINI BEACH PARK. The golden sands of 'Anini Beach line the coast for nearly 2 mi. A long reef fringes the narrow sand beach, creating a wide, shallow lagoon of clear water. Swimmers frolic at the eastern end of the beach, while local boat owners, surfers, and windsurfers occupy the waters to their left. County campgrounds, complete with spacious beachfront sites and full facilities, are available (see **Camping**, p. 370). The lawn backing the county park features pavilions and picnic tables aplenty. The flat shore and incredibly calm waters make 'Anini one of Kauai's safest swimming beaches, and the warm lagoon provides the perfect windsurfer's paradise.

Shallow turquoise waters and the warm offshore breeze invite young and old alike to try their hand at the sailing boards. A veteran windsurfer with 17 yr. of teaching experience, Celeste at **Windsurf Kauai** takes small groups (up to six) out on the lagoon. A 3hr. introductory lesson, open to competent swimmers ages 5 and up, includes 1hr. on a land simulator before the remaining two on the water. Those who catch the windsurfing bug can take a second lesson that focuses on advanced skills and qualifies students for certification. Rentals and surfing lessons also available. *(To reach the beach, head makai (toward the ocean) on the 2nd (western) Kalihiwai Rd., between the 25 and 26 mi. markers, and turn left on 'Anini Rd., which runs north to the shore, and then west the length of the beach. Windsurf Kauai ☎ 828-6838; windsurfkauai@aol.com. 3hr. lesson, including all equipment, $75.)*

👁 🎵 SIGHTS AND ENTERTAINMENT

Kilauea's green bluffs shelter a wildlife refuge and secluded beach; the surrounding land is dotted with farms. In addition, the quiet town is home to one of Kauai's few cinemas. The **Kilauea Theater** (☎ 828-0438), next to the Farmers' Market, has one screen that plays independent and big-budget films. Two films are usually played per day, one at about 5pm and the other at about 8pm; call for specific showtimes.

KILAUEA POINT NATIONAL WILDLIFE REFUGE. The two main features of the refuge are the historic **Kilauea lighthouse** and the wild bird population. Kilauea Lighthouse was built in 1913 to guide commercial boats on their journey to the Orient. Despite being decommissioned in 1976, the 52 ft. lighthouse still features a giant clamshell lens and an unbeatable view of the frothing blue ocean from 217 ft. above sea level. Visitors are allowed into the first floor of the lighthouse, but not up the stairs. The old communications building alongside the light has a historical display, a video, and reference books and articles about the lighthouse and the refuge's ecology.

The various species of birds that inhabit the refuge during the year include red-footed boobies (a year-round resident, and the most visible species in the refuge), great frigate birds (year-round fishermen), the endangered *nene*, or Hawaiian Goose (the official state bird, visible all year), the Laysan Albatross (Dec.-July), Pacific Golden Plovers (Aug.-Apr.), and Tropic birds and Wedge-tailed Shearwaters in the summer. In the winter, humpback whales are commonly seen from shore, as well as spinner dolphins, monk seals, and sea turtles.

Just offshore is **Moku'ae'ae Rock,** a small rock that forms an island about 100 yd. north of the point, inaccessible to man and a favorite hangout for birds. An old story (recorded in the reference section of the communications building) claims that Moku'ae'ae Rock was the first American possession in Hawaii, lost by King Kalakaua in a poker game to the American Ambassador long before Hawaii became the 50th state.

The visitor-accessible part of the refuge consists of a ¼ mi. sidewalk from the parking lot to the lighthouse, as well as a Visitors Center. The refuge is run by the US Fish and Wildlife Service, who have built educational signs along the paths and dioramas in the visitor's center, and also have workers walking about the grounds answering questions and loaning binoculars. A small bookstore in the visitor's center is run by the non-profit Kilauea Point Natural History Association, and sells books and souvenirs. Hikes to Crater Hill have been discontinued indefinitely because they disrupt wildlife, but the views from the walkway and the point are spectacular. (At the end of Kilauea Rd. Refuge administration ☎828-1413, Bookstore ☎828-0168; www.kilauea-point.com. Refuge open daily 10am-4pm. $3.)

GUAVA KAI. Fans of the sweet, pink fruit will enjoy a stop at Guava Kai, a plantation and agronomical engineering center dedicated to perfecting guava production. The Visitor Center stocks guava products galore, sells souvenirs, and shows a video illustrating the life of a plantation-grown guava. A few displays detailing the cultivation process are located next to a small table laden with all sorts of guava-flavored sauces and spreads, as well as a dispenser of guava juice, free for tasting. Harvested by hand, the plantation's guava trees have been engineered to produce a year-round harvest—as opposed to biannual wild trees—that is maintained by cyclical fertilization and pruning, as well as simulated seasonal conditions. A short nature walk features tropical flowers and a picturesque pond. When guava is being harvested, visitors can watch the assembly line from a designated viewing area as workers inspect each fruit. A small snack shop adjacent to the Visitor Center serves slices of fresh guava fruit, guava floats and other chilly treats (ice cream $2-4), plus heartier items such as *saimin* ($2.50) and cheeseburgers ($3.30). Visitors can also wander the orchards and pick one guava fruit from the trees for themselves. (On Kuawa Rd., which runs mauka (toward the mountain) from Hwy. 56 just south of the 23 mi. marker. ☎828-6121. Open daily; summer 9am-6:30pm, winter 9am-5pm. Free.)

PRINCEVILLE

Robert Crichton ("R.C.") Wyllie, a visiting merchant who caught the attention of King Kamehameha III, served as the king's Minister of Foreign Affairs for more than two decades. Settling on Kauai's North Shore, the grandly ambitious Wyllie began buying up large parcels of land on which to build a posh and splendid manor like those in his native Scotland. Wyllie was absolutely devoted to the royal family and planned to bequeath his lands to Prince Albert, the charming infant son of Kamehameha IV and Princeville's namesake. Sadly, Albert died at the age of four, followed within a year by Wyllie himself, whose estate, though divided and sold, retains its royal name to this day. Modern Princeville is a meticulously planned resort community where golf courses, condominiums, and the island's most luxurious hotel make up for the town's overall lack of personality.

✈ 🛈 ORIENTATION AND PRACTICAL INFORMATION

Located 28 mi. north of Lihue on Hwy. 56, Princeville is a resort community. **Ka Haku Road** is the main artery through town; it begins by branching off Hwy. 56 north toward the ocean at the 28 mi. mark to the immediate east of Princeville Shopping Center, and is marked by a huge fountain about 50 yd. from the main highway. It bends to the left (west) and extends 1-2 mi. until it ends at the Princeville Hotel. The only other access to the town from Hwy. 56 is via **Hanalei Plantation Road,** which is west of Ka Haku Rd. Hanalei Plantation Rd. ends in a dead end, but not before **Lei O Papa Road** branches off to the right and leads to Ka Haku Rd. in the center of the town. A gate that allows cars to turn onto Lei O Papa Rd. from Hanalei Plantation Rd. closes nightly at 9pm.

Princeville Center, situated at the 28 mi. marker, houses numerous real estate offices, and all of the following. **Bank of Hawaii** (☎826-6551) is next to the post office, and **First Hawaiian Bank,** 4280 Kuhio Hwy. (☎826-1560), is at the eastern end of the shopping center. (Both open M-Th 8:30am-4pm, F 8:30am-6pm with **24hr. ATMs.**) The **Princeville Public Library,** 4343 Emmalani Dr., is across the street and has 3 computers with **Internet access** for cardholders. (☎826-4310. 3 mo. card $10. Open T and Th-F 9am-5pm, W noon-8pm, Sa 10am-5pm.) Princeville's **post office,** 4280 Kuhio Hwy., mails coconuts and more. (☎828-1721. Open M-F 10:30am-3:30pm, Sa 10:30am-12:30pm.) **Postal Code:** 96722.

ACCOMMODATIONS

Built into a bluff at the eastern end of Hanalei Bay is the glorious **Princeville Hotel** ❺, 5520 Ka Haku Rd., at the end of the road. The crown jewel of the resort community, the hotel's floors are a series of tiers that maximize its stunning vistas. The ninth floor lobby sits atop the bluff, and the first floor opens out to a swimming pool and Pu'u Poa Beach. Although becoming an official guest of the hotel costs a minimum of $425, the Princeville Hotel's restaurants, *luau,* spa, and fantastically posh lobby provide non-hotel guests with affordable opportunities to taste the good life. The floor-to-ceiling lobby windows offer unmatched views of aquamarine Hanalei Bay and a verdant backdrop of cliffs, cascading waterfalls, and Bali Hai, a mountain peak visible to the west of Hanalei Bay. (☎800-325-3589 or 826-9644; www.princeville.com. Reserve 3-6 mo. in advance. Rooms $425-4800.)

A slightly less extravagant, but still very luxurious, stay in Princeville can be had at the **Hanalei Bay Resort** ❺, 5320 Honoiki Rd. From Ka Haku Rd. westbound, take a left onto Liho Liho Rd., and an immediate right on Honoiki Rd.—the resort is at the end of the road. Pools, tennis courts, beautiful views, and more. Ask about special rates and rooms and you might strike a deal. (☎826-6522 or 800-827-4427; www.hanaleibayresort.com. Rooms $185-390.)

FOOD

Within the Princeville Hotel, three restaurants and a posh cocktail lounge serve a variety of casual and haute cuisine to meet a range of tastes and budgets. A more affordable option is **Foodland,** located in Princeville Shopping Center, a market featuring an extensive deli (sandwiches $4) that also sells fried chicken and deli counter pasta salads. (☎826-9880. Open daily 6am-11pm.)

The Beach Restaurant, located poolside above the sparkling bay water and accessible via the first floor of the Princeville Hotel or the path that leads to Pu'u Poa Beach (see p. 397), serves standard lunchtime fare. Sandwiches with chips (turkey, avocado, and bacon $14), angus burgers ($15), and salads (grilled chicken Caesar $15) taste even better at the swim-up bar, where underwater stools are accessible to hotel guests only. Non-guests can eat and drink on the other side of the bar, on dry land, where humans were meant to eat. Bar open daily 10:30am-sunset, food served 11am-5:30pm. ❸

Cafe Hanalei, the Princeville Hotel's main dining room, features *al fresco* dining on a pleasant terrace overlooking the bay, tall waterfalls and majestic Bali Hai, giving it one of the best views of any restaurant on the island. Serves continental cuisine with an Asian flair and fresh island ingredients. Breakfast selections include french toast with macadamia nuts ($9), eggs benedict ($13), and a buffet (continental $18, full $25; M-Sa 6:30-10:30am, Su 6:30-9:30am). Salads and sandwiches ($12-18) dominate the lunch menu, which also offers a few seafood specialties (*unagi* platter $19). Su brunch buffet ($38, ages 3-12 $2 per year of age; 10am-2pm), F night seafood buffet ($46, children $3 per year of age; 5:30-9:30pm). Reservations recommended for dinner (☎826-9644). Breakfast daily 6:30-10:30am, lunch 11am-2:30pm, dinner 5:30-9:30pm. ❺

The Living Room, with plush couches and a relaxed ambience, provides a wonderful setting for high tea or a few drinks. An outdoor lanai overlooks the bay and makes for an excellent place to watch the sun set. High tea daily 3-5pm. Sushi bar, *pupus,* and desserts daily 5-9:30pm. Demonstrations of traditional Hawaiian hula and chant Su and Th at 6:30pm. Live music nightly 7:30-10:30pm, and entertainment Sa-Su 3:15-5:15pm. Beverage service nightly until midnight. ❹

La Cascata, accessed through a set of antique gates that transport diners to an Italian coastal village with pretty murals and hanging ivy, specializes in upscale Mediterranean and Italian cuisine. Named for the towering waterfalls that dominate its view, the restaurant is worth the splurge. Live acoustic guitar featuring contemporary classical and jazz, W-Su 7:30-9:30pm. Entrees $24-38. Three-course meal $52. Reservations recommended (☎826-9644). Dinner nightly 6:30-10pm. ❺

◪ BEACHES

Princeville's bluff-top location affords excellent views of Hanalei Bay and tall waterfalls, but sharp drops mean steep (and sometimes slippery) descents to the resort's secluded beaches. All resort beaches are open to the public.

QUEEN'S BATH. A deep lava rock pool carved by Mother Nature, Queen's Bath is a unique swimming and snorkeling spot. Over a ½ mi. stretch of shoreline in Princeville, waves splash ocean water over the black rock walls, and a series of pools and inlets provide swimming holes for visitors as well as fish and sea turtles. The largest of these pools is known as Queen's Bath, but in the summer when the surf is down, other pools and inlets are sometimes swimmable, too. Take caution, though, because even calm-looking seas can bring deceptively strong currents and big waves, especially in the winter when high tide and heavy surf make it too dangerous to enter the water in any of the pools. In good weather, though, the bath is one of the most enjoyable sights to see and experience on the whole island. A hike along the lava rocks yields views of pool after beautiful pool, until about a ½ mi. west of the end of the dirt trail the lava rocks become impossible to traverse on foot. Bring shoes, not sandals or slippers, for the walk from your car to the bath, and when hiking around the lava rocks, be mindful of endangered monk seals who have been known to doze off for a few hours among the rocks—they need their space. *(From Ka Haku Rd., turn toward the ocean on Punahele, which curves to the right to form a loop with Kapiolani. Just past the base of the loop, there is room to park a dozen cars, and a trail leads down toward the ocean. A small waterfall flows to the right of the trail, which ends 5min. from the road at a wide lava rock shelf. Turn left and walk across the rocks for another 5min. to Queen's Bath.)*

HIDEAWAYS BEACH. Also known as Pali Ke Kua Beach, Hideaways is a beautiful—albeit short—stretch of coarse gold sand with amazingly clear water and exceptional snorkeling. Although swimming is usually considered safe here, winter sometimes brings high surf and unpredictable tides. *(Park in the tiny public lot wedged between the Princeville Hotel lot and the Pu'u Poa condos. From there, Hideaways is 10min. down the narrow trail that runs between the lot and the tennis court. Wet weather can make the walk dangerous; use caution, and walk down in sturdier footwear than beach sandals.)*

PU'U POA BEACH. Fronting the Princeville Hotel and extending south into Hanalei Bay, Pu'u Poa is the resort's longest beach. A broad stretch of sand slopes gently to shallow and transparent water, and a long fringe reef protects a wide swath of tranquil water, where even the littlest *keiki* (children) can safely swim and snorkel the afternoon away. *(Park in the tiny public lot wedged between the Princeville Hotel lot and the Pu'u Poa condos. Accessible from a marked path that begins to the left of the Princeville Hotel's gatehouse and leads down to the beach. Use caution on the walk down.)*

HANALEI

Situated in a deep, green valley surrounded by sheer cliffs and towering waterfalls, Hanalei's natural splendor is matched by its welcoming, relaxed vibe. Within the diverse community, local *taro (poi)* farmers rub elbows with affluent mainland refugees, and everyone flocks to the colorful downtown shopping centers to socialize. The name Hanalei translates to *"lei* valley" or "crescent-shaped bay," and indeed, stunning rainbows often hang like *leis* in the rain-soaked sky. The pristine bay makes a wonderful backdrop for photographs and romantic moments; its sparkling shore also served as the inspiration for Peter, Paul and Mary's classic song about a dragon named Puff who lived by the sea.

ORIENTATION AND PRACTICAL INFORMATION

Hanalei lies just a few miles west of Princeville's manicured lawns and sprawling condominium complexes. Two retail centers, brimming with enticing restaurants and shops, face each other across the highway in the center of town. On the *mauka* (mountain) side, **Hanalei Center** features a pleasant lawn dotted with stands and picnic tables, and consists of a number of buildings. Across the way, the **Ching Young Center,** whose more closely connected buildings form an outdoor sidewalk with shops on both sides, has restrooms, payphones, and a mermaid cutout to stick your head through.

At the western end of Ching Young, **Big Save** sells groceries and has an **ATM.** (☎826-6652. Open daily 7am-9pm.) **Internet access** is available at Java Kai and at **Discount Activities,** located on the east corner of Hwy. 56 and Aku St., across from Zelo's. Discount Activities has four computers with DSL and a place to connect your own laptop to the net; $2 per 10min. They also book activities around the island. (☎826-1913. Open daily 9am-8pm.) Hanalei's **post office,** 5226 Kuhio Hwy., is immediately west of Ching Young Center. (☎800-275-8777. Open M-F 9am-4pm, Sa 10am-noon.) **Postal Code:** 96714.

Hanalei town has most of the North Shore's **equipment rental** and activity shops. **Pedal 'n Paddle,** in Ching Young Center, rents a quality selection of kayaks (single $20/80 per day/week, double $35/140 per day/week), as well as snorkel gear, body boards, bikes, and camping gear at reasonable prices. (☎826-9069; www.pedalnpaddle.com. Open daily 9am-6pm.) On the *makai* (ocean) side of the highway on the way into town from the east, **Kayak Kauai** (☎800-437-3507 or 826-9844; www.kayakkauai.com) has an even bigger selection of gear, including surfboards, at slightly higher prices, and also offers tours (see **Activities,** p. 400). **Hanalei Surf Company** (☎826-9000), in Hanalei Center, stocks all kinds of surfing gear, and rents snorkel gear, body boards, and surfboards at reasonable prices (surfboards $65 per week). The **Snorkel Depot,** 5075 Kuhio Hwy. (☎826-9983), located across the street from Kayak Kauai on the east end of town, also has decent prices on surfboards, body boards, snorkel gear, bikes, and even golf clubs.

FOOD

Nearly all of the North Shore's restaurants are located along the highway in Hanalei, and serve local and global cuisine in comfortable, and usually intimate, surroundings. For a healthy snack or wholesome groceries, visit the small, family-run **Hanalei Natural Foods,** in the Ching Young Center. (☎826-6841. Open daily 8:30am-6pm.) Their mobile **Aloha Juice Bar ❶,** parked in the lot, blends smoothies and fresh organic juices (from $3.50) and sells prepared sandwiches. (☎826-6919. Open daily 8:30am-6pm.) The **Hanalei farmers market,** where you can find fresh fruits and crafts, goes on every Sa from 9:30-11:30am in a field on the south side of Hwy. 56, about ¼ mi. past the Hanalei Center, next to the soccer fields.

Zelo's Beach House (☎826-9700), at Aku Rd. next to Ching Young Center. The recently revamped menu, which now features primarily Mexican food, still makes Zelo's one of Hanalei's top draws. In addition to the usual tacos, burritos, and quesadillas, Zelo's offers Tequila lime baby back ribs ($21), and a simple cheeseburger ($9). One of Kauai's most extensive beer lists (domestic $3, drafts $4) complements a wide variety of mixed drinks, most notably the Party Margarita: a massive 52 or 72 oz. margarita that comes in a huge glass with, thankfully, lots of straws ($16/21 for 52/72oz.). Happy Hour daily 3:30-5:30pm. Open M-Sa 11am-10pm, Su 11am-9pm. ❸

The Hanalei Dolphin Restaurant and Fish Market (☎826-6113), located on the north side of the road, in the first building after you cross the 1-lane Hanalei Bridge coming from the east. Indoor and outdoor seating afford great views of the mountains enclosing Hanalei Valley. Local fish is caught daily and is the feature of this popular seafood restaurant ($16-33). The lunch menu consists mostly of salads (fish salad $9) and burgers (fin burger, fresh fish of the day charbroiled $9). Veggie options, too. The fish market, whose entrance is around back behind the restaurant, also serves salads and sandwiches to go, as well as plenty of fresh fish. Open daily for lunch 11am-3:30pm, dinner 5:30-10pm. Fish market open from 10am-5pm. MC/V. ❹

Tropical Taco (☎827-8226), in the long green building past Kayak Kauai. A Hanalei institution, this former food truck has moved indoors to accommodate the lunchtime rush for its homemade corn tortillas and beer-battered fish burritos ($6.75). Huge beef taco $6.75, veggie burrito $5.50. Open M-Th and Sa 11am-7pm, F 11am-3pm. ❶

Neide's Salsa and Samba (☎826-1851), in Hanalei Center. Enjoy spicy Mexican *antojitos* or authentic Brazilian cuisine in the casual yet intimate dining room, or relax on the wooden lanai. Locals rave about the house special *muqueca* (fresh catch with coconut sauce, shrimp, and Brazilian rice; market price). Most of the Mexican entrees can be made vegetarian. Fish tacos $12. Nachos grande $9. Huevos rancheros $9. Open daily 11:30am-2:30pm and 5-9pm. MC/V. ❸

Java Kai (☎826-6717; www.javakai.com), in Hanalei Center. Savor fabulous *aloha* bars (made with shortbread, coconut, macadamia nuts, and chocolate) in the plush armchairs. Early birds can enjoy a sweet Kauai waffle (topped with banana, papaya, macadamia nuts, and whipped cream $8) or a fruit-filled papaya boat on the lanai. Open daily 6:30am-7pm. Breakfast until 11am. 1 computer with Internet access, $2.50 per 15min., 1st 15 min. free with a $10 purchase. AmEx/D/MC/V. ❶

Hanalei Mixed Plate (☎826-7888), in Ching Young Center. Locals and tourists alike queue up for big portions of hearty local food, and then eat on the small lanai or make a picnic of it elsewhere. Plate lunches include entrees such as *shoyu* ginger chicken, *kalua* pork, and veggie stir-fry (1 entree $7, 2 entrees $8, 3 entrees $9). Less ambitious eaters can munch on salads, sandwiches, and burgers (tempeh burger $7, cheeseburger $7, delicious corn dog $5). Open M-Sa 10:30am-8:30pm. ❶

◢ BEACHES

Postcard-pretty **Hanalei Bay** attracts beachgoers by the dozens with its soft, sandy shores. Swimming is usually considered safe during the summer, but tides from the surrounding ocean sometimes sneak into the wide bay, creating fabulous winter surf and unpredictable sea conditions. From June to August, novice surfers learn to ride the baby swells that gently graze the shallow shoreline, but in winter experienced wave riders paddle to the mouth of the bay in search of the perfect wave.

BLACK POT BEACH. A pleasant place for an evening picnic, Black Pot has a lawn with full facilities, and a sturdy pier that juts into the bay. While the picnic tables and pier provide great sunset views, the beach itself is nothing special. Named for the communal cooking pot used by campers, the flat beach blends into the sandy parking lot and slopes very gradually into slightly cloudy water. For information on camping at Black Pot, see **Camping,** p. 370. (From the highway, turn makai (toward the ocean) on Aku Rd., next to Zelo's. Take a right where Aku ends at Weke Rd. and continue to the parking area at the end of the road.)

HANALEI PAVILION BEACH PARK. Shady trees and wooden benches dot the wide lawn, and a huge pavilion shelters a few picnic tables. *Keiki* (children) play in the gentle waves that break right along the sandy shore and young body boarders try their luck in the surf as a lifeguard looks on. A great place for a picnic. (From Aku Rd., turn right on Weke. The parking area will soon appear on the left. Restrooms and showers are located alongside the pavilion.)

WAI'OLI BEACH PARK. Nicknamed "Pinetrees" by the local surfers who rest beneath the shade of the tall ironwoods, Wai'oli is a long, wide stretch of beach that forms the bottom of Hanalei Bay. Less crowded than Hanalei Pavilion, the eastern end of Wai'oli Beach features similar rolling waves. The western half is more exposed to ocean currents and consequently more popular with surf and kite board instructors. Constant summertime swells provide the perfect learning environment, but winter surf here is strictly for the experienced. Volleyball nets toward the western end offer water-free fun, and a lifeguard stand, restroom, and shower are located at the eastern end of the beach. (From Aku Rd., turn left on Weke and then right down He'e, Ama'ama, or Anae Rd. to small dirt parking areas.)

WAIKOKO BEACH. Narrower than other Hanalei Bay beaches, Waikoko is visible from the highway between the 4 and 5 mi. markers. The near-shore waters are a little too shallow for swimming, but local fishermen and savvy snorkelers find the calm, reef-protected beach perfect for their purposes. Farther west of town, Waikoko's ribbon of fine sand provides a nice place to sit and admire the scenery. (Park anywhere along the road after the 4 mi. marker and walk down to the beach. Immediately west of the 4 mi. marker are parking spaces shaded by trees that front the eastern end of the beach. A few turnouts offer minimal parking farther west along the beach, where short trails lead from the road to the water.)

🛶 ACTIVITIES

Kayak Kauai (see p. 398) offers kayaking and hiking tours (including a 17 mi., 13-14hr. ocean kayak trip along the Na Pali Coast for $175 from May-Nov.), as well as surfing lessons in Hanalei Bay ($50, daily 10am, 2pm; reserve 24hr. in advance). Wannabe surfers looking for the best value and the most personal attention should call ▨**Learn to Surf.** Most lessons are given by the very friendly, very knowledgeable, and very tall Cliff, who will meet students at whichever beach has the best surf that day. Their flexibility and friendly attitude make for a great introduction to surfing. (☎826-7612. 1½hr. lessons for up to 2 people $35; 3 or more people $30.) In Ching Young Center, **(H.S.C.) Backdoor** has surfing lessons with Australian pro Russell Lewis. (☎826-1900. 2hr. lesson, daily 10am, 1pm, in Hanalei Bay, $50. Open daily during summer 8am-9:30pm, in winter 8am-9pm.)

👁 SIGHTS

HANALEI NATIONAL WILDLIFE REFUGE. Many years ago, ancient Hawaiians settled the valleys of Hanalei, cultivating *taro (poi)* in the fertile wetlands. Today, part of that tradition is preserved in the refuge, visible from a highway **overlook**

slightly west and to the *mauka* (mountain) side of the Princeville Shopping Center. The small turnout provides a bird's-eye view of the postcard-perfect patchwork ponds and fields that cover the valley floor, as well as the meandering Hanalei River. Established to protect the endangered populations of native waterbirds, including the gallinule, coot, *koloa* duck, and black-necked stilt, the refuge also hosts migrant birds who winter in the warm valley. Through a partnership with the refuge, local Hawaiian farmers work the *taro* ponds on a rotating cycle. Early growth ponds make nourishing feeding sites for the resident waterbirds, while later growth ponds provide protection from inclement weather and potential predators. The man-made *taro* ponds also serve as the birds' primary nesting area, sheltering delicate eggs from human and animal interference. Although most of the reserve is closed to visitors, narrow **Ohiki Road** runs through the valley for a couple of miles. *(To reach Ohiki Rd., turn left immediately after the Hanalei Bridge at the entrance to the valley. A marked, dirt parking area, ¾ mi. down Ohiki Rd. on the left, provides access to a trail across the road that begins with a wooden bridge and winds uphill through the refuge. About ¼ mi. in, there is a mediocre overlook into the valley. About ½ mi. in, the trail reaches a small peak where power lines are maintained. From there, the trail switches back to the left and follows the ridge for another 1½ mi., affording spectacular views of the valley the whole way. The trail ends when it reaches a small plateau.)*

HAENA

Cruising through on their way to golden beaches, few visitors venture into the heart of Haena proper. Completely devoid of commercial establishments, Haena is less a town than a small residential community comprised of narrow roads and fancy beachfront homes.

ORIENTATION AND PRACTICAL INFORMATION

Leaving Hanalei, **Route 560** ascends parallel to the western shore of Hanalei Bay before dropping into the miniscule town of **Wainiha** and following the coast through Haena to **Ke'e Beach.**

The only convenience store west of Hanalei is the **Wainiha General Store,** on the left after the Wainiha Bridge. In addition to stocking drinks, snacks, and sunblock, it's also the last place to rent snorkel gear on the way to the beaches at the end of Hwy. 560. (☎826-6251. Open daily 10am-7:30pm.) The tiny **Bradda Lou's Sandwich Shack ❶** next door makes tasty sandwiches that are great for beach picnics. (Veggie wrap $7, *kalua* pork sandwich $6.75. Build-your-own sandwich $6.50. Open daily 10am-3pm.) The very last place to grab a bite to eat on Hwy. 560 is **A Taste of Paradise ❶,** a food truck parked at Haena Beach. Assorted sandwiches (chicken $5), burgers ($3.50), hot dogs ($2.00), snacks and smoothies comprise the surprisingly extensive menu. (Open daily 9:30am-5:30pm.)

ACCOMMODATIONS AND CAMPING

A number of vacation rentals line the narrow streets of Haena, and those with cash to burn can enjoy the opulence. A quick online search or a call to a rental agent will turn up many appealing, though pricey, options. Less affluent travelers needn't despair, as Haena is also home to the North Shore's only budget accommodation, **YMCA Camp Naue ❶,** which is located right by the 8 mi. marker at the western end of Alealea Rd. The not-for-profit camp, equipped with hot showers and located on the beach, sleeps 56 people in its 5 bunkhouses, and can accommodate tents on its grassy lawn. During the summer the camp is typically reserved for large groups from youth organizations and schools, and is closed to the public, so the best time to find a bunk here is from mid-September to mid-April. Reservations are not accepted, so to check availability, visit the campsite—a sign on the front gate will indicate whether or not the camp is currently open for drop-in travelers. Please respect the privacy of campers when the site isn't open to the public. (☎ 826-6419. No linens. Tents $10 per person; bunks $12.)

▶ BEACHES

Haena's beaches are strikingly beautiful—from the stark black lava rocks of Lumahai to the lush cliffs of Ke'e. Despite their soft sands and endless winter surf, the beaches of Hanalei Bay pale in comparison to the series of glorious golden beauties that pave the shoreline to the west.

■ **LUMAHAI BEACH.** Considered by many to be Kauai's most beautiful beach, a picture of Lumahai can be found on almost every rack of postcards on the island. Divided into two stretches of sand by a mass of volcanic rock that protrudes into the ocean halfway down the beach, Lumahai is a joy to explore. The western half of the beach, bounded by a stream, is one of the widest stretches of beach on Kauai, but also vulnerable to the unpredictable forces of Pacific tradewinds. Devastating surf and powerful currents make swimming here **unsafe** year-round; the ocean has claimed more than one human victim. Sunbathers and fans of *South Pacific* frequent the picturesque beach, and families with *keiki* (children) sometimes take a dip in the stream. Although it may appear calm, the clear stream is subject to the occasional flash flood from neighboring waterfalls or ocean tides, and swimming is not advised. The eastern half of Lumahai, also known as **Kahalahala Beach,** is even more picturesque than its western counterpart. Visitors who want to do more than just look will revel in the calm summertime waters at this end of the beach. Powerful winter tides can turn the tranquil waters into a dangerous spot. Popular with locals and visitors, the eastern end of Lumahai can get crowded by Kauai standards, but there is enough sand for all who make the trek. Both halves of Lumahai are accessible from the other—one can hike over the giant rocks that separate the sands, or walk on a path behind them. *(To access the western end of the beach, an opening in the trees leads to a dirt parking lot ¾ mi. after the 5 mi. marker. The eastern end is accessible via a short (100 yd.) trail that leads from a highway turnout down to the beach. Leaving Hanalei, the highway takes a U-curve toward the sea before the 5 mi. marker. Long turnouts lined with parked cars hug the base of the curve, and a short marked trail leads down to the beach from the 2nd turnout.)*

KEPUHI BEACH. This long, narrow ribbon of sand hugs the shoreline, hidden from the highway behind a series of residential roads. Few visitors ever come to Kepuhi, and even locals tend to pass it over in favor of Tunnels (see below) in the west. Crazed snorkelers battle for tight parking spots up the road, while Kepuhi's long reef is all but ignored. Although it is not quite as protected as its neighbor, the sloping beach provides good snorkeling during calm surf, but currents sometimes penetrate the breaks in the reef. Local surfers and kite boarders frequent the western end of the beach during the summer. *(Access from a marked pathway on either end of Alamoo Rd. From the highway, turn right on One-one Rd. between the 7 and 8 mi. markers just after Hanalei Colony Resort; turn left on Alealea and then right on Alamoo, which curves left to parallel the beach for about ½ mi. Access paths are at both ends of Alamoo.)*

■ **TUNNELS BEACH.** A wide horseshoe reef encloses the fine, and often hot, sand of the North Shore's premier **snorkel** and **shore dive** locale. On calm summer days, Tunnels' crystalline waters and intricate reef outshine the competition. Despite its fame for complex underwater topography, the beach's name actually describes its characteristic curving winter surf break. Trees back the long sandy beach, providing much-appreciated shade, and limited parking translates into plenty of space for snorkelers. A lifeguard sits at the western end, which also affords fabulous views of the surrounding mountains. There are no facilities, but Haena Beach Park is just a 10min. stroll to the west. *(Access is via 2 unmarked dirt roads. The 1st is ½ mi. west of the 8 mi. marker, just before a "Weight Limit 10 Tons" sign, and the 2nd is ¼ mi. further. The 2nd dirt road is slightly longer, and offers a few more parking spaces, but also leads to a steeper slope to the beach.)*

HAENA BEACH PARK. Popular with the Winnebago set and backpackers on their way to the Kalalau Trail, Haena boasts a huge lawn, usually full of tents. Picnic, bathroom, and shower facilities, along with the semi-permanent food truck, **A Taste of Paradise** (see p. 401), and the **Maniniholo Dry Cave** (see p. 404) directly across the street make the beach park a destination that can host a full afternoon's worth of activities. A lifeguard keeps watch over the lovely, unprotected beach. Due to its exposure to ocean currents, and the steepness of the beach itself, Haena is known to be **dangerous for swimmers.** The western end of the beach, though, is used by experienced surfers, who call it **Cannons.** *(2 parking areas are located on the highway just before the 9 mi. marker and across from Maniniholo Dry Cave.)*

KE'E BEACH. At the end of the road, Ke'e features soft sand, brilliant blue water, and towering cliffs. Kalalau dayhikers (see **Kalalau Trail,** p. 406), beachgoers, and cave explorers share the sprawling parking lot, which forks right to restrooms and payphones. During the summer months, experienced snorkelers can explore the area just outside of the reef, where an amazing variety of fish swim alongside sea turtles. The sandy shore stretches east to Haena Beach, but most visitors stick to the area just west of the parking lot, where the beach can get pretty crowded with families. Here, a jumble of lava rocks leads west around the bend to stunning views of the Na Pali cliffs—and a very popular spot for sunset photographers. A trail heads uphill from the western end of the beach to the remains of **Ka-ulu-a-Paoa,** an ancient *heiau* (temple) where the island's best hula students were trained in the ancient arts of dance and chant. The trail begins behind the trees that back the western end of the beach, and soon forks. The right fork parallels the coastline and eventually leads out over some rocks to a small patch of very secluded sand about ¼ mi. west of Ke'e Beach. The left fork leads to the *heiau,* which consists of at least two lawns bounded by rock walls, the second of which lies at the end of a 5min. uphill hike and offers a wonderful view of the ocean. *(At the end of the highway. Additional parking can be found about a ½ mi. before the end, on the makai (ocean) side of the highway, in a lot marked as "Visitor Parking" to Haena State Park.)*

SIGHTS

LIMAHULI GARDEN. The final link in Kauai's trio of **National Tropical Botanical Gardens** (see p. 414), Limahuli Garden features a comprehensive collection of native plants as well as traditional rock-wall terraces, used for *taro* farming, that date back over 700 years. Nestled in the foothills of the Na Pali cliffs, the garden's primary goals are educating the public and reestablishing native plants among more aggressive introduced flora. Limahuli's focus on conservation complements the themes of art and science advocated by its sister gardens, the Allerton and McBryde Gardens in the Lawai Valley. A sometimes steep and uneven trail meanders through the terraces and climbs up a bluff to a perch with outstanding views of the soft green mountains and bright blue ocean. *(Mauka (toward the mountain) between the 9 and 10 mi. markers. ☎826-1053; www.ntbg.org. Open Tu-F and Su from 9:30am, last entry at 4pm. Guided tours 10am by reservation only, $15. Self-guided tours, including guidebook filled with history and legend, $10.)*

KAUAI

AS SURE-FOOTED AS A WHAT?

Having hiked the Kalalau Trail once before, I knew this time I would be hiking through wild goat country. I didn't, however, remember exactly how closely I would interact with the furry inhabitants of the Na Pali Coast. Hopefully this short guide-within-a-guide will prepare you for your Kalalau Trail experience.

Rule #1: It's OK to be startled. No matter how many times you've hiked the trail, the first goat you see will startle you. You will be around the 4 mi. marker, having become accustomed to the solitude of the trail, taking in the fresh air and the awe-inspiring coastal views, when—CRASH!—no more than 20 yd. away a goat will appear out of nowhere. Heedless of the obstacles before it, the goat will shatter your peaceful world. Take a deep breath and don't worry; soon this type of occurrence will seem as commonplace as prime time commercials.

Rule #2: If wild goats scare you, make a game out of it. One fun game is "I'm a wild goat!" Best played with a friend, in this game you dress up as a wild goat, scream out, "I'm a wild goat! Baaaaaah!" and launch yourself off the trail down a steep slope. This crazy game is a great cure for the 7 mi. blues, when the beach seems far away. However, don't play during goat-hunting season weekends in Aug. and Sept.).

MANINIHOLO DRY CAVE. More of a landmark than an attraction, Maniniholo Dry Cave is a large crevice carved out of the soaring rock walls. Legend attributes the origin of the cave to a tribe of *menehune* led by a fisherman named Maniniholo who dug into the rock to capture an evil spirit who had been stealing their catches. In the 1950s, a tsunami closed up much of what was once a huge cave. *(Across the street from Haena Beach Park. Parking available in the beach lot.)*

WET CAVES. Just west of the dry cave lies the boundary of **Haena State Park,** which encompasses Ke'e Beach and the legendary wet caves. Scientists estimate that the caves were formed 4000 years ago, during an earlier geological period that was marked by a higher sea level. Hawaiian lore offers a different story, crediting the fire goddess Pele with creating the two water-filled caverns. Scouring the islands for a hot, dry home to suit her needs, **Pele** came across the North Shore of Kauai but quickly left when her subterranean explorations yielded water. Of the two caves, **Waiakapala'e,** the eastern cave, is the more impressive. A short hike leads down from the highway to the huge cave, where the water is relatively clear, and the recesses can't be seen from the water's edge. The cave is said to be home to a water-loving lizard goddess, and the graying water of the cavern supposedly reflects her aging hair. The other, smaller, murkier cave, **Waikanaloa,** is visible from the road, just a few hundred yards west of Waiakapala'e. Linked to the ocean below ground, the level of the two freshwater caves fluctuates with the tide, and divers sometimes explore the upper cave. *(A grassy parking lot on the makai (ocean) side of the highway provides access to the short trail across the street that leads to Waiakapala'e. Farther up the highway, just before the Ke'e parking lot, is Waikanaloa.)*

MAKANA. The towering green peak that dominates North Shore vistas is known to the world as **Bali Hai.** The name comes from the landmass' famous appearance in the movie *South Pacific,* but the mountain's true name is *Makana* (gift). Anchoring the northern end of the Na Pali cliffs, Makana has long been respected by the Hawaiian people. In ancient Hawaii, the soaring summit hosted sacred fire-throwing *'oahi* (ceremonies) that honored visiting *ali'i* (royalty) or marked special occasions like the graduation of hula students at Ka-ulu-a-Paoa (see **Ke'e Beach,** p. 403). Trained fire-throwers would ascend the mountain carrying narrow logs of *papala* and *hau*. As the moon rose and darkness descended, they lit their makeshift spears and hurled them out over the ocean. Buoyant trade winds held the flaming logs aloft, carrying them far, far out to sea, and the fiery arcs stretching from Makana Mountain to the ocean were visible for miles around. *(One good view of the peak is from Tunnels or Haena Beach, as you look west along the shore. The peak can also be seen from Keʻe beach, by looking straight up at the mountains.)*

NA PALI COAST

Comprised of 15 rugged miles of jagged cliffs and pristine coastline, the Na Pali Coast stretches from Keʻe Beach (p. 403) in the north to Polihale State Park (p. 431) in the south. There is no way to drive through this part of Kauai; visitors can journey either by foot or by boat. Those who do gain access to the coast's hidden treasures will encounter steep lava rock walls, lush green valleys, secluded sandy beaches, and cascading waterfalls.

The steep Na Pali ("the cliffs") tower up to 4000 ft. above the ocean; at one time, however, the terrain sloped gradually from the ancient volcanic dome to the sea. Powerful winter surf gradually wore away the aging volcanic rock, eroding its foundations and causing massive landslides. Slowly, the coast's prominent cliffs and narrow canyons were formed. Simultaneously, streams of water flowing down from the peak of Mt. Waiʻaleʻale carved out Na Pali's valleys. As they continued on to the sea, the streams formed the curtain of narrow waterfalls that stretches along the coast.

The five large valleys strung between Kalalau and Miloliʻi are fertile agricultural lands that once sustained hundreds of inhabitants. Reliable water flow provided easy irrigation for *taro (poi)* farms where the valley communities cultivated their staple food. Native fishermen reaped abundant catches in the waters offshore, and the moist, rich soil proved perfect for cultivating Polynesian crops such as banana, sweet potato, coconut, and breadfruit. Today, these trees continue to flourish alongside the more recently introduced mango, passion fruit, guava, and Java plums that have all but conquered the ancient rock terraces. The simple life of farming and fishing was standard in the Na Pali valleys for hundreds of years, until the beginning of the 20th century, when many residents began to abandon their remote settlements

Rule #3: Watch your step. Wild mountain goats trot along the edges of cliffs as nervously as you or I stroll through the local indoor shopping mall. As you watch countless goats leap away from you and disappear over a ledge, you will ask yourself, "Where did that goat go?" and "How do goats do that without falling?" The truthful answers to these questions are 1) We don't know, and 2) Sometimes unsuccessfully. I myself witnessed the fall of one goat, from a steep rock face to a dense thicket of shrubs 10-20 ft. below. Needless to say, it was disturbing—I not only wished the best for the fallen goat, but I also snapped out of my daydream and planned my next few steps more carefully. I felt like I had seen something that I wasn't supposed to see, like I was walking by at the exact moment that the door of the dressing room blew open, and Mother Nature was changing inside. Equally disturbing was the fact that other nearby goats didn't appear alarmed—they just went about their business chewing on grass and other plants. It's not that I expected a group of wild goats to rush over to their friend and check to see that he was alright, but at least that would have reassured me that this type of thing was indeed a rare event. Instead, I was left feeling as if goats lose their footing all the time, and that it might happen to me pretty soon, too. So, as you negotiate the narrow, twisting, Kalalau Trail, be sure to watch your step, even if you're as sure-footed as a mountain goat.

-Kenny Shirley, 2003

for the flourishing towns of Waimea and Hanalei. By the 1920s, the coast's only inhabitants were grazing herds of cattle, until a sudden wave of camping hippies took over in the late 1960s. Unhappy with this turn of events, the state worked to control the burgeoning tent cities and protect the wild coast from sanitary disaster. Beginning with the Kalalau Valley, the establishment of the Na Pali Coast State Park has strictly regulated human access and allowed the coastline to regain most of its natural splendor.

KALALAU TRAIL

Long ago, a series of trails stretched all the way from Polihale to Haena, but hundreds of years of winds and waves have erased the fragile dirt paths, and now only the ▧Kalalau Trail remains. Originally cleared by Hawaiian traders who traveled the coast by canoe and on foot, the trail was widened in 1860 to allow for the transport of coffee, oranges and cattle from Na Pali's valleys to markets in Hanalei.

Today, adventurers from around the globe come to Kauai to experience the Kalalau Trail, traveling 11 mi. southwest along the Na Pali Coast. It crosses five major valleys (from northeast to southwest: Hanakapi'ai, Hoolulu, Waiahuakua, Hanakoa, and Kalalau), at least half a dozen streams. In general, the trail alternates between exposed oceanside cliffs and ridges with outstanding views of the coastline, and sheltered, quiet stretches through valleys with shade and streams. Mile markers are posted throughout the trail, although they are low, brown, and one-sided (facing northeast), to the inconvenience of tired hikers on their way back to Ke'e Beach. There are three shorter side trails that branch off the Kalalau Trail, all with posted signs: the **Hanakapi'ai Falls Trail** (2 mi.), the **Hanakoa Falls Trail** (¼ mi.), and the **Kalalau Valley Trail** (2 mi.).

The condition and composition of the Kalalau Trail varies greatly with respect to the season and, more importantly, current weather conditions. The trail is 1-2 ft. wide, and rarely is it either completely flat or so steep that it requires hikers to use their hands to climb or steady themselves. Wet weather makes parts muddy, and stone stretches can be hazardous, so hiking boots with ankle support are helpful. It's wise to wait until high waters recede before attempting to cross streams.

In ideal weather conditions, a physically fit hiker can make it from Ke'e Beach to Kalalau Beach without any stops or side hikes in 5-6hr. However, rather than planning on being this person, be ready for wet weather, hot weather, flooded streams, or any number of other obstacles out of your control that will slow you down. By leaving early in the morning, you'll stand a chance of avoiding day hiker traffic on the first 2 mi., and you can afford to rest more often as you hike the dry, exposed last 3-4 mi. under the scorching midday sun. The two campsites along the way (Hanakapi'ai Beach, at the 2 mi. marker and Hanakoa Stream, at the 6 mi. marker) are equipped with restrooms and a sheltered picnic table or two. Some hikers cover the entire 22 mi. round trip in 2 days, but most people allow up to 5 days to enjoy the stunning vistas and pristine beaches along the way.

▧ HIKES

There are basically four different types of hikes on Na Pali Coast: a day hike from Ke'e Beach to Hanakapi'ai Beach and back, a multi-day hike to the end of the Kalalau trail, a hike all the way to Kalalau Beach in one day, or the side hikes.

KE'E BEACH TO HANAKAPI'AI BEACH. (2 mi. Trailhead: Ke'e Beach parking lot. Level: moderate.) The hike from Ke'e Beach to Hanakapi'ai is the section of the trail least likely to induce vertigo. A popular day hike for both visitors and locals,

HIKING NA PALI COAST

The following list is a rough guideline of the important things to consider before hiking the Kalalau Trail—keep in mind this preparation checklist is a bare minimum!

1. Permits: A state park camping permit is required of all campers as well as dayhikers who hike beyond Hanakapi'ai Beach. Permits cost $10 per night per camper, and can sell out up to a year in advance for the summer months, although check with the Division of State Parks Office for last-minute cancellations even a few days before a potential hike (see p. 370).

2. Parking: Parking is not recommended at the trailhead at remote Ke'e Beach (about 1½hr. from Lihue), where rental cars may be broken into. Instead, park down the road at the Haena State Park lot, across from the first wet cave.

3. Gear: The lighter you pack, the happier you'll be. A tent or tarp is recommended, though in the summer caves on the beach are accessible and offer shelter. You may also want to bring a cooking stove, fuel, and biodegradable soap.

4. Clothing: Dress lightly and bring rain gear. Wearing as little as possible is the typical strategy; toward the end of the trail and around Kalalau Valley and Beach you may even run into hikers wearing nothing at all (although nudism is illegal).

5. Footwear: Sturdy, comfortable hiking boots are a necessity in wet weather.

6. Drinking Water: All water taken from streams should be boiled or treated with iodine tablets before drinking, since leptospirosis can be found in Na Pali's streams.

7. Food: Don't count on finding anything edible along the trail. That beef jerky in the bottom of your backpack will taste like filet mignon by the third day on the trail.

8. Your Skin: Wear sunscreen and bug repellent. Most visitors are unaccustomed to the direct sunlight of the tropics, and can suffer from sunburns and heat exhaustion.

9. Stream Crossings: Be patient; avoid crossing quickly-flowing or swollen streams.

10. Ocean swimming: During the winter, ocean swimming is extremely dangerous at Hanakapi'ai and Kalalau Beaches. In the summer, carefully observe ocean conditions for 10-15min. before swimming, as powerful undertows and longshore currents exist.

11. Tsunamis: Try to avoid them. Seriously though, often a tsunami (a tidal wave caused by an underwater volcanic eruption) is preceded by a sudden drop in ocean level. Immediately climb to higher ground if you see or sense one coming.

12. Goat Hunting: The goat-hunting season is weekends in August and September. Keep out of the hunters' way and protect the environment—stay on the trail.

13. Preservation: Practice leave-no-trace camping; pack out *everything* you pack in.

traffic on the trail can be downright congested during the summer, especially along the first mile and at Hanakapi'ai Beach. The first mile of the trail, laden with rocks slippery in wet weather, climbs steadily uphill, affording panoramic views of Ke'e and the verdant cliffs. Less ambitious hikers can walk a short but strenuous ½ mi. and enjoy the view. A few hundred yards before reaching Hanakapi'ai, a striped pole marks the elevation below which hikers would be in danger during a tsunami—and yes, the pole is surprisingly far above sea level. A wide, glorious stretch of sand in summer, Hanakapi'ai Beach all but disappears during the winter. Totally exposed to the forces of the ocean, it is Kauai's most dangerous beach, a fact hikers are reminded of by a memorial sign on the side of the trail approaching the beach, listing the names and dates of recent drownings. Powerful longshore currents from the north and pounding surf make winter swimming here extremely dangerous. Although the beach can be calm and inviting in summer, swimmers are nonetheless cautioned to evaluate ocean conditions before jumping in. Besides swimming in the ocean, Hanakapi'ai Beach and the surrounding area offer outhouses, campsites, a few scattered picnic tables, and plenty of big boulders to sit on and sunbathe or enjoy a snack. The beach is accessible by bearing to the right after crossing the stream where it meets the Kalalau trail. For hikers not stopping at the beach, the Kalalau Trail bears to the left after crossing the stream, and continues uphill behind the beach.

HANAKAPI'AI FALLS SIDE HIKE. (2 mi. one-way. Level: challenging.) Many dayhikers combine this spur trail with the hike from Ke'e, which together form a strenuous 8 mi. round-trip. From Hanakapi'ai Beach, allow 3hr. to make the 4 mi. round-trip hike to the falls and back, which covers terrain more challenging than most, if not all, of the Kalalau Trail itself. The Falls trail splits off from the Kalalau Trail about 30 yd. past the stream crossing, and is marked by a sign with an arrow. After rock-wall *taro (poi)* farms, bamboo stands, the remains of an old coffee mill once operated by *haole* (white) planters, and crossing the stream three times, weary hikers are rewarded with a picturesque waterfall. Due to falling rocks, swimming is not recommended, though visitors are known to take a dip. The trail is not steep, but because it is rocky, uneven, and usually wet, it is difficult. It is a good hike for those who aren't camping overnight along the Kalalau Trail, and are thus restricted to a day hike. Otherwise, save time and energy and see a great waterfall by hiking the shorter, easier Hanakoa Falls side hike later along the trail.

HANAKAPI'AI BEACH TO HANAKOA VALLEY. (4 mi. Level: challenging.) A grueling ascent out of Hanakapi'ai Valley toughens hikers for the hardest part of the trail: an endless series of steep switchbacks that leads 800 ft. uphill. About 3½ mi. in from Ke'e, the trail passes between a cliff on the left and a huge boulder on the right, opening up to a beautiful view of Hoolulu Valley, the second of the five major valleys the Kalalau Trail crosses. Having left behind Hanakapi'ai Valley and the dayhikers that crowd it, Hoolulu Valley introduces hikers to the real Kalalau Trail: wild, isolated, and scenic. The trail is gentle as it passes the 4 mi. marker, proceeds along the other side of Hoolulu, and leads into the next hanging valley, Waiahuakua. Somewhere around 5¾ mi., the trail suddenly leaves the ocean behind and in a matter of a few steps, takes hikers from the windy, exposed cliffs into the quiet, shady, and lush Hanakoa Valley, whose entrance is marked by a sign posted to a tree on the right side of the trail. The 6 mi. marker is about a hundred yards short of Hanakoa Campground. Campsites appear, with an outhouse and a sheltered picnic table. The trail then crosses Hanakoa Stream at the point where the two branches of the stream meet—the crossing can be tricky when the water level is high. Across the stream are more campsites and another picnic table.

HANAKOA FALLS SIDE HIKE. (1½ mi. one-way. Level: easy.) The Hanakoa Falls Trail branches off the Kalalau Trail about 30 yd. up the slope past the stream crossing on the Kalalau Beach side, and continues up the left fork of the valley about ½ mi. A small sign on the shelter next to the Kalalau Trail points the way to the trail. The first 100 yd. of the trail are the most difficult to follow, as it crosses back over the right branch of the stream and winds its way through a few campsites. Bear left, and you will stay roughly on track—eventually all paths lead to the falls trail, anyway, and it is marked by pink and orange ribbons every 50 yd. for most of its length. The trail is not very steep, although often wet. It crosses two side streams on its way to a ridge that overlooks the stream, which it then follows for a few hundred yards to the falls. The cliffs surrounding the falls form a 270° arc that puts Hanakoa Falls in the middle of a natural amphitheater, making it one of the most breath-taking views on the entire coast, and its remote location means you will probably have the place all to yourself. The trip is easily worth the side hike.

HANAKOA VALLEY TO KALALAU BEACH. (5 mi. Level: moderate.) After ascending the ridge out of Hanakoa Valley, the conditions of the trail change instantly. The lush lowland valleys and abundant trees are replaced by arid terrain. The dry heat of the West Shore and the lack of tree cover make this segment of the trail very sweaty, but spectacular views of the surrounding cliffs and coast make up for the discomfort. After the trail exits Hanakoa Valley, it winds its way down a series of steep switchbacks and into one of the more nerve-wracking sections of the trail. Narrow and rocky, the trail between the 7 and 9 mi. markers traverses a number of cliff edges that require extra concentration to pass safely. A glance down to the frothy, churning sea below provides hikers with a peek at a few gorgeous sea caves and arches, as well as a sobering reminder of why not to fall. This section of trail also affords the first, albeit distant, view of Kalalau Beach during the summer, though in winter the high surf obscures the view of the beach from here. Shortly after the 9 mi. marker, hikers "officially" enter magnificent Kalalau Valley, whose impossibly steep walls, lush plant life, and sheer size may make the other valleys along the trail look like the drainage ditch on your front lawn. A sign marks the entrance to the valley, and sets the tone for the rest of the hike, saying first in Hawaiian, and then in English: "This is sacred land. Give it your utmost care, respect, and leave knowing you have preserved it for future generations." The last 1½ mi. of the trail are the easiest yet. The 10 mi. marker is at the crossing of Kalalau Stream, and the final mile is a nearly flat footpath along the shore to the beach.

KALALAU BEACH. Few beaches in Hawaii change as dramatically from season to season as Kalalau. In the summer, the beach stretches nearly ½ mi. along the coast; in the winter, the southwestern end is completely taken over by surf that pounds the cliff walls, making the caves inaccessible, and at the northeastern end the waves crash all the way up to the boulders. There is a strong undertow and powerful shoreline break year-round—safe swimming is only an option in the summer, and with extreme caution. The Kalalau Trail finally ends at a small waterfall at the end of the campground, where hikers often bathe. There are two outhouses, a sheltered picnic table, a grassy lawn, and dozens of small campsites. Sand campsites are on the ocean side of the trail, only a few feet from the beach, while dirt campsites lie on the valley side of the trail, hidden in the trees that cover most of the land between the trail and the looming cliffs.

KALALAU VALLEY SIDE HIKE. (2 mi. one-way. Level: easy.) This spur trail only takes about 1hr. to hike, and is a pleasant way for multi-day campers to escape the midday sun. The trail begins just past the 10 mi. marker, a few yards up the slope on the southwest bank of the Kalalau Stream, where the Kalalau Trail forms a T. To the right is the ocean, and the last mile of the trail that leads to Kalalau Beach; to the left is the valley trail, which gently climbs the valley for 2 mi. until it reaches a series of pools in the stream, known to some as "Big Pools." The valley trail passes through quiet, shady country dotted with guava and mango trees, bamboo, and agricultural terraces originally built by Hawaiians who grew *taro (poi)* in the valley until the 1920s. Other, smaller trails branch off the main trail and often lead to the campsites of some of the valley's semi-permanent residents, throwbacks to the 1960s when hippies made Kalalau Valley their home, much to the displeasure of the state and the Department of Land and Natural Resources. The trail makes two easy stream crossings, and offers at least one unforgettable view of the valley from a small stretch of trail that meanders out into a small, rocky, open field. Here, hikers get their most close-up and awe-inspiring view of the 1000 ft. sheer cliffs that enclose the valley, and it becomes immediately clear why Kalalau Valley is inaccessible from anywhere but the ocean. The trail ends when it runs into the stream at Big Pools. The lower pool is about 6 ft. deep—a wonderful spot for a dip.

KAUAI

WEST OF KALALAU

From Kalalau Valley south to Polihale, the cliffs of the Na Pali Coast are too steep and fragile for hikers. Those who wish to explore this part of the coast must do so by boat or helicopter, and countless companies of both types advertise all over the island. More adventurous travelers can tour the coast by kayak, either alone or as part of a guided trip; **Kayak Kauai** (see p. 398) leads 14hr. sea kayak tours of the coast that include transportation back from Polihale. Most kayakers travel the coast only one way—launching at Ke'e, following the currents from north to south, and making their final landing at Polihale. Those planning to go it alone should check weather forecasts before departing, as a slackening of the dominant tradewinds or strong Kona winds can make paddling more than difficult.

By sea, the nearly 1½hr. hike to **Hanakapi'ai Beach** from Ke'e becomes a quick 5min. paddle, but because the beach is so popular with dayhikers, boat landings are prohibited. Cruising past the trail-accessible section of the shoreline, boaters and kayakers pass Kalalau Beach and arrive at Honopu, the second of five major valleys stretching from **Kalalau** in the northeast to Miloli'i in the southwest. Although the hanging valley of Honopu lies far above ocean travelers, its scenic beach, divided by an arch, makes for a pretty photograph. Continuing west for ¼ mi., **Awa'awapuhi Valley** winds through a deep canyon 3000 ft. below the sheer, green cliffs. A strenuous trail in **Koke'e State Park** ends at a steep ridge overlooking this same valley (see p. 426). Nine miles west of Ke'e Beach, the beach at **Nu'alolo** is sheltered by a wide reef, so landing there is much easier than along the exposed coast. It is another 2 mi. from Nu'alolo to Miloli'i, where a reef provides safe landing at the very secluded beach. (For information about camping at Miloli'i, see p. 370.) A few more miles of plunging cliffs and amazingly clear water separate the Na Pali Coast from **Polihale State Park** (p. 431), where, exhausted from rowing and dizzy from the stunning views, tired kayakers can crash on the beach.

Not surprisingly, most visitors to Kauai forgo the kayaks and view the Na Pali Coast from the relative comfort of power **catamarans** that cruise the waters daily or helicopters that crisscross the Na Pali sky. Countless boat tour operators leave from the West Shore, and a few from the North, most offering half-day **snorkeling** and **sight-seeing** trips.

SOUTH SHORE

The southern shore of Kauai draws the greatest concentration of the island's tourists with a luxuriant garland of sandy beaches. The laid-back shoreline fronts the calmest water of the island year-round, and is the only recommendable place to swim in winter. Po'ipu Beach takes its throngs of adoring fans in stride, and Koloa still harbors a small-town ambience amidst the growing presence of tourism.

PO'IPU

The southernmost town on Kauai, Po'ipu is known for its sunny skies and white sand beaches. Huge resorts and pricey restaurants hover above clear aquamarine waves and sandy shores. Sea turtles and colorful fish also favor the warm southern waters, which offer excellent opportunities for snorkeling and scuba diving. The town itself is overshadowed by the stunning coast; downtown is really little more than a shopping center facing a wall of condominiums and vacation rentals.

KAUAI

✦ ORIENTATION

From Lihue, **Highway 50** runs 7 mi. until **Highway 520** branches off to the south. At this intersection, and continuing for a full mile along Hwy. 520, is the well-known Tree Tunnel, a section of road along which grows a row of Eucalyptus trees on both sides that shade the highway and create the so-called tunnel. Hwy. 520 leads south toward Po'ipu and Koloa, whose boundaries can be tricky, especially along the coast. So, for simplicity's sake, all of the sights and beaches lining the ocean are hereby located in Po'ipu. Five miles after leaving Hwy. 50, Hwy. 520 passes Po'ipu Plaza and forks left to **Po'ipu Road** where most of the area's resorts and condominiums are concentrated, and right to **Lawai Road** and **Spouting Horn.**

🛈 PRACTICAL INFORMATION

Composed primarily of resorts and beaches, Po'ipu does not offer a range of services. However, nearby Koloa can supply anything that Po'ipu lacks. A small branch of **Bank of Hawaii,** 2360 Kiahuna Plantation Dr., in Po'ipu Shopping Village, has a **24hr. ATM.** (☎742-6800. Open M-Th 8:30am-4pm, F 8:30am-6pm.) **Kukuiula Store,** 2827 Po'ipu Rd., in Po'ipu Plaza, is the town's biggest grocery store. (☎742-1601. Open M-F 8am-8:30pm, Sa-Su 8am-6:30pm.)

⚑**Kauai Nature Tours,** 1770 Pe'e Rd., is at the top of the hill. Geologist Chuck and his son, Rob, lead small group adventures to some of Kauai's most fascinating natural wonders. Tours range in difficulty, from easy coast walks along Maha'ulepu to strenuous day treks of the Na Pali Coast, Waimea Canyon, and Sleeping Giant. Full-day hikes include lunch, water, and snacks. (☎888-233-8365 or 742-8305; www.kauainaturetours.com. Tours $82-97, children 5-12 $49-64.) For conveniently located and fairly priced **snorkel and beach gear,** visit **Nukumoi Surf Company,** on Ho'one Rd. across from Brennecke's Beach. (☎742-8019. Snorkel sets or boogie boards $5 per day, $15 per week. Open daily 7:45am-6:30pm.) **Outfitters Kauai,** 2827A Po'ipu Rd., in Po'ipu Plaza, rents **kayaks** (singles $30-40 per day, doubles $45-65 per day) and **bikes** ($20-40 per day). They also offer a variety of active **tours** including a downhill bicycle ride from the rim of Waimea Canyon and a one-day sea kayak along the Na Pali Coast. (☎888-742-9887 or 742-9667; www.outfitterskauai.com. Tours $80-165, children under 14 permitted on certain tours for a reduced rate. Open daily 8am-5pm, phone lines until 9pm.)

🍴 FOOD

Eating out can be a costly habit in touristy Po'ipu, but there are also sandwich shops and cheap burrito stands. High-end restaurants abound, but the two upscale establishments listed below stand out for their food and relaxing atmospheres.

⚑ **Beach House Restaurant,** 5022 Lawai Rd. (☎742-1424; www.the-beach-house.com), next to Lawai Beach. Endless views (including surfers and sunsets) and the best location on the South Shore keep this casually elegant beachfront restaurant packed. The sophisticated menu blends international flavors with local seafood and vegetables. One delicious appetizer is the fish nachos with refried black Thai rice, roasted Hawaiian corn and chili salsa, and mango *chipotle* sauce ($10). Entrees include the Crusted Macadamia Nut mahi mahi ($28), and the tasty Kiawe Grilled Filet Mignon ($28). The limited vegetarian options are not quite as spectacular. Reservations strongly recommended. Lounge open daily 5-10pm. Dinner Oct.-Apr. 5:30-10pm; May-Sept. 6-10pm. ❺

KAUAI

■ **Puka Dog** (☎ 635-6354; www.pukadog.com), in Po'ipu Shopping Village. The menu is simple, and the food is delicious. A puka dog (sausage or veggie $6), a Hawaiian-style Hot Dog, inserted lengthwise into a roll via a hole cut into the end, and embellished with your choice of relishes and sauces. One solid choice is the Kekaha special (named for the West Shore town that was home to the original Puka Dog stand), which features mango relish and garlic lemon secret sauce. Lemonade $2. Open M-Sa 11am-6pm. ❶

Roy's Po'ipu Bar and Grill (☎ 742-5000), in Po'ipu Shopping Village. Hawaii's celebrity chef, Roy Yamaguchi, has attracted a loyal following with his "Hawaiian-fusion" cuisine. The ever-changing menu features an entire page of nightly specials, including fresh island fish (blackened island *ahi* $28) and plenty of red meat (Parmesan-crusted lamb shank $21), as well as dim sum-style appetizers, fresh local salads, and *imu*-baked pizzas. Reservations recommended. Open daily 5:30-9:30pm. ❺

Brennecke's Deli (☎ 742-1582, www.brenneckes.com), on Ho'one Rd., across from Po'ipu Beach Park, serves made-to-order deli sandwiches ($4-5) to hungry beachgoers as well as picnickers and adventurers who take their food to go. Also found here are some of the biggest servings of shave ice on the island ($3), and a small convenience store with snacks, drinks, beer, and most other beach essentials. Upstairs is **Brennecke's Beach Broiler** (☎ 742-7588, www.brenneckes.com), a steak and seafood restaurant that offers a beautiful sunset view over Po'ipu Beach. Deli open daily 8am-9pm, MC/V. Broiler open 11am-10pm, with Happy Hour 3-5pm daily (draft beer pitchers $7 or $10). Deli ❶/Broiler ❹

Taqueria Nortenos, 2827A Po'ipu Rd. (☎ 742-7222), a hole-in-the-wall in Po'ipu Plaza, this Mexican food stand serves up huge portions for tiny prices. Burritos are a bit soggy, but stuffed so full you can't wrap your hand around them. Burritos (meat or veggie), tacos, *tostadas, chalupas,* and nachos all $3-4. Open M and Th-Su 11am-10pm. ❶

◢ BEACHES

Recently recognized as "America's #1 Beach" by Steve "Dr. Beach" Leatherman (see **Dr. Beach on Hawaii's Beaches,** p.448), sunny Po'ipu Beach and the host of neighboring coves that line Kauai's southern coast boast excellent snorkeling, safe swimming, crystal-clear waters, and spectacular sea cliffs. The beaches below are listed from west to east, and all lie on or just off Lawai Rd. or Po'ipu Rd.

LAWAI BEACH. Its proximity to nearby condos, as well as the occasional monk seal sighting, make this short and very narrow stretch of sand and rocks a daytime hotspot. Body boarders ride the inshore waves, while experienced surfers favor the larger swells behind the Beach House. Swimming is usually safe, and snorkelers troll the shallow waters just west of the restaurant. High tides obscure nearly all of the sand, but the pleasant lawn around the Beach House provides a consistent and comfortable cushion for sunbathers and a great view of Kauai's famous sunsets. *(On Lawai Rd., about 1 mi. west of the fork and next to the Beach House Restaurant. Public parking available in a small lot across the street in front of the Lawai Beach Resort.)*

PK'S. A tiny patch of sand, PK's (short for Prince Kuhio's) is surrounded by rocks that do their best to make entry difficult. Early risers can take advantage of relatively calm waters for excellent snorkeling and private time with the big sea turtles that thrive in the often intimidating waves. PK's is also an excellent, and uncrowded, place for non-snorkelers to catch a glimpse of turtles bobbing with the tide. *(On Lawai Rd. across from Prince Kuhio Park.)*

BABY BEACH. Hidden behind Ho'one Rd., a narrow ribbon of fine sand fronts a calm, shallow pool protected by a wall of black lava rocks. Away from shore, the sand soon gives way to rock, and full-sized beachgoers will have to squat rather than swim—this one is definitely for the *keiki* (children). *(On Ho'one Rd. The best access is about a 2min. walk east from PK's to a marked beach access—look for the red handrail just past a big brown stone house.)*

KOLOA LANDING. Once the largest port on Kauai, Koloa Landing is now the South Shore's premier scuba diving spot. Local dive shops, including **Fathom Five** (see **Koloa,** p. 416), often bring entry-level shore divers here, and the waters can get downright crowded. An old boat ramp provides very easy access to the slightly cloudy near-shore water that clears up away from land. A handful of snorkelers can usually be found kicking about the western end of the rocky inlet. *(Down a 1-lane driveway from Ho'onani Rd. From Lawai Rd. eastbound, turn right on Ho'onani and park in the dirt clearing half a block up on the right. More parking is found down the driveway to the left, but space is limited.)*

PO'IPU/KIAHUNA BEACH. Running from the Sheraton to the Kiahuna Plantation Resort, this long crescent beach is backed by resorts its entire length, and a neat row of tall, swaying palms. If you thrive on activity, wedge your towel into an available spot of sand or join the throngs of body boarders. Surfers can use Kiahuna Beach or Po'ipu Beach Park to paddle out to the offshore swells that roll in between the two beaches. *(On Ho'onani Rd. The 1st of 2 public parking lots sits just west of the entrance to the Sheraton, a 5min. walk from the beach; another more crowded lot is at the eastern end of the road, directly behind the beach.)*

■ **PO'IPU BEACH PARK.** Extensive facilities, including picnic tables, showers, restrooms, a large grassy lawn, playgrounds, and a lifeguard station, attract a diverse crowd to Po'ipu's most popular beach. At low tide, sunbathers can walk all the way out to the point, but high tide submerges the pathway. Swimming is safe on both sides of the point, but snorkelers prefer the shallow area just west of the point. Po'ipu Beach is also home to one of the South shore's better surf breaks, especially in the summer, and it's a cinch to rent a board across the street at **Nukumoi Surf Shop.** Sand space is at a premium, and late arrivals will probably be relegated to the western end, where the beach narrows and the gently lapping waves are bigger. *(Access from the southern end, at Hoowili Rd. From eastbound Po'ipu Rd., turn right at the "Po'ipu Beach" sign a few blocks past Po'ipu Shopping Village. 2 large parking lots lie at the end of the road directly across from the beach.)*

BRENNECKE'S BEACH. A small, semi-protected patch of sand bordered by rocks, Brennecke's is best known for its tantalizingly large, yet still safe, body boarding and body surfing waves. The rocky shore and breaking waves also host a population of friendly sea turtles. *(From Po'ipu Beach Park, walk east just a couple hundred yards to the end of the grassy area and Brennecke's will be right in front of you.)*

SHIPWRECK BEACH (KEONILOA BAY). Po'ipu's widest beach fronts the grand Hyatt Regency. Surprisingly few hotel guests venture into this beautiful—but slightly windy—natural beach, preferring the artificial sand-ringed pools and comfy lounge chairs behind the hedge. Makawehi Point, the striking cliff to the east, recently made its Hollywood debut as a diving platform for Harrison Ford in *6 Days/7 Nights.* Healthy-sized waves crash here in the summer, ideal for body boarding and limited surfing. *(Turn right on Ainako from Po'ipu Rd. immediately after the Hyatt. A big parking lot is located right behind the sand.)*

■ **MAHA'ULEPU BEACHES.** These two pretty, relatively deserted beaches offer great kite surfing, peaceful sunbathing, limited swimming, pole-fishing galore, and a wonderful place for walking. From west to east, the first stop on the road is long, narrow **Gillin's Beach,** with little shade and choppier waves. The eastern end of Gillin's provides some swimming space, and ideal winds for kite surfers. For slightly calmer waters, either drive or walk along the coast to **Kawailoa Bay,** a pleasant half-crescent of white sand most often visited by picnicking locals. The rocky outcroppings just east of the bay are a popular pole-fishing spot. The area also boasts a few shady trees and some of Maha'ulepu's best swimming. An eastbound stroll from Kawailoa Bay to the fence along the shore offers grassy fields, beautiful views, and a very small, secluded stretch of sand where the waters are unswimmable. Both Maha'ulepu beaches are located on privately owned land, so please respect the natural surroundings and refrain from giving the owners any reason to suspend access. *(Continue down Po'ipu Rd. as it turns into dirt past the Hyatt, and turn right 1½ mi. later at the dead end. The parking area for Gillin's Beach is in another ½mi. The beach is a short walk down any of the overgrown trails from the lot, or to the right of the lot. To reach Kawailoa Bay, turn left out of the parking area and drive until the road runs along the ocean. A parking area on the right is marked by a line of boulders. Open 7:30am-7pm.)*

◎ SIGHTS

It's worth a quick drive west along **Lawai Road** for this trio of outdoor activities.

NATIONAL TROPICAL BOTANICAL GARDEN (NTBG). A verdant valley sheltered by steep cliffs, **Lawai Valley** holds two of the NTBG's five gardens (a third, Limahuli Garden, is located near Haena). A tram, the only way to get to the gardens, transports plant enthusiasts from the Visitor Center and parking lot to the valley, winding along a private road and stopping at a high coastal vista of pristine (and private) Lawai Kai Beach. Dedicated to science, the **McBryde Garden** is divided into four short walking tours, featuring native Hawaiian plants, palm trees, food and spice plants, and canoe plants. A self-guided tour of the 1 mi. loop links the four walks. Butterflies, wild chickens, and croaking frogs may well be your only company. The only way to see the **Allerton Garden**, the more aesthetic of the two, is on a guided walking tour. Volunteer naturalists share their knowledge and admiration of the garden, laid out by Robert Allerton in a series of outdoor "rooms." Children and movie fans will appreciate a stop at the three towering Moreton Bay fig trees that hid a giant cracked eggshell in *Jurassic Park*. The tour ends at the Allerton Family home on Lawai Kai, where a cottage once inhabited by Queen Emma faces a beach frequented by egg-laying sea turtles. The Visitor Center contains informative displays and a gift shop. *(4425 Lawai Rd., 2 mi. west of the fork, across the street from Spouting Horn. ☎ 742-2623; www.ntbg.org. Trams depart from the Visitor Center to the gardens every hour on the ½hr.; check in 15min. in advance. McBryde Garden self-guided tours daily 9:30am-2:30pm $15. Allerton Garden 2½hr. guided tours M-Sa 9, 10am, 1, 2pm; reservations required; $30. Visitor Center open daily 8:30am-5pm. Free.)*

SPOUTING HORN BEACH PARK. Beneath a securely fenced viewing area, a thin shelf of lava rock extends outward from the coast. Waves breaking over the shelf move water into the narrow spaces between the rocks, forcing a giant plume of water to spout skyward to the delight and applause of camera-toting onlookers. Mini spouts surround the large central plume, while another opening in the lava contributes the "horn" by spouting only air. The overlook provides a pretty view of Kukuiula Harbor to the east, a small lawn dotted with picnic tables, and a row of outdoor gift shops near the restrooms. *(On the makai (ocean) side of Lawai Rd., immediately west and across the street from the NTBG Visitor Center.)*

🎵 ENTERTAINMENT

Pub crawlers and dancing queens may be disappointed with Po'ipu's rather mellow evening scene, and those looking for a late night should catch the next shuttle to Honolulu. After a long day at the beach, most travelers are happy

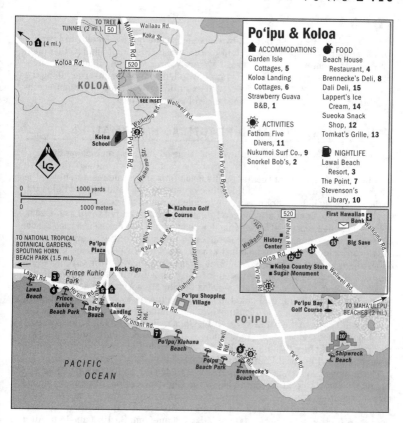

Po'ipu & Koloa

🏠 **ACCOMMODATIONS**
Garden Isle
  Cottages, **5**
Koloa Landing
  Cottages, **6**
Strawberry Guava
  B&B, **1**

☀️ **ACTIVITIES**
Fathom Five
  Divers, **11**
Nukumoi Surf Co., **9**
Snorkel Bob's, **2**

🍴 **FOOD**
Beach House
  Restaurant, **4**
Brennecke's Deli, **8**
Dali Deli, **15**
Lappert's Ice
  Cream, **14**
Sueoka Snack
  Shop, **12**
Tomkat's Grille, **13**

🍸 **NIGHTLIFE**
Lawai Beach
  Resort, **3**
The Point, **7**
Stevenson's
  Library, **10**

just to slather on aloe and crawl into bed. If you must have a drink, **The Point** (☎742-1661) at the Sheraton offers fantastic vistas of Po'ipu Beach to the east and the setting sun to the west. (Live music M-Th 8:30-11:30pm, Sa 9:30pm-12:30am. DJ and dance party F 9:30pm-1:30am. Open M-Th and Su 11am-midnight, F 11am-1:30am, Sa 11am-1am.) The opulent **Stevenson's Library** (☎742-1234) at the Hyatt features a *koa* wood bar, pool and chess tables, and a pleasant terrace. The Hyatt also hosts the South Shore's only *luau*, the **Drums of Paradise Luau.** (☎742-1234. Open bar. Reservations recommended 1 wk. in advance. Su and Th 6pm, also Tu in summer. $65, ages 13-20 $50, ages 6-12 $32.50, under 5 free. Show only $38, young adults and children $18, under 5 free.) Lastly, Kauai's only **mini-golf** course can be found at the **Lawai Beach Resort,** 5017 Lawai Rd., across the street from Lawai Beach and The Beach House Restaurant. Built as part of the Lawai Beach Resort's recreation center, the course sits inside a chainlink fence atop the resort's four-story parking garage, a long way from any natural grass, but a little closer to the stars. Don't let its gruff exterior fool you—deep down it's a simple, yet challenging course that leaves very little to blind luck. Remember to use plenty of club on the signature hole, the par-3 11th, to safely carry the course's only water hazard. (Public parking for golfers available on third floor of garage. www.lawaibeach.org. Open 10am-9pm. $5.)

KAUAI

KOLOA

Hawaii's oldest sugar plantation town has undergone quite a facelift to keep up with neighboring Po'ipu's constant influx of tourists. Historic buildings that once housed barber shops and bathhouses have been spruced up and filled with souvenirs and beachwear, and a charming raised wooden boardwalk now runs along the main street. Underneath its tourist-coated exterior, however, Koloa retains a comfortable small-town feel and a strong sense of pride in its past.

◪ ⧉ ORIENTATION AND PRACTICAL INFORMATION

Koloa is located about 10 mi. southwest of Lihue—7 mi. west on **Highway 50** and 3 mi. down **Highway 520,** which leads right to the center of town. Most of the town's commercial establishments center on **Old Koloa Town** shops and restaurants, at the intersection of Po'ipu and Koloa Rd., while others line the south side of Koloa Rd. to the east of Po'ipu Rd. Koloa is a couple miles north of the coast.

First Hawaiian Bank, 3506 Waikomo Rd., at the eastern end of town, has a **24hr. ATM.** (☎742-1642. Open M-Th 8am-4pm, F 8:30am-6pm.) The **Koloa Public and School Library,** on the west side of Po'ipu Rd. about ½ mi. south of the Chevron station, offers cardholders high-speed **Internet access,** and a huge video collection. (☎742-8455. Open M-Tu and Th-F 8:30am-5pm, W noon-8pm. A visitor card gives its holder 3 mo. of full library privileges for $10.) Those without library cards can check their **email** over a coffee at the **Koloa Country Store.** (Internet access $5 min. charge for 30min., $2 for each additional 10min. Printing $0.75 per page. Open M-Sa 8am-8:30pm, Su 9am-5pm.) Parking is at a premium in front of **Big Save Market,** on Koloa Rd. next to the bank. (☎742-1614. Open daily 7am-11pm.) Koloa's weekly **Sunshine Market** is held Mondays at noon at the Koloa Ball Park, north of downtown. The **post office,** 5485 Koloa Rd., is across from Big Save. (☎800-275-8777. Open M-F 9am-4pm, Sa 9-11am.) **Postal Code:** 96756.

The knowledgeable folk at **Fathom Five Divers,** 3450 Po'ipu Rd. (☎800-972-3078 or 742-6991; www.fathomfive.com), behind the Chevron station, offer scuba diving and snorkel rental as well as a variety of boat and shore dives. Shore dives leave from Koloa Landing on the South Shore or Tunnels Beach in the north, while boats depart from Kukuiula Harbor. (Open M-Sa 7:30am-5pm, Su 10:30am-4pm. After hours, call for availability and weather conditions. 2-tank shore dive $80, boat dive $100, certification courses for ages 10 and up, 4-5 days, $395-495.) For bargain basement snorkel gear, check out **Snorkel Bob's,** 3236 Po'ipu Rd., on the east side of Po'ipu Rd. just north of the library. Snorkel Bob's boasts free inter-island and 24hr. gear return. (☎742-2206. Snorkel sets from $2.50 per day or $9 per wk. Body boards from $4.50 per day or $15 per wk. Open daily 8am-5pm.)

⌂ ACCOMMODATIONS

Most of the South Shore's accommodations are in Koloa. Countless condominium developments and a few resort hotels line Lawai Rd. and Po'ipu Rd.; a quick online search will uncover a multitude of options. Visitors wishing to save a few hundred dollars a night may want to focus their searches on privately owned and listed condos or vacation homes. Numerous cottages and inns also offer a good value.

◪ **Koloa Landing Cottages,** 2704B Ho'onani Rd. (☎800-779-8773 or 742-1470; www.koloa-landing.com), on the left side of Ho'onani Rd., about 100 yd. after it branches off Lawai Rd. 4 colorful cottages, ranging from studios to a 2-bedroom house, all boast full kitchens and lanais. Another 2-bedroom "budget" house near the center of Koloa town, as well as a 3-bedroom house and 1-bedroom ocean-view cottage near

Brennecke's, round out the offerings. Units are cheerful, airy, and clean, and the friendly owners do their best to make you feel at home. Discounts may be negotiated for longer stays. Units $85-200. ❹

Garden Isle Cottages, 2660 Puuholo Rd. (☎800-742-6711 or 742-6717; www.ocean-cottages.com), on the left if you turn south from Lawai Rd. 4 luxurious and tasteful oceanfront 1-bedroom cottages, each with a private lanai overlooking a rocky cove and the ocean beyond. Fully equipped with washer/dryer facilities, telephone, and full or mini kitchens. 2-night min. stay. High-season $170, low-season $149; plus tax. Weekly rates available in low season. ❺

Strawberry Guava Bed and Breakfast (☎332-7790), in Lawai. From Hwy. 50 westbound, turn right onto Kua Rd. After about 1 mi., turn right up an unmarked steep hill and drive about ¼ mi. to the 3rd driveway on the right. Turn in and bear right at the "The Sullivans" sign at the fork. Small and out-of-the-way, Strawberry Guava's biggest perk is its super-low price tag. Suites are well-furnished and come with refrigerators, but not kitchenettes. Ask for the suite with mountain views—the other looks out at a yard and purple bougainvillea. Breakfast included. Rooms $75. ❸

🔾 FOOD

Sueoka Snack Shop, 5392 Koloa Rd. (☎742-1112), behind Sueoka Store. Lots of choices, quick service, rock bottom prices, and great fries make this little stand a local favorite. Hamburgers $1.20. *Saimin* $1.75. Plate lunches $4-4.50. Open summers daily 9am-3pm. The rest of the year, Tu-Sa 9am-3pm, Su 9:30am-3pm. ❶

Dali Deli, 1, 5492 Koloa Rd. (☎742-8824), across from the post office. A comfortable and modern cafe, Dali Deli provides a relaxing setting for your morning cappuccino. The limited breakfast menu includes bagelwiches ($6), and a tasty breakfast burrito ($8). Lunch features hot and cold sandwiches ranging from tuna salad ($6.25) to cheese steak ($8) and portobello mushroom ($8.75). Breakfast served until 11am. By night Dali Deli becomes **Cafe Cara,** a sophisticated but casual Italian restaurant. *Bistecca* (herb-stuffed, rolled tenderloin; $17) and Tuna on Polenta ($15) are among the gourmet dishes served for dinner, in addition to a variety of salads, pastas, and appetizers. Open M-Sa 8am-3pm. Cafe Cara open Tu-Sa 5:30pm-9pm. MC/V. ❷-❸

Lappert's Ice Cream (☎742-1272), in the middle of downtown, is a bright ice cream parlor with 25+ flavors and lots of icy goodness. Made right here in Kauai, many of the options feature island flavors. A coffee and espresso bar, plus plenty of baked goods, make for a tasty breakfast. Ice cream $3.10 per scoop. Open daily 6am-10pm. ❶

Tomkats Grille, 5404 Koloa Rd. (☎742-8887), near the middle of the downtown storefronts. Although the "kat" theme and the menu full of words misspelled with a "k" may make any intelligent kustomer want to skream, this breezy patio-style restaurant boasts a big menu and tasty food. Sheltered tables surround a sunken, outdoor garden. Nibblers include crab-stuffed mushrooms ($7.50) and jalapeño poppers ($6.25). Entrees feature fish, steak, and sandwiches ($6.25-25.50), with vegetarian options limited to salad or a Garden Burger ($7.25). "Kitten" meals $3.50-4. Happy Hour daily 3-6pm; Mai Tais $4, beer $2. Restaurant open daily 11am-10pm, bar until 12:30am. MC/V. ❸

🔾 SIGHTS

Koloa ("long cane") was established in 1834 as a commercial center for the plantation community. Home to a sugar plantation and the major sea port of Koloa Landing, the town soon developed into a hub of activity. As quickly as they had arrived, throughout the 19th century, oranges, sweet potatoes, and sugar left Koloa Landing for California. Ever proud of its key role in Hawaii's history, Koloa markets itself as Old Koloa Town.

KAUAI

A **History Center,** next to the Country Store, presents a life-size diorama of plantation life with interpretive plaques. Across the street, at the corner of Koloa Rd. and Hwy. 520, a grassy field immortalizes the plantation tradition. Koloa's **Sugar Monument,** a registered national historical landmark, features a circular concrete sculpture that represents a mill stone opened to show seven bronze figures, each signifying one of the main ethnic groups—Hawaiian, Puerto Rican, Chinese, Korean, Japanese, Filipino, and Portuguese—who played a role in Hawaii's history. A plaque facing the monument describes an eighth figure as well, a Caucasian overseer on horseback, whose image was omitted at the last minute in response to heavy criticism. The accompanying plaques will teach you more about the sugar industry than you ever desired to know.

WEST SHORE

Though the region maintains the sense of a small-town community, authenticity is tempered by the inevitable appearance of vacation rentals and extravagant houses. The towns of the West Shore serve as gateways to the grand parks farther north—Waimea Canyon State Park, Koke'e State Park and Polihale State Park. According to Hawaiian myth, the souls of the dead followed the path of the sun west, departing the world in a blaze of glory in the famed sunsets at Polihale.

KALAHEO

A quiet one-light town, Kalaheo doesn't offer much in the way of tourist attractions, but a couple of solid accommodations make the town worth a stop.

■♦ ◪ **ORIENTATION AND PRACTICAL INFORMATION.** Kalaheo is located 11 mi. west of Lihue on **Highway 50** and nearly all of the establishments listed below line the highway. The **post office,** 4489 Papalina Rd. (☎800-275-8777), behind Kalaheo Coffee Company, is open M-F 8am-4pm, Sa 8-10am. **Postal Code:** 96741.

◪ **ACCOMMODATIONS.** Kalaheo has two excellent accommodations for the traveler on a budget. To get to ◪**Classic Vacation Cottages ❷,** 2687 Onu Pl., turn right on Puuwai Rd. just after entering Kalaheo and stay to the right. Onu Place will be on the left. Tucked away from the main road, but still just a minute or two from the center of Kalaheo, the 12 units are all unique and range from studios to a four-bedroom house; some of the studios have kitchenettes, the larger units all have full kitchens.

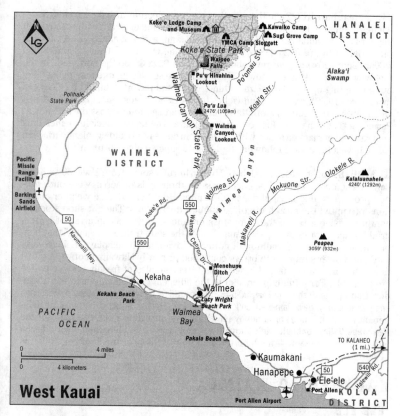

West Kauai

The owners have stocked enough beach, picnic gear, and sporting equipment (including bikes, tennis racquets, and golf clubs) in their garage to make Wal-Mart jealous. Charcoal grills, a six-person Jacuzzi, and free use of the Kiahuna Tennis Club facilities (in Po'ipu) round out the fun. (☎332-9201; fax 332-7645; clascot@hawaiian.net. Free laundry on-site. Studios from $45; cottages and houses $75-$100. Discounts can be negotiated for longer stays. Ask about off-site cottages, which have been recently added to the offerings and have similar facilities and price tags.) Another good value is the **Kalaheo Inn ❸**, 4444 Papalina Rd. Turn south onto Papalina Rd. at the stoplight where it intersects Hwy. 50; the inn will be one block up on the left. Plain but sparkling clean, the 15 suites with kitchens are arranged in tidy rows. There is laundry on-site, a small collection of beach and sports equipment free for borrowing, and free use of the Kiahuna Tennis Club facilities. (☎888-332-6023 or 332-6023; www.kalaheoinn.com. 2-night min. stay. Units range from $55-135; 20% discount for month-long stays.)

◘ **FOOD.** Outstanding Italian food, a friendly coffee shop, juicy hamburgers, and the island's best pizza make Kalaheo the hidden gem of Kauai dining. **Kalaheo Coffee Company & Cafe ❶**, on the *makai* (ocean) side of the highway just past Papalina Rd., is a popular local meeting spot. Breakfast features egg dishes (from

KAUAI

$5), a great burrito ($7), and a mouth-watering selection of baked goods. Sand-wiches dominate the lunch menu (grilled cajun tofu and eggplant with roasted bell peppers $7.25), and taste even better with a foaming cup of chai. Parking in back off Papalina Rd. (☎332-5858; www.kalaheo.com. Open M-F 6am-2:30pm, Sa-Su 6:30am-2pm.) *Kama'aina* rave about **Brick Oven Pizza ❷,** on the north side of the highway on the east end of town. The small table service charge may make take-out a tempting option. The pizza is thin-crusted and flavorful, but a bit pricey (15 in. cheese $19.50), with hot sandwiches from $7 and salads ($3.25-7). (☎332-8561. Open Tu-Su 11am-10pm.) More Italian cuisine can be found across the highway at **Pomodoro ❹,** on the 2nd floor of Rainbow Plaza. The house specialties, including veal sauteed in marsala sauce with fresh mushrooms ($20) and eggplant parmesan ($18), have a loyal local following. (☎332-5945. Open daily 5:30-10pm.)

◩ SIGHTS. Just west of Kalaheo, Hwy. 540 runs south from Hwy. 50 to **Kauai Coffee.** The oceanfront fields, encompassing thousands of acres, were once pro-lific producers of sugar and macadamia nuts. However, adverse weather condi-tions prompted the switch to coffee about a decade ago. The gift shop stocks a comprehensive array of the company's products, as well as an array of coffee-drinking accessories. A covered lanai divides the shop from a "museum" that hon-ors the long Hawaiian tradition of coffee cultivation. The displays include early MJB and Folger's tins—both brews contained primarily Hawaiian coffee. A video illustrates the coffee-making process, and free samples of freshly-brewed coffee are available. For a full cup, check out the adjacent coffee bar, which has a win-dow that opens to the lanai (☎800-545-8605 or 335-0813; www.kauaicoffee.com. Gift shop and museum open daily 9am-5pm, coffee bar 9am-4pm. Free.) A short drive west of Kala-heo, at the 14 mi. marker, a newly paved turnout provides a place to park for the **Hanapepe Valley Lookout.** High above the valley, the well-maintained vista offers a wide, impressive view—much better than that of the previous lookout, which is obscured by overgrowth.

KALAHEO TO WAIMEA

'ELE'ELE

A residential community situated along the western shore of the Hanapepe River, across from the 16 mi. marker, 'Ele'ele contains a noteworthy sight and a surpris-ingly comprehensive cluster of businesses. The **'Ele'ele Shopping Center** houses fast food outlets, a **Big Save** (open M-Sa 6:30am-10pm, Su 6:30am-9pm), a branch of **First Hawaiian Bank** (open M-Th 8:30am-4pm, F 8:30am-6pm, **24hr. ATM**), a **laundro-mat** (open 24hr.), and a small **post office** (open M-F 8am-4pm, Sa 9am-11am). Two popular restaurants cater to locals and Waimea Canyon-bound tourists. ◪**Toi's Thai Kitchen ❷,** features a huge menu of delicious entrees, all served with papaya salad, a choice of rice, and dessert (house specialty Toi's Temptation $12-17). Those wary of new flavors can order from the "American plate" section, which includes honey dip chicken and french fries. (☎335-3111. Open M-Sa 10:30am-2pm and 5:30pm-9pm. Karaoke Sa 9:30pm-1:30am. AmEx/MC/V.) At the far end of the shop-ping center, ◪**Grinds Cafe and Espresso ❶** offers a basic menu of baked goods ($1.25), pizza (15 in. cheese $12.50; slice $3), and breakfast all day (from $4). Din-ner is still affordable (mahi mahi $7.50; chili and rice $4.50), but slightly more sophisticated. Cushy seats in the corner make a comfy place to sip coffee. (☎335-6027; www.grindscafe.net. Open daily 5:30am-9pm. AmEx/D/MC/V.)

Continuing south from the 'Ele'ele Shopping Center, Hwy. 541 (Waialo Rd.) forks right to Port Allen and left to the unique sands of **Glass Beach.** From Waialo, turn left on Aka Ula and right onto the dirt road. Glass Beach is just below, before

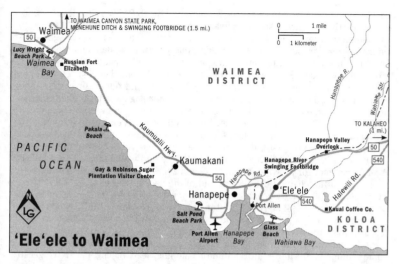

'Ele'ele to Waimea

the road turns left. You can park in a dirt turnout on the right side of the road where it runs into the beach. Named for its once-famed shores, made up of sea glass particles washed ashore from fishing boats and auto parts, Glass Beach has deteriorated. A decade ago, the black lava rocks, green cliffs, and crashing blue surf highlighted the sparkling multi-hued beauty of the beach. Today, the beach still shines, but mostly clear or brown, against its industrial backdrop of oil silos. Once a hidden gem, Glass Beach's "discovery" led to its downfall—each visitor, dazzled by the glistening shore, pocketed a tiny handful of its beauty.

HANAPEPE

The "biggest little town" on Kauai, Hanapepe entices visitors with art galleries, gourmet vegetarian cuisine, and a unique bridge. Less than ¼ mi. past the 'Ele'ele Shopping Center, a few signs on the right side of the highway mark the turn for Hanapepe Rd. The road swings to the north of Hwy. 50 and creates a mile-long loop that hosts Hanapepe's historic downtown area. In addition to the usual general stores and banks, the horseshoe-shaped downtown is lined with storefronts featuring the works of local painters, artisans, and designers. Erratic hours sometimes frustrate would-be gallery browsers, and true art-lovers would be best off visiting the town on Friday evenings. From 6 to 9pm, over half-a-dozen galleries celebrate **Art Night** (a.k.a. Art Walk), during which, besides staying open late, many galleries offer drinks, snacks, and occasional live entertainment. A darling of earth-crunchy food connoisseurs island-wide, the **Hanapepe Cafe ❸**, 3830 Hanapepe Rd., satiates veggie-craving tummies with healthy breakfasts (tofu scrambler $9.75), lunches (grilled vegetable sandwich $9), salads (from $6), and flavorful pastas (southwestern lasagne $18.75) from its entirely vegetarian menu. (☎335-5011. Open Tu-Sa 9am-2pm, dinner served F 6-9pm.) A visit to the ⬛**Green Garden Restaurant ❸**, won't disappoint. Located on the north side of Hwy. 50 just below the eastern end of downtown, it has a garden-like atmosphere, indeed. Won tons and spring rolls are among the appetizers, while entrees include *ahi* or *ono* ($17), a delicious, juicy filet mignon ($21), the seafood special (mahi mahi fillet, scallops, oysters, and fried shrimp; $14.25), and a few veggie options, like the veggie kabob ($14). All entrees come with soup or salad from a basic, but tasty, salad bar.

KAUAI

(☎335-5422. Open for dinner M and W-Su 5-9pm. AmEx/MC/V.) For dessert, look no further than the **Kauai Kookie Kompany** factory, 3959 Kaumualii Hwy. (Hwy. 50), located on the north side of Hwy. 50 on the western end of town. A small gift shop offers visitors free samples of the cookies, many with Hawaiian-inspired flavors. On some mornings, a brief tour of the factory is possible; ask for details. (☎800-361-1126; www.kauaikookie.com. Shop open M-F 8am-4pm, Sa-Su 9am-4pm.)

A slightly unsteady, but thrilling, view of the hills and fields surrounding the town can be had from the middle of Hanapepe's **swinging footbridge.** The bridge is near the eastern end of town, behind a gravel parking lot just west of a big green building, about 100 yd. after the road through downtown curves to the left. "No diving off bridge" signs are posted for the safety of the insane few. Just west of Hanapepe, a left turn past the 17 mi. marker onto Lele Rd. leads south to one of Kauai's best-kept secrets. *Kama'aina* of all ages and walks of life treasure **Salt Pond Beach Park** for its wide curving bay and soft sands. The park gets its name from the salt flats behind the eastern end of the beach, where locals still harvest salt by letting the sun dry ocean water. Signs warn visitors not to interfere with the salt-gathering process, so resist the temptation to trespass. Gentle swells make their way over the rocky bar that encloses the uncrowded waters, which are perfect for swimming and not bad for snorkeling. Restrooms, showers, and grills make for a great picnic site. On the eastern end of the beach, a grassy field welcomes campers. For more information on camping, see **Camping,** p. 370. To get to the beach, turn south onto Lele Rd. from Hwy. 50 just west of the 17 mi. marker, and then follow signs which direct you to take a right onto Lolokai Rd.

KAUMAKANI TO MAKAWELI

Most drivers cruise right by the small dirt roads that lead into the sugar plantation towns of Kaumakani and Makaweli, and the Robinson family probably prefers it this way. The close-knit plantation community of Makaweli, which boasts more than a few emigrants from mysterious Ni'ihau, keeps tourists away with a number of "Private Property" signs. The sugar cane fields that dominate this stretch of highway belong to **Gay and Robinson,** the only operating family-run sugar plantation left on the islands. The Visitor Center, on Kaumakani Ave., has displays of sugar history and plantation life. The Olokele tour takes visitors north to the Olokele Ditch, which is the water source for the plantation. The Field and Factory Tour includes a walk through the sugar processing factory and the sugarcane fields. (Turn left off westbound Hwy. 50 right after the 19 mi. marker. ☎335-2824. Tour reservations recommended. Both tours offered M-F 9am, 1pm. Field and Factory Tour 2hr. $31, children 7-15 $21. Children under age 7 are not allowed on the factory portion of the tour. Olokele Tour 3½hr. $60. For tours, wear closed-toe shoes and clothes that can get dirty. Visitor Center open M-F 8am-4pm, Sa 11am-3pm.)

Also along this stretch of highway is **Pakala Beach,** one of the west shore's best surf spots. The beach is nicknamed "Infinities," because the breaks here are some of the longest-lasting on the island. The muddy water and narrow beach are poor for swimming or sunbathing, and there are no facilities here, making it almost exclusively a surfing destination (for experienced surfers only). A 5min. walk along a short path leads from Hwy. 50 to the beach. The path is located past the west end of the guardrail on the south side of the highway, immediately west of the 21 mi. marker, where there is plenty of room to park on both sides of the road.

WAIMEA

Once an important agricultural port, Waimea was the first stop for many visitors to Hawaii, including Christian missionaries, Russian emissaries, and the legendary Captain Cook. The historic wooden buildings that line Waimea Rd. downtown

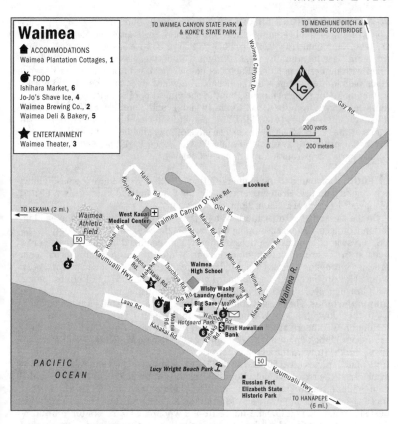

Waimea

🏠 ACCOMMODATIONS
Waimea Plantation Cottages, **1**

🍎 FOOD
Ishihara Market, **6**
Jo-Jo's Shave Ice, **4**
Waimea Brewing Co., **2**
Waimea Deli & Bakery, **5**

⭐ ENTERTAINMENT
Waimea Theater, **3**

TO WAIMEA CANYON STATE PARK
& KOKE'E STATE PARK

TO MENEHUNE DITCH &
SWINGING FOOTBRIDGE

Waimea Canyon Dr.

Gay Rd.

0   200 yards
0   200 meters

■ Lookout

Keopewa St.

Haina Rd.

Nele Rd.

Oioi Rd.

TO KEKAHA (2 mi.)

Waimea
Athletic
Field

West Kauai ✚
Medical Center

Waimea Canyon Dr.

Haina Rd.

Maule Rd.

Kanu Rd.

Menehune Rd.

Oma Rd.

Huakai Rd.

Kaumualii Hwy.

Waena Rd.

Makeke Rd.

Tsuchiya Rd.

Waimea
High School

Nima Pl.

Ape Pl.

Alanai Rd.

Waimea R.

Laau Rd.

Wishy Washy
Laundry Center

Big Save

Ola Rd.

Maile Rd.

Moana Rd.

Kahakai Rd.

Waimea Rd.

Hofgaard Park

Parako Rd.

First Hawaiian
Bank

PACIFIC
OCEAN

Lucy Wright Beach Park

50

Kaumualii Hwy.

Russian Fort
Elizabeth State
Historic Park

TO HANAPEPE
(6 mi.)

---

date back to the town's colorful past. Nowadays, Waimea's dusty streets and swinging doors call forth images of spaghetti Westerns with high-noon show-downs. There's no shortage of genuine hospitality, however; the few tourists who lounge over a picnic in Hofgaard Park or take in a movie at the fabulous Waimea Theater are warmly welcomed into the community.

■₽ ORIENTATION AND PRACTICAL INFORMATION. The biggest town on the West Shore, Waimea lies 23 mi. west of Lihue on **Highway 50**. After crossing the Waimea River just beyond Fort Elizabeth, the highway runs through the center of town. Most services and restaurants lie right along the highway or on Waimea Rd.

The stately **First Hawaiian Bank,** 4525 Panako Rd., has a **24hr. ATM.** (☎338-1611. Open M-Th 8:30am-4pm, F 8:30am-6pm.) **Waimea Library,** 9750 Kaumualii Hwy., is a good place to catch up on the news or surf the **Internet.** (☎338-6848. Open M and W noon-8pm, Tu and Th 9am-5pm, F 10am-5pm. Visitor Cards, $10, give 3 months of full library privileges.) Wash the red dirt out of your shorts at **Wishy Washy Laundry Center,** on Waimea Rd., across from the monument. (Wash $1, dry $0.50. Open 24hr.) Other services include: the **police** (☎338-1831), on the *mauka* (mountain) side of the highway, across Menehune Rd. from Big Save; the **West Kauai Medical Center,** 4643 Waimea Canyon Dr. (☎338-9431); and the **post office,** 9911 Waimea Rd. (☎800-275-8777. Open M-F 8:30am-4pm, Sa 8:30-10:30am.) **Postal Code:** 96796.

⛺ ACCOMMODATIONS AND CAMPING. Originally built to house sugar plantation workers at the beginning of the 20th century, the **Waimea Plantation Cottages ❹**, 9400 Kaumualii Hwy #367 (☎800-922-7866 or 338-1625; www.waimea-plantation.com), are located just west of town. The cottages have been restored and filled with modern amenities. Each has its own lanai overlooking either the spacious palm-dotted grounds or the ocean. The windy dark-sand beach and murky waters make for poor swimming, but the oceanfront pool is a pleasant place for a dip. Units range from the Hotel Room (which is still a cottage, $115-130, to studios with kitchenettes ($130-145), and lastly to the very luxe five-bedroom manager's estate ($545-625). On the eastern edge of town, by the mouth of the Waimea River, **Campsites** are available in Lucy Wright Beach Park (see **Sights**, p. 424), a county park. For permit information, see **Camping**, p. 370.

🍴 FOOD. Compared to the limited offerings of other West Shore towns, Waimea is a diner's paradise. Grab groceries at the **Big Save**, on the corner of Hwy. 50 and Waimea Rd. (Open M-Sa 6am-10pm, Su 6am-9pm.)

On the west edge of town, located along the same driveway as the Waimea Plantation Cottages, **⬛Waimea Brewing Company ❸**, the western-most brewery in the US, serves good food at big prices. A roomy, high-ceilinged interior gives diners a peek at the microbrewery behind the bar, while the outdoor patio provides a breezier setting for a meal. The casual menu features hearty sandwiches (*ahi poke* wrap $11; ½ lb. burger $9) and standard *pupus* (onion rings $7.25). Entrees (penne with Portuguese sausage and grilled chicken $19; strip steak $20) appeal to the truly carnivorous. They've got some of the best burgers around—for a challenge, try to take down the 1 lb. Waimea Canyon Burger ($16). Over half-a-dozen tasty, locally brewed beers are named after different parts of the island. (Open daily 11am-9pm.) Stock up for a big day of hiking at **⬛Ishihara Market ❶**, 9894 Kaumualii Hwy., *makai* (toward the sea) and across from the Cook Monument. Everything—from plate lunches ($6-6.50) and sushi ($3) to sandwiches ($4) and salads ($3)—is available at the extensive deli. No indoor seating, though. (☎338-1751. Open M-F 6am-8:30pm, Sa-Su 7am-8:30pm. MC/V.) **⬛Jo-Jo's Shave Ice ❶**, on the *makai* (ocean) side of the highway, across from the high school, has been crowned the best shave ice ($2) on Kauai. Choose from a whopping 60 flavors for your ultra-fine ice. (Open daily 11am-6pm.) Locals rave about the delicious sandwiches served at the **Waimea Deli and Bakery ❶**, 9875 Waimea Rd. Gourmet made-to-order sandwiches feature mahi mahi or *ahi* ($6.50), *kalua* pork ($5.50), or a homemade *taro* burger ($5.50) served on just-baked sweetbread, which is the best part of all. Fresh juices and baked goodies full of local fruits complement lunch or breakfast, which you can take out for a picnic or enjoy at one of the three or four tables in the small dining room. (☎338-1950. Open M and W-Su 6:30am-4pm.)

🔷🎵 SIGHTS AND ENTERTAINMENT. On the way into town from the east, just before Hwy. 50 crosses the Waimea River, lie the remnants of **Russian Fort Elizabeth.** An information board near the parking lot provides a brief history of the fort, guide maps, and a map of the ruins outlining a path that tours the interior and exterior of the fort. Unfortunately, the real path is confusing and only remotely resembles its mapped version. Although as a tourist attraction the fort has room for improvement, it may be enjoyable for the history buff who appreciates the story as well as the strategic implications of the site and the structure of the fort.

Two sites commemorate **Captain James Cook,** the British explorer who discovered the Hawaiian islands and who first landed at Waimea in 1778. The triangle of grass that separates Waimea Rd. from the highway is **Hofgaard Park,** a monument to the captain. At the southern end of Alawai Rd., a small dirt parking lot faces the mouth of the Waimea River and a solitary boulder directly to the south, in **Lucy Wright Beach Park.** A small plaque (now decorated with graffiti) that is embedded in the rock memorializes Capt. Cook's landing spot. The park also has a baseball field and a grassy area available to campers, with showers, restrooms, picnic tables and a pavilion. The beach is small and relatively unused.

Long before Captain Cook's arrival, the *menehune* constructed their own monuments in Waimea. Off the beaten path, along the western bank of the Waimea River, 1½ mi. north of the highway, a narrow ditch runs along the left side of Menehune Rd. Many years ago, Hawaii's legendary little people dug this ditch to divert the flow of the river, and it still functions to this day. Much of the ancient **Menehune Ditch** has been obscured by road construction and development, but sections of the rock wall are still visible. Right across the street from where the **swinging footbridge** crosses the river, a plaque honors the *menehune* and their miraculous building skills. About 20 yd. down the road, the ditch enters a tunnel carved into the mountain, an impressive display of ancient rock carving.

Originally housed in an Art Deco building that boasted the first electric marquee on Kauai, the restored ⬛**Waimea Theater,** 9691 Kaumualii Hwy., is still a local landmark. The large screen and modern sound system don't detract from the charm of the "loge"—two rows of roomy rattan armchairs that put standard movie theater seats to shame. (☎338-0282 for show times. $6, students, seniors over 55, and military $5, children 5-12 $4. Films Tu-Su 7:30pm, and some weekends at 2:30, 5pm.)

WAIMEA CANYON STATE PARK

Brilliant red cliffs plunge into a lush green valley, carved by streams and faults millions of years ago. Soaring birds, fragrant flowers, and the constant buzz of tourist-laden helicopters complete the scene. After a visit, you'll see why Waimea Canyon State Park has been nicknamed "The Grand Canyon of Kauai."

👁 LOOKOUTS

From central Waimea, Waimea Canyon Dr. slowly winds its way up to the rim of the canyon, joining the much more relaxed—but not nearly as scenic—Koke'e Rd. after just under seven glorious miles. Every one of the road's turns has a great view. About ½ mi. past the 10 mi. marker, a driveway on the right leads to a huge parking lot that welcomes you to the Waimea Canyon Lookout. A commanding view of the colorful canyon lies just beyond the green railing. Back on the road, the next official lookout is Pu'u Hinahina, between the 13 and 14 mi. markers. A short path, heading away from the restrooms, leads to a Ni'ihau viewpoint. Between these two lookouts are a number of smaller lookouts without parking lots, but the numerous dirt turnouts make it easy to reach any of them.

🥾 HIKES AND TRAILS

If you looked out over Waimea Canyon and thought there couldn't possibly be any way to get down to its base, think again. From the edge of the canyon between the 8 and 9 mi. markers, the **Kukui Trail** begins its 2000+ ft. descent into the canyon, ending at the Waimea River. The 2½ mi. trail is well-defined and well-marked (it has markers every ¼ mi., although many are obscured by growth on the side of the trail), but rather strenuous because of its steepness. The first ¾ mi. is full of switchbacks as the trail quickly drops down the side of the canyon, making its way through shrubs and other low vegetation. The stretch of trail from the ¾ mi. marker to the 1¾ mi. marker is largely exposed to the sun—it traverses a ridge that first points into the canyon, and around the 1¼ mi. marker, turns left

GIVING BACK

HELP THE PARK

Koke'e State Park is one of Kauai's most popular destinations. It's hard not to fall in love with the beauty of its 40+ mi. of trails and its incredible location at the junction of swamp, cliffs, and canyon. But it can only remain such a magnificent place with the help of volunteers like you. If you are interested in helping, there are a number of options out there.

Museum Shop Interpreters are volunteers who spend their time in the Koke'e Museum answering visitors' questions and helping them find their way around the museum and park, or supporting the museum's day-to-day operations by answering the phone or stocking shelves. This position requires 2-4 days of work per month.

Volunteers on the **Trail, Grounds, and Facilities Crew** are needed for 2 or more days per month, and take care of all construction in the park, like building a new trail sign or landscaping the grounds outside the museum.

A new initiative called the **Koke'e Resource Conservation Program (RCOP)** focuses on eliminating alien species that threaten to overgrow native plants in Koke'e's forests. On the first Saturday of each month, volunteers pull weeds, beginning at 8:30am.

The museum is at the 15 mi. marker of Hwy. 550. Call ☎ 335-9975 or go to www.aloha.net/ ~kokee to volunteer.

and heads up the canyon, parallel to the river below. The trail becomes less well-defined here, but stick to the wide stretch of red dirt atop the ridge. If you look up across the canyon to the top of the eastern edge, you can see Waialae Falls. After about 1¾ mi., the trail turns right, back down toward Waimea River, and enters a wooded area. As the trail approaches the river, it flattens out, and an outhouse comes into view on the left, and a sheltered picnic table of **Wiliwili Campground.** The Kukui Trail hits a T here: to the right lies the **Waimea Canyon Trail**, which leads downriver past Waialae Canyon all the way to Waimea; to the left is a ½ mi. stretch of trail which leads upriver to the **Koaie Canyon Trail**. This short stretch tiptoes along the western shore of the Waimea River until it crosses the river about ½ mi. upstream, and passes another picnic table and outhouse. A hundred yards later, another sign indicates **Koaie Canyon.** This 3 mi. trail leads to **Lonomea Camp.** Be careful; the Koaie Canyon trail is vulnerable to flash floods in wet weather. Take a break before you head back up the Kukui Trail; it seems twice as long on the way up. MM 8–9

A much easier hike that still gives visitors a taste of Waimea Canyon is the **Iliau Nature Loop.** Beginning at the same place the Kukui Trail does, The loop is ¼ mi. long, and offers hikers great views of Waimea Canyon as well as a lesson on native flora, given by a number of small, informational signs along the trail.

To get to either trail, park in one of the dirt turnouts about ¾ mi. past the 8 mi. marker on Waimea Canyon Road. A sign on the canyon side of the road indicates where the two trails begin. Scramble up the slope to the **Iliau Nature Loop.** A turn to the left will lead you around the loop. To the right leads around the loop, too, but also, after about 100 yd., the Kukui Trail is marked by a sign

KOKE'E STATE PARK

Continuing up the road, past the 14 mi. marker, Waimea Canyon State Park gives way to Koke'e State Park. The cool upland forests of Koke'e present a marked contrast to the lush valleys below, and temperatures here are often 10-15° cooler than at sea level. The sprawling trails of Koke'e present spectacular—and comfortable—hiking adventures. Most of the park's 45 mi. of trails feature stunning vistas and peaceful forests, but Koke'e also has the muddy, fascinating **Alaka'i Swamp.**

⑦ PRACTICAL INFORMATION

For trail information and advice, head to the **Koke'e Natural History Museum** (☎335-9975; www.aloha.net/ ~kokee), on the left after the 15 mi. marker. Interesting and comprehensive displays present general information about Kauai's ecology, geology, and the hunting and fishing opportunities and indigenous birds and plants of the park. Lastly, historical photographs give a glimpse of the park as it appeared to early explorers, and a fascinating one-room display details the destruction wrought by Hurricane Iniki, as well as the park's slow but encouraging recovery. Books, short guides to popular trails, maps, and gift items are for sale. The simple Koke'e Trails Map ($1.50) will satisfy the needs of most casual hikers, while the amazing **Earthwalk Press Northwestern Kauai Recreation Map** ($10) might be a worthwhile investment for those planning to stay a few days in the Koke'e State Park area. The much larger Earthwalk Map encompasses the coastal region between Hanalei, Polihale State park, and Mt. Wai'ale'ale, including inset maps of the Na Pali Coast State Park, and detailed descriptions of Koke'e State Park trails and the Kalalau Trail. (Museum open daily 10am-4pm. Free admission—donations accepted. AmEx/D/MC/V.)

Next door, the **Koke'e Lodge** stocks gifts and snacks and maintains **public restrooms. A window ❶** at the back sells tasty and filling food that can be eaten at the indoor tables. Although crowded at lunch time, the lodge's long windows provide a pleasant setting for a meal. The breakfast menu includes quiche ($6.75), hot cornbread ($3), and fruit ($3.25). Lunch features sandwiches ($6.50) on yummy 12-grain bread, hot dogs ($3), meaty or vegetarian chili ($6.25), and plenty of alcohol for those celebrating the completion of a tough hike. (Lodge and gift shop open until 4pm; food served daily 9am-3:30pm. AmEx/D/MC/V.)

CABINS AND CAMPING

The lodge acts as the rental office for the 12 wooden cabins located along the road to the south. The cabins, ranging from studios to two-bedrooms, some of which can accommodate up to six people, come equipped with kitchens, hot showers, linens, and wood-burning stoves. There is a maximum stay of 5 days. Reservations are recommended 2-4 months in advance, or 1 year for holiday weekends. For reservations or more information, write or call Koke'e Lodge, P.O. Box 819, Waimea, HI 96796 (☎335-6061). **Cabins ❷** range from $35 to $45. Koke'e also has four campgrounds. Across the meadow from the museum, the beautiful (and state park-operated) Koke'e campground is a series of spacious, grassy sites along a dirt road, with restrooms, drinking water, and picnic tables. Three forest reserve campgrounds, **Kawaikoi, Sugi Grove,** and **Camp 10,** are to the east, on the 4WD-only Mohihi-Camp 10 Rd. For information on obtaining a permit see **Camping,** p. 370.

YWCA Camp Sloggett ❶ (☎335-6060 for the caretaker's home, or 245-5959 for group reservations and booking) is located down Mohihi-Camp 10 Rd., directly opposite the lodge (a Camp Sloggett sign points the way at the road's beginning), and has affordable indoor accommodations. Large groups sometimes take over the camp, which includes a lodge that can sleep 10, a bunkhouse, and tent-camping sites. At other times, however, the long bunkhouse, lined with rows of metal twin bunks and anchored at either end by a private studio with kitchen, makes a decent hostel. Two bathrooms are provided for guests; tent-camping facilities are limited to showers. A caretaker lives on-site and welcomes phone calls or walk-ins until 8pm. Bunks are $20 and tents are $5-10 per person per night. Rates are negotiable for groups or weekday stays.

LOOKOUTS

The Koke'e lookouts provide expansive views of the wild **Na Pali Coast** and the endless Pacific Ocean. Across from the 18 mi. marker, the **Kalalau Lookout,** over 4100 ft. above sea level, presents a postcard-perfect view of the **Kalalau Valley.** The lookout is in the southern corner of the valley, giving visitors an especially good

KAUAI

view of the northeastern wall of the valley and a waterfall halfway up the valley's wall. Vets of the Kalalau Trail will get an extra kick out of seeing the valley they crossed on foot from thousands of feet above.

Many travelers stow their cameras and turn around here, but another less popular (but equally stunning) vista awaits at the end of the road. Free of massive tour buses and chatty guides, the **Pu'u o Kila Lookout** has a magnificent view of Kalalau's green cliffs and lush river basin. Unfortunately, perhaps due to the lighter tourist traffic, a growing wall of shrubbery encroaches on the sights. A sign to the east points toward Mt. Wai'ale'ale, and Pu'u o Kila also serves as the starting point for trails into the Alaka'i Swamp.

From time to time, the road from the Kalalau Lookout to the Pu'u o Kila Lookout is closed to vehicles. This requires tourists to make the roughly 1 mi. trek from one lookout to the next. Although cool temperatures make hiking more comfortable, the breezy lookouts can be chilly. Since fog can sometimes roll in, make the lookouts your first stop of the day in Koke'e State Park for the best chance of a view.

⬛ HIKING

The main attraction of Koke'e State Park is without a doubt its network of one-of-a-kind trails. Over 40 mi. of trails criss-cross the park, from short forest walks through groves of Methley plums to heart-pounding balancing acts across narrow, rocky ridges. Before visiting Koke'e for a hike, it's important to be familiar with the roads that provide access to many of the park's trails, as well as the guided hikes that are offered, and the steps it takes to prepare for a hike through the park.

A few trails begin from Hwy. 550, but the majority of the trailheads are located along the handful of 4WD dirt roads that head east from Hwy. 550. Three such dirt roads that are important to hikers are the **Mohihi-Camp 10 Road, Kumuwela Road, and Halemanu Road.** Mohihi-Camp 10 Rd. is the longest of the 4WD dirt roads that make their way through the park, and is also the road with the most trailheads. It begins across the street from the Koke'e Lodge, and extends about 4 mi. east of the highway until it reaches its final destination, forestry reserve Camp 10. A sign at the beginning of the road says "Kumuwela Rd." because it *leads* to Kumuwela Rd. Although Mohihi-Camp 10 Rd. is officially considered a 4WD-only road, the stretch from the highway to about ¼ mi. past the Kumuwela Rd. intersection is passable in 2WD, but only in dry weather. Kumuwela Rd. itself branches to the right from Mohihi-Camp 10 Rd. about 1½ mi. in from Hwy. 550, and heads south for over 2 mi. Rarely can any part of it be driven in a 2WD car. The third road, Halemanu Rd., branches to the east of Hwy. 550 near the 14 mi. marker and meanders about 1½ mi. into the forest. On good days, the first ¾ mi. of Halemanu Rd. is passable in 2WD, providing access to a couple popular trailheads. Otherwise, there is room to park on the side of Hwy. 550 where Halemanu Rd. begins.

Another option is to take advantage of the park's **Wonderwalks.** Led by park employees or local naturalists, these guided hikes are informative and accessible. State vehicles transport the 4WD-less to otherwise unreachable trailheads, while knowledgeable leaders lead hikers through a wide range of hikes. Wonderwalks are generally given only on summer weekends, and are free. Call ☎ 335-9975 or stop by the museum for a schedule to find out exactly which trails will be covered on a given Wonderwalk. Reservations are recommended, some hikes have limited capacities. All Wonderwalks leave at 12:30pm from Koke'e Museum. In the winter, visitors can call to arrange a custom guided hike, for a fee.

Anyone hiking in the park should carry sufficient water; leptospirosis, a bacteria that can sneak through most water filters, is a constant concern. Hikers should also avoid attempting the trails during wet and rainy weather; many of the canyon and Na Pali view hikes include extremely steep drops and narrow ledges.

The trails of Koke'e State Park cover roughly four different types of terrain: The Na Pali Coast, Waimea Canyon, the forests of Koke'e, and Alaka'i Swamp. Of the dozens of trails in Koke'e State Park, the six trails/loops listed below represent the full range of terrain and difficulty.

■ **CANYON TRAIL** (1¾ mi., 2-3hr. round-trip. Trailhead: 0.8 mi. down Halemanu Rd. from Hwy. 550, and then 0.1 mi. down the dirt road that branches to the right off Halemanu Rd. (the same trailhead as Cliff Trail). Level: moderate.) Deservedly Koke'e Park's most popular hike, the Canyon Trail skirts the edges of the Waimea Canyon, revealing breathtaking views at every corner. After guiding travelers through verdant native forest brimming with *koa* trees and blackberry bushes, the trail passes over an old sugar plantation ditch. A quick climb out of the forest leads to a broad ridge with an exhilarating view of the valley below. From here, the trail descends to Waipo'o Falls, about 1 mi. from the trailhead. Most hikers turn back at this point; continue on to escape some of the crowds. To the left, a short spur takes adventurers to a small swimming hole that is only safe when water is running. More breathtaking views await atop Kumuwela Ridge, before the trail ends at the lower end of Kumuwela Rd.

LG: Wouldn't that scare people from going in the water?

A: Maybe it would. In Hanakapi'ai, there have been 24 drownings in 27 years—14 bodies never recovered. If you put up a sign that emphasized this...I think that would be more effective than "Swim at your own risk."

LG: Did you find any strange patterns?

A: Well, the main thing that has saved lives on Kauai have been 2 hurricanes. Fewer people came, so fewer people were able to drown.

LG: What is the relative danger of drowning here as opposed to the other islands?

A: Actually, there are more drownings on the other islands, but Kauai is much higher for visitors drowning. The state spends tons of money to promote tourism here, but they do relatively little to keep people safe. You get this local attitude, "Ah, another stupid *haole* drowned on the North Shore."

LG: If people get in trouble what should they do?

CB: The correct response is to stay calm, and breathe. I always tell people before they go in the water to use the 10min. rule. Sit on the beach and watch the water for 10 min., because within 10min. you're going to see the biggest waves and the smallest waves, because every few minutes you get a swell coming in. You have to be aware. The biggest hazard is ignorance.

■ NU'ALOLO-NU'ALOLO CLIFF-AWA'AWA'PUHI LOOP. (8¼ mi., about 4-7hr. round-trip. Trailheads: Nu'alolo trailhead, 100 yd. south of the lodge road; 'Awa'awa'puhi trailhead, just past the 17 mi. marker, on the left. Level: very challenging.) The Nu'alolo-Awa'awa'puhi Loop is a combination of three hikes, all of which are difficult in their own regard. Together, they form a grueling trek that loops from the highway to and from the majestic Na Pali Coast, and should satisfy any hard-core hiker's hunger for adventure. Start early, and on a sunny day—wet weather can make a few stretches of trail extremely dangerous. The **Nu'alolo Trail** gradually descends 3¼ mi. from the highway toward the ocean through dry upland forests dominated by towering *koa* trees, flowering shrubs, and a grassy meadow. Shortly after the 2¼ mi. marker (the entire loop is marked every ¼ mi., although some of the markers are difficult to see or missing), hikers get their first good view of the Pacific Ocean. After about 3¼ mi., hikers reach a junction. Here they can choose to continue on the loop by turning right onto the 2 mi. Nu'alolo Cliff Trail, or hike an extra ½ mi. toward the ocean to the Lolo Vista, which is the end of the Nu'alolo Trail. Lolo Vista is a must-see, and easily one of the most breathtaking views of the Na Pali Coast that one can reach by land. The Nu'alolo Cliff Trail tiptoes precariously atop the rim of Nu'alolo Valley for about 2 mi. and connects the Nu'alolo Trail and the Awa'awa'puhi Trail. The Nu'alolo Cliff Trail traverses stretches of stretches of bare cliffs with wide-open views, ventures into lush green forest, and happens upon an exposed ridge with picnic tables and a stream crossing. One-quarter mile from the intersection of the Nu'alolo Cliff Trail and the Awa'awa'puhi Trail, the cliff trail crosses another stream and passes by a small but picturesque waterfall. The Awa'awa'puhi Trail extends for 2¾ mi. from the highway to its junction with the Nu'alolo Cliff Trail, and then an additional ¼ mi. to another lookout on the Na Pali Coast. Don't skip it. The three-trail loop measures 8¼ mi., but including round trips to and from both vistas, and the 1½ mi. hike along Hwy. 550 from one trailhead to the other, hikers could be in for an 11¼ mi. journey. Bring plenty of water on this hike, and no matter which trailhead you start on, be prepared for a 1500+ ft. climb from the Nu'alolo Cliff Trail to Hwy. 550.

CLIFF TRAIL. (500 ft., 15min. round-trip from trailhead. Trailhead: ¾ mi. down Halemanu Rd. from Hwy 550, and then 500 ft. down the dirt road that branches to the right off Halemanu Rd.; same trailhead as Canyon Trail. Level: easy.) Halemanu Rd. winds its way from Hwy. 550 to the trailhead, passing through *koa* and *'o'hia* trees, fragrant *Kahili* ginger, and other flowering plants. The cliff trail itself is a short, wide, dirt path that leads to a stunning lookout over Waimea Canyon. The lookout is actually just the last 50 yd. of the trail, which emerges from the forest to the edge of the canyon, where hikers enjoy the expansive view from behind the long guardrail. The lookout is about as close to the headwall of Waimea Canyon as you can get, and is roughly across the canyon from the Pu'u Hinahina lookout. For those who don't drive down Halemanu Rd. to the trailhead, the hike from Hwy. 550 to the lookout at the end of the trail is about 1 mi. long, and is still a worthwhile and relatively easy hike for those without a lot of time in the park.

PU'U KA 'OHELO-BERRY FLATS LOOP. (2 mi., 1hr. round-trip. Trailheads: Pu'u Ka Ohelo trailhead, about 1 mi. down Mohihi-Camp 10 Rd., then about ¼ mi. down a dirt trail fork to the left that leads to a small group of private cabins (a sign at the trailhead says "State Park Area"); Berry Flats trailhead, ¾ mi. farther down Mohihi-Camp 10 Rd., past Kumuwela Rd., about 100 yd. before a wide section of the road and a left turn. Level: easy.) This pleasant hike wanders through a forest shadowed by tall *koa* trees and lacy ferns. The constant struggle between indigenous and introduced plants is evident—flowering honeysuckle, beautiful but destructively invasive, lines the path. The Berry Flats end of the loop is dominated by Japanese *sugi* pines and California redwoods, which have prevented native plants from taking root. Along the loop, two trails branch off to the side. About ½ mi. into the Pu'u Ka 'Ohelo Trail, The Water Tank Trail forks to the left and leads about 1 mi. back to Hwy. 550 across the street from the Koke'e Campground. About 1 mi. later on the loop, the trail makes a sharp turn to the right, where the Pu'u Ka 'Ohelo trail ends and meets the Berry Flats Trail. Here a short path forks to the left and leads to a dead end. The loop is a gentle hike through beautiful, old-growth forest, and is great for families. If you park your car at one trailhead and plan on hiking the loop, don't forget to factor in the ¾ mi. hike along the road.

KALUAPUHI TRAIL. (1½ mi., 1hr. round-trip. Trailhead: An overgrown grassy slope with room for one car to park on the right side of the road, a little less than ¼ mi. past the Awa'awa'puhi trailhead (17 mi. marker), at the beginning of a sharp left turn in the highway. Level: easy to moderate.) Due to the elusive trailhead, you may very well have the path to yourself. The well-maintained trail travels inland, through native upland forest, ending just a couple hundred yards past the **Kalalau Lookout.** With a change in elevation of only 120 ft., the peaceful stroll can be enjoyed by all, especially families with children. Native Hawaiian flora and fauna prevail here; indigenous birds swoop down from above the forest canopy of *'o'hia*, and strawberry guava grows in abundance. At the T-intersection in the grove, take the left fork—the right fork leads to a dead-end hunting trail. The trail ends in an orchard of Methley plums, harvested by locals in early summer. If you choose to walk back to your car via the highway, it's about 1 mi. from trailhead to trailhead.

PIHEA TRAIL TO ALAKA'I SWAMP TRAIL. (3¾ mi., 3-4hr. round-trip. Trailhead: to the right of the Pu'u o Kila Lookout, at the end of Waimea Canyon Dr. Level: challenging.) Just about the only way to get to the Alaka'i Swamp without 4WD is via the Pihea Trail, which is a pretty memorable trail in its own right. The first section of the Pihea Trail features sweeping views of the Na Pali cliffs and valleys. Hovering around 4000 ft., this stretch follows the course of an old, attempted road across the top of Kalalau Valley. The road was intended to link Koke'e State Park with the highway at Haena, but failed, leaving a badly eroding scar in its place. Parts of this section of trail are shaded by *'o'hia* trees that form a leafy roof overhead and attract a steady stream of native birds. After about 1 mi., the trail forks, and a steep offshoot to the left leads to **Pihea Vista.** The Pihea Vista really isn't any more impressive than the half-dozen great vistas that line the first mile of the trail, and it certainly isn't worth the steep scramble up the side trail that leads to it. Meanwhile, the Pihea Trail turns right at the fork, and leaves the Na Pali Coast behind to enter the Alaka'i Swamp. After about ¼ mi., the trail becomes a narrow boardwalk, and descends gradually for another ½ mi. until it reaches a junction. This is about 1¾ mi. into the Pihea Trail, where it crosses the Alaka'i Swamp Trail. Straight ahead, the Pihea Trail continues for almost 2 mi. until it reaches its other end, at Kawaikoi Camp, along Mohihi-Camp 10 Rd., 3¾ mi. from Pu'u o Kila Lookout. To the right are the first 1½ mi. of the Alaka'i Swamp Trail, whose trailhead is also along Mohihi-Camp 10 Rd. To the left are the last 2 mi. of the Alaka'i Swamp Trail, which ends at the Kilohana Lookout. These last couple miles of the Alaka'i Swamp trail are a fascinating hike along a boardwalk through havens for endemic birds and plants. The Kilohana Lookout has an amazing, but usually cloudy, view of the North Shore, offering proof that the island is indeed circular.

KEKAHA

Once a sugar town where everything centered around the big (and now rusting), mill, modern-day Kekaha functions mainly as a gateway to **Koke'e State Park** (see p. 426) to the north or **Polihale State Park** (see p. 433) to the west. Although Kekaha doesn't have much to offer in the way of services or nightlife, its miles of remote,

KAUAI

THE ORIGINS OF THE HAU

The delicate blossoms of the native *hau* tree, a type of hibiscus, bloom a brilliant yellow in the morning, then turn deep orange by afternoon and bright red by the end of the day before they fall from the tree. Besides beautifying gardens, the trees are used to build fish net floats, outriggers for canoes, and the tough bark is shaped into rope, nets, or hula skirts.

At least two legends circulate about the origins of the *hau*. In one story, a man named Hi-Hi-Aka-La-La-Hau fell in love with Poliahu, the goddess of the sacred *heiau* (temple) along the Wailua River. Failing in his quest to win her love by scaling a massive cliff overnight, the man was turned into a tree that grew twisting in every direction. A series of storms first carried the tree to the top of Mt. Wai'ale'ale, and then tore it to pieces and washed it down through Kauai's five rivers into the ocean, and farther to the other islands where the pieces took root and grew into many, many *hau* trees. The *hau* tree's magical origins are apparent in its round leaves which feature a central ridge, representing Mt. Wai'ale'ale, and five veins spreading outward, the five rivers of Kauai flowing into the ocean.

uncrowded beach and spacious public parklands make it a super place to relax and get away from the crowds and traffic of other west shore towns.

⚠ PRACTICAL INFORMATION. The western-most town in the United States, Kekaha lies 26 mi. west of Lihue on **Highway 50. Kekaha Road** branches right from the highway between the 24 and 25 mi. markers and runs nearly parallel to Hwy. 50, about two blocks north of the highway, for 2 mi. west to **Waimea Canyon Plaza** at the base of Koke'e Rd. The plaza has a few standard tourist shops stocked with *aloha* shirts and beach towels, as well as the last place to fill your tummy—or your picnic basket—before heading north to Koke'e or west to Polihale.

🍴 FOOD. Kekaha doesn't have any restaurants, but there are a couple nice lunch spots and a convenience store to stock up on snacks and basics, all three of which are located in the Waimea Canyon Plaza. The **Menehune Food Mart ❶** has a good selection of the basics plus Icees, prepared sandwiches ($3), and sliced fruit bowls ($3). There is also an **ATM** inside. (☎237-1335. Open daily 5am-8pm. AmEx/MC/V.) **Obsessions Cafe ❶** offers a basic breakfast menu with the usual pancakes, omelettes, and the "Complete Breakfast," (2 pancakes, meat, egg, and coffee; $6), as well as a lunch menu which includes salads, wraps, sandwiches, and burgers, all for under $7. (☎337-2224. Open M-F 8:30am-6pm, Sa-Su 6:30am-6pm; breakfast M-F 8:30am-11am, Sa-Su 6:30am-noon. MC/V.) The **Waimea Canyon Snack Shop ❶** sells sandwiches ($3.75-6), salads, and Lappert's ice cream ($2.75 per scoop) to fuel you for a day outside. (☎337-9227. Open daily 8am-4:30pm.)

🏖 BEACHES. Across Kekaha Rd. from the Plaza, and between the elementary school and the ocean, the sprawling **Faye Park,** complete with track, baseball fields, tennis courts, basketball court, playground, picnic tables, pavilion, and grills, has hosted many a neighborhood *luau.* There are restrooms behind the pavilion and an outdoor shower at the other end of the park (right on the highway facing the beach). Every Saturday morning at 9am, a **Sunshine Market** sets up shop next to the tennis courts. Kekaha's main attraction, the glistening white **Kekaha Beach Park,** runs alongside the town between the highway and the ocean for 1-2 mi., and offers sunbathers and swimmers plenty of chances to find their own secluded stretch of sand. However, like other

West Side beaches, pretty Kekaha hides strong rip currents, and swimmers should be aware of surf conditions before entering the water. Families with young *keiki* (children) favor the eastern end of the beach, where a small, reef-fringed pool (just east of the church) creates safer waters. Small waves break virtually the entire length of the beach, making Kekaha Beach Park a decent spot for body boarders and, though rarely, surfers. The sand actually continues uninterrupted along the coast 15 mi. to the north all the way to Polihale, but much of it lies within the bounds of Barking Sands Airfield and Pacific Missile Range—not a safe place for the *keiki*.

⚠ OUTDOORS. Outside of Kekaha, **Polihale State Park** is well worth a trip. Hwy. 50 ends 5 mi. out of Kekaha; following the signs to Polihale, veer right at the fork and turn left onto the first dirt road. While trucks full of local teenagers careen merrily down miles of potholes, bumps, and rocks to the park, visitors in modest rental cars may have a more difficult—but definitely worthwhile—ride. Ease off the gas, avoid braking suddenly, and shift into low gear as you navigate your way through the cane fields. About 3½ mi. later, the road forks to the right at a big monkeypod tree, and runs another 1½ mi. to the north end of Polihale Beach. Along these 1½ mi. a dirt loop branches off toward the ocean and is the access road for a number of campsites. More campsites await beyond the loop toward the northern end of the road; and the whole area is lined with facilities that include multiple restrooms, showers, drinking water fountains, and pavilions. For more information, see **Camping** p. 370. The left fork at the monkeypod tree leads south about ½ mi. to a small parking area that sits at the northern edge of Polihale's famous dunes, and provides access to the southern end of Polihale Beach. The beach itself is an absolute wonder: up to 50 yd. wide, the white sands stretch for 3 mi. along Kauai's western coast, from the military base on the south to the southwestern corner of the Na Pali Coast on the north. Powerful waves smash the shoreline the whole length of the beach, and the water is crystal clear. One nice place to swim is Queen's Pond, the only section of Polihale protected by a reef. It is a small bay about 100 yd. to the north of the parking area reached by taking a left at the monkeypod tree. The rest of the beach is constantly pounded by the surf; swimming is possible (not for children) but requires caution.

Even without entering the water, Polihale will leave a strong impression on visitors. At the north-

A second legend tells the story of a young girl, Hina-hau-kaekae, who was not allowed outside the walls of a *heiau* by night, according to a promise made to her mother by her sisters, who cared for her. To help Hina-hau-kaekae, her mother gave her a flower that changed color during the day, from yellow in the morning to red at dusk, so that when she was outisde during the day, she could always look at the color of the flower to be sure she made it back to one of her sister's *heiaus* by nightfall. One day Hina-hau-kaekae was out walking when she encountered a series of villagers struggling with their daily tasks because they lacked a tree with light, strong wood and supple, strong bark that would allow them to build what they needed. Each time she ran across one of these people, Hina-hau-kaekae promised them that she knew of such a tree, and would look for it and tell them when she found it. As dusk approached, Hina-hau-kaekae was within sight of the *heiau* where she would spend the night, but unhappy because she had not found the tree that she sought, and had left many promises unkept. As she stood there, turning toward the *heiau* and then back toward the people she had met, undecided about what to do, her feet took root and her twisted form became a *hau* tree, the very tree she was searching for all day. Now her wood and bark could be put to use by all the people of the village, and her blossoms would mark the passage of each day.

ern end of the beach, past the campsites, an ancient *heiau* (temple) is nestled at the base of Polihale Cliff. According to legend, the souls of the ancient dead used the cliff as a departure point, floating away from the earth and into the glorious setting sun. As one stands at Polihale, isolated from the rest of Kauai, gazing out over thousands of miles of unbroken Pacific, it's not hard to imagine why Hawaiians considered this a spiritual place. The world-famous **Polihale sunset** is best seen from the northern end, where the blazing orange sun sinks below crashing waves, and the forbidden isle of **Ni'ihau** sits 20 mi. offshore, providing a perfect backdrop for a romantic picnic.

NI'IHAU

LAND

Ni'ihau lies 18 mi. southwest of Kauai and is the western-most of Hawaii's eight major islands. Only 70 sq. mi. in area, Ni'ihau is the smallest of the inhabited Hawaiian islands. While Mt. Wai'ale'ale on neighboring Kauai is the rainiest spot on earth, Ni'ihau's average rainfall is a mere 12 in. per year, giving it a flat, arid landscape. Because it lacks the lush tropical vegetation that characterizes the other islands, Ni'ihau, with its grassy lowland topography, is well-suited for grazing by the herds of animals that today outnumber people on the island.

HISTORY

Ni'ihau was never conquered during **Kamehameha I's** campaign to unite all of the Hawaiian islands under one rule in the late 1700s. Rather, it joined the kingdom of its own volition in 1810.

In 1863, **Eliza Sinclair,** a Scottish widow turned New Zealand farmer, moved to Honolulu, where **King Kamehameha V** offered to sell her a parcel of land on Oahu stretching from Honolulu Hale to Diamond Head. (Not a bad deal, considering this area is some of the most lucrative real estate in the world today.) Sinclair did not think this land was suitable for farming, however, and instead purchased the entire island of Ni'ihau, along with all of its inhabitants, for $10,000. Sinclair established the **Niihau Ranch** on the island, where she raised cattle and other livestock, enlisting the island's residents and her own family as employees. After her death in 1892, Sinclair's grandson, **Aubrey Robinson,** took over the ranch.

The island is highly isolated and uninvited visitors have been forbidden on Ni'ihau since its purchase in the 19th century—hence its nickname, **"The Forbidden Isle."** One memorable intruder, a Japanese pilot, crash-landed on the island after the attack on Pearl Harbor in 1941. After a week spent sporadically dispensing machine gun fire from the wreckage of his plane, the pilot was eventually subdued by Ni'ihau native **Benehakaka Kanahele.** Kanahele received the Congressional Medal of Honor for his bravery.

Ni'ihau

Kaulakahi Channel

Lehua

PACIFIC OCEAN

Lehaua Landing

Kii

Keawanui Bay

Mt. Paniau
1281' (390m)

Kaeo
1018' (310m)

Puuwai

Pueo Point

Halulu Lake

Nonopapa Lake

Halali Lake

Ni'ihau

Kamalino

Kawaihoa Point

Kaumuhonu Bay

N

0   4 miles
0   4 kilometers

The island is famous for the hand-strung **shell *leis*** that native women have produced for hundreds of years. Tiny *Laiki*, *Kehelelani*, and *Momi* seashells wash up on Ni'ihau during certain seasons of the year, and they are then collected and strung into intricate necklaces. **Captain James Cook** returned from his first expedition to Hawaii with one of these *leis*, which is now the property of the British Museum. Many of these beautiful necklaces have become treasured heirlooms in Hawaiian families, and can fetch four figures in antique shops throughout Hawaii.

TODAY

Ni'ihau is still owned by the Robinson family, and today Eliza Sinclair's great-great-grandsons, **Keith and Bruce Robinson,** manage the ranch. Nowadays the island is home to about 250 people (all employed by the ranch in some capacity), 2000 head of cattle, 3000 wild turkeys, and 12,000 sheep.

There is no electric power on the island, with the exception of that produced by the occasional privately-owned generator. There are also no telephones and no paved roads. There is one school on the island, which provides instruction up to eighth grade. Students who wish to pursue a secondary education commute to schools on Kauai or Oahu.

Hawaiian is the primary language spoken on Ni'ihau, and residents of the island are known for their insularity and staunch opposition to Western ways of life. In addition to the widespread rejection of modern conveniences that would allow for greater contact with the outside world, Ni'ihau was the only island that voted against Hawaiian statehood in 1959.

Although uninvited visitors are prohibited, residents are free to come and go as they choose. However, the inhabitants, including the Robinson family, are highly committed to preserving traditional Hawaiian culture, and therefore most choose to stay on the island.

VISITING THE ISLAND

Technically, nobody is allowed to visit Ni'ihau unless they are invited by a resident. However, **helicopter tours** are permitted on the island, which are run by **Niihau Helicopters.** Flights leave from Kauai, and trips include an aerial tour of the island, half a day at a secluded beach, and lunch. Reservations are required, and tours are often booked months in advance. (P.O. Box 690370, Makaweli, HI 96769. ☎877-441-3500; www.hawaiian.net/~niihauisland/heli.html. $280 per person; group and charter rates available.) **Niihau Safaris** have recently begun running hunting trips to The Forbidden Isle. Trips include air transportation to Ni'ihau, as well as a guide, lunch, two kills, and trophy care in the field, among other things. Reservations are required. (P.O. Box 690370, Makaweli, HI 96769. ☎877-441-3500; www.hawaiian.net/~niihauisland/safaris.html. $1650 per day per hunter, 4 hunters max. per group. $1200 per day for a hunting spouse, $1000 per day for a hunting minor with hunting parent. ($400 per day per observer, 3 observers max. per group. All parties limited to 5 except by special charter. Family rates available.)

FURTHER INFORMATION

Niihau: The Last Hawaiian Island, by Ruth M. Tabrah. This book is based on the author's experiences in Ni'ihau, and is a good source for general information about the island.

Niihau Incident, by Allan Beekman. An account of the Japanese fighter pilot who landed on Ni'ihau in 1941 and terrorized the island's residents.

A Chronicle and Flora of Niihau, by Juliet Rice Wichman. An illustrated volume documenting wildlife on Ni'ihau.

GLOSSARY

COMMON HAWAIIAN WORDS AND PHRASES

WORDS		
'aina	eye-nah	land, earth
alelo	ah-lay-low	tongue, language
ali'i	ah-lee-ee	Hawaiian chiefs, royalty
aloha	ah-low-ha	love, hello, goodbye
aole	ah-oh-lay	no
halau	hah-lau	school
hale	hah-lay	house
haole	how-lay	caucasians
hapa	hah-pah	half, part
hauoli	how-oh-lee	happiness
heiau	hey-ee-au	temple
hui	hoo-ee	club, association, or group
hula	hoo-lah	Hawaiian dance
imu	ee-moo	underground oven
kahuna	ha-hoo-na	priest
kalua	kah-loo-ah	to bake underground
kane	kah-nay	man
kapu	kah-poo	keep out
keiki	kay-kee	child
ki	kee	plant in daily activities, also an ancient symbol of power
koa	ko-ah	valuable endemic Hawaiian lumber tree
kokua	ko-koo-ah	help, aid, relief
koloa	ko-low-ah	Hawaiian duck
kumu	koo-moo	teacher, tutor
kupuna	koo-poo-nah	grandparent, ancestor
lanai	lah-nye	porch
lei	lay	garland, wreath of flowers
lomi lomi	low-me low-me	massage
luau	loo-ow	Hawaiian feast
mahalo	mah-hah-low	thank you
ma'ika'i	mah-ee-kah-ee	good, fine
makai	mah-kye	in the direction of the sea
makaainana	mah-kah-ay-nah-nah	common people
makua	mah-koo-ah	parent, parent generation
malama	mah-lah-mah	to take care of, attend to
mauka	mah-ow-kah	toward the mountains; inland
mele	meh-leh	a song, chant, or poem
menehune	meh-neh-hoo-neh	legendary race of little people
muumuu	moo-moo	loose gown, dress

nalu	nah-loo	wave, surf
nani	nah-nee	beautiful
nui	noo-ee	big
ohana	oh-hah-nah	family
'ohia lehua	oh-hee-ah leh-hoo-ah	native Hawaiian plant
'olelo	oh-leh-loh	language, speech, word
ono	oh-no	delicious
pali	pah-lee	cliff
paniolo	pah-nee-oh-low	Hawaiian cowboy
pakololo	pah-kow-low-low	marijuana
pau	pow	finished
pule	poo-leh	prayer or incantation
pupu	poo-poo	hors d'oeuvre
pupule	poo-poo-lay	crazy
ukelele	oo-keh-leh-leh	"jumping flea," Hawaiian instrument
wahine	wah-hee-nay	woman, girl, female
wai	why	water, liquid or liquor
wiki wiki	wee-kee-wee-kee	fast, speedy, to hurry

PHRASES		
aloha'aina	ah-low-hah eye-nah	love of the land
aloha ahiahi	ah-low-hah ah-hee-ah-hee	Good evening
aloha kakahiaka	ah-low-hah kah-kah-hee-ah-kah	Good morning
aloha kakou	ah-low-hah kah-koo	Greetings, everybody
'a'ole pilikia	ah-o-lay pee-lee-kee-ah	no problem, no trouble
kama'aina	kah-mah-ay-nah	"child of the soil," native-born or long-time resident
kanaka maoli	kah-nah-kah mah-oh-lee	full-blooded Hawaiian person
kipa mai	kee-pah mah-ee	You're welcome
mahalo nui loa	mah-ha-low new-ee low-ah	Thank you very much
ma'i ka'i	mah-ee kah-ee	I am fine
'olelo no'eau	oh-lay-low no-ee-ah-oo	proverb, wise saying
owai kau inoa	oh-why kah-oo ee-no-ah	What is your name?
pehea 'oe	pay-hay-ah oh-ay	How are you?
pau hana	pow hah-nah	end of the work day

LOCAL FOODS AND DISHES

adobo: pork or chicken in a vinegar and garlic sauce
'ahi: yellowfin tuna
arare: crisp rice crackers seasoned with soy sauce
azuki: sweetened red or black beans
crack seed: popular snack of preserved fruits mixed with salt, sugar, and seasonings
dim sum: Chinese brunch of appetizer-size food (often dumplings) dispensed from carts
haupia: coconut pudding
huli huli chicken: chicken barbequed on spits over an open grill
lau lau: meat and fish wrapped in leaves (usually taro or ti) and then baked or steamed
li hing mui: dried seasoned plum, a type of crack seed
lilikoi: passion fruit
limu: edible seaweed
loco moco: a fried egg on top of a hamburger, served over rice and smothered in gravy
lomi salmon: sushi-type salmon mixed with Maui onion, and seasoned

kalua pig: barbequed pork, cooked whole in an imu
katsu: pork or chicken deep-fried and served with a soy-based dipping sauce
kim chee: heavily seasoned pickled vegetables
kona coffee: coffee from beans grown in the upcountry Kona District of The Big Island
kulolo: dessert made of baked taro root mixed with coconut milk and honey or sugar
mahi mahi: dolphin fish
malasadas: sweet Portuguese doughnuts
mochi: balls of cooked, pounded sweet rice
musubi: rice ball wrapped in dried seaweed
nori: dried, compressed seaweed
onaga: red snapper
ono: similar to mackerel or tuna
opakapaka: pink snapper
opihi: limpet (a shellfish delicacy)
plate lunch: two scoops white rice, macaroni salad, and a local-style meat or seafood entree
poi: paste-like food made of pounded taro root
poke: appetizer consisting of cubed raw fish, marinated and served with raw seaweed
puna goat cheese: rich creamy cheese from organically-raised goats in the Puna District of The
    Big Island, used in many regional cuisine dishes
saimin: Japanese noodle soup
shave ice: shaved ice topped with syrup, lighter and flakier than a snow cone
shoyu: Japanese word for soy sauce
spam: spiced ham in a can
'ulu: breadfruit
wasabi: green, Japanese-style horseradish

LOCAL SPEAK

Auntie: respectful address for a female elder
an den: "What's up?" or expression of boredom
ass why: "That's the reason"
any hine: anything
bang 'em: to cause a collision
boo: pronoun, equivalent to man, guy etc...
brah: friend, bro
braddah: brother
broke da mout: delicious
buggah: a chap or a fellow
charge it: to assail a problem or obstacle (ex: a formidable wave)
chicken skin: goose bumps
choke: many, a large amount
choke cars: traffic
cockaroach: to steal
cruise/cruisin': to take it easy; to stay or rest where one is
da cute: how precious!
da kine: the kind (versatile pidgin phrase, can mean almost anything)
foa: used instead of "to" in "to do something"
grind: to eat
grinds: good food
hana hou: once more, again, encore
Hele on: "Let's go" (common phrase in hula dancing)
Howzit?: condensation of the greeting, "How is it going?"
kay den: all right
Like beef?: equivalent of asking someone if they want to fight
moke: very large local (derogatory)
no can: unable to
shoots: ok ("Why not?")
slippah: flip-flop sandals, slippers
shaka: greeting in the form of a hand gesture ("Hang loose")
sistah: sister
stink eye: dirty look, sideward glance
talk stink: say something bad about somebody, gossip
talk story: chit chat, casual conversation
titah: brutish local woman, female moke (derogatory)
Uncle: respectful address for a male elder

A Brief History

The hula dance and hula dancers are arguably some of the most recognized icons of Hawaiian culture, but the images adorning postcards and photo books represent a more modern form of the dance. This modern variety grew out of an ancient oral tradition, that of a chant accompanied by pantomimed movements.

For the ancient Hawaiians, the hula dance was of secondary importance; the chant was the main part of the hula. While there are many different forms of hula dance which vary depending on the implements used, the chant remains constant throughout these variations. In its most basic form, a beat is created by thumping a hollow gourd (*ipu*) on the ground, and drumming on it with the palm of the hand. This creates the basis for the pantomimed movements, while the chanting over the sound of the beat gives the movement meaning and conveys cultural stories. Many such stories celebrated the volcano goddess Pele, while others described historic events as a mode of preserving Hawaiian history. Through chant and pantomimed movements, hula dance served as a vehicle for oral history to be passed from generation to generation.

Chant and hula dance were not performed on their own, however, but were merely part of a more elaborate religious practice that occurred in the *heiau*—a temple where religious rites were performed. The dance itself took place in the *halau*, a portion of the *heiau* reserved especially for it. The *halau*, in addition to being a structure devoted to hula dance was also a term denoting a school for hula instruction which would be associated with a *heiau*—a definition that continues to this day, although the religious significance has all but disappeared.

The arrival of Western missionaries in the late 18th and early 19th centuries marks the beginning of hula's dark ages. The missionaries viewed the hula dance as a heathen practice and sought to eliminate it from Hawaiian culture first by limiting its practice, and eventually by banning it altogether. The hula dance saw a revival under the reign of King Kalakaua—nicknamed the Merrie Monarch—and Queen Kapiʻolani during the late 19th century. These two monarchs legalized the dance, and in fact held several hula festivals during their twenty year reign. Kalakaua's important role in the revitalization of the hula dance is honored every April during the Merrie Monarch Hula Festival, held on the Big Island, which showcases both ancient and modern hula styles.

It was under Kalakaua and his successor Queen Liliuokalani that the hula began to evolve and take on the more modern form that most would recognize today. The early 20th century saw the introduction of the ukulele, borrowed from Portuguese immigrants, and the use of band music and Western rhythms to accompany the hula dance. With the beginning of the tourist boom in the mid 20th century, the hula dancer was transformed into the common image that most think of today—complete with grass skirt, flower *lei* and ukulele.

Christine Yokoyama, whose family hails from Oahu, is the map editor for Let's Go: Hawaii 2004, Let's Go: Australia 2004, Let's Go: Boston 2004, *and* Let's Go Road Trip USA: 2005. *Despite having extensively researched the hula dance, she does not hula, save for one horribly awkward experience at Waiamea Falls.*

The Hawaiian Islands are America's tropical paradise. All the beaches in Hawaii are public, and even the most exclusive resorts must provide public access below the high tide level.

The beaches in Hawaii run the gamut in size, shape, sand color, and wave conditions. The white sand beaches are composed primarily of coral, crushed and ground up by powerful waves. This organically derived sand can range from slightly coarse to super fine. On some islands, especially the Big Island and Maui, volcanic sand varies in color from black to red and even green. These sands are exotic, but can be quite hot to walk on, particularly the heat-absorbing black sand.

Hawaii's climate is perfect for beaching, as average temperatures vary little throughout the year, and even when it is rainy on one side of an island, the other side can be sunny. Summer rains are of short duration, making for terrific single and double rainbows.

Few people seem to watch the weather forecast as it is often the same day after day—gorgeous. The real news is the waves, particularly the huge swells that come rolling in during the winter months. The largest ridable surfing waves in the world are found on the North shore of Oahu at Waimea Bay (p.160), where professional surfers ride waves that are several stories high. The good news is that beaches exist at every point on the compass so that you can pick your beach according to your desired activity.

The most visited beach in Hawaii is Waikiki Beach (p.128) in downtown Honolulu, on Oahu. The water temperature at this world-famous beach is always comfortable, ranging from 77 to 82°, winter to summer. This is where surfing on long boards was invented by Hawaii's kings and first witnessed by European sailors. This may be the best place for a surfing lesson or to ride the waves on an outrigger canoe, as Waikiki Beach is protected by an offshore, fringing coral reef. Breakers on the reef provide good surfing conditions, and at the same time, knock down the big waves, making the nearshore waters safe for year-round swimming. Also on Oahu, Ala Moana Beach (p.104) was carved out of coral reef rock for a boat basin so that the shallow water drops off to a deep channel; the sand was imported to create the beach. Kailua (p.153) and Laniki (p. 154) are National Winners in my annual survey of America's Best Beaches (see www.drbeach.org).

On Maui, Kapalua Bay Beach (p.218) was the first National Winner, and 4 mi. Kaanapali (p.217) is Maui's best-known beach. The coral sand is divided into sections by points of lava rock, providing varying wave conditions. To the south, Wailea is one of Hawaii's newest luxury beach resort destinations. Adventurous beach enthusiasts will want to visit the Makena area to swim at Big Beach (p.201) and perhaps to climb over the cinder cone to catch a view at Little Beach (p.202), known for its nudists.

The Hanalei Bay area (p.370) on the north coast of Kauai boasts the most famous beach on this island—the classic movie "South Pacific" was filmed here. Nearby Lumahai Beach (402) is one of the most scenic and photographed in Hawaii, but it is better for viewing than swimming due to the dangerous waves and currents. At Po'ipu Beach (p.201), a sand spit has grown in the protective lee of offshore rocks, forming one of the few tombolo beaches in America, so that the conditions range from flat water, perfect for swimming and snorkeling, to the pounding waves for surfers.

The Big Island is still growing, as witnessed by the frequent volcanic eruptions, tremendous lava flows, and ground-shaking earthquakes. The sand at Hapuna (p.334) beautifully contrasts with the black lava that bounds this half-mile long pocket beach. Nearby Mauna Kea Beach (p.334), known to Hawaiians as Kaunaoa Beach) has sparkling clear waters for swimming and snorkeling, except during the winter storm season.

Many Hawaiians choose to vacation in Lanai to "get away from it all" and to enjoy the cooler weather on this high island, while Molokai provides a more rural and native experience. Both islands have beautiful beaches; Hulopoe Beach on Lanai is a past National Winner. So whatever your taste in beaches, you are sure to find one (or more likely, many) to suit your desires in the tropical paradise of the Hawaiian Islands.

Dr. Stephen P. Leatherman, a.k.a. "Dr. Beach," has written 18 books and more than 200 scientific articles about beaches. He is a professor and Director of the Laboratory for Coastal Research at Florida International University in Miami. See www.drbeach.org for more information about beaches in Hawaii, and www.nhbc.fiu.edu for information on the National Healthy Beaches Campaign.

INDEX

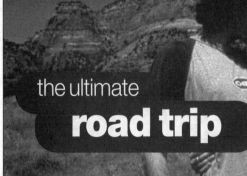

the ultimate
road trip

don't trip out planning your big road trip.
put contiki in the driver's seat with a hassle-free vacations designed for 18 to 35 year olds. make new friends, enjoy your free time and explore the sights in a convenient vacation that gives you more bang for your buck... **from only $70/day** including accommodations, sightseeing, many meals and transportation. with contiki leading the way, you can leave the road map at home!

> 7 days **eastern discovery**
new york, washington d.c., us naval academy, kennedy space center

> 10 days **canada & the rockies**
vancouver, calgary, banff national park

> 13 days **wild western**
san francisco, grand canyon, las vegas, yosemite national park

*prices subject to change, land only.

for more info on our trips...
see your travel agent
call 1-888-CONTIKI
visit www.contiki.com

contiki
VACATIONS for 18-35 year olds

CST# 1001728-20

> europe > australia > new zealand > america > canada

MAP INDEX

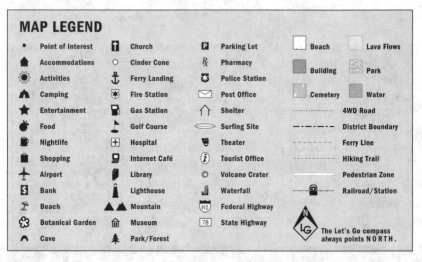

MAP LEGEND

▪ Point of Interest	🏠 Church	🅿 Parking Lot	Beach / Lava Flows
🏠 Accommodations	○ Cinder Cone	℞ Pharmacy	Building / Park
☼ Activities	⚓ Ferry Landing	✚ Police Station	
⛺ Camping	✳ Fire Station	✉ Post Office	Cemetery / Water
★ Entertainment	⛽ Gas Station	⌂ Shelter	.... 4WD Road
🍴 Food	⛳ Golf Course	Surfing Site	—·—·— District Boundary
🍷 Nightlife	✛ Hospital	🚩 Theater	--------- Ferry Line
🛍 Shopping	💻 Internet Café	ⓘ Tourist Office	----------- Hiking Trail
✈ Airport	📖 Library	○ Volcano Crater	Pedestrian Zone
$ Bank	🗼 Lighthouse	Waterfall	🚂 Railroad/Station
⚲ Beach	▲▲ Mountain	H1 Federal Highway	
🌸 Botanical Garden	🏛 Museum	78 State Highway	The Let's Go compass always points NORTH.
⋀ Cave	🌲 Park/Forest		

450